Constructing the World

David J. Chalmers constructs a picture of reality on which all truths can be derived from a limited class of basic truths. The picture is inspired by Rudolf Carnap's construction of the world in *Der logische Aufbau Der Welt*. Carnap's *Aufbau* is often seen as a noble failure, but Chalmers argues that a version of the project can succeed. With the right basic elements and the right derivation relation, we can indeed construct the world.

The focal point of Chalmers' project is scrutability: the thesis that ideal reasoning from a limited class of basic truths yields all truths about the world. Chalmers first argues for the scrutability thesis and then considers how small the base can be. The result is a framework in "metaphysical epistemology": epistemology in service of a global picture of the world.

The scrutability framework has ramifications throughout philosophy. Using the framework, Chalmers defends a broadly Fregean approach to meaning, argues for an internalist approach to the contents of thought, and rebuts W. V. Quine's arguments against the analytic and the a priori. He also uses scrutability to analyze the unity of science, to defend a sort of conceptual metaphysics, and to mount a structuralist response to skepticism.

Based on Chalmers' 2010 John Locke lectures, *Constructing the World* opens up debate on central philosophical issues concerning knowledge, language, mind, and reality.

David Chalmers is Professor of Philosophy at New York University and Distinguished Professor of Philosophy at the Australian National University.

Constructing the World

David J. Chalmers

OXFORD
UNIVERSITY PRESS

OXFORD
UNIVERSITY PRESS

Great Clarendon Street, Oxford, ox2 6DP,
United Kingdom

Oxford University Press is a department of the University of Oxford.
It furthers the University's objective of excellence in research, scholarship,
and education by publishing worldwide. Oxford is a registered trade mark of
Oxford University Press in the UK and in certain other countries

First published 2012
First published in paperback 2014

Impression: 1

Published in the United States of America by Oxford University Press
198 Madison Avenue, New York, NY 10016, United States of America

British Library Cataloguing in Publication Data
Data available

ISBN 978–0–19–960857–7 (Hbk.)
ISBN 978–0–19–960858–4 (Pbk.)

Printed in Great Britain by
CPI Group (UK) Ltd, Croydon, CR0 4YY

For David and Steffi Lewis

Contents

Acknowledgments

I am grateful to the University of Oxford for the invitation to give the John Locke Lectures. That invitation helped me to write this book well before I might have otherwise. I am also grateful to All Souls College and to many Oxford philosophers and others for their warm hospitality during a memorable Oxford spring.

I have presented and discussed versions of the material in this book four times: in a reading group at the Australian National University in March–April 2009, in a graduate seminar at New York University in September–December 2009, in a course of lectures at the University of Barcelona in April 2010, and in the lecture series at Oxford in May–June 2010. I received valuable feedback on all of those occasions.

For discussion at ANU, I am grateful to Jens Christian Bjerring, David Bourget, Peter Fritz, Alan Hájek, Frank Jackson, Ole Koksvik, Stephan Leuenberger, Fiona Macpherson, Dan Marshall, Kelvin McQueen, Martine Nida-Rümelin, Brian Rabern, Gabriel Rabin, Jonathan Schaffer, Susanna Schellenberg, Wolfgang Schwarz, Nico Silins, Declan Smithies, Daniel Stoljar, Mike Titelbaum, Clas Weber, and Tobias Wilsch, among others.

For discussion at NYU, I am grateful to Eli Alshenatsky, Max Barkhausen, Ned Block, Hartry Field, Camil Golub, Paul Horwich, Robert Howell, Uriah Kriegel, Farid Masrour, Tom Nagel, Chris Peacocke, Jeff Russell, Raul Saucedo, Stephen Schiffer, Erica Shumener, Ted Sider, Jonathan Simon, Matthew Smith, Andy Snyder, Michael Strevens, and Jared Warren, among others.

For discussion at Barcelona, I am grateful to Oscar Cabaco, José Díez, Manuel García-Carpintero, Carl Hoefer, Max Kölbel, Josep Macià, Genoveva Martí, Manolo Martínez, Josep Prades, Sven Rosenkrantz, Josefa Toribio, and Dan Zeman, among others.

For discussion at Oxford, I am grateful to Frank Arntzenius, Anita Avramides, Tim Bayne, Corine Besson, John Broome, Troy Cross, Cian Dorr, Antony Eagle, Philip Goff, Anandi Hattiangadi, John Hawthorne, Kelvin McQueen, Maria Lasonen-Aarnio, David Mathers, Ian Phillips, Simon Saunders, Nick Shea, Walter Sinnott-Armstrong, Maja Spener, Scott Sturgeon, David Wallace, Tim Williamson, Alastair Wilson, and Juhani Yli-Vakkuri, among others.

For correspondence about the manuscript, thanks go to Stephen Biggs, Darren Bradley, Adrian Currie, Eric Dietrich, Edward Elliott, Jonathan Kvanvig, Noa Latham, Paul Livingston, Anna-Sara Malmgren, Robert Rupert, Joe Salerno, and Chris Tucker, as well as to many of those mentioned above. For detailed written comments on the manuscript, thanks go to John Bengson, Berit Bro-gaard, Zoe Drayson, Melissa Ebbers, Philip Goff, Dan Greco, Ole Koksvik, Dan Korman, Kelvin McQueen, Angela Mendelovici, Adam Pautz, Chris Pincock, Brian Rabern, Gabriel Rabin, Wolfgang Schwarz, Susanna Schellenberg, Susanna Siegel, Jonathan Simon, and Robbie Williams. For useful feedback, thanks also to Farid Masrour, Sarah Moss, and participants in their seminars discussing the book manuscript at Harvard and Michigan. I am especially grateful to Kelvin McQueen for in-depth comments and discussion through this process and for compiling the index.

Thanks also go to four reviewers for Oxford University Press and to Peter Momtchiloff for his editorial guidance. Thanks to Ole Koksvik and Brian Rabern for their terrific editing. Thanks also to Zoe Drayson for suggesting the term 'excursus' and for convincing me that it is not too pretentious to use. I am grateful to too many others to mention for useful conversation about these issues.

Parts of chapter 1 and chapter 3 are based on parts of 'Conceptual Analysis and Reductive Explanation', co-authored with Frank Jackson and published in *Philosophical Review* 110: 315–61, 2001. Chapter 5 is closely based on 'Revisability and Conceptual Change in 'Two Dogmas of Empiricism'', published in *Journal of Philosophy* 108: 387–415, 2011. I am grateful to Frank Jackson and to the two journals for their permission to use this material.

I am grateful to Stephen Yablo for pointing out affinities between some ideas in my first book and Carnap's research program in 'Modal Rationalism Meets Logical Empiricism' (presented at a conference in Buffalo in 1999), and to Paul Livingston for pointing out others in his 2004 book *Philosophical History and the Problem of Consciousness*. I am indebted to Magdalena Balcerak Jackson, Brendan Balcerak Jackson, Ben Blumson, Yuri Cath, and Daniel Stoljar for their part in a memorable reading group on the *Aufbau* at ANU in 2005. I presented an early version of some of these ideas as a presidential address on 'From the *Aufbau* to the Canberra Plan' to the Australasian Association of Philosophy in 2006, and subsequently as a talk on a number of occasions. I am grateful to audiences on those occasions for their feedback. Thanks also to the Australian Research Council for a Federation Fellowship and two other grants that have supported work on this book.

When David Lewis died in 2001, Steffi Lewis gave me his copy of the *Aufbau*. That book has been my companion in writing this one. David's philosophical influence on this book will be obvious. I am enormously grateful to him and to Steffi for their friendship and support. This book is dedicated to both of them.

Introduction

In his 1814 *Philosophical Essay on Probability*, Pierre-Simon Laplace wrote:

> An intellect which at a certain moment would know all forces that set nature in motion, and all positions of all items of which nature is composed, if this intellect were also vast enough to submit these data to analysis, it would embrace in a single formula the movements of the greatest bodies of the universe and those of the tiniest atom; for such an intellect nothing would be uncertain and the future just like the past would be present before its eyes.

Laplace suggests that given the right basic information, and sufficiently powerful reasoning, all truths about the universe can be determined. For Laplace, this basic information included truths about the fundamental laws of physics and truths about the location of all fundamental entities at a time. Let us call these the *Laplacean truths*. The reasoning requires an idealized 'vast enough intellect', which we might call a *Laplacean intellect*. A Laplacean intellect who knows all the Laplacean truths is a *Laplacean demon*.

The key claim in Laplace's text is that a Laplacean demon would be uncertain of nothing. In effect, Laplace is saying that for any proposition that the demon can entertain, the demon will not be uncertain about that proposition. Or in a small variation: for any proposition the demon can entertain, the demon will be in a position to know whether it is true.

Suppose that there will be an election tomorrow. I can entertain the proposition that the left-wing candidate will win, the proposition that the right-wing candidate will win, and the proposition that the third-party candidate will win. If Laplace's thesis is right, a Laplacean demon in my shoes will be able to know which if any of these propositions is true. If the left-wing candidate will win, the demon will be in a position to know it; if the right-wing candidate will win, the demon will be in a position to know it; if the third-party candidate will win, the demon will be in a position to know it.

Laplace's thesis is an instance of what I call a *scrutability* thesis. It says that the world is in a certain sense comprehensible, at least given a certain class of basic truths about the world. In particular, it says that all truths about the world are *scrutable* from some basic truths. This means roughly that there is a connection in the realm of knowledge between the basic truths and all the rest: given the basic truths, the rest of the truths can be determined.

We might then put a version of Laplace's thesis as follows:

Laplacean Scrutability: For all true propositions *p*, a Laplacean intellect who knew all the Laplacean truths would be in a position to know that *p*.

In the years since Laplace wrote, Laplace's demon has come in for something of a battering. But I think that there remains much value in Laplace's pregnant idea. One can extract some of the value by examining the problems that arise for Laplace's thesis, and by reformulating the scrutability thesis in a way that avoids them.

One sort of problem arises from the information that Laplace allows in the base. Most famously, the apparent failure of determinism in quantum mechanics suggests that the demon could not predict the future just from facts about physical laws and about the present. It may be, for example, that futures in which the left-wing candidate, the right-wing candidate, and the third-party candidate win are all left open by these facts. All three futures could evolve from the present state of the world given the right sort of quantum-mechanical evolution.

There are other limitations. Many have argued that complete physical information is not enough to know all truths about the mind: if Laplace's demon has never experienced colors, for example, it will not know what it is like to see red. Others have argued that complete objective information is not enough to determine perspectival truths about the current time, or one's own identity: even given complete physical information, Laplace's demon might not know that today is Tuesday. Others find gaps for mathematics, morality, and other areas.

To avoid these problems, however, we need only give Laplace's demon more information than Laplace allows. To accommodate nondeterminism, we might give the demon full information about the distribution of fundamental physical entities throughout space and time. To handle problems involving the mind and the self, we might give the demon information about consciousness or the principles governing it, along with information about its own location in spacetime. If there are gaps for mathematics or morality, we can give Laplace's demon mathematical and moral principles as well. It is not clear precisely what information is required, but here the key claim is that there is *some* limited class of base truths that will allow Laplace's demon to do its work.

We might say that a *compact* class of truths is a set of truths that involves only a limited class of concepts and that avoids trivializing mechanisms such as coding the entire state of the world into a single number. I will elaborate on this rough characterization in the first chapter. For now, we can say that the class of physical truths will be a compact class, as will the expanded class of truths suggested above. We can then put a generalized Laplacean thesis as follows:

Inferential Scrutability: There is a compact class of truths such that for all true propositions *p*, a Laplacean intellect who knew all the truths in that class would be in a position to know that *p*.

Inferential Scrutability allows a broader class of base truths than Laplacean Scrutability, but otherwise it shares a similar form. In both theses, the idea is that if the demon knew all the basic truths, it could come to know all the truths, perhaps by inference from those basic truths. For the demon to know all the basic truths, they must be true in the demon's own world. So Inferential Scrutability in effect requires that the demon inhabits our world or one very much like it, knows all the basic truths about it, and comes to know all truths from there.

This requirement gives rise to a second sort of problem for Laplace's demon. In the actual world, we may suppose, one truth is that there are no Laplacean demons. But no Laplacean demon could know that there are no Laplacean demons. To avoid this problem, we could require the demon to know all truths about its own modified world rather than about the actual world. But now the demon has to know about itself, and a number of paradoxes threaten. There are paradoxes of complexity: to know the whole universe, the demon's mind needs to be as complex as the whole universe, even though it is just one part of the universe. There are paradoxes of prediction: the demon will be able to predict its own actions and then try to act contrary to the prediction. And there are paradoxes of knowability: if there is any truth q that the demon never comes to know, perhaps because it never entertains q, then it seems that the demon could never know the true proposition that q is a truth that it does not know.

To avoid these paradoxes, we can think of the demon as lying outside the world it is trying to know. Or better, we can think of the demon as contemplating the universe conditionally: *if* the Laplacean truths obtain, *then* this is what follows. Even if our own world does not contain a demon, we can still ask what a demon in some other world could come to know about our world, if it were given the relevant information in conditional form. Such a demon need not contemplate its own existence. What results is a conditional version of the scrutability thesis.

Conditional Scrutability: There is a compact class of truths such that for all true propositions p, a Laplacean intellect would be in a position to know that *if* the truths in that class obtain, then p.

We can make one final change. A key element of Laplace's idea is that the Laplacean truths are *all* the truths that the demon needs. No other empirical information is needed for the demon to do its job. Here, the idea is that to know the conditional above—*if* the basic truths hold, then p holds—the demon does not need any further empirical information in the background. That is, to know the conditional, the demon need not rely on a posteriori sources such as perception, introspection, or testimony. The demon can know the conditional a priori, or with justification independent of experience. We might put this as follows.

A Priori Scrutability: There is a compact class of truths such that for all true propositions p, a Laplacean intellect would be in a position to know a priori that if the truths in that class obtain, then p.

The three preceding theses are all scrutability theses. They say that there is a compact class of basic truths from which all truths can be determined, given sufficiently powerful reasoning. The A Priori Scrutability thesis is the most important for my purposes, so I will sometimes refer to it as simply 'the scrutability thesis'. But the other theses above will also play a role.

All sorts of questions immediately arise. How can these scrutability theses be made precise? Why should we believe them, and how can one argue for them? Just which truths are among the basic truths, and how small can the basis be? What about hard cases, such as knowledge of social truths, or moral truths, or mathematical truths? What does the scrutability framework tell us about language, thought, knowledge, and reality? All of these questions are pursued in this book.

I suspect that to many readers, the scrutability theses just discussed will seem obvious. I hope that they at least seem plausible to many more. But to paraphrase Russell, philosophy is the art of moving from obvious premises to interesting conclusions. Even if scrutability theses are obvious, there are many interesting conclusions downstream from them. Of course theses requiring only a compact base do not do everything that Laplace's stronger thesis could do. If a demon is given a full specification of how basic physical entities are distributed throughout space and time, for example, then its ability to predict the future is less impressive than it would have been for Laplace's original demon. I think that nevertheless, the weaker thesis is powerful, because of its many applications.

Applications to epistemology, the study of knowledge, are perhaps the most obvious. For example, the scrutability thesis is at least a cousin of the knowability thesis, the thesis that all truths can be known. In addition, I will argue later that a version of the scrutability thesis can help with the problem of skepticism about the external world.

There are also applications in many other areas. In metaphysics, specific versions of the scrutability thesis can be used to help determine what is true and what is fundamental. In the philosophy of science, the scrutability thesis can be used to shed light on reductive explanation and the unity of science. In the philosophy of mind, the scrutability thesis can be used to help understand primitive concepts and the content of thought. And perhaps most importantly, the thesis has powerful applications in the philosophy of language, helping us to analyze notions of meaning and content that are tied to thought and knowledge.

In fact, the scrutability framework bears directly on many of the central debates in philosophy. One version of the thesis can be used to defend a Fregean approach to meaning (an analysis of meaning grounded in rationality and the a priori) over a purely Russellian approach (an analysis grounded in reference and the external world). Another can be used to defend internalism about mental content, defining a sort of content that is largely intrinsic to the subject, against a strong externalism on which all content depends on the environment. Another can be used as a key premise in an argument against materialism about consciousness. Another can be used to deflate many traditional skeptical arguments about knowledge. Another can be used to support a version of structural realism about science.

Different versions of the scrutability thesis are relevant to different applications, so the issues do not all stand and fall together.[1] But in different ways, scrutability provides a powerful fulcrum through which we can gain leverage on these issues. In some cases, one can make related arguments without a direct appeal to scrutability, so the conclusions are not wholly beholden to the scrutability framework and can be cast in different terms. But in every case, thinking in terms of scrutability reframes the issues in a way that can make old, murky problems a little clearer.

The scrutability framework tends in a direction contrary to a number of trends in post-1950 philosophy: trends including direct reference theories of meaning, externalism about mental content, and rejection of the analytic/synthetic distinction. In various respects, it helps to support ideas from an earlier era in philosophy. It supports Gottlob Frege's distinction between sense and reference, and helps provide a concrete account of what Fregean senses are. It coheres well with Bertrand Russell's ideas about constructions of the external world and about the role of acquaintance in thought and knowledge. And above all, it provides support for many key ideas of the great logical empiricist, Rudolf Carnap.

In many ways, Carnap is the hero of this book. Like the other twentieth-century logical empiricists, he is often dismissed as a proponent of a failed research program. But I am inclined to think that Carnap was fundamentally right more often than he was fundamentally wrong. I do not think that he was right about everything, but I think that many of his ideas have been underappreciated. So one might see this project, in part, as aiming for a sort of vindication.

The title of this book is a homage to Carnap's 1928 book *Der logische Aufbau der Welt*, usually translated as either *The Logical Construction of the World* or *The Logical Structure of the World*. The title (like Carnap's?) should be heard as self-consciously absurd. I am not really constructing the world. But one can see the

---

[1] The application to Fregeanism requires a generalization of the A Priori Scrutability thesis already stated, while the other four applications respectively involve what I later call Narrow, Fundamental, Nomic, and Structural Scrutability respectively. The first application is outlined in the eleventh excursus, and the other four applications are discussed in and around chapter 8.

current book as trying to carry off a version of Carnap's project in the *Aufbau*: roughly, constructing a blueprint of the world, or at least constructing a blueprint for a blueprint, by providing a vocabulary in which such a blueprint can be given, and making a case that the blueprint would truly be a blueprint for the world. More specifically, the aim is to specify the structure of the world in the form of certain basic truths from which all truths can be derived. To do this, I think one has to expand Carnap's class of basic truths and change the derivation relation, just as we had to for Laplace. But with these changes made, I think that the project is viable and that some of the spirit of the *Aufbau* remains intact.

I did not set out to write a Carnapian book. Instead, the connections between my project and Carnap's crept up on me to the point where they could not be ignored. The connections to Carnap go beyond the *Aufbau*. The approach to Fregean sense in terms of intensions is very much a descendant of Carnap's approach in *Meaning and Necessity*. The reply to Quine in chapter 5 can be seen as an adaptation of Carnap's analysis in 'Meaning and Synonymy in Natural Language'. My approaches to the unity of science, to ontology, to skepticism, to inferentialism, and to verbal disputes all have something in common with different elements of Carnap's work. In some cases I was not conscious of the connection to Carnap until well into the process, but his presence here is clear all the same.

I should not overstate the extent to which my views and my motivations are Carnap's. I am not a logical empiricist or a logical positivist. I do not share Carnap's sometime inclination toward verificationism and phenomenalism. Where Carnap invokes a semantic notion of analyticity, I invoke an idealized epistemological notion of apriority. Logic plays a less central role for me than for Carnap, and unlike him, I eschew explicit definitional constructions. Carnap would not have approved of my views on the mind–body problem. Where Carnap saw the *Aufbau* as an attempt to make the content of science wholly objective and communicable, vindicating science serves less as a motivation for me, and my version of the project has subjective and nonstructural elements right in the base.

So this book picks up only on certain strands in Carnap, and not on his project as a whole. To oversimplify, one might say that where Carnap leans toward empiricism, I lean toward rationalism. The project as a whole might be seen as a sort of Carnapian rationalism. To some, that label might seem oxymoronic, but this just brings out that there is more to Carnap than traditional caricatures may suggest.

That said, I would like to think that those who share more of Carnap's empiricism than I do will find that there are still many elements of the current picture that they can accept. Later in the book, I discuss ways in which a version of this project might be used to vindicate something quite close to the Carnapian picture, coming as close as possible to the structural and definitional picture in the *Aufbau*.

Here is roughly what happens in this book. Chapter 1 introduces the project using the *Aufbau* as a guide. I go over various objections to the *Aufbau*, and sketch a version of the project that has the potential to overcome all these objections. This chapter in effect motivates and gives an overview of the project of the book as a whole. Chapter 2 goes over preliminaries, formulating scrutability theses in detail and addressing a number of other preliminary issues.

Chapters 3 and 4 mount the core arguments for scrutability. I argue for a limited scrutability thesis concerning the scrutability of all 'ordinary truths' from a certain base. Chapter 3 focuses on Inferential and Conditional Scrutability, using a hypothetical device, the Cosmoscope, to make things vivid. Chapter 4 extends these arguments to A Priori Scrutability. Many epistemological issues come up along the way in these chapters, and numerous objections are addressed.

Chapter 5 uses the framework to respond to Quine's arguments against analyticity and apriority, by providing an analysis of conceptual change. Along the way, it develops a notion of meaning inspired by Carnap and grounded in the scrutability framework. Chapter 6 extends the arguments of chapters 3 and 4 to the scrutability of all truths, by considering various 'hard cases' such as mathematical truths, normative truths, intentional truths, ontological truths, and many others.

Chapters 7 and 8 investigate the character of a scrutability base. Chapter 7 tries to whittle down the base to the smallest possible class, proceeding through various domains to see whether they involve primitive concepts and need to be in the base or whether they can be eliminated. Chapter 8 builds on this to investigate the prospects for certain principled scrutability theses, in part to see to what extent the projects of Carnap and Russell can be vindicated, and in part to develop various applications. I see these two chapters as perhaps the central chapters of the book. Chapter 7 goes over many important issues concerning what should be in the base, while chapter 8 gives a sense of the upshot and rewards of the project. A summation after chapter 8 reviews the prospects for *Aufbau*-like projects, arguing that projects in the spirit of Carnap and Russell look surprisingly good.

Along the way, a series of excursuses after each chapter explore all sorts of connected issues. 'Excursus' is usefully ambiguous between 'a detailed discussion of a particular point in a book, usually in an appendix' and 'a digression in a written text.' Some of my excursuses are detailed discussions of points within the framework. Some of the more important excursuses in this group are the third (on sentential and propositional scrutability), the fifth (on insulated idealization), and the fourteenth (on epistemic rigidity and super-rigidity). Others are digressions that draw connections to the philosophical literature or develop applications. The more important excursuses in this group include the eleventh (on meaning), the fifteenth (on skepticism), and the sixteenth (on metaphysics).

The excursuses can be read in order along with the rest of the book, but they can be read in many different ways, and they can also be skipped as the reader pleases.

I originally intended that this book would contain a ninth chapter on verbal disputes, bringing out a way to use the scrutability framework to help resolve philosophical debates and shedding more light on primitive concepts and the analytic/synthetic distinction. The approach taken there also conveys a more flexible and dynamic version of the framework, without as much philosophical baggage as the earlier chapters. In the end I have left that chapter out: the book is long enough already, and that chapter (which has been published as a separate article) is not quite essential to the overall narrative. Still, I think of that chapter as part of this book in spirit, and it can be found online as part of an extended edition of this book. The same goes for four additional excursuses that I have ended up omitting: on inferentialism and analyticity, Twin-Earthability and narrow content, reference magnets and the grounds of intentionality, and conceptual analysis and ordinary language philosophy.

I have been asked a few times what area of philosophy this book falls into. The answer is not obvious, even to me. The book is an unholy stew of epistemology, philosophy of language, metaphysics, and philosophy of mind, with some philosophy of science and metaphilosophy thrown in along the way. But it approaches each of these areas in a distinctive way and with the other areas in mind.

Scrutability theses concern knowledge, so epistemology is at the heart of the project. But the analysis of knowledge, justification, and related notions, which form the core of contemporary epistemology, are only occasionally in focus here. Rather, I am doing a sort of *metaphysical epistemology* (or should that be epistemological metaphysics?): roughly, epistemology in service of a global picture of the world and of our conception thereof.

The metaphysical epistemology in this book breaks down into a number of components. To a first approximation, the early chapters (especially 3 and 4) focus on *global epistemology*: articulating and supporting general theses about what can be known and about the epistemological relations between truths about the world. The middle part of the book (especially chapter 5 and thereabouts) focuses on *epistemological semantics*: understanding notions of meaning and content that are tied to epistemological notions such as rationality and the a priori. The latter part of the book (chapter 7 onward) focuses on *conceptual metaphysics*: roughly, investigating the structure of our conception of reality, with one eye on how well this structure corresponds to reality itself.

The global epistemology in the early chapters serves as the motor that drives the arguments for scrutability for those who are skeptical. Scrutability theses can be seen as global epistemological theses akin to knowability theses and the like. I start by articulating these theses, and then try to argue for them in detail.

Along the way, a lot of epistemology takes place: epistemological issues about warrant, self-doubt, idealization, skepticism, conditionalization, evidence, recognitional capacities, inference, and the a priori take center stage.

The conceptual metaphysics of chapters 7 and 8 serves as the culmination of the book, giving a sense of the full picture that emerges for those who are sympathetic. Here the aim is to boil down our conception of reality to its most basic elements, isolating primitive elements in which our concepts are grounded, and to draw out consequences for mind, language, and reality. The sixteenth excursus draws out the application to issues in metaphysics, fleshing out the projects of conceptual metaphysics and connecting the epistemological notion of scrutability to the related metaphysical notions of supervenience and grounding.

The epistemological semantics of chapter 5 and the excursuses that follow gives a sense of one important application of the framework. Chapter 5 serves to motivate the framework of epistemically possible scenarios and intensions defined over them. The tenth excursus develops the modal framework in more detail. The eleventh excursus develops the semantic framework a little further and argues that the intensions so defined can play many of the key roles of Fregean senses. In chapter 8, I argue that these intensions can serve as a sort of narrow content of thought.

I sketch semantic applications only briefly in this book, but I develop the semantic applications much further in a forthcoming companion volume, *The Multiplicity of Meaning* (and also in various existing articles on which that book is partly based). Where this book starts with Carnap, that book starts with Frege, developing a Fregean approach to language and an internalist approach to thought. There the framework of epistemic two-dimensional semantics, which is itself grounded in the framework of scrutability, plays a central role. The books are written so that either can be read independently of the other, but I think that they work especially well together. They can be read in either order, proceeding either from epistemological foundations to semantic applications or vice versa.

I expect that there will also be a third book at some point, exploring related issues about modality and metaphysics. That book will develop the framework of epistemically possible scenarios, explore its relationship to the space of metaphysically possible worlds, and explore connections to related metaphysical issues. Between them, these three books can be seen as forming a sort of trilogy on the three vertices of the 'golden triangle' of reason, meaning, and modality.

The ideas in these books have grown indirectly out of some ideas in my 1996 book *The Conscious Mind*. An early version of the scrutability thesis is explored in chapter 2 of that book, as is a version of the two-dimensional semantic framework that plays a central role in *The Multiplicity of Meaning*. Some of the central themes in the early chapters got their initial airing in the 2001 article 'Conceptual Analysis and Reductive Explanation', co-authored with Frank

Jackson, an article that was at least putatively driven by issues about the mind–body problem.

Despite this connection, it would be a mistake to think of this book as intended mainly to provide a foundation for arguments about the metaphysics of consciousness. If I had been trying to bolster those arguments, I would have written a very different book. In this book, purely metaphysical issues (conceptual metaphysics aside) are most often in the background, while epistemological and semantic issues are in the foreground. In a few places I have articulated theses that might connect the epistemology to the metaphysics (notably the Fundamental Scrutability, Apriority/Necessity, and Conceptual/Metaphysical theses), but I have not tried to argue for them at any length. I have devoted much more energy to arguing for weaker scrutability theses that even thoroughgoing physicalists can accept. The stronger theses and associated metaphysical issues come into focus briefly in chapter 8 and the sixteenth excursus, but they will be more central in the book on modality mentioned above.

It would be somewhat closer to the mark to think of this book as intended to provide a foundation for the ideas about two-dimensional semantics that I have developed in other work. It has gradually become clear to me that the key issue here is scrutability: once an appropriate scrutability thesis is accepted (as I argue in the eleventh excursus), a version of the epistemic two-dimensional framework follows. In fact, this book started its life as a chapter or two in *The Multiplicity of Meaning*, before taking on a life of its own. Still, by now I think that the scrutability thesis has interest for all sorts of purposes, and that while the applications to the theory of meaning and content are important, there are certainly many others as well.

I have tried not to assume too much in the way of theoretical principles from the start. Instead, I have tried to proceed by working through cases and mounting arguments to see what sort of theses emerge at the other side. In this way my approach differs from that of Carnap in the *Aufbau*, who starts with a strong structuralist thesis. I was tempted to write another version of this book, one that first articulates one of the principled scrutability theses in chapter 8 and then uses it to drive a construction from the ground up while also defending it from objections. That principled approach would have been more theoretically elegant and cohesive. But the relatively unprincipled approach of the current book has the advantage of letting the chips fall where they may. This way, by the end of the book we are in a position to judge the prospects for numerous different principled approaches.

Of course I do not proceed with complete philosophical neutrality. There is no such thing, and the discussion here is inevitably filtered through my own philosophical sensibilities. Still, I have tried to acknowledge alternative viewpoints where I can, to find a way for opponents to come at least part of the way with me if possible, to argue against them where I can, and to see where they will get off the bus if they must.

My philosophical sensibilities play a role when I consider some of the most famous arguments in recent philosophy: Quine's arguments against analyticity and the a priori, Kripke's arguments against Fregean views, Putnam's and Burge's arguments against internalism. I use the scrutability framework to rebut some of these famous arguments and to limit the consequences of others, thereby defending key elements of the traditional views (internalism, Fregeanism, belief in the a priori, and so on) against which these arguments are directed. I generally take it that the traditional views here have a sort of default status, so that if they are to be rejected it must be on the basis of argument. Because of this way of proceeding, I do not know how much I will do to bring around someone who is entirely unsympathetic with the traditional views, not as a matter of argument but as a matter of starting point. But I am happy enough for now with the conclusion that if these views (or the versions of them that I accept) are wrong, it is for reasons that are interestingly different from the familiar reasons that I argue against.

More generally, it will not surprise me if some of the key conclusions in this book are wrong. Even if ideal reasoners can be certain of the philosophical truth, I am not an ideal reasoner. But I hope that if I am wrong, it is not for old reasons, or not only for old reasons, but also for new and interesting reasons that lead to new and interesting philosophy.

That said, I think of scrutability as supporting a sort of philosophical optimism. Conditional on knowledge of certain fundamental truths and ideal reasoning, everything can be known. In particular, this means that any failures of philosophical knowledge can be ascribed either to the non-ideality of our reasoning or to our ignorance of fundamental truths. Now, it is far from clear to what extent the fundamental truths are knowable, and it is far from clear to what extent we approach the ideal in relevant respects. Still, it is also far from clear that fundamental truths are beyond our grasp, and it is far from clear that reasoning that is needed to determine philosophical truths is beyond our grasp. Philosophy is still young, and the human capacity for reasoning is strong. In a scrutable world, truth may be within reach.

How to Read This Book

It is certainly possible to read this book straight through from start to finish, but the book is long enough that I cannot expect most readers to do that. Some guidance may be helpful, though readers should feel free to ignore it.

Everyone should read the introduction and chapter 1, which introduce the project, and at least browse chapter 8, which discusses conclusions and some applications. For a minimal path in between, it is possible to read just the first section or two of each of the intervening chapters, especially chapters 2, 3, and 7. The remainder of chapters 2–4 formulate and argue for scrutability theses in considerable detail, and it is quite possible to skip this detail on a first reading, although readers who are skeptical about scrutability theses might want to focus here. Chapters 6 and 7 (and to some extent 8) focus on the question of just what needs to be in a scrutability base. Chapter 7 is the more important of the two (and provides useful background to chapter 8), but readers should feel free to skip to the cases that are most interesting to them. Chapters 5 is not essential to the central narrative, but it goes into important foundational issues about the a priori while also developing the application of the framework to the analysis of meaning. Everyone should read the summation after chapter 8, which sums up some main conclusions.

Readers should feel free to dip into the excursuses as they like. Many of them can be read on their own, at least given chapter 1 as background, although there is usually some connection to the preceding chapter. A few of the excursuses (especially 3–7 and 14) go into details that are in principle essential to the theses and arguments of the book, but that in practice can be skipped by those who are not too concerned with the relevant issues. Some others (1–2, 8–9, 13) develop connections to related literature. Further excursuses (especially 10–12 and 15–16) develop applications of the framework to issues about modality, meaning, the unity of science, skepticism, and metaphysics. A number of further applications are outlined in chapter 8.

The six John Locke lectures correspond roughly to portions of chapters 1 (along with the introduction), 3, 4, 5, 6, and 8 (along with the summation) respectively, with some elements of chapters 2 and 7 thrown in along the way, and with almost none of the material from the excursuses.

The extended edition, containing an additional chapter (on verbal disputes) and four additional excursuses (on inferentialism, reference magnets and the grounds of intentionality, conceptual analysis and ordinary language philosophy, and Twin-Earthability) can be found online by searching for 'Constructing the World: Extended Edition'. I have developed a number of relevant points further in various articles, usually cited in the text with just an article title. All of these articles are also available online.

Readers without a background in philosophy will probably find this book hard going, but some relatively accessible material includes the introduction and chapter 1, the material on the Cosmoscope in chapter 3, the first half of chapter 5, and intermittent sections of chapters 6 and 7. A glossary at the end of the book provides a guide both to expressions and theses that I have introduced and to some commonly used philosophical expressions that I deploy.

Issues in many areas of philosophy are discussed in this book. Here I have indicated where to find material especially relevant to certain areas. In what follows '1' stands for chapter 1, '1.1' stands for section 1 of chapter 1, '1.1–2' stands for sections 1 and 2 of chapter 1, 'E1' stands for the first excursus, and so on. Some of these abbreviation formats ('1.1', 'E1') are also used for cross-referencing throughout the book.

Informal epistemology: 2.3, 3.3–4, 3.7, 4, 8.5, E1, E4, E7, E8, E15.
Formal epistemology: 2.4, 4.2, 5.6, 5.7, E5.
Metaphysics and modality: 1.5, 6.4, 6.6, 6.16, 7.3, 7.9, 8.6, E6, E10, E16.
Philosophy of language: 1.1, 1.3, 1.4, 2.2, 5, 6.9-13, E2, E3, E9, E11, E14.
Philosophy of mind: 1.1, 3.7, 6.7, 6.14, 7.4–5, 7.7, 8.3–7, E9, E17.
Philosophy of science: 6.2, 6.15, 7.3, 7.5, 7.8, 8.7, E9, E12.
Carnap and logical empiricism: 1, 3.1, 5, 8, E1, E10, E12, E15.

1

Scrutability and the *Aufbau*

1 Primitive concepts

What are the basic elements of thought? It is common to hold that thoughts, such as *Galahs are pink*, are composed of concepts, such as *galah* and *pink*. It is also common to hold that many concepts are composed from simpler concepts. For example, Aristotle held that 'man' can be defined as 'rational animal'. This suggests that the concept *man* is a complex concept built out of the simpler concepts *rational* and *animal*.

In his manuscript 'De Alphabeto Cogitationum Humanarum', Leibniz suggests that there is a level of concepts so simple that they make up an alphabet from which all thoughts can be composed:

> The alphabet of human thoughts is a catalog of primitive concepts, that is, of those things that we cannot reduce to any clearer definitions.[1]

In *An Essay Concerning Human Understanding*, John Locke develops such a picture. He introduces complex ideas (or concepts) as follows:

> As simple ideas are observed to exist in several combinations united together, so the mind has a power to consider several of them united together as one idea; and that not only as they are united in external objects, but as itself has joined them together. Ideas thus made up of several simple ones put together, I call complex;—such as are beauty, gratitude, a man, an army, the universe. (Locke 1690, book 2, chapter 12)

Locke held that all of our perception and thought derives from simple ideas. At one point in the *Essay* (book 2, chapter 21), he suggests that the most basic ideas come down to eight. Three are ideas of matter that come to us through our senses: *extension*, *solidity*, and *mobility* (the power of being moved). Two are ideas

---

[1] Translated from Leibniz's 'De Alphabeto Cogitationum Humanarum' (A 6.4.270), written around 1679–81. Thanks to Brandon Look for the translation.

of mind that come to us through reflection: *perceptivity* (the power of perception or thinking) and *motivity* (the power of moving). The last three are neutral ideas that come to us both ways: *existence, duration*, and *number*.

The same theme can be found in some parts of contemporary cognitive science. The linguist Anna Wierzbicka, for example, has argued that every expression in every human language can be analyzed in terms of a limited number of 'semantic primes' that occur in every language. In her 1972 book *Semantic Primitives*, Wierzbicka proposed 14 semantic primes, but by her 2009 book *Experience, Evidence, and Sense* these had expanded to the following list of 63 primes.

Substantives: *I, you, someone, something/thing, people, body.*
Relation substantives: *kind, part.*
Determiners: *this, the same, other/else.*
Quantifiers: *one, two, some, all, much/many.*
Evaluators: *good, bad.*
Descriptors: *big, small.*
Mental predicates: *think, know, want, feel, see, hear.*
Speech: *say, words, true.*
Actions and events: *do, happen, move, touch.*
Existence, possession: *to be (somewhere), there is, to have, to be (someone/something).*
Life and death: *live, die.*
Time: *when/time, now, before, after, a long time, a short time, for some time, in a moment.*
Space: *where/place, here, above, below, far, near, side, inside.*
Logic: *not, maybe, can, because, if.*
Augmentors: *very, more.*
Similarity: *like.*

Wierzbicka's methods have been used to analyze an extraordinary range of expressions in many different languages. To give the flavor of the project, a sample analysis (from Goddard 2003, p. 408) runs as follows.

X *lied* to Y =
X said something to person Y;
X knew it was not true;
X said it because X wanted Y to think it was true;
people think it is bad if someone does this.

In twentieth-century philosophy, this sort of framework was developed most systematically by Bertrand Russell and Rudolf Carnap.[2] Russell suggested that

---

[2] Russell engaged in numerous different projects of analysis and construction. Some central works concerning analysis into primitives involving acquaintance include 'Knowledge by Acquaintance and Knowledge by Description' (1911), *The Problems of Philosophy* (1912), and 'Theory of Knowledge' (1913). He pursued related projects of constructing the world from primitives

all concepts are composed from concepts of objects and properties with which we are directly acquainted. For Russell, these concepts included concepts of sense-data and certain universals, and at certain points in his writings, a concept of oneself. All other concepts were to be analyzed as constructions out of these concepts. For example, concepts of other people and of objects in the external world were to be analyzed as descriptions built up from these basic elements.

In *Der logische Aufbau der Welt*, Carnap pushed the project of analysis to its limit. Carnap argued that all concepts can be constructed from a single primitive concept, along with logical concepts. Carnap's primitive concept was a concept of the relation of phenomenal similarity: similarity in some respect between total experiences (roughly, momentary slices of a stream of consciousness) had by a subject at different times.[3] For example, if a subject has two experiences both involving a certain shade of red, the experiences will stand in this relation of similarity. Using this simple concept, Carnap gave explicit constructions of many other concepts applying to experiences. For example, concepts of specific sensory qualities, such as that of a certain shade of red, are defined in terms of chains or circles of similarity between experiences.

In Carnap's framework, these concepts are used to build up all of our concepts of the external world. Spatial and temporal concepts are defined in terms of sensory qualities. Properties of external bodies are defined in terms of spatial and temporal properties. Behavior is defined in terms of the motion of bodies. Mental states of other people are defined in terms of behavior. Cultural notions are defined in terms of these mental states and behavior. And so on.[4]

Carnap's project, like most of the other projects above, is committed to what we can call a *Definability* thesis. Like the other theses I discuss in this chapter, this thesis is cast in terms of expressions (linguistic items such as words) rather than in terms of concepts (mental or abstract items) for concreteness.

Definability: There is a compact class of primitive expressions such that all expressions are definable in terms of that class.

I will say more about compactness later, but for now we can think of this as requiring a small class of expressions. For most of the *Aufbau*, the class of primitive expressions included an expression for phenomenal similarity and

---

in numerous later works, such as 'The Philosophy of Logical Atomism' (1918). Also worth mentioning is Ludwig Wittgenstein's conception of the world as the totality of atomic facts in his *Tractatus Logico-Philosophicus* (1921), although Wittgenstein says less than Carnap and Russell about the character of his primitives and about the construction of ordinary concepts.

[3] In this book 'phenomenal' always means 'experiential': roughly, pertaining to conscious experiences.

[4] It must be acknowledged that the details are sometimes sketchy. See the start of chapter 6 for an illustration of Carnap's treatment of culture.

logical expressions ('not', 'and', 'exists', and the like). Late in the *Aufbau*, Carnap went on to argue that phenomenal similarity is itself dispensable: it can itself be defined in logical terms. If so, then primitive expressions can be restricted to logical expressions, and all other expressions can be defined in terms of these. Of course the general program of definability is not committed to as strong a claim as this.

We can say that an expression E is definable in terms of a class of expressions C if there is an adequate definition statement with E on the left-hand side and only expressions in C on the right hand side. We then need to say what a definition statement is, and what it is for such a statement to be adequate.

A definition statement connects a left-hand side involving a defined expression E to a right-hand side, with a logical form that depends on the grammatical category of E. Various different logical forms might be required, but the differences will not matter for our purposes. As an example, definition statements for singular terms, general terms, and predicates might be required to specify the extension of E (roughly, the entity or entities in the world that E applies to) in a form akin to the following: 'For all x, x is Hesperus if and only if x is the brightest object visible in the evening sky'; 'For all x, x is a bachelor if and only if x is an unmarried man'. If such definition statements are adequate, then 'Hesperus' is definable in terms of 'brightest', 'evening', and so on, and 'bachelor' is definable in terms of 'unmarried', 'man', and so on.

What is it for a definition statement to be adequate? Here, there are various possible criteria. Certainly one should require at least *extensional* adequacy: that is, definitions of the sort above must be true, so that the extensions of the relevant expressions on the left and right sides are the same. But typically more is required. Suppose that as it happens, all bachelors in our world are untidy men and vice versa. Then 'For all x, x is a bachelor if and only if x is an untidy man' is true, and the definition statement is extensionally adequate. Still, this statement does not seem to give an adequate definition of 'bachelor'.

To handle these cases, it is common to require some form of stronger-than-extensional, or *intensional*, adequacy for a definition. For example, it is often required that a definition statement be analytic (true in virtue of meaning), a priori (knowable without justification from experience), and/or necessary (true in all possible worlds). A definition of 'bachelor' in terms of 'untidy man' does not meet these conditions: 'all bachelors are untidy men' is not true in virtue of meaning, one cannot know a priori that all bachelors are untidy men, and it is not true in all possible worlds that all bachelors are untidy men. But it is at least arguable that a definition of 'bachelor' in terms of 'unmarried man' meets these conditions.

A surprising and often-overlooked feature of the *Aufbau* is that Carnap there requires only that definitions be extensionally adequate. Carnap intended the *Aufbau* to shed light on knowledge and on meaning, but it is questionable whether definitions that are merely extensionally adequate can fulfill these epistemological and semantic goals. For example, while a definition of 'bachelor' as 'unmarried man' may shed some light on the meaning of 'bachelor' and on how we come to knows truths about bachelors, the same does not seem true of a definition as 'untidy man', even if that definition is extensionally adequate. In the preface to the second edition of the *Aufbau*, Carnap says that this is the greatest mistake in the project, and says that definitions should be held to a stronger, intensional, criterion of adequacy. Certainly much of the *Aufbau* can be read with a stronger criterion of adequacy in mind.[5]

The stronger criteria of analyticity, apriority, and necessity ensure that an expression and its definition are connected semantically (that is, in the realm of meaning), epistemologically (in the realm of knowledge), and modally (in the realm of necessity and possibility). Further potential criteria include psychological criteria, to the effect that a definition somehow reflects the psychological processes involved in understanding and using an expression; formal criteria, to the effect that definitions have a certain limited complexity; conceptual criteria, to the effect that the expressions used in the definition express concepts that are more basic (in some relevant sense) than the concept expressed by the original expression; and so on.

Definitions allow us to connect sentences in different vocabularies. Given a definition of bachelors as unmarried men, truths such as 'John is a bachelor' will be logically entailed by truths such as 'John is an unmarried man' along with the definition. More generally, given certain assumptions about the language,[6] any statement containing 'bachelor' will be logically entailed by a corresponding sentence containing 'unmarried man' in place of 'bachelor' (with the rest of the sentence as before), along with the definition. Given these assumptions, the Definability Thesis leads to the following thesis:

Definitional Scrutability: There is a compact class of truths from which all truths are definitionally scrutable.

---

[5] Carnap sometimes explicitly invokes stronger criteria in the *Aufbau*. For example (as Chris Pincock pointed out to me), in section 49 he suggests a method according to which constructional definitions for scientific objects are determined by their epistemological 'indicators'.

[6] We can assume that every natural-language sentence has a *regimentation* into an equivalent sentence with a clarified logical form. One can then apply definitional and logical machinery to regimented sentences in the first instance, and derivatively to unregimented sentences. If definitions are required only to be extensionally adequate, it suffices to assume that the language and the logic are extensional: that is, the logic allows one to substitute coextensive expressions (given a statement of coextensiveness), and this substitution will not change truth-values in the language. If definitions are required to be intensionally adequate, it suffices to assume that the language and the logic are intensional to the same degree (definitions will then need to contain a statement of cointensiveness, such as 'Necessarily, bachelors are unmarried men'). The language may also be hyperintensional, so that cointensive expressions are not intersubstitutable in certain contexts, as long as these contexts can themselves be defined in an extensionally/intensionally adequate way ('For all x, x believes that such-and-such if...').

Here, a truth is a true sentence.[7] A compact class of truths, to a first approxi-mation, is a class of truths involving only a small class of expressions. A sentence S is definitionally scrutable from (or definitionally entailed by) a class of sen-tences C if S can be logically derived from some members of C and some ade-quate definition sentences. For example, given the relevant assumptions, sentences involving 'bachelor' are definitionally scrutable from sentences involv-ing 'unmarried man'. If we repeat this process for every definable expression, we can eventually translate every sentence of the language into a sentence in the primitive vocabulary, and the original statement will be entailed by the trans-formed sentence conjoined with a number of definitions.

On the *Aufbau* view, all truths are definitionally scrutable from a class of truths about the phenomenal similarity relation. In fact, Carnap holds that there is a single *world-sentence* D that definitionally entails all truths. The world-sen-tence says that there exist entities that are related in such-and-such fashion by the phenomenal similarity relation R. If there are just two dissimilar total experi-ences in the world, then the world-sentence will be a sentence saying that there are two entities that stand in R to themselves but not to each other: $\exists x, y \, (Rxx \,\&\, Ryy \,\&\, {\sim}Rxy \,\&\, {\sim}Ryx \,\&\, \forall w \, (w = x \lor w = y) \,\&\, {\sim}(x = y))$. If there are more total experiences than this, then there will be a longer world sentence, specify-ing the similarity relations that do and do not hold among the total experiences.

According to Carnap's stronger view late in the *Aufbau*, the previous world-sentence D is definitionally entailed by an even more austere world sentence D', using purely logical vocabulary. To get from D to D', Carnap defines away the single nonlogical vocabulary item R as that relation that makes the previous world-sentence D true.[8] If this is correct, then the highly austere truth D' defini-tionally entails all truths.

If we require that adequate definitions are a priori (knowable independently of experience), as is common, then Definitional Scrutability entails the following thesis:

A Priori Scrutability: There is a compact class of truths from which all truths are a priori scrutable.[9]

---

[7] The choice of sentences rather than propositions here is discussed in 2.2. A subtlety here (discussed at length in the third excursus) is that not all sentences are true or false independent of context. For example, there may be no context-independent fact of the matter about whether a sentence such as 'I am hungry' or 'John is tall' is true. Where context-dependent sentences are concerned, we can talk instead of the scrutability of sentences in contexts.

[8] For the world-sentence just specified, R will be defined as that relation R' such that: $\exists x, y \, (R'xx \,\&\, R'yy \,\&\, {\sim}R'xy \,\&\, {\sim}R'yx \,\&\, {\sim}\forall w \, (w = x \lor w = y) \,\&\, {\sim}(x = y))$. Then the new world-sentence will be the resulting of replacing R everywhere in the world-sentence above by this definition. Or more straightforwardly, the world-sentence can simply say $\exists R', x, y \, (R'xx \,\&\, R'yy \,\&\, {\sim}R'xy \,\&\, {\sim}R'yx \,\&\, {\sim}\forall w \, (w = x \lor w = y) \,\&\, {\sim}(x = y))$.

[9] A more elaborate definition of a priori scrutability is given in 2.5, and a more elaborate dis-cussion of what it is for a sentence to be a priori is in 4.1.

We can define a priori scrutability in parallel to definitional entailment: a sentence S is a priori scrutable from (or a priori entailed by) a class of sentences C if S can be logically derived from some members of C along with some a priori truths. Given weak assumptions,[10] the right-hand side is equivalent to the claim that there is a conjunction D of sentences in C such that the material conditional 'If D, then S' (which is equivalent to '$\sim(D \,\&\, \sim S)$') is a priori.

One can characterize Analytic and Necessary Scrutability theses in a parallel way. If we require that adequate definitions are analytic or necessary respectively, then these theses will follow from Definitional Scrutability.

It is theses such as A Priori and Analytic Scrutability that give the definitional program its epistemological bite. To a first approximation, these theses suggest that knowledge of the base truths about the world might serve as a basis for knowledge of all truths about the world.

To make this vivid: suppose that Laplace's demon is given all the base truths about our world. Given Definitional Scrutability, then as long as the demon knows all the definitions and can engage in arbitrary logical reasoning, then the demon will be able to deduce all truths about the world. Given A Priori Scrutability, then as long as the demon can engage in arbitrary a priori reasoning, then it will be able to deduce all truths about the world. For example, if Carnap is right, then the demon should be able to derive all truths about the world from a world sentence such as D or D'.

2 Objections to the *Aufbau*

The *Aufbau* is widely held to be a failure. It is also widely held that no project like it can succeed. These doubts have a number of sources. Perhaps the best-known problems for the *Aufbau* are arguments that Carnap's primitive vocabulary cannot do the work it needs to do. Two of these are specific criticisms of Carnap's constructions from phenomenal vocabulary, while another two are general criticisms of constructions from phenomenal vocabulary or from logical vocabulary.

First: In *The Structure of Appearance* (1951), Nelson Goodman argued that Carnap's definition of sensory qualities in terms of the primitive of recollected

---

[10] In one direction, it suffices to assume that all conjunctions are logically derivable from their conjuncts (this is trivial in the finite case, but slightly less trivial if infinite conjunctions are allowed, as may be necessary for some purposes). In the other direction, it suffices to assume that when B is logically derivable from a set A of premises, a conditional 'If D then B' is a priori, where D is a conjunction of the premises in A, and that a priori conjuncts can be detached from the antecedents of a priori conditionals without loss of apriority.

phenomenal similarity is unsuccessful, as there can be circles of similarity among total experiences that do not correspond to a single sensory quality. One problem raised by Goodman is that of 'imperfect community': a similarity circle can satisfy Carnap's definition of a sensory quality even when some members of the circle share one quality (phenomenal redness, say) and others share another quality (phenomenal blueness). Another problem is that of 'companionship': if two distinct qualities always occur together in total experiences, Carnap's definition will not distinguish them.

Second: In 'Two Dogmas of Empiricism' (1951), W. V. Quine argued that Carnap's definition of spacetime points in terms of the phenomenal field is unsuccessful, as it requires nonphenomenal notions that violate his own criteria of adequacy. Carnap defined 'Quality q is at x, y, z, t' by specifying certain principles for assigning qualities to spacetime points that must be obeyed as well as possible, but this does not yield a definition that can be cast entirely in terms of phenomenal notions and logic.

Third: In 'The Problem of Empiricism' (1948), Roderick Chisholm gives a general argument against phenomenalism: the view that statements about the external world can be definitionally analyzed in purely phenomenal terms. On a phenomenalist view, 'There is a doorknob in front of me' (P) must be analyzed as a complex conditional along the lines of 'If I had certain experiences, certain other experiences would follow' (R): for example, 'If I experience a certain sort of attempt to grasp, I would experience a certain sort of contact'. Chisholm argues that no such R is entailed by P, as one can always find a further sentence S (e.g. specifying that one is paralyzed and subject to certain sorts of delusions of grasping that are never accompanied by experiences of contact) that is consistent with P such that $S \& P$ entails $\sim R$. If so, no phenomenalist analysis of P can succeed.

Fourth: In 'Mr. Russell's Causal Theory of Perception' (1928), the mathematician Max Newman pointed out a general problem for the more ambitious project of reducing the primitive vocabulary to logical structure alone. The problem was pointed out simultaneously by Carnap himself late in the *Aufbau*.[11] Given a purely logical vocabulary, the ultimate world-sentence (like D' above) will specify simply that there exist certain objects, properties, and relations that stand in certain patterns of instantiation and co-instantiation. Newman and Carnap observe that as long as we are liberal enough about what we count as a property or a relation, this world-sentence will be satisfied almost vacuously.[12] Carnap responds by suggesting that the properties and relations in question must be

---

[11] Carnap marks these sections of the *Aufbau* (153–55) 'can be omitted', quite remarkably given the centrality of these sections to the logical structure project. For further discussion of Newman's problem and the *Aufbau*, see Demopolous and Friedman 1985.

[12] In particular, as long as there is a property corresponding to any set of objects, and a relation corresponding to any set of ordered pairs, then the world-sentence S will be satisfied by any set of

restricted to 'natural' (or 'founded', or 'experiencable') properties and relations. This requires an expansion of the primitive vocabulary, which Carnap justifies by suggesting that 'natural' is a logical term. Few have found this latter suggestion convincing, however.

Still, it is clear that criticisms of this sort threaten only *Aufbau*-style projects that involve phenomenal and/or logical bases. To avoid the problems, one need only expand the primitive basis. One can avoid Newman's problem by allowing almost any nonlogical vocabulary. One can avoid Goodman's problem by allowing expressions for specific sensory qualities. One can avoid Quine's and Chisholm's problems by allowing spatiotemporal expressions into the basic vocabulary directly, or perhaps by allowing expressions for causal relations.[13]

One might wonder whether expanding the base like this is in the spirit of the *Aufbau*. For many years, the popular conception of logical empiricism has focused on a commitment to phenomenalism and verificationism (views on which a phenomenal base is central), and the *Aufbau* has been regarded as a paradigm of that tradition.[14] In reality, these views do not play a central role in the *Aufbau*. A much more important role is played by Carnap's commitment to structuralism and objectivity in developing a language for science. Carnap himself says that the choice of a phenomenal basis in the *Aufbau* is somewhat arbitrary, and that he could equally have started with a physical basis. A base with expressions for specific sensory qualities or specific physical properties (such as

---

the right size. To see this, suppose that one set A of size n satisfies S, and let A' be any other set with the same size. Take a group of properties and relations that relate the members of A in the pattern specified by S. Map those properties and relations to a corresponding set of properties and relations on A' by a one-to-one mapping. (Any one-to-one mapping will do; the liberalness claim will ensure that every property maps to a property, and so on.) Then the resulting properties and relations will relate the members of A' in the same pattern. So S will be satisfied by A. It follows that S cannot entail any truths that specify features of the world beyond its cardinality.

[13] Even while retaining a phenomenal base, Carnap has some options in avoiding the first three problems. Carnap's construction is defended against Goodman and Quine by Thomas Mormann (2003, 2004), while a different construction from an expanded phenomenal base is explored by Hannes Leitgeb (2011).

[14] The distortions in the popular conception of the *Aufbau* and logical empiricism are explained partly by simplified versions promulgated by A. J. Ayer and W. V. Quine, and partly by a post-*Aufbau* period in the Vienna Circle in which phenomenal reductions involving protocol sentences played a more crucial role. Within a few years of that period (for example, in his 1932 work 'The Physical Language as the Universal Language of Science') Carnap had moved on again to a view on which physical language rather than phenomenal language plays the crucial role in reduction. In recent years, the flourishing scholarly literature on the *Aufbau* and logical empiricism, including Alberto Coffa's *The Semantic Tradition from Kant to Carnap* (1985), Michael Friedman's *Reconsidering Logical Positivism* (1999), Alan Richardson's *Carnap's Construction of the World* (1998), and Thomas Uebel's *Overcoming Logical Positivism from Within* (1992), among other works, has painted a picture that is much more nuanced than the popular caricature.

spatiotemporal properties) might not fully vindicate Carnap's structuralism, but as I discuss in chapter 8, there are other bases that come even closer to fulfilling Carnap's goals. In any case, expanded bases have the potential to fulfill many of the more general aims of a project of definability, while avoiding the criticisms above.

Other doubts about the project of the *Aufbau* are driven not by Carnap's basic vocabulary but by his construction method: that is, by his method of deriving nonbasic truths from basic truths using definitions. A number of doubts about definitions have been influential.

First: In 'Verifiability' (1945), Friedrich Waismann argued that purported definitions of ordinary expressions are subject to the problem of *open texture*: these definitions are always subject to correction, as we cannot foresee all possibilities to which they might apply. Every definition 'stretches into an open horizon', and no definition of an empirical term will cover all possibilities. Waismann's argument was especially directed at definitions in the style of logical empiricism that appeal to methods of verification, but his underlying point applies quite generally.

Second: In the *Philosophical Investigations* (1953), Ludwig Wittgenstein suggested that when we apply a term such as 'game' to some things, there is no single condition that they all satisfy. 'Game' is a family resemblance term, with different sorts of games resembling each other in various respects and with no common core. There is merely a 'complicated network of similarities, overlapping and criss-crossing'. Many have taken this idea to suggest that there are no definitions giving necessary and sufficient conditions associated with ordinary expressions of this sort.

Third: In 'Two Dogmas of Empiricism' (1951), Quine gave a critique of the notion of definition and more generally of the analytic/synthetic distinction He argued that standard understandings of these notions are circular and that the notions are based on a misconceived picture of language and its relation to the world. This critique has led many to doubt that a substantial distinction between the analytic and the synthetic, or between the a priori and the a posteriori, or between the definitional and the nondefinitional, can be drawn. If these doubts are correct, then any *Aufbau*-like project that involves these notions must fail.

Fourth: In *Naming and Necessity* (1980), Saul Kripke argued against descriptivism: the thesis that names are equivalent to descriptions. Kripke's modal argument makes a case that for an ordinary name (e.g. 'Aristotle') and an associated description (e.g. 'the teacher of Alexander'), the name and the description are not necessarily equivalent. Kripke's epistemic argument makes a case that for an ordinary name (e.g. 'Gödel') and an associated description (e.g. 'the man who proved the incompleteness of arithmetic'), the name and the description are not a priori equivalent. If these arguments succeed, then it appears that no *Aufbau*-like definitional project that applies to names and that invokes necessity or apriority as a condition of adequacy can succeed.

These criticisms mainly threaten an *Aufbau*-style project whose construction relation requires definitions of nonbasic expressions. Just as we can get around the first class of problems by expanding the base, we can get around the second class of problems by weakening the construction relation.

Before doing that, however, it is useful to look more closely at the source of the problems. At least three of the critiques (Waismann's, Wittgenstein's, and Kripke's) turn on a common problem: the problem of *counterexamples*. (Quine's critique turns on somewhat different issues, and I return to it in Chapter 5.) For many terms in English, it seems that every definition that has ever been offered is subject to counterexamples: actual or possible cases to which the original term applies but the purported definition does not, or vice versa, thereby showing that the definition is inadequate.

The most famous case is the case of 'knowledge', traditionally defined as 'justified true belief'. In his 1963 paper 'Is Knowledge Justified True Belief?', Edmund Gettier pointed out counterexamples to this purported definition. Suppose that Smith has a justified belief that Jones owns a Ford, and deduces that Jones owns a Ford or Brown is in Barcelona. And let us say that Jones has recently sold his Ford, and that Brown is in fact in Barcelona, though Smith has no information about either of these things. Then Smith has a justified true belief that Jones owns a Ford or Brown is in Barcelona, but this justified true belief is not knowledge. So knowledge cannot be defined as justified true belief.

In Gettier's wake, others attempted to modify the definition of knowledge to avoid these counterexamples, for example suggesting that knowledge can be defined as justified true belief that is not essentially grounded in a falsehood. But other counterexamples ensued: if I see the one real barn in an area of fake barns, and form the belief that I am seeing a barn, then this is a justified true belief not essentially grounded in a falsehood, but it is not knowledge. A parade of further attempted definitions and further counterexamples followed (Shope's *The Analysis of Knowing* gives an exhaustive summary). Eventually definitions with fourteen separate clauses were proffered, with no end to the counterexamples in sight.

What goes for 'knowledge' seems to go for most expressions in the English language. Given any purported definition of 'chair', or 'run', or 'happy', it is easy to find counterexamples. For some scientific terms such as 'gold' or 'electron', there may be true definition statements ('Gold is the element with atomic number 79'), but these do not appear to be a priori. For Wierzbicka's definition of 'lie', above, counterexamples are not hard to find: I can tell a lie even if I do not care whether the hearer believes me.[15] And even in the case of 'bachelor',

---

[15] A philosopher will find possible counterexamples to many or most of Wierzbicka's definitions. Wierzbicka's intended criteria of adequacy for definitions almost certainly differ from philosophers' criteria, so it is not obvious to what extent the existence of counterexamples is a problem for Wierzbicka's project.

there are unmarried men who do not seem to be bachelors, such as those in long-term domestic partnerships. The only clearly definable expressions appear to be derived expressions (such as 'unhappy' and 'caught'), which can arguably be defined in terms of the expressions ('happy' and 'catch') that they are derived from, along with some technical expressions that have been introduced through definitions, and a handful of others.

The philosophical flight from definitions has been paralleled by a similar flight in cognitive science. Contemporary psychologists almost universally reject the so-called classical view of concepts, according to which most concepts are associated with sets of necessary and sufficient conditions. A major influence here is work by Eleanor Rosch (1975) and others on concepts such as that of a bird, suggesting that subjects classify various creatures as birds in a graded way according to their similarity to various prototypes rather than by necessary and sufficient conditions.[16] By and large, the classical view has been supplanted by views on which concepts involve prototypes, exemplars, and theories, among other views. On few of these views is it required that concepts are associated with definitions.

It remains possible that for these expressions, there exists an adequate definition that has not yet been found. In philosophy, the search for definitions typically runs out of steam once purported definitions reach a certain length. In psychology, it is not out of the question that prototype theories and the like might be used to deliver something like a definition, perhaps cast in terms of weighted similarities to certain prototypes or exemplars. Likewise, theory-based accounts of concepts might yield definitions of various concepts in terms of clusters of associated theoretical roles. Still, it is far from obvious that such definitions will exist, and even if they do exist, they will be so unwieldy that they will be quite unlike definitions as traditionally conceived. As a result, the definitional program has been put to one side in most areas of philosophy and psychology in recent years.

3 From definitional to a priori scrutability[17]

Even if Definitional Scrutability is false, there remains a strong case for other scrutability theses. For example, even if expressions such as 'knowledge' and 'chair' are not definable in terms of more primitive expressions, it remains plausible that there is some strong epistemological relation between truths

---

[16] A distinct anti-definition influence in psychology derives from psycholinguistic arguments for the conclusion that lexical concepts are primitive by Jerry Fodor et al. (1980).

[17] This section overlaps in part with Chalmers and Jackson 2001.

involving these expressions and truths involving more primitive expressions. In particular, it is striking that in many cases, specifying a situation in terms of expressions that do not include 'knowledge' or its cognates (synonyms or near-synonyms) enables us to determine whether or not the case involves knowledge. Likewise, correctly describing an object in terms of expressions that do not include 'chair' or its cognates may enable us to determine whether or not it is a chair. And so on.

For example, in the Gettier situation we are told something like:

'Smith believes with justification that Jones owns a Ford. Smith also believes that Jones owns a Ford or Brown is in Barcelona, where this belief is based solely on a valid inference from his belief that Jones owns a Ford. Jones does not own a Ford, but as it happens, Brown is in Barcelona.'

Let the conjunction of these sentences be *G*. *G* does not contain the term 'know' or any cognates. But when presented with *G*, we are then in a position to determine that the following sentence *K* is false:

'Smith knows that Jones owns a Ford or Brown is in Barcelona.'

Something like this happens throughout philosophy, psychology, and other areas. We are given a description *D* of a scenario without using a key term *E*, and we are asked to determine whether and how the expression *E* applies to it. This is the key method for experimental work on concepts in psychology: an experimenter presents a description (or perhaps a picture) of a case, subjects are asked to classify it under a concept, and they usually can do so. The same goes for conceptual analysis in philosophy: one considers a specific case, considers the question of whether it is a case of an *F*, and one comes to a judgment. Often we have no trouble doing so.

In fact, this method of cases is precisely how counterexamples to definitions are often generated. When someone suggests that *E* can be defined as *F* ('bachelor' is defined as 'unmarried man', say), someone else suggests a scenario *D* (involving long-term gay couples, say) to which *F* applies but *E* does not, or vice versa. The Gettier case fits this pattern perfectly. Despite the absence of definitions, there is some form of scrutability present in these cases: once we know *G*, we are in a position to know ~*K*, and so on.

In many cases, it is plausible that the scrutability is a priori. For example, in the Gettier case, it is plausible that one can know the material conditional 'If *G*, then ~*K*' a priori. Someone who knows that *G* is true and who has mastered the concepts involved in *K* (in particular the concept of knowledge) is thereby in a position to know that *K* is false, even if they lack any further relevant empirical information. That is, mastery of the concept of knowledge (along with a grasp of the other concepts involved) and rational reflection suffices to eliminate the possibility that both *G* and *K* are true.

On the face of things, Gettier's argument was an a priori argument, in which empirical information played no essential role, and its conclusion is a paradigmatic example of a non-obvious a priori truth. The argument proceeds by presenting the hypothesis that *G* holds, and appealing to the reader's possession of the concept of knowledge to make the case that if *G* holds, ~*K* holds (and *J* holds, where *J* is a corresponding positive claim about Smith's justified true belief). Empirical information plays no essential role in justifying belief in this conditional, so the conditional is a priori. The a priori conditional itself plays an essential role in deriving the a priori conclusion.

This brings out a key point: a priori scrutability does not require definability. One might think that for a sentence *B* to be a priori entailed by a sentence *A*, the terms in *B* must be definable using the terms of *A*. However, this thesis is false. The a priori entailment from 'There exists a red ball' to 'There exists a colored ball' is one counterexample: 'colored' cannot be defined in terms of 'red' and the other terms involved. But the case above is another counterexample. At least once general skepticism about the a priori is set aside, 'If *G* then ~*K*' is a central example of an a priori truth. But at the same time, we have seen that there is little reason to think that there is an adequate definition of 'knowledge', whether in the terms involved in *G* or any other terms.

As before, it could be that there is an adequate definition that has not yet been produced, or that has been produced but overlooked. Someone might even hold that all these a priori conditionals are underwritten by our tacit grasp of such a definition. But even if so, it seems clear that the a priori entailment from *G* to ~*K* is not dialectically hostage to an explicit analysis of knowledge that would support the entailment. That is, we can have reason to accept that there is an a priori entailment here even without having reason to accept that there is an explicit analysis that supports the entailment.

If anything, the moral of the Gettier discussion is the reverse: at least dialectically, the success of a definition itself depends on a priori judgments concerning specific cases, or equivalently, on a priori judgments about certain conditionals. The Gettier literature shows repeatedly that purported definitions are hostage to specific counterexamples, where these counterexamples involve a priori judgments about hypothetical cases. So a priori conditionals seem to be prior to definitions at least in matters of explicit justification. Our judgments about a priori conditionals do not need judgments about definitions to justify them, and are not undermined by the absence of definitions.

It might be suggested that our conditional judgments here require at least explicit *sufficient* conditions for knowledge or its absence: for example, the condition that a belief based solely on inference from a false belief is not knowledge. It is trivial that there is a sufficient condition in the vicinity of such an entailment (the antecedent provides one such), so the claim will be interesting only if the complete set of sufficient conditions for knowledge is not huge and open-ended. But the Gettier literature suggests precisely that the set of sufficient conditions for knowledge is open-ended in this way; if it were not, we would have a satisfactory definition. And as before, the a priori entailments are not dialectically hostage to the proposed sufficient conditions. Rather, at least in common practice, proposed sufficient conditions are hostage to a priori intuitions about specific cases.

It may even be that there are no short nontrivial sufficient conditions for knowledge. That is, it may be that any reasonably short condition not involving 'know' or cognates is compatible with the absence of knowledge.[18] Not every expression is like this. For example, there are plausibly short sufficient conditions for *not* knowing that p: the condition of not believing that p, or of believing that p based solely on inference from a false belief. But it may be that for many expressions, there are at least hypothetical cases for which there is no reasonably short nontrivial sufficient condition (perhaps even no finite sufficient condition) obtaining in that case. In such a case, a nontrivial sufficient condition must be a long one: in the limit, a fully detailed specification of such a scenario, perhaps in the language of a scrutability base. All this is quite consistent with A Priori Scrutability, but it does bring out the need for idealization in understanding the thesis.

An opponent of A Priori Scrutability may hold that there are not even long nontrivial sufficient conditions for knowledge and the like, or that any sufficient conditions here do not yield a priori scrutability. These remain separate substantive issues, distinct from the standard objections to Definability and addressed in the arguments for A Priori Scrutability in later chapters. For present purposes, it suffices to observe that the standard objections to Definability are not objec-

---

[18] See Williamson 2000 for discussion of this point in the context of knowledge. Williamson 2007 suggests that common descriptions of Gettier cases do not suffice for the absence of knowledge, for example because there are deviant cases compatible with these descriptions in which subjects have other evidence for the relevant p (see Malmgren 2011 and Ichikawa and Jarvis 2009 for discussion). G above may escape this charge by including the 'based solely on' clause. But the point still applies to justification: there will be deviant possible cases that satisfy G but not J because extraneous factors undermine Smith's justification for believing the relevant proposition. Deviant cases undermine conclusive a priori scrutability (in the sense of 2.1) of J from G and may undermine any short nontrivial a priori sufficient condition for justification, but they do little to undermine the weaker scrutability claim that J is nontrivially a priori scrutable from a full enough specification of the case. An analogy: deviant cases undermine necessitation of J by G and may undermine any short nontrivial modally sufficient condition for justification, but they do little to undermine the weaker supervenience-style claim that J is nontrivially necessitated by a full enough specification of the case.

tions to A Priori Scrutability and that A Priori Scrutability remains an attractive thesis in the face of them.

4 From descriptions to intensions[19]

At this point we can take a leaf from Carnap's later work, especially his 1947 book *Meaning and Necessity*, and understand the meaning of expressions not in terms of definitions but in terms of *intensions*. Here the intuitive idea is that an intension captures the way an expression applies to possible cases of all sorts. For example, the Gettier case brings out that whether or not there is a good definition for 'know', we can classify different scenarios as involving knowledge or as not involving knowledge. An intension is a way to represent those classifications.

The intension of an expression can be identified with a function from scenarios to extensions, mirroring speakers' idealized judgments about the extension of the expression in the scenario. The intension of a sentence (as used in a context) is a function from scenarios to truth-values. For example, the intension of 'Smith knows that Jones owns a Ford or Brown is in Barcelona' is false in a Gettier scenario. The intension of a subsentential expression such as 'bachelor' is a function from scenarios to sets of individuals. In any given scenario, its intension picks out the people who are bachelors if that scenario is actual. An expression's intension will often depend on its context of use, but for simplicity I will set aside this context-dependence for now.

For our purposes, we can think of these scenarios as *epistemically possible* scenarios: roughly, highly specific ways the world might turn out that we cannot rule out a priori. (Here and throughout, I work with an idealized notion of epistemic possibility that is tied to what cannot be ruled out a priori.) For a given scenario w and a given sentence S, we can consider the hypothesis that w actually obtains and judge whether if w obtains, S is the case. If yes, the intension of S is true at w. If no, the intension of S is false at w. I give a fuller definition of scenarios and intensions in the tenth excursus, but for now we can work with this intuitive understanding.

On this model, speakers can grasp an expression's intension without grasping a corresponding definition. Instead, the grasp corresponds to a *conditional ability* to identify an expression's extension, given sufficient information about how the world turns out and sufficient reasoning. That is, a sufficiently rational

---

[19] This section presupposes a little more philosophical background than the rest of the chapter and can be skipped without too much loss by nonspecialists. There is a somewhat gentler introduction to the framework of intensions in chapter 5, sections 3–5. A more precise account is in the tenth excursus.

subject using expressions such as 'bachelor', 'knowledge', and 'water' will have the ability to evaluate certain conditionals of the form 'If E, then C', where E contains relevant information about the world (typically not involving the expression in question) and where C is a statement using the expression and saying whether a given case fall into its extension (e.g. 'John is a bachelor', 'Sue knows that p', 'Water is H_2O'). And in order that it is not an accident that subjects can do this in the actual world, subjects will also be able to do this given specifications of many different scenarios.

For some expressions, we can capture the intension of the expression in the form of a definition. In other cases, we will merely be able to approximate an intension with an *approximate definition*. For example, 'justified true belief' can be seen as an approximate definition for 'knowledge': it gets most cases right, in an intuitive sense of 'most'. 'Justified true belief not essentially grounded in a falsehood' is even better. In the face of counterexamples, one can refine definitions yielding longer and longer definitions that cover more and more cases. If there is no finite definition that gets all possible cases right, there may be a converging series of definitions: a series of longer and longer approximate definitions such that for any given case, there is some point in the series after which all definitions get that case right. In all these cases, however, the definitions are beholden to the intension rather than vice versa.

Arguments from counterexample can make a case against definitions, but they cannot make a case against the claim that expressions have intensions. Such arguments themselves proceed by considering scenarios (say, a Gettier scenario), and by making the case that the extension of an expression E ('S knows that P') with respect to that scenario differs from the extension of a purported definition D ('S has a justified true belief that P'). To capture the intuitive data on the intensional model, we need only suppose that the intension of the expression picks out the intuitive extension at that scenario (in this case, false) rather than the intuitive extension of the definition (in this case, true).

All this applies equally to Kripke's arguments against descriptivism, which are also arguments from counterexample. In fact, Kripke deploys two different sorts of arguments from counterexample. We might say that *modal* arguments from counterexamples are used to oppose the claim that 'N is the D' is necessary (for a name N and a description D), while *epistemic* arguments from counterexample are used to oppose the claim that 'N is the D' is a priori. In the case of knowledge, the Gettier counterexample serves as the basis of both a modal argument and an epistemic argument, showing that it is neither necessary nor a priori that knowledge is justified true belief. In Kripke's arguments against descriptivism, modal arguments and epistemic arguments from counterexample are employed separately.

Modal arguments from counterexample require exhibiting a *metaphysically possible* situation (roughly, a situation that might have obtained) of which the equivalence is false. Kripke's modal argument against descriptivism fits this template. It focuses on a metaphysically possible situation in which Aristotle did not go into pedagogy, and makes the case that if this situation had obtained, then it would not have been the case that Aristotle was the teacher of Alexander. It follows that it is not necessary that Aristotle was the teacher of Alexander.

Epistemic arguments from counterexample require exhibiting an *epistemically possible* scenario (that is, a scenario not ruled out a priori) of which the equivalence is false. Kripke's epistemological argument against descriptivism is an argument from counterexample of this second kind. It focuses on an epistemically possible situation in which the proof of the incompleteness of arithmetic was stolen, and makes the case that if that situation actually obtains, then Gödel is not the prover of incompleteness. It follows that it is not a priori that Gödel is the prover of incompleteness.

In effect, modal arguments from counterexample show that the *modal profile* of an expression (the way it applies across metaphysically possible worlds) is not identical to that of a purported definition. Such an argument is clearly compatible with the claim that the modal profile can be represented as an intension, however. As usual, we need only choose an intension that respects the counterexample. The modal profile of 'know' can be represented as an intension that classifies Gettier cases as cases in which knowledge is absent. Likewise, the modal profile of 'Aristotle' can be represented as an intension that picks out Aristotle in the situation in which he never went into pedagogy, rather than picking out Alexander's teacher.

Similarly, epistemic arguments from counterexample show that the *epistemic profile* of an expression (the way that it applies across epistemically possible scenarios) is not identical to that of a purported definition. Again, such an argument is clearly compatible with the claim that the epistemic profile of an expression can be represented as an intension.[20] The epistemic profile of 'knows that P' can be represented as an intension that classifies Gettier cases as cases in which knowledge is absent. Likewise, the epistemic profile of 'Gödel' can be represented as an intension that picks out the stealer in Kripke's stolen-proof scenario rather than the prover.

---

[20] In the case of an expression such as 'knowledge', the epistemic and modal profiles appear to be more or less the same, so one intension will suffice to represent both. In the case of names such as 'Aristotle' and 'Gödel', the epistemic and modal profiles may be quite distinct, so one needs distinct intensions to represent them. These are just the primary and secondary intensions of two-dimensional semantics (discussed in 5.5 and E10). The intension over epistemically possible scenarios discussed in the text is the primary intension, which is the most important for present purposes.

Like Gettier's argument from counterexample, Kripke's arguments from counterexample pose no problem for A Priori Scrutability. Kripke's modal argument does not pose even a prima facie problem: it concerns what is metaphysically possible and necessary, whereas A Priori Scrutability concerns what is a priori and a posteriori. Kripke's epistemological argument suggests that 'Gödel' is not a priori equivalent to a description such as 'the prover of incompleteness', but it gives no reason to deny that sentences such as 'Gödel did not prove incompleteness' are themselves scrutable from a specification of the relevant scenario. Given a specification of the stolen-proof scenario, we can certainly determine that if the scenario is actual, Gödel did not prove incompleteness.

Likewise, Kripke's epistemological argument cannot refute *approximate descriptivism*: the thesis that for every name (as used by a speaker) there is a converging series of descriptions such that for every scenario, there is some point in the series such that all descriptions after that point give the same result as the name in that scenario. An approximate definition that works fairly well for 'Gödel' is 'The actual person called 'Gödel' by those from whom I acquired the name'.[21] As usual the approximation will be imperfect and there will be counterexamples (cases where one misheard the name, perhaps), but refinements will gradually remove the counterexamples as they converge on the name's intension. In any case, these counterexamples pose no more of a problem for A Priori Scrutability or for the intensional model than the Gettier case.

Much follows from these observations. Kripke's arguments are often thought to undermine broadly Fregean analyses of meaning and content. But we will see shortly (and in more detail in the eleventh excursus), an appropriate scrutability thesis can itself be used to support a broadly Fregean analysis of meaning and content, by defining intensions over epistemically possible scenarios. The resulting intensions can do much of the work that descriptions or Fregean senses are often held to do.

We can put things as follows. If the scrutability thesis is correct, a Fregean view of meaning and content is viable. Kripke's arguments give us no reason to reject the scrutability thesis. So Kripke's arguments should not lead us to reject a Fregean view of meaning and content. The scrutability thesis therefore suggests that Kripke's arguments are much more limited in scope than is often supposed. Of course there is more to say here, but this at least makes an initial case that the seemingly innocuous scrutability thesis may have highly significant consequences.

---

[21] For more on approximate descriptivism, see 8.2. For more on intensions and approximate definitions in the 'Gödel' case, see the discussion of Kripke's epistemological argument in 'On Sense and Intension'.

5 The scrutability base

A *scrutability base* is a class of truths from which all truths are scrutable, for a given notion of scrutability.[22] What sort of truths might go into a scrutability base?

At the end of the *Aufbau*, Carnap embraces what we might call Logical Scrutability: the view that there is a scrutability base using only logical expressions. Some phenomenalists accept Phenomenal Scrutability, holding that there is a scrutability base using only phenomenal expressions (expressions for the character of conscious experiences) and logical expressions. Some physicalists accept Microphysical Scrutability, holding that there is a scrutability base using only microphysical expressions (expressions used in fundamental physics) and logical expressions.[23] For our purposes, all of these views are strong and interesting scrutability theses (versions of all of them are entertained by Carnap in the *Aufbau*), but the current project is not committed to any of them. Our working scrutability thesis is what we might call Compact Scrutability: there is a compact class of truths from which all truths are scrutable. Given that logical, microphysical, and phenomenal bases count as compact, then Logical, Phenomenal, and Microphysical Scrutability entail Compact Scrutability. But less austere bases than these may still be compact.

What is compactness, exactly? As I characterized compactness earlier, a class of truths is compact if it uses only a small class of expressions. A little more precisely, we can say that compactness requires that a class of truths uses only expressions from a small number of *families* of expressions. If it turns out that all truths are scrutable from phenomenal truths, but that an infinite number of phenomenal expressions are required to capture the diversity of possible phenomenal qualities, this would still be a strong enough scrutability thesis for our purposes. We can stipulate that the class of phenomenal expressions counts as a single family, as does the class of microphysical expressions, the class of logical expressions, the class of mathematical expressions, and so on. The intuitive idea here is that expressions in the same family should share a common domain. (So the class of spatiotemporal expressions counts as a family, while the class of singular terms does not.) Beyond this I will leave the notion of a family intuitive.

---

[22] I will speak of sets and classes interchangeably. For some purposes it might be useful to admit classes of sentences that are too large to form a set, but for most of our purposes set-sized classes will be adequate. I discuss this issue further toward the end of E3.

[23] In principle, these views concerning a scrutability base can be combined with different scrutability relations (such as definitional or a priori scrutability), yielding such theses as Definitional Phenomenal Scrutability, A Priori Microphysical Scrutability, and so on. When the scrutability relation is not specified, a thesis involving a priori scrutability should be understood. For more on the conventions here, see 2.1.

How small is small? We can leave this notion vague. But to give a rough idea, I would say that fewer than ten or so families would be ideal, that twenty would be acceptable, but that more than a hundred would be pushing things. One could also stipulate that a compact class of truths will exclude the great majority of terms used in natural languages: there will be few or no ordinary proper names ('London', 'George Bush'), natural kind terms ('water', 'kangaroo'), artifact terms ('car', 'table'), and neither will there be cognate terms in a different language, constructions from such terms, and so on. The idea is that truths involving terms like this should all be scrutable from truths in a more primitive vocabulary. I will not build this into the official definition, but one can see this as part of the spirit of the thesis.

It is worth noting that while a compact class of truths must use only a limited vocabulary, it need not include *all* truths that use a given vocabulary. For example, there is a compact class of truths that includes all microphysical truths but not all mathematical truths. Stating the microphysical truths may require mathematical vocabulary, but many truths that use only mathematical vocabulary will not be included.

We also need to require that a compact class of truths avoids *trivializing mechanisms*. There are certain sorts of base truths that threaten to render the scrutability thesis trivial. One such is a base consisting of the family of expressions for *propositions*, along with 'is true'. It is not implausible that every sentence is scrutable from a sentence saying that a corresponding proposition is true, but this result is not interesting. Likewise, one could perhaps code all truths of English into a single real number ϕ, via an appropriate coding scheme: then it is not implausible that all such truths are scrutable from the single truth that ϕ equals such-and-such. But again, this thesis is not interesting. There is a clear sense in which these proposals involve trivializing mechanisms, by somehow directly coding a large number of truths from different families into a single truth or a single family of truths. I will not attempt to define this notion, but it should be understood that compact classes cannot include sentences of this sort.

So a class of sentences is compact if it includes expressions from only a small number of families and includes no trivializing mechanisms. Of course this notion is vague and has not been precisely defined. But in practice, this will not matter. The sort of specific scrutability claims I will discuss and defend will all involve highly restricted vocabularies that are clearly small enough to be interesting. In most cases, there will be no threat of a trivializing mechanism, and when there is such a threat, it can be discussed directly.

How small can a scrutability base be? Let us say that a *minimal* scrutability base is a class of sentences C such that C is a scrutability base and no proper subclass of C is a scrutability base. (In order to ensure that C uses a minimal vocabulary, one could also require that there is no scrutability base using only a proper subclass of the expressions used in C.)

Three proposals about minimal scrutability bases correspond to the theses of Logical Scrutability, Phenomenal Scrutability, and Microphysical Scrutability. I think that there are good reasons to reject these proposals, however. In part for reasons we have already discussed, it is plausible that many physical truths are not a priori scrutable from logical or phenomenal truths. Conversely, it is plausible that many phenomenal truths are not a priori scrutable from a microphysical base. For example, it appears that no amount of a priori reasoning from microphysical truths will settle what it is like to see red (Jackson 1982). This suggests that many phenomenal truths (truths concerning the character of conscious experiences) are not a priori scrutable from microphysical truths. It also appears that no amount of a priori reasoning from microphysical truths will enable one to know such perspectival truths as 'It is now March', or such negative truths as 'There are no ghosts'.

Still, this leaves more liberal scrutability theses on the table. I will argue (in chapters 3, 4, and 6) that all ordinary macroscopic truths are a priori entailed by a class *PQTI* (physics, qualia, that's-all, indexicals) that includes both truths of physics *and* phenomenal truths, as well as certain indexical truths ('I am such-and-such', 'Now is such-and-such') and a totality or 'that's-all' truth (on which more in 3.1 and E5). If so, then *PQTI* can serve as a scrutability base. There may be even smaller bases. For example, microphysical truths may themselves be scrutable from a base involving phenomenal expressions and nomic expressions (such as 'law' or 'cause'), perhaps along with spatiotemporal and/or mathematical expressions. If so, then (as I argue in chapter 7) a scrutability base might need to involve only phenomenal, nomic, logical, indexical, and totality expressions,[24] perhaps along with spatiotemporal and/or mathematical expressions. On some views (explored in chapters 7 and 8), the base may be smaller still.

A few principled scrutability bases are worthy of attention. One base, in the spirit of Carnap's own view, yields the thesis of Structural Scrutability: all truths are scrutable from structural truths. If structural truths are restricted to a logical vocabulary, this view falls prey to Newman's problem. But we might understand structural truths more expansively, to let in truths about fundamentality or naturalness (as on Carnap's own final view), or about laws and causation, for example. I explore the viability of views of this sort in chapter 8.

Another principled scrutability thesis, perhaps less in the spirit of Carnap's view, is Fundamental Scrutability: the thesis that all truths are scrutable from

---

[24] Throughout this book, I count as 'indexical expressions' just a limited class of perspectival expressions: 'I', 'now', and perhaps certain heavily constrained demonstratives. In this sense, indexical expressions count reasonably as a family. I use 'context-dependent' for the broader class of expressions whose content depends on context.

metaphysically fundamental truths (plus indexical truths and a that's-all truth, if necessary). The metaphysically fundamental truths are those that serve as the metaphysical grounds for all truths: they might involve attributions of fundamental properties to fundamental entities.[25] On a standard physicalist view, the metaphysically fundamental truths are microphysical truths. On a standard property dualist view, metaphysically fundamental truths may include microphysical and phenomenal truths.

Another thesis, in the spirit of Russell's quite different constructions of the world, is Acquaintance Scrutability: all truths are scrutable from truths about entities with which we are directly acquainted. Another, in the spirit of the thesis about concepts with which we started this chapter, is Primitive Scrutability: all truths are scrutable from truths involving only expressions for primitive concepts. Yet another, relevant to debates about internalism and externalism about meaning and content, is Narrow Scrutability: all truths are scrutable from truths whose content is determined by the internal state of the subject.

In chapter 8, I will make a case for all three of the theses just mentioned, as well as a tentative case for Fundamental Scrutability. I will also connect each of these theses to philosophical applications. For the purposes of many applications, it is these specific scrutability theses rather than Compact Scrutability per se that matters. Compactness plays a role in some applications, but where it does not, it can be seen as playing a sort of guiding role en route to the specific theses, ensuring that our scrutability bases are small enough that those theses are plausible.

Some potential scrutability bases are less austere than others. For example, someone might think that we need normative expressions ('ought') in the base, or that we need expressions for secondary qualities ('red') in the base, or that we need intentional notions ('believes') in the base. If a scrutability base needs to be expanded to include these expressions, then the base will plausibly go beyond the structural or the metaphysically fundamental, but it will still be small enough that we will have a strong and interesting scrutability thesis.

There are many scrutability bases. For a start, as long as scrutability is monotonic (if S is scrutable from C, S is scrutable from any set of truths containing C) adding truths to any scrutability base will yield a scrutability base, and substituting a priori equivalent synonyms within a scrutability base will also yield a scrutability base. Even if we restrict ourselves to minimal scrutability bases (scrutability

---

[25] Metaphysical fundamentality should be distinguished from conceptual primitiveness. One might reasonably hold that spin and charge are metaphysically fundamental without holding that the concepts *spin* and *charge* are primitive. Likewise, one might hold that the concept *I* is primitive without holding that the self is anything metaphysically fundamental. Still, there may be an attenuated relation between the two; see E16, and also 8.4 and 8.6.

bases of which no proper subclass is a scrutability base and for which there is no scrutability base using only a proper subset of the expressions) and factor out synonyms, a diversity of bases is possible. For example, given a minimal scrutability base involving predicates F and G, there will also be a minimal scrutability base involving four new predicates H, I, J, and K, corresponding to conjunctions of F, G, and their negations. One can also obtain multiple bases from the familiar idea that there can be a priori equivalent formulations of a physical theory in different vocabularies. It is even not out of the question that on some views, both a microphysical vocabulary and a phenomenal vocabulary (or a phenomenal vocabulary combined with a nomic or spatiotemporal vocabulary) could yield minimal scrutability bases.

For most of our purposes, the existence of multiple scrutability bases is not a problem. Carnap himself held a pluralistic view on which there are many equally privileged bases that we can choose between only on pragmatic grounds. Still, the phenomenon does suggest that the mere fact that an expression is involved in a minimal scrutability base does not suffice for the expression to express a primitive concept in an interesting sense. And there remains an intuition that some scrutability bases are more fundamental than others. For example, in the case above, it is natural to hold that predicates F and G stand in certain conceptual, epistemological, and psychological priority relations to H, I, J, and K. Likewise, one might hold that phenomenal and nomic expressions stand in certain conceptual, epistemological, and psychological priority relations to microphysical expressions. This will be especially clear if one holds that microphysical expressions are definable in terms of phenomenal and nomic expressions, but even if one rejects the definitional claim, one might still accept some priority claims.

I take the moral here to be that a priori scrutability is a relatively coarse-grained relation among classes of truths. One might react to this by postulating a more fine-grained relation of conceptual or epistemological dependence among truths. Whenever one class of truths depends on another in this sense, truths involving the former will be scrutable from truths involving the latter, but not vice versa. On this way of doing things, many scrutability bases will not be dependence bases, and it is not out of the question that there might be just one minimal dependence base (at least up to equivalence through synonymy).[26]

---

[26] This reaction is an epistemological or conceptual analog of a familiar metaphysical line of thought concerning supervenience, leading some to postulate relations of ontological dependence or grounding that are finer-grained than the coarse-grained relation of supervenience. We could think of the more fine-grained relation as conceptual dependence or conceptual grounding. For more on these issues, see E16.

This line of thought immediately raises the question of how the fine-grained dependence relation in question should be understood. If one accepts the definitional model, one might suggest that the relation is just definitional scrutability, and that the dependence base will involve all and only the undefinable expressions. But if one rejects the definitional model, the correct understanding is less clear. I discuss such fine-grained relations and their relation to scrutability later in the book (and also in the companion chapter, 'Verbal Disputes').

For now, I will concentrate on a priori scrutability and related coarse-grained notions. These have the advantage of being better-understood than more fine-grained notions, so that arguing for scrutability theses of this sort is more straightforward. A number of the scrutability bases I will consider will also be plausible candidates to be dependence bases, so that the expressions involved will be plausible candidates to be primitive concepts. But even in the absence of claims about dependence and primitiveness, these scrutability theses have significant consequences.

6 Reviving the *Aufbau*

If the A Priori Scrutability thesis is correct, it offers a vindication of something like the project of the *Aufbau*.[27] There are two significant differences: the very limited bases (logical and/or phenomenal) of the *Aufbau* are replaced by somewhat less limited bases here, and the role of definitional entailment in the *Aufbau* is played by a priori entailment here. The expansion of the base allows us to avoid Goodman's, Quine's, and Chisholm's objections to the phenomenalist base, and Newman's objection to the purely logical base. The move from definitions to a priori entailment allows us to avoid the central problems for definitions and descriptions, including the problem of counterexample, and Kripke's modal and epistemological arguments against descriptivism.

Of course there are challenges to the *Aufbau* that also apply to the scrutability framework. Most notably, Quine's critique of the analytic/synthetic distinction is often thought to generate an equally significant critique of the a priori/a posteriori distinction, and so has the potential to undermine the A Priori Scrutability thesis. In chapter 5, however, I will suggest that an analysis in terms of scrutability provides the materials required to show where Quine's arguments go

---

[27] A quite different project in a similar spirit, attempting to vindicate something like the *Aufbau*, is carried out by Hannes Leitgeb in his important article 'New Life for Carnap's *Aufbau*?' (2011). Leitgeb retains a phenomenal basis, although he gives it more structure than Carnap allowed. He also retains definitional entailment by imposing a relatively weak criterion of adequacy according to which definitions must involve 'sameness of empirical content'. On this criterion, definitions can be false. Because of this, I think that Leitgeb's version of the *Aufbau* will not play the semantic, metaphysical, and epistemological roles that I am interested in, but it may well be able to play other roles.

wrong. I will address a number of other challenges to the scrutability framework in chapters 3 and 4.

One might ask: does A Priori Scrutability have the potential to satisfy some of the ambitions of the *Aufbau*? These ambitions included an analysis of meaning and concepts, an epistemological optimism, a metaphysical deflationism, and a language that might help to unify science. These elements were supposed to jointly yield a sort of blueprint for scientific analysis and philosophical progress. The *Aufbau* is widely held to have failed in these ambitions, and I will not try to put anything so strong in their place. Still, the scrutability thesis has consequences in many different areas of philosophy, consequences that share at least some of the flavor of Carnap's ambitions in the *Aufbau* and other works.[28]

1. *Knowability and skepticism*. In the *Aufbau*, Carnap used his construction to argue that there is no question whose answer is in principle unattainable by science. This is a version of the notorious Knowability Thesis in epistemology, often associated with the programs of logical empiricism and verificationism, which holds that all truths are knowable. This thesis is now widely rejected, for both formal and intuitive reasons. I argue shortly (E1) that scrutability theses capture at least a plausible relative of these theses, and can play some parts of the role that the knowability thesis has been used to play. Furthermore, certain scrutability theses offer a distinctive response to skepticism (E15).

2. *Modality*. Carnap's *Aufbau* project yields a basic vocabulary that can be used not just to characterize the actual world, but also other possible states of the world. This leads directly to Carnap's later project in *Meaning and Necessity* (1947), in which he analyzes possibility and necessity in terms of state-descriptions for other possible worlds. While this sort of construction is now often used to understand metaphysically possible worlds, the scrutability framework allows such a construction to yield a space of epistemically possible worlds, or scenarios (E10). One can use a generalized scrutability thesis to define epistemically possible scenarios in terms of maximal a priori consistent sets of sentences in a scrutability base. These are analogous to Carnap's state-descriptions, and behave

---

[28] For more on these applications, see E1 and E15 (knowability and skepticism, respectively), E9 and E10 (modality and meaning), 8.3 and 8.4 (primitive concepts and narrow content), 8.6 and E16 (metaphysics), 8.7 and E12 (structuralism and the unity of science), and 6.5 (metaphilosophy). It should be noted that many of these applications require specific scrutability theses. For example, the reply to skepticism requires Structural Scrutability or a variant thereof. The analysis of narrow content requires Narrow Scrutability. Central applications to metaphysics require theses such as Fundamental Scrutability. The crucial applications to meaning and modality require less, but they work better if one at least has scrutability from a compact base consisting of non-context-dependent expressions and primitive indexicals, and better still if one has a version of Acquaintance Scrutability. See chapter 8 for a discussion of most of these matters.

in a more Carnapian way than possible worlds on the usual contemporary understanding. For example, a posteriori sentences such as 'Hesperus is Phosphorus' are true in all metaphysically possible worlds, but they are false in some epistemically possible scenarios, as one might expect. So these scenarios can play a role in analyzing epistemic possibility analogous to the role of possible worlds in analyzing metaphysical possibility.

3. *Meaning.* Carnap's construction in *Meaning and Necessity* was intended to support a Fregean analysis of meaning, by understanding meanings as intensions defined over possible worlds. As discussed in chapter 5 and the eleventh excursus, the scrutability framework can be used to help vindicate this Fregean project by defining intensions over epistemically possible scenarios as above. For example, one can define the (epistemic or primary) intension of a sentence as the set of scenarios in which it is true. Then two sentences will have the same intension if and only if they are a priori equivalent. One can go on to define intensions for other expressions, such as singular terms, such that a and b will have the same intension if and only if $a = b$ is a priori. So 'Hesperus' and 'Phosphorus' will have different intensions. If the scrutability thesis is true, intensions of this sort will behave in a manner reminiscent of Fregean sense.

4. *Concepts and mental content.* In the *Aufbau*, Carnap put much emphasis on the construction of concepts. We can use the scrutability framework to associate intensions not just with linguistic items such as sentences but with mental items such as thoughts. As in the case of language, these intensions will serve as contents that reflect the epistemological properties of thoughts. Under some reasonable assumptions (outlined in the discussion of Narrow Scrutability in chapter 8), these intensions can also serve as *narrow* contents of thought: contents that are wholly determined by the intrinsic state of the thinker. These contents, grounded in a priori inferential relations to thoughts composed of primitive concepts, can go on to ground wide contents in turn. This approach to content naturally leads to a view in which primitive concepts play a grounding role with respect to all intentionality, and suggests that the path to naturalizing intentionality may proceed through the naturalization of the content of these primitive concepts.

5. *Metaphysics.* Carnap's philosophy was known for its anti-realism about metaphysics: many metaphysical questions do not have objective and determinate answers. With specific scrutability theses in hand, the current framework can be used to argue for realism, anti-realism, or metaphysical primitivism about a given subject matter. For example, given Fundamental Scrutability (the thesis that all truths are scrutable from fundamental truths), then if ontological sentences (about the existence of composite objects, say) are not scrutable from more fundamental truths, then they are either themselves fundamental or they are not true. In the domain of ontology, one might use this method to argue for

a sort of anti-realism.[29] In other domains (that of consciousness, say), one can use this method to argue for an expansion in the metaphysically fundamental truths. We can also use scrutability as a guide in various projects of conceptual metaphysics, discussed in the sixteenth excursus.

6. *Scientific analysis.* The unity of science was one of the major concerns of the logical empiricists, and Carnap hoped that the *Aufbau* program might contribute to this unity by showing how all scientific notions could be analyzed in terms of a common basic vocabulary. If the scrutability thesis is true, then all scientific truths are at least scrutable from a common base. Furthermore, it can be argued that when scientific truths are scrutable from other truths of which there is a scientific account, this account can be used to provide an explanation of the scrutable truths. If so, then (as I argue in E12), scrutability might yield a relatively unified account of all scientific truths. Scrutability also helps to analyze the prospects for structuralist views of science (8.7).

7. *Metaphilosophy.* The scrutability thesis entails that all philosophical truths are scrutable from base truths. So even philosophical ignorance can be localized to our ignorance of base truths or the non-ideality of our a priori reasoning (6.5). An extension of the scrutability thesis ('Verbal Disputes') suggests a way of reducing all philosophical disagreements to disagreements over base truths.

The analysis of meaning and concepts that one gets from this project is more open-ended than in the ambitions of the *Aufbau*, the epistemological optimism is attenuated, and any metaphysical deflationism is more limited. Still, the consequences are strong and striking enough that the scrutability thesis is certainly worthy of investigation.

---

[29] This application is restricted to distinctions between realism and anti-realism that can be drawn in terms of truth and falsity. The framework does not bear so directly on distinctions that are drawn differently: for example, arguments of this sort will not easily distinguish moral realism from varieties of moral anti-realism that allow that 'Such-and-such is good' is true. The framework itself is largely neutral on the nature of truth and its grounds in various domains. While I lean toward a correspondence view of truth myself, the arguments of this book are compatible with many different analyses of both realist and anti-realist flavors.

Scrutability and Knowability

The scrutability thesis is related to a number of widely discussed theses in analytic philosophy. In this excursus, I discuss the relation to the knowability thesis and its cousin the verification principle. In the next excursus, I discuss its relation to Quine's thesis of the inscrutability of reference. Doing so can help to indirectly motivate the scrutability thesis, by showing how it avoids problems for related theses while still capturing something of their flavor.

First, the Knowability Thesis.

Knowability Thesis: For any truth *S*, it is possible that someone knows *S*.[1]

This thesis is often doubted, for both intuitive and formal reasons. Intuitively, it seems that there may be truths concerning the distant past, the far away, and the very small, that it may be impossible for anyone to know. Formally, the thesis gives rise to what is often known as the Paradox of Knowability, first published by Frederick Fitch in his 1963 article 'A Logical Analysis of Some Value Concepts'.[2]

Fitch in effect gives a disproof of the Knowability Thesis, arguing from the weak assumption that some truth is not *known* to the conclusion that some truth is not knowable. Let *P* be a truth such that in the actual course of history, no one ever knows *P*. Let *Q* be '*P* and no one knows that *P*'. Then *Q* is true, but *Q* is unknowable. If someone were to know *Q*, then they would know *P*, but if someone were to know *P*, then *Q* would be false. So no one can know *Q*.

The scrutability thesis is closely related to the knowability thesis. It does not say that every truth is knowable, but it does say that every truth is scrutable, or derivable from a limited class of basic truths. One might thereby wonder

---

[1] I cast the thesis in terms of knowing sentences rather than knowing propositions for continuity with later discussion (see 2.2 for more on this). The present issues are much the same either way.

[2] Fitch attributes the result to an anonymous referee. Joe Salerno's 'Knowability Noir: 1945–1963' locates the source in a 1945 referee report by Alonzo Church. The relevant material can be found in Salerno's *New Essays on the Knowability Paradox* (2009).

whether scrutability theses are liable to similar problems. In the introduction, we saw briefly that Inferential Scrutability is liable to problems related to Fitch's paradox, problems that I discuss at more length in 2.4 and 3.5. However, Conditional and A Priori Scrutability avoid both sorts of problems.

Concerning the intuitive problem: the truths in a scrutability base C may well include relevant truths about the distant past, including perhaps the spatiotemporal configuration of physical particles then, and so on. Even when S is an intuitively unknowable truth about the distant past, there is no corresponding intuitive problem with the idea that one can know that *if* the sentences in C are true, then S is true. Likewise there is no corresponding intuitive problem with the idea that one can know a priori a material conditional connecting a conjunction of all the truths in C to S. Something similar applies to truths about the far away and the very small. So there is no intuitive objection to the scrutability thesis here.

As for the paradox of knowability: even though Q above is unknowable, there is no formal problem with the claim that one can know that *if* the sentences in C are true, then Q is true. Indeed, as long as P itself and claims about knowledge of P are both scrutable from C, then 'P and no one knows that P' will be straightforwardly scrutable from C. This goes for both A Priori and Conditional Scrutability.

One might suggest that the Scrutability Thesis entails the Knowability Thesis, at least if we grant that the conjunction of all truths in C is itself knowable. By knowing this conjunction D (empirically) and by knowing $D \rightarrow Q$ (a priori), one could thereby come to know Q. However, there is no reason to believe that D is itself knowable. In fact, there is good reason to believe that it is not, both for intuitive and Fitch-style reasons. The intuitive reasons are obvious: D may involve information about the distant past and the far away that no one will ever know. As for the Fitch-style reasons: assuming that no one in the actual history of the world believes D, then D specifies a world in which no one believes D. If someone came to believe D, they would live in a world quite different from ours, one in which their belief would be false. So no one can know D.

One might think that one can define a factive operator 'scry' such that one scries P iff one derives P from base truths.[3] One might then try to generate a Fitchian paradox, by taking P to be any truth that one does not actually scry, and taking Q to be 'P and I do not scry that P'. By Fitch's reasoning, if scrying is factive, then Q is an inscrutable truth. However: the notion of scrying above is ambiguous. If to scry P is to derive P from C, where C are the base truths of the

[3] 'Scry' is the preferred verb form of 'scrutable', having the advantage of both being more euphonious than the unlovely term 'scrute' and already being a word of English with a somewhat appropriate meaning. 'Scry: to divine, esp. by crystal gazing' (Collins English Dictionary).

actual world (or of any specific world) then scrying is not factive: there will be worlds in which P is scried but false. If to scry P is to derive P from the base truths of the world one is in at the time of scrying, then 'P and I do not scry that P' is indeed inscrutable. But this does not yield a counterexample to the A Priori or Conditional Scrutability theses above, as these require only that truths be derivable from the base truths of the worlds in which they are true, not the worlds in which they are so derived.

It may be that scrutability theses can do some of the work that knowability theses have been intended to do, or that they capture some of the intuitions that have led theorists to express sympathy with the knowability thesis. For example, Dorothy Edgington (1985) suggests that it is intuitive that if P is true in the actual world, then it is possible that one can come to know, in some different world, that P is true in the actual world. Of course this raises questions about what it is to know in a different world that P is true in the actual world. One suggestion is that to do this requires specifying the actual world with a canonical sentence D, and coming to know that if D were the case, P would be the case. Transposing this counterfactual claim into an epistemic mode (if D is the case, then P is the case), the resulting claim is not too far from the conditional scrutability thesis.

Another problem for the knowability thesis concerns cases of indeterminacy. (This problem is raised by Hawthorne (2005) for the case of omniscient knowers, but the problem generalizes.) Suppose that 42 is a borderline case of a small number, and let S be '42 is a big number'. On most views of vagueness, S is neither determinately true nor determinately false. On some such views, the statement $S \vee \sim S$ will be true all the same. If so, one could reason disjunctively: if S, then S is true, so S is knowable; if $\sim S$, then $\sim S$ is true, so $\sim S$ is knowable. So either S is knowable or $\sim S$ is knowable. But if S is (necessarily) indeterminate, this conclusion is implausible. One can raise a parallel problem for the scrutability thesis, yielding the conclusion that for all S, either S is scrutable (from a relevant D) or $\sim S$ is scrutable. Once again, this conclusion is implausible when S is indeterminate.

One could resist this conclusion by rejecting the law of the excluded middle and refusing to accept that $S \vee \sim S$ is true when S is indeterminate, or by holding that when S is indeterminate, it is likewise indeterminate whether S is scrutable. But perhaps the most straightforward way to avoid the problem is to understand the scrutability thesis as applying to *determinate* truths. That is, the thesis will say that when S is *determinately* true, or when $det(S)$ is true, then S is scrutable from D. On the relevant sort of view, the disjunction $det(S) \vee det(\sim S)$ will not be true in cases of indeterminacy, so the problem here will be avoided.

One might worry about cases of higher-order indeterminacy, where it is indeterminate whether $det(S)$ or $\sim det(S)$. In such a case, the best thing to say is that it is indeterminate whether *S* is scrutable from *D*. Given the presence of vagueness in language, one should expect that scrutability can be vague too. On this view, implication by base truths goes along with determinacy, and vagueness of implication goes along with vagueness of determinacy.[4]

One can extend the scrutability thesis to the thesis that for all *S*, the truth-value of *S* is scrutable from *D*, whatever this truth-value may be. To obtain the extended thesis, one could simply apply the original thesis to the statement '*S* has truth-value *T*', or better, one could apply the thesis to a statement such as '~*S*', '*indet* (*S*)', and other statements which are true iff *S* has a relevant truth-value. As in the cases above, then if one adopts the view of indeterminacy outlined above, these statements will be scrutable only when they are determinately true. So, for example, the claim will be that if *indet* (*S*) is determinately true, then it is scrutable from *D*.

A final worry related to these matters arises from cases analogous to the Liar Paradox. Say that *S* is 'This sentence is not scrutable from *D*'. Then if *S* is true, it is inscrutable, and if *S* is false, it is scrutable. Either way we have a counterexample to the thesis that a sentence is true if and only if it is scrutable.

This worry is an instance of a general worry for any thesis holding that a sentence is true iff it has property ϕ. Whether 'This sentence does not have ϕ' is true or false, it generates a counterexample to the thesis. I do not think it is reasonable to infer that no such thesis can be true. If this were correct, the Liar Paradox would generate a counterexample to 'Every sentence is true iff it is true'. Instead, it seems best to say that sentences like 'This sentence does not have ϕ' should be handled by whatever mechanism best handles the Liar Paradox. Indeed, one might take it to be a constraint on solutions to the Liar Paradox that they should also apply to sentences like this.

The most obvious thing to say is that in cases like this, '*S* does not have ϕ' is indeterminate. Given the discussion above, 'This sentence is not scrutable from *D*' is slightly more complicated, as the relevant thesis says that a sentence is *determinately* true iff it is scrutable. This renders the sentence at issue more closely analogous to the Strengthened Liar, 'This sentence is not determinately true'. So a proponent of the Scrutability Thesis should say that the sentence has

[4] This view is analogous to the view that knowability goes along with determinacy, and vagueness of knowability goes along with vagueness of determinacy, suggested on behalf of the supervaluationist by Hawthorne 2005. There is an alternative view (Dorr 2003) on which the vagueness of knowability goes along with the vagueness of truth rather than the vagueness of indeterminacy. Transposed to the key of scrutability, this approach yields a view on which *S* is true iff *S* is scrutable and *S* is indeterminate iff it is indeterminate whether *S* is scrutable. If we accept the law of the excluded middle, this view will most naturally be combined with a view on which it is always the case that either *S* is scrutable or ~*S* is scrutable (cases apparently in the middle will be borderline cases of each).

the same truth-value of the Strengthened Liar, whatever that truth-value is (perhaps involving some sort of higher-order indeterminacy). Saying more requires an adequate treatment of Liar paradoxes in general, but that is a problem for everyone, and not for the scrutability thesis in particular.

Finally, the scrutability thesis is in some limited respects reminiscent of the logical empiricists' verification principle, which says that only verifiable statements are meaningful. The scrutability thesis, rephrased, says that only scrutable statements are true, where a statement is scrutable if it is implied by certain base statements. Perhaps scrutability here might be seen as a sort of idealized verifiability, conditional on those statements in the base. One might then wonder whether any of the famous problems for the verification principle will apply here.

Most traditional worries about verifiability are removed by the extension of the base. Scrutability is much weaker than verifiability, not least because the base statements may include truths that are not themselves verifiable. For example, they may include truths about the distant past, the far away, about other minds, and about the extent of the universe. Because of this, there is no problem for scrutability generated by distinct empirically equivalent theories in physics, for example, or by statements about the past, or by the possibility of unverifiable ghosts.

Another famous problem is: is the verification principle itself verifiable? One might likewise ask: is the scrutability thesis itself scrutable? I will argue later that certain general versions of the scrutability thesis are themselves a priori, and are therefore scrutable. Other versions, such as scrutability from a specific base, are a posteriori. But we will later see that as long as a 'that's-all' sentence is included in the base, the scrutability thesis itself will follow. In some cases this 'that's-all' sentence will itself be akin to a scrutability thesis, but this just brings out a way in which the scrutability thesis is far more flexible than the verification principle.

It is also worth noting that where the logical empiricists offered the verification principle in a prescriptive spirit, I am not inclined to offer the scrutability thesis in this way. Instead, in the first instance I am simply arguing for its truth. Perhaps downstream from these arguments, it can be used prescriptively, as a check on realism about certain subject matters that are not scrutable from base truths. Much here will depend on what one antecedently allows into the base, so the matter is not cut and dried. But in any case, it seems clear that the standard reasons for doubt about the verification principle do not apply to the scrutability thesis.

....

The Inscrutability of Reference and the Scrutability of Truth

In his 1960 book *Word and Object*, W. V. Quine put forward the thesis of the Inscrutability of Reference. This thesis says very roughly that there is no fact of the matter about what a given expression refers to, because there are too many equally good candidates. This thesis is a metaphysical rather than an epistemological thesis: it concerns the existence and determinacy of reference, rather than our knowledge of reference. Perhaps because of this, and because the term 'inscrutability' suggests an epistemological thesis, Quine later came to think that this name for the thesis was suboptimal. In his 1990 book *Pursuit of Truth* he renamed it the thesis of the *indeterminacy of reference*.

My scrutability theses, unlike Quine's, are epistemological. We can bring out a connection between the two, however, by considering epistemological theses in the vicinity of Quine's. In particular, Quine's metaphysical thesis of the indeterminacy of reference can be seen as a challenge to an epistemological thesis about reference. If we start from this thesis, and modify it to meet Quine's challenge and other challenges, this motivates something like the scrutability theses I have discussed.

To start with: if we follow Quine's later practice and reserve 'scrutability' for broadly epistemological theses, one might call the following thesis the *scrutability of reference*.

The Scrutability of Reference: For any referring expression *E*, once we know enough about the world, we are in a position to know what *E* refers to.

The thesis has commonsense appeal. At the beginning of enquiry, we may not know what a term such as 'Hesperus', or 'Jack the Ripper', or 'arthritis' refers to. But once we discover enough about the world—which heavenly bodies are where, who murdered whom, which diseases have which properties—then we are in a position to know the referents of these terms. I have suggested a picture like this informally in section 4 of chapter 1.

Still, there are various potential problems with the thesis as it stands. One problem is that it is not clear just what counts as knowing what an expression refers to. One might suggest that to know what 'Hesperus' refers to, one must know, of some object, that 'Hesperus' refers to it. But it is notoriously hard to give a precise content to the notion of (*de re*) knowledge of an object. Arguably, one expresses *de re* knowledge by saying ''Hesperus' refers to *that*', looking in the sky, or perhaps even by saying ''Hesperus' refers to Hesperus'. But this sort of knowledge is much easier to obtain than the more substantial knowledge of reference envisaged in the scrutability thesis, such as the knowledge that we have after we do some astronomy. Alternatively, one might suggest that to know what 'Hesperus' refers to, one must have knowledge expressible in the form ''Hesperus' refers to *X*', where *X* is a special sort of canonical designator. But here it is not clear what counts as a canonical designator of an object. For example, if 'Venus' is a canonical designator, does this mean that any user of 'Venus' knows what 'Venus' refers to?

Another problem is Quine's indeterminacy thesis. If reference is indeterminate, so that there is no fact of the matter about what our expressions refer to, then we cannot know what our expressions refer to. Quine argues that there are multiple ways of assigning referents to our terms that make sense of all available data (including data about our judgments concerning whether sentences containing those terms are true), and that there is no fact of the matter about which assignment is correct. Even if one has doubts about the generality of Quine's argument, many have made similar arguments concerning specific domains. For example, Paul Benacerraf (1965) argues that many different sorts of entities are equally well-qualified to be the referents of number terms, all yielding the same truth-values for numerical statements. In a related way, David Lewis (1993) argues that we can take various different entities to be the referent of 'cat', while Terence Horgan (1986) argues that we can take various different sorts of entities to be the referent of 'symphony'. In all of these domains, it is often held that reference is indeterminate.

Strikingly, both of these problems can be bypassed if we move from the scrutability of reference to the scrutability of truth.

> *The Scrutability of Truth* (informal version):[1] For any truth *S*, once we know enough about the world, we are in a position to know that *S* is true.

The scrutability of truth captures much of the force of the scrutability of reference. The former thesis implies that for *any* true claim of the form 'Hesperus is X', then once we know enough about the world, we are in a position to know that 'Hesperus is X' is true. So we are in a position to know the truth-value of 'Hesperus is Venus', 'Hesperus is the second planet from the Sun', and so on for any designator at all. Most of the intuitive backing behind the scrutability of

---

[1] For a perfect analogy with the scrutability of reference, this should really be the scrutability of truth-value. But the shorter label works just as well.

reference (e.g. that given enough qualitative information, we can know who Jack the Ripper is) is reflected in the scrutability of truth (e.g. that given enough qualitative information, we can know whether Jack the Ripper was Prince Albert Victor).

In the reverse direction, it is arguable that the scrutability of reference entails the scrutability of truth. If one holds with Frege that sentences are referring expressions that refer to their truth-values, then the entailment is immediate. Even if one rejects this claim, it is not hard to construct a referring expression that functions to refer to the truth-value of a given sentence: we might just use 'the truth-value of S', or perhaps better (in order to avoid semantic ascent), we might stipulate an operator 'whether' such that 'whether S' behaves this way. Then applying the scrutability of reference to these expressions yields the scrutability of truth.

Furthermore, the first problem concerning knowledge of reference has no parallel in the case of knowledge of truth. Truth is canonically presented under the concept *true*. To know that E is true, it suffices to have knowledge of the form *E is true*, deploying this concept. Further, if one knows the truth of 'Hesperus is X' for all relevant X, then it seems reasonable to say that one knows what Hesperus refers to.

Importantly, Quine's central case for the inscrutability of reference causes no problems for the scrutability of truth. This case starts by assuming that the truth-values of sentences are fixed, and makes the case that there are multiple assignments of reference that yield the same truth-values. Even if this argument makes a case for the indeterminacy of reference, it does not make a corresponding case for the indeterminacy of truth: while reference varies between the multiple assignments, truth-values do not. One might suggest that if reference is indeterminate, truth must then be indeterminate too, but this is far from obvious: if one accepts Quine's picture here, one will presumably accept a picture on which determinate truth-values do not require determinate referents (perhaps denying that truth-value is determined by referents, or perhaps holding that truth-value is determined by supervaluating over possible assignments of reference). In any case, there is certainly no direct argument for the indeterminacy of truth-value here.

Quine has other arguments for the indeterminacy of truth-value, tied to his arguments for the indeterminacy of translation. These arguments do not start by holding fixed the truth-value of all sentences, but only the truth-value of certain observational sentences. In this case, multiple assignments of reference are put forward in a way that makes a difference to the truth-value of non-observational sentences. This is a case for the indeterminacy of reference that also makes a case for the indeterminacy of truth-value. But these arguments concerning the indeterminacy of translation are usually held to be distinct from the central arguments concerning the inscrutability of reference. Further, these arguments are often held to be much more problematic than the arguments concerning the inscrutability of reference, because they rest on much stronger verificationist or behaviorist assumptions. If this is right, Quine's best case for the indeterminacy of reference does not undermine the scrutability of truth.

As for related arguments, such as Benacerraf's, these have at best minor implications for matters concerning truth. In these arguments, as with Quine's, the multiple assignments of reference are usually chosen precisely so that they preserve the truth-values of first-order sentences (such as '2 + 2 = 4' and 'There are an infinite number of primes') in the domain in question. If so, almost all of the indeterminacies will drop out when it comes to the truth-values of statements. An exception may be quasi-philosophical statements such as 'the number two is a set of sets', and the like. But now the issue is restricted to a few isolated sentences in the metaphysical domain, and these can be handled in the same way that one handles other sentences with indeterminate truth-value. The highly limited indeterminacy here contrasts with the issue concerning reference, which potentially affects every use of the relevant words, thereby rendering the scrutability of reference either false or useless.

The moral is that the inscrutability of reference is quite compatible with the scrutability of truth. Even if one is inclined to accept the arguments for the inscrutability of reference (I am not), one does not have corresponding reasons to reject the scrutability of truth.

Of course the thesis of the scrutability of truth is still informal and unclear in certain respects. We need to clarify 'know enough about the world', for example so that this does not typically allow the trivializing knowledge that S is true. The obvious thought is that the relevant information about the world should be restricted to a limited (compact) vocabulary, and that the relevant class of truths is limited (compact) in a similar way.

So clarified, the thesis now becomes:

> *The Scrutability of Truth* (second version): There is a compact class C of truths such that for all truths S, once we know enough truths in C, we are in a position to know that S is true.

This version of the thesis is quite close to the Inferential Scrutability thesis. It is subject to the Fitch-style problems discussed in the first excursus, but as discussed there, one can get around these by changing the scope and using a conditional formulation. This yields a version of Conditional Scrutability: there is a compact class of truths such that we are in a position to know that *if* these truths are true, then S is true.

This line of motivation does not yet get to A Priori Scrutability, but one might get there by a certain clarification of 'in a position to know'. One natural thought is that being in a position to know such-and-such should involve being able to know such-and-such, given ideal rational reflection and without further empirical information. Furthermore, it is natural to interpret the second version of the thesis above as holding that the compact class of base truths contains all the empirical information that is required to know the truth in question. In the conditional version of the thesis, all this information is built into the antecedent of the conditional. So it is natural to require that this conditional can be known (on ideal rational reflection) without any further empirical information at all; that is, that it can be known a priori. This yields the following.

> *Scrutability of Truth* (final version): There is a compact class of truths such that for all truths S, there is a conjunction D of truths in this class such that 'If D, then S' is knowable a priori.

This is a version of the A Priori Scrutability thesis. In this fashion, A Priori Scrutability can be motivated by starting from claims about the scrutability of reference and by modifying them to avoid the most pressing objections.

2

Varieties of Scrutability

1 Scrutability theses

Scrutability theses can take a number of different forms. Some are restricted scrutability theses: one such thesis holds that all mental truths are scrutable from physical truths, for example. Most of the scrutability theses I am interested in will be unrestricted theses, however, saying that all truths are scrutable in some way.

The general form of an unrestricted scrutability thesis is: all truths are scrutable from base truths. This leaves three things to be clarified further: 'truths', 'scrutable from', and 'base'. All three elements correspond to important dimensions of variation.

What are 'truths': true propositions, true sentences, or something else? In the introduction, scrutability theses were formulated in terms of propositions. In chapter 1, they were formulated in terms of sentences. I discuss this issue in section 2 and in much more detail in the third excursus, following this chapter.

What are 'base truths'? These might be a class of truths, such as the class of physical truths, phenomenal truths, or fundamental truths. If so, a scrutability thesis will say that all truths are scrutable from that class. Alternatively, 'base truths' might stand for a type of class of truths, such as the type: compact classes of truths. If so, a scrutability thesis will say that all truths are scrutable from some class of truths of that type. One important constraint on base truths is compactness (as characterized in section 5 of chapter 1), but numerous other candidates will be discussed. I characterize an initial class of base truths in the first section of chapter 3, and focus on minimal classes of base truths in chapters 7 and 8.

What is 'scrutable from'? We have already encountered numerous scrutability relations: inferential scrutability, conditional scrutability, a priori scrutability, definitional scrutability, and so on. I will adopt the convention of using lower case for these scrutability relations ('inferential scrutability'), while using upper case for corresponding scrutability theses ('Inferential Scrutability').

In principle one can mix and match different values for each of these three dimensions (scrutability relations, base elements, sentences or propositions), yielding many different scrutability theses such as A Priori Fundamental Sentential Scrutability, Conditional Physical Propositional Scrutability, and so on. My convention will be that the default values are A Priori, Compact, and Sentential. So Scrutability (simpliciter) says that all true sentences are a priori scrutable from a compact class of true sentences. Fundamental Scrutability says that all true sentences are a priori scrutable from the class of fundamental true sentences. Conditional Propositional Scrutability says that all true propositions are conditionally scrutable from a compact class of true propositions. And so on.

Where scrutability relations are concerned, the three most important are those outlined in the introduction: inferential, conditional, and a priori scrutability. There I laid out corresponding theses in propositional form, but for present purposes it is useful to define the relations themselves and to do so in sentential form. Put this way, they will be relations between a sentence S and a class of sentences C for a subject s.[1] The basic characterization of these three notions is as follows.

S is inferentially scrutable from C for s iff, if s were to come to know C, s would be in a position to know S.

S is conditionally scrutable from C for s iff s is in a position to know that if C, then S.

S is a priori scrutable from C for s iff s is in a position to know a priori that if C, then S.

What is it to know a sentence S is discussed in the next section. To know a class of sentences C is to know all sentences in C, or to know a conjunction of all sentences in C. For ease of discussion, I adopt the convention that when a name for a class of sentences appears in a context where a sentence would be more appropriate (such as after 'if' or 'know'), it stands for a conjunction of the sentences in the class.[2] In all three cases, 'in a position to know' should be understood as involving an idealization, with the rough idea being that the

---

[1] Strictly speaking, scrutability is always relative to a time and a world as well as to a subject, in part because of differences in what subjects are in a position to know at different times and in different worlds. So we should say that S is scrutable from C for a subject s at time t in world w. To avoid clutter, I will usually mention only s and leave the relativization to time and world implicit. Where context-dependent sentences are concerned, we can also relativize scrutability to a context in order to reflect differences in what the sentences express in different contexts, as discussed later.

[2] For such a conjunctive sentence to exist when C is infinite, C must be sufficiently disciplined and the language must allow infinite conjunctions (see the end of E3 for more on related issues). For most purposes the appeal to these conjunctive sentences is just a convenience, and we could also formulate the theses without them (e.g. in terms of knowing all sentences in C rather than in terms of knowing their conjunction).

subject could come to know these things through sufficiently ideal reasoning if they were capable of such reasoning. I flesh out all of these notions and the nature of the idealization later in this chapter.

Of the three relations, a priori scrutability theses are the most important for our purposes. Conditional scrutability plays an important role in arguing for a priori scrutability theses and also provides a useful fallback thesis that is available even to those who are skeptical about the a priori. Inferential scrutability plays a less essential role and is also more problematic in some respects, but I have included discussion of it both because it can help to motivate the other theses and because its problems are interesting in their own right.

For each of these scrutability relations, there is a corresponding *conclusive* scrutability relation concerning not knowledge but certainty. The conclusive relations can be defined by replacing 'know' in the definitions above by 'know with certainty'. For example, conclusive inferential scrutability requires that if s came to know C with certainty, s would be in a position to know S with certainty, while conclusive conditional scrutability requires that s is in a position to know with certainty that if C, then S. Certainty is sometimes understood in a psychological sense, as requiring absolute confidence, or degree of belief 1. Here it should be understood in an epistemological sense as requiring justified absolute confidence, or rational degree of belief 1. (These notions are discussed at more length later in this chapter and in the seventh excursus.) Knowledge with certainty is a particularly strong sort of knowledge: intuitively, it requires absolutely eliminating all hypotheses on which S is false. It is plausible that we cannot be certain of ordinary empirical claims, such as 'There is a table in this room', but it is at least arguable that it is possible to be certain of some claims: perhaps 'All cats are cats' and 'I am conscious'.

There will then be conclusive variants of the scrutability theses we are concerned with: Conclusive A Priori Scrutability, for example. In some cases (certainly for Conditional Scrutability, and arguably for the others) the conclusive variant will be stronger than the original thesis. But many of the reasons for believing the original theses are also reasons for believing the conclusive theses (it is notable that Laplace himself talked of certainty), and the conclusive theses are important for a number of applications. So I will keep an eye on both the original theses and the conclusive theses in what follows.

Some conveniences: when S is a priori scrutable from C, I will also say that C *a priori entails* S. We can define conditional entailment, inferential entailment, and conclusive versions of all three in an analogous way. I will sometimes say that C *implies* S when C a priori entails S. I will occasionally use the language of scrutability and entailment for relations between sentences: when T is a priori scrutable from the class containing only S, we can say that T is a priori scrutable from S, that S a priori entails T, or that S implies T.

In what follows, I discuss the objects of scrutability in section 2, the three main scrutability relations in 3 through 5, generalized scrutability in section 6, and issues about idealization in sections 7 and 8. These sections clarify a number of foundational issues regarding the formulation of scrutability theses. Many of these clarifications are not essential to following the later discussion, so it is possible to skip the remainder of this chapter on a first reading or to read only those sections that are of interest. For many readers, it may work best to look briefly at the following section and then move directly to Chapter 3, coming back to this chapter when necessary.

2 Sentences or propositions?

Many different sorts of things are sometimes said to be truths: true propositions, true beliefs, true sentences, true utterances. Which of these are most relevant to scrutability theses?

Truths are most commonly understood as true propositions, where propositions are entities that are independent of any particular language, and that are the things we assert and believe. My own view is that if propositions and scrutability are understood correctly, then all true propositions are indeed scrutable from a compact class of propositions. However, the nature of propositions is strongly contested, and different conceptions of propositions will yield quite different results for scrutability.

On a *possible-worlds* view of propositions, the proposition expressed by a sentence is the set of possible worlds where the sentence is true. On this view, all necessary truths express the same proposition (the set of all worlds), a proposition that is itself knowable a priori. If so, then if it is necessary that water is H_2O, it follows that the proposition that water is H_2O is itself knowable a priori.

On a *Russellian* view of propositions, the proposition expressed by a sentence is a structure involving those objects and properties that are the extensions of parts of the sentence. On this view, not all necessary truths express the same proposition, but the proposition that Hesperus is a planet and the proposition that Phosphorus is a planet are identical.

On a *Fregean* view of propositions, the proposition expressed by a sentence is a structure of senses expressed by parts of a sentence, where senses are fine-grained entities reflecting the epistemic and cognitive significance of various expressions. On this view, not all necessary truths express the same proposition, and the proposition that Hesperus is a planet and the proposition that Phosphorus is a planet are distinct.

On an *eliminative* view of propositions, there are no propositions at all. There are only sentences and utterances, and perhaps acts of thinking and states of believing. But sentences do not express propositions, and thinking and believing do not involve relationships to propositions.

It is clear that if we antecedently assume one or another of these views of propositions, there will be very different results for a scrutability thesis cast in terms of propositions. On the possible-worlds view, all necessary truths will automatically be a priori scrutable from any basis. On the Russellian view, necessary truths will not usually be a priori scrutable from arbitrary bases. But some, such as the proposition that Hesperus is Phosphorus (if they exist), will arguably be scrutable from any basis, and there will be no epistemological differences between propositions expressed by pairs of sentences involving 'Hesperus' and 'Phosphorus' respectively. On a Fregean view, necessary truths will not automatically be scrutable, and epistemological differences between sentences involving 'Hesperus' and 'Phosphorus' will be preserved. On an eliminative view, the thesis that all propositions are scrutable will be vacuously true.

My own purposes include the analysis of fine-grained epistemological properties of sentences and thoughts. For this purpose, a Fregean view of propositions is the most promising. But I cannot simply assume such a view at the outset. It is controversial whether there are Fregean propositions, and even among sympathizers, it is controversial just what sort of thing they might be and how they behave. Further, one of my purposes is to use scrutability theses to provide support for a Fregean view of propositions. If I were to assume such a view at the outset, there would be some circularity here. Perhaps some support for the view would accrue from demonstrating coherence and power in the resulting picture, but a flavor of assuming the conclusion and of begging the question against opponents would remain.

At the same time, it will not do to assume one of the other views of propositions. And it does not make sense to cast things in terms of propositions but stay neutral between these views, as the views yield very different results in evaluating scrutability theses.[3] One can certainly cast scrutability theses in terms of all three notions of propositions, but scrutability bases for each of the three may look very different.

So I will set aside propositions for now. That being said: if one accepts Fregean propositions, or if one is at least prepared to allow that propositions are sufficiently fine-grained to reflect differences in cognitive significance as well as differences in reference, then one might well construe scrutability theses in terms

---

[3] I think that the arguments in the next two chapters can in principle make the case for scrutability of all truths (or at least all truths expressible by the subject) from the relevant base even if Russellian or possible-worlds propositions are involved. But I do not expect many Russellians to agree (see E11 for more on this); and while possible-worlds theorists might agree, they might also take the conclusion to be a weak one. And in practice, casting scrutability theses in terms of propositions of this sort, or in a neutral way, would lead to too many complications arising from disagreements among theorists about how to treat the epistemology of these propositions.

of propositions. That way many of the added complexities that come from appealing to sentences can be dispensed with, and much of what I say later will still apply. So those who accept fine-grained Fregean propositions should feel free to translate what I say into propositional terms (though a couple of obstacles to a perfect translation are noted in the third excursus).

It is not out of the question to cast a scrutability thesis in terms of mental states such as thoughts or beliefs, holding for example that for any thought one might entertain, the truth or falsity of the thought could be inferred from a certain class of (potential) basic thoughts. But the individuation of thoughts and beliefs is also nontrivial, and it is more awkward to speak of mental items than of linguistic items, so I will set these aside too, although later I will give a role to thoughts in interpreting scrutability claims.

Instead, I will take the truths at issue to be linguistic items such as *sentences*: both sentence types (abstract sentences such as 'The cat sat on the mat') and sentence tokens (sentences as uttered on a given occasion). It is somewhat awkward to speak of knowing sentences, and this manner of speech is certain less familiar than talk of knowing propositions or facts. But it is not hard to motivate belief-like and knowledge-like relations between speakers and linguistic items, not least through considerations about sincere assertion, knowledgeable assertion, and so on. Doing so brings out certain dialectical advantages of proceeding this way, compared to proceeding via propositions.

To see this, consider the Russellian about propositions who holds that the proposition that Hesperus is Hesperus and the proposition that Hesperus is Phosphorus are identical, so that there can be no psychological or epistemological differences between these propositions. Even if the Russellian is right, the *sentences* 'Hesperus is Hesperus' and 'Hesperus is Phosphorus' are not identical, and likewise utterances of these sentences are quite distinct. So it is at least open to the Russellian to associate different psychological and epistemological properties with these sentences. Furthermore, there are very good reasons for the Russellian to do so.

One way to bring this out is through what we might call the *argument from assertion* against Russellian views of propositions. Suppose that Sue knows that the morning star is a planet but believes that the evening star is not a planet. Like others in her community, she associates 'Hesperus' with the evening star and 'Phosphorus' with the morning star. Intending to deceive John, she says 'Hesperus is a planet'. We can then argue as follows:

1. Sue's assertion is not sincere.
2. An assertion is sincere iff the speaker believes the proposition asserted.
3. Sue asserts the proposition that Hesperus is a planet.
4. If the Russellian view is correct, the proposition that Hesperus is a planet is identical to the proposition that Phosphorus is a planet.

5. Sue believes the proposition that Phosphorus is a planet.

6. The Russellian view is not correct.

This argument has some force. Premise 1 cannot be plausibly rejected: it is clear that insofar that there is a sincerity norm on assertion, for example, Sue's utterance violates it. Premise 2 is a standard way to understand sincerity, and a standard Russellian view is committed to premises 3–5.[4] Still, it is not a knock-down argument against the Russellian view. Russellians will typically reject premise 2, giving an alternative account of sincere assertion. They might hold, for example, that an assertion is sincere if the speaker believes the proposition asserted under the guise under which it was asserted, or if the speaker believes that the assertion expresses a true proposition.

It is reasonable enough for a Russellian to understand sincerity in this way, but their doing so makes the point that is relevant here. To save the data about sincere assertion, the Russellian needs a way to associate cognitive properties with acts of assertion that is not determined simply by the speaker's cognitive relations to the asserted propositions. Indeed, a reformulated version of the argument, with premise 2 omitted, leads to the conditional conclusion that if the Russellian view is correct, it is not the case that an assertion is sincere if and only if the speaker believes the proposition asserted.

One can make a similar point using notions such as knowledgeable assertion and justified assertion. It is clear that Sue's assertion is not a knowledgeable assertion. It is also clear that Sue's assertion is not a justified assertion. But on a standard Russellian view, Sue knows the proposition that she asserts, and she is justified in believing the proposition that she asserts. So standard Russellians need to distinguish a knowledgeable assertion from assertion of a proposition that the speaker knows.[5] They also need to distinguish making a justified assertion from asserting a proposition that the speaker is justified in believing.

We need some language to distinguish these notions. I will say that when an assertion of a sentence S is a sincere assertion (or a believed assertion, as in footnote 4), the speaker believes S. When an assertion of a sentence S is a

---

[4] A nonstandard Russellian view suggested by Soames (2002) holds that in cases like these, speakers assert propositions that are not semantically expressed by the asserted sentence. This view will deny premise 3, but the upshot will be much the same as in the text. Making a sincere assertion will come apart from believing the proposition semantically expressed, and utterances that semantically express the same proposition can nevertheless have different epistemic properties.

[5] The case of sincerity is more complicated in some respects than the case of knowledgeable and justified assertion, as there are arguably other cases in which one might tease sincerity apart from believing the proposition asserted. For example, if Sue says something that she believes to be true but that she knows will mislead John, then arguably her assertion is not sincere. To avoid these complications one could use the somewhat more constrained (if somewhat less familiar) notion of a believed assertion instead.

knowledgeable assertion, the speaker knows S. When an assertion of a sentence S is a justified assertion, the speaker is justified in believing S. The same goes for other properties such as being a justifiable assertion, being an a priori justifiable assertion, and so on. When S is a context-dependent sentence type ('He is ready'), it is best to relativize knowledge to context: so the speaker knows or believes S relative to the current context, or knows or believes the current token of S.

This analysis is developed further in the third excursus. The key idea there is to analyze the epistemic status of a sentence S in terms of epistemic properties of mental states that S expresses or is apt to express. For example, one knows S when one has knowledge that is apt to be expressed by S. Likewise, one knows S a priori when one has a priori knowledge that is apt to be expressed by S, and one believes S when one has a belief that is apt to be expressed by S. This allows the notion of knowing a sentence to be extended to the case in which the sentence is not uttered. The language of believing and knowing sentences is somewhat nonstandard, but it provides an efficient way to capture the association of doxastic and epistemic properties with sentences and assertions, and not just with propositions.

This account of knowing a sentence makes no appeal to the notion of knowing a proposition. Given a positive theory of propositions, there will presumably be some connection between knowing a sentence and knowing a proposition, as any such theory needs some way to capture the data about sincerity, knowledgeable assertion, and so on. But different theorists of propositions will make the connection in different ways. It is open to a Fregean to simply hold that a speaker knows S if and only if she knows the proposition expressed by S. Russellians (such as Nathan Salmon in *Frege's Puzzle*) who allow that propositions are presented under guises might say that the speaker knows a sentence S when she knows the proposition expressed by S under the guise associated with S. Other Russellians might say that the speaker knows S when she knows some ancillary proposition that is not semantically expressed by S but is otherwise associated with S.[6]

It might be suggested that one knows S iff one knows that S is true. On a literal reading of 'knows that S is true', this involves a certain sort of metalinguistic knowledge about S, in which case the equation between the two is not plausible. It seems clear that Sue might knowledgeably assert 'Phosphorus is a

---

[6] If associated propositions or guises can vary between utterances of a sentence, then one can relativize these connections to contexts: one knows S in a context if one knows the proposition associated with S in that context, perhaps under the guise associated with S in that context. Alternatively, one can make the connection at the level of sentence tokens: one knows a sentence token S if one knows the proposition expressed by S, perhaps under the guise associated with S.

planet' in a case such as the above without having any metalinguistic beliefs about her assertion: all that is required is the right sort of astronomical beliefs. Still, there is a looser reading of 'knows that S is true' that does not require any metalinguistic knowledge, and that comes to a simple rephrasal of the claim that one knows S in the sense from two paragraphs ago. I will sometimes use this locution, as it is more idiomatic and convenient for some purposes than the alternative. It should be understood, though, that to know that S is true is not to have metalinguistic knowledge: it is just to know S in the sense above. On this usage, to know that 'bachelors are unmarried' is true is just to know 'bachelors are unmarried', which as characterized above is more akin to knowing that bachelors are unmarried than to knowing something about the word 'bachelor'.

In the third excursus, following this chapter, I discuss issues about sentential and propositional scrutability in much more detail. I spell out an account of knowledge of sentences in terms of thoughts expressed by those sentences; I discuss complications arising from context-dependence; I go into the precise formulation of sentential scrutability theses; and I analyze the relationship between sentential scrutability theses and propositional scrutability theses. Those who are interested in those issues should feel free to skip to the excursus now. Those details are complex, however, and they are not crucial to following the remainder of this chapter, so other readers should feel free to proceed to further issues.

In the remainder of this chapter, I discuss the formulation and interpretation of inferential, conditional, and a priori scrutability theses. Most of these issues apply to both propositions and sentences, but I will typically assume a formulation in terms of sentences.

3 Inferential scrutability

As defined in section 1, S is inferentially scrutable from C for s when, if s were to come to know C, s would be in a position to know S. The notion of inferential scrutability is not essential to the present project, but it plays a useful motivating role.[7] It is useful in part because it avoids technical notions such as apriority and analyticity, and in part because the inferential scrutability thesis lacks the rationalist flavor of other scrutability theses. If anything, it has an empiricist flavor, saying that one could come to know a great many things by knowing certain (largely

---

[7] One way to simplify the path through this book is to ignore all material on inferential scrutability (mainly in this chapter and the next). The problems for Inferential Scrutability are interesting in their own right, especially if one is interested in Fitch-style issues, and the thesis plays a minor role in motivating Conditional and A Priori Scrutability, but the latter two theses play a more central role in the following chapters.

empirical) truths. So it provides a good entry point to scrutability theses for one who is skeptical of rationalism and the a priori.

Inferential scrutability differs structurally from the other two sorts of scrutability. Conditional and a priori scrutability involve knowledge of conditionals, while inferential scrutability involves knowledge of unconditional sentences, given knowledge of other sentences.[8] As we saw in the introduction, this distinctive form raises distinctive problems for inferential scrutability theses that do not apply to the other two. I discuss these problems and some potential solutions later in this section.

Typically, inferential scrutability will involve knowledge by inference: if s came to know C, s would be in a position to know S by inference from C. The definition does not require knowledge by inference, however, so it can be satisfied in cases where S is in a position to know C some other way: perhaps s knew S already, or perhaps S is a theorem that s can prove independently of C. It is arguable that in any such case, s is also in a position to infer S from C (perhaps s could start with C, conjoin S after recalling or proving it, and then drop C). But even if this does not count as inference, we can simply note that inferential scrutability does not require inferrability. The label 'inferential' is imperfect, but it captures the idea that transitions from knowledge states to knowledge states (rather than knowledge of conditionals) are central here.[9]

The Inferential Scrutability thesis says (to a first approximation): there is a compact class of truths C from which all truths are inferentially scrutable for all subjects.[10] That is: there is a compact class C of truths such that any subject who came to know C would be in a position to know S.

Here the stipulation that the subject knows C is best understood as a stipulation that the subject knows the sentences in C and continues to know them, insofar as this is possible. Without this stipulation, some subjects who are on the point of inferring S from C might respond by rejecting C instead, perhaps because they disbelieve S. But for our purposes we are really interested in the

---

[8] That is, the first two can be represented as $PK(C \rightarrow S)$ and $PKA(C \rightarrow S)$, while inferential scrutability can be represented as $K(C) \Rightarrow PK(S)$. Here K, PK, and PKA stand for 'knows', 'is in a position to know', and 'is in a position to know a priori' respectively, '$\rightarrow$' is an indicative (or perhaps material) conditional connective, and '$\Rightarrow$' is a counterfactual connective.

[9] In earlier versions of this work I used 'empirical scrutability', because of the empiricist flavor discussed below, but that name misleadingly suggests a parallel to a priori scrutability with a defining role for a posteriori knowledge.

[10] As discussed in the third excursus, this characterization of Inferential Scrutability (and other scrutability theses) requires a small adjustment to accommodate indexicals such as 'I' and 'now' in the base. The amended version says: there is a compact class of sentences C such that for all subjects s, all truths (relative to s) are inferentially scrutable from the truths (relative to s) in C. This amendment does not seriously affect the main issues under discussion here, and for simplicity I will ignore it in the body of this chapter.

consequences of knowledge of C where this knowledge is held fixed. Alternatively, we can require in the antecedent that the subject knows C with certainty. In this case, it is arguable that subjects should never respond by rejecting C (at least given that they are not certain of $\sim S$, which they will not be if they are rational and S is true).

A subject s at time t is in a position to know S when it is possible that s comes to know S at some later time t', starting from s's position at t and without acquiring any further empirical information.[11] The process of coming to know S need not involve a priori reasoning alone, as it can use any empirical beliefs that the subject has at the time of utterance, but it cannot involve new empirical discovery (based on perception, testimony, and so on) after this point. There are various notions of possibility, but for our purposes it is most natural to appeal to metaphysical possibility here. This makes for a significant idealization, allowing possible futures in which the subject manifests reasoning capacities that are not present at t, but such an idealization is needed for our purposes in any case.

One can illustrate the thesis by first selecting a scrutability base. Let us say as in chapter 1 that $PQTI$ is the class of all truths of physics, phenomenal truths, along with certain indexical truths and a that's-all truth saying that the world is a minimal world in which the previous truths obtain (more details can be found in chapter 3). For present purposes not much depends on this choice of basis: we could use any class that stands a chance of serving as a scrutability base for all truths.

It seems clear that *if* a subject knew all truths in $PQTI$, then she would thereby be in a position to know many more truths about the world. And it does not seem immediately out of the question (at least setting aside the problems discussed below) that for any truth S, she would be in a position to know S. If so, all truths would be inferentially scrutable from $PQTI$.

Of course $PQTI$ is an enormous set of truths about all of spacetime. As stated, the thesis requires considering a scenario in which the subject comes to know all these truths. To do this, the subject would need to have cognitive capacities greater than any actual human subject. So as before, we need to idealize to make sense of this scenario.

There is a worse problem than idealization, however. For the inferential scrutability thesis to be true, the base class C (such as $PQTI$) will have to be sufficiently encompassing that its truths are jointly true of this world and this world alone. But then, assuming that no one actually knows C, it will be impossible to

---

[11] Bringing in worlds: A subject s at time t in world w is in a position to know S iff there is a world w' (possible relative to w) and a time t' (later than t) such that s is in the same position at t in both w' and w and such that s comes to know S at t' in w'. I will typically leave the world-relativization tacit, with the note that 'starting from their position at t' always invokes the position in the original world. I will not try to analyze the notion of position, but it will probably suffice for w and w' to be duplicates at all times up to t.

know C. Any world in which someone knows C will differ from the actual world and will therefore be a world in which C is false. But there are no worlds in which someone knows C and C is false. So no one can know C. If so, then the Inferential Scrutability thesis is vacuously true (if counterfactuals with impossible antecedents are vacuously true), or at least hard to assess (if not).

This problem is closely related to Fitch's paradox of knowability, discussed in the first excursus: if there is a truth S that no one ever knows, there is a truth S_1 = 'S and no one knows S' that no one can possibly know (if someone knew S_1, they would know S, so S_1 would be false). If we take S to be a conjunction of the sentences in C, we obtain a sentence S_1 that is unknowable for much the same reason that C is unknowable. The general version of Fitch's paradox poses a related problem for the Inferential Scrutability thesis. On the face of it, Inferential Scrutability entails that all truths can be known, at least if C can be known. But we know that not all truths can be known. So either Inferential Scrutability is false or C cannot be known. If we choose C so that Inferential Scrutability is true, as in the previous paragraph, we are then faced with the worry that the thesis is vacuously true or at best unclear.

The remainder of this section is devoted to a number of possible responses to this Fitch-style problem. First, one might try construing 'being in a position to know' in terms of warrant rather than in terms of possible knowledge, as in the fourth excursus. On such a construal, inferential scrutability of S from C requires that knowing C would provide a warrant for believing S. This might arguably help with the case of the Fitch sentence S_1: it is arguable that if one knew all the truths in C, one would have warrant for each conjunct of S_1 and therefore for S_1 itself, even though one could not use this warrant to know S_1. But it does not obviously help with the worry that it is impossible to know all the truths in C. At this point one could try allowing that counterfactuals with impossible antecedents are not always vacuously true. Then one might allow (nontrivially) that *if*, impossibly, one came to know all truths in C, then one would have warrant for sentences such as S_1 above. This strategy is not uninteresting, but I will set it aside in what follows.

Second, one could address the problem concerning the knowability of C by weakening the notion of inferential scrutability. We can say that S is inferentially scrutable from a class C for s if there is a knowable *subclass* of C such that if s were to come to know that subclass, s would be in a position to know S. In most cases, the required subclass will be much smaller than C itself. This helps to avoid the problem arising from the unknowability of C and also requires a less demanding idealization.

I will adopt this useful amendment in what follows, as it at least allows that some truths are clearly inferentially scrutable. But there remain obvious problems with the corresponding Inferential Scrutability thesis. One worry is that it weakens the thesis considerably.[12] For many truths S, there will be some C-truths such that knowing these truths justifies belief in S, but such that knowing *further* C-truths would justify rejecting S. For this reason one will have to be careful in making inferences from these weakened inferential scrutability claims to other scrutability claims.

Another problem for the amended thesis is that the Fitch sentence S_1 yields a counterexample to the thesis, at least on a modal understanding of being in a position to know. Because S_1 is unknowable, no knowable subclass of C can be such that knowing C would put a subject in a position to know S_1. There are related problem cases: say that S_2 is 'I know no sentences in C', uttered by a subject who has beliefs about some sentences in C but does not know them, and is not now in a position to know that she does not know them. Then S_2 is true, but the subject is not in a position to know it by coming to know any subclass of sentences of C. To solve these problems, further work is needed.

A third way of dealing with the Fitch-style problems stems from the observation that in all these cases, it is not ruled out that one can come to know *whether* the sentence S is true (where knowledge of whether S is true is the natural generalization of knowledge that S is true as explained above). It is just that the very process of coming to know whether S is true (by the procedure of coming to know C-truths) will render S false.

We might call truths like this *Fitchian* truths, because Fitch's unknowable truth 'P and I don't know P' is a paradigm. We might define a Fitchian truth as an *alethically fragile* truth: a truth S such that properly investigating the truth-value of S will change the truth-value of S. Here to investigate the truth-value of S is to investigate whether S is true, and to do so properly is, roughly, to do so as well as could be done. There are numerous different methods by which one might come to know the truth-value of S, so one might also say that S is Fitchian with respect to a method when properly investigating the truth-value of S by that method will render S false. Then S_1 above is Fitchian with respect to any method, as is the conjunction of all truths in C, while S_2 is Fitchian with respect to the method of determining truth-value via knowledge of sentences in C.[13]

---

[12] Another worry concerns the scrutability of negative truths, which as discussed in the next chapter may require the use of a 'that's-all' sentence. On some formulations of the that's-all sentence, knowing it will entail knowing all the other sentences in the class. Then the considerations here suggest that the that's-all sentence will be unknowable; but then remaining subclasses will not allow scrutability of negative truths. To avoid this problem one would have to use other formulations of the that's-all sentence or restrict scrutability theses to positive truths, as in the next chapter. Thanks to Wolfgang Schwarz for discussion here.

[13] Likewise, the sentence 'There is no Laplacean demon', discussed in the introduction, is alethically fragile with respect to the method of knowledge by a Laplacean demon. The solution of moving to 'know whether' is in effect a version of the move suggested there, requiring the demon to know about its own modified world rather than the actual world. Versions of the paradoxes of complexity and prediction still arise; I discuss a way to handle these in 3.5.

One might then suggest a modified thesis saying that for any truth S (or perhaps for any truth-apt sentence S), there is some subclass of C such that if one were to come to know this subclass, one would be in a position to know *whether* S is true. Or better, one can suggest that there is some subclass such that if one were to come to know whether the sentences in this subclass are true, one would be in a position to know whether S is true. This latter formulation allows for the possibility that the process of coming to know the sentences may also change the truth-value of sentences in C, as well as the truth-value of S.

This modified thesis is not threatened by Fitchian truths or by any of the cases above. There are some residual worries. One worry is that in cases where one cannot know that S is true without knowing whether a very large subclass of C-sentences is true, worlds where one knows that subclass may be so different from our world (in the cognitive capacity they allow, for example) that they are nomologically impossible. In such a world, knowing whether S is true might require knowing about alien features of that world not described by C-sentences. If so, then no knowledge of C-sentences will put one in a position to know whether S is true. It is unclear whether this scenario can arise. But a milder version of the worry applies more generally. For any truth S such that one can know the truth-value of S only by knowing some (actual) truths in C to be false, then the inferential scrutability relation between S and C does not tell us directly about the status and grounds of S in the actual world. Correspondingly, one will not be able to use inferential scrutability to argue directly for the scrutability of the truth of S from the truth of C in the actual world. So the force of the scrutability thesis is weakened somewhat. Still, this modified inferential scrutability thesis remains interesting and important.

A fourth strategy is simply to exclude Fitchian cases, and require only that all non-Fitchian truths (with respect to the method of inferential scrutability from C-truths) are inferentially scrutable from C-truths. (For some purposes one will need to modify this thesis further, for reasons I discuss in section 3.5.) This strategy loses the universal scope of the thesis, of course, and it may appear somewhat ad hoc. Nevertheless, this strategy can help in supporting other scrutability theses. In the next chapter, I will argue that all non-Fitchian truths (of a certain sort) are inferentially scrutable. If inferential scrutability entails conditional scrutability, and if conditional scrutability is not subject to worries about Fitchian cases, then there is at least a reasonable prima facie case that all truths (of the relevant sort) are conditionally scrutable.

A fifth fix, and perhaps the most natural, is to move to conditional scrutability, as discussed below.

I revisit these problems for Inferential Scrutability and offer a different way to approach them in section 5 of chapter 3. In any case, these problems will not matter too much for my purposes. Inferential Scrutability is mainly valuable for its role in helping to argue for other scrutability theses, such as Conditional and A Priori Scrutability, and in providing initial motivation for these scrutability theses for those who may be skeptical about them. As long as the Fitch-style problems for Inferential Scrutability do not affect the other theses, then the Inferential Scrutability thesis can still play these roles reasonably well.

4 Conditional scrutability

A sentence S is conditionally scrutable from a class of sentences C for a subject s when s is in a position to know that *if* the members of C are true, then S is true. The Conditional Scrutability thesis says that there is a compact class of truths C from which all truths are conditionally scrutable for all subjects. As we saw in the first excursus, the conditional formulation avoids the Fitchian problems above. Even if S is unknowable, there is usually no problem knowing that if some other sentence T is true, then S is true. And in the cases above, there seems to be no problem with the idea that the relevant subjects are in a position to know (on idealized reflection) that *if* the sentences in $PQTI$ are true, then S_1 and S_2 are true.

This thesis uses the notion of conditional knowledge: that is, knowledge of conditionals such as 'If P, then Q'. Such claims are common in English: it would be natural to say that I know that if it rains today, then my car will get wet. Such claims are about as common as claims about conditional belief, as when I say that I believe that if Australia bats first in the cricket match, Ricky Ponting will score a century. It is natural to hold that conditional knowledge stands to conditional belief much as knowledge stands to belief.

The correct analysis of conditional belief and conditional knowledge is nontrivial. It is implausible that conditional belief and conditional knowledge, at least as ordinarily understood in English, simply involve belief in or knowledge of a material conditional, for which 'If P, then Q' is true whenever P is false or Q is true. For example, I might know that it is not raining, and thereby know (and believe) the material conditional 'If it is raining, then my car is dry'. But if my car is out in the open, it is intuitively incorrect to say that I know (or believe) that if it is raining, then my car is dry.

It is somewhat more plausible to say that conditional belief and knowledge involve belief in and knowledge of an *indicative* conditional. For reasons analogous to those above, most theorists deny that indicative conditionals are equivalent to material conditionals: intuitively, for an indicative conditional such as 'If it is raining, then my car is dry' to be acceptable, then there must be a stronger connection (perhaps an epistemological connection) between the antecedent and the consequent than the material conditional requires. But it is still not entirely clear what belief in or knowledge of an indicative conditional involves. For example, David Lewis (1976) gives good reason to think that conditional belief cannot simply be a matter of believing or knowing a *proposition*, at least while preserving one's epistemological intuitions. If so, then if conditional belief is belief in an indicative conditional, indicative conditionals cannot be understood as propositions.

The most common view of conditional belief, associated especially with Frank Ramsey (1931), holds that a subject believes that if p, then q (for propositions p and q) if and only if the subject's *conditional credence* in q given p, $cr(q \mid p)$, is sufficiently high. Here we adopt a view on which subjects have credence between 0 and 1 in various propositions: $cr(p) = 1$ when the subject is certain of p, $cr(p) = 0$ when the subject rejects p with certainty, $cr(p) = 0.5$ when the subject is entirely agnostic between the two, and so on.[14] If p is the proposition that the dice will come up double six, then my credence $cr(p)$ might be 1/36. In cases where the subject believes that p, then $cr(p)$ will be well over 1/2. To a first approximation, we can say that a subject believes that p when $cr(p)$ is sufficiently high. It is plausible that the threshold for belief is context-dependent, vague, and differs between different propositions: for example, a credence of 0.999 may suffice for belief in some cases (belief that it will rain today) but not in others (belief that one will lose the lottery). But we can understand 'sufficiently high' to be context-dependent, vague, and variable between propositions in a similar way.

Subjects can also have conditional credences in one proposition given another. For example, if p is the proposition that two dice will come up double six and q is the proposition that the red die will come up six, then my conditional credence $cr(p \mid q)$ might be 1/6. In cases where $cr(q)$ is greater than zero and where the subject is fully rational, $cr(p \mid q)$ will be equal to $cr(p \& q)/cr(q)$. But for familiar reasons (Hájek 2003), it is reasonable to hold that subjects can have a conditional credence $cr(p \mid q)$ even in some cases where $cr(q) = 0$. For example, if p is as above, and q is the proposition that a randomly thrown dart lands exactly at position π on an interval, then $cr(q)$ might reasonably be 0, while $cr(p \mid q)$ might nevertheless reasonably be 1/36. So a subject's conditional credence in p given q should not in general be understood as deriving wholly from the subject's credences in p, q, and $p \& q$. Rather, it should be understood as capturing some more complex cognitive dependence between the subject's attitudes to p and to q.

Just as we can say that a subject believes that p when her credence $cr(p)$ is sufficiently high, we can likewise say that a subject believes that if p then q when her

---

[14] Ordinary subjects do not usually have precise credences, but it is plausible that they at least have credence ranges, as described below. I do not take it to be a constraint that credences (or credence ranges) must obey the probability axioms. For example, a non-ideal subject might have a low credence in a logical truth. However, the probability axioms may well be constraints on *rational* credences as characterized below.

conditional credence $cr(q \mid p)$ is sufficiently high. Of course, much more needs to be said about just what 'sufficiently high' involves. As before, we should expect that the threshold for conditional belief will be context-dependent, vague, and will differ for different pairs of propositions. But it is not implausible that what goes for unconditional belief also goes for conditional belief.

What about knowledge? In the case of unconditional knowledge that p, the justification requirement on knowledge plausibly corresponds to a claim that the subject is justified in having a sufficiently high credence $cr(p)$. This requires that a subject's credences are subject to normative assessment and in particular that they can be justified (that is, that a subject can be justified in having a certain credence). Some radical subjectivists reject this claim, holding that all credences in nonlogical propositions are equally reasonable; but this path leads easily to skepticism. If one holds that beliefs can be justified, it seems reasonable to hold that credences can be justified too. Of course unconditional knowledge also requires that the proposition be true, and that some sort of anti-Gettier condition be satisfied, requiring for example that one's justification for the proposition is appropriately connected to the truth of the proposition.

Conditional knowledge that if p, then q also plausibly requires that the subject is justified in having a sufficiently high conditional credence $cr(q \mid p)$. Insofar as unconditional credences can be justified, it is also reasonable to hold that conditional credences can be justified. A difficult question concerns whether there is a truth requirement on conditional knowledge. It is not at all clear what it means to say that the conditional 'If p, then q' is true, as opposed to being acceptable for a subject. Still, there are plausibly cases in which the subject has a high justified conditional credence $cr(q \mid p)$, but does not know that if p, then q. This can happen if p is true and q is false, or if the subject infers q from p only with the aid of a false but justified belief in R, for example. So the question of just what needs to be added to justified conditional belief to obtain conditional knowledge remains open.[15]

For present purposes, it might suffice to rely on our intuitive understanding of conditional knowledge, just as philosophers often rely on their intuitive understanding of knowledge even without an analysis of what an anti-Gettier condition involves. But an alternative way to proceed is to stipulate that for the purposes of the Conditional Scrutability thesis, what matters is justified conditional belief, not conditional knowledge. That is, we can modify the definition of scrutability so that conditional scrutability of S from C requires only that the subject be in a position to have a justified conditional belief that if the sentences in C are true, then S is true. And we could understand this notion in turn by

[15] Sarah Moss's 'Epistemology Formalized' discusses closely related issues about probabilistic knowledge and offers a proposal for dealing with them.

saying that the subject is in a position to be justified in having a sufficiently high conditional credence in S given C. (Here the notion of being in a position to be justified can be understood in terms of the existence of a justification, as in the fourth excursus.)

In what follows, I will move back and forth between these related conceptions of conditional scrutability. The official thesis will be cast in terms of conditional knowledge, but I will often analyze things in terms of conditional credence. This is justified in part by the plausible thesis that conditional knowledge *requires* a sufficiently high justified conditional credence. When moving in the reverse direction, we can explicitly attend to the possibility of high conditional credence without conditional knowledge when it is relevant.

I will also adopt the idea that for at least some subjects and some propositions, there is a *rational* credence for the subject to have in the proposition, the credence that the subject ideally *ought* to have in the proposition. Or better, I will assume that for some subjects and propositions, there is a rational range of credences, in that one or more credences are rational, and some credences are irrational. If a subject is not ideally rational, her rational credence in a proposition may differ from her actual credence in that proposition. We can say that the rational credence for a subject in a proposition is high when only high credences in the proposition are rational for the subject. As before, if we deny that subjects have high rational credences in some propositions, it is not easy to avoid skepticism.

We can then say that p is conditionally scrutable from a class of propositions c, for a subject, when the subject's rational conditional credence $cr'(p \mid c)$ is high, where $cr'(p \mid c)$ is stipulated to be $cr'(p \mid cc)$, where cc is a conjunction of all the propositions in c. Here the notion of rational conditional credence in a pair of propositions is understood in a way parallel to the understanding of rational unconditional credence in a single proposition, above.

We can also define notions of *conclusive* knowledge and scrutability, involving knowledge with certainty. Intuitively, knowledge with certainty of p requires that one is justified in having credence 1 in p, so that one's rational credence in p is 1. Likewise, conditional knowledge of p given q requires that one's rational credence in p given q is 1. We can then say that p is conclusively conditionally scrutable from c for s when $cr'(p \mid c) = 1$.[16] This relation is stronger than the nonconclusive

---

[16] It is arguable that credence 1 does not suffice for certainty. I might have credence 1 that a the value of a random real number between 0 and 10 is not π, without being certain of it. Some will say that the credence here is infinitesimally less than 1, or at least that it is not 'true 1'. Alternatively, we could represent true certainty as credence '1*' in order to distinguish it from cases like this. But in any case, rational credence 1 is plausibly a necessary condition for certainty, and the notion of conclusive scrutability defined this way is at least a good approximation to conclusive conditional scrutability. As before we can attend to the possibility of exceptions as they come up.

conditional scrutability relation, but it is also better defined and better behaved, and it will be useful for some purposes.

What about credences and conditional credences in sentences? We might define these directly, for example in terms of the rational betting odds associated with sentences and with pairs of sentences for a subject. They can also be defined in terms of the thoughts apt to be expressed by the relevant sentences. I spell this sort of analysis out in the third excursus. For now, for ease of discussion, we can take it that a subject's credence $cr(S)$ in sentence S (in a context) is the subject's credence in the proposition that S expresses (relative to that context), or perhaps the subject's credence in the proposition that S expresses under the guise associated with S (in that context). A subject's rational credence $cr'(S)$ in S is the subject's rational credence in the proposition expressed by S (under the guise, in the context). With appropriate modifications, the same goes for a subject's conditional credence $cr(S_1 \mid S_2)$ and the subject's rational conditional credence $cr'(S_1 \mid S_2)$ in a sentence S_1 conditional on another sentence S_2.

We can then say that S is conditionally scrutable from C (for a subject s at time t) when $cr'(S \mid C)$ is high for s at t, where $cr'(S \mid C)$ is stipulated (following the convention in 2.1) to be $cr'(S \mid CC)$ where CC is a conjunction of all sentences in C. The Conditional Scrutability thesis says that there is a compact class C of truths from which all truths are conditionally scrutable for all subjects and times.[17] (A slightly modified version to accommodate context-dependence is given in the third excursus.) We can likewise define conclusive versions of the conditional scrutability relation and the corresponding thesis, by replacing 'high' by '1' in the definition.

It has taken a while to unpack the Conditional Scrutability thesis, but it remains plausible. In particular, it remains plausible that given such a class as *PQTI* above (or some disciplined subclass of it), then for at least many truths S, ideal reasoning would support a high conditional credence in S given the hypothesis that all the sentences in *PQTI* are true.

In many cases, when S is inferentially scrutable from C for a subject, it will be plausible that S is conditionally scrutable from C for that subject. This follows from a version of the Bayesian principle of conditionalization (discussed in chapter 4), at least if we assume that C is the total relevant evidence that the subject acquires. This assumption may be false in some cases: for example, in coming to know p one may come to know that one believes p. But one might instead appeal

---

[17] Whereas other scrutability theses trivially rule out the possibility that false sentences are scrutable from truths, this is not quite so trivial for conditional scrutability. So one might consider explicitly making the thesis a biconditional, saying that S is true if and only if it is conditionally scrutable from C. Still, this claim plausibly follows from the original version, along with the claim that when S_1 and S_2 are incompatible, $cr(S_1 \mid C)$ and $cr(S_2 \mid C)$ cannot both be high.

to a mildly strengthened Inferential Scrutability thesis: if one were to come to know the truths in C and use no additional evidence other than the truths in C, one could thereby come to know S. This strengthened thesis remains plausible in the core cases, and leads more directly to conditional scrutability.

So there is good reason to accept that in the core cases in which Inferential Scrutability holds, Conditional Scrutability holds. Furthermore, even in the Fitchian cases in which Inferential Scrutability fails, there is no corresponding reason to think that Conditional Scrutability fails. So if Inferential Scrutability is true of all non-Fitchian cases, then there is a good case for thinking that Conditional Scrutability holds in general. The relationship between Inferential and Conditional Scrutability is discussed further in chapter 3.

One concern about Conditional Scrutability is that the idealization involved in it is not as easy to attenuate as with other scrutability theses. In the case of Inferential Scrutability, we attenuated the idealization by moving to a notion on which S is inferentially scrutable from C if there is some *subclass* C' of C such that knowing C' would put one in a position to know S. One might correspondingly move to a notion on which S is conditionally scrutable from C if there is some subclass C' of C such that $cr'(S \mid C')$ is high. The trouble with doing this is that for almost any S, including false S, this definition will be satisfied. For most false S, there are some truths that taken collectively would constitute strong misleading evidence for S. If C contains such sentences, constituting a subclass C', then $cr'(S \mid C')$ will be high, and S will be conditionally scrutable from C even though S is false.

A version of this problem arose for inferential scrutability, but it was not nearly as acute: it is impossible to know a false sentence, so no false sentence is inferentially scrutable. To avoid this worry in the case of conditional scrutability, it is best not to employ the weaker subclass-involving notion of conditional scrutability. This means that to make an inference from inferential scrutability to conditional scrutability one will also have to employ the stronger notion of inferential scrutability that avoids subclasses. One might still use the weaker sort of inferential scrutability to help make the case for the stronger sort, however.

Where conditional scrutability is concerned, there is no getting around the need for a strong idealization at some point. In fact, the idealization needs to be subtly modified to handle problems tied to self-doubt, in which subjects are not confident of their own reliability. I discuss this modification in the fifth excursus.

5 A priori scrutability

The A Priori Scrutability thesis says that there is a compact class of truths from which all truths are a priori scrutable. The informal characterization in section 1 says that S is a priori scrutable from C for s if s is in a position to know a priori that if C, then S (where the antecedent should be read as involving a conjunction of all the sentences in C).

The parallel with conditional scrutability might suggest that a priori scrutability is defined in terms of conditional knowledge, as in the last section, with the added requirement that the knowledge is a priori. But in the case of a priori scrutability we can avoid the complex issues about conditional knowledge entirely. Instead, we need require only that a material conditional 'If C then S' can be known a priori. Using material conditionals would trivialize conditional scrutability, but it does not trivialize a priori scrutability. While we can know the material conditional 'If C then S' just by knowing S, we cannot know the material conditional a priori in any such simple way. (One can know it a priori by knowing S a priori, when S is a priori knowable, but this is the right result for a priori scrutability.)

This leads to the definition of a priori scrutability in the last chapter: S is a priori scrutable from C (for s) when a material conditional from C to S is a priori (for s). We can also say that S is a priori scrutable from C when there is some conjunction D of sentences in C such that the material conditional $D \rightarrow S$ is a priori. Near-equivalently, S is a priori scrutable from C when S can be logically derived from some sentences in C and some a priori truths.

Apriority of a sentence is discussed in the third and seventh excursuses. To a first approximation, we can say that S is a priori when it is a priori knowable: that is, when it is metaphysically possible for someone to know S a priori. On the analysis in the third excursus, one knows S a priori if one has a priori knowledge that is apt to be expressed by S. Alternatively, one can say that S is a priori when there is an a priori warrant for S, as discussed in the fourth excursus. The definition in terms of warrant has the advantage that it is not hostage to claims about what is metaphysically possible, and that it extends more naturally to the case of propositions while avoiding the difficulties about semantic fragility discussed at the end of the third excursus.

We can relativize apriority of a sentence to a subject if we want to: S is a priori for a subject when it is metaphysically possible for the subject to know S, or when there is an a priori warrant for the subject to believe S. This yields a notion of a priori scrutability that is itself subject-relative. We could then state an A Priori Scrutability thesis that quantifies over subjects (as Inferential and Conditional Scrutability do): there is a compact class C such that for all subjects, S is a priori scrutable from C. But if the relevant sentences are restricted to context-independent sentences (see the third excursus), then a sentence is plausibly a priori for one subject if and only if it is a priori for all subjects, so this relativization is not really necessary. When S is a priori scrutable from C in the non-subject-relative sense, it follows that S is a priori scrutable from C for some subject, so (given the previous sentence) S is a priori scrutable from C for all subjects. If so, the A Priori Scrutability thesis that does not mention subjects is equivalent to the one that quantifies over all subjects. I discuss the extension to context-dependent sentences, where some relativization to subjects or contexts is needed, in the third excursus.

Note that a priori scrutability, unlike conditional scrutability, requires that S be epistemically related to *some* conjunction of members of C, rather than to the conjunction of all members. We could define it the latter way, but the two definitions are near equivalent. If S is a priori scrutable from C in the latter sense, it is trivially a priori scrutable in the former sense (as the conjunction of all members is a conjunction of members). If S is a priori scrutable from C in the former sense, then as long as the conjunction of all members of C exists, S is a priori scrutable from C in the latter sense. The second step here parallels the observation that if a material conditional $A \rightarrow S$ is a priori, then so is any material conditional $A \& B \rightarrow S$ because the former conditional entails the latter. As before, this attenuates the required idealization somewhat: to establish a priori scrutability of S from C, we need not always consider the conjunction of all members of C. Scrutability from a proper subclass of C will suffice.

A priori scrutability is clearly not subject to the Fitchian problems that arose for inferential scrutability. It also involves much less subject-relativity than conditional scrutability. In a number of respects, a priori scrutability is better behaved than the other sorts of scrutability, and it is the notion that I will concentrate on the most. The main downside of the notion compared to the others is that it invokes the more theoretical and controversial notion of the a priori. So it is useful to have the other notions too, to help motivate and argue for scrutability claims. Still, a priori scrutability will be the central focus.

6 Generalized scrutability

Scrutability theses need not be restricted to the actual world. If the a priori scrutability thesis is true, then it is plausible that it still would have been true if the world had turned out differently. To see this, note that we can evaluate the truth of various sentences even given *hypothetical* information about ways the world might be. For example, in the Gettier case, it is irrelevant whether Smith's case is actual: a subject can know that *if* Smith's case as described is actual, then Smith does not know that someone owns a Ford. Or in the case of water, given an appropriate specification of the distribution, behavior, and appearance of clusters of XYZ molecules (information analogous to the information we have about H_2O in the actual world), a subject is in a position to conclude that *if* the specification is correct, then water is XYZ.

One might formulate a stronger scrutability thesis by requiring that the A Priori Scrutability thesis be necessary, or better, by requiring that it be a priori. If A Priori Scrutability is itself a priori (and conclusive a priori, in the sense outlined in chapter 4), then it will be true however the world turns out. That is, for every epistemically possible scenario, it will be a priori that if the scenario obtains, then A Priori Scrutability is true. So for every scenario, it will be a priori that truths (with respect to that scenario) are scrutable from a compact class of truths (with respect to that scenario). This would require that there is a compact scrutability base for each scenario, although there might be entirely different scrutability bases for different scenarios.

For my purposes, it is useful to formulate a somewhat stronger thesis still, according to which there is a single scrutability base that applies to all scenarios. We can formulate such a thesis as follows. Let us say that a sentence S is epistemically possible when S is truth-apt and $\sim S$ is not a priori, and that a class of truths is epistemically possible when every conjunction (finite or infinite) of truths in that class is epistemically possible.[18]

Generalized Scrutability: There is a compact class C of sentences such that for all sentences S, if S is epistemically possible, then there is an epistemically possible subclass C' of C such that S is scrutable from C'.

In effect, the generalized scrutability thesis says that there is a compact vocabulary that will serve to make up a scrutability base *however* the world turns out. The relevant compact class in effect yields a scrutability base for each scenario in epistemic space. For example, if *PQTI* is a scrutability base for one's actual scenario, related classes *PQTI** will serve as scrutability bases for many nearby scenarios. False but epistemically possible sentences such as 'Oswald did not kill Kennedy' will plausibly be scrutable from some classes of this form.

There will be more distant scenarios that involve all sorts of alien properties that are not present in the actual world. As a result, a scrutability base for the entire space of such scenarios will go far beyond *PQTI* and may involve many more families of expressions than a scrutability base for the actual world. So for the purposes of generalized scrutability, the understanding of 'compactness' may need to be weakened significantly, compared to the understanding that is required for actual-world scrutability. Perhaps we might even need to allow an infinite number of families in the base, for example if there are infinitely many sorts of fundamental alien properties. But the hope is that some interestingly limited class will suffice all the same.

---

[18] As always in this book, this use of 'epistemically possible' is stipulative and does not reflect the ordinary usage of the expression, according to which S is epistemically possible roughly when one does not know $\sim S$. See 'The Nature of Epistemic Space' for more on the relations between the notions.

In principle, one can formulate generalized versions of A Priori Scrutability, Conditional Scrutability, and Inferential Scrutability. Where the latter two are concerned, one needs to invoke subject-relativization in the statement of the thesis, requiring that for all subjects s, S is scrutable from C' for s. Where Generalized A Priori Scrutability is concerned, though, the subject-relativization is arguably redundant, just as it is for the ungeneralized version. Generalized A Priori Scrutability will be the most central for our purposes.

7 Idealization

Laplace's scrutability thesis, discussed in the introduction, appealed to an intellect 'vast enough' to know all the physical truths and to 'submit these data for analysis'. In effect, Laplace is invoking an idealization of cognitive capacities, allowing capacities far greater than normal human capacities.

All of our central notions of scrutability involve such an idealization. Inferential scrutability appeals to what it is metaphysically possible for a subject to know. Conditional scrutability appeals to what a subject ideally ought to believe. A priori scrutability appeals to what it is metaphysically possible for a subject to know a priori.

These idealizations, like Laplace's, have at least two dimensions. First, they idealize thoughts. Second, they idealize reasoning. The idealization of thought is required to allow subjects to entertain base truths and dependent truths, both of which may involve new concepts and great complexity. The idealization of reasoning is required to allow the subjects to make connections between the two.

The idealization of thought involves two fairly clear dimensions in turn. The first is the idealization of concepts: this allows subjects to possess any concept that it is possible to possess, regardless of whether they actually possess it or whether any humans possess it. Such concepts are needed to entertain both base truths and dependent truths, both of which may involve new concepts. For example, such concepts may be needed to entertain truths about what it is like to be a bat. The second is the idealization of complexity, or of storage. This allows subjects to entertain thoughts whose complexity is far beyond normal human capacity: the conjunction of all base truths, for example. This may extend even to infinitary thoughts (such as conjunctions of an infinite number of finite thoughts), if the world is infinite in extent.

The idealization of reasoning has less clear dimensions. One aspect of it is idealization of calculation: arbitrary numbers of steps of reasoning are allowed, allowing proofs of enormously complex mathematical theorems, for example. Another aspect is idealization away from mistakes: idealized reasoners never make missteps in reasoning. A third is idealization of judgment: ideal reasoners are sensitive to all relevant reasons and evidence in their possession, and make judgments appropriately grounded in the reasons and evidence. A fourth is ide-alization of processes: ideal reasoners can use any possible reasoning processes, regardless of whether humans actually use these processes.

We need not dictate what counts as reasoning. Any process by which someone comes to know something (or by which someone comes to know something a priori) is good enough for our purposes. As far as I can tell, however, the specific idealized forms of reasoning that I invoke in this book all involve natural exten-sions of familiar sorts of human reasoning (deduction, induction, inference, intuition, and various others), perhaps extended to arbitrary complexity or to infinitary processing. Given some epistemological views on which knowledge is cheap, one may have to constrain the allowed forms of reasoning to avoid trivial-izing scrutability theses (as discussed briefly in what follows), but on my own views this is not necessary. So while I will appeal to idealizations of calculation, of error, and of judgment, I will not need to directly appeal to idealization of processes beyond these.

One could in principle define non-idealized analogs of the idealized notions of scrutability, perhaps in terms of what it is practically possible for subjects to know, or in terms of what a subject ought to believe in an ordinary non-idealized sense. But scrutability theses corresponding to the theses we have considered would then be much less plausible. For example, it is not practically possible for most subjects to entertain enormous world-descriptions; likewise, it is not clear that subjects ought to believe complex mathematical theorems in any ordinary non-idealized sense. It is not out of the question that by building more into the base (all mathematical truths, for example), the required idealization on reason-ing might be diminished; and it is not out of the question that by reformulating scrutability theses in an appropriate way, the required idealization on entertain-ing thoughts might be diminished.[19] But at least for a version turning on a priori entailment of all truths from base truths, an idealization is hard to avoid.

The idealized scrutability theses that I appeal to all involve *idealization facts*: facts about what ideal reasoning dictates. Idealization facts can be cast in at least three different ways for our purposes. First, there are *modal* idealizations, cast in terms of what it is metaphysically possible for a subject to know or believe. Sec-ond, there are *normative* idealizations, cast in terms of what subjects ideally ought to believe. Third, there are *warrant* idealizations (discussed in the fourth excur-sus), cast in terms of what there is an (ideal) warrant for subjects to believe.

In principle, a given scrutability thesis can be cast in any of these three ways. We can say that a sentence is a priori, for example, when it is possible for some-one to know it a priori, or when someone who cares about its truth and is

---

[19] One less idealized thesis is discussed in 'Verbal Disputes'.

restricted to a priori reasoning ideally ought to believe it, or when there exists an ideal warrant for someone to believe it.

For example, given a complex mathematical theorem M and a non-ideal subject Fred, it is metaphysically possible that Fred come to know M, although it is not practically possible. Fred ideally ought to believe M, at least if he were to consider it and to care about it, although it is not the case that he ought to believe M in a less idealized sense. There is an ideal warrant for Fred to believe M, deriving from the proof of M, but Fred does not *have* this warrant to believe M.

The relation between these three sorts of idealization is complex. One might think that normative idealizations are answerable to modal idealizations (because ought implies can) or that warrant idealizations derive from normative idealizations. For my part, I think that warrant idealizations are the most fundamental. When someone ideally ought to believe p, this is because there is a warrant for them to believe p. When someone is in a position to know p, again this is because there is a warrant for them to believe p.

Modal idealizations are perhaps the most familiar of the three, but they have some disadvantages. One is the problem of semantic fragility, discussed at the end of the third excursus. Another is that if we define apriority and the like using a modal idealization, claims about apriority are then hostage to certain theoretical views about modality. For example, some hold that there are brute constraints on metaphysical modality. If cognitive capacities beyond a certain size are metaphysically impossible, for example, then certain apparent apriorities, such as mathematical theorems that require enormous proofs, will not count as a priori. But there may still be an ideal a priori warrant for such a theorem, in virtue of there being a proof for the theorem. Related constraints may arise from views on which anything nomologically impossible is metaphysically impossible. I do not think that metaphysical modality is constrained in this way, but someone who holds that there are such constraints should appeal to warrant idealizations (or perhaps normative idealizations, invoking ideal norms for which ought does not imply can) instead of modal idealizations.

In this book I appeal more often to modal idealizations than to normative and warrant idealizations, mainly because the notions involved (possibility and knowledge) are more familiar than those of ideal norms and ideal warrants. But granted an understanding of normative idealizations or of warrant idealizations, it is certainly possible to interpret most of what I say in this book using those idealizations alone.

8 Objections from idealization

The idealization facts involved in scrutability theses involve a large idealization from ordinary human cognitive capacities. The idealization allows possession of arbitrary concepts, thoughts of infinite complexity, arbitrary amounts of calcula-tion, no missteps in reasoning, and ideal judgment throughout. Idealizations of this sort are sometimes apt to provoke an incredulous stare, or at least a raised eyebrow.

When the raised eyebrow evolves into an argument, it seems that there are four sorts of especially salient objections. There are objections from *coherence*, arguing that there are no idealization facts: the idealization is not well-defined, or the definition involves notions about which there is no fact of the matter. There are objections from *knowledge*, holding that we could never know the idealization facts: one would have to be an idealized reasoner to know those facts, and we are not. There are objections from *triviality*, which hold that the appeal to idealization makes scrutability theses trivially true. And there are objec-tions from *applicability*, holding that idealization facts (and therefore the ideal-ized scrutability theses) have very little application in understanding non-ideal creatures such as ourselves. I will take these one at a time.

Regarding objections from coherence: insofar as idealization facts are defined in terms of what it is possible to know, then these facts will be as well-grounded as facts about knowledge and possibility. Perhaps one might be an epistemic or modal anti-realist who questions such facts, but short of this anti-realism there is no problem for idealization facts here. Something similar goes for idealization facts characterized in terms of what certain subjects can know by some possible reasoning process (or by some possible a priori reasoning process). Perhaps some-one might argue that where infinitary thought is concerned, our ordinary notions of knowledge and justification break down: there is no fact of the matter about which infinitary thought processes lead to knowledge and justification. But I do not see much reason to believe this, and it is natural for an epistemic realist to hold that there are facts of the matter here, whether or not we are in a position to know those facts.

What about idealization facts cast in terms of norms or warrants? In this case, perhaps there is some question about what these idealized norms or war-rants consist in. Someone might hold that there is no single ideal 'ought' but many different 'oughts', some of which are more idealized than others. Still, one can plausibly at least compare the goodness of various reasoning processes, and hold (for example) that one ideally ought to believe *p* if and only if some good reasoning process warrants belief in *p* and all equally good or better rea-soning processes also warrant belief in *p*. Similarly, one can consider which propositions really do support other propositions. An epistemic anti-realist might question whether there are such facts, but otherwise the facts seem to be on reasonably solid ground.

Regarding objections from knowledge: the scrutability theses, and the argu-ments for them given here, do not require that we non-ideal theorists can know the idealization facts. All that is required is that there is an appropriate relation between what is true and what is (ideally) scrutable. To argue for this thesis I do not appeal to premises such as '*M* is ideally knowable'. What matters are conditional claims such as the claim that *if M* is true, then *M* is scrutable. That said, I think it is plausible that we know some idealization facts: we know that it is possible to know that all objects are self-identical and that it is not possible to know that 2 + 2 = 5, for example. Someone might object that our knowledge of certain truths (say, grass is green) is more secure than our knowledge that the truths in question are ideally scrutable from base truths; but I certainly do not require that knowledge of these truths is in any way mediated by knowledge of idealization facts. Someone might also object that we cannot rule out the possibility that idealized reasoning will tell us that grass is not green, after all; but to the extent that we take this hypothesis about idealized reasoning seriously, we should equally take seriously the hypothesis that grass is not green. So idealized facts are not worse off than non-idealized facts here.

Regarding objections from triviality: one objection here suggests that a truly ideal reasoning process is a godlike process that upon entertaining any proposition immediately determines whether it is true. If so, one might think that at least Inferential Scrutability is trivial (any truth will be knowable using ideal reasoning, with or without prior knowledge of base truths), and perhaps Conditional and A Priori Scrutability too (ideal reasoning will automatically deliver knowledge of the relevant true conditionals).

Now, it is not clear that such a reasoning process is possible. But even if it is possible, it does not trivialize the theses, as these theses invoke strong constraints on the kind of knowledge involved. For Inferential Scrutablity, for example, the relevant knowledge must be obtained without appeal to any further empirical information over and above background beliefs that the speaker possesses at the time of utterance. I think the godlike reasoning process in question certainly counts as generating empirical knowledge, so it is ruled out here. And once such empirical processes are ruled out, there does not seem to be a potential trivialization of this sort in the offing. Something very similar goes for Conditional Scrutability and A Priori Scrutability. There are very strong constraints on what can be known a priori. I do not think that anyone could know a priori that there is a table in this room, for example. For this reason, the claim that certain conditionals can be known a priori may be true, but it is far from trivial.

An important objection from triviality turns on reliabilism about knowledge and justification.[20] If all it takes to have knowledge is a mechanism that

---

[20] I understand reliability here in a broad way that subsumes related notions such as safety and sensitivity, and I understand reliabilism in a broad way to subsume epistemological views cast in terms of these related notions.

reliably produces true beliefs, then possible knowledge may be easy to have. For any domain at all, there will be a metaphysically possible reasoner who reliably gets facts about that domain right, perhaps by magic. Like the godlike processes in the previous paragraph, this sort of sensitivity to the external world will usually count as empirical, so that scrutability will not be trivialized. But there may also be non-empirical reliable processes of this sort, even in apparently empirical domains.

To see this, consider a sentence S that is reliably true in a creature's environment: a sentence stating a law of nature, for example, or a robust contingent truth about local conditions. For most such sentences we can imagine an innate process, perhaps produced by natural selection, that reliably brings about belief in S independently of the creature's experience. (This sort of case is discussed further in the eighth excursus.) Then on many reliabilist views this belief will count as knowledge, and presumably as a priori knowledge. If so, then S will be a priori scrutable from any base, and will be inferentially and conditionally scrutable from many bases, including empty bases. While this is not a complete trivialization of scrutability, it certainly allows scrutability to encompass much more than one might have intended.

I reject strongly reliabilist views of this sort. But if someone holds that reliability suffices for knowledge, we need not engage a potentially verbal issue about how the word 'knowledge' is to be used. Instead, we can stipulate a notion that is subject to further constraints.

Most obviously, we can appeal to conclusive knowledge, or epistemological certainty. It is plausible that even completely reliable knowledge of laws of nature by a process such as the above will not deliver certainty: it will not justify absolute confidence in the laws of nature. It is arguable that no creature could have certainty in such matters: one will never be justified a priori in ruling out alternative hypotheses about laws of nature with absolute confidence. In fact, I have argued elsewhere (in *The Conscious Mind* and 'The Content and Epistemology of Phenomenal Belief') that reliability alone never delivers certainty. If either of these points is correct, then our stipulated notion of conclusive knowledge avoids trivialization by reliabilism.

Even where nonconclusive knowledge is concerned, we can stipulate a notion that is subject to nonreliabilist constraints. For example, we might stipulate a notion of e-knowledge ('evidentialist knowledge') such that all knowledge requires support by a constrained class of basic evidential states, where support is not understood in terms of reliability. Then one can argue that in cases such as the above, this sort of support is absent, so e-knowledge is absent. If so, then e-knowledge avoids trivialization by reliabilism.

At this point, some reliabilists might respond either by denying that the notions of conclusive knowledge or e-knowledge are coherent and nontrivial (perhaps rejecting the notion of grounding in evidence, or of certainty) or by arguing that these notions can themselves be explained in reliabilist terms (perhaps explaining evidential grounding in terms of reliable connections between evidence and belief and explaining certainty in terms of completely reliable processes).

Here we can distinguish different sorts of reliabilism. Moderate reliabilism allows that there are epistemic notions that can be understood in nonreliabilist terms (perhaps in traditional internalist terms), while holding that knowledge and/or justification should not be understood that way. One sort of moderate reliabilist allows that some epistemic expressions ('reason', 'evidential support', or 'certainty' for example) express these notions. Another sort allows that while existing epistemic expressions express reliabilist notions, the nonreliabilist notions are at least coherent, nontrivial, and satisfiable. In practice, many reliabilists are moderate reliabilists, and certainly the best-known arguments for reliabilism support only moderate reliabilism.[21] If moderate reliabilism is true, we can formulate a scrutability thesis in terms of nonreliabilist notions that will avoid the objection here.

Extreme reliabilism holds that there are no interesting epistemic notions that can be understood in nonreliabilist terms: alternative epistemic notions are incoherent, trivial, or never satisfied. If extreme reliabilism is true, then we cannot formulate a useful scrutability thesis in terms of nonreliabilist notions. It is not out of the question that we could exclude trivializing counterexamples in some other way, perhaps by defining a notion akin to conclusive knowledge or evidentialist knowledge in reliabilist terms, or perhaps by imposing restrictions on the relevant sort of cognitive processes. But it is not obvious whether this is possible, and it may well depend on the character of the reliabilism.

At this point, I simply note that the major arguments for reliabilism all tend to support moderate reliabilism rather than extreme reliabilism. Some of these arguments make a case that there are instances of knowledge and justification (in unreflective thinkers, for example) that do not meet alternative 'internalist' constraints, including accessibility constraints and guidance-deontological constraints. These arguments conclude that the alternative notions do not explain knowledge, but they do nothing to suggest that the alternative notions are

---

[21] Alvin Goldman, the originator of reliabilism, appears to be a moderate reliabilist: he does not suggests that nonreliabilist analyses are incoherent or trivial, and (in Goldman 2011) he even allows nonreliabilist elements, such as a notion of a belief's 'fitting' evidence in his analysis of justification. Of course 'moderate' here just captures one dimension of moderation that is relevant for present purposes. We might also cast these issues in terms of internalism and externalism, and speak of moderate and extreme externalism, but standard ways of cashing out the internalist/externalist distinctions do not quite fit my purposes (some reliabilist views will also qualify as internalist, for example). Thanks to Alvin Goldman for discussion here.

incoherent. Another well-known argument holds that nonreliabilist views lead to external-world skepticism, because the alternative constraints are hard to satisfy. These arguments certainly do not establish that the alternative notions are incoherent or never satisfied, however, and they do not obviously apply to the a priori knowledge we are centrally concerned with here.

Following the methodology outlined in the introduction, in the absence of a strong argument that undermines nonreliabilist ('internalist') epistemological notions entirely, I will take it that these notions are at least coherent and that extreme reliabilism is incorrect. If so, we can invoke nonreliabilist constraints to avoid trivialization. Complete philosophical neutrality is impossible, but at least on a wide variety of epistemological views, scrutability theses remain interesting and nontrivial.

Regarding objections from applicability: these are perhaps the most important objections from idealization. The force of such an objection clearly depends on the application in question. In some cases, there is obviously a problem. For example, one cannot use an idealized scrutability thesis to argue for a non-idealized epistemological optimism that holds that ordinary humans can know almost any truth. In other cases, there is obviously no problem. For example, one might use the scrutability thesis to localize the sources of our ignorance, arguing that any limits of our knowledge correspond to either limits in our knowledge of base truths or non-ideality of our reasoning. Such an application is clearly not undermined by the idealization.

Other cases are intermediate. Take a metaphysical application in which one uses Fundamental Scrutability along with the claim that truths in one class (mental truths, say) are not scrutable from truths in another class (physical truths, say) to conclude that truths in the second class do not exhaust the fundamental truths. In this case, the idealization might make us worry about whether we have really established the nonscrutability claim: perhaps truths in the first class seem inscrutable for us but in fact are scrutable for a more ideal reasoner. Still, at least in some cases, we can have good grounds for a nonscrutability claim even when it is idealized. Given such grounds and the scrutability thesis, the idealization will cause no further problem for the application.

Perhaps the most important application for my purposes is to the study of meaning, using scrutability to define intensions that can play some of the roles of Fregean senses and narrow contents (as discussed in chapter 1, chapter 5, and the eleventh excursus). In this case, idealization has some impact on the application but does not undermine it. For example, the idealization entails that the intensions in question are not as fine-grained as Fregean senses: two expressions 'a' and 'b' can be cognitively distinct but equivalent given ideal a priori reasoning, in which case they will have the same intension although different Fregean senses. Still, the intensions have many sense-like properties, and they will still differ for a posteriori distinct expressions such as 'Hesperus' and 'Phosphorus'. Furthermore, they can be used to define more fine-grained semantic values in turn, as in the eleventh excursus.

A cruder worry here is that insofar as these intensions are defined in terms of what subjects should accept under ideal reasoning conditional on vast hypotheses such as *PQTI* that they could never entertain, we cannot expect these intensions to be any sort of guide to the cognitive life of an ordinary non-ideal reasoner. For example, ideal reasoning might dictate that a complex mathematical sentence has an intension that is true at all scenarios; but if a non-ideal reasoner can never perform the reasoning, then the fact that the intension is true everywhere rather than false everywhere will tell us nothing about the role of the mathematical sentence or thought in the thinker's cognitive and linguistic life.

Here, one should sharply distinguish the relevance of idealization of complexity and idealization of reasoning. In these cases, idealization of complexity alone does little to undercut the relevance of these intensions. Even if the thinker could never entertain *PQTI*-specifications, the intension may nevertheless serve as a good guide to the inferential role of the thought or sentence. This is brought out in the next chapter in which a special device is used to store *PQTI*. This device, the Cosmoscope, handles much of the idealization of complexity. Even a non-ideal reasoner may be quite good at using a Cosmoscope to determine whether a given sentence is true or false.

Even without such a device, a typical human thinker will be disposed to accept or reject certain thoughts on coming to know that the world is or is not a certain way (through a limited partial description well short of *PQTI*). Assuming the thinker is reasonably competent, and assuming that heavily idealized reasoning is not required in order to come to a correct inference in these cases, then the thinker's inferences here will typically be correct. We could in principle capture this inferential role in something like a partial intension, defined over partial scenarios described in limited detail. The full intension is then just a more fine-grained analog of this inferential role. It may have more detail than is required, but it will nevertheless provide a good guide to the role of the thought or the sentence for the thinker. In effect, the intension provides a useful representation of the sort of scenarios that the thinker takes to verify the sentence and the sort that the thinker takes to falsify it.

Now, to the extent that idealized reasoning (as opposed to idealized complexity) makes a difference here, things may differ. If the ideal judgments about a scenario (even a partial scenario) differ significantly from a subject's disposition to judge, then the intension will be less good as a guide to the relevant inferential role. Something like this is going on in the mathematical case, for example. Still, my own view is that cases where ideal reasoning makes a difference of this magnitude are relatively rare. In most cases, if one has a good human reasoner making inferences from partially specified scenarios and the like, their inferences will be good ones and their results will not differ greatly from those of ideal reasoning. This is brought out by the fact that we are reasonably good at determining the truth of sentences given information about the external world. To determine whether there is a cat on the mat or water in the glass, for example, ideal reasoning is typically not needed.

Now, someone might argue that ideal reasoning will tell us that in fact no cats exist, in which case the idealized intension will come apart from the non-ideal inferential role. In this case, though, many semantic values (such as the extension of 'cat' and the truth-value of the sentence) will be no better off as guides to the state of the thinker. And if I am right that ideal reasoning about ordinary truths rarely undercuts merely competent reasoning in this way, then the problem will not arise.

Of course, to the extent that a given thinker is more and more non-ideal, the intensions in question will serve as ever more divergent guides to their psychology. Still, one can see the intensions as reflecting something about the thinker's thoughts: they yield a sort of truth-condition, for example, and they correspond to a sort of normative inferential role, the role that the thought should have even if it does not. Even this much allows the intensions to play an explanatory role in various projects, although perhaps not so much in modeling the psychological dynamics of the thinker.

Overall, I am inclined to say that while idealization can raise reasonable questions about applicability, some applications are not affected at all by the idealization, and others are affected only to a limited extent. The idealization of complexity does little to undercut most applications. Idealization of reasoning affects some applications, but the effect is limited. A fuller assessment of objections of this sort requires a detailed case-by-case treatment of the relevant applications.

Sentential and Propositional Scrutability

In section 2 of chapter 2, I introduced the notion of knowing a sentence, and suggested that scrutability theses might be formulated in terms of it. In what follows, I analyze this notion in more detail. I also formulate the sentential scrutability theses that result, and discuss their relations to propositional scrutability theses, along with associated issues about context-dependence, semantic fragility, propositional warrant, and the persistence of thoughts.

Sentences and thoughts

In chapter 2, I suggested various ways of understanding the notion of knowing a sentence that are available to theorists of various different stripes. Different theorists can say that to know S is to know the Fregean proposition that it expresses, or to know the Russellian proposition that it expresses under the guise of expression, or to know that S is true. Here I will develop another way to understand the notion that is available to theorists of many different stripes. This understanding is not obligatory, but it helps to give an idea of just how the notion works.

The approach taken here relies on connections between utterances and mental states of the speaker. Recall the example in 2.2, in which Sue knows that the morning star is a planet, believes that the evening star is not a planet, and associates 'Phosphorus' with the morning star and 'Hesperus' with the evening star. Intuitively, when Sue utters 'Phosphorus is a planet', her utterance is associated with a mental state—a specific state of entertaining the proposition that Phosphorus is a planet—that is itself a state of belief and a state of knowledge. When Sue utters 'Hesperus is a planet', her utterance is associated with a very different sort of mental state—a specific state of entertaining the proposition that Hesperus is a planet—that is neither a state of belief nor a state of knowledge.

To make this more precise, let us say that *entertaining* is the maximally general propositional attitude (occurrent or non-occurrent) with a mind-to-world direction of fit. So when one believes that p, knows that p, expects that p, hypothesizes that p, or supposes that p, one entertains p. Now let us say that a *thought* is a specific state of entertaining. This notion is parallel to that of a belief (a specific state of believing), a supposition (a specific state of supposing), a knowing (a specific state of knowing), and so on.

Wherever there is a belief, there is a thought. Likewise, wherever there is a knowing, there is a thought. The thought is intimately related to the belief and the knowing. On some views, the thought, the belief, and the knowing are all identical to each other. On another view, they are distinct states, but they stand in some other strong relation to each other: a relation of coincidence or realization, for example. I will not adjudicate this question here, but I will say that when this relation holds, the thought *constitutes* the belief and *constitutes* the knowing. When a thought constitutes a belief or constitutes a knowing, we can also say more simply that the thought constitutes belief or that the thought constitutes knowledge (as with my current thought that 2 + 2 = 4, for example). We can also say that a thought constitutes justified belief iff it constitutes a justified belief, and that a thought constitutes a priori knowledge if it constitutes an item of a priori knowledge: that is, a knowing whose justification is independent of experience.

I will be especially (although not only) concerned with *occurrent* thoughts. In this special case, thoughts are not mere dispositional states, as with beliefs that are currently dormant. Instead, we can take occurrent thoughts to be specific acts of entertaining occurring in a subject's stream of thought. These acts will themselves constitute acts of judging, of supposing, and so on. I take it that acts of judging can at least sometimes constitute states of believing and knowing, so that occurrent thoughts can also constitute states of believing and knowing. I will not restrict the notion of thoughts to occurrent thoughts, and non-occurrent thoughts will sometimes be relevant, but occurrent thoughts will play the central role.

We can then appeal to the idea that utterances of truth-apt sentences typically *express* thoughts (and indeed occurrent thoughts). Sincere utterances typically express beliefs, and correlatively express thoughts. Insincere utterances do not express beliefs, but they nevertheless typically express thoughts (when I insincerely assert *p*, I do not believe *p*, but I typically at least entertain *p*). Note that expression is here construed as a relation between utterances and mental states, and should not be confused with the different notion of expression construed as a relation between utterances and propositions. However, there is a close relationship between the notions. Intuitively, an utterance and the thought it expresses have the same propositional content. I will not build this in as a definitional constraint, as there may be views on which thoughts and utterances have contents of different sorts. But it is at least a constraint that when an utterance expresses a thought, the utterance and the thought have the same *truth-value*, and it is natural to hold that they must have the same *truth-conditions* as well. These are not the only constraints on the notion: there must also be a causal link between the thought and the utterance, and an appropriate psychological relation. I will not try to define these things here, and will take the notion as an intuitive primitive (unanalyzed at least for now) instead.

There are weaker notions on expression that do not have this constraint. For example, according to a weaker notion, one could express a true thought with a false utterance by misusing a word, or merely by conveying the content of the thought while literally asserting something else. To use an example of Keith Donnellan (1966): one may utter 'Smith's murderer is insane' to express (in a weaker sense) a thought such as *Jones is insane*, so that if one is wrong about whether Jones murdered Smith, the utterance and the thought will have different truth-values. According to the stronger notion I am using here, these do not qualify as cases of expression. Rather, the thought expressed in this case is a thought such as *The murderer of Smith is insane*. One can think of expression as a relation that comes with an a priori guarantee of truth-preservation (roughly as deductive inference might), so that the utterance is guaranteed to have the same truth-value as the thought.

It may be that there are some utterances that do not express thoughts. One might absent-mindedly utter a sentence by rote, without entertaining its content at all. If one is grasping for words, one might use a word whose content is not that of a thought. But at least for typical utterances, it is plausible that they express thoughts. So we can take utterances that express thoughts to be our paradigm cases for initial analysis.[1] Insofar as there are utterances that do not express thoughts, we can handle these derivatively.

In the reverse direction, we can say that when an utterance expresses a thought, the thought *endorses* the utterance. Such a thought will not be metalinguistic thought about the utterance: rather, if the utterance is about bachelors (say), the thought will be about bachelors. It is possible in principle even for a thought that follows an utterance to endorse that utterance, although understanding this idea properly requires appeal to the notion of persistence discussed below.

For present purposes, we can start with a subject who is making a fully competent utterance of a sentence S (one in which the expressions in S are used correctly and nondeferentially). We can say that if the utterance expresses a thought

---

[1] This restriction will affect only the analysis of context-dependent sentences below, not the analysis of context-independent sentences. In particular it will affect the analysis of what it is to be in a position to know a sentence in a context. In the first instance we can restrict attention to contexts in which a sentence is uttered expressing a thought. To handle other contexts, we can appeal to the notion of having warrant to accept a sentence in a context, along the lines of the following excursus, or we can appeal to possible thoughts that endorse the utterance.

that constitutes belief, the subject believes S. If the utterance expresses a thought that constitutes knowledge, the subject knows S. This fits naturally with the accounts of these notions in terms of sincere and knowledgeable assertion: it is plausible that an assertion is sincere precisely when it expresses a thought that constitutes belief, and that it is knowledgeable precisely when it expresses a thought that constitutes knowledge. Then in the case of Sue, it is plausible that Sue knows 'Phosphorus is a planet' but not 'Hesperus is a planet': the thought expressed by her utterance of the former constitutes knowledge (and belief), but the thought expressed by her utterance of the latter does not.

This analysis is available to many different theorists of propositions. The argument from assertion earlier strongly suggests that there are different mental states associated with Sue's utterances of 'Hesperus is a planet' and 'Phosphorus is a planet'. Whatever one's account of propositions, it is hard to deny that there are distinct thoughts (acts of entertaining) associated with Sue's utterances of 'Hesperus is a planet' and 'Phosphorus is a planet', and that these thoughts have relevant psychological and epistemological differences (one constitutes an act of belief and an act of knowledge, the other does not). Rather than denying these claims, it is more plausible for a Russellian to deny that a thought constitutes knowledge iff the subject knows the proposition that is the content of the thought. In cases such as the above, the subject may have two thoughts with the same content, one of which constitutes knowledge and the other one does not. The same goes for belief.

Here it might help to briefly adopt a common model according to which thoughts correspond to sentence tokens in the language of thought. Each token has some content. When such a sentence token is in the 'belief box', it corresponds to a belief in the content. When the token is in the 'desire box', it corresponds to a desire in the content. When a token in the belief box was brought about by the right sort of process, it constitutes a justified belief. When further conditions are met, it constitutes knowledge. In a case such as the above, Sue's utterance of 'Hesperus is a planet' might be triggered by the sentence '$\phi(H)$' in her language of thought, while her utterance of 'Phosphorus is a planet' might be triggered by the sentence '$\phi(P)$' in her language of thought. The second sentence will be in the belief box, will meet the relevant further conditions, and will constitute knowledge. The first sentence will not be in the belief box, so it will not constitute belief or knowledge.

Of course the model involving a language of thought and belief boxes may be a fiction. But it remains plausible that thoughts correspond to specific states of a cognitive system, playing specific functional roles. If the state plays the right sort of role, the corresponding thought will be a belief, and so on. Even without a language of thought, Sue's two utterances are plausibly brought about by quite different states, one of which plays the functional role of a belief and the other one of which does not. So one state corresponds to a belief, and the other to a thought that is not a belief. All of this is so far quite compatible with a view on which these two thoughts have the same content.

We can extend the thought-based analysis to sentences that the speaker is not currently uttering by saying: a subject knows (or knows a priori, or believes) a sentence S iff the subject has a thought apt to be expressed by S and that constitutes knowledge (or a priori knowledge, or belief). Here, a thought is apt to be expressed by a sentence type S if it could be expressed by a fully competent utterance of S. In this case, unlike the case where the thought is actually expressed, the thought may well be non-occurrent. Furthermore, knowing and believing a sentence type S does not require that the subject is competent with the expressions in S: a French speaker who believes $2 + 2 = 4$ believes 'Two plus two equals four', in virtue of having a belief apt to be expressed by the sentence, if the subject were competent in English.

One can define credences in sentences in a similar way. We can assume that thoughts are at least sometimes associated with credences $cr(T)$ and conditional credences $cr(T_1 \mid T_2)$. We can then say that a value x is in the credence range $cr(S)$ for a subject at a time iff x is in the range $cr(T)$, where T is a thought by s at t that is apt to be expressed by S. Likewise, we can analyze $cr(S_1 \mid S_2)$ in terms of $cr(T_1 \mid T_2)$, where T_1 and T_2 are apt to be expressed by S_1 and S_2 respectively. The same goes for rational credences $cr'(S)$ and $cr'(S_1 \mid S_2)$ (and also the insulated rational credences $cr^*(S)$ and $cr^*(S_1 \mid S_2)$ discussed in the fifth excursus).[2]

Some philosophers are doubtful about the very idea of token thoughts. David Lewis (1994) suggests that 'beliefs' is a 'bogus plural'. On this view, subjects can certainly believe that p for various p, but there are no token entities called beliefs to undergird this believing, except perhaps for trivial derivative entities such as the instantiation of the property of believing that p. Presumably Lewis would take a similar view of thoughts. For someone with this view, the current definitions of key notions such as knowing a sentence will be problematic.

It is worth noting that some of the doubts about token beliefs apply less clearly to occurrent thoughts. I think that it is an introspective datum that there are acts of judging and acts of entertaining a hypothesis. Given that there are

---

[2] This definition requires that there is a thought corresponding to any sentence with a credence, so unless we are very liberal about thoughts, the model will lead to undefined credences in many sentences. An alternative model says that $cr(S)$ is the credence one would have if one harmlessly entertained S—that is, entertained S without disturbing any existing thoughts. This model is subject to certain counterexamples, for example involving sentences such as 'I am entertaining a sentence about entertaining'. As I discuss later, these counterexamples do not arise for insulated rational credences, and can be avoided in the case of non-insulated rational credences by giving a warrant-based analysis.

such acts, it is hard to deny that there are at least occurrent thoughts. Furthermore, it is then very plausible that when someone sincerely asserts p, they typically judge that p, and that when they insincerely assert that p, they typically entertain p. Still, some philosophers may reject these claims, either denying that there are thoughts at all or denying that assertions typically express thoughts.

For someone who denies these claims, the key notions such as that of knowing a sentence S (and the apriority of S, discussed below) will have to be understood differently. If the theorist takes a fine-grained view of propositions, so that 'Hesperus is Hesperus' and 'Hesperus is Phosphorus' express distinct propositions, it will suffice for present purposes for them to understand knowledge of S as knowledge of the proposition it expresses. If the theorist takes a coarse-grained view of propositions but allows that there are guises, it will suffice for them to understand knowledge of S as knowledge of a proposition under the guise associated with S, as above. If the theorist accepts none of these notions, an alternative approach will be needed. But in any case, the intuitive distinction between the statuses of various utterances is clear, and any theory that cannot explain it is an incomplete theory. So I will take it that even for theorists who reject all of the notions just mentioned, some way of understanding the key notion of knowing or believing a sentence can be found.

It is also not out of the question that one could take the notion of a thought as a useful fiction for motivating an intuitive idea of the apriority or scrutability of an utterance, and leave that notion unanalyzed in the short term. Once one has motivated scrutability theses and the like in this way, one can use them to motivate a Fregean notion of proposition, and of the propositional content of a sentence. With this done, one could return to a characterization of apriority in terms of Fregean propositions.

Sentential scrutability and context-dependence

How do we formulate scrutability theses in terms of sentences? We need to say what it is for a sentence to be (inferentially, conditionally, a priori) scrutable from a class of sentences for a subject, and then plug these notions into the general form of a scrutability thesis. I will start with context-independent sentences, which are fairly straightforward, and then move to complications raised by context-dependence.

Inferential scrutability for sentences was defined in section 2.3 in terms of possible knowledge of sentences. The definition of knowledge of a sentence S given above can be plugged into this definition straightforwardly. Conditional scrutability of sentences was defined in section 2.4 in terms of a subject's rational credences $cr'(S_1 \mid S_2)$, in certain sentences S_1 given sentences S_2. The definition of rational credences in sentences given above can be plugged in here (subject to a modification discussed in the next section). A priori scrutability for sentences was defined in section 2.5 in terms of the apriority of sentences. Using the framework laid out above, one can say that S is a priori when it is possible that someone comes to know S a priori, and that S is a priori for a subject when it is possible that that subject comes to know S a priori.

In the first instance, we can take the sentences here to be context-independent sentence types in any possible language.[3] The thesis that results has roughly the scope of a propositional scrutability thesis, at least if we assume that for every proposition, there is some possible sentence that expresses p context-independently. For this assumption (discussed in the next section) to have a chance of being true, we must quantify over more than just English sentences or sentences in languages that are actually spoken. The restriction to context-independent sentences simplifies things while still allowing considerable power.

For some purposes, we need to apply scrutability theses to context-dependent sentences. After all, many sentences in natural language are context-dependent, and we would like to be able to apply scrutability theses to them. This is particularly important if we want to use scrutability to define a sort of content for utterances of such sentences, as I do. In general, the content of a sentence is defined in terms of what that sentence is scrutable from, and when a sentence is context-dependent, we should expect both the content and the scrutability of the sentence to vary with context.

Here, sentences in the dependent class and in the base class need to be treated somewhat differently. Sentences in the base class need not include natural-language sentences: the project of the *Aufbau* does not require that there is a natural-language expression for recollected similarity, for example. So we can allow that the sentences in the base class be sentences in a merely possible language, if appropriate natural-language sentences are not available. We can also largely allow that base sentences be restricted to context-independent sentences, apart from (as we will see) a couple of exceptions such as 'I' and 'now'.

The sentences in the dependent class must include sentences of natural language, however, at least for purposes such as defining the content of those sentences. When these sentences are context-dependent, the truth of these sentences will be context-dependent, as will their scrutability. For example, there may be

---

[3] I will be neutral on just what sort of abstract object a sentence type is, but I will take it that they are structures composed from simpler expression types such as words. I will take it that expression types belong to their languages essentially, so that the same expression type cannot recur in English and French. I will also take it that where there are ambiguous strings such as 'bank' there is more than one corresponding expression type in English. It follows that expression types are more than uninterpreted strings.

no context-independent fact of the matter about whether '87 is a large number' is true, or whether it is scrutable from a certain base.[4]

Furthermore, there are cases in which scrutability is context-dependent even if truth is not. Ordinary proper names are often used with different modes of presentation in different contexts. For example, Leverrier might have used 'Neptune' solely under a mode of presentation characterizing it as whatever perturbs the orbit of Uranus, while later speakers might not. Then the truth of 'Neptune is a planet' is not context-dependent. But nevertheless, it seems reasonable to say that 'Neptune is a planet' is scrutable from 'A planet perturbs the orbit of Uranus' on Leverrier's usage, but not on later usage. One can get the same behavior with any ordinary proper name. Any such name can be associated with different modes of presentation for different speakers and occasions: for example, the name 'Adolf Hitler' will involve a different mode of presentation for Hitler's mother and for a student today. We can expect that this difference in mode of presentation will give rise to differences in scrutability.

We might put this by saying that these expressions are *epistemically context-dependent*, even if they are not *extensionally context-dependent*.[5] Officially, an expression E is epistemically context-dependent when there exists a sentence S containing E such that S is a priori scrutable from some base sentences in one context and not in another, wholly in virtue of a difference in the use of E in those contexts.[6] E is extensionally context-dependent when the extension of E can vary between contexts (where the extension of a singular term is the entity it refers to, and the extension of a predicate or general term is the associated property).

---

[4] Knowledge of and belief in context-dependent sentence types can still be defined as in the previous section, but it will not yield useful results, because the definition will put only weak constraints on what is required to know or believe S. For example, any belief about the location of an object is apt to be expressed by 'It is there', so almost any subject will believe this sentence. Likewise, almost any subject will believe 'It is not there'. For useful results, we need to relativize to context somehow.

[5] On a standard Russellian view of content, names have the same content relative to all contexts. On such a view epistemic context-dependence will not be a form of semantic context-dependence, where semantic context-dependence requires that an expression has different contents relative to different contexts. But not all forms of context-dependence are semantic, and even a Russellian should acknowledge the epistemological variations between different utterances of names.

[6] The relevant contexts here should be restricted to those in which S is uttered with full competence. For the definition of scrutability in a context, see below. An awkward consequence of the official definition of epistemic context-dependence is that someone who rejects apriority (or rejects a priori scrutability for names from any base) will then be committed to the claim that no expressions (or no names) are epistemically context-dependent. I argue against these views later, but given a view on which they are correct, it is probably best to replace the appeal to a priori scrutability in the definition by an appeal to conditional scrutability, or to understand epistemic context-dependence in some other way.

When an expression is not epistemically context-dependent, we can say that it is *epistemically invariant*. For example, 'I' is plausibly epistemically invariant. That is, 'I' is associated with a canonical first-person mode of presentation, and at least in standard uses there is no associated context-dependence in its scrutability from various bases. The same goes for 'now', at least if we ignore any context-dependence associated with whether it refers to an instant or a longer span of time. 'I' and 'now' are both extensionally context-dependent, though, in that they can refer to different referents on different occasions of use. Expressions such as 'tall', 'ready', and 'that' are arguably both epistemically and extensionally context-dependent. Expressions such as 'zero' and 'conscious' are arguably both epistemically and extensionally invariant. Expressions such as 'Gödel' and 'water' are arguably epistemically but not extensionally context-dependent.

When an expression is extensionally context-dependent, the truth of sentences containing it will depend on context. When an expression is epistemically context-dependent, the scrutability of sentences containing it will depend on context. So if scrutability theses are to accommodate such expressions, we need them to accommodate this sort of context-dependence.

To do this, we can apply scrutability not just to sentence types but also to utterances, sentence tokens, or sentences in contexts. The sentences discussed so far are sentence types: abstract expressions such as 'The cat sat on the mat', not anchored to any specific occasion of utterance. By contrast, different utterances of 'The cat sat on the mat' are made by different speakers and by the same speaker at different times. It is natural to say that there are different sentence tokens here. For present purposes we should not understand sentence tokens as inscriptions (concrete objects such as ink patterns or sound waves), as there would then often be multiple tokens per utterance, Instead, we can understand a sentence token as an ordered pair of a sentence S and an utterance of S. Perhaps better, we can understand it as an ordered pair consisting of a sentence S and a context of utterance of S, where such a context of utterance is a centered world centered on an utterance of S: that is, an ordered pair consisting of a possible world and an utterance of S within that world.

Equivalently, we can relativize scrutability of a sentence type S to a context (again, a centered world centered on an utterance of S).[7] For example, 'Neptune

---

[7] Different models of contexts and context-dependence are available. On a standard view of extensional context-dependence, contexts involve sets of parameters (speakers, times, salient individuals, standards of strictness, and so on), and the extension of an expression depends on some formal way on those parameters. It is not obvious how to generalize this model to epistemic context-dependence, however. We could suppose that there are some parameters on which an expression's epistemic role depends. But it is not obvious what the parameters are and how to represent epistemic roles. One might take Fregean senses themselves to be parameters (and/or to be epistemic roles), but then we have gained little over working directly with Fregean propositions. The centered-world understanding of context has the advantage that the world itself fixes all the

is a planet' might be scrutable from a given base relative to Leverrier's context but not relative to a later context. In practice I will move back and forth between talk of utterances, sentence tokens, and sentences in contexts. Sentence tokens and sentences in contexts are identical as defined, and they correspond one-to-one to utterances (in worlds). For ease of discussion, I will sometimes speak of a sentence token S rather than of a token of a sentence S, and will speak of a token expressing a thought when the corresponding utterance expresses a thought.

We can first define knowledge of sentence tokens or sentences in contexts. A subject who utters a sentence S knows the relevant token of S (or knows S relative to the context of utterance) if the utterance of S expresses a thought that constitutes knowledge. More generally, a subject who utters a sentence S at time t_1 knows the relevant token of S (or knows S relative to the context of utterance) at time t_2 if the utterance of S at t_1 expresses a thought that constitutes knowledge at t_2. (Persistence of thoughts over time is discussed later in this excursus.) We will not need to characterize knowledge of a sentence token by a subject other than the original speaker. Corresponding definitions can be given for a priori knowledge and for belief. For our purposes, these definitions need not be restricted to fully competent utterances; they also apply to deferential and incompetent utterances.

We can then define scrutability for sentence tokens or sentences in contexts. For example: a token of S is inferentially scrutable from a class C of (context-independent) sentence types (or: S is inferentially scrutable from C relative to the context c of utterance) iff, were the speaker to know all the true sentences in C, she would be in a position to know the token of S (or: to know S relative to c). The corresponding inferential scrutability thesis will then say: there is a class of (context-independent) sentences C from which all sentence tokens are inferentially scrutable. I discuss the (inferential, conditional, a priori) scrutability of sentence tokens in more detail later in this excursus.

This scrutability thesis for sentence tokens is weaker in some respects than a scrutability thesis for sentence types or for propositions. As it stands, the thesis is restricted to tokens of sentences that are uttered in the actual word, so its truth depends on which sentences are uttered. The less that is said in the actual world, the easier it is for the thesis to be true! Still, this thesis is strong enough to be applied to all actual utterances, say for the purposes of defining content. For a stronger thesis, one can require that the thesis holds not just in our world but in

features of context. Restricting these centered worlds to worlds in which the speaker at the center is uttering the sentence in question allows the association between utterance and thought to fix an epistemic role and consequently to fix facts about scrutability. I do not rule out other models of context for analyzing scrutability, but the centered-world model will suffice for our purposes here. (It should be noted that the use of centered worlds to represent contexts is quite distinct from their use to represent epistemically possible scenarios.)

all nearby worlds, and perhaps in all nomologically possible worlds (all worlds with the same fundamental properties and laws as ours). We could in principle extend it to all metaphysically possible worlds (including those with alien properties and laws), but such a strengthening would be stronger than is needed for initial purposes.

In any case, we still have scrutability theses for sentence types to capture the central intended force.[8] Theses for sentence tokens can be thought of as auxiliary devices to handle the application to utterances of context-dependent sentences.

A final issue arises from extensional context-dependence. Where this arises in the dependent class, we can handle it as above. However, a residual issue concerns extensional context-dependence in the base. Base sentences typically need to contain the indexicals 'I' and 'now'. These sentences are not true and false absolutely (in the actual world): 'I am hungry now' can be true relative to one subject at one time, and false relative to another subject or another time. For this reason, we cannot require that base sentences be true absolutely. Rather, they must be true or false relative to a subject at a time. Given that our key theses concern the scrutability of truths from truths, we need to allow the relevant class of base truths to be different for different subjects and different times. On a moment's reflection, this is just what one should expect, if the base truths include a specification of the subject's place in the world.[9]

We might try formulating the thesis by saying: for all subjects s at all times t, there is a compact class of truths (true relative to s and t) such that all truths (relative to s and t) are scrutable (for s at t) from that class. This works when the dependent truths are sentence types, but if the dependent truths are restricted to sentence tokens, this formulation threatens to trivialize the thesis. It may be that every true sentence token is scrutable from a *single* truth (namely itself, or its counterpart in the base language). If so, then as long as subjects can produce

---

[8] Someone might object that whether an expression is context-dependent will depend on what counts as the content of an utterance of an expression, which depends on one's theory of propositions. A Fregean theory may count 'Neptune' as context-dependent where a Russellian theory does not, for example. However, the sorts of context-dependence that matter here are extensional and epistemic context-dependence. These notions are not defined in terms of propositional content, and are available irrespective of whether one is Fregean or Russellian. Both views can utilize the notion of an expression's extension in a context, and both views can utilize the notion of an expression's epistemic role in a context. It is true that given a Fregean view, epistemic context-dependence will correspond at least roughly to context-dependence of Fregean content (likewise for extensional context-dependence and Russellian content). But the notion of epistemic context-dependence does not presuppose a Fregean theory of content.

[9] Note that this relativization of truth of sentences to subjects should be distinguished from relativization of scrutability of sentences to subjects. The discussion in chapter 2 suggests that inferential and conditional scrutability of a sentence from a class of sentences is always relativized to a subject and a time, and that a priori scrutability can be so relativized but need not be so relativized.

only a finite number of tokens at one time, then for any s and t, there will be a finite class of truths from which the true tokens (relative to s and t) are scrutable.

In light of all this, one can formulate the thesis more generally (for both sentence types and tokens) by saying that there is a compact class C of *sentences* such that for all subjects s and all times t, all sentences that are true relative to s and t are scrutable (for s at t) from the subclass of sentences in C that are true relative to s and t. If dependent truths are restricted to sentence tokens, the thesis can be put more simply by saying that there is a compact class C of sentences such that every true sentence token S (uttered by subject s at time t) is scrutable (for s at t) from the subclass of sentences in C that are true relative to s and t. We can also extend this thesis to all nomologically possible sentence tokens, as suggested above, if we also relativize truth to the world of utterance.

In what follows, for simplicity, I will typically suppose that we have chosen an (arbitrary) subject and time, and will allow arbitrary sentence types or sentence tokens to be in the dependent class. (When those tokens have not actually been uttered, we can adopt the fiction that they have been uttered.) Then we can consider the question of whether there are sets of base truths from which all truths are scrutable; the relativization to the subject will often be left implicit.[10]

Scrutability of sentence tokens and the persistence of thoughts

A residual issue concerns the scrutability of sentence tokens from sentence types. In defining scrutability of a sentence type S from a class of sentence types C, we have used notions such as: if s came to know the sentences in C, s would be in a position to know S (inferential scrutability); s is in a position to know that if D,

---

[10] Another worry about extensional context-dependence is that knowledge takes time, and that an indexical sentence type such as 'It is now t' that is true at t will not be true after t, so cannot be known after t. This worry especially affects Inferential Scrutability: here we might modify our understanding of 'in a position to know S at t'' to require not possible knowledge at a later time t' of thoughts apt to be expressed by S at t', but instead possible knowledge at t' of thoughts apt to be expressed by S at t. This requires an appeal to the persistence of thoughts, as discussed in the next section. The worry is not so bad for A Priori Scrutability, as long as we recognize that conditional sentences such as '$D \rightarrow$ It is now t' (where D may itself contain 'now') can come to be known a priori at a time t' after t. It is a delicate question whether this should require a thought at t' (constituting a priori knowledge) that is apt to be expressed by the conditional at t' or at t; I think there is a case for the latter (so that the relevant thought in effect involves *It was then* . . . rather than *It is now* . . . on both sides), but either claim is plausible. The issue does not arise for Conditional Scrutability, which is understood normatively rather than modally. Perhaps this is another point in favor of the view that normative or warrant-based understandings of apriority and the like are more basic than modal understandings.

then S (conditional scrutability); and $D \to S$ is a priori (a priori scrutability). However, it is not obvious how to apply these definitions to sentence tokens, or to sentences in contexts.

One option here involves understanding these notions in terms of warrant, as discussed below: for example, being in a position to know a sentence token S would involve there being a warrant for the thought expressed by S. This option will not raise the issues that follow. However, we may also want to understand these notions in broadly modal terms. A modal account needs further analysis.

In the case of inferential scrutability, we want to analyze what it is for a speaker to be in a position to know a sentence token S, both at the time of uttering S and at certain later times (such as after coming to know truths in C). The natural suggestion, following the modal account for sentence types, is that at time t, the speaker is in a position to know S iff it is possible that she later comes to know S, starting from her position at t and without acquiring further empirical information.

This analysis invokes the notion of knowing a sentence token S at a time after the time of utterance. To define that notion, we can say that the speaker of a sentence token S, uttered at time t_1, knows S at some later time t_2, if the thought expressed by S at t_1 constitutes knowledge at t_2. As discussed shortly, this requires reidentification of thoughts over time. Here the idea is that there is some possible process of reasoning that starts from the subject's thought at t and justifies that thought, ending with the thought constituting knowledge. For the analysis of being in a position to know, the reasoning process need not involve a priori reasoning alone, as it can use any empirical beliefs that the subject has at the time of utterance, but it cannot involve new empirical discoveries.

This analysis yields a straightforward analysis of inferential scrutability: a sentence token S is inferentially scrutable from C iff there is some subclass of C such that if the speaker came to know the sentences in that subclass, she would be in a position to know S. What about a priori and conditional scrutability?

We can say that a thought is *a priori* iff it is possible that on (perhaps idealized) reflection, the thought comes to constitute a priori knowledge. A sentence token S is a priori (equivalently: one is in a position to know S a priori) iff it expresses an a priori thought. We can then say that a sentence token S is a priori scrutable from a class C when there is a possible thought T', apt to be expressed by some conjunction of sentences in C, such that T' *implies* T, where T is the thought expressed by S. For thoughts T_1 and T_2 had by the same subject, T_1 implies T_2 when a disjunction of T_2 with a negation of T_1 is a priori.

Likewise, S is conditionally scrutable from C when T' *rationalizes* T, where T is the thought expressed by S and T' is the thought one would have if one harmlessly entertained the conjunction of all sentences in C.[11] For thoughts T_1 and T_2 had by the same subject, T_1 rationalizes T_2 when a conditional thought in T_2 given T_1 is rational, according to the standards of ideal insulated rationality.

These definitions invoke certain relations between thoughts. One thought can be a negation of another, intuitively when it is formed by negating the former thought. One thought can be the conjunction of some others, or the disjunction of some others, intuitively when it is formed by conjoining or disjoining those thoughts. A conditional thought can be the conditionalization of one thought on another, intuitively when it is formed by accepting the latter conditional on the former. I think we have a clear intuitive grasp of these notions. Given the notion of persistence in the next paragraph, all we really need here is a synchronic relation: the idea that a thought can be a negation of a simultaneous thought, or a disjunction, a conjunction, or a conditionalization of two simultaneous thoughts.

These definitions presuppose that thoughts can be reidentified over time, or that thoughts can persist over time. The notion of persistence enters into the analysis of being in a position to know when we say 'the thought expressed by S at t_1 constitutes knowledge at t_2'. It enters into the analysis of apriority of a thought when we say that it is possible that a thought 'comes to constitute a priori knowledge'. It also enters tacitly into the analysis of a priori and conditional scrutability in that the relevant conditional or disjunctive thoughts involving T (the thought expressed by S) may arise later than the original time of utterance of S.

This notion of persistence over time might give rise to objections. What is it for a thought at t_1 to persist as a thought at t_2? One might suggest that this is simply for the thought to have the same content. But then one's conclusions about potential knowledge and apriority will be hostage to one's theory of content, and it is not clear that they can then be used to ground a theory of content.

However, persistence should not be understood as sameness of content. First: on a fine-grained Fregean view of content, persistence may not require sameness of content. For example, my thought that I am hungry now might persist as my

---

[11] This analysis is of a piece with the claim that $cr'(S) = cr'(T_1)$ and that $cr'(S_1 \mid S_2) = cr'(T_1 \mid T_2)$, where T_1 and T_2 are the thoughts one would have if one harmlessly entertained S_1 and S_2. This claim about non-insulated rationality is not quite right: for example, if S_1 is 'I am entertaining S_2', then $cr'(S_1 \mid S_2)$ may intuitively be low while $cr'(T_1 \mid T_2)$ may be high. (When thinking T_2, one will entertain S_2 and will plausibly thereby be in a position to know that one is entertaining S_2.) Fortunately this problem does not arise for the insulated rational credence $cr^*(S_1 \mid S_2)$, which is what is relevant to rationalization and conditional scrutability, because here $cr^*(T_1 \mid T_2)$, will be low due to the barring of introspection. To handle non-insulated rational credences, one can define $cr'(S_1 \mid S_2)$ in terms of there being warrant for having a certain credence $cr(S_1 \mid S_2)$, as discussed at the end of the fourth excursus.

thought that I was hungry then, which arguably has a different fine-grained Fregean content.

Second: even on a Russellian view of content, cases of semantic fragility (discussed at more length shortly) suggest a possible gap between persistence and sameness of content. Suppose that I express a thought T with 'Snow is white iff actually snow is white', but I do not reflect on T or attempt to justify it. Then T does not express a priori knowledge, but it is natural to say that T is justifiable and expresses potential a priori knowledge. But if I had followed through, the content of the ensuing a priori knowledge would have been q iff q-in-w, whereas the actual content of T is q iff q-in-@. So it appears that T is justifiable in virtue of a later possible thought with a different content being justified. One way to put this is to say that T could have persisted as a later thought with a different content. If we say this, we also need to say that T itself could have had the different content q iff q-in-w. This leads to a picture on which the relevant thoughts are themselves semantically fragile: if one had investigated them, they would have had different contents. So one might take these cases to motivate a view on which thoughts do not have their Russellian contents essentially.

The alternative for a Russellian is to say that if one had engaged in the relevant investigation, one would not have had T at all, but instead would have had a different thought with a different content. This preserves the individuation of thoughts by contents, but makes it harder to associate properties such as justifiability with the relevant thoughts. On this view, T is not justifiable at all by the process in question: only a counterpart thought will be justified. To capture the phenomenon, one will end up saying something like: a thought is quasi-justifiable iff it is possible that a counterpart thought is justified. The upshot for present purposes will be much the same as on the previous view: to understand the phenomena of justifiability and potential a priori knowledge, one needs to appeal to a relation between a thought and possible future thoughts that does not require sameness of content.

Third: on almost any view of content, sameness of content does not entail persistence: if I think that p at t_1, and at t_2 I have a causally independent thought that p, then the latter does not persist as the former. This applies even on a Fregean view, but is particularly clear on a Russellian view of content: when Sue has thought T_2 (expressed by 'Phosphorus is a planet') shortly after T_1 (expressed by 'Hesperus is a planet'), these thoughts may have the same content, but T_1 certainly does not persist as T_2.

Persistence requires an appropriate continuity between thoughts over time. It is plausible that this continuity requires some sort of relatedness of content, perhaps involving common or related guises, but this relatedness of content does not suffice for persistence. Causal and psychological continuity is also required. I will not attempt to define the notion of persistence here, but will leave the notion unanalyzed. For present purposes, the most essential applications of the notions of persistence (in the case of a priori scrutability) can be restricted to occurrent thoughts within a single brief stream of thought: we can imagine an idealized thinker entertaining the thought, and coming moments later to justify it.

Most importantly, persistence is an intuitive notion that everyone needs, whatever they think about the theory of content. Anyone who believes in thoughts should allow that a thought can come to be justified, or that it can come to be confirmed by evidence. Making sense of these notions requires the notion of persistence. The notion, along with the related notions of negation, disjunction, and conjunction in thought, are also crucial to understanding the notion of *inference* in thought. Suppose one reasons: A, B, therefore $A \& B$. For this to be a valid inference in thought, conferring immediate justification of the conclusion, one's initial thought that A must be appropriately related to one's later thought $A \& B$, intuitively acting as a conjunct of that thought. If one formed an independent thought with the same content, then this thought would not acquire the same sort of immediate justification. So an appeal to the notion of persistence does not presuppose commitment to any theoretical account of content, or to any technical notions such as apriority. The notion is already manifest in our ordinary notions of justification, confirmation, and inference in thought.

Sentential vs. propositional scrutability

There are at least three potential differences in strength between sentential and propositional scrutability theses. One potential difference arises from a course we have considered already: differences between theories of propositions. We have seen that on Fregean accounts, there will plausibly be a close link between sentential scrutability as defined here and propositional scrutability: roughly, a sentence S will be scrutable from a class C of sentences iff the proposition expressed by S is scrutable from the class of propositions expressed by sentences in C (though see below for limitations of scope and exceptions). On a Russellian or possible-worlds theory of propositions, however, there will not be such a close parallel. For example, 'Hesperus is a planet' is not a priori scrutable from 'Phosphorus is a planet', but the associated Russellian propositions are identical, so the first is a priori scrutable from the second.

On a Russellian or possible-worlds account, one might bring propositional scrutability theses into a closer alignment with sentential scrutability theses by replacing propositions in the scrutability thesis by proposition/guise pairs. Then it is attractive to hold that a sentence (type or token) is scrutable from a class of sentences if the corresponding proposition is scrutable from the corresponding class of propositions, under the guises associated with the sentences.

A second difference arises from the phenomenon of *inexpressibility*: propositions that cannot be expressed by sentences. If there are inexpressible propositions, then it may happen that all expressible propositions are scrutable from a certain base but some inexpressible propositions are not. If so, an unrestricted sentential scrutability thesis may be true: sentences express only expressible propositions, so all sentences are scrutable. But an unrestricted propositional scrutability thesis is false: some inexpressible propositions are inscrutable. If we grant that sentences are scrutable from each other iff the propositions they express are scrutable from each other (as perhaps on a Fregean view of propositions), sentential scrutability theses are akin to propositional scrutability theses restricted to expressible (or entertainable) propositions. A thesis cast in terms of guise/proposition pairs may in effect have the same restriction, at least if we assume that there are no guises associated with unentertainable propositions.[12]

The issues here depend on just how we understand the scope of a sentential scrutability thesis. One could attempt to avoid the problem by stipulating an ideal language with a sentence for every proposition. But it is not obvious that such a language is possible, and it is less obvious that it could be spoken or that we could align the language with thoughts as we need to for present purposes. For our epistemological purposes, a sentential scrutability thesis needs to be restricted to possible languages that could be spoken, and to sentences in those languages that are apt to express thoughts. This means that there is room for sentences and propositions to come apart.

For example: in chapter 7 (section 9), I discuss a view on which certain intrinsic properties (quiddities) of matter cannot be grasped or expressed. If these properties are involved in propositions, then on such a view there may well be propositions that are not expressible or thinkable. These propositions may then yield counterexamples to propositional scrutability theses without corresponding counterexamples to sentential scrutability theses.

Another inexpressibility issue will arise if there are propositions expressible by sentence tokens but not expressible by any context-independent sentence types. For example, suppose that object-involving propositions can only be expressed in a spoken language using ordinary proper names and that ordinary proper names are always epistemically context-dependent. Then object-involving propositions fall under the scope of a propositional scrutability thesis, but no corresponding sentence falls under the scope of a sentential scrutability thesis for

---

[12] If graspability of Fregean propositions varies between subjects, as on Frege's own view of first-person propositions, one might also want to relativize to subjects and times, saying: for all subjects s and times t, all true propositions graspable by s at t are scrutable from a compact class of propositions graspable by s and t. On a Russellian view, one could do much the same for guise-proposition pairs.

context-independent sentence types. On my own view, this case cannot arise: for any sentence token there is some possible epistemically invariant sentence type all of whose tokens behave like the original token (perhaps by stipulation). Even on other views, a token expressing the proposition in question will at least fall into the scope of scrutability theses cast in terms of sentence tokens. But the case is worth keeping in mind.

A third inexpressibility issue concerns the limited complexity of languages. If the scrutability thesis is limited to a language with only finite sentences and a countably infinite vocabulary, then there will be only a countably infinite number of sentences, while there may be enormously more propositions. It is arguable that infinitary languages with more sentences than this could be spoken. Even then, though, it is still arguable that there will be more propositions than sentences. If so, there will be many inexpressible propositions.

Admitting infinitary sentences into the scope of the scrutability thesis raises many tricky issues concerning just what sort of infinite complexity is allowed. Set-theoretic paradoxes lurk nearby, including David Kaplan's paradox of cardinality (Kaplan 1995; I discuss these issues in 'The Nature of Epistemic Space'). To avoid these complications, I will mostly assume that the truths in the dependent class in a sentential scrutability thesis are restricted to finite sentences. Truths in the idealized language in the base class can in principle be infinite, although in practice the sentences I consider will mostly be finite. I will occasionally invoke infinitary sentences (such as the conjunction of all sentences in a scrutability base) in an auxiliary role, but these sentences are not themselves among the dependent sentences in the scope of the scrutability thesis. The restriction to finite dependent sentences means that there will be a considerable amount of inexpressibility, but the scrutability thesis will still have unrestricted application to the spoken natural languages that we know about. Where relevant, I will occasionally consider relaxations of this restriction.

A third difference between sentential and propositional scrutability theses (in addition to those arising from Russellian propositions and inexpressibility) arises from the phenomenon of semantic fragility. A sentence S is semantically fragile when investigating whether S is true can change the proposition that S expresses.[13] One example is 'Snow is white iff actually snow is white'. On one common view, this sentence S expresses a proposition p involving the actual world @. Now, suppose that no one actually ever investigates S. Then it is still

---

[13] I discuss semantic fragility at more length in 'Actuality and Knowability'. In cases of semantic fragility, investigating S changes the proposition it expresses, while in cases of alethic fragility (discussed in section 2.3), investigating S changes its truth-value. The Fitch sentence is alethically fragile without being semantically fragile. 'Snow is white iff actually snow is white' is semantically fragile without being alethically fragile.

possible that someone comes to know that S is true. But if someone did so, S would express a proposition different from the one that it actually expresses. It would express a proposition p' involving a different world w: the world in which S is investigated and known. For example, p may be the proposition q *iff q-in-@* while p' is the proposition q *iff q-in-w*, where q is the proposition that snow is white.

It is natural to say that in this process, the subject would come to know S. But she would not come to know p, the proposition S actually expresses; instead she would come to know p'. In these cases, we need to distinguish knowledge of a sentence from knowledge of the proposition that it actually expresses. Rather, knowledge of a sentence in a world should be knowledge of the proposition that the sentence expresses relative to that world (perhaps under the guise associated with that sentence in that world).

In 2.2, I discussed two reasons for distinguishing sentential from propositional knowledge: dialectical reasons and reasons based on the argument from assertion. The phenomenon of semantic fragility constitutes a third reason. Its force is slightly different. The argument from assertion suggested that knowledge of p does not suffice for knowledge of a sentence S expressing p, at least on coarse-grained views of propositional content. The argument from semantic fragility does the reverse: it suggests that knowledge of S (in counterfactual worlds) does not suffice for knowledge of p, at least on object-involving views of propositional content.

Semantic fragility drives a wedge between sentential and propositional scrutability. In cases such as the above, it can happen that S is scrutable from some base when p is not. In fact, in the case above, it is plausible that S is a priori knowable, so that it is a priori scrutable from any base. But p may not be a priori knowable: if one does not actually know S, then any world in which one knows S will be a world in which S does not express p. So even if one comes to know S a priori, one will not thereby come to know p a priori. I have argued in 'Actuality and Knowability' that in some such cases, p is not knowable at all. If so, then p is not a priori scrutable from any base. So a priori scrutability of a sentence can come apart from a priori scrutability of the proposition it expresses.

Another example: say I introduce 'Bigthink' as a name for the most powerful reasoner in the world. Let us suppose that the most powerful reasoner is in fact Einstein, and let S' be 'Bigthink is German'. Assume a view on which S' expresses a proposition p' involving Einstein. Then my utterance of S' may well be a priori scrutable from a giant world-sentence G, in that 'If G, then S'' is knowable a priori. But if I were to come to know this (extraordinarily complex) conditional a priori, I would be the most powerful reasoner in the world. If so, 'Bigthink' would refer to me. So in deriving S' from G, I would not derive the proposition p' (involving Einstein) that S' actually expresses, but a different proposition involving me. So S' is scrutable from G by this method, but p' is not. On a Russellian view where p' is the same as the proposition that Einstein is German, p' may be scrutable under a different guise, but on a Fregean view where both guises and objects are built into propositions, p' may not be scrutable at all. Once again, the semantic fragility of S' leads to a difference between sentential and propositional scrutability.

Semantic fragility tends to suggest that many propositional scrutability theses will be false where corresponding sentential scrutability theses are true. For the overarching Scrutability thesis, for example, there may be no compact base of true propositions from which all true propositions are a priori scrutable: if a proposition such as p is not actually derived a priori from base sentences, it may be impossible to derive it. One might take this as a further reason to formulate scrutability theses in sentential rather than propositional terms.

Alternatively, to avoid the problem posed by semantic fragility, and to hold onto propositional scrutability theses in the spirit of the introduction one can try to understand propositional scrutability and propositional apriority in nonmodal terms: that is, not in terms of what it is possible to know, or to know a priori. An alternative nonmodal understanding in terms of warrants is developed in the next excursus.

Warrants and Support Structures

So far, I have often cast notions such as apriority, scrutability, and knowability in modal terms: that is, in terms of what it is possible to know or to know a priori. We have seen that modal idealizations can lead to difficulties in some circumstances: they cause problems for propositional apriority and scrutability in cases of semantic fragility (see the end of the third excursus), and they cause other problems if there are brute modal constraints on possible reasoners (see section 2.7). It is also arguable that modal idealizations are not explanatorily fundamental: even when a scrutability thesis involving a modal idealization is true, it derives from more fundamental epistemological facts. So it is worth exploring nonmodal ways of understanding these notions.

In the introduction, scrutability theses are cast in terms of what one is in a position to know. This notion can be cashed out in modal terms, but it can also be cashed out in other ways.

In particular, a relevant notion of one's being in a position to know p can be cashed out in terms of there being a *warrant* for one to believe p. A warrant is a knowledge-apt justification, or a justification suitable for knowledge. There can be a warrant for one to believe p even if one does not in fact know or believe p. For example, when there exists a proof of p, this yields a warrant for believing p regardless of whether anyone proves p. These warrants are a form of *propositional justification*: a justification that supports belief in p for a subject, whether or not the subject believes p. This notion is standardly distinguished from *doxastic justification*: justification on which someone's justified belief in p is based.

On one notion of propositional warrant, one says that a subject *has* a propositional warrant to believe p when the warrant is (in some sense) within the subject's grasp. In this sense, the mere existence of a complex proof for p does not entail that a mathematically ignorant subject has a warrant for believing p. For our (idealized) purposes, however, this notion is too strong. The more relevant notion for our purposes is that of there *being* a propositional warrant for a subject to believe p (or more briefly, there being a propositional warrant for p), whether or not the subject has that warrant. This notion does not come with the requirement that the warrant is within the subject's grasp. There can be a warrant for one to believe *p* even when knowing or believing *p* is beyond one's cognitive capacities. For example, even when a proof of *p* is enormously complex, it yields a warrant for a mathematically ignorant subject to believe *p*. We might call the first sort of warrant a *non-ideal warrant*, and the second sort an *ideal warrant*.[1]

The framework of warrants makes a difference in cases of semantic fragility.[2] When *p* is the proposition expressed by the semantically fragile sentence *S* discussed at the end of the third excursus ('Snow is white iff actually snow is white'), one can argue that there exists a proof of *p* even though it is impossible to use it to prove *p*. In particular, there exists an abstract proof of *S* using the logic of 'actually'. *S* expresses *p* in the actual world, so this abstract proof of *S* is also an abstract proof of *p*. But if one were to *use* the proof to prove *S*, *S* would express *p'* rather than *p*, so one would not prove *p*.

What goes for proof goes also for warrant. In this case, there exists an (ideal a priori) warrant for believing *p* even though the warrant cannot be used to know *p*. This warrant is a propositional warrant that cannot be used as a doxastic warrant. If the subject is sophisticated and the proof is easy, the subject may even *have* a (non-ideal a priori) warrant for believing *p*, even though the subject cannot use that warrant to believe *p*. This last issue depends on precisely how one understands the conditions for having a (non-ideal) warrant, but either way, there will certainly *be* an a priori warrant for believing *p*. So there can be an a priori warrant for a subject to believe *p* even when it is not possible to know *p* a priori.

This suggests a nonmodal conception of propositional apriority: *p* is a priori in the nonmodal sense when there is an a priori warrant for some subject to believe *p*. Propositions expressed by semantically fragile sentences such as '*S* iff actually *S*' above may be a priori in this sense even if they are not a priori in the modal sense. Likewise, this suggests a nonmodal conception of knowability: *p* is knowable by a subject in the nonmodal sense if that subject has warrant for believing *p*.

One can define nonmodal apriority and knowability for sentences in a similar way: *S* is nonmodally a priori if there is an a priori warrant for some subject to believe *S* (where believing *S* is understood as in the third excursus), while *S* is nonmodally knowable for a subject if there is a warrant for that subject to believe *S*. Unlike the propositional versions, these nonmodal notions of sentential

---

[1] One might require that even an ideal warrant is within a subject's idealized grasp (in some nonmodal sense), where the idealization involves idealization of reasoning. So non-ideal and ideal warrants could both be seen as providing 'subjective' reasons (reasons for a subject that are in some sense available to the subject), although the latter is a highly idealized variety. Thanks to John Bengson, Jon Kvanvig, Nico Silins, and Chris Tucker for discussion of warrant.

[2] The next few paragraphs will make most sense in light of the last few paragraphs of the previous excursus, on semantic fragility (or alternatively, in light of 'Actuality and Knowability'). Readers can either read that material first or alternatively skip directly to 'What is a warrant, exactly?' below.

apriority and knowability will not come apart from modal apriority and knowability in cases of semantic fragility. They may still come apart if there are brute modal constraints on possible thinkers, however. For example, if no possible thinker can carry out a proof that involves more than a million steps, then certain true mathematical sentences (and propositions) will be a priori in the nonmodal sense but not in the modal sense.

One can also appeal to warrant to define nonmodal notions of scrutability. For example: q is inferentially scrutable from p when knowing p would provide a warrant for q; q is conditionally scrutable from p when one has a warrant for accepting *if p, then q*; and q is a priori scrutable from p when there is an a priori warrant for accepting *if p, then q*. These definitions are unaffected by semantic fragility. In the cases from the third excursus on which a semantically fragile sentence P is scrutable from Q on a modal definition of scrutability, the corresponding proposition p is not scrutable from q on a modal definition of propositional scrutability, but p will plausibly be scrutable from q on the nonmodal definition of propositional scrutability.

I often cast notions such as apriority and scrutability in modal terms elsewhere in this book, in part because modal analyses of notions such as apriority are more familiar than those in terms of warrant, and partly because the problem of semantic fragility does not affect sentential scrutability. But it is reasonable to hold that the warrant-based notions are more fundamental than the corresponding modal notions. When it is possible to know p a priori, this is typically possible because there is an a priori warrant for p. Likewise, when S is scrutable from C in a modal sense, this is typically because S is scrutable from C in a warrant-based sense.

What is a warrant, exactly? A warrant is plausibly a sort of justification: a justification suitable for knowledge. But what is a justification? On some views, there is no particular entity that is a justification, but simply a relation between subjects and propositions misleadingly labeled 'There is a justification for s to believe p.' For our purposes, however, it is useful to develop a more substantive understanding.

I will develop an understanding of warrants and justifications as *support structures*. This understanding is inspired by the special case of proof. When belief in p is warranted by a proof, the corresponding warrant for p derives from the structure of propositions in the proof, with support relations corresponding to logical steps. We can count this structure as a support structure. More generally, a support structure will involve directed graphs of labeled propositions with support relations between them, capturing the justification for a proposition.

It is more common in the epistemological literature to view warrants and justifications as propositions or perhaps as sets of propositions. But these propositions only play their role in virtue of their position in a support structure, and for various purposes it is useful to make this structure explicit. The case of a proof suggests that there can sometimes be a warrant (in an intuitive sense) for someone to believe a proposition even though there is no clear proposition or set of propositions that constitute the warrant. It does not seem right to say that the warrant is the proposition expressed by the first step of the proof or that it is the proposition expressed by the penultimate step. It is also not perspicuous to say that it is the set of all propositions in the proof thrown together, as so many of these propositions are themselves supported by other propositions in the set. Viewing warrants as support structures avoids these problems. This view need not involve a substantive disagreement with those who view warrants as propositions: to be fully explicit we could call these structures 'warrant structures' instead of warrants, and likewise for justifications. The details of this framework are not crucial for addressing the problem of semantic fragility, but they will play a role for other epistemological purposes in chapters 3 and 4. So I will develop the framework in some detail.

We can start with doxastic justification. Take any justified belief that p. Something (a belief or an experience, for example) *justifies* belief in p when it supports p or provides evidence for p in a way that yields prima facie justification for the belief that p. It *directly justifies* belief in p when it justifies belief in p and does not justify belief in p wholly in virtue of justifying something else that justifies belief in p.[3]

A *direct justification* for p can be represented as a graph consisting of a node for p along with nodes for elements (if any) that directly justify belief in p, with arrows from those nodes to p. For example, when a belief in p is justified inferentially, it will be directly justified by inference from one or more other justified beliefs: a belief that q, a belief that r, and so on. Here we can say that these other beliefs, collectively, provide a direct justification for the belief that p. A direct justification can here be represented as a node for p with nodes for q, r, and so on, with arrows from them to p. If the justification is redundant, so that the belief that q suffices on its own to inferentially justify the belief that p, there will also be a direct justification consisting of a node for q with an arrow to a node for p.

When a belief in p is justified non-inferentially, either it will be directly justified by some evidence distinct from the belief (e.g. perceptual evidence) or it will be justified by no such evidence (as on some views of basic belief). In the first

---

[3] The justification relation is an epistemic grounding relation, and should be distinguished from the metaphysical and conceptual grounding relations discussed in the excursus on grounding and elsewhere. For something to stand in this relation to p is not for it to be the metaphysical grounds for the belief that p or the metaphysical grounds for the justification of the belief that p. For example, on a reliabilist view, a reliable process might serve as metaphysical grounds for the justification of a basic belief that p, but this process will not itself stand in the epistemic grounding relation to the belief that p. When a belief that p directly justifies a belief that q, however, it is plausible that their standing in this support relation (or the metaphysical grounds of their standing in this relation) will serve as part of the metaphysical grounds for the justification of the belief that p.

case, we can say that p is justified non-inferentially and evidentially. Here a direct justification for the belief that p can be represented as a node for p with arrows from nodes for any directly justifying evidence. In the second case, we can say that the belief that p is justified non-inferentially and non-evidentially. Here a direct justification for p can be represented by a node for p alone, with p labeled as a basic belief. If the belief that p is self-justifying (if this is possible), the graph will include an arrow from p to itself. If there are beliefs that are justified both inferentially and non-inferentially, then both sorts of support can be included in the structure; though as above, in cases where the justification is redundant, there will also be direct justifications that exclude redundant elements.

An *indirect* justification for p will include a direct justification for p and also justifications for one or more elements in the structure that supports p. A *justification* for p is a direct or indirect justification for p. A *full* justification is a justification that includes a justification for every belief in the structure. A *partial* justification is a justification that is not a full justification.[4]

For example, when belief in p is inferentially justified by belief in q, and belief in q is inferentially justified by belief in r, and belief in r is non-inferentially justified by evidence e, a direct justification will include only a link from q to p. A full justification p will include links from e to r to q to p. There will also be an indirect partial justification with links from r to q to p.

If there can be circles of justificational support (e.g. from p to q to r to p), then justifications can include these circles. If there can be infinite chains of support, then justifications can include these chains. When there are no such circles or infinite chains, we can say that a justification is *classical*. The *grounds* of a classical justification are its initial elements. When a belief that p has a classical justification (whether partial or full), we can say that the grounds of that justification *ground* belief in p. When a belief that p has a full classical justification, we can say that the grounds for the justification *fully ground* belief in p. The grounds of a full classical justification will be *basic evidence*: these may include basic beliefs and/or basic nondoxastic evidence.[5]

For simplicity, I will adopt a model on which evidence always involves propositions. So introspective evidence might involve the proposition that one is in a

---

[4] Note that a partial justification is partial in the sense that it omits some elements that play a justifying role, but not in the sense that it yields support that merely weighs in favor of p without justifying belief in p. I am taking it that all of the justifications I consider here are strong enough to justify belief in p. The elements omitted in a partial justification will either be redundant elements (whose contribution is not required for justification) or indirectly justifying elements (whose contribution is mediated by another element).

[5] Even when there is no full classical justification for p, there may still be a partial classical justification for p. For example, when full justification involves an infinite chain, there will always be a partial justification without such a chain. Even when full justification involves a circle, it may be that there is a partial justification without a circle.

given mental state: for example, the introspective evidence for the belief that one is in pain may be the proposition that one is in pain. Likewise, perceptual evidence may involve the propositional contents of perceptual experience: for example, the perceptual evidence for the perceptual belief that there is something red in front of one may be the (perceptually represented) proposition that there is something red in front of one.[6] Something similar may go for evidence provided by (for example) intuition, memory, and testimony, if one thinks that these involve sources of non-inferential justification distinct from perceptual or introspective evidence.

To distinguish the different roles for various propositions here, the structure will label a proposition p as a belief proposition (p is believed), perceptual evidence (p is the content of a perceptual state), introspective evidence (p is introspectively experienced, or perhaps need only be true), and so on. So in the case above, the justification might look like: e (experienced) $\rightarrow p$ (believed) $\rightarrow q$ (believed) $\rightarrow r$ (believed). This can be read as saying that experience as of e justifies belief in p, which justifies belief in q, which justifies belief in r. The model can easily be adapted to views on which evidence and the relata of the support relation are mental states rather than propositions. On such a view the nodes in the structure will be mental states such as beliefs that p or even nonpropositional mental states such as pains. The model can also be adapted to views on which some of the relata are facts (or perhaps property instances or other entities) rather than propositions.

All this is a sketchy and incomplete picture of support structures. For completeness, the picture should be elaborated in various ways. Importantly, one can also allow support relations themselves to be supported or defeated by evidence. As I discuss in the section on empirical inference in chapter 4, an inferential relation between s and t (say, a direct inference from someone's being a bachelor to his being untidy) can itself be grounded in prior perceptual evidence e. This can be represented by an arrow from e to the arrow between s and t. Similarly, as discussed in chapter 3, an empirical recognitional capacity connecting a perceptual experience e to a recognitional belief b (e.g. recognizing a certain shape as an iPhone) may itself be grounded in prior evidence e' (say, evidence that iPhones have that shape). As I also discuss there, it is even possible to allow that perceptual experiences can sometimes be supported by prior evidence (so that seeing a person as angry may be grounded in prior evidence that they look that way when angry). If so, experiences can sometimes occupy non-initial positions in support

---

[6] I am using 'evidence' in a broad sense on which all epistemic grounds count as evidence, as opposed to a sense on which only justifiers that are true or that are known count as evidence. Whatever one says about 'evidence', I think it is plausible that false propositions can serve as direct justifiers: for example, a belief that p or an experience as of p can justify a belief that q whether p is true or false.

structures. Adding structure to support relations is also possible, for example to indicate that p and q conjointly support $(p \& q) \vee r$ while r supports it separately.

A propositional justification is the same sort of item as a doxastic justification, with the difference that there can be a propositional justification for a subject to believe p even without the subject believing the belief propositions in the justification. It is still plausibly required that for any perceptual and introspective evidence specified in the support structure, the subject must have (or at least have had) corresponding mental states. (If we understand the nodes of the support structure as mental states, the evidential nodes will be mental state tokens while the supported nodes will be mental state types.) A propositional justification yields a doxastic justification when the subject has all the relevant beliefs, and when the beliefs are properly based on each other and on the evidence in a way that reflects the support relations in the structure.

A (propositional or doxastic) warrant is a (propositional or doxastic) justification that meets certain further conditions to make it knowledge-apt for the subject. These arguably include the conditions that all the included propositions be true, that any initial belief propositions (especially in a doxastic warrant) be known, and that there are no defeaters and no Gettier circumstances. These conditions might be varied or extended, but I will stay neutral on the precise conditions required.[7]

The model has a foundationalist flavor to it, but it does not presuppose foundationalism. As long as a view acknowledges the distinction between inferential and non-inferential justification (even if it holds that all justification falls on one side), the model will be coherent. Coherentist and infinitist views will allow nonclassical justifications, and may or may not give a role to basic evidence. Reliabilist and other externalist views may sometimes find non-inferential

---

[7] What is the relation between these notions and the standard notions of subjective and objective reasons for belief? Let us say that a *reason structure* is a justification freed of the requirement that the subject have states corresponding to the relevant perceptual and introspective evidence. Then a reason structure provides subjective reason to believe p roughly when the subject either has mental states corresponding to the initial elements in the structure or perhaps when the subject is in a position to have them (at least where these elements correspond to a priori beliefs). A reason structure provides objective reason to believe p when all the initial elements are true. All of the justifications I have talked about yield at least subjective reasons (although these may be idealized subjective reasons in some cases). Warrants yield both subjective and objective reasons. Here reason structures are roughly analogous to valid arguments, subjective reasons are roughly analogous to valid arguments whose premises are justifiably believed, objective reasons are roughly analogous to sound arguments (valid arguments whose premises are true), and warrants are roughly analogous to sound arguments whose premises are known. (The fact that experiences need not be objects of justification complicates the analogy, however, as does the fact that not every argument transmits justification.) One might also develop a more general notion of a 'basing structure', analogous to an argument (whether valid or invalid): such a structure might reflect only the basing (or potential basing) of certain beliefs on others, whether or not this basing goes along with justification.

justification where other views find inferential justification, and may or may not give a role to non-inferential evidential justification. (If a view does not recognize the notion of non-inferential evidential justification, we can count it as classifying all non-inferential justification as non-evidential.) Speaking for myself, I think it is enormously plausible that there is much inferential justification and much non-inferential evidential justification, so I think that full justifications will often be quite complex.

We can use this framework to help analyze the distinction between a priori and a posteriori justification. At least among full classical justifications, an a posteriori justification will be one with some empirical grounds, while an a priori justification will be one with no empirical grounds. Empirical grounds will include all perceptual and introspective evidence, and perhaps other basic evidence depending on one's views. If one accepts (as I do) that all basic empirical evidence is perceptual or introspective evidence, we can say more simply that a justification is a posteriori iff its grounds include perceptual or introspective evidence. If one holds that there are other sorts of basic empirical evidence, one will need further criteria for classifying basic evidence as empirical or non-empirical. If there are full nonclassical justifications, one will need further criteria to classify these as a priori or a posteriori; here the existence of an empirical ground will serve at least as a sufficient condition for such a justification to be a posteriori.[8]

To analyze a priori doxastic justification, we can then say that a subject's belief is justified a priori if it has an a priori doxastic justification. To analyze a priori propositional justification, we need only invoke the idea that there is an a priori justification for a subject to believe a proposition. We can make parallel claims about a posteriori justification, and about a priori and a posteriori warrant. We can distinguish a special class of conclusive a priori and conclusive a posteriori justifications—that is, justifications for certainty rather than for mere belief—by requiring conclusive basic evidence and conclusive support relations in a justification.

We can also distinguish some a priori warrants as *conceptual* warrants, where a conceptual warrant for *p* is a conclusive a priori justification that derives from the concepts involved in *p*. I develop one way of understanding this notion, on an inferentialist model of concepts, in the seventeenth excursus. We might then

---

[8] When support relations are themselves empirically supported, as with empirical inferences, the relevant empirical evidence will count as grounds and the resulting beliefs will be a posteriori. There are tricky cases discussed at the end of E8 involving processes (perhaps innate processes) that are not obviously grounded in experience but that are not traditionally a priori either. A further option to handle these cases is to label some support relations as a priori relations (perhaps based on the positive character of the support) and to require that an a priori justification involve only a priori support relations.

see an analytic truth as one that expresses a proposition for which there is a conceptual warrant.

We can straightforwardly extend the current analysis to warrant for sentences and for thoughts. One can also extend the current model to analyze cases in which prima facie justification is defeated or in which support is only partial. Finally, one can extend it to analyze justification for having certain credences in propositions (or sentences or thoughts), based on credences in other propositions (or sentences or thoughts) and evidence. The last analysis can yield a warrant-based analysis of rational credences, helping to avoid the problems for modal analyses discussed in the previous excursus.

Insulated Idealization and the Problem of Self-Doubt

Some important epistemological problems arise from cases of *self-doubt*: cases in which subjects have evidence that their own belief-forming processes are unreliable, and cases in which subjects cannot rule out the possibility that their belief-forming processes are unreliable. Cases of the former sort raise difficult questions about what subjects should believe when they have such evidence. If I have evidence that I am a poor mathematical reasoner, should I accept any mathematical conclusions? Cases of the latter sort threaten a sort of overarching meta-cognitive skepticism: if I cannot be certain that my belief-forming processes are reliable, then arguably I cannot be certain of the beliefs that they produce.

The problem of self-doubt raises a significant issue for scrutability theses, and it has consequences for the nature of the idealization we must invoke. Addressing these issues helps to shed some light on the problem of self-doubt more generally. I will discuss these cases first as a problem for Conditional Scrutability. I will then draw some more general conclusions and evaluate related problems for Inferential and A Priori Scrutability.

Say that John has recently been given an anti-arithmetic drug that is known to render users incompetent at doing arithmetic: any arithmetical belief of his will have (let us say) at most a 50 percent chance of being true. Let M be '57 + 65 = 122', which we can suppose has just been uttered by John. Let U be 'My arithmetic judgments are unreliable' (or more specifically, 'My judgments about M have at most a 50 percent chance of being correct'). Suppose that John comes to know that he was recently given the anti-arithmetic drug, so that he comes to know U. What should he then judge about M? There is at least a strong intuition that John should adopt a credence of at most 0.5 in M, or perhaps suspend judgment about M. To continue believing M in light of the evidence about his unreliability seems irrational.

Now suppose that John has not been given the drug, but that he cannot rule out the possibility that he has been given it. What should John judge about M, conditional on the assumption that he has been given the drug? That is, what is the ideally rational credence for him to have in M given U? As in the case above, it is plausible that this credence $cr'(M \mid U) \leq 0.5$. Even if John is in fact an ideal reasoner, he should suspend judgment when he conditionalizes on the hypothesis that he is unreliable.

If this is right, a problem for Conditional Scrutability immediately threatens. There are subjects in the actual world who are unreliable about mathematics. For them, an analog of U is true. Suppose that $PQTI$ is a conditional scrutability base for those subjects. Then U is conditionally scrutable from $PQTI$, so that $cr'(U \mid PQTI) = 1$. Given that $cr'(M \mid U) \leq 0.5$, and given that $PQTI$ does not contain information beyond U that changes the conditional judgment about M, then $cr'(M \mid PQTI) \leq 0.5$. If so, M is not conditionally scrutable from $PQTI$. But M is true. So not all truths are conditionally scrutable from $PQTI$, contradicting the assumption that $PQTI$ is a conditional scrutability base. If this reasoning applies to all putative scrutability bases, then the Conditional Scrutability thesis is false.

Someone might resist by holding that a scrutability base may contain relevant further information beyond M that changes the conditional judgment about M. Most obviously, the base might contain M itself. Still, given a paradigmatic scrutability base with only a posteriori truths, such as $PQTI$, it is hard to see how the rest of C will change the conditional judgment. So at the very least this problem forces us to expand the base considerably. Furthermore, one can raise an analogous problem involving an anti-scrutability drug (one that disrupts scrutability reasoning) or an anti-reasoning drug (one that disrupts all reasoning). Or one can simply note that many actual-world inhabitants are unreliable at reasoning and scrutability, so that analogs of U such as 'I am an unreliable reasoner' are true for them. It is then arguable (as discussed below) that even an ideal reasoner should suspend judgments that are conditional on U, and likewise should suspend all judgments that are conditional on bases from which U is scrutable. If so, there will be no base from which U and all other truths are conditionally scrutable.

Alternatively, one might respond that the ideally rational credences $cr'(M \mid U)$ and $cr'(M \mid PQTI)$ are 1: if John were ideally rational, then even on the supposition that $PQTI$, his ideal reasoning would allow him to know M with certainty. But this does not seem quite right. It is plausibly *irrational* to accept simultaneously that one's belief in M is unreliable and to be certain that M. (The statement 'It is raining and my judgment that it is raining is unreliable' seems to manifest a sort of irrationality that is reminiscent of Moore's paradoxical sentence 'It is raining and I do not believe it is raining'.) If I were to learn U (and to acquire no other new evidence), then rationality would require that if I do not question U, I should suspend judgment about M. So even before learning U, my credence $cr(M \mid U)$ should not be high. Even for an ideally rational being, $cr(M \mid U)$ will not be high. Although U is false in an ideally rational being's context, such a being may well have some tiny positive credence in U, perhaps because they have a tiny positive credence that they have been given an anti-reasoning drug. That area of their credence space will be divided more or less evenly between M and $\sim M$. It follows that for each of us—whether or not we are ideally rational, and whether or not we have recently been given such a drug—$cr'(M \mid U)$ will not be high. The same goes for John. So the counter-example stands.

Someone might suggest that if one is reasoning ideally, one can know with certainty that one is reasoning well: perhaps by introspecting the quality of one's reasoning, or perhaps simply by introspecting one's judgments and then re-using the reasoning to determine that they are correct. This conclusion will be incompatible with U, at least if U says that one reasons poorly in every instance (as we may as well stipulate that it does). Then the objection will say that ideal reasoning can rule out U with certainty, so that $cr'(U) = 0$, and $cr(PQTI) = 0$ when U is scrutable from $PQTI$. Now, I am very doubtful that one can ever rule out U with certainty. But even if we can, this leaves open the question of what $cr(M \mid U)$ and $cr(M \mid PQTI)$ should be, especially if we allow credences conditional on hypotheses with credence zero (as I think one should). In general, a supposition (such as U) trumps any empirical evidence, including introspective evidence, that it conflicts with. So it is natural to say that under the supposition of U, any conflicting evidence deriving from introspection that tends to undermine U will be rendered irrelevant. If so, this evidence will not affect the values of $cr'(M \mid U)$ and $cr'(M \mid PQTI)$, and these credences should still be low.

This sort of problem affects much more than conditional scrutability. David Christensen (2007) has observed that a problem of this sort affects even our knowledge of logical truths. It is commonly held that if L is a logical truth, the rational credence $cr'(L)$ is 1. But it may well be rational to have a small positive credence in the thesis U that one is unreliable about logic: after all, one cannot exclude with certainty the hypothesis that one has recently been given an anti-logic drug. For the reasons above, $cr'(L \mid U)$ cannot be high. It follows that $cr'(L)$ cannot be 1.

The best way to handle this problem is to disentangle various different principles of rationality. It is clear that the principle of rationality invoked above is quite different in kind from ordinary principles of rational inference and the like. We might call it a level-crossing principle: it is a principle by which one's higher-order beliefs about one's cognitive capacity are used to restrain one's first-order beliefs about a subject matter. This principle governs how one should reason in a way quite different from standard principles of theoretical reason. In the case above, standard principles support believing M, but the level-crossing principle support suspending judgment about M, and in this case the second principle wins.

We can imagine a cognizer—call him Achilles—who is at least sometimes insensitive to this sort of level-crossing principle. On occasion, Achilles goes into the mode of *insulated cognition*. When in this mode, Achilles goes where first-order theoretical reasoning takes him, entirely insulated from higher-order beliefs about his cognitive capacity. He might acquire evidence that he is unreliable about mathematics, and thereby come to believe 'I am unreliable about arithmetic', but he will go on drawing conclusions about arithmetic all the same. We might say that in the insulated mode, his reasoning is *practically self-confident*, even if it is not *theoretically self-confident*. That is, any self-doubt manifests itself only in what Achilles believes, and not in how he goes about believing.

What if Achilles comes to believe that he has been taking a falsity pill, so that all of his mathematical beliefs are false? Then he will believe 'All my mathematical beliefs are false'. At the same time, through introspection he may figure out 'I have the mathematical belief that FLT is true' (where FLT is Fermat's Last Theorem). From these he would infer, by ordinary theoretical reasoning, that FLT is false. To avoid this result, we need to stipulate that when in the insulated mode, Achilles is also incapable of introspection.[1] In fact, to avoid indirect evidence of his beliefs through observing his behavior, we can stipulate that in the insulated mode, he is incapable of perception, too.

There is plausibly some sense in which insulated cognition is irrational, but it is a limited sort of irrationality. Suppose that Achilles is otherwise fully rational. And suppose that at a certain point of time, he might either engage in insulated reasoning or fully rational reasoning, where we stipulate that in both cases this involves armchair reasoning (without perception or introspection) that may exploit existing beliefs. Then insulated cognition will yield at least as many true beliefs as the fully rational mode, and in some cases (those in which Achilles has misleading evidence for his irrationality) it will yield more. It is only if Achilles has independent sorts of theoretical irrationality that his cross-level irrationality will be a problem, causing him to keep forming false beliefs where a fully rational creature would be restrained.

Insofar as it is reasonable to postulate ideal cognizers at all, there seems to be no bar to postulating *insulated ideal cognizers*: cognizers whose rational processes are practically insulated from higher-order beliefs, as Achilles' processes are, but

---

[1] What if Achilles also has a prior belief, formed before he entered insulated mode, that he will believe FLT? One could attempt to exclude such beliefs by requiring that Achilles disregard all evidence and beliefs from before he entered insulated mode, or at least that he disregard all empirical evidence and beliefs. But this would be too close to restricting Achilles to a priori reasoning, which would have the undesirable effect of making the notion of conditional scrutability depend on the notion of apriority. Instead, one can rely on the observation that if Achilles believes or supposes that he has been taking the drug, this will have the effect of undercutting his prior grounds for believing that he will believe FLT, or at least of rendering any such belief uncertain. So his insulated reasoning in support of FLT will overwhelm these defeated grounds for denying FLT.

are otherwise ideal. As we have seen, insulated ideal cognizers are in some ways more successful cognizers than fully ideal cognizers, at least where non-empirical reasoning is concerned, because their cognition is never affected by misleading self-doubts. For example, a fully ideal cognizer may have some small positive credence in its own unreliability (it cannot exclude with certainty the hypothesis that it has recently been given the drug above), so it will correspondingly never be absolutely certain of anything, even of logical truths. By contrast, there is no corresponding bar to an insulated ideal cognizer's being certain of logical truths.

Rational idealizations need not be cashed out in terms of ideal cognizers.[2] More fundamentally, they involve ideal norms or ideal warrants. One can cash out an insulated idealization in normative terms, speaking of what one ideally ought to believe (starting from one's current state) if cross-level principles are set aside. We might even define a notion of what one 'ought*' to believe that works in this way, and a corresponding notion of one's 'rational*' credence in a sentence, $cr^*(S)$. For example, where L is a logical truth, then even if one's ordinary rational credence $cr'(L)$ is less than 1 for the reasons above, it may be that the insulated rational credence $cr^*(L)$ is 1.

One can also cash out an insulated idealization in terms of warrant. An insulated warrant is a warrant that gives no role to level-crossing principles of support. It is arguable that even after John has taken the anti-arithmetic drug, there exists an insulated warrant for John to believe M, and even for John to be certain in M. A proof of M provides such a warrant, for example. It is just that John is not in a position to take advantage of that warrant. Likewise, before taking the drug, there is an insulated warrant for John to have conditional credence 1 in M given U. We can then say that $cr^*(P)$ is the credence in P for which there is an insulated warrant. It is arguable that any warrant is an insulated warrant. On this view, level-crossing principles do not play any role in ordinary warrants, so that there is an ordinary warrant for John to be certain in M in the case above (a lower credence may be rational, but it is not warranted). I will not try to adjudicate this matter here, but if this view is correct, it may be another place where warrant can play an especially basic role.

---

[2] Still, a bonus of the insulated idealization is that it overcomes one familiar problem in appeals to ideal cognizers. Typically, one cannot simply identify one's rational credence in P with the credence one would have in P if one were to become an ideal cognizer, as this would entail that everyone has an overly high rational credence that they are ideal cognizers, and so on. However, this problem does not arise on the insulated idealization, because of the bar on introspection. So this problem does not exclude the thesis that one's rational credence in P is the credence one would have in P if one were to become an insulated ideal cognizer (starting from one's current state). I will not rely on this thesis, in part because it is not obvious that there could be a truly ideal cognizer, as opposed to a series of more and more ideal cognizers. (A propositional version of the thesis, like other theses involving modal idealizations, also runs into trouble in cases of semantic fragility.) But the thesis may occasionally be a useful aid in thinking about insulated credences.

We can then say that S is conditionally scrutable from C if the *insulated* rational credence $cr^*(S \mid C)$ (which is identical to $cr^*(S \mid CC)$, where CC is a conjunction of the sentences in C) is high. Understood this way, the drug case poses no problem for the Conditional Scrutability thesis. In this case, although $cr'(M \mid U)$ is not high, $cr^*(M \mid U)$ is still plausibly high. The belief that one is unreliable about arithmetic has no impact on one's insulated rational credence in M, and likewise the supposition that one is unreliable has no impact on one's insulated conditional rational credence. So Conditional Scrutability is unthreatened.

I think that for many purposes involving theoretical rationality, insulated rational credence is often the most useful notion. Certainly, insulated rational credence seems to better reflect the sort of claims that theorists often make about rational credence. Where non-insulated rational credences are concerned, even tiny empirical self-doubts will infect the analysis of all sorts of otherwise well-behaved matters, in ways that are hard to regiment, and that will render many standard claims of formal epistemology false. (Logical truths will not have rational credence 1, Sleeping Beauty will not have rational credence 1/3, and so on.) The insulated idealization keeps the focus on first-order theoretical reasoning, allowing a more straightforward analysis of theoretical reason. Of course when it is relevant one can still invoke a non-insulated idealization, in order to see how first-order and higher-order reasoning interact, and to determine what it is rational (simpliciter) for a subject to believe.

The insulated idealization allows us to take seriously the thesis of Conclusive Conditional Scrutability. Here S is conclusively conditionally scrutable from C iff $cr^*(S \mid C) = 1$, and the thesis holds that $cr^*(S \mid C) = 1$ for all truths S and for the appropriate compact C. Where ordinary rational credences are concerned, a thesis as strong as this is out of the question for reasons discussed above. But for insulated rational credences, the thesis may well be correct. I will return to this matter in the next chapter.

What about Inferential Scrutability? There are presumably some domains about which I am actually unreliable: that is, there are classes U of sentences such that my beliefs about sentences in that class are only 50–50 likely to be true. Let S be the sentence: 'I am unreliable about the sentences in U'. Then S is true. S will presumably be inferentially scrutable from the right sort of scrutability base C: that is, if I came to know the sentences in C, I would come to know S. But if I knew (or even believed) S, then I should rationally suspend judgment about the sentences in U, so I could not know the sentences in U. So it appears that these sentences will not be inferentially scrutable from C. Still, one could argue that this is a Fitchian case: properly investigating S requires ideal reasoning, so that a proper investigation would render S false. This allows that if I properly came to know enough sentences in C, I would come to know the true sentences in U. So it is not obvious whether self-doubt causes a problem for Inferential Scrutability. If it turns out that it does, however, we can invoke an insulated idealization as above.

What about A Priori Scrutability? If M is a mathematical truth, then given that M is a priori, any material conditional $D \rightarrow M$ will also be a priori. For similar reasons it follows that M is a priori scrutable from any base, even a base specifying a world where the subject has been given an anti-arithmetic drug. At worst, the Achilles worry suggests that a subject cannot come to be certain of M by a priori reasoning, for reasons akin to those discussed earlier in the case of logic. If one is interested in conclusive a priori knowledge, which requires certainty, one can invoke an insulated idealization in one's definition of apriority: for example, S is a priori if insulated ideal a priori reasoning could bring about psychological certainty in S. Or perhaps best, one can say that S is a priori when there is a conclusive (insulated) a priori warrant for believing S, where a conclusive warrant is one that supports certainty.

3

Adventures with a
Cosmoscope

1 A Scrutability Base

To argue for scrutability theses, as I do in this chapter and the next, we first need a potential scrutability base. I will start with a reasonably generous base. In later chapters (6 and 7) I will consider whether it needs to be augmented and whether it can be narrowed down.

In the *Aufbau*, Carnap's main base was a phenomenal base, consisting just of logical expressions plus an expression for phenomenal similarity (similarity of conscious experiences). This base was rejected by Goodman on the grounds that it does not definitionally entail all truths about specific phenomenal qualities of experience, and by Quine on the grounds that it does not definitionally entail physical truths about spatiotemporal location in the external world. More generally, it is commonly believed that no set of phenomenal truths a priori entails all truths about the external world. If so, a scrutability base must involve more than phenomenal truths.

Carnap suggests in the *Aufbau* that he might instead have used a physical base. In a 1927 letter to Moritz Schlick (see Coffa 1985, p. 403), he says that he plans to publish two *Aufbau*-like books, one with a phenomenal base and one with a physical base. He says that in some ways the second book would even better deserve the title *The Logical Structure of the World*, while the first book (the actual *Aufbau*) might more accurately be called *The Logical Structure of Knowledge*. All this suggests some sensitivity to the limitations of a phenomenal base and openness to a physical base, presaging the physicalist orientation of his work in the 1930s.

A physical base would have avoided Goodman's and Quine's problems, but it would have had other problems. Just as a phenomenal base has trouble accounting for physical truths, a physical base has trouble accounting for phenomenal truths. In particular, it is arguable that phenomenal truths ('Someone is conscious',

'Such-and-such is what it is like to see red') are not a priori entailed by physical truths. This is often held to be one of the main morals of Frank Jackson's thought-experiment concerning Mary, the neuroscientist who knows all the physical truths about color processing but still does not know what it is like to see red. It is at least arguable that no amount of a priori reasoning can lead Mary from the physical truths to full knowledge of the phenomenal truths.

Carnap seems to be moved by related problems in at least one stage of his work. In his 1923 article 'On The Task of Physics and the Application of the Principle of Maximal Simplicity' (section III), he discusses Laplace's demon explicitly and suggests that knowing standard physics is not enough to know everything:

> How are we to imagine such an ideal physical system? What can it do, and what sort of propositions does it contain? Evidently it would have to be able to accomplish the feat of 'Laplace's Demon', who is able to calculate every future and past event. He would need three kinds of knowledge for this; the completed representation of physics consists, metaphorically speaking, of three volumes. [...] The entire knowledge content of the first volume resides entirely in the axioms themselves. These consist in the fundamental propositions of space determination, time determination, and the dependence of processes on one another. [...] The second volume establishes a connection between the domain of perception and the domain which constitutes the object of physical theory. That these two realms are entirely distinct cannot be emphasized sharply enough. The first contains the contents of sensation: colors, tones, tastes, pressures, sensations of heat, and so on, which, strictly speaking, do not occur in theoretical physics at all. [...] The third volume contains the description of the physical state of the world at any two points in time.

In effect, Carnap suggests that Laplace's demon would need not only a specification of fundamental physical laws (the first volume) and physical boundary conditions (the third volume), but also 'psycho-physical' connecting principles that connect physical theory to the phenomenal domain (the second volume). At a later stage of his work (e.g. in his 1932 article 'Psychology in Physical Language'), he attempted physical (largely behavioral) definitions of mental concepts, suggesting that a second volume is not required any more than it is required for other definable concepts. But for our purposes we can follow the earlier Carnap and appeal to multiple 'volumes', if only to make sure that we have a generous initial base that falls on the safe side.[1]

---

[1] Thanks to Chris Pincock for pointing me to this article. Of course Carnap's and Jackson's concerns differ in many respects. Carnap officially focuses on the perceptual domain (the colors of objects, and so on) rather than the mental domain, though he also talks of 'psycho-physical facts' here. He is just as concerned with the inference from phenomenal to physical as with the reverse step. He calls the second volume a 'dictionary', which might suggest a conceptual reduction, though his talk of distinctness suggests a weaker relation. He sets aside any questions about the ontological significance of the two domains. Still, his discussion of Laplace's demon is too marvelous to omit.

We may need further volumes still. A purely physical (or physical and phenomenal) base has at least two further limitations. First, some indexical truths ('I am David Chalmers', 'It is now 3 a.m.') are not scrutable from objective physical truths alone. Second, some negative truths ('There is no nonphysical ectoplasm') are not scrutable from positive physical truths alone. In principle a perfect a priori reasoner could have a complete physical characterization of the world cast in positive and objective terms, without being in a position to know these indexical truths or these negative truths.

To avoid these problems, we can appeal to a combined base $PQTI$ with four volumes. There is a volume for physical truths (P), one for phenomenal truths (Q), one for certain indexical truths (I), and one for a negative 'that's-all' truth (T). Expanding the base in this way does not prejudge the question of whether a smaller base might also work, but it allows us to put off that problem until later.

P is the class of physical truths, including microphysical truths (truths about fundamental physical entities in the language of a completed fundamental physics) and macrophysical truths (truths about any entities, including macroscopic entities, in the language of classical physics). I take the language of classical physics (that is, pre-relativistic and pre-quantum physics) to include expressions for spatiotemporal properties (relative locations, velocity, shape, and so on), mass, and related properties. The language of a completed fundamental physics is not known, but it might be helpful to conceive of it as involving expressions for relativistic spatiotemporal properties, quantum-mechanical properties, and properties such as mass, spin, and charge.[2] Macrophysical truths (for example, 'There exists an object of such-and-such shape and size at such-and-such location') may well be scrutable from microphysical truths, but it is convenient to include them for now. We can also allow P to include any microphysical laws (so it in effect subsumes Carnap's first and third volumes) as well as any other statements of lawful regularities and counterfactual dependence among microphysical and macrophysical truths.

Q is the class of phenomenal (or experiential) truths: truths about what it is like to be a given entity. Phenomenal truths will take the form 'There exists an

---

[2] I use 'microphysical' to mean 'fundamental physical' throughout. There is no commitment to smallness here: for example, it is possible that a microphysical truth could specify the wavefunction of the whole universe. Nevertheless, I will set aside issues that are specific to quantum mechanics until later, by assuming that there are classical truths at a low enough level for present purposes. For now, it might help to assume a Bohmian interpretation of quantum mechanics, on which there are fundamental particles with classical properties; I return to quantum mechanics toward the end of chapter 6. If it turns out that there is no completed fundamental physics because levels descend forever (Schaffer 2003), then P can include a conjunction of all truths below a certain low level.

entity with such-and-such phenomenal properties at such-and-such time', where phenomenal properties are properties specifying what it is like to be an entity. Phenomenal properties will be picked out using expressions for pure phenomenal concepts, concepts that pick out phenomenal properties by their phenomenal character: intuitively, a pure phenomenal concept of a phenomenal property is the sort of concept that would be deployed in knowledge of what it is like to have that property. Our language lacks expressions for many pure phenomenal concepts (concepts for what it is like to be a bat, perhaps), so we need to assume an idealized language here. For simplicity, we can follow Carnap and restrict these truths to truths attributing *total* phenomenal properties (those fully specifying what it is like to be a subject at a time). We can also allow Q to include any psychophysical truths (akin to Carnap's second volume): truths concerning lawful regularities and counterfactual dependence between the phenomenal truths above and microphysical or macrophysical truths.[3]

I includes at least two indexical truths. We can suppose that we have picked out a subject s and time t relative to which we are assessing scrutability (see E3). Then I will include truths of the form 'I am D_1' and 'Now is D_2', where D_1 and D_2 are descriptions in the vocabulary of P and Q satisfied by s and t. These will typically be identifying descriptions, picking out s and t uniquely (the precise constraints on these identifying descriptions are discussed in the sixth excursus). When I takes this form, we can say that $PQTI$ specifies s and t. The indexical expressions such as 'I' and 'now' used in I are the *primitive indexicals*. In chapters 6 and 7 I will discuss whether further primitive indexicals are required, but for now these two will suffice.

T is a single totality sentence, saying that our world is a *minimal* scenario satisfying P, Q, and I. T is needed in order to render scrutable certain negative truths about the world, such as 'There are no ghosts'. T says in effect 'that's all': the world is no bigger than it needs to be to accommodate the truth of P, Q, and I. One can formalize T in various ways, but perhaps the best for our purposes is to understand it as saying that all positive truths are a priori entailed by PQI, the union of P, Q, and I. Here, a positive sentence is intuitively one that cannot conceivably be rendered false by *adding* something to a world: so 'There are more than five particles' is a positive sentence, while 'There is no nonphysical

---

[3] Pure phenomenal concepts are discussed at length in 'The Content and Epistemology of Phenomenal Belief'. Including Q in the base does not prejudge questions about materialism and dualism. The most common materialist view (type-B materialism) explicitly allows that phenomenal truths are not scrutable from microphysical truths, while holding that this epistemological gap does not yield an ontological gap. On this view, a base will need to include Q or something like it. Other (type-A) materialists hold that phenomenal truths are scrutable from microphysical truths, so that there is not even an epistemological gap. On this view, a base need not include Q, but there is no harm in including it.

ectoplasm' and 'All life is made of DNA' are negative sentences. Of course, if the scrutability base for positive truths needs to be expanded, then T will need to be modified correspondingly. The correct understanding of T (and also of I) is discussed at length in the sixth excursus.[4]

It is not out of the question to add further truths. For example, one could add the class of mathematical truths, or chemical truths, or truths about secondary qualities, or intentional truths (truths about subject's having propositional attitudes such as beliefs and desires). I will not do so, as I think that these truths are themselves scrutable from the truths I have discussed. But if one disagrees, one can add these to the base class while retaining a compact base. (In the case of intentional truths, one needs to be careful to avoid trivializing mechanisms, for reasons discussed in chapter 6.)

Let $PQTI$ be the union of P, Q, I, and the singleton set containing T.[5] We can suppose we have chosen an arbitrary subject s and time t where $PQTI$ specifies s and t. $PQTI$ is plausibly a compact class of truths: it involves vocabulary from a limited number of families, and it does not appear to involve any trivializing mechanisms (though I will discuss a potential trivializing mechanism involving phenomenal truths in chapter 6).

In this chapter and the next, I will argue for the thesis that for all ordinary subjects, all ordinary macroscopic truths are scrutable from $PQTI$. More precisely: for all subjects s and times t, if s is an ordinary subject at t, and if M is an ordinary macroscopic truth in the context of s at t, then M is scrutable (for s at t) from $PQTI$, where $PQTI$ specifies s and t.

An ordinary subject is a normal adult human subject, with normal capacities and background knowledge. We can be vague about just what normality involves here, given that scrutability idealizes so much in any case, but the restriction avoids worrying about infants, alien creatures, and the like for now.

Ordinary macroscopic truths include truths like 'Water is H_2O', 'Water boils at such-and-such temperature', 'There is such-and-such amount of water on our planet', 'Life on our planet is based on DNA', 'Platypuses are egg-laying mammals', 'The temperature of the atmosphere is n degrees warmer than it was a century ago', and so on. This class excludes hard cases such as mathematical,

[4] Note that insofar as P or Q are infinite classes, T will be an infinite sentence. To maintain some discipline, we can restrict the sentences in P and Q to finite sentences, perhaps along with any infinite sentences needed to specify fundamental microphysical truths and laws and to specify phenomenal character and psychophysical principles.

[5] Note that this $PQTI$ differs from the $PQTI$ described by Chalmers and Jackson in 'Conceptual Analysis and Reductive Explanation' in that it includes macrophysical truths and truths involving counterfactuals, and in that it is a class of truths rather than a single conjunctive truth (although following the usual convention, '$PQTI$' in sentential position stands for the conjunctive truth).

mental, metaphysical, modal, and moral truths. I will also set aside proper names for now, as well as truths associated with social domains. To avoid issues about context-dependence and unpossessed concepts, we can focus on sentences that have been uttered by the subject at the relevant time. Utterances of expressions used deferentially or incompetently are excluded, and any utterances involving borderline cases of vague expressions are excluded. I will return to all of these cases in chapter 6.

I will be arguing for versions of Inferential Scrutability and (especially) Conditional Scrutability in this chapter before arguing for A Priori Scrutability in the next chapter. This has the advantage of not needing to engage controversial issues about the a priori at the initial stage of the argument. In all these cases, subjects can use idealized reasoning from the information provided in $PQTI$. For inferential scrutability and for conditional scrutability, although not for a priori scrutability, they can also use any empirical background knowledge that they have at the relevant time. I will not rely heavily on this background knowledge, however, and in the next chapter I will argue that it is inessential for scrutability, as is any other justifying role of perceptual experience. Doing so will make a case for A Priori Scrutability.

One complication of proceeding this way is that the notion of the a priori is invoked in T, at least on certain formulations, for reasons discussed in the sixth excursus. If so, the a priori cannot be entirely avoided even in discussing inferential and conditional scrutability from $PQTI$. To avoid invoking apriority at this point, I will proceed by first dispensing with T, and arguing for versions of the thesis that all *positive* ordinary macroscopic truths are scrutable from PQI. This thesis is strong enough for our purposes, and it allows us to consider the issue of Inferential and Conditional Scrutability without invoking the notion of the a priori. Once we extend these arguments in the next chapter to make the case that all positive ordinary macroscopic truths are a priori scrutable from PQI, one can argue from there to the thesis that all ordinary macroscopic truths are scrutable from $PQTI$. For convenience, I will henceforth abbreviate 'positive ordinary macroscopic truth' as 'ordinary truth'.

A couple of other minor worries about P and Q are worth addressing. One worry is that some expressions in P, such as 'charge', may be epistemically context-dependent in that different speakers may associate them with different modes of presentation, perhaps tied to different aspects of the 'charge'-role. In principle this violates the requirement that expressions in the base class should be epistemically invariant and opens up the possibility that a sentence S may be scrutable from PQI in one context but not in another. The arguments in this chapter are robust over most reasonable choices of guise, however. To avoid any problems, one can simply stipulate a guise, perhaps by giving a Ramsey-style definition of 'charge' in terms of its role in physical laws.

Another worry pertains to the variety of phenomenal concepts involved in Q: these may specify not just what it is like to be a human but what it is like to be a bat or a Martian. The alien phenomenal concepts involved here will not be relevant to the scrutability of ordinary truths, but they will be relevant to the scrutability of other truths, for example about the character of other minds. Here the idealization of concepts discussed in section 7 of the previous chapter takes care of the basic worry. A more specific worry, though, is that possession of some phenomenal concepts may be incompatible. Suppose that for two incompatible properties (being intelligent and unintelligent, perhaps), one has to have the property in order to possess a phenomenal concept of what it is like to have the property. Then no one can possess both concepts at once, and if both are involved in Q, no one can entertain all of PQI. In response, I think that there are no concepts whose possession is mutually incompatible. The supposition just mentioned cannot obtain: in these cases there is usually no bar to having a phenomenal concept of what it is like to have a property through imagination even without having the property. In any case, this worry will not affect scrutability from PQI when this is understood in terms of a warrant-based idealization (see 2.7 and E4) rather than a modal idealization.

2 The Cosmoscope argument

In arguing for scrutability from PQI, it will be helpful to invoke a hypothetical virtual reality device that I call a Cosmoscope.[6] A Cosmoscope is a device that stores all the information in PQI and makes it usable. In particular it contains (i) a supercomputer to store the information and to perform any necessary calculations; (ii) tools that use P to zoom in on arbitrary regions of the world, and to deliver information about the distribution of matter in those regions; (iii) a virtual reality device to produce direct knowledge of any phenomenal states described in Q; (iv) a 'you are here' marker to convey the information in I; and (v) simulation devices that deliver information about counterfactuals, exhibiting the physical and phenomenal states that will be produced under various counterfactual circumstances specified in PQI above.

On the first component: this may require a supercomputer with infinite storage, at least if our universe is infinite. It seems likely that a physical Cosmoscope

---

[6] As Gabriel Rabin pointed out to me, a device akin to the Cosmoscope is the central element of Piers Anthony's science fiction novel *Macroscope*. For a picture of a Cosmoscope, see http://consc.net/cosmoscope.html. The name is partly inspired by Terence Horgan's classic 1984 article 'Supervenience and Cosmic Hermeneutics'. Horgan's cosmic hermeneutics is itself a sort of scrutability and an important precursor of the current analysis. One difference is that Horgan's hermeneutic process, unlike the present notion of scrutability, allows direct appeals to a posteriori entailments arising from rigid designation. See also Alex Byrne's 'Cosmic Hermeneutics' (1999) for critical discussion.

THE COSMOSCOPE ARGUMENT   115

that accurately describes our world could not exist in our world. But for the purposes of A Priori and Conditional Scrutability, we can think of the Cosmoscope as inhabiting some other world, perhaps one markedly different from our own, and as containing a specification of this world. (Inferential Scrutability requires special adjustments that I discuss in section 5.) The Cosmoscope need not be nomologically possible—it need only be conceivable. So the computer can have infinite storage, infinite parallel processing, and so on.

On the second component: for the display of macrophysical information, the Cosmoscope renders information about the spatial character of some region of the world in geometrical form.[7] For example, for a specified mass density, the Cosmoscope might display color-coded regions in which the density exceeds that threshold. This display could be rendered more efficient by using three-dimensional holographic display rather than two-dimensional screens. For even greater efficiency, it could induce imaginative states in the user with spatial content representing the spatial character of the world. We can stipulate ancillary tools for selecting different regions of the world at many different scales, locations, and times, and for displaying information of many different sorts: mass density, chemical composition, and so on. Given a classical microphysical world, the same sort of display will work at that level. Given a nonclassical microphysical world, one will need a different sort of display for that level, but all sorts of tools to render microphysical information in a useful way are conceivable.

On the third component: there will first be a device for the user to select a conscious individual at a time, perhaps by selecting a corresponding physical entity or region as long as there is no more than one individual per region. If the same individual can have both physical and phenomenal properties, the Cosmoscope can rely on truths about the co-instantiation of such properties; if not, it can rely on nomic or counterfactual connections between them. If this does not work (perhaps because there are disembodied or co-located minds), one can select from a space of such minds in some other way (perhaps indexing by phenomenal properties in one case and physical properties in the other). One *could* think of the Cosmoscope as then simply inducing the relevant experiences (that is, phenomenal states) in the user. After appropriate warning, the user's brain and mind would be manipulated in order to induce the experiences had by a specified conscious being at a specified time: perhaps another person, or a bat,

---

[7] One could think of this rendering as a more powerful version of Google Maps or Google Earth: Google Cosmos, if you like. Of course Google Maps (on satellite view) includes information about color as well as space. It would be easy to supplement *PQI* to include truths about color (and perhaps other secondary qualities too), thereby allowing an all-the-more convenient display, without affecting any of the arguments in this chapter. But information about the phenomenal states of individuals looking at these objects is probably good enough, even without color information built in. In chapter 6 I argue that truths about color are scrutable from the narrower *PQI*.

or an alien. But there may be difficulties: if we are simulating certain states of anger or of stupor, entering such a state may undermine the capacity for reasoning. So it is best to think of the Cosmoscope as inducing imaginative states, analogous to the states we have when we imagine certain color experiences, say, without actually having those experiences. There is no obvious objection to the conceivability of imaginative states corresponding to arbitrary experiences. And when we have such states, we are certainly able to reason about the imagined experiences.

On the fourth component: a particular individual will be highlighted as one-self. Depending on the descriptions used in I, either a particular physical entity may be highlighted, or a particular slice of a stream of experience.

On the fifth component: as well as tools for selecting regions of spacetime and conscious individuals, one will be able to specify antecedents of counterfactuals in physical terms, perhaps by specifying new physical properties using geometrical tools, or perhaps by entering antecedent sentences directly. The Cosmoscope will then go into counterfactual mode: insofar as there are determinate counterfactual truths with these antecedents and physical or phenomenal consequences, the Cosmoscope will display the corresponding physical and phenomenal results.

Of course the Cosmoscope is a highly fanciful device. But its purpose here is simply to make vivid what an idealized reasoner who entertained the hypothesis of PQI would be able to do. Such a reasoner could certainly imagine the relevant spatial configurations, imagine the specified phenomenal states, identify themselves, perform complex calculations, perform simulations, and so on. The Cosmoscope simply offloads some of the work from ourselves onto the world. In effect, the Cosmoscope takes the burden of storage and much of the burden of calculation. These tools, along with tools for selection and simulation, mean that even a non-ideal reasoner can get a long way with a Cosmoscope. But all the Cosmoscope is doing is conveying and manipulating information that is included in PQI.

The Cosmoscope need not itself engage in reasoning. Likewise, it need not possess concepts or understand language. It is simply an extremely sophisticated device for calculation and for the display of information. For most purposes, the Cosmoscope need not traffic in natural language at all. For example, instead of supplying users directly with the sentences in PQI, it instead uses its display devices to enable the user to entertain elements of PQI.[8] It may occasionally be

---

[8] Strictly speaking, perceiving the PQI display devices is incompatible with the no-perception rule for insulated reasoning (E5). To address this worry we can invoke a version of the Cosmoscope that works entirely by engaging the subject's imagination and allow introspection limited to these imaginative states. Also: to entertain or know PQI, the user need not use or even be competent with the sentences in PQI. As defined in the third excursus, entertaining and knowing PQI require only having mental states that are apt to be expressed by utterances of the relevant sentences (if the subject were fully competent with them).

useful for it to produce linguistic or mathematical elements of P as outputs, to convey microphysical truths that are hard to convey geometrically or imaginatively. It may also be useful for the Cosmoscope to be able to take sentences such as PQI as input, for example to specify non-actual states of the world in counterfactual or conditional mode. But these uses of language are not obviously essential, and in any case they do not require language understanding on the part of the Cosmoscope, any more than processing textual inputs and outputs in existing computers requires such understanding.

There are two ways that one can use a Cosmoscope. One can use it in *empirical mode*, as a guide to the world one is in when using the Cosmoscope. In this mode the Cosmoscope will tell one about the character of one's own world. One can also use it in *conditional* mode, as a guide to a scenario that may or may not correspond to the world one is in when using the Cosmoscope. In this mode the Cosmoscope will enable you to reason about how things are *if* that scenario obtains. The first mode is especially relevant to Inferential Scrutability (although one needs some care to handle Fitchian truths, those whose truth-value is changed by the attempt to investigate them). The second mode is especially relevant to Conditional and A Priori Scrutability.

As with any mapping device, use of a Cosmoscope will be governed by certain conventions for interpreting its outputs. Users of a Cosmoscope will first need to know these conventions. For example, if the Cosmoscope produces two-dimensional or three-dimensional states on a display, the conventions will govern the mapping from states of this display to beliefs or suppositions involving physical concepts. If the Cosmoscope produces imaginative states in the user, the conventions will govern an analogous mapping. Certain imaginative states will be marked (perhaps by a prior or simultaneous signal) as representing phenomenal states, other states as representing physical states, so that the user will be able to endorse these states in such a way as to yield beliefs or suppositions about physical or phenomenal states of affairs. Users will also know whether the Cosmoscope is operating in empirical or conditional mode, so that they know whether to form beliefs or suppositions on the basis of its outputs.[9]

---

[9] I set aside here the questions of how the Cosmoscope in empirical mode gets its information and of why the user should trust it. We can suppose that the information is obtained by magic and that prior to use the user is given extremely convincing evidence that the Cosmoscope is accurate. These questions do not really arise for a Cosmoscope in conditional mode (by far the more important mode for our purposes), which traffics in hypothetical representations whose source is irrelevant. In the general case (relevant to generalized scrutability theses), these representations need have no tie to the actual world. To evaluate non-generalized conditional and a priori scrutability theses, we are interested in the special case where the conditional Cosmoscope accurately represents the actual world. There is no need for users to believe that the Cosmoscope accurately represents the actual world, however (they need merely suppose this), so it suffices to consider a scenario where the conditional Cosmoscope describes the actual world as a matter of luck.

Given any sentence, one could use a Cosmoscope to investigate its truth. For current purposes we can start with a subject in the actual world who has just uttered a sentence M.[10] We can then imagine a nearby world in which just after the utterance, the subject is given a Cosmoscope and asked to determine the truth of M. The Cosmoscope could work in empirical mode, conveying information about the character of the new world w' (some obvious complications here are discussed in section 5), or it could work in conditional mode, conveying information about the character of the original world w. The subject does not feed the sentence M to the Cosmoscope: instead, she uses the Cosmoscope as a tool and determines the status of M for herself. In empirical mode, the subject's task will be to determine the truth of M (the sentence uttered a moment ago) in the world she is now in. In conditional mode, the subject's task will be to determine whether, under the supposition that things are as the Cosmoscope describes them (that is, as they were in the original situation), M is true.

It is clear that with the aid of a Cosmoscope (in empirical mode, say), even an ordinary subject could come to know a lot. A Cosmoscope will deliver a sort of supermovie of the world. In fact, it will deliver multiple supermovies. It will deliver many phenomenological supermovies, exhibiting the life history of experience for any experiencer, and more still by simulating what these experiencers would have experienced if they had been located differently. In this way, the Cosmoscope will tell us just how the world looks from any number of perspectives. It will deliver a geometrical supermovie: using macrophysical truths, it can deliver various 3D displays of just what is happening in arbitrary locations and times and levels of scale. And it will deliver a microphysical supermovie, in the more mathematical language of a fundamental physics. There are few aspects of the world that will escape the reach of a Cosmoscope.

A reasonably intelligent subject could use a Cosmoscope to answer many questions: who was Jack the Ripper, will there be a Third World War, is there life on other planets? Of course there may be limits on what ordinary intelligent subjects could do here. Even with a Cosmoscope, they may not be able to determine the truth of the Riemann hypothesis (too much mathematical reasoning required), or the number of particles in the universe (too much use of the Cosmoscope required). But these are not ordinary truths in the sense defined above. And we are also entitled to suppose that in answering these questions, our subject uses idealized reasoning capacities, which might well overcome these barriers. In

---

[10] Starting with a subject in the actual world helps to handle the scrutability of context-dependent sentences, by fixing the context of utterance; for context-independent sentences the restriction is unnecessary. Note that the subject-plus-Cosmoscope are still be akin to Laplace's demon in the introduction in that they are outside the actual world (and in conditional mode are outside the world they are analyzing), assuming that the actual world contains no Cosmoscope.

any case, it is not unreasonable to suggest that with sufficiently good reasoning, one could use a Cosmoscope (in conditional mode, say) to come to know any ordinary truth about the world.

At the same time, there is a strong connection between what we can know with a Cosmoscope and what is scrutable from *PQI*. The Cosmoscope is simply storing and conveying truths in *PQI* and doing some calculation that could in principle be done by an ideal reasoner. When the Cosmoscope is used properly, it is intended to produce some specific thoughts concerning physical and phenomenal properties: specific states of knowledge, if used in empirical mode, or some specific suppositional states, if used in conditional mode. Each of these thoughts either has content corresponding to elements of *PQI*, or is a priori derivable in principle from elements of *PQI*. We can call these thoughts the states canonically delivered by a Cosmoscope. Likewise, we can call the calculation tools provided by the Cosmoscope the canonical tools of the Cosmoscope.

This suggests the following *Cosmoscope argument*:

1. All ordinary truths are scrutable from a Cosmoscope.
2. If a truth is scrutable from a Cosmoscope, it is scrutable from *PQI*.

3. All ordinary truths are scrutable from *PQI*.

Here, a truth *M* is scrutable from a Cosmoscope iff *M* is scrutable from the canonical deliverances of the Cosmoscope. (One could also stipulate an idealization that allows use of the canonical tools of the Cosmoscope, though this is not essential.) We can define scrutability of sentences from thoughts just as we defined scrutability of sentences from sentences in the third excursus, where scrutability for sentences is defined in terms of associated thoughts in any case. In the case of inferential scrutability, this comes to the claim that if one came to have certain canonical knowledge from a Cosmoscope, one would be in a position to know *M*. In the case of conditional scrutability, this comes to the claim that one can have knowledge of *M* conditional on the canonical suppositions delivered by the Cosmoscope. In the case of a priori scrutability, this comes to the claim that the canonical suppositions delivered by the Cosmoscope imply the thought expressed by *M* (where implication is a priori entailment between thoughts, as in the third excursus).

The argument above can be read in three different versions, depending on whether scrutability is understood as inferential, conditional, or a priori scrutability. I am inclined to endorse all three versions, with one qualification. In the case of inferential scrutability, premise 1 and the conclusion need to be modified to exclude Fitchian truths: those truths, discussed in the previous chapter (2.4), whose truth-value is changed by the attempt to investigate them (and in particular by the attempt to determine them using *PQI* or a Cosmoscope). So here the relevant versions of 1 and 3 will say that all ordinary non-Fitchian truths are scrutable from a Cosmoscope and from *PQI* respectively.

Premise 2 is reasonably straightforward. The canonical deliverances of a Cosmoscope are themselves thoughts apt to be expressed by *PQI* or else are derivable from such thoughts, so scrutability from these deliverances entails scrutability from *PQI*. The Cosmoscope simply provides the information in *PQI* in a convenient way and performs calculations that could equally be performed by ideal reasoning. If one could come to conditionally know a truth with the aid of a Cosmoscope, then that truth is conditionally scrutable from *PQI*. If a truth is implied by the deliverances of a Cosmoscope, then that truth is implied by *PQI*. Finally, if one would be in a position to know a non-Fitchian truth given sufficient knowledge delivered by a Cosmoscope, then one would also be in a position to know it given sufficient knowledge in *PQI*.

We have already seen that premise 1 has significant antecedent plausibility. We know that maps, television, and interactive software can convey an enormous amount of information about the natural world. Our experience with these tools makes especially plausible the claim that an extended version of them, such as a Cosmoscope, could provide knowledge of all ordinary truths. For any given truth, such as the truth that water is H_2O or that the moon orbits the earth, it is not hard to see how an idealized reasoner could use the Cosmoscope to verify the truth in question. This is just a prima facie case that needs much defense and supplementation, and it makes more of a case for inferential and conditional scrutability than for a priori scrutability, but it carries at least some initial weight.

As I noted earlier, the Cosmoscope mainly serves as a device for making vivid what an idealized reasoner who entertains *PQI* would be able to do. So the prima facie support for premise 1 of the Cosmoscope argument is simply making vivid a certain prima facie case that all ordinary truths are scrutable from *PQI*. Those who find the prima facie case compelling can feel free to move on for now, while those who do not can read the following sections for more substantial arguments. Two detailed arguments are given in the next two sections. Each of these can in principle be construed as an argument that all ordinary truths are scrutable from a Cosmoscope, thereby supporting premise 1 of the Cosmoscope argument. For the most part, however, I will present them as arguments that all ordinary truths are scrutable from *PQI*, thereby providing arguments for scrutability in their own right.

3 The argument from elimination

Suppose that I am given all the information in *PQI*, either directly or through a Cosmoscope. I then start making inferences about what else is the case. How far can I get? In particular, for an arbitrary ordinary truth *M*, can I infer the truth of *M*? The argument from elimination makes a case that one can do so by eliminating hypotheses on which *M* is false.

The initial set-up can be adapted to each of Inferential, Conditional, and A Priori Scrutability. Under Inferential Scrutability, my being given the information in *PQI* will amount to being given knowledge of all truths in *PQI* (or of as many of these truths as can be known), and my inferring *M* amounts to coming to know *M* on that basis. Under Conditional Scrutability, my being given the information in *PQI* amounts to hypothetically supposing *PQI*, and my inferring *M* amounts to hypothetically concluding *M* from that supposition by armchair reasoning. Under A Priori Scrutability, my being given the information that *PQI* amounts to hypothetically supposing *PQI*, and my inferring *M* amounts to deducing *M* from *PQI* alone by a priori reasoning.

In what follows, I will proceed in a way compatible with each of these understandings, though it is perhaps most natural to keep Conditional Scrutability in mind. In later sections and in the next chapter, I will consider issues specific to each understanding.

Given *P* alone, I could get some distance. *P* gives me a map of physical structure throughout space and time. For every object that exists, *P* will specify its shape, size, composition, mass distribution, and so on, in a physical vocabulary. So *P* tells me a great deal about the contours of the physical world. On the other hand, *P* alone seems to leave open many questions about the mental. It also arguably leaves open many questions about the way that microphysical objects appear: their colors, sounds, and tastes, for example.

I could also get some distance using *Q* alone. Combining the complete phenomenal information in *Q* with the indexical information in *I* puts me in a position to infer the phenomenal character of my current experiences, and of my experiences throughout my lifetime. This will include in particular the phenomenal character of a lifetime of perceptual experiences. This information serves as an epistemic guide to many macroscopic truths, just as it does in ordinary life. If *V* is a specific phenomenal character of a visual experience as of a large object in front of me, then from the information that I am now having an experience with phenomenal character *V*, I might reasonably infer that there is a large object in front of me. The same goes for many other perceptual experiences.

Still, *Q* leaves many questions open. There is a vast class of truths about which my perceptual experience gives no guidance: truths concerning unperceived objects, for example. And even for truths *M* about which my perceptual experience gives guidance, it remains epistemically possible (in the broad sense) that I have these perceptual states but that *M* is false. Such epistemic possibilities range from traditional skeptical scenarios concerning the non-existence of the external world to a wide range of scenarios involving perceptual illusions, false inductive inferences, and so on.

These open questions can be settled by further information. Truths about which my perceptual experience gives no guidance can often be settled by further information; and skeptical scenarios can often be ruled out by further information. Adding Q to P rules out numerous skeptical scenarios about other minds. Adding P to Q rules out numerous skeptical scenarios about the external world. The residual question is whether the information in PQI suffices to infer all of the unknown truths, and to rule out all the skeptical scenarios.

Here the information in P will play a crucial role. In effect, it gives us a sort of X-ray vision for what is going on in the external world: a route that is quite different from the perceptual route given by Q, and that can give us guidance even when Q is misleading. P yields a complete geometric characterization of the world, in terms of shape, position, mass, dynamics, and so on. It also contains complete information about microphysical composition. This information suffices to give us access to all sorts of unknown truths, and to rule out all sorts of skeptical scenarios.

Further, PQI contains rich information about the regularities connecting the physical and phenomenal domain. If there are certain regularities by which other physical systems in the world affect my perceptual phenomenal states, then P, Q, and I will yield information about those regularities. So although information about the external causes of perceptual phenomenal states is not built in to Q, PQI will yield information about these causes. It will also yield information about the perceptual phenomenal states that various external systems are disposed to cause when appropriately situated: that is, about the perceptual appearance of these systems.

Overall, PQI yields complete information about the (geometrically characterized) structure and dynamics of macroscopic systems and objects in the world, their spatiotemporal distribution and microstructural composition, and their actual and potential perceptual appearances. This information puts a subject in a position to conclusively know (on rational reflection) the truth or otherwise of any ordinary macroscopic claim M. Complete knowledge of perceptual appearances yields the information that members of our community rely on in coming to know macroscopic truths; and complete structural, dynamic, distributional, and compositional information contains all the information that we need to settle the truth of claims that perceptual information does not settle.

For example, suppose I am trying to settle the truth-value of 'There is water in front of me', when in fact water is in front of me. PQI will give me full information about the way the substance appears to me (through Q), about its microphysical composition (through P), about its macroscopic shape (through P), about the ways it behaves and appears in various conditions (through the counterfactuals in P and Q), and about its physical relationship to me (through P and I). This will enable me to know that in front of me is a substance that looks watery, that behaves in a certain fluid way, and that has a certain molecular structure. Further use of *PQI* (with a Cosmoscope, say) can reveal to me that the same molecular structure is present in most other substances that look watery in my environment.

All this information enables me to determine that the substance is water. I need not invoke a definition of 'water' in more basic terms. Instead, just as in the discussion of 'know' in chapter 1, this is a case where sufficient information enables me to apply the underlying concept to the case directly. Once I know the appearance, behavior, and composition of a certain body of matter in my environment, along with complete information about the appearance, behavior, and composition of other bodies of matter in the environment, and knowledge of their relationships to myself, I am in a position to infer (on rational reflection) a conclusion about whether the original system is a body of water.

The same goes for knowledge of whether the system is gold, whether it is alive, whether it boils at a certain temperature, or whether it is found in the oceans. And the same applies to ordinary macroscopic truths M in general: complete knowledge of structure, dynamics, composition, distribution, and appearance puts one in a position to infer that M is true.

Importantly, the information in *PQI* serves to conclusively eliminate arbitrary skeptical hypotheses under which M is false. Hypotheses involving perceptual illusions or hallucinations are eliminated by full structural and dynamical information. Hypotheses concerning differences in the past and the future are eliminated by full distributional information. Hypotheses concerning differences in underlying causal or compositional structure are eliminated by full compositional information. Even skeptical hypotheses concerning differences in others' minds are plausibly eliminated by full phenomenal information. Further skeptical hypotheses that turn on the subject's own relation to these systems are removed by the indexical information in *PQI*. This conditional elimination of skeptical hypotheses by *PQI* does not help much in answering the skeptic, as the skeptic will simply question whether we can know *PQI* itself. But it makes a strong case for scrutability.

One important class of skeptical hypotheses that remains involves doubts about one's own reasoning capacities: for example, doubts about whether one is reasoning well in inferring truths from *PQI*. These skeptical hypotheses are removed by the insulated idealization discussed in the fifth excursus, however, so we can set them to one side.

A relevant skeptical hypothesis would have to be one in which the structure, dynamics, distribution, composition, and appearance of objects and systems across space and time is preserved (along with indexical information), but on which M is false. There do not seem to be any such (once hypotheses turning on self-doubt are set aside). For example, if one's actual environment contains trees, there is no coherent skeptical hypothesis according to which one's environment is exactly as it is in microphysical and macrophysical respects (including appearances and global history) but in which there are no trees. It is no accident that there is a skeptical problem of other minds but not of other trees.

What about a Twin Earth scenario? If a Cosmoscope tells us only that there is a watery liquid made of H_2O, we cannot thereby conclude that water is H_2O, as we cannot rule out a hypothesis on which the Cosmoscope is showing us a distant planet with H_2O and on which water (our water) is XYZ. However, this sort of hypothesis will be ruled out by indexical truths fixing our relation to the objects. Given these truths, we can determine that the H_2O we are seeing is in our own environment and that H_2O has been the relevant liquid in our environment all along. The same goes for skeptical hypotheses according to which there are macrophysically tree-like objects that are not trees but 'fool's trees', because they have the wrong makeup or history. The information in *PQI* enables us to determine their makeup and history and compare it to that of the dominant tree-like objects in our environment, thereby enabling us to decide whether or not these objects are trees just as we might decide similar cases in the actual world.

What about defeaters? In the spirit of Chisholm's objection to phenomenalism (chapter 1), one could worry that for almost any ordinary truth M that we say is a priori scrutable from *PQI*, one can find a further claim D that defeats an inference from *PQI* to M. This requires that D that is consistent with *PQI* and that *PQI* & D either entails $\sim M$ or at least is clearly consistent with $\sim M$. For example, where M is 'Heat is molecular motion', Block and Stalnaker (1999) suggest a defeating hypothesis D on which there is nonphysical 'ghost heat' that plays the heat role even better than molecular motion. D is arguably consistent with *PQI*, and if *PQI* & D is true, M is arguably false. If so, M is not conclusively scrutable from *PQI*.

Objections of this sort are handled by the that's-all clause T and the requirement of positiveness. In Block and Stalnaker's case, D is ruled out by adding T to *PQI*. Furthermore, the argument requires that M is not a positive truth, so that it does not fall into the scope of the thesis currently at issue. An opponent may reply that almost no ordinary truths are positive because almost all can be defeated in this way. I think that this claim is implausible, but even if it is correct, it remains the case that *PQTI* rules out the defeating hypotheses.[11]

---

[11] To see this intuitive point formally, one can use the argument in the sixth excursus (from principles (i)–(iii) there) to establish that if *PQTI* is true, then *PQTI* implies all truths. Assuming that D is in fact false, then either *PQTI* implies $\sim D$ or *PQTI* is false. Given that *PQI* is true, the remaining possibility is that T is false: some positive truths are not scrutable from *PQI*. But then the opponent will require independent failures of scrutability for positive truths.

A metaphysically inclined opponent might suggest distinctively ontological skeptical hypotheses. For example, someone might suggest an ontological hypothesis on which there are microscopic but not macroscopic objects, so that there are atoms but no trees. Given that *PQI* builds in macrophysical truths, however, then as long as there are actually trees, *PQI* will specify that there are macroscopic objects with exactly their macrophysical properties. So this hypothesis will be ruled out. Someone might suggest a 'sparse' ontological hypothesis on which there are only macrophysical objects that have their spatiotemporal properties essentially, whereas trees have their spatiotemporal properties contingently, so that there are tree-shaped macroscopic objects but no trees. This is perhaps the best route for an opponent. I think that conditional on the assumption that only macrophysical objects of this sort exist, we should accept that trees are among them, but some ontologists think otherwise. In any case, ontological hypotheses are treated as a hard case in chapter 6, and the diagnoses there will also apply to the case at hand here. For now, if someone thinks that there is a coherent ontological hypothesis here, they can simply assume that correct general ontological principles that settle the issue between the relevant sparse and liberal ontologies are also built into *PQI*.

Once this is done: then given that there are actually trees, there do not seem to be any coherent skeptical hypotheses according to which everything in *PQI* is preserved (along with a that's-all claim, and invoking an insulated idealization to remove hypotheses tied to self-doubt) and in which there are no trees. We are in a position to rule out any hypothesis of this form with certainty. If so, truths about trees are scrutable from *PQI*. The same reasoning applies to ordinary truths in other domains.

In fact, this reasoning supports a stronger conclusion: all ordinary truths are *conclusively* scrutable from *PQI*. I am not just in a position to infer *M* from *PQI*. I am in a position to infer *M* with certainty (at least given an insulated idealization). That is, in the case of Inferential Scrutability, if I am certain of the relevant truths in *PQI*, I should be certain that *M*. In the case of Conditional Scrutability, my rational credence $cr^*(M \mid PQI)$ should not just be high; it should be 1. In the case of A Priori Scrutability, I am in a position to be certain of the material conditional '$PQI \rightarrow M$'. I will not rely on these claims in everything that follows, but I will return to them from time to time.

4 The argument from knowability

The argument from knowability uses considerations about knowability to argue for scrutability. Let *s* be the subject for whom we are assessing scrutability. Let us say that a sentence *M* is *s*-knowable when it is possible that *M* is known by *s* through a process that starts from their state at the relevant time and that allows

normal sorts of perception, introspection, and action (but not further knowledge by testimony), along with idealized reasoning.

The argument from knowability runs as follows.

1. All ordinary truths are *s*-knowable or *s*-unknowable.
2. All *s*-knowable ordinary truths are scrutable from *PQI*.
3. If all *s*-knowable ordinary truths are scrutable from *PQI*, all
   s-unknowable ordinary truths are scrutable from *PQI*.

---

4. All ordinary truths are scrutable from *PQI*.

Here scrutability is scrutability for the subject *s*, though as usual I have not
made that relativization explicit. Scrutability can be understood as any of inferential, conditional, or a priori scrutability, although for present purposes conditional scrutability is perhaps the most important. When scrutability is understood
as inferential scrutability, the premises and conclusion should be restricted to
non-Fitchian ordinary truths.

One can support premise 2 as follows. It is plausible that any truth knowable
by *s* directly through perception or introspection is scrutable by *s* from a Cosmoscope (at least setting aside Fitchian truths, in the case of inferential scrutability),
as the Cosmoscope's movies arguably provide everything that perception or
introspection by *s* could provide. In cases where the knowability requires that *s*
gains perceptual knowledge by acting in counterfactual ways, scrutability will
require the use of counterfactual scenarios provided by the Cosmoscope, but this
is allowed (see the discussion of the objection from counterfactuals later in this
chapter). Further, anything knowable through reasoning (broadly construed to
include intuition and memory as well as inferential reasoning), or through a
combination of perception, introspection, and reasoning, will also be scrutable
from a Cosmoscope, as the reasoning will be available either way. Given that
everything that is *s*-knowable is knowable through perception, introspection,
and reasoning, it follows that all knowable ordinary truths are scrutable from a
Cosmoscope, and so from *PQI*.

One can support premise 3 as follows. The clear cases of ordinary truths that
are not *s*-knowable for a subject *s* can be divided into Fitchian truths and what
we might call remote truths: those associated with the far away, the past, the very
small, black holes from which information cannot escape, and other physical
barriers between the subject and the relevant domain. As discussed in the last
chapter, the Fitch problem poses an obstacle at most to inferential scrutability
from *PQI*, and not to conditional or a priori scrutability. Remoteness poses no
special problem for scrutability from *PQI*, as the Cosmoscope carries information about what is on the other side of all the relevant barriers. Non-ideal reasoning may also pose an obstacle to knowability in an ordinary sense (an ordinary
subject may be unable to know certain ordinary scientific truths knowable by

Einstein), but given that we are idealizing reasoning and allowing normal human action (including scientific investigation), this is no obstacle to knowability or scrutability in our sense. Given that the only obstacles to s-knowability of ordinary truths derive from Fitchian and remote truths, and that these are not obstacles to scrutability from PQI, it plausibly follows that if all knowable ordinary truths are conditionally scrutable from PQI, then all unknowable ordinary truths are conditionally scrutable from PQI. The same goes for a priori scrutability and (with an exception for Fitchian truths) inferential scrutability.

From these premises (on the various interpretations), it follows that all non-Fitchian ordinary truths are inferentially scrutable from PQI, and that all ordinary truths are conditionally and a priori scrutable from PQI.

We can extend the argument in some respects. First, the restriction to ordinary truths plays no role here, except perhaps for the worry that non-ordinary truths might generate new sorts of unknowable truths (as discussed in the next paragraph). So one might at least suggest that the argument gives reason to hold that all knowable truths, ordinary or not, are scrutable from PQI. Second, one can argue that where ordinary methods yield knowledge, the Cosmoscope has the capacity to yield *certainty*: conditional certainty, if used in conditional mode, and empirical certainty (at least if we are certain that the Cosmoscope is accurate) in empirical mode. Here the idea, as in the last section, is that various forms of doubt that are relevant to ordinary knowledge can be ruled out by a Cosmoscope, because of all the information it provides. The results would be the conclusive versions of Conditional and Inferential Scrutability, involving certainty.[12]

Of course there is more to say about the argument, and numerous potential objections to address. Regarding premise 3, one could object that there may be unknowable ordinary truths that are not remote or Fitchian truths. Most extremely, an external-world skeptic may hold that almost all ordinary truths are unknowable. But even granted external-world skepticism, it is clear that as for remote truths, the relevant obstacles to knowability are not obstacles to (conditional or a priori) scrutability from a Cosmoscope.

There are numerous other potential sources of unknowability in specific domains, including mathematics, metaphysics, negative truths, and so on. The

---

[12] Because ordinary knowledge does not involve certainty, the argument from knowability is in the first instance an argument for nonconclusive scrutability theses, where the argument from elimination is in the first instance an argument for conclusive scrutability theses. Still, the two reinforce each other. Many objections to conclusive scrutability theses (and to the argument from elimination) are also objections to nonconclusive scrutability theses, and the argument from knowability can help to overcome these. Likewise, the argument from elimination helps us to see how the conclusion of the argument from knowability might be extended to a stronger conclusion concerning conclusive knowledge, by exploiting the extra material that is available in PQI, compared to ordinary knowledge.

most obvious such sources do not involve ordinary truths, though. Perhaps one might argue that unknowable truths in such domains might give rise to unknowable ordinary truths. For example, if it is unknowable whether metaphysical nihilism (only particles exist) is true or false, then ordinary utterances of 'There are trees' will arguably count as unknowable as well. Still, *PQI* will build in truths about the existence of macrophysical as well as microphysical objects, so *PQI* is not neutral on truths of this sort, and it is arguable that any ordinary truths of this sort will be scrutable from *PQI*. In any case, if certain domains (such as metaphysics or mathematics) provide other potential sources of unknowable truths (whether ordinary or not), then we can count these as 'hard cases', to be covered not by the arguments in this chapter but by the discussion in chapter 6.

What about knowledge by testimony? This sort of knowledge was excluded from *s*-knowability because including it would make premise 2 more questionable: it is not obvious that if *s* could know *M* through testimony after *t*, then *M* would also be scrutable from a Cosmoscope. We cannot simply assume that a Cosmoscope will give access to any testimony, as we are setting aside for now questions about whether social, linguistic, and intentional truths are scrutable from *PQI*. But excluding testimony raises a new sort of worry about premise 3, by introducing a potential new sort of *s*-unknowable truth: truths that *s* could know through testimony but not any other way. Certain truths about the past, for example, may be knowable in the present only through testimony. Still, it is plausible that *s*-unknowable sentences in this class all involve varieties of remoteness (non-remote ordinary truths knowable by *s* through testimony are also knowable by *s* without testimony), and so do not pose obstacles to scrutability.

One could also object to premise 2 and to the argument I have given for it. One objection says that there are truths that are not knowable through perception, introspection, and reasoning alone but are knowable though alternative sources of knowledge. The most obvious alternative source is testimony, but this has been explicitly excluded from *s*-knowability. Other candidates that might be proposed are intuition and memory, but for our purposes these are subsumed under reasoning (broadly construed): anything the subject can know using intuition and memory will be equally available when the subject is using a Cosmoscope. Likewise, any innate knowledge, like all knowledge that the subject already has at *t*, will be available when the subject uses a Cosmoscope.

Another sort of objection to premise 2 suggests that there are truths knowable through perception, introspection, and reasoning that are not scrutable from *PQI*. One such objection involves intentional truths known by introspection. One might hold that the phenomenological information in *PQI* suffices for knowledge of one's experiences, but not for knowledge of one's beliefs and desires. Now, truths about one's beliefs and desires are not ordinary truths on the current understanding, and are discussed further in chapter 6. Still, one might in principle hold that knowledge of these non-ordinary truths plays a role in knowledge of ordinary truths. If so, one can either stipulate for present purposes that the relevant intentional truths are built into Q along with truths about experience, or one could use the considerations in chapter 6 to make the case that these truths are scrutable from PQI.

Another objection of this sort holds that perception plays a special epistemological role that cannot be played by knowledge or by reasoning from a supposition. For example, someone might hold that *perceiving* a red cube in front of one can ground further knowledge in a way that merely *knowing* or *supposing* that there is a red cube in front of one cannot. If so, there may be knowledge grounded in perception that is not scrutable from PQI. In response: for the purposes of inferential scrutability, we are entitled to assume *certainty* of the truths in PQI, and therefore of the relevant perceptual truths. Even if perceptual knowledge is unusually strong, it is hard to see how it involves something stronger than certainty. Likewise, for the purposes of conditional scrutability, one can at least conditionally suppose the truths in PQI with certainty. This is enough to conditionally know the relevant perceptual truths with certainty. On the face of it, this conditional knowledge will be as efficacious in generating further conditional knowledge as was the unconditional knowledge in the case of inferential scrutability. If so, there will be no objection to the inference from perceptual knowability to scrutability here.

Someone might suggest that perception of a red cube can engage certain processes that mere knowledge or supposition concerning a red cube will not. However, full PQI-style knowledge or supposition will put one in a position to at least imagine the red cube in fully vivid detail: here we can count the transition from knowledge or supposition concerning color and shape to imaginative states concerning those qualities as a capacity of idealized reasoning (or at least idealized imagination, which is good enough for present purposes). And it is also plausible that any conclusions that can be reached by ideal reasoning from a perceptual state can equally be reached by ideal reasoning from a corresponding imaginative state, at least if it is accompanied by knowledge or supposition that what is imagined obtains. If seeing a certain experimental result enables one to infer conclusions about hidden causes, for example, imagining the same result enables one in principle to infer those conclusions under the supposition that what is imagined obtains. Someone might argue that this connection between perception and imagination breaks down where certain high-level recognitional capacities are concerned. I think that this is not clear, but in any case I argue later in the chapter that any (non-Fitchian) truth that can be known using such a capacity is also knowable without using such a capacity. If this is right, then they do not pose an objection to premise 2.

To approach further objections to premise 2 (especially objections from further alternative routes to knowledge), it is useful to first set out a version of a traditional foundationalist thesis that if true, would support premise 2.

Core Evidence Thesis: Necessarily, all knowledge is grounded in core evidence.

Here, core evidence is to be understood as including (i) subjects' introspective evidence about their own phenomenal states (and their own intentional states if necessary, as above), and (ii) perceptual evidence about the distribution of primary and secondary qualities in the environment. As before, I will take evidence to be propositional, though I will be neutral on whether evidence must be believed or known. An item of knowledge K is grounded in (or ultimately warranted by) a set of empirical evidence propositions E when there is a doxastic warrant for K (as defined in the fourth excursus) whose empirical grounds include only elements of E.[13] Throughout this book, I take primary qualities to be mass properties and spatiotemporal properties, and I take secondary qualities to be colors and analogous properties in other modalities.

When K is inferentially justified, its grounds will include the grounds for all the items of knowledge on which it is inferentially based. When K is non-inferentially justified, it will either be grounded in some distinct evidence E or it will be its own ground. For example, if K is introspective knowledge (e.g. that one is in pain) it will plausibly be grounded in introspective evidence E (that one is in pain). If K is perceptual knowledge (e.g. that there is a red cube in front of one) it will plausibly be grounded in perceptual evidence E (the content of a perception as of a red cube in front of one).

A strong foundationalist thesis says that all knowledge is grounded in introspective evidence alone. For present purposes, we do not need such a strong thesis. The Core Evidence thesis allows that perceptual evidence about primary and secondary qualities may play a role too. In effect this leaves room for a 'dogmatist' version of foundationalism on which perceptual experience as of a red square object provides direct evidence that there is a red square object in front of one, without this role being mediated by introspective evidence. However, the Core Evidence thesis excludes grounding in evidence with richer contents than this. This excludes both perceptual evidence with rich contents (concerning matters over and above primary and secondary qualities) and also non-inferential empirical beliefs with rich contents that are not grounded in perceptual or introspective evidence at all.

---

[13] A priori knowledge will be vacuously grounded in core evidence, on this definition, as it will have a warrant with no empirical grounds (any a priori grounds are set aside as irrelevant for current purposes). For more on warrants and on grounding, see the fourth excursus. Note that the sort of grounding that is relevant here is epistemic grounding, as opposed to the sort of metaphysical grounding that is discussed in some other places in this book.

To use the Core Evidence thesis to support premise 2, one can argue that (i) if s can know M with the knowledge grounded in core evidence E, then M is (inferentially and conditionally) scrutable from E for s, and (ii) if M is scrutable from core evidence E, it is scrutable from PQI. I discuss principles analogous to these shortly. But first there is a worry about the Core Evidence thesis to deal with.

Many reject the Core Evidence thesis on the grounds that there are sources of knowledge and justification that go beyond core evidence. Some of these potential alternative sources include (i) recognitional capacities, as when chicken-sexers may come to know the sex of a chicken by direct recognition, or in which a savant comes to have reliable hunches about the weather; (ii) high-level perception, in which high-level features such as being happy are directly perceived by subjects and arguably constitute part of a subject's basic perceptual evidence; (iii) high-level empirical inference, where a subject uses empirically grounded inference mechanisms that do not derive from core evidence and a priori reasoning alone; (iv) unconscious perception, as when blindsight subjects come to know what is in front of them without consciously perceiving it; (v) testimony, on views where testimonial knowledge is not grounded in perceptual knowledge.[14]

In all of these cases, one could try to make the case that the knowledge is grounded in core evidence. In cases (i) and (ii), one could suggest that inference from core perceptual evidence is always operative, or at least that the recognitional capacities that are being used are themselves grounded in prior core evidence. In case (iii), one could suggest that the empirical inference mechanisms will themselves always be grounded in prior core evidence. In case (iv), one could suggest that unconscious perception equally involves core perceptual evidence (e.g. unconscious perception of colors and shapes), even though the perceptual states are unconscious. In case (v), one can argue that testimonial knowledge is always grounded in (current and prior) perceptual evidence. These matters are highly arguable, however.

Fortunately, the argument from knowability does not require the Core Evidence thesis. It suffices to have something like the following:

Core Knowability Thesis: All knowable (non-Fitchian) ordinary truths are knowable with grounds in core evidence.

The Core Knowability Thesis is consistent with the existence of knowledge (by recognition, high-level perception, unconscious perception, testimony, and

---

[14] Cases (i) and (iii) might be seen as involving grounds beyond core evidence, or alternatively might be seen as involving special processes in the transition from core evidence to belief that undermine the step from Core Evidence to Conditional or A Priori Scrutability. Either way, they need to be addressed.

so on) that is not grounded in core evidence. It simply requires that any (non-Fitchian) truths known this way can *also* be known in principle with the knowledge grounded in core evidence.[15]

The case of unconscious perception can be handled by noting that any non-Fitchian truths knowable using unconscious perception can also be known using conscious perception (or introspection, in the case of introspective knowledge of unconscious perception itself). Likewise, the case of testimony can be handled by noting that any non-Fitchian truth knowable using testimony can also be known without using testimony. The latter is a consequence of the claim that testimony is not a means of originating knowledge: testimonial knowledge requires prior knowledge, which will originate in nontestimonial knowledge. (In any case testimony is excluded from *s*-knowability, so the objection from testimony is irrelevant for applying Core Knowability to the argument from knowability.)

The cases of high-level recognitional capacities and high-level perceptual evidence can likewise be handled by arguing that any non-Fitchian truth that can be known using these can also be known without using them, and instead by using core evidence and inference alone. This case is complex, however, so I discuss it separately later in this chapter under the objection from recognitional capacities.

Finally, the case of high-level empirical inference can be handled by arguing that what can be known using empirical inference mechanisms can also be known using a priori inference along with core perceptual evidence, including past evidence. In any case, this phenomenon does not really yield an obstacle to conditional or inferential scrutability: if *s* has certain capacities for high-level empirical inference from core evidence, these capacities can be used for the purposes of conditional and inferential scrutability from *PQI*. The phenomenon may yield an objection to a priori scrutability, however, so I discuss it in the next chapter, under the objection from empirical inference.

---

[15] The restriction to non-Fitchian truths is required in order to avoid a class of Fitch-style potential counterexamples of the form '*p* and *p* is not known with grounds in core evidence'. (Thanks to Tim Williamson for pointing these out.) Such claims are not knowable with grounds in core evidence: if the first conjunct were known in this way, the second conjunct would be false. But if there are alternative methods of knowledge, there will arguably be cases in which such claims are true and knowable: perhaps one might know the first conjunct in the alternative way and the second conjunct in a standard way. The conjunctive claim is Fitchian with respect to the method of reasoning from core evidence, so to rule these cases out, it suffices to exclude Fitchian truths of this sort. This exclusion does not affect the argument as a whole, as we know that Fitchian truths do not pose any special obstacle to scrutability.

One might also restrict the principle to context-independent truths, to avoid worries about differences in usage between subjects, but this restriction is unnecessary for the subject-specific version discussed below.

The Core Knowability thesis also has a subject-specific version: what is s-knowable is s-knowable with grounds in core evidence. The case for the subject-specific version parallels the case for the general version above. Some extra worries come up in considering the cases. In the case of unconscious perception, we need s's capacities for unconscious perception to be paralleled by capacities for conscious perception; but this will be so in a normal subject. The case of testimony delivers knowability by other subjects but not obviously knowability by s, but fortunately our notion of s-knowability excludes testimonial knowledge in any case. The cases of recognitional capacities and empirical inference may involve grounding in inference from long-past perceptual evidence, which may not now be available for the purposes of s-knowability. However, such evidence will certainly be available for the purposes of scrutability by s, so for present purposes we can simply extend the notion of s-knowability by idealizing away from imperfect memory and allowing that s has access to all of her past evidence.

Using the subject-specific Core Knowability thesis, we can support premise 2 of the argument from knowability: the claim that any s-knowable ordinary truth is scrutable from PQI for s. This needs the further claims that (i) if M is s-knowable with grounds in core evidence E, M is scrutable from E, and (ii) if M is scrutable from core evidence E, M is scrutable from PQI.

Regarding (i): this claim is most straightforward when the possible knowledge of M grounded in E is grounded in inference from knowledge of E. This suggests that knowledge of E puts s in a position to know M, and that supposition of E will yield conditional knowledge of M given E. If knowledge of M is grounded in perceiving or introspecting E, rather than knowing E, then perceiving or introspecting E puts s in a position to know M. Then we can argue, as in the discussion of the special epistemological role of perception above, that knowledge is just as powerful as perception when it comes to grounding further knowledge (and likewise for supposition and conditional knowledge).

Regarding (ii): E includes truths about phenomenal states and about primary and secondary qualities. Truths about phenomenal states and primary qualities are built into PQI. Truths about secondary qualities are plausibly scrutable from PQI, as I argue in chapter 6; if they are not, we can simply build them in. So if M is scrutable from E, M should be scrutable from PQI, at least given the reasonable claim that the rest of PQI does not contain defeaters for the knowledge of M.

A tricky issue arises here from the possibility that E is core evidence in a counterfactual world (the world in which s knows M) but is not even true in the actual world. If this were so, scrutability from E would not yield scrutability from PQI. To exclude such cases, we can restrict the relevant notion of 's-knowability with grounds in core evidence' to s-knowability with grounds in *actual* core evidence. This requires that E is true of the actual world that satisfies PQI, so that (ii) above will go through. Claim (i) above will also be unaffected.

The cost of this restriction is that potential exceptions to subject-specific Core Knowability will be introduced: ordinary truths M that are s-knowable using counterfactual core evidence (evidence that s might counterfactually obtain by moving through the world) but not using actual core evidence. For example, let M be 'There has existed a green thing', and assume that the only actual green thing is in the distant past, so that M is not s-knowable from actual core evidence. M might still be s-knowable using counterfactual evidence, for example evidence that s might obtain by building a green thing and looking at it. Still, it is plausible that such exceptions will involve special obstacles—remote truths, Fitchian truths with respect to the method, truths requiring knowledge of counterfactuals about core evidence—that are not themselves obstacles to scrutability. If so, then the argument for scrutability will still go through.

I conclude that the argument from knowability provides at least a prima facie case for inferential and conditional scrutability. The argument so far does not establish a priori scrutability, because we have allowed the subject to use empirical background knowledge. Still, one can extend the argument by applying the reasoning above to background knowledge itself. For any background truth T known nontestimonially by s, one can argue that insofar as T was known through perception, introspection, and reasoning, T is itself scrutable from core evidence, using background knowledge that does not use T and does not use any other background knowledge unavailable to the original subject. Where a background truth T is known testimonially by s, one can make a case that T is knowable nontestimonially by someone. It may be that testimonial knowledge of some further T' is involved in this nontestimonial knowledge of T, but T' will also be knowable nontestimonially. Pushing this back, any particular piece of testimonial knowledge can be seen to be inessential to knowing M, and one can make a case that knowledge of M is ultimately grounded nontestimonially and therefore in core evidence, albeit perhaps in the core evidence of many individuals. As long as reasoning from core evidence that is available to those subjects is also available to s, then M will be a priori scrutable (for s) from core evidence, and therefore from PQI. This suggests that all empirical background knowledge is dispensable from the scrutability process in principle, yielding a case for a priori scrutability. This case is developed further in the next chapter.

5 Inferential scrutability with a Cosmoscope

The inferential scrutability thesis under discussion says that all ordinary truths are inferentially scrutable from PQI. That is, for all ordinary truths M, if the subject were to come to know sufficiently many truths in PQI, the subject would be in a position to know M.

As before, Inferential Scrutability is less important for my purposes than Conditional and A Priori Scrutability, and I am not inclined to defend it to the death. It is not crucial for establishing conditional and a priori scrutability, and it raises some distinctive difficulties. But the thesis and the difficulties are interesting in their own right, and the thesis can also play a useful if non-essential supporting role in arguing for Conditional and A Priori Scrutability. So I will discuss some distinctive issues that arise for the thesis here.

The distinctive difficulties for the thesis are mainly tied to Fitchian truths: those whose truth-value would be changed by the attempt to determine their truth-value from PQI. In the Cosmoscope scenario, these are truths that would be rendered false by the introduction and use of a Cosmoscope: for example, 'There is no Cosmoscope'. This is a negative truth, so is excluded from the scope of the thesis, but there will be positive Fitchian truths: in fact, P and Q themselves are good candidates to be Fitchian truths. It may be that numerous ordinary truths about our world are Fitchian, perhaps because they would be false in a world in which there is widespread inference from PQI, or perhaps because they would be false in a world with a Cosmoscope.

For the purposes of the Cosmoscope argument, one can at least minimize the number of Fitchian truths by specifying the right sort of Cosmoscope. We can think of the Cosmoscope as a nonphysical device that interacts with the physical and phenomenal world at only one spatiotemporal location. We can suppose that an individual is locked up in a room, that the Cosmoscope ensures that everything outside that room goes on as it would have if the Cosmoscope had not been used, and that the Cosmoscope afterwards removes all traces of its use, so that the future is just as it would have been without the Cosmoscope. We can even minimize the physical impact of the Cosmoscope by supposing that it is a *mental Cosmoscope*: one that conveys information by directly producing certain imaginative states in the subject, and that receives information by monitoring the subject's mental states. Of course this will still involve changes to Q, compared to a world with no Cosmoscope. If physicalism about the mind is true, this will also involve changes to P, including some violations of the physical laws that hold otherwise.[16] It may also involve changes to I. But at least the changes will be minimal.

---

[16] Whether one is a dualist or a physicalist, the key question here is whether it is conceivable that we could have disembodied thought: thoughts without correlated physical activity. Many but not all dualists will accept this, and many but not all physicalists will deny it. If one accepts this, a mental Cosmoscope need involve no change to P. If one denies it, a mental Cosmoscope will involve some change to P, so there is less to be gained by moving from a holographic Cosmoscope in a room to a mental Cosmoscope. One might think that a strong dualist can leave both P and Q intact by stipulating an extra nonphysical thinker. Here the trouble is that the user of the Cosmoscope must be identical to the original subject (who uttered the sentence), in order to get indexical truths and others right. Perhaps there is a way to use scrutability by a disembodied subject of this sort as a premise to yield conclusions about the original subject, but this is not obvious.

There are now two ways we can think of a Cosmoscope used in empirical mode. A *complete* Cosmoscope will convey information about PQI^*, the version of PQI that is true in its world at the time of use. An *incomplete* Cosmoscope will convey information about $PQI-$, the component of PQI that is true in both its world and ours. The difference between these Cosmoscopes may be small, given the previous paragraph, but it will be significant. Each has advantages and disadvantages for our purposes.

One advantage of the complete Cosmoscope is that there is at least a chance that all ordinary truths might be scrutable from it. Another advantage is that PQI^* is relevantly similar in form to PQI. A disadvantage is that PQI^* includes sentences that are false in our world. A related disadvantage is that scrutability from PQI^* does not immediately entail conclusions about scrutability from PQI. Still, it is arguable that if we can establish that for any given sentence, we can at least determine its truth-value *in the world of use of the Cosmoscope at the time of use*, we can use this to argue for conditional scrutability of such truths from PQI^*. One could then go on to argue that given that PQI^* and PQI are relevantly similar where conditional scrutability is concerned, all ordinary truths are conditionally scrutable from PQI.

Another worry about a complete Cosmoscope in empirical mode is that it must enable one to monitor one's own current and future states, leading to potential paradoxes. If the Cosmoscope monitors one's own current phenomenal state E, it will feed in an imaginative recreation of E—but it is far from clear that any phenomenal state can include an imaginative recreation of itself. It would seem that we would need an imaginative recreation of the imaginative recreation, and so on, leading to an infinite chain. Perhaps that is not out of the question. Another way to deal with this issue would be to stipulate that the Cosmoscope does not need to convey information about one's current state, as one will have access to that state by introspection in any case. This requires a certain confidence in the powers of introspection, though, and may also cause problems when combined with the insulated idealization in the fifth excursus, which disallows introspection. A related worry concerns paradoxes of prediction: if one is given information about what one will do a moment later, could not one act in such a way as to falsify the prediction? So it is at least arguable that a Cosmoscope that conveys such future information is impossible.[17]

---

[17] What of the third paradox for Laplace's demon that arose in the introduction, the paradox of complexity? (A formal cousin of this paradox is presented by Wolpert (2008), who argues that no universe could contain two Laplacean demons.) This paradox is largely avoided by rendering the Cosmoscope nonphysical, so that it need not carry information about itself: PQI^* will be a correct description of the Cosmoscope's world (as the that's-all clause T is not present) but not a complete description. There will be a problem only when the thinker needs to entertain all (or most) of the information in PQI^* at once in order to ascertain some ordinary truth. If we assume a mental Cosmoscope and disembodied thought, a version of the stipulation in the text may help with this case.

It is best, then, to appeal to an incomplete Cosmoscope, conveying information about *PQI–*. The incompleteness will be minor, pertaining mostly to one's own phenomenal and perhaps physical states in a short period surrounding the present. Given that use of the Cosmoscope takes time, the indexical 'now is' component of *PQI–* cannot convey the same specific time conveyed in the original *PQI*, on pain of it being false at some times of use. We could either stipulate that *PQI–* contains imprecise temporal information that is true both of the original situation and the Cosmoscope world, or we can stipulate that it contains constantly updated information about the time of use in the Cosmoscope world. The second option allows more precise temporal information to be scrutable, at cost of raising issues akin to those in the paragraph before last. For present purposes, the first option will suffice.

With the incomplete Cosmoscope, we avoid worries about recreation of current states, and we also avoid paradoxes of freedom: while the Cosmoscope will make predictions about the future, one will never be in a position to falsify them. The disadvantage is that some ordinary truths about the actual world, as well as some ordinary truths about the Cosmoscope world, will not be scrutable using *PQI–*: in particular, truths about the subject's physical and phenomenal states around the relevant time, and truths about the current time. Still, it is clear than an enormous number of truths will be scrutable from *PQI–*. Information about one's own present physical and phenomenal states seems to be irrelevant for the scrutability of *most* ordinary truths outside one's immediate environment. Precise temporal information is relevant for many 'now'-involving truths, but from imprecise information we can at least get to corresponding 'around now'-involving truths. Let us call those to which the extra information is not relevant *nonlocal* ordinary truths.[18]

We can then focus on the thesis that all nonlocal ordinary truths are inferentially scrutable from *PQI–*. We do not need to explicitly rule out Fitchian truths here, as all Fitchian truths (relative to this method) are either non-ordinary (because negative) or local. For example, '*p* and I don't know that *p*' is local, while '*p* and no one knows that *p*' is both local and negative.

Once Fitchian worries have been set aside, the thesis that all nonlocal ordinary truths are inferentially scrutable from a Cosmoscope involving *PQI–* is very

---

[18] The definition of nonlocality is probably best left at the intuitive level given here. One might say that a truth is nonlocal when it is inferentially scrutable from *PQI–* if it is inferentially scrutable from *PQI**, but this will raise the issues about scrutability from *PQI** above. An analogous definition in terms of conditional scrutability will avoid these issues. Note that nonlocality should not be defined in terms of supervenience on or necessitation by nonlocal elements of *P* and *Q*, as there may be truths that supervene nonlocally but still require local information for scrutability: for example, 'Someone a mile away is having an experience identical to my current actual experience'.

plausible for the reasons given earlier. Here we can appeal to the basic Cosmoscope argument and the arguments from elimination and from knowability to argue for the thesis. One can also use these arguments to argue directly, as in the previous sections, that all non-Fitchian ordinary truths are inferentially scrutable from *PQI*.

6 Conditional scrutability

The conditional scrutability thesis that I am arguing for in this chapter says that all ordinary truths are conditionally scrutable from *PQI*. That is: for all ordinary true sentence tokens *M*, the speaker is in a position to know (on ideal reflection) that *if PQI* is true, then *M* is true. This requires crucially that the subject's insulated rational credence $cr^*(M \mid PQI)$ is high.

The arguments in sections 2–4 work straightforwardly as arguments for Conditional Scrutability. For example, if one uses a Cosmoscope to suppose *PQI* in conditional mode, the arguments from elimination and knowability suggest that under ideal reflection, one can infer *M*. In this case, Fitchian worries are irrelevant: we need not suppose that the world in which one supposes *PQI* is itself a world in which *PQI* is true. Likewise, even though the world contains no Cosmoscope, if there were to be a Cosmoscope one could use it in conditional mode to reason about *PQI*, which holds in our world. It remains plausible that if supposing that the Cosmoscope is correct should lead one to conclude *M*, then likewise supposing that *PQI* is correct should lead one to conclude *M*. Either way, *M* is conditionally scrutable from *PQI*.

Alternatively, if one has already accepted a version of Inferential Scrutability, then Conditional Scrutability follows naturally. Suppose that *M* is inferentially scrutable from *PQI*, so that if one were to come to know *PQ*, one would come to know *M*. This suggests that even before coming to know *PQI*, one could know that *if PQI*, then *M*. It is true that in coming to know *PQI*, one may also acquire additional evidence, such as knowledge that one is entertaining *PQI* or knowledge that one is using a Cosmoscope. So one might think that this evidence needs to be factored into the antecedent as well. But it is plausible that this evidence is either extraneous to knowing *M* (as in the former case), or relevant only in virtue of its role in supporting *PQI* (as in the latter case). If so, then we need not build this evidence into the antecedent, and it remains the case that one could know beforehand that if *PQI*, then *M*.

Now suppose that we have established, as argued earlier, that all non-Fitchian ordinary truths are inferentially scrutable from *PQI*. If this is right, then the considerations in the last paragraph suggest that all non-Fitchian truths are conditionally scrutable from *PQI*. We have seen that Fitchian obstacles to the inferential scrutability of broadly Fitchian truths do not provide any obstacle to their conditional scrutability. So unless, implausibly, there is some other obstacle to conditional scrutability that is associated only with broadly Fitchian truths, it follows that all ordinary truths are conditionally scrutable from *PQI*.

Likewise, suppose we have established, as discussed in the last section, that all ordinary nonlocal truths are inferentially scrutable from *PQI*–. If this is right, then the considerations above suggest that all ordinary nonlocal truths are conditionally scrutable from *PQI*–. The Fitchian obstacles to the inferential scrutability of local truths from *PQI* do not provide any obstacle to the conditional scrutability. So unless, implausibly, there is some other obstacle to conditional scrutability that is associated only with local truths, it follows that all ordinary truths are conditionally scrutable from *PQI*.

A residual issue is that in the world of supposition, the subject may be certain that *PQI* is false, for example because she is certain that her course of experiences differs from that specified by Q. So here she must suppose something that she is certain is false. Making such a supposition is a little unusual, but it is nevertheless coherent. We have already seen that a conditional credence $cr^*(A \mid B)$ can be well defined even when $cr^*(B) = 0$. This applies even when one is certain that *B* is false. In effect, the supposition that *B* is false simply overrides ones knowledge that *B*, leaving the latter inoperable. In the case of *PQTI*, the supposition of Q will override any existing beliefs about the character of the subject's experience, leaving the subject free to reason as in section 2. In any case, we can avoid this issue if we operate with the insulated idealization in the fifth excursus, so that during the reasoning process the subject will be blind to introspective and perceptual evidence. In this mode, the subject will have no grounds for certainty that *PQTI* is false, so the issue will not arise.

7 The objection from recognitional capacities[19]

An important objection appeals to the recognitional capacities embodied in high-level perception and high-level recognition. Let us say that *core* properties are phenomenal properties and primary and secondary qualities. *Noncore* properties are any other properties: the property of being a chair, for example. In high-level perception, subjects directly perceive noncore properties: for example, they might see an object to be a chair or a banana. Here noncore properties are part of the content or the object of a perceptual experience. It is controversial whether high-level perception of this sort exists.[20] But whether or not noncore

---

[19] Thanks to Nick Shea, Susanna Siegel, and Tim Williamson for discussion of this objection.
[20] In *The Contents of Visual Experience* (2011), Susanna Siegel argues that the content of perceptual experience involves noncore properties including natural kind properties (such as being a pine tree) and causation.

properties are *perceived*, they are certainly *recognized*. High-level recognition involves the non-inferential detection of noncore properties, whether or not these properties are part of the content of perception. For example, even if the content of perception involves just color and shapes, one can still recognize a seen object non-inferentially as a tree.

Let us say that a *high-level recognitional capacity* is a capacity to detect noncore properties non-inferentially through high-level perception or through high-level recognition.[21] We saw earlier that high-level recognitional capacities pose a challenge to the argument from knowability. They can be seen to pose a challenge to scrutability theses more generally. An opponent might hold that ordinary truths are not scrutable from a limited base precisely because knowledge of them rests essentially on these recognitional capacities. Two slightly different challenges are posed by high-level perception and high-level recognition respectively.

First, if knowledge of chairs requires high-level perception of chairs, then 'chair'-truths will not be inferentially or conditionally scrutable from *PQI*. Given *PQI* alone, we would be unable to find the chairs. Even an imaginative state with the relevant spatial and color content (as provided by a Cosmoscope, for example) would fall short of what is needed: it would not involve experience as of a chair, so we would not recognize chairs in the image of the external world. Perhaps this would be akin to the experience of some forms of agnosia or of Sartrean nausea. If a Cosmoscope provided a screen or a hologram, then perhaps we might be able to recognize the chairs (as we do when we watch television), but this would be only because we would be using perceptual capacities that could not be used in reasoning from *PQI*.

Second, if our knowledge of chairs requires high-level recognition but not high-level perception, then 'chair'-truths will arguably not be a priori scrutable from *PQI*. Without using high-level recognition, we would once again be left with a sort of agnosia that prevents us from detecting the presence of chairs. Unlike the previous case, this case is not obviously a problem for inferential and conditional scrutability. The high-level recognitional capacity allows us to move from a low-level perceptual experience (with spatial and color content, say) to recognition of chairs. If so, it will presumably also allow us to move from an analogous low-level imaginative experience to recognition of chairs. If so, then inferential and conditional scrutability can proceed by transitions from *PQI* to such an imaginative experience (as discussed in section 4) and then to judgments about chairs. But it is arguable that some of these recognitional capacities are

---

[21] Here and throughout I construe inference as a relation between judgments or judgment-like mental states such as suppositions. The recognitional capacities in question cannot involve inference in this sense, but they may involve quasi-inferential transitions whose relata include experiences or subpersonal representational states.

grounded in experience, so that this process does not yield a priori scrutability. While inferential and conditional scrutability are the main foci of this chapter, it is useful to address both sorts of objection at once.

One might respond to the first version of the objection by saying that Q tells us what it is like to have the relevant high-level perceptual experiences: for example, that one is having an experience as of a chair. But it is not obvious how to get from introspective knowledge about experiences of chairs to knowledge about chairs themselves. Given a traditional foundationalist view on which all perceptual knowledge is grounded in knowledge of experience, then perhaps one could exploit that route here. But given a dogmatist view on which perceptual knowledge is grounded directly in perceptual experience (Pryor 2000; see also Pollock 1974, White 2006, Wright 2007), it is not obvious that knowledge about experience can play the same role. An additional premise that these experiences are usually caused by chairs might help, but it is not obvious why that premise is justified. In any case, this line of defense is not available for the second version involving high-level recognition without high-level perception. Here the phenomenology may be restricted to core experiences as of colors, shapes, and the like, so that Q will build in no distinctive phenomenology of seeing chairs.[22]

Instead, I will respond by arguing for a dispensability thesis: every truth M that is knowable using a problematic recognitional capacity (that is, one whose use could not figure in scrutability from PQI) is scrutable from $PQTI$ without using such a capacity. To illustrate: the thesis says that if we can know that chairs are present using a problematic high-level capacity along the lines above, we can also use a Cosmoscope to determine that chairs are present without using that capacity (perhaps instead using inference from the structure and use of relevant objects), and indeed without using any high-level recognitional capacities at all. In practice, it is easier to argue for the weaker thesis that every truth knowable using a specific problematic recognitional capacity is scrutable without using that very capacity: so one can know that chairs are present without using the chair capacity though perhaps using a recognitional capacity for something else such as wood. If we can also avoid circles of dependence (where knowledge of chairs requires the wood capacity and knowledge of wood requires the chair capacity, for example), then we can eliminate problematic recognitional capacities one at a time to obtain the original thesis.

One can also proceed by arguing for a dispensability thesis about knowability rather than scrutability: any (non-Fitchian) truth knowable using problematic recognitional capacities is also knowable without using them. It follows from

---

[22] The second version of the objection will work best on a view of experience (as developed e.g. in Jesse Prinz's *The Conscious Brain*) on which there is no high-level perceptual phenomenology and also no nonsensory experience of recognition or judgment.

this that if knowability entails scrutability for knowledge not involving these capacities, knowability entails scrutability across the board. To illustrate the thesis: an expert might use high-level perception to perceive electrons in a bubble chamber diagram, but it is also possible to ascertain whether electrons are present without using this capacity, instead using painstaking analysis. A chicken sexer might use high-level recognition to recognize the sex of a chicken, but it is also possible to ascertain the sex of a chicken without using this recognitional capacity, instead detecting certain core features, comparing them to the core features of male and female chickens, and inferring the sex of the chicken. The idea here is that the relevant recognitional capacities may speed things up, but they do not introduce knowledge of a new class of truths.[23]

To argue for the dispensability theses, it is useful to make some distinctions among recognitional capacities and the associated concepts. Let us say that a recognitional capacity *involves* a concept when it is a capacity to apply that concept to instances. I will take it that every recognitional capacity involves a concept. In cases of *recognitional concepts*, possession of the concept derives from a recognitional capacity. For example, one might come to recognize a given person repeatedly and thereby come to form an associated recognitional concept *that person*. In cases of *nonrecognitional concepts*, possession of the concept does not derive from a recognitional capacity. A recognitional capacity may involve a nonrecognitional concept, but possession of the concept will have some other grounds. For example, one might have a prior concept of *gay* (based on a definition, say) and later come to acquire a capacity for recognizing gay people. These two cases raise different sorts of issues for scrutability, so I will consider them separately.

First, we can consider recognitional concepts and the recognitional capacities that they derive from. Examples might include recognitional concepts of people or of plants or of musical sounds. One might express these concepts using a demonstrative such as 'that person' or a made up name such as 'triffid' for a plant or 'blizz' for a sound. One may in some cases find that there is an existing word for the thing one is recognizing ('Joe' or 'cactus' or 'diatonic', say) and associate

---

[23] An alternative general argument for this dispensability thesis starts from the empirical premise that all perceptual and recognitional knowledge is produced by transitions from core representations: sensory representations of core properties, as in early vision (or in the case of high-level recognition, as in core perceptual experience). It combines this with the premise that any knowledge produced this way can also be produced in principle by inference from corresponding core perceptual knowledge with the same content. This yields the required conclusion. Of course the premises of this causal argument might be questioned. The first premise might be questioned by anti-representationalists about vision, for example, and the second premise might be questioned by someone who denies that the causal transition in question can be converted into rational inferential transitions. I think that one might respond to these doubts, perhaps by articulating appropriately modified premises, but this would clearly require some work.

that word with the concept—but here I am interested in a concept that derives 'purely' from the recognitional capacity, setting aside possible contributions from a linguistic community.

Most often, recognitional concepts are *response-dependent* concepts: they are concepts of whatever is bringing about the recognition response, and in particular of whatever is bringing about the application of the recognitional concept. For example, a *that person* recognitional concept typically functions to pick out the person (if any) who is triggering the response. A *that sound* concept typically functions to pick out the sort of sound that triggers the response. Response-dependent concepts do not cause any special problems for scrutability. At least if we are given information about when the response itself is present (about when a subject judges *that person is over there*, for example), we can then determine the referent of the concept by determining what typically triggers this response.

Suppose one has a recognitional concept *triffid* of a certain sort of plant. In real life, one might get tentative evidence that a triffid is present by recognizing something as a triffid, and one might get stronger evidence by examining the plant that triggers the response and determining that it is of the same kind as other plants that have triggered the response. Correspondingly, using a Cosmoscope, one might get tentative evidence that a triffid is present by noting that one has triffid-recognizing response, and one might get stronger evidence by examining the plant that triggers the response and determining that it is of the same kind as other plants that have triggered the response. So when one knows that a triffid is present using the recognitional capacity, the presence of a triffid is also scrutable from a Cosmoscope without using the recognitional capacity.

A few objections might be made here. A dogmatist about recognition might say that the justification we get from simply recognizing a triffid is greater than the justification we get from noting that one has a triffid-recognizing response and inferring that a triffid is present. If so, this justification may also be greater than corresponding justification from a Cosmoscope. Still, in all these cases justification is inconclusive and tentative (one might be seeing a fake triffid, after all), and even the direct recognitional belief is best confirmed by examining the plant as above. This stronger sort of justification is certainly available from the Cosmoscope. One might also object that the Cosmoscope will not tell us whether the recognition response is present, or that it will not tell us what sort of plant is causing the response. But these are potential obstacles to scrutability that have nothing to do with the recognitional concept in question: one involves mental concepts, the other involves theoretical biological concepts and causal concepts. So assuming that there are no other obstacles to scrutability, scrutability for recognitional concepts such as *triffid* will not pose an obstacle.

It is arguable that some special recognitional concepts are not response-dependent but qualitative, functioning to directly pick out certain qualities. For example, it may be that our concept of *consciousness* is recognitional in that it derives from a capacity to introspectively recognize conscious states. But it is arguably not response-dependent: rather, we are directly presented with a certain quality, understand what that quality is, and refer to it. One could suggest that the same goes for perceptual concepts of color and shape, at least on some views of perception. I think these are special cases, though, restricted to phenomenal qualities and to primary and secondary qualities directly presented in perception and to complex properties deriving directly from these (a recognitional concept of a brown rectangle, perhaps). In these cases, the relevant information will be directly available in *PQTI*.

One might then wonder: could there be analogous qualitative concepts for high-level properties such as *triffid*? On examination the answer seems to be no: even if there is high-level perception, concepts such as *triffid* serve to pick out an underlying kind that brings about the relevant response, and whose referent is correspondingly scrutable.[24] There may be some hybrid qualitative/response-dependent concepts: a recognitional concept of a green triffid, perhaps. It may even be that many high-level recognitional concepts are hybrid in this way, involving qualitative constraints as well as a response-dependent element. But as with qualitative concepts and response-dependent concepts taken alone, these hybrid concepts will pose no problem for scrutability.

Second, we can consider nonrecognitional concepts, for which possession of the concept does not derive from a corresponding recognitional capacity. More broadly, I will consider recognitional capacities involving concepts whose possession does not derive from that capacity: they might be nonrecognitional concepts, or they might be recognitional concepts whose possession derives from some different recognitional capacity. Capacities of this sort divide into two groups: conceptual and empirical recognitional capacities.

---

[24] In the framework of E13: where response-dependent concepts are epistemically nonrigid, with a primary intension that picks out whatever causes a relevant response in a given scenario, qualitative concepts are epistemically rigid, with a primary intension that picks out the same property in every scenario. In the terminology of chapter 8, we might also say that qualitative concepts are acquaintance concepts. The difference between *triffid* and *conscious* here corresponds to the fact that we have an epistemically rigid concept (or an acquaintance concept) for consciousness but not for triffidity. It is arguable that we also have epistemically rigid nomic and normative concepts, so one might wonder whether these might also count as qualitative recognitional concepts. I am inclined to think that they do not, as recognition does not play the same role in concept possession in these cases. In any case I discuss the place of these concepts with respect to scrutability elsewhere, in chapters 6 and 7. For another angle on qualitative and response-dependent recognitional concepts, see Stephen Yablo's discussion of 'oval' in 'Coulda, Woulda, Shoulda' and my response in 'Does Conceivability Entail Possibility?'

Conceptual recognitional capacities are processes of a priori recognition in which the capacity to recognize instances derives directly from possession of the concept. We saw in chapter 1 that concepts come along with conditional abilities to apply the concept to fully specified cases. These abilities can be seen as conceptual recognitional capacities in a broad sense: broad in that these capacities may involve inference and reasoning and may be applied to hypothetical cases. When these abilities are applied non-inferentially to actual cases, they count as conceptual recognitional capacities in a narrower sense. Consider the concept *has more than two parts*. In recognizing an object as having more than two parts, one might simply deploy this concept in an immediate way in perception or recognition, recognizing the object as having more than two parts not on the basis of contingently associated features, but rather on the basis of grasping the concept itself.

Because conceptual recognition is a sort of a priori process, it poses little threat to scrutability: conceptual recognition is itself available for the purposes of a priori scrutability. One might worry about cases in which conceptual recognition is deployed in perception, yielding a high-level perceptual experience of an object as having more than two parts, say. We saw earlier that insofar as we have to rely on high-level perceptual experience, there is a potential threat to conditional and a priori scrutability from *PQTI*. But for any such deployment in perception, there will be a corresponding case in which the capacity is deployed postperceptually in high-level recognition. This use of the capacity then yields conditional and a priori scrutability.

Perhaps the hardest cases involve *empirical* recognitional capacities. These involve nonrecognitional concepts deployed recognitionally, not simply a priori on the basis of a grasp of the concept, but empirically on the basis of associated features. For example, a subject might have a pre-existing concept of *computer* or *astronaut* or *gay*, and acquire a capacity to recognize exemplars of the concept based on various associated features. For example, one might have a concept of an astronaut as someone who goes into space, and a capacity to recognize astronauts based on their distinctive spacesuits.

Crucially: where any empirical recognitional capacities for noncore properties are concerned, there is an alternative route to identifying instances of the property that does not involve the recognitional capacity. Insofar as the recognitional capacity can be used to gain knowledge about instances of the properties, the alternative route can also be used to gain the same sort of knowledge. For example, it is possible to recognitionally identify astronauts on the basis of spacesuits, but it is also possible to identify astronauts in other, more conclusive ways, for example by examining their histories and their capabilities. It is plausible that any truths that are knowable the first way are knowable the second way. In some cases, the alternative route will be a conceptual recognitional capacity, perhaps in the broad sense involving reasoning and inference. In other cases it will be another empirical recognitional capacity that relies on fewer contingently associated features than the original capacity. If something like this is always the case, then any given empirical recognitional capacities will be dispensable. By repeating the process, one can ultimately dispense with arbitrary empirical recognitional capacities.

In fact, an alternative route of this sort appears to be involved in the acquisition of almost any empirical recognitional capacity. Any empirical recognitional capacity for a target property—say, for being an astronaut—involves sensitivity to certain associated features (say, wearing a spacesuit). Acquiring the capacity involves connecting the features to the target property. Making this connection will almost always involve some prior way of identifying the target property. If so, there will be an alternative route to identifying the target property that does not involve the empirical recognitional capacity.

This does not yet tell us that the alternative route is a good route. But we might extend the argument above as follows. Let us say that an empirical recognitional capacity is *justifying* when it generates justified recognitional beliefs. Typically, when a justifying recognitional capacity is acquired, there will be prior evidence that things with the associated features usually have the target property. Let us say that when such evidence exists, the capacity is *grounded*.[25] So typically, when an empirical recognitional capacity is justifying, it is grounded. When a capacity is grounded, it is dispensable: one has an alternative route to knowledge of the target property. In particular, any knowledge that can be obtained using the recognitional capacity can instead be obtained by identifying the associated features and using the prior evidence to infer the presence of the target property.

One might respond here by saying that a capacity can be justifying without being grounded. If one holds a reliabilist view of justification, one might hold that a capacity could come to be reliable (and therefore justifying) even though it is entirely a matter of luck that the capacity is reliable. However, these cases are likely to be rare: for every lucky reliable capacity, we should expect many unreliable capacities. So given that most of our recognitional capacities are reliable, we should expect that most are grounded. Perhaps there will be a small minority of

---

[25] If one talks of belief-forming processes being justified, as I do in 4.9, it is natural to say that when the capacity is grounded in prior evidence in this way, the recognitional process is justified by the prior evidence. In this way certain recognitional judgments might themselves be seen as justified by the relevant prior evidence. Where high-level perception is concerned, we might even see the perceptual experience produced by such recognitional processes as justified (or proto-justified in the sense of E15) by the prior evidence. (See also E4, and Siegel forthcoming on the epistemological impact of the etiology of experience.) None of these epistemological claims are required for the current response, however. Likewise the response does not need the epistemological claim that for a capacity to produce justified beliefs it must itself be justified or grounded.

ungrounded reliable recognitional capacities, but even in these cases it is natural to expect that a grounded capacity for the same property will at least be possible, insofar as the (ordinary macroscopic) property involved is of a piece with those involved in grounded capacities. If there are special cases involving non-ordinary properties (luckily reliable recognitional capacities for ghosts or other minds, say), these will fall under the scope of the hard cases considered in chapter 6.

It might be suggested that natural selection could produce an innate reliable capacity, weeding out unreliable capacities and thereby providing a non-lucky basis for the remaining reliable capacities. I think that it is likely that if there are innate concepts at all, the great majority of innate concepts involved in recognitional capacities are recognitional concepts. Where nonrecognitional concepts are involved, we can expect that in typical cases the evolutionary environment will contain evidence of a connection between the recognized property and the associated features, evidence that could also be exploited in using a Cosmoscope. The same goes for other selection and feedback mechanisms that might play a role in the grounding of a reliable capacity. As before, exceptions are imaginable, but insofar as the properties involved are similar in kind to those involved in grounded capacities, we can expect that grounded capacities will also be possible here.

In some cases, the alternative route will involve testimony: for example, a child acquires a recognitional capacity for astronauts by initially being told that certain people are astronauts. But as discussed in section 5, the testimony itself will ultimately have to be grounded in some distinct nontestimonial route. So once again an alternative nontestimonial route to knowledge will always be available. Using this reasoning, we can eliminate high-level empirical recognitional capacities one at a time in favor of alternative routes, avoiding potential circles if we step back far enough. This makes a case that all such capacities are dispensable in favor of conceptual recognitional capacities, capacities involving recognitional concepts, and nonrecognitional capacities.

Putting the pieces together: where does this leave the dispensability argument from earlier? I have argued that empirical recognitional capacities are dispensable in scrutability from *PQI*. Conceptual recognitional capacities may not be dispensable, but their use is consistent with a priori scrutability so they are not problematic. Capacities involving qualitative recognitional concepts are not problematic and are also dispensable as *PQI* supplies the relevant information. Capacities involving response-dependent recognitional concepts are dispensable in the sense that their results are scrutable from information about the responses they provide, information that will also be scrutable from *PQI*. If this is right, any problematic capacities here are dispensable for the purposes of scrutability, and the capacities in question do not pose an obstacle to scrutability.

Furthermore, it is reasonable to hold that all recognitional capacities involve fall into these classes. Some recognitional capacities may involve a combination of two or three of them: a capacity to recognize chairs may well involve an element of all three, for example. But when a combination is involved, combined reasoning along the lines above will establish that scrutability is not threatened.

The arguments I have given here are not knockdown arguments, but I think they suffice to put the burden onto the proponent of the objection. In particular, an opponent needs to exhibit an ordinary (non-Fitchian, nonremote) truth that can be known only by using a problematic high-level recognitional capacity. I think that given the ubiquity of alternative routes, it will be very hard to do this. For any truth that we come to know using a high-level recognitional capacity, we could also come to know it by puzzling over a Cosmoscope and reasoning using the concepts involved. If this is right, then high-level recognitional capacities do not pose a threat to scrutability.

8 The objection from counterfactuals

A pressing objection holds that scrutability of many ordinary truths will give a central role to knowledge of counterfactuals. To determine whether an object is red, for example, one may need to determine what sort of experiences it produces under certain counterfactual circumstances. To know whether a glass is fragile, one arguably needs to know whether it would break if it were hit in the right way. An opponent might then object that the truth of the relevant counterfactuals is not scrutable from *PQI*.

Now, some counterfactual truths are certainly scrutable from *PQI*. Truths about counterfactual dependence among physical properties and between physical and phenomenal properties have been explicitly built into *PQI*. So one can certainly know truths of the sort: if an object with such-and-such macrophysical properties were placed in such-and-such a position, it would move at such-and-such rate. And one could easily enough come to know truths such as: if there were to be such-and-such microphysical configuration [in my brain], I would have such-and-such experience. More generally, let us say that *PQI*-counterfactuals are counterfactuals that use only the vocabulary used in *PQI*. Then it is plausible that all *PQI*-counterfactuals are scrutable from *PQI*. But the objector might hold that knowledge of *PQI*-counterfactuals will not suffice for knowledge of many ordinary counterfactual-involving truths.

To evaluate the objection, we may assume that all ordinary non-counterfactual-involving truths are scrutable from *PQI*. In fact, we may as well assume a generalized version of this thesis, so that given a *PQI*-style description of various nearby worlds (perhaps along with *PQI* itself as a description of the actual world), we can determine the truth-value of arbitrary ordinary non-counterfactual-involving sentences there. We can then consider an ordinary counterfactual truth of the form 'If A were the case, C would be the case'. Given our assumptions, the truth-values of A and C are scrutable from PQI in the actual world, and from related descriptions in other nearby worlds. One might think that if one combines this with the scrutability of PQI-counterfactuals, these counterfactuals will straightforwardly be scrutable. But matters are not quite this clear.

The first worry arises from the grain of the antecedent A. If A is maximally precise, so that it is satisfied in only one nearby world, there will be no problem: with the aid of the Cosmoscope we can find the world, determine its PQI-description, and from there determine the truth or falsity of C in that world. But A will typically be satisfied in an enormous (perhaps infinite) number of nearby worlds. Given any one of these worlds, we could use the Cosmoscope to determine whether C is true or false in it. But it might take an infinite amount of work to determine precisely which A-worlds are C-worlds. And even given that information, it takes work to move from there to facts about the truth or falsity of the original counterfactual, and it is not entirely obvious that the Cosmoscope can do this work.

Things are most straightforward if we (i) assume a Lewis-Stalnaker semantics for counterfactuals, according to which the counterfactual 'If A then C' is true iff C is true in all of the nearest A-worlds, and (ii) if we assume that we or the Cosmoscope can determine which A-worlds are closest to our own, and (iii) if we assume that either we or the Cosmoscope can determine whether all the worlds in that class are C-worlds. Regarding (ii) and (iii), it is not clear that we are entitled to assume that the Cosmoscope can do this work for us, as closeness may be a context-dependent relation that is not antecedently programmable into the Cosmoscope, and scrutability of ordinary truths such as C is typically done by the user rather than the Cosmoscope. So we may require an idealization that allows the user to examine an infinite number of worlds at once here. Still, large idealizations such as this are already needed for certain purposes, as we have seen, and there is no problem in principle with having the user determine closeness. As for (i), it is not obvious that the Lewis-Stalnaker semantics is correct, but it is arguable that a similar method will work even if it is not. All we need is the claim that the truth-value of counterfactuals is scrutable from facts about the distribution of the truth-values of C and A across worlds, and from facts about certain relations between those worlds and ours, where the relevant facts about worlds are themselves scrutable from PQI descriptions. Such a claim is reasonably plausible.

There is one important residual issue. It is arguable that to determine the truth-value of many ordinary truths, one has to determine the truth-value of counterfactuals whose antecedents concern *action*. For the case of colors, one arguably needs to know how things will look if one looks at them. For a tactile predicate, one needs to know how something will feel if one touches it. Furthermore, the argument from knowability relies on the claim that one *could* come to know certain truths, presumably by undergoing a certain course of action. But now, it is not clear that truths about action are themselves scrutable from *PQI*. They are certainly not included among ordinary truths, and raise various distinctive issues. If they are not so scrutable, then the argument in the previous paragraph does not apply. So it may seem that without establishing that truths about action are scrutable from *PQI*, we cannot establish that various ordinary truths are scrutable from *PQI*.

Now, I will consider the scrutability of truths about action in chapter 6. I will argue that such truths are in fact scrutable from *PQI*. But if they are not, then *PQI* needs to be supplemented in any case, perhaps directly by truths about action, or perhaps by some intermediary such as intentional truths. Either way, then, even before getting to issues about counterfactuals, we will have a base from which truths about action are scrutable. Given this much, the argument above will establish that the relevant counterfactuals are scrutable too.

In light of all this, one might wonder just how or whether one might realistically use a Cosmoscope to ascertain the relevant truths. Of course the original idealized thesis does not require realism: if infinitary reasoning and perhaps an expanded base can do the job, that is good enough. But it remains interesting to ask: is there any hope for an ordinary subject using a version of the original Cosmoscope? I am inclined to think that there is, at least if we assume that there is a reasonably substantial phenomenology of action. Where counterfactuals involving action are concerned, one might get the subject to imagine performing the action in question (or perhaps simply to perform it, within a convincing enough holographic recreation). One could then suppose that the Cosmoscope can determine the phenomenology of the action itself from the subject's imaginative act. This is roughly the reverse of the process in which a Cosmoscope induces an imaginative recreation of phenomenal states in the subject, and is justified on the grounds that any subject that can correctly imagine performing an action can know what it is like to perform that action. The Cosmoscope could then determine the truth-value of *PQI*-counterfactuals such as: if the subject were to have that action experience, such-and-such *PQI*-consequences would ensue. Given this much, it could then display relevant consequences for the subject, enabling the subject to determine whether the consequent is true or false, or perhaps indeterminate.

A tricky residual issue is that the truth-value of this sort of *PQI*-counterfactual may be context-dependent. For the Cosmoscope to do the job, we may need to fix the relevant contextual parameters (a closeness relation between worlds, say) in advance, which may limit its usefulness in different contexts. Still, even a fixed closeness relation will give us considerable guidance concerning counterfactual situations. So one may be able to get a long way with a Cosmoscope of this sort, even without appealing to the idealized reasoning suggested earlier.

Totality Truths and Indexical Truths

A ny scrutability base needs to provide a base for negative truths, such as 'There are no ghosts', and indexical truths, such as 'It is now 2012'. For reasons that we have seen, bases consisting of ordinary positive truths, such as P and Q, do not suffice for the scrutability of these truths. I have handled this matter by adding a totality sentence T, and a small class of indexical sentences I, to the scrutability base. Here I will discuss the correct formulation of T and I.

The totality sentence T is essentially a 'that's-all' truth, or a 'stop clause': it says that the world contains no more than it needs to in order to accommodate the other elements. Such a truth is familiar from debates over physicalism and supervenience. One might try formulating physicalism as the thesis that microphysical truths necessitate all truths: that is, for all truths S, $P \to S$ is necessary (where here we understand P as the conjunction of all microphysical truths). But this is not quite right. Where S is 'There are no ghosts', then even if physicalism is true and S is true, $P \to S$ is not necessary. The truth of physicalism about our world is consistent with the existence of other possible worlds in which there are nonphysical ghosts as well as the physical character specified by P.

To handle this, one can suggest instead that physicalism requires that for all truths S, $PT \to S$ is necessary, where T is a totality sentence (or proposition), saying 'that's all'. In effect, T has the form $T(P)$. (More generally, a totality statement will usually have the form $T(F)$, for some sentence or proposition F.) One can think of $T(P)$ as saying that our world is a *minimal* world in which P is true.[1]

Here the idea is that we have a partial ordering relation among worlds. We might say that a world w_1 *outstrips* another world w_2 if w_1 includes a duplicate of w_2 as a proper part. For example, a P-world in which there are ghosts

[1] For ease of discussion, I set aside the fact that one also wants physicalism to be true in some worlds where P is false, and I set aside doubts about whether supervenience suffices for physicalism, as these issues are largely irrelevant to the current issue of defining T. One could equally speak of 'supervenience physicalism' or 'supervenience P-physicalism' for present purposes.

outstrips a purely physical P-world. Likewise, a P-world in which some people are conscious outstrips an otherwise identical P-world in which there is no consciousness, assuming both sorts of world are possible. We can then say that a minimal P-world is a P-world that outstrips no other P-world. The ghost world is not a minimal P-world, so it is not a world in which PT is true. So even though 'There are no ghosts' is not necessitated by P, it may well be necessitated by PT.

One can also proceed in other ways. For example, one can say that S is a *positive* sentence iff for all w, if S holds in w, S also holds in all worlds that outstrip w. (Note that a positive sentence here should not be understood just as one that does not contain a negation. For example, 'All life is made of DNA' and 'The universe has such-and-such mass' are probably not positive on the sense I have defined, as they could be falsified by adding something to the world.) One could then stipulate that T is the thesis that all positive truths are necessitated by P. This T is somewhat weaker than the previous formulation (it does not require the truth of P), but given weak assumptions, it still has the crucial property that if PT is true, PT necessitates all truths.

(Here it suffices to assume (i) the S5 principle that when S is possible, it is necessary that S is possible, (ii) the thesis that if S is positive, it is necessary that S is positive, (iii) the thesis that all truths are necessitated (entailed) by positive and anti-positive truths. Here an anti-positive truth is a true negation of a positive sentence. To see this, first note that PT entails that if S is positive and not entailed by P, S is false. Further, given (i) and (ii), when S is positive and not entailed by P, it is necessary that S is positive and not entailed by P. So when S has this property, PT entails $\sim S$. Now when PT is true and $\sim S$ is an anti-positive truth, S has this property. So if PT is true, PT entails all anti-positive truths (by this result) as well as all positive truths (by definition of T). So by (iii), if PT is true, it entails all truths.)

Physicalism (at least when restricted to our world, in which P is the complete microphysical truth) could then be formulated as the thesis that PT necessitates all truths, or simply as the thesis that P necessitates all positive truths. Note that given P, T is equivalent to the truth of physicalism itself. In essence, physicalism is equivalent to the thesis that the conjunction of microphysical truths with the truth of physicalism necessitates all truths.

In this definition of T and the previous one, the notion of outstripping is taken as basic. Alternatively, one can take the notion of a positive sentence as basic, and define outstripping in terms of it: w_1 outstrips w_2 iff all positive sentences true of w_2 are true of w_1 but not vice versa. This has the advantage that the basic notion does not require the framework of possible worlds. It is arguable that we have an intuitive grasp of the notion of a positive sentence that is independent of that framework. But in any case, in this area, as in related areas such as the question of defining intrinsic properties, it appears that one has to take some notion as basic.[2]

Where scrutability rather than supervenience is concerned, analogous issues arise. PQ does not imply 'There are no ghosts', but PQT might imply 'There are no ghosts'. The residual question is how to formulate T. One might try taking T to be exactly the same as one of the versions of T suggested above, holding for example that our world is a minimal P-world. This *might* work: it is reasonably plausible that 'There are no ghosts' (and so on) is a priori scrutable from the claim that our world is a minimal PQ-world. But one might worry that one has imported an extraneous modal element into the otherwise epistemological scrutability thesis. And one can imagine philosophical views on which things could go wrong. For example, some views of modality have the consequence that one cannot rule out a priori that it is metaphysically necessary that if PQ obtains, there are ghosts. Given such a view, it is not ruled out a priori that a minimal PQ-world contains ghosts, so the scrutability claim above will fail. I think that such views are false (and indeed can be ruled out a priori), but it is probably best to avoid this issue by removing the modal element from T.

The obvious alternative is to convert all modal elements to epistemic elements in the characterization of T. So T could say that the actual scenario is a minimal PQ-scenario, one that is outstripped by no other PQ-scenario. One worry here is that the notion of a scenario, the epistemic analog of a possible world, is not as familiar or as well-understood as the notion of a possible world, and it might be preferable not to assume it at this point. So it is probably best to go with a version of the alternative above, with T saying that all positive truths are implied by PQ.

As before, instead of defining positiveness in terms of worlds or scenarios, one can take the notion of a positive sentence as basic and intuitive. But the essential idea, for our purposes, is that a positive sentence is one that could not *conceivably* be falsified by adding something to the world while leaving the rest of the world as it is. It might be that on some views this will come apart from the notion of a positive truth defined in terms of worlds. For example, if it is necessary that there is an omniscient being, then 'There are no omniscient beings' will be positive in the modal sense: if true in a world, it will be true in all worlds that outstrip that world. But if it is also conceivable that there is no omniscient being, then 'There are no omniscient beings' will not be positive in the current sense. Formally, it can be true in a scenario while false in an outstripping scenario. Intuitively, it is conceivable that the sentence could be falsified by adding character to the world while leaving the rest of the world as it is.

---

[2] One might also define positive sentences as those that attribute only intrinsic properties. This notion is somewhat stronger than the previous notion, and requires some unpacking, but it is arguable that a version of T invoking this notion will suffice for our purposes.

From *PQT* in this sense, it follows from reasonable assumptions that all truths are a priori scrutable from *PQT*. The assumptions required here are analogs of those in the case of necessitation above. They are (i) the S5 thesis that if *S* is not a priori, it is a priori that *S* is not a priori, (ii) the thesis that all truths are a priori scrutable from positive and anti-positive truths, (iii) the thesis that if *S* is positive, it is a priori that *S* is positive. The proof is as before. The S5 thesis is reasonably plausible given the idealized notion of apriority, although not completely obvious.[3] Without the S5 thesis, the resulting counterexamples to (ii) will require that the positive truths in the base be expanded by further negative truths, and not just by *T*.

Of course *T* is itself a scrutability thesis. In fact, given *PQ* and the assumptions above, *T* is equivalent to the original scrutability thesis, holding that all truths are scrutable from *PQT*. This parallels the case of physicalism, in which (given *P*) *T* was itself equivalent to the thesis of physicalism. One might think that building the scrutability thesis itself into the base somehow trivializes the thesis, but it does not do so in this case any more than in the case of physicalism. If *D* does not imply all positive truths, then *DT* will not imply all positive truths either. Of course *DT* implies that *DT* implies all truths (where 'all truths' has narrow scope), but this thesis must be distinguished from the thesis that for all truths *S*, *DT* implies that *DT* implies *S* (where 'all truths' has wide scope). Only the wide-scope thesis would suggest a trivialization of the scrutability thesis (it would immediately lead to the thesis that for all truths *S*, *DT* implies *S*), but

---

[3] The S4 thesis that $Ap \rightarrow AAp$ (where *A* is an apriority operator) is very plausible: when a priori reasoning leads one to *p*, then sufficient reflection (even without introspection) will indicate a priori that a priori reasoning can lead one to *p*. Nothing as simple as this works for the S5 thesis: a corresponding method would have to involve surveying all a priori reasoning processes and coming to know that they do not lead to *p*. There are obvious problems with the idea that an a priori reasoning process could survey all a priori reasoning processes, especially if there is a series of ever-more-powerful such processes with no maximal element.

Still, for most empirical truths (external-world truths such as 'There are chairs', for example) it is very plausibly a priori that one could not know a priori that *p*, even without surveying all a priori reasoning processes. In these cases there are clear positive scenarios in which *p* is false (in which there are no chairs) and it is plausible that we can grasp their coherence in a way that enables us to know that they cannot conclusively be ruled out a priori. In effect, the non-apriority of *p* is accompanied by the positive conceivability of ~*p*, which enables us to know that *p* is not conclusive a priori. If this connection between non-apriority and positive conceivability holds in general (as I have suggested in 'Does Conceivability Entail Possibility?'), it may give us reason to accept the S5 principle.

In the case of mathematical truths, one might worry that apriority is the same as provability, and we know that the S5 thesis fails for provability. Given Gödel's theorem and consistency, there are unprovable truths (in a given system) that are not provably unprovable. But as I will argue in chapter 6, idealized apriority should not be equated with provability, and Gödelian reasons for believing in unprovable mathematical truths do not generate reasons for believing in non-apriori mathematical truths. So the reasons for doubting S5 here do not generalize to apriority.

whereas the narrow-scope thesis is true for all D, the wide-scope thesis is false for almost all D. So there is no trivialization worry here.

One might worry about the vocabulary needed to formulate T, including such notions as apriority, positiveness, and that of a sentence. Do we need to use all these in a minimal scrutability base? One can dispense with quantifying over sentences if one treats apriority and positiveness as operators (A, pos) rather than metalinguistic predicates: so T could be a conjunction of all sentences of the form $(S \mathrel{\&} pos(S)) \to A(PQ \to S)$, or perhaps all sentences of the form $(S \to A(PQ \to S))$ where S is positive. One might get rid of positiveness in favor of the notion of intrinsicness, but here we are still in the same vicinity. One might get rid of apriority in favor of a notion such as necessity, at least if one thinks that there are a priori ties between necessity and apriority (as I do). One could also attempt to invoke a primitive 'that's-all' operator T, as in $T(PQ)$, but it is at least arguable that our grip on T (at least on the sort of T required to do the relevant work) depends on our grip on notions such as positiveness and of apriority.

A promising strategy is to dispense with both positiveness and apriority in favor of a notion of fundamentality. Here T might say that such-and-such are all the fundamental truths. If one accepts that it is a priori that all positive truths are scrutable from fundamental truths, and if T itself (or other versions of a that's-all clause) is not a fundamental truth, then this version of T will suffice for our purposes. Here one could understand fundamentality as metaphysical fundamentality, if one holds that Fundamental Scrutability is a priori (as I do). Another strategy understands fundamentality as conceptual fundamentality, although this strategy may require replacing P by other base sentences that are more plausibly conceptually fundamental (as in chapter 7). One might try further to dispense even with the notion of fundamentality, and of any other notion in the vicinity, but I do not presently see how this would be done.

One might also worry that T makes P and Q redundant, as T implies the other three. This is so for some formulations of T, for example as the claim that ours is a minimal PQ-scenario. But if formulated as the claim that all positive truths are implied by PQ, T does not itself imply P and Q: T could be true in an empty scenario or a scenario with physics and no consciousness, for example. In any case, there would be no real problem if the base were to consist of the single complex sentence $T(PQI)$ instead of the large class $PQTI$, but for various purposes (especially those formulations of scrutability in which we appeal to subclasses of the base class) it is useful to have the larger class available.

Another issue concerns the relative priority of T and I. In the case of supervenience, there is no need to use I to define T, but in the case of scrutability I plays a more central role. The reason is that indexical truths are plausibly necessitated by non-indexical truths, but are usually not implied by them. For example, given that 'I am David Chalmers' is necessary and a posteriori, 'I am Australian' is necessitated but not implied by 'David Chalmers is Australian'. Correspondingly, it is reasonably plausible that 'I am Australian' is necessitated by PQ, but it is not implied by PQ. Given that this indexical truth (or something like it) is positive, not all positive indexical truths are implied by PQ. If so, a version of T that says that PQ implies all positive truths is false. One could modify T so that it says that all positive truths are implied by PQI. But defining T in terms of I leads to a worry about circularity, given that I is constrained by T, as discussed shortly. Perhaps the best solution is to instead modify T so that it says that PQ implies all positive non-indexical truths. Here 'indexical' needs to be understood in a broad way to include terms such as 'water', given that 'water is H_2O' is arguably implied by PQI but not by PQ. The simplest way to handle this is to characterize non-indexicality as semantic neutrality, where this notion is defined in the fourteenth excursus.[4]

As for I, this will consist of at least two sentences of the form 'I am the D_1' and 'Now is the D_2'. Here 'The D_1' and 'The D_2' are non-indexical definite descriptions (ideally in the vocabulary of P and Q) that are uniquely satisfied by the subject and the time, if there are such descriptions. We should also require that 'There is exactly one D_1' is scrutable from PQT alone. Then as long as non-indexical truths of the form 'The D_1 is D_2' are themselves scrutable from PQT, then further truths such as 'I am D_2' will be scrutable from $PQTI$.

If the actual world has certain symmetries, appropriate descriptions D_1 and D_2 may not exist. If the world involves an eternal recurrence, or a sort of mirror symmetry, then there may be no non-indexical description D_1 that uniquely picks out a given subject: any such description will also pick out the subject's counterparts in the other cycle or component. There will be uniquely identifying indexical descriptions (e.g. 'The owner of my house'), but these may not help with scrutability. In this case, the best one can do is use a non-uniquely identifying description, 'I am a D_2' that is satisfied by only me and the relevant counterparts. Then any truth of the form 'I am F' will be scrutable, as long as truths of the form 'Every D_2 is F' are scrutable. The symmetries pose no obstacle to the latter, so they pose no obstacle to the former. The same goes for truths of the form 'Now is G', and other indexical truths deriving from these. So even if the world contains symmetries of this sort, the scrutability thesis is unthreatened.

---

[4] Alternatively, one could try making I entirely prior to T by requiring that where I consists of 'I am the D_1' and 'Now is the D_2', the sentence 'There is exactly one D_1 and one D_2' is scrutable from PQ, rather than from PQT. But it is unclear that this negative truth will be scrutable from the positive PQ. As a third alternative, one could require that T and I mutually constrain each other by requiring that 'There is exactly one D_1 and one D_2' is scrutable from PQT, where T says that all positive truths are scrutable from PQI. There is a danger of trivialization for some choices of D_1 and D_2, but an appropriate choice of these should still do the job. This path has the advantage of not requiring an explicit appeal to the notion of semantic neutrality.

4

The Case for A Priori Scrutability

1 From Conditional to A Priori Scrutability

The arguments in the previous chapter—the Cosmoscope argument, the argument from elimination, and the argument from knowability—were primarily put forward as arguments for a restricted version of Conditional Scrutability: all ordinary truths are conditionally scrutable (whether nonconclusively or conclusively) from $PQTI$. In this chapter I will assume that those arguments are successful, and will argue from there to a corresponding version of A Priori Scrutability.

The relevant version of A Priori Scrutability says that for all ordinary truths M, it is a priori that if $PQTI$, then M. More precisely: for all ordinary subjects s at times t, and for all ordinary truths M in the context of s at t, the material conditional $PQTI \rightarrow M$ (where $PQTI$ specifies s and t) is a priori for s at t.[1]

To say that a sentence S is a priori for s at t is to say, roughly, that at t, s is in a position to know S with justification independent of experience. Here 'independent of experience' excludes justification from empirical sources such as perception and introspection. So A Priori Scrutability claims that one can know the conditional $PQTI \rightarrow M$ without empirical justification. As usual, 'in a position to know' allows idealization away from contingent cognitive limitations. As discussed at the start of chapter 2, one can distinguish conclusive a priori knowledge, which requires being in a position to know S a priori with certainty, from nonconclusive a priori knowledge, which is neutral on certainty. In this chapter I will argue for both conclusive and nonconclusive versions of A Priori Scrutability.

---

[1] Throughout this chapter I follow the convention established at the start of chapter 2: when an expression for a set of sentences occurs in a context where a sentence would be appropriate, such as in the antecedent of a material conditional, it stands for a conjunction of all the sentences in that set.

I discuss these matters and other issues concerning the definition of the a priori at greater length in the seventh excursus.

One might initially argue from Conditional Scrutability to A Priori Scrutability as follows. If Conditional Scrutability is true, then one is in a position to know from the armchair that if *PQTI*, then *M*. If one can know from the armchair that if *A*, then *B*, one can also know from the armchair that it is not the case that *A* is true and *B* is false. It follows that one can know the material conditional *PQTI* → *M* from the armchair. So one can know it a priori.[2] One can argue from Conclusive Conditional Scrutability (involving knowledge with certainty) to Conclusive A Priori Scrutability in the same way.

Here the obvious worry is that armchair knowledge does not entail a priori knowledge. Conditional Scrutability allows that the justification of a conditional belief (and rational conditional credences) may depend on a subject's existing empirical evidence and beliefs. So any corresponding knowledge of the material conditional *A* → *B* may likewise depend on existing empirical evidence or beliefs. The conditional will be knowable from the armchair, in that the subject need not go out and acquire new empirical evidence, but it need not be knowable a priori. So one cannot make a direct inference from Conditional Scrutability to A Priori Scrutability.

In their arguments against theses akin to A Priori Scrutability, Ned Block and Robert Stalnaker (1999) emphasize this gap. They suggest that although conditionals from scenario specifications to truths such as 'water is H_2O' are knowable from the armchair, they are not knowable a priori. They hold that knowledge of these conditionals depends essentially on considerations about simplicity (leading us to identify water with a natural kind, for example), and that these considerations depend essentially on background empirical knowledge: for example, knowledge that the world is simple.

In what follows, I build on the arguments for Conditional Scrutability to yield arguments for A Priori Scrutability. I will do this by arguing that justification for the conditional knowledge that if *PQTI*, then *M* is not essentially empirical. That is, one is in a position to have a priori conditional knowledge that if *PQTI*, then

---

[2] In the inference from conditional knowledge to knowledge of the material conditional, one might worry about cases where one has a high rational credence in *B* given *A* without knowing *A* → *B*: for example, a case where *A* = 'I have one ticket in a fair lottery with *n* tickets' and *B* is 'I will not win the lottery'. But these are equally cases in which one lacks conditional knowledge that if *A* then *B*. If we formulate Conditional Scrutability in terms of high rational credence, there is no problem as long as we understand 'high' as 'high enough for conditional knowledge' (where the threshold may depend on the case). Something similar goes for the inference from conditional certainty to certainty in the material conditional. If we formulate Conclusive Conditional Scrutability by requiring rational credence of 1 in *B* given *A*, then the inference to Conditional A Priori Scrutability may break down in cases where credence 1 does not reflect certainty: say *A* = '*x* is a randomly chosen real number' and *B* = '*x* is irrational'. But the arguments in the last chapter for credence 1 in *M* given *PQTI* were also arguments for certainty.

M. The same goes for conditional knowledge with certainty. If this is right, then by the reasoning above it follows that one is in a position to know the material conditional $PQTI \to M$ a priori, and indeed to know it with certainty.

In the next section, I argue that in the case for Conditional Scrutability, existing empirical beliefs play no essential justifying role. In section 3, I argue that even if empirical beliefs do play such a role, they can be incorporated into a base that will then support a priori conditional knowledge. In section 4, I offer a diagnostic to help determine whether putative empirical evidence (such as evidence that the world is simple in the case above) plays a merely causal role, a mediating role, or a justifying role in knowledge of a scrutability conditional. In later sections I discuss Generalized A Priori Scrutability and address objections.

2 The argument from suspension of belief

An initial, somewhat flat-footed argument extends the arguments in chapter 3 as follows. Before supposing $PQTI$, one could engage in a Cartesian suspension of all empirical beliefs. Even under such a suspension, the arguments in chapter 3 will still go through. That is, these arguments suggest that upon supposing $PQTI$ while suspending empirical belief one could rationally conclude M on that basis just as well as one could have without the suspension. For example, one could use a Cosmoscope while suspending all empirical beliefs (or at least all except those pertaining to the Cosmoscope) to come to know that if $PQTI$, then M. One could likewise run the argument from elimination with a subject who has suspended empirical beliefs. As for the argument from knowability, any core evidence required to know M will itself be scrutable from $PQTI$, so that it will in effect be available to a subject who suspends empirical belief.

If one can be justified in the conditional belief (that if $PQTI$, then M) even while suspending empirical beliefs, this strongly suggests that empirical beliefs play no essential role in justifying the conditional belief.

It remains possible that one's conditional belief in M given $PQTI$ is justified by experiences rather than by empirical beliefs. To handle this issue, we can note that the justifying role of experiences is plausibly screened off by its role in justifying certain perceptual beliefs and introspective beliefs. So if one suspends judgment concerning all perceptual and introspective beliefs, then one will remove the justifying role of experience. Perhaps there are ways to suspend these beliefs that allow a role for experience to persist, for example in directly justifying nonperceptual beliefs that perceptual beliefs might have justified. But we can stipulate that a full suspension of empirical belief disallows this, in that it removes all perceptual and introspective roles for experience in justifying beliefs. It remains plausible that under such a full suspension of empirical belief, one could have a justified conditional belief in M given $PQTI$. If so, experience plays no essential role in justifying the conditional belief.

I think that this argument gives at least prima facie support to A Priori Scrutability. It is not entirely conclusive, though, as we may be fallible in our reasoning about what counts as suspending all empirical belief. Perhaps the situation that we imagine when we imagine suspending all empirical beliefs is really one in which we suspend a proper subset of empirical beliefs. Perhaps some of the beliefs that are purportedly suspended are still playing a subterranean role in justifying one's reasoning in this scenario. Or perhaps there are empirical beliefs that we do not suspend because we do not realize that they are empirical beliefs.

Still, I think that at least the following is plausible. For any *obviously empirical* belief E, one could suspend judgment in E, and one could still come to be justified in accepting the conditional belief that if $PQTI$ then M, and in accepting the material conditional $PQTI \rightarrow M$. The same goes for any class of obviously empirical beliefs. These will include beliefs about most of the things that are most commonly invoked as empirical evidence: conscious experiences, qualitative properties of objects in the external world, and so on. At most, what is left is a possible role for empirical beliefs that are not obviously empirical.

For example, suppose that someone thinks that some or all of the following beliefs are empirical: two is greater than one, all bachelors are male, everything is self-identical. It is not obvious that one could suspend judgment in *these* beliefs and still be justified in inferring M from $PQTI$ (though it is also not obvious that one could not). So the argument here does not immediately rule out the hypothesis that the inference is justified by empirical beliefs of this sort. Nevertheless, I do not find it plausible that these beliefs are empirical, and empirical justification of this sort would be very different from empirical justification as usually conceived. So if the rest of the argument is successful, then it makes a strong prima facie case against empirical justification.

What if reasoning from perceptual or introspective evidence is itself empirically justified by background experience? If the reasoning survives suspension of one's current empirical background beliefs, this suggests that it is not essentially empirically justified by those beliefs. A remaining possibility is that the reasoning is justified by long-forgotten experience or long-forgotten empirical beliefs, so that suspending current empirical beliefs will not affect the reasoning. I discuss this possibility later in the chapter, under the objection from empirical inference.

3 The argument from frontloading

The most important argument for A Priori Scrutability proceeds by 'frontloading' any empirical evidence E that might play a role in conditional scrutability into the antecedent of one's conditional knowledge.

Suppose that one has conditional knowledge that if *PQTI*, then *M*. Suppose also that this knowledge is justified by some empirical evidence *E*. Then one is plausibly in a position to know that if *PQTI* & *E*, then *M*. Furthermore, *E* will not play an essential role in justifying this conditional knowledge: there is no need for it to do so, as *E* is built into the antecedent, and its justifying role in reaching the conditional conclusion that *M* from the supposition of *PQTI* can be played just as well by supposing it as by believing it. Perhaps the knowledge that if *PQTI* & *E*, then *M* is itself justified by some further evidence, but then one can repeat the process by conjoining this evidence to the antecedent. If one repeats this process for all relevant empirical evidence, one will eventually end up with a large conjunction *F* of evidence statements such that one can know that if *PQTI* & *F*, then *M* without justification from any empirical evidence. That is, one can know 'If *PQTI* & *F*, then *M*' a priori.

This reasoning is especially natural in a Bayesian framework. Suppose that $cr^*(M \mid PQTI)$ is high, and that this credence is justified by some class of empirical evidence sentences *E*. Then $cr^* (M \mid PQTI \,\& \,E)$ will also be high. By an extension of the Bayesian principle of conditionalization (which I will discuss shortly), if acquiring total evidence *E* enables one to have a high rational credence $cr^*(M \mid PQTI)$, then even before acquiring evidence *E*, one is in a position to have a high rational credence $cr^*(M \mid PQTI \,\& \,E)$. So it is plausible that *E* plays no essential role in justifying one's high rational credence $cr^*(M \mid PQTI \,\& \,E)$. By repeating this process, one will end up with a large class of evidence sentences *F* such that a high rational credence $cr^*(M \mid PQTI \,\& \,F)$ is justified a priori.

If our basic empirical evidence (the empirical evidence in which all empirical justification is grounded) consists in phenomenal states, then *F* will itself be implied by *Q*. If so, it follows that a high rational credence $cr^*(M \mid PQTI)$ is justified a priori. If our basic empirical evidence consists in claims about external states of affairs that are implied by *P* (or by *PQTI*), the same applies. If our basic empirical evidence consists in more than this, then *PQTI* & *F* will go some distance beyond *PQTI*. And repeating this process for arbitrary *M* may lead to a larger class *PQTI* & *F** that goes further beyond *PQTI*. But as long as the relevant empirical evidence is itself constrained in form, then *PQTI* & *F** will be a compact scrutability base from which all ordinary truths are a priori scrutable. Only if basic empirical evidence is open-ended—for example, if one must make irreducible appeal to evidence sentences about water, kangaroos, trees, and so on—will there be a problem for scrutability.

At this point, one might appeal to the Core Evidence thesis from chapter 3. This thesis holds that all knowledge is grounded in core evidence: evidence about phenomenal states and primary and secondary qualities. However, as in chapter 3, we do not need a thesis as strong as this, or as strong as the claims in the previous paragraph. Instead we can again appeal to the Core Knowability thesis, which holds that all knowable (non-Fitchian) truths are knowable with grounds in core evidence. It is easy to use the arguments in chapter 3 to extend the Core Knowability thesis to conditional knowledge. We can also argue for a subject-specific version: when s is in a position to know A conditional on B, then s is in a position to know A conditional on B with this knowledge grounded in core evidence.[3]

These versions of the Core Knowability thesis enable an argument from Conditional Knowability to A Priori Scrutability. From Conditional Scrutability, it follows that s is in a position to know M given $PQTI$. The Core Knowability thesis above entails that s is in a position to know M given $PQTI$, with the knowledge grounded in core evidence E. So by the reasoning above (discussed more below), s is in a position to know M given $PQTI$ & E, with justification independent of E. But E was the total relevant empirical evidence, so this justification independent of E will be justification independent of all empirical evidence. So M is a priori scrutable from $PQTI$ & E. Furthermore, $PQTI$ & E is certainly compact, and E is plausibly a priori scrutable from $PQTI$. If so, M is a priori scrutable from $PQTI$.

This argument requires what we might call a *frontloading* principle. A simple frontloading principle holds: if one knows M with justification from E (construing M and E now as sentences), then one can have conditional knowledge of M given E with justification independent of E. Strictly speaking, we need a slightly more complex frontloading principle: if one has conditional knowledge of M given N, with justification from E (perhaps along with other sources F), then one can have conditional knowledge of M given N & E with justification that is independent of E (and that involves no sources outside F). I will focus on the simpler version for ease of discussion, but everything below applies to the more complex version.

We can also put these principles in the probabilistic framework. Simple version: if having a high credence $cr^*(M)$ is justified by E, then having a high conditional credence $cr^*(M \mid E)$ is justified independently of E. Complex version: if having a high credence $cr^*(M \mid N)$ is justified by E, then having a high conditional credence $cr^*(M \mid N$ & $E)$ is justified independently of E.

These frontloading principles have strong intuitive support. One can argue for the simple frontloading principle as follows. Given that E justifies M, then one could in principle (i) suspend judgment concerning E, (ii) suppose (for the purposes of conditional reasoning) that E, (iii) conclude (under this supposition)

[3] It is arguable that there is no analog of Fitchian phenomena for conditional knowledge from $PQTI$. On the analysis in 2.3, Fitchian phenomena are tied to alethically fragile sentences: cases where M is true but properly investigating M would render M false. In a case where if $PQTI$, then M, it is hard to see how properly investigating this conditional could render it false.

that M, with justification provided by E's support for M, and (iv) discharge the supposition, yielding a justified conditional belief in M given E. This conditional belief is justified even though one has suspended judgment concerning E, so that E played no non-suppositional role in its support. So the conditional belief in M given E is justified independently of E.

This argument requires an appeal to suspension of judgment, but here it is just a single act of suspension of judgment concerning a clearly empirical truth, so that many of the concerns in the previous argument do not apply. The main question concerns step (iii): could it be that E's support for M itself somehow depends on E, in a way such that suspending judgment about E also undermines the epistemic connection between E and M? This would be at least odd. Typically, if P's support for Q itself depends on support from some further claim R, then one can combine these elements of support, yielding a combined support by $P \& R$ for Q that does not depend on R's support in this way. On the face of it, in this fashion one could combine all the ways that E provides support into a single support relation that does not depend on E. And typically, we take it that evidential support can be provided equally whether the evidence is accepted (to support a conclusion) or merely supposed (to conditionally support a conclusion).

Indeed, something like this claim is at the foundation of the Bayesian principle of conditionalization. The ordinary principle of conditionalization says (in the relevant version):

Conditionalization: If $cr^*(M \mid E) = \phi$ at t_1, and if one acquires total relevant evidence E between t_1 and t_2, then $cr^*(M) = \phi$ at t_2.

One might think that Conditionalization entails a reverse principle:

Reverse Conditionalization: If $cr^*(M) = \phi$ at t_2, and one acquires total relevant evidence E between t_1 and t_2, then $cr^*(M \mid E) = \phi$ at t_1.

If this principle were correct, then it could be used to support the frontloading argument. Let us take it that rational credences are justified. It would follow that having $cr^*(M \mid E) = \phi$ could be justified independently of E, as the credence is rational at t_1 and one does not possess evidence E then. And the principle has a certain plausibility. After all, if $cr^*(M \mid E)$ had a value other than ϕ at t_1, then conditionalization itself would be violated.[4]

However, reverse conditionalization is not entailed by conditionalization alone. The gap between the two theses arises because it is compatible with

---

[4] It should be noted that if one moves to a framework (such as Jeffrey Conditionalization) on which $cr^*(E)$ can be less than 1 for evidence statements, then one will have to restate the consequent of reverse conditionalization principles to say that $cr^*(M \mid E) \geq \phi$ at t_1. This will still be good enough for the purposes of the argument.

conditionalization that $cr^*(M \mid E)$ at t_1 is undefined. Some versions of Bayesianism require that all conditional and unconditional credences are defined, and these versions will be committed to reverse conditionalization. But there is room in logical space for exceptions. For example, an opponent might suggest that an exception will arise if the subject is unable to even entertain E at t_1 because they lack crucial concepts. Here one might imagine that E specifies a certain sort of color experience, such that one could not even possess the concepts prior to having a relevant sort of experience.

It is not clear that exceptions of this sort threaten the argument from frontloading, however. For a start, it is not clear that there are concepts of this sort. In the case of color, someone could plausibly come to have any phenomenal color concept through brain surgery, without having had the relevant experiences. If so, then we can change events prior to t_1 so that the subject has the concepts in this way, without any relevant new evidence. Then the obstacle to a conditional credence in E given M will be removed, and on acquiring evidence E the subject will presumably come to have the same $cr^*(M)$ at t_2 as before. Here it is plausible that $cr^*(M \mid E)$ will be high and justified independently of E.

To be more precise, we can appeal to a weaker principle:

Diachronic Frontloading: If $cr^*(M) = \phi$ at t_2, and one acquires total relevant evidence E between t_1 and t_2, and $cr^*(M \mid E)$ is defined at t_1, then $cr^*(M \mid E) = \phi$ at t_1.

Diachronic Frontloading is weaker than Reverse Conditionalization, because of the extra requirement that $cr(M \mid E)$ is defined at t_1. Because of this extra requirement, Diachronic Frontloading is certainly entailed by Conditionalization. Furthermore, in the case just mentioned, it appears that $cr^*(M \mid E)$ will be defined: certainly any obstacle due to the possession of concepts will be removed. Then Diachronic Frontloading entails that $cr^*(M \mid E)$ will be high, and justified independently of E. This suggests strongly that $cr^*(M \mid E)$ is justifiable independently of E in the original case.

If there are concepts whose possession requires having certain experiences, the last observation will not go through. But even here, the observation merely suggests an *enabling* role for E in entertaining the conditional belief in M given E. Nothing here suggests a *justifying* role, which is what an opponent of the current argument needs.

Furthermore, one can extend the thesis to cover any remaining cases. Given Diachronic Frontloading, the following closely related Synchronic Frontloading principle is extremely plausible.

Synchronic Frontloading: If $cr^*(M \mid E) = \phi$ at t_2, and one acquires total relevant evidence E between t_1 and t_2, and if $cr^*(M \mid E)$ is defined at t_2, then $cr^*(M \mid E) = \phi$ at t_2, with justification independent of E.

Here we simply change t_1 to t_2 in the latter parts of the statement of Dia-chronic Frontloading. In this case, the conditional probability $cr^*(M \mid E)$ will be *temporally* posterior to the acceptance of evidence E. But the same reasons as before suggest that it is *epistemically* prior to the acceptance of E, and can be supported even without the assumption of E. If so, the argument goes through.

Of course it is formally possible to deny the frontloading principles. One worry about frontloading principles arises from applying them to ordinary knowledge (not conditional knowledge) of truths M such as 'There are electrons' or 'The sun will rise tomorrow'. Suppose I know M, so that $cr^*(M)$ is now high, on the basis of total evidence E. Then the principles suggest that even before acquiring E, $cr^*(M \mid E)$ was high. But E is my total evidence, so this entails that before obtaining any empirical evidence, $cr^*(M \mid E)$ was high. If we are doubtful about Diachronic Frontloading for the reasons above, even Synchronic Front-loading suggests that in one's current state, having a high rational credence $cr^*(M \mid E)$ is justified a priori.

This line of reasoning tends to lead to a view on which there are substantive constraints on the rationality of 'ultimate priors', that is, credences prior to or independent of any empirical evidence. These constraints are substantive in that they go well beyond requiring credence 1 in logical truths, mathematical truths, and other traditional a priori truths. For example, there may need to be con-straints requiring higher credences in various inductively or abductively simple hypotheses compared to corresponding complex hypotheses. A common strand of Bayesian thinking, radical subjectivism, denies that there are any such con-straints on ultimate priors: roughly, any distribution of ultimate priors is equally rational, as long as it involves credence 1 in logical truths (and perhaps mathe-matical truths, analytic truths, and the like). So frontloading principles seem to be in tension with the combination of an anti-skeptical claim (the rational cre-dence in M in our current circumstances is high) and radical subjectivism.

I reject radical subjectivism. I think there are substantive constraints on the rationality of ultimate priors arising from considerations of simplicity and sym-metry, among other sources. Furthermore, if I were a radical subjectivist, I would reject the anti-skeptical principle (as many radical subjectivists do), holding that it is equally rational to accept or reject the relevant truths M, at least if doing so mirrors one's ultimate priors.

The option of rejecting frontloading principles is also available, but it is less attractive, not least because it seems to require rejecting conditionalization. Radical subjectivism suggests that prior to acquiring E, $cr^*(M \mid E)$ will be some-thing like the interval from 0 to 1 (inclusive or exclusive). The anti-skeptical principle says that after acquiring total evidence E, $cr^*(M \mid E)$ is high. This vari-ation in rational credences violates conditionalization. The violations might be motivated in one of two different ways. One could take a coherentist or epistemic conservative line where merely coming to have a certain credence in a hypothesis tends to rationalize that credence. Or one could hold that evidence plays roles that go beyond conditionalization. For example, one could hold that the introduction of new evidence fundamentally reconfigures the support relation between sentences, in a way that was not antecedently present as conditional support.[5]

These denials of conditionalization are at least uncomfortable, however. The coherentist or conservative denial tends to lead in a skeptic-friendly direction: there is nothing less rational about the person who coherently rejects M (including claims about theoretical entities and the future) in light of total evidence E than the person who accepts M. The denial involving new roles for evidence leads to trouble with diachronic Dutch books. In these cases, the role of evidence will typically be knowable, so that it will be predictable before acquiring evidence E that if one acquires E, one's rational credence $cr^*(M)$ will be high. If so, then one will be vulnerable to a diachronic Dutch book, where one initially places a conditional bet on $\sim M$ given E at 1:2 odds (losing \$2 if E & M, gaining \$1 if E & $\sim M$) and later, if E occurs, placing a bet on M at 1:2 odds (gaining \$1 if M, losing \$2 if $\sim M$). Neither bet will be irrational by one's lights at the time (assuming that high credences must be above 2/3), but one will be guaranteed to lose money if the bet pays off at all. One can also devise a variant in which one loses a very small amount at the first stage if $\sim E$, so that one is guaranteed a loss come what may. The second bet seems unproblematic given the anti-skeptical thesis, so to avoid the guaranteed loss it seems that one must reject the first bet. But this suggests that there are rational constraints on $cr(M \mid E)$ prior to acquiring E after all.

Furthermore, it is not clear that the reasons for worrying about substantive a priori constraints on priors translate into reasons for worrying about the apriority of conditionals involving $PQTI$. In the inductive and abductive cases, where sentences are neither certain nor uncertain, it is natural to hold that many prior probabilities are equally reasonable. In the $PQTI$ case, by contrast, there is a reasonable case that the conditional from $PQTI$ to M can be known with certainty. Where these probabilities of 1 are concerned, the reasons for concern about frontloading and conditionalization do not apply. The credence in this conditional does not appear to depend on the assignment of prior probabilities to uncertain sentences. It is more akin to credence in logical, mathematical, and

---

[5] Brian Weatherson (2007) and James Pryor (unpublished) have developed non-Bayesian frameworks on which evidence plays roles that go beyond conditionalization as standardly understood, in order to accommodate dogmatism about perception. Weatherson's framework is driven by doubts about substantive a priori knowledge, while Pryor allows that there can be substantive a priori knowledge but holds that this apriori knowledge is explained by the nature of experience. Weatherson's framework will reject frontloading principles, as will some versions of Pryor's framework.

analytic truths, which are not threatened by radical subjectivism. So I think that these uses of the frontloading principle are on fairly firm ground.[6]

4 Causal roles, mediating roles, and justifying roles

A third analysis yields not so much a conclusive argument for A Priori Scrutability as a sort of diagnostic tool that helps to determining the status of purported empirical evidence that plays a role in conditional knowledge of M given $PQTI$.

For example, I noted earlier that Block and Stalnaker (1999) hold that our conditional knowledge of various truths about water (given a specification of underlying states of the world) is itself justified by empirical background knowledge, such as our knowledge that the world is simple. This knowledge may play a central role in our taking water to be a natural kind rather than a superficial kind, for example.

Here we need to distinguish a number of roles that empirical information might play in knowing these conditionals. There is no question that empirical information can play a *causal* role in acquiring conditional knowledge. For example, empirical information often plays a causal role in the acquisition of concepts with certain a priori connections, and it sometimes plays a role in triggering changes in the a priori connections associated with a term. In these cases empirical information plays a causal role in the possession of concepts that underwrite conditional knowledge. For example, the simplicity of the world might play a causal role in our coming to have concepts whose a priori connections work in the way that is distinctive of 'water'.

There is also no question that empirical truths E could play a *mediating* role in conditional knowledge. It might be that E is itself implied by $PQTI$ and that one can then use E in combination with $PQTI$ to deduce M. In the case of simplicity, it is very plausible that $PQTI$ describes a simple world, so that 'The world is simple' is implied by $PQTI$. This claim might then be used in turn to help deduce that water is H_2O.

However, in neither of these cases does E play a role in *justifying* the conditional knowledge of M given $PQTI$. In fact, I think that in all cases where E plays

---

[6] The objection from lost evidence in the previous section might still be raised: when a belief in M is justified by long-forgotten evidence E, one may no longer have high credence in E and suspending judgment in it may have no effect. Still, in such a case, if E supports M, $cr(M \mid E)$ *should* be high. Furthermore, the high credence should be justifiable independently of E, for much the same reason as above. We can also invoke a counterpart ideal reasoner who has access to the past evidence E. If E plays a justifying role for an agent who has forgotten it, it will equally play a justifying role for an agent who remembers it. The argument from frontloading will then constrain the justifying role of E for the agent who remembers it, and we can use this conclusion to constrain the justifying role for the agent who has forgotten it.

a role in conditional knowledge of M given $PQTI$, it plays a causal role or a mediating role rather than a justifying role.

One can attempt to diagnose the matter as follows. Let us start by assuming that we have established not just Conditional Scrutability but Generalized Conditional Scrutability, so that the truth-value of ordinary macroscopic truths M is scrutable from many other $PQTI$-style sentences describing alternative scenarios and not just from $PQTI$ itself.

If E plays a causal role in conditional knowledge of M given $PQTI$, then one expects that E plays the same sort of role in other conditionals involving the same concepts and different scenarios. In particular it will play a role even in knowledge conditional on those X such that $\sim E$ is conditionally scrutable from X. If a belief that the world is simple plays a causal role in our acquiring a certain concept of water, then we expect that this role will affect our judgments about both simple and non-simple scenarios.

If E plays a mediating role in conditional knowledge of M given $PQTI$, then one expects that E plays the same role only for some conditionals involving the same concepts and different scenarios. In particular it will play a role in knowledge conditional on those X such that E is conditionally scrutable from X, but not for those X such that $\sim E$ is conditionally scrutable from X. If the claim that the world is simple plays a mediating role in our judgments about water, we expect that this role will affect our judgments about simple scenarios but not about nonsimple scenarios.

So to diagnose the matter: given an E that is said to play a role in conditional knowledge of M given $PQTI$, one can ask: does E play the same role in knowledge conditional on X, for some X such that $\sim E$ is conditionally scrutable from X? For example: does simplicity play the same sort of role in our judgments about simple scenarios and about nonsimple scenarios?

If yes: then this role for E is almost certainly a causal role and not a justifying role. If $\sim E$ is conditionally scrutable from X, then E cannot justify conditional knowledge of N given X for any N. If one came to accept X, one would accept N and rationally reject E, so that E could play no justifying role in accepting N. Even if one only supposes X, one can conclude N by the same reasoning process, so E will play no essential justifying role here either. For example, if one came to accept that we are in a nonsimple scenario, the belief that the world is simple could not play a role in justifying further beliefs about water. Our conditional beliefs about water given a nonsimple scenario will be justified by a similar reasoning process, so the belief that the world is simple will not play a role.

If no: then this role for E is very likely a mediating role. Given a no answer, E plays a justifying role only for knowledge conditional on X for which E is itself conditionally scrutable from X. This strongly suggests a mediating role. If E were to play a justifying role in only these cases, one has non-uniformity in the justifying factors across the various cases. A picture on which the same factors justify conditional knowledge of M given $PQTI$ and (for example) $\sim M$ given $PQTI^*$, where the latter is another $PQTI$-style sentence from which $\sim E$ is conditionally scrutable, is much more attractive. For example, if the belief that the world is simple played a justifying role only in judgments about simple scenarios, then there would be an odd non-uniformity in our judgments, whereas if it plays a mediating role, this non-uniformity is to be expected.

This is not a knockdown argument. An opponent can always deny Generalized Conditional Scrutability, and in particular Generalized Conditional Scrutability from $PQTI$-sentences. It might be that empirical evidence E justifies knowledge of M given $PQTI$, but given that E is unavailable to justify inferences from $PQTI^*$, conditional scrutability from $PQTI^*$ fails completely. At best one will have conditional scrutability from a base larger than $PQTI^*$, and then it will not be as surprising that E is not involved in the justification.[7]

Still, if an opponent grants a uniform sort of conditional scrutability, then these considerations make their view uncomfortable. And certainly, if one already has the reasons for accepting A Priori Scrutability laid out in the previous arguments, then these considerations can help us to classify purportedly relevant empirical sentences as playing either a causal role or a mediating role.

In the case of simplicity, we asked: does simplicity play a role in judgments concerning scenarios that are not simple themselves? If yes, then it seems that the role of simplicity cannot be a justificatory role, for the reasons given above. At best it might play a causal role in the acquisition of a concept whose application-conditions across scenarios involve simplicity. If no, then it is plausible that simplicity plays its role because the truth that the world is simple is itself conditionally scrutable from $PQTI$. On this view, it appears that simplicity may play a mediating role in reasoning from $PQTI$ to simplicity to M, but it is not essentially required to justify conditional belief in M given $PQTI$. Either way, a posteriori evidence regarding simplicity plays no essential role in justifying the conditional itself. So the role of this evidence is no obstacle to a priori scrutability.[8]

5 Generalized A Priori Scrutability

If the arguments of this chapter (and chapter 6) work, we have made a case for A Priori Scrutability: there is a compact class of truths from which all truths are a priori scrutable. Let us assume that this class is $PQTI$. If all truths are a priori

---

[7] I think that a version of this reply can also be given to the earlier version of this argument presented by Chalmers and Jackson (2001).

[8] For more on the various possible roles of empirical evidence, see the discussion of Williamson in the eighth excursus.

scrutable from *PQTI*, then *PQTI* is epistemically complete: that is, there is no *H*
such that *PQTI* & *H* and *PQTI* & ~*H* are both epistemically possible (where
PQTI is the conjunction of sentences in *PQTI*, and *S* is epistemically possible
iff ~*S* is not a priori).[9]

What can we then say about Generalized A Priori Scrutability, the thesis that
there is a compact class of sentences such that all epistemically possible sentences
(whether true or false) are a priori scrutable from sentences in that class? If this
thesis is right, then this compact class can be used to generate epistemically complete classes that can play the same role with respect to other scenarios as *PQTI*
does for the actual scenario.

If my argument for A Priori Scrutability were itself entirely a priori, then we
would have good reason to accept some version of Generalized A Priori Scrutability. But the argument is not obviously a priori. It appears to rely on various a
posteriori claims about the character of actual-world truths: that there are microphysical truths and phenomenal truths, for example, and that macroscopic
truths have a certain character.

That said, there is good reason to believe that the argument applies to more
than the actual world. The argument does not turn on the precise microphysical
truths specified by *P*, or the precise phenomenal truths specified by *Q*: it could
not, as I do not know most of these truths. So the argument would still go
through if *P* and *Q* were somewhat different. This already suggests that there will
be many *PQTI*-like classes that can play the role of *PQTI*. If *PQTI* is epistemically complete, so are many analogous classes *PQTI**. Then for many false sentences *M*, such as 'There is water in this cup', *M* will be a priori scrutable from
some *PQTI**.

We can extend things further. The argument turned on very little that was
specific about *P*, except that it enabled us to recover information about the spatiotemporal and mass properties of arbitrary objects. It is arguable that for many
different hypotheses about the character of fundamental physics, the argument
will still go through. Likewise, the argument will go through for many different
hypotheses about the distribution of conscious experiences (including everything from solipsistic to panpsychist hypotheses). So one can extend the argument to a very broad variety of epistemically possible hypotheses, making the
case that these are scrutable from *PQTI*-style classes specifying a physics and a
distribution of phenomenology that is quite different from the actual world.

Of course there are epistemic possibilities that are more distant than this. It is
arguably epistemically possible that nothing has spatiotemporal properties,
or that nothing has conscious experience. There will be no straightforward

---

[9] For more on these notions and for a discussion of indeterminacy in this context, see the tenth
excursus.

PQTI-style scenario corresponding to these hypotheses. One might also think that it is epistemically possible that the world has a sort of complexity that goes far beyond what can be specified by a *PQTI*-style sentence. To handle hypotheses of this sort, the appeal to *PQTI*-style classes in a Cosmoscope argument gets little grip.

Still, it remains plausible that for such hypotheses, there will be some analog of a Cosmoscope that could deliver information from which the truth of the hypothesis is conditionally scrutable: such a Cosmoscope would serve in effect as a guide to the character of a scenario in which the hypothesis is true. The Cosmoscope might be very different from an actual-world Cosmoscope, but as long as it works by storing and conveying information of certain constrained sorts, and thereby allows a sufficiently ideal user to determine the truth-value of arbitrary hypotheses, an analogous case for a scrutability thesis will go through.

As discussed in chapter 2, it is not obvious that we can have generalized scrutability from a base that is compact in absolute terms: there may be too many alien properties in other scenarios for that. But there remains good reason to believe in generalized scrutability from a base that is relatively compact relative to possible languages as a whole. For example, many of the arguments in chapter 6 suggesting the a priori scrutability of truths involving names, social truths, mathematical and moral truths, and so on are a priori in character, suggesting that truths of this sort are a priori scrutable from truths not of this sort however the world turns out to be. If so, there are certainly generalized scrutability bases that are relatively compact.

I cannot claim to have settled the status of Generalized A Priori Scrutability here, but I think these considerations at least make the generalized thesis a highly attractive one. I will return to the thesis in chapter 8.

6 Objections from self-knowledge

There are a number of objections that might be made to the A Priori Scrutability thesis. I have in effect considered a few of them already: objections from the absence of definitions in chapter 1; objections from knowability, indeterminacy, and Liar-like paradoxes in the first excursus; objections from idealization in chapter 2; objections from self-doubt in the fifth excursus; and objections from recognitional capacities and counterfactuals in chapter 3. I discuss objections from Quinean skepticism about the a priori in chapter 5, objections from conceptual change in the ninth excursus, and objections from specific sorts of truths—mathematical, moral, metaphysical, and so on—in chapter 6.

In the remainder of this chapter I focus on some further objections. I start with two objections that turn on a role for self-knowledge in a priori scrutability.

First: Janice Dowell (2008) and Andrew Melnyk (2008) have suggested that scrutability claims and related methods in conceptual analysis rest on an over-confident empirical claim about self-knowledge. This is the claim that we can know how we *would* react to discovering that *PQTI* is true (for example, whether we would then say that *M* is true or false), simply by considering now the hypothesis that *PQTI* is true and observing our reaction. According to the objection, this claim may well be false: as a matter of psychological fact, our reactions on discovering that *PQTI* is true may be quite different from our reaction on merely considering the hypothesis that *PQTI* is true.

In response: nothing in the arguments I have given requires this empirical claim. Claims about how we would react on making a certain discovery play no role in the arguments. The closest thing to such a claim arises in the case of Inferential Scrutability, with the thesis that were the relevant subject to come to know *PQTI*, he or she could come to know *M* (on ideal reflection). But even this thesis does not make any empirical claims about how the subject *would* react, let alone about how we ourselves would react. In the case of Conditional and A Priori Scrutability, there is nothing even as close as this. The former concerns an (idealized) conditional credence $cr^*(M \mid PQTI)$, and the latter concerns knowability of a material conditional $PQTI \rightarrow M$. Claims about one's own future reactions are irrelevant here. A high conditional credence in $cr^*(M \mid PQTI)$ is certainly not equivalent to a belief that one would accept *M* if one accepted *PQTI*, for example.

Translated into the current framework, perhaps the nearest counterpart of the objection would run as follows. A subject might now accept the conditional claim that if *A*, then *B*, but then later on learning *A* (and only *A*), might never-theless reject *B*. If so, conditional scrutability and inferential scrutability will come apart, so both cannot be a guide to the truth. In response: certainly there can be such a subject. But as with the previous objection, standard Bayesian principles entail that such a subject cannot be fully rational throughout, or else must have engaged in conceptual change. So as long as we characterize scrutabil-ity so that both require a rational idealization, and so that inferential scrutability requires no conceptual change, then conditional and inferential scrutability can-not come apart in this way.

Second: David Henderson and Terence Horgan (2000) have argued that alleged a priori knowledge depends on introspective observation of our own judgments. Correspondingly, Stephen Yablo (2002) suggests that scrutability inferences from *PQTI* to *M* may depend on considering *PQTI* and then intro-spectively observing (or 'peeking' at) our own reactions. If so, the inference is not a priori.

In response: in the arguments I have given, there is little reason to think that self-observation plays a role. In the case of inferential scrutability of *M* from

PQTI, self-observation plays no more role than in any other case of inference. Likewise, in the case of conditional scrutability of *M* from *PQTI*, self-observation plays no more role than in any other conditional credence. And in the case of knowledge of the material conditional *PQTI* → *M*, self-observation plays no more role than with any other material conditional. If self-observation is not needed to justify an empirical inference from knowing *PQTI* to knowing *M*, it is likewise not needed to justify conditional belief in *M* given *PQTI*, or to justify belief in the corresponding material conditional. In each of these cases, one needs to deploy the concepts involved in *M*, but one need not observe their deployment.

That said, there are certainly some expressions such that in order to determine their extension, one needs to observe one's own reactions. Perhaps one determines what is green by determining what causes green experiences, or one determines what is funny by determining what one finds funny. In cases like these involving response-dependence, however, the relevant observations should be seen as packed into the antecedent. In the case of inferential scrutability of claims involving 'green', one's green experiences will be specified by *Q*, and knowledge of this part of *Q* will be part of what enables one to know what is green. Likewise in the case of conditional scrutability, one's conditional credence in 'X is green' given 'X causes green experiences' will be high: the relevant experiences are built into the antecedent, and play no role in justifying the conditional credence itself. Correspondingly, they play no role in justifying the corresponding material conditional.[10]

7 Objections from theories of concepts and reference

A common objection holds that certain theories of concepts or certain theories of reference are incompatible with a priori scrutability. On certain atomist theories of concepts (e.g., Fodor 1998), for example, the referent of a concept such as *water* or *horse* is held to be quite independent of its inferential role. Likewise, some hold a version of the causal theory of reference on which the referent of an expression is determined by what an expression is causally connected to, quite independent of its role in cognition and thought. On these views, our a priori inferences about reference in a scenario may tell us little about an expression's actual referent.

Relatedly, Philip Goff (2011) argues against theses akin to A Priori Scrutability by suggesting that concepts can be 'radically opaque', revealing neither essential

---

[10] I think that a similar diagnosis applies to what Yablo calls 'response-enabled' concepts in his 'Coulda Woulda Shoulda' (2002). See my reply in 'Does Conceivability Entail Possibility?'

nor accidental properties of their referents. For example, on a traditional descriptivist picture, *Hesperus* is associated a priori with (or reveals) the property of being the evening star, and picks out Venus in virtue of its having that property. If concepts can be radically opaque, referents can float free of a priori associated properties and of a priori inferential role. If so A Priori Scrutability may be threatened, as subjects will not have sufficient grip to identify a referent a priori in a scenario.

In the current context, a proponent of this sort of objection needs to say where the arguments for A Priori Scrutability go wrong. I think that such a proponent will naturally end up denying Conditional and Inferential Scrutability too. Once Inferential Scrutability (or even limited versions of it in specific cases) is granted, we then have the materials for an argument to Conditional and then to A Priori Scrutability. Furthermore, even a weak form of Inferential Scrutability—say, the claim that there are underlying non-'water'-truths such that knowing those truths suffices for us to know that water is H_2O—gives us enough of a connection between reference and inferential role that the force of the objection is blunted.

So a proponent of this objection needs to deny even these weak forms of Inferential Scrutability, holding (for example) that knowledge of non-'water'-truths does not suffice for us to know that water is H_2O. For example, knowledge of the appearance, behavior, composition, and distribution of H_2O in our environment (as well as its relation to us) does not suffice to know that it is water. Perhaps the most consistent form of this objection holds that our judgments about reference, even given full relevant information about the actual world and good reasoning, are not a reliable guide to actual reference. On this view, it could turn out that we have been wrong all along about water's being H_2O: after all, our judgments are not a reliable guide to reference.

At this point I think the objection loses plausibility. The fact that we are able to identify referents for typical expressions given enough empirical information is something of a datum that theories of concepts and reference need to accommodate. Indeed, the paradigm arguments *for* the causal theory of reference rest partly on judgments about reference in cases. Once granted, this datum automatically yields some sort of link between reference and inferential role. If certain theories cannot accommodate this datum, then this is much more of a problem for the theories than for the datum. I think that this datum is indeed a problem for certain overly simplistic forms of the causal theory of reference, and for certain overly simplistic theories of concepts, but that more sophisticated versions of these can probably accommodate it. In any case, I do not think that there is a serious objection to a priori scrutability here.

A related objection appeals to recently popular 'reference magnet' theory of reference (Lewis 1984), which appeals to the naturalness of potential referents rather than to causal connections. It might be thought that this view renders reference radically opaque in a way that undermines scrutability. I think that this objection can be subjected to the same sort of dilemma as causal theories: does the reference magnet theory yield verdicts incompatible with our reflective judgments about cases (including full information about the naturalness of properties in those cases)? If yes, then the view loses plausibility. If no, then there is no problem for scrutability. Certainly I think that the most plausible and well-motivated versions of reference magnet theories are entirely compatible with scrutability. I develop this analysis at much greater length in the additional excursus on 'Reference Magnets and the Grounds of Intentionality'.

Another objection holds that the scrutability of truths such as 'water is H_2O' from *PQTI* is grounded in our tacit acceptance of a certain theory of reference, and that the correct theory of reference may be empirical rather than a priori, in which case we should expect A Priori Scrutability to fail. There are a number of things wrong with this objection. First, it does not say where the arguments for A Priori Scrutability go wrong, unless it denies Inferential and Conditional Scrutability as well. Second, even if the correct theory of reference is knowable only empirically, *PQTI* or a Cosmoscope in effect supply relevant empirical materials, and the arguments in the previous chapter suggest that if the theory can be known empirically, it can be known using *PQTI* or a Cosmoscope. Third, and perhaps most important, there is little reason to think that scrutability judgments presuppose a theory of reference.

To see the last point, note first that in using *PQTI* or a Cosmoscope to ascertain whether water is H_2O, the subject need not reason metalinguistically about the *word* 'water' at all: they need only use the word, or make inferences using the concept it expresses. (Recall that we have excluded deferential users, who might have to reason about the use of the word by others.) The theory of reference centrally involves metalinguistic claims, so if metalinguistic reasoning is inessential to scrutability reasoning here, so is acceptance of a theory of reference. And in practice, the situation is reversed: our nonmetalinguistic judgments about whether water is H_2O in effect serve as inputs to a theory of reference.

An opponent might suggest that although we do not reason explicitly about words, metalinguistic reasoning involving a theory of reference lies underneath the surface of our reasoning here. But the judgments here are similar in kind to those made by actual subjects trying to decide whether water is H_2O, and indeed those made by actual subjects trying to decide whether p is true, for all sorts of p, in light of empirical evidence. So this line leads to an implausible view on which metalinguistic reasoning underlies most apparently first-order reasoning.

An opponent might also suggest that although our reasoning does not presuppose a theory of reference, it nevertheless can be defeated by a theory of reference. For example, we might decide in light of nonmetalinguistic reasoning that water is X, but then general metalinguistic reasoning about reference might convince us that in fact 'water' refers to Y, leading us to conclude that water is Y. I am doubtful about whether metalinguistic reasoning can trump ideal nonmetalinguistic reasoning in this way (though it might sometimes be useful as a shortcut, for example allowing us to use insights derived from the case of 'water' to apply to the case of 'gold'). But even if one accepts this picture, it does not pose any problem for A Priori Scrutability, as long as the theory of reference (along with the disquotational claim ''water' refers to water') is itself scrutable from $PQTI$.

A residual position is that the correct theory of reference is unknowable, or at least inscrutable from $PQTI$ and related compact bases, and that as a result A Priori Scrutability, Conditional Scrutability, and Inferential Scrutability all fail. For example, it might be that on discovering relevant truths about H_2O and the like, ideal reasoning (both about language and about the world) leads us to the view that water is X, but in fact the true theory of reference dictates that 'water' refers to Y, so water is Y. This view leads easily to the unattractive view that the true theory of reference may well undermine most of our judgments about the world in light of empirical evidence and reasoning.

At this point, I think we should recall Humpty Dumpty's dictum: Words are our servants, not our masters. To invoke a theme from 'Verbal Disputes': once we know enough underlying facts about substances in non-'water'-language, we know how those substances are, and further debate about whether or not a given one of those substances counts as water is in a certain sense verbal. The opposing view here elevates shallow verbal issues into sources of deep and essential ignorance about how things are in the world. But language is merely our tool, and we can use it to divide the world up as we please, without thereby creating deep and essential ignorance of how things are in the world. So I think that a view on which the theory of reference is a source of inscrutability should be rejected.

8 Objections from acquaintance and from nonpropositional evidence

Some important objections to A Priori Scrutability proceed by making proposals about what sort of evidence empirically justifies the conditional beliefs we have considered. One objection holds that my arguments can be evaded by appealing to empirical evidence that is nonpropositional in form. Another appeals more specifically to acquaintance, claiming for example that our conditional beliefs about water are empirically justified by our acquaintance with water. I will consider these objections in turn.

On nonpropositional evidence: some of my arguments for a priori scrutability proceed by assuming that evidence can be encapsulated in propositional form.

In these arguments, evidence is represented by an evidence statement E, and the epistemological force of the evidence is captured by knowledge of the statement's truth. This fits a conception of evidence as something believed or known. But it may be held that evidence can also be nonpropositional.

Most obviously, evidence might consist in an *experience*. An opponent might hold that the epistemological force of an experience is not captured by the epistemological force of belief in any corresponding evidence statement, whether the statement that the experience occurs, or the statement that some perceived state of affairs obtains. So the arguments for a priori scrutability do not exclude the possibility that relevant knowledge is justified by experience in this way.

In response: there is some intuitive plausibility in the claim that an experience as of a red cup can give one a sort of justification for belief in the presence of a red cup, justification that goes beyond that given by the mere knowledge that there is an experience as of a red cup. I do not think that there is the same intuitive plausibility in the claim that this can justify further beliefs that cannot be justified by knowledge that there is a red cup at a certain location (or by knowledge of whatever the contents of experience might be). Someone might suggest that the content of experience cannot be captured in any set of sentences. Even if so, it is plausible that the epistemic role of experience is screened off by its role in directly justifying certain beliefs about the external world (such as the belief that there is a cup of a certain shape, size, and color in a certain location). So I think that by considering evidence statements of the latter sort, I am in effect considering evidence at least as strong as the evidence provided by experience.

Someone might suggest that all the same, experiences are not subject to the same epistemic principles as beliefs. Perhaps experiences are not subject to conditionalization: it may be that upon having an experience, one is thereby justified in having a certain credence in M, but there is no corresponding evidence statement E such that one is antecedently justified in having the same credence in M conditional on E. And perhaps while suspension of judgment in a belief precludes any justificatory role for that belief, one cannot suspend judgment in an experience in the same way.

Now, I think it is implausible that experiences are not subject to conditionalization, and I think there is at least a form of suspension of judgment such that suspending judgment about whether one had a given experience is incompatible with a justificatory role for that experience. But in any case, the arguments for scrutability go through if we take the relevant evidence statement to be E', a sentence expressing a conjunction of any beliefs that might be directly justified by the experience. If one can suspend judgment in E', and still come to know that M, then the experience does not play an essential role in justifying M. And if having an experience allows one to learn M, then even before having the experience, one's conditional credence in M given E' should be high. The same sort of analysis applies to other sorts of nonpropositional evidence that someone might appeal to.

On objections from acquaintance: The objection can be motivated by the general thesis that any knowledge we have concerning a natural kind such as water is justified by our acquaintance with the kind, with a central role for perceptual experience and for causal links. If so, then even conditionals such as 'If *PQTI*, then water is H_2O' are justified in this way, and cannot be known a priori. This objection in effect concedes Conditional Scrutability (at least for subjects who have the relevant acquaintance) but rejects A Priori Scrutability, on the grounds that the relevant conditional beliefs are empirically justified by acquaintance.

In response: It is not out of the question that to possess the *concept* of water, and to use the English expression 'water', one must stand in some causal acquaintance relation to water. Perhaps there are counterexamples involving someone who comes to form the concept in unusual ways, perhaps through thinking about hydrogen and oxygen, but I will set those aside here. But it is a familiar point about the a priori that we must distinguish what is required to possess the concepts involved in a belief from what is required to justify that belief. I do not think it is plausible that acquaintance plays any essential role in justifying a belief in 'If water exists, water is water' or 'If nothing exists, then water does not exist', for example. The arguments already given suggest that the same goes for 'If *PQTI*, then water is H_2O'.

We can start by asking how acquaintance does its justifying work. As with the previous objection, it is natural to suppose that one's acquaintance with water does its epistemic work by first supporting perceptual beliefs: for example, the belief that there is something with such-and-such appearance in the environment, or perhaps even the belief that there is water over there with certain properties. But it appears that one could suspend judgment in these perceptual beliefs, and indeed in any other positive beliefs involving the presence of water in the environment, and still have justified conditional beliefs connecting *PQTI* and water here. If so, then acquaintance is not playing its justifying role in conditional belief in virtue of its role in supporting these empirical beliefs. Perhaps acquaintance is supposed to directly support the conditional belief, not in virtue of supporting the perceptual beliefs, but it is very unclear how this might work. Alternatively, the proponent of this objection might hold that suspension of belief undermines justification even of the conditional belief, but they then owe us a story about why this is so.

One can also apply the diagnostic tool from section 4, asking whether acquaintance also justifies conditional beliefs concerning *PQTI*-style scenarios in which acquaintance with water is missing. For example, on the face of it I am justified in believing that *if* I am in a Twin Earth scenario (where XYZ has always been the watery stuff in the oceans and lakes around me), then water is XYZ; and I am justified in believing that *if* I am in a Dry Earth scenario (with no watery stuff at all), then water does not exist. Intuitively a conditional belief is justified in each case. But in the Twin Earth and Dry Earth scenarios, there is no water and I am not acquainted with it. And for reasons discussed in section 4, it is implausible that acquaintance with water can justify credences conditional on hypotheses in which there is no such acquaintance and no water. So the diagnostic reasoning there strongly suggests that acquaintance is merely playing a causal role in enabling us to possess the concept and not a justifying role.

The objection from acquaintance parallels a familiar line among Russellians (such as Keith Donnellan, Nathan Salmon, and Scott Soames) who reject Kripke's claims about contingent a priori knowledge.[11] We can take the case of 'Julius', introduced by stipulating that it is a name for the inventor of the zip, if anyone invented the zip (here 'invent' should be understood as 'uniquely invent' throughout). The Kripkean line is that 'Julius invented the zip (if anyone did)' is contingent a priori, known a priori in virtue of the stipulation. Now, Russellians typically hold that this sentence expresses a singular proposition about William C. Whitworth, who actually invented the zip. Russellians who reject the Kripkean line hold that no one could know this proposition a priori, as no one could know a priori of Whitworth that he invented the zip (if anyone did). Instead, anyone who knows this proposition knows it a posteriori, justified in part by their direct or indirect acquaintance with Whitworth. Here I assume that we have some sort of acquaintance with Whitworth in virtue of our acquaintance with zips; analogous cases without acquaintance are discussed below.

Now, on the current understanding of apriority, we cannot simply equate the apriority of the sentence with the apriority of the singular proposition. Still, the claim that the knowledge expressed by 'Julius invented the zip (if anyone did)' is empirical is a more general one that deserves attention. Anyone who takes this line will also hold that conditional sentences such as 'Whitworth invented the zip → Julius is Whitworth' are not knowable a priori, and it will be natural for them to take a similar line on '*PQTI* → water is wet'. So it is worth addressing the familiar Russellian line from within the current framework.

As before, I think the argument from suspension of judgment gives good reason to hold that the relevant knowledge in these cases is not empirical. Even if one has the relevant sort of acquaintance with Whitworth, one can engage in Cartesian suspension of belief about the external world, including suspension of one's beliefs in the deliverances of perception. Under such suspension of belief, one cannot be justified in believing 'There are zips', 'Someone invented zips',

----

[11] See Donnellan 1979, Salmon 1988, and Soames 2004.

'Whitworth exists', or 'Julius exists'. But on the face of it, assuming that one uses 'Julius' in a way governed by the original stipulation, one is still perfectly justi-fied in believing 'Julius invented the zip (if anyone did)', and indeed, this belief constitutes knowledge. One's justification for this claim cannot be constituted by perceptual evidence concerning zips, and indeed by any perceptual evidence, as the justificatory role of evidence of this sort is undermined by the Cartesian suspension of belief. And introspective justification does not seem to the point here (certainly the putative acquaintance-based justification was not supposed to be introspective). So prima facie, one's justification here is a priori.

A related but different sort of case is posed by 'Newman 1', introduced as a name for the first child born in the 22nd century. In this case, we can suppose that the introducer lacks any empirical acquaintance with the individual who is the referent. All the same, an utterance of 'Newman 1 is the first child born in the 22nd century (if anyone is)' appears to be true, appears to be justified, appears to express knowledge, appears to express armchair knowledge, and in this case there is no obvious empirical justification anywhere in the vicinity. So there is a very strong prima facie case that this utterance expresses a priori knowledge. At this point, the Russellian may hold that there is a discontinuity between descrip-tive names used with and without acquaintance:[12] for example, perhaps the former are disguised descriptions rather than names (so that utterances involving them do not express singular propositions, and may well be a priori), while the latter are truly names (so that utterances involving them express singular propo-sitions and are not a priori). But the argument from suspension of judgment suggests that even if Russellians are right about this semantic claim, it does not yield a difference at the epistemic or mental level. The arguments in this chapter strongly suggest that even if acquaintance with Julius enables us to possess a certain sort of concept of him, it is not essential to justifying our belief in 'Julius invented the zip (if anyone did)'.

Other Russellians hold that descriptive names are always disguised descrip-tions and are never names, whether used with or without acquaintance.[13] These Russellians may hold that cases involving descriptive names such as 'Julius' are no guide to cases involving ordinary proper names such as 'Gödel'. Even if they

---

[12] Marga Reimer (2004) takes a version of the line on which acquaintance transforms content of a name from something descriptive to something referential (although her line holds that if a descriptive name relies on description rather than acquaintance to fix reference even after acquaint-ance, the name is still semantically descriptive). Salmon (1998) and Soames (1995) take related views on which although the content of a descriptive name pre-acquaintance is still its referent, the acquaintanceless user of the relevant name is unable to fully grasp propositions involving this referent.

[13] This sort of view is also associated with Gareth Evans (1979), although Evans' version of the view is not Russellian.

are right, however, the bulk of what I have said about the case of 'Julius invented the zip' also applies to cases such as '$PQTI \to$ Gödel discovered incompleteness'. In particular, the argument from suspension of judgment, the argument from frontloading, and the diagnostic tool all suggest that this case is a priori, just as before. So the natural moral once again is that acquaintance plays at most an enabling role in enabling us to entertain conditional beliefs about Gödel, and not a justifying role.

9 The objection from empirical inference

A remaining objection turns on the idea that our reasoning from $PQTI$ to M may be grounded in past experience without being mediated by any current empirical beliefs. The case where past experience justifies a current empirical belief that supports the reasoning was discussed in sections 3 and 4. But there remains the possibility that reasoning involves *empirical inference*: inference that is grounded in past experience without the role of that experience being mediated by its justifying a current belief. If so, one might hold although the inference from $PQTI$ to M is not a priori, suspension of judgment and frontloading will not pick up on the epistemological role of experience.

Empirical inferences are reminiscent of the empirical recognitional capacities discussed in section 7 of chapter 3. Empirical recognitional capacities, such as the capacity to recognize an astronaut from superficial features, typically operate within perception or between perception and belief. Empirical inferences are similar, but operate between beliefs, or suppositions or related cognitive states. I argued in the last chapter that empirical recognitional capacities are dispensable for the purposes of scrutability, so they do not pose an objection to a priori scrutability. The same goes for empirical inferences.

The paradigmatic empirical inferences are *associative inferences*: non-deductive inferences from a premise to a conclusion based in some sort of experienced association. For example, one might make a justified inference from 'He is a bachelor' to 'He is untidy', based on past correlations between bachelors and untidiness in one's environment, without ever believing that all or most bachelors are untidy. The past correlations might simply have disposed one to infer from bachelorhood to untidiness in an unmediated way. One might respond to such a case by holding that there is always at least a tacit belief that all or most bachelors are untidy, so that the inference is indirect. Depending on what one means by a tacit belief, this claim might even be trivial. Still, it is not clear that such a tacit belief could be said to mediate the inference, and it is not obvious that tacit beliefs are the kind of thing that can easily be suspended. If there is not a mediating tacit belief, on the other hand, then it is even less clear how an inferential disposition can easily be suspended.

Let us allow for the sake of argument that there are inferences (that is, acts of inferences) in this vicinity that are not mediated by current empirical beliefs. Despite the lack of mediation, one can certainly distinguish between justified and unjustified inferences here. And among those unmediated inferences that are justified, one can distinguish between those that are justified by experience and those that are not. For example, the inference above from 'He is a bachelor' to 'He is untidy' is plausibly justified by experience: one's past experience of situations involving correlation between bachelorhood and untidiness. An unmediated inference from 'X is a bachelor' to 'X is male', on the other hand, may be justified a priori: there need be no essential role for experience here.

This requires talking of justified and unjustified acts of inferences, rather than merely justified and unjustified beliefs, and of a priori and empirical acts of inference, rather than merely of a priori and empirical beliefs. But this is a natural enough way of talking. For example, it is natural enough to say that there can be a justified act of inference from an unjustified belief p, yielding an unjustified belief q. This brings out that justified acts of inference are not just those that result in justified beliefs.

The justificatory status of any given act of inference, on a specific occasion, is plausibly inherited from the justificatory status of an inference type that it falls under. The relevant inference types here are akin to inference rules, but they need not be formally specifiable: for example, a complex gestalt-style associative inference pattern might yield a justified inference type. (We might also speak of justified inferential processes here.) For example, the a priori status of an inference by modus ponens is inherited from the a priori status of the modus ponens inference rule. When an inference type is epistemologically grounded in experience, any inferences of this type will be empirical; when the inference type is not grounded in experience, any inferences of that type will be a priori.[14]

The objection now comes to the claim that the inference from $PQTI$ to M may involve an empirical inference. Such inferences will not be affected by the suspension of empirical belief, but may be empirical all the same, so the argument from suspension of judgment will not get a grip here. The argument from frontloading still applies, however. When an inference from $PQTI$ to M involves an empirical inference justified by past experience encapsulated in an evidence sentence E, it seems that the antecedent credence $cr(M \mid PQTI \& E)$ should be

---

[14] More generally, it is natural to talk about the justificatory status not just of individual beliefs but of belief-forming processes. There can be justified processes, a priori justified processes, and so on. Inference types are one example of such a process, but one might also talk this way about (for example) recognitional capacities, as in chapter 3. Note that to talk this way is not to be committed to the strong general claim that every belief-forming process is assessible for justification or that a belief is justified only if it is formed by a justified process.

high. Likewise, it is plausible that one should have a high posterior credence $cr(M \mid PQTI \& E)$, with justification independent of E. If so, the argument still goes through.

One can also respond to the objection by arguing, much as in the case of recognitional capacities, that everything that can be known using empirical unmediated inference can be known without it. After all, whether or not the inference from bachelorhood to untidiness is mediated by a belief that most bachelors are untidy, there is certainly a closely related pattern of reasoning from the same premise to the same conclusion using an inference that is mediated by such a belief. And when the first inference is empirically justified, the second will be mediated by a justified empirical belief. We can then apply the original arguments for A Priori Scrutability to the new case, and the objection from unmediated inference will fall away.

Someone might offer a more radical view of the role of experience in inference, so that this role cannot be mirrored in a case involving mediating empirical beliefs, and is not reflected in conditionalization. For example, one might hold that experience plays a role in shaping an inferential disposition that is inaccessible to reflection, so that conditionalizing in advance on the experience would yield entirely different results, and so that inference from a belief corresponding to the experience would also go in a different direction. If there are such cases, they would appear to involve counterexamples to conditionalization, and (as discussed in the next chapter) I think are best seen as involving conceptual change or irrationality.

As with recognitional capacities, someone might also hold that an unmediated inference simply needs to be reliably truth-preserving to do its justifying work. For example, one might simply by luck come to be disposed to infer from bachelorhood to untidiness, in a way that is not grounded in correlations between bachelorhood and untidiness but that is reliably truth-preserving all the same. One might hold that this mechanism could yield justified belief in M (given $PQTI$ as a premise) even though a corresponding case in which one just by luck forms the mediating belief that most bachelors are untidy would not yield justified belief in M. One might also hold that this is a case in which a justified inference from $PQTI$ to M holds without there being a nearby justified conditional belief in M given $PQTI$, giving a sort of violation of conditionalization. If so, the inference from Inferential Scrutability to Conditional Scrutability and/or A Priori Scrutability may not go through.

I am skeptical that such an ungrounded reliable inference should count as justified. But if someone disagrees, I will once again stipulate higher standards of strong knowledge and justification that excludes ungrounded reliable inferences. As in the case of recognitional capacities, one can argue that cases of ungrounded reliable inference will be rare. And as in that case, one can argue that what can be known using these inferences can be known without them. We can then run the argument from knowability (for inferential and conditional scrutability) using the notion of strong knowability, and the premises remain equally plausible. It follows that one is in a position to have strong conditional knowledge of *M* given *PQTI*. The inference to A Priori Scrutability then goes through, unaffected by worries about ungrounded reliable inferences.

Varieties of Apriority

The notions of a priori knowledge and justification play a central role in this work. There are many ways in which one can understand the a priori, so in this excursus I will go into more detail about just how I am understanding it.

I have said that a sentence S is a priori for a subject s if s is in a position to know S with justification independent of experience. This characterization of apriority differs from some standard conceptions in that it predicates apriority of sentences and also in that it involves potential knowledge rather than knowledge. Other aspects of the definition, such as 'justification independent of experience' and the strength of the relevant sort of knowledge, need to be clarified.

In order to clarify my conception of the a priori, I will go over issues concerning sententiality, idealization, experience-independence, and conclusiveness. My aim is not to show that this is the one true conception of the a priori. Rather, my aim is to set out a stipulative conception that is the most useful for my purposes, and to show how it differs from other conceptions.

I will not try to give a positive account of the a priori in the sense of answering the question 'How is a priori knowledge possible?' I do not have a positive account to offer any more than I have a positive account of empirical knowledge. I have instead adopted the approach of clarifying what I mean by the a priori, and of answering important challenges. I take it to be antecedently fairly obvious that there is a priori knowledge (in logic and mathematics, for example), so I take it that absent strong arguments to the contrary, we have good reasons to believe that a priori knowledge is possible. I address Quine's famous challenge to the a priori in the next chapter, and I address two recent challenges in the next excursus.

Sententiality

Standardly, the notion of apriority applies most fundamentally to knowledge and justification, and perhaps derivatively to propositions. Typically, one says that a subject knows a priori that p when she knows that p with justification independent of experience. A subject knows a posteriori (or equivalently, knows empirically) that p when she knows that p with justification that depends on experience. One can then say that p is knowable a priori, or more simply that p is a priori, when it is possible that someone knows a priori that p.

It is less standard to associate apriority with sentences.[1] One could start with the definitions above and simply say that a sentence S is a priori when it expresses an a priori proposition. But because the nature of propositions is contested, as discussed in section 2 of chapter 2, doing this will not serve my purposes. Instead, I ground the apriority of sentences in the apriority of associated thoughts, where thoughts are mental states such as beliefs.

A thought is *a priori justified* when it is justified independently of experience. A thought constitutes *a priori knowledge* when it is a priori justified and constitutes knowledge in virtue of that justification. A thought constitutes *potential a priori knowledge* when it is possible that on (perhaps idealized) reflection, it can come to constitute a priori knowledge. In this case, we can also say more simply that the thought is *a priori*.

We can then define the apriority of sentences in terms of the apriority of thoughts. For a context-independent sentence S, S is *known a priori* by a subject when the subject has a thought that constitutes a priori knowledge and is apt to be expressed by S. S is *justified a priori* when S expresses a thought that is justified a priori. S is *knowable a priori* or just *a priori* when it is possible that someone knows S a priori.

When S is context-dependent, its apriority may depend on context. For example, it may be that 'bald' is context-sensitive in such a way that 'Someone is bald iff they have no hairs on their head' is a priori in some contexts but not others. We can say (as in the third excursus) that S is known a priori in a context (in which S is uttered) if the utterance of S in that context expresses a thought that constitutes a priori knowledge. (Equivalently, a sentence token is a priori if it expresses such a thought.) S is justified a priori in a context when it expresses a thought in that context that is justified a priori. S is knowable a priori, or just a priori, in a context when it expresses in that context a thought that constitutes potential a priori knowledge.

The stipulated conception of apriority helps to bypass the debate between Fregeans and Russellians about the nature of propositions and about which sentences express propositions that are knowable a priori. Fregeans typically endorse the intuitive view that 'Hesperus is Phosphorus' expresses a proposition that cannot be known a priori. Russellians (e.g. Salmon 1986; Soames 2002) typically hold that the sentence expresses a trivial singular proposition (that Venus is Venus) that can be known a priori. For this reason, a Russellian might classify

---

[1] It is worth noting, though, that in *Naming and Necessity* (e.g. pp. 65–6), Kripke often casts his discussion of apriority in terms of the apriority of a sentence for a speaker.

the sentence as a priori. This debate concerns a conception of apriority distinct from the one I am concerned with, however.

On the current definition of apriority, 'Hesperus is Phosphorus' is not a priori in a typical context. The thought expressed by a typical utterance of 'Hesperus is Phosphorus' clearly cannot be justified independently of experience. There is no process of reasoning that starts with this very mental state and ends with its constituting a priori knowledge. At best, a different thought (one expressible by 'Hesperus is Hesperus', for example) associated with the same singular proposition can be so justified.

It might be objected that if expression of a thought by an utterance requires only that the thought and the utterance have the same content, and if the contents of both are singular propositions, then 'Hesperus is Phosphorus' might express a thought that Venus is Venus, which is a priori. Likewise, it might be objected that if persistence of a thought over time requires merely sameness of content, then a thought that Hesperus is Phosphorus might become justified a priori in virtue of persisting as a thought that Hesperus is Hesperus. In response, we can note that the notions of expression and persistence (discussed in the third excursus) require more than sameness of content: they require appropriate causal, psychological, and inferential connections, of a sort that are absent in the purported case of expression and persistence above.

On the current definition, the apriority or non-apriority of a sentence is not simply a function of the referents of the parts of the sentence. For example, although 'Hesperus is Phosphorus' above is not a priori in a typical context, and the same goes for 'If Hesperus exists, Hesperus is Phosphorus', 'If Hesperus exists, Hesperus is Hesperus' is plausibly a priori in all typical contexts.[2] On this approach, as on the intuitive understanding, apriority is sensitive to modes of presentations. The last two sentences differ in apriority despite the expressions used having the same referents, and differing only in the way that those referents are presented. We do not need to make any explicit stipulations about modes of presentation to obtain this result. The phenomenon in question results from the stipulation that the apriority of a sentence in a context depends on the epistemic properties of the thought expressed by an utterance of the sentence, where these epistemic properties are tied to the inferential role of the thought in cognition. There is no doubting that the thoughts associated with the two sentences above are associated with quite different inferential roles.

[2] Perhaps there are atypical contexts in which someone has acquired the name 'Hesperus' from two different sources and in which a speaker uses 'If Hesperus exists, Hesperus is Hesperus' to express an empirical thought that they are not in a position to know a priori. If so, the sentence is not a priori in that context. Likewise, there perhaps are atypical contexts in which a speaker uses 'Hesperus' and 'Phosphorus' entirely interchangeably (perhaps taking it as stipulative that both refer to Venus). Then 'If Hesperus exists, Hesperus is Phosphorus' is a priori in that context.

It is worth noting, though, that Russellians who accept guises or modes of presentation can define something close to the current notion by appeal to these entities. For example, Salmon (1993) allows that a proposition is *w-apriori* relative to a given way of taking it if the proposition can be known a priori under that way. One could then suggest that a sentence S is a priori in a context (in which S is uttered), in the current sense, if the proposition it expresses is w-apriori relative to the way the proposition is presented in the utterance of S in that context. The apriority of a thought could be defined in a similar way. In this sense, even on a Russellian view 'Hesperus is Phosphorus' will certainly not be a priori in typical contexts.

To say that sentence S is a priori in a context centered on speaker A is not to say that a knowledge ascription of the form 'A knows a priori that S' (or 'A can know a priori that S') is true. Clearly 'If I exist and am located, I am here' may be a priori for a speaker even if that speaker cannot know a priori that if I exist and am located, I am here. The criteria may also come apart in cases where ascriber and ascribee use the expressions in S with different modes of presentation. The current construal of apriority requires no commitment on the semantics of attitude ascriptions (although in 'Propositions and Attitude Ascriptions', I have argued for a Fregean treatment of these ascriptions). What I have said here about the non-apriority of 'Hesperus is Phosphorus' is even consistent with a Russellian semantics for attitude ascriptions on which 'A knows a priori that Hesperus is Phosphorus' is true.

My account of sentential apriority presupposes the notions of thoughts, expression, and persistence. If one rejects these notions, one will have to define the apriority of a sentence in some other way. One could appeal to Fregean propositions, or to associated guises, or perhaps to ancillary propositions. But again, at least once general skepticism about the a priori (discussed in the eighth excursus and in the next chapter) is dismissed, it is something of a datum that utterances of sentences such as 'Hesperus is Hesperus (if it exists)' correspond to a priori knowledge in a way that typical utterances of 'Hesperus is Phosphorus (if it exists)' do not. So any satisfactory theory will have to give an account of this distinction.

Idealization

The current notion of apriority involves an idealization away from a speaker's contingent cognitive limitations, and even away from contingent human limitations. A sentence token (of a complex mathematical sentence, for example) may be a priori even if the speaker's actual cognitive capacities are too limited to justify the corresponding thought a priori. To a first approximation, what matters is that it is *possible* that the corresponding thought be justified a priori.

On a second approximation one can dispense with the modal definition. As we saw earlier (E3), that definition leads to problems both with semantic fragility and with views on which certain conceivable cognitive capacities are not metaphysically possible. For example, if it turns out that no possible being can construct a proof with more than a million steps, then a statement whose proof requires more steps than this will not be knowable a priori by any thinker. But it will still count as a priori in the idealized sense I am invoking here.

One might invoke a normative idealization here, understanding apriority in terms of what a thinker ideally ought to accept. But perhaps the best option is to understand the apriority of a sentence in terms of the existence of an a priori warrant for that sentence (as in E4). We can say that context-independent sentence *S* is a priori when there exists an a priori warrant for it (for some possible speaker), and that a context-dependent sentence *S* is a priori in a context when there is an a priori warrant for accepting it for the speaker of that context. In the mathematical case above, for example, there exists a proof for the sentence, even if it is impossible that the proof be used to prove the sentence. Correspondingly, one can say that there exists an a priori warrant for the sentence, even if it is impossible that the warrant be used to justify the sentence. One can argue that all a priori knowledge is grounded in an a priori warrant, so that a priori warrant is the more fundamental notion here.

In principle, we can understand the apriority of both sentences and propositions in terms of a priori warrants. If we do so, the notion will be unaffected by brute constraints on the metaphysical possibility of a priori knowledge. As a bonus, this construal gives us a notion of propositional apriority that is unaffected by the problems of semantic fragility discussed earlier (E3): the propositions expressed by relevant sentences of the form 'S iff actually S' may not be knowable a priori, but there exist proofs for these propositions, and the propositions still have an a priori warrant.

Non-experiential justification

The definition of apriority says 'justified independent of experience'. Here, what is excluded is a justifying role for experience. It is a familiar point that even in a priori knowledge (say, knowledge of 'Red is red'), experience may play an enabling role in giving one the concepts that are required for this knowledge. Furthermore, in a priori deduction of one logical claim from another, it is not out of the question that the experience of thought plays a causal role in the inference process. Apriority is compatible with enabling roles and other causal roles for experience: only a justifying role is ruled out. One could capture this notion more precisely in the framework of support structures by saying 'has a non-experiential justification', where a justification is non-experiential (to a first approximation) when it is not grounded in experiential evidence.

The paradigm cases of experiential justification are cases in which a subject's phenomenal experience serves as evidence. For example, a belief that there is a red cube in front of one can be justified by perceptual experience as of a red cube, and an introspective belief that one is in pain can be justified by the pain experience. But there are tricky cases that do not obviously involve an evidential role for phenomenal experience: what about beliefs produced by unconscious perception, or by non-experiential introspection? These should count as a posteriori for our purposes. (On some conceptions, introspective knowledge counts as a priori, but it does not on mine: we do not want 'I believe that I am Australian' to be a priori scrutable for me from any base just because I can know it by introspection.) So one might instead stipulate that an experiential justification is one grounded in perceptual or introspective evidence, where this leaves open whether conscious experience per se is involved.

In principle one might also count other sources of justification as experiential: testimonial justification, for example. I will not explicitly include this, as I think that perceptual justification is always involved in testimonial justification, but if someone disagrees, these can be included too. More generally, we might have a category of basic empirical evidence (as in E4) and say that a justification is a posteriori when basic empirical evidence plays a justifying role and a priori when it does not. Basic empirical evidence includes at least perceptual and introspective evidence, but the definition leaves open that it includes more. This question is revisited at the end of the eighth excursus.

Conclusiveness

It is often held that a priori knowledge must meet higher standards than those ordinarily invoked for empirical knowledge. For example, it is sometimes held that a priori knowledge must meet the sort of conclusive standard associated with proof and analysis, rather than the weaker standard associated with induction and abduction. On this conception, an inductive generalization from instances each of which is known a priori—say, generalizing to the truth of Goldbach's conjecture on the grounds that all even numbers so far examined are the sum of two primes—does not yield a priori knowledge, even though there is some sense in which it is justified as well as most empirical inductive knowledge, and justified a priori. Likewise, an abductive conditional from total evidence to a conclusion that is grounded in and goes beyond the evidence might have some sort of a priori justification, but on the conception in question it will not yield a priori knowledge.

This conception is that of the *conclusive* a priori, since it requires that one can conclusively rule out (in a certain intuitive sense) the possibility that the relevant conclusion is false. In the cases above, although one may have non-experiential justification for believing a conclusion, one is unable to conclusively rule out the possibility that the conclusion is false. This standard is higher than the standard typically invoked for empirical knowledge, where one typically allows that induction and abduction can yield knowledge, even though one cannot conclusively rule out (in the same intuitive sense) the possibility that the relevant conclusion is false.

There is some intuitive force to the idea that a priori knowledge requires conclusiveness (or at least potential conclusiveness), but we need not adjudicate this matter here. Instead, we can stipulate a notion of the conclusive a priori, which builds in a requirement of conclusiveness, and a notion of the nonconclusive a priori, which does not. Both notions are useful for different purposes, including my own purposes. On the face of it, A Priori Scrutability remains a strong and interesting thesis if it is cast in terms of nonconclusive apriority. Still, for some of my purposes (notably the modal and semantic purposes discussed in the tenth and eleventh excursuses), conclusive apriority is the most important notion, and a scrutability thesis cast in terms of it will play an important role.

It is natural to understand conclusive knowledge as *certainty*, as we did in section 1 of chapter 2. We might take this notion as primitive, or understand it as requiring a justified credence of 1, or understand it intuitively as knowledge beyond skepticism: knowledge that enables one to absolutely exclude any skeptical scenarios in which the relevant belief is false. This epistemological notion should be contrasted with mere psychological certainty, which requires something like full confidence without requiring justification. We might say that certainty in the epistemological sense is justified psychological certainty.

On a traditional view, processes such as induction, abduction, and perception do not yield certainty, but other processes such as deduction, introspection, and perhaps conceptual analysis can yield certainty. For example, it is widely held that a priori reasoning can yield certainty of mathematical claims. Perhaps it is not obvious that we non-ideal reasoners can be certain here, but there is some appeal to the idea that idealized reasoning about logic and mathematics could yield certainty. Likewise, it is arguable that there is at least an ideal warrant for being certain of various mathematical truths.

One complication is that even with ideal a priori reasoning, certainty can be undermined by self-doubt concerning one's cognitive capacities, as discussed in the sixth excursus. To handle this, one might suggest that conclusive knowledge is knowledge that falls short of certainty at most in virtue of this sort of self-doubt. Or perhaps better, one might invoke the insulated idealization discussed in the sixth excursus, and hold that a thought is conclusively a priori if insulated idealized reflection on the thought would lead to its being accepted with psychological certainty (or: if there is an insulated ideal warrant for its being accepted with psychological certainty).

Even setting aside self-doubt, someone might argue that there cannot be epistemological certainty even for ideal reasoners. It might be held that even logical truths are not certain in this way, even on an insulated idealization. Given such a view, one will need to characterize conclusive knowledge in other terms (perhaps by example). Speaking for myself, I think it is reasonably plausible that there can be certainty under an idealization, and I think that scrutability conditionals are in principle knowable with this sort of certainty. But I leave open the possibility that conclusive knowledge can be defined in some other way.

Recent Challenges to the A Priori

I have appealed freely to the notion of a priori justification: justification independent of experience. I have also appealed freely to derivative notions such as
a priori knowledge, a priori knowability, a priori sentences, a priori inferences, and
so on. While these notions have a venerable history in philosophy, they have also
attracted some skepticism. The most prominent source of skepticism arises from
Quine's critique of the analytic/synthetic distinction, which is the focus of the next
chapter. In this excursus, I focus on some more recent doubts about the a priori,
articulated by John Hawthorne in his article 'A Priority and Externalism' (2007)
and by Timothy Williamson in his book *The Philosophy of Philosophy* (2007).

Hawthorne raises doubts about a priori knowledge tied in the first instance to
externalist constraints on knowledge. He first stipulates a strongly internalist
notion of a priori knowledge: x's believing p is a case of a priori knowledge iff for
any possible intrinsic duplicate y, the counterpart in y of x's belief that p is a case
of knowledge. Here the idea is that a priori knowledge is knowledge that depends
only on features intrinsic to a subject. He also assumes that knowledge requires
safety: to know that p, it should be the case that there are no close worlds in
which one makes a mistake about p. (Strictly: there are no close worlds in which
one makes a mistake that is relevantly similar to one's actual belief that p.)

Hawthorne then argues that given these two constraints, there can be no a
priori knowledge. For any subject with a belief that p that putatively counts as a
priori knowledge, there will be an intrinsic duplicate whose belief that p is not
safe, and therefore is not knowledge. The key case involves 'a priori gas': a gas
that if inhaled causes the subject to make all sorts of mistakes in a priori reasoning. If one is surrounded by a priori gas, then one's beliefs are not safe: even if
one has not inhaled the gas, there are nearby worlds in which one inhales the gas
and makes mistakes. And for any subject, there is an intrinsic duplicate subject
who is surrounded by a priori gas. So for any subject, there is an intrinsic duplicate subject whose beliefs are not safe, and who therefore (by the safety criterion)
lacks a priori knowledge. So no belief by any subject satisfies the definition of a
priori knowledge above.

Now, I think this definition of a priori knowledge should clearly be rejected.
I think there are possible subjects who have a priori knowledge enabled by

extrinsic conditions (see the discussion in the thirteenth excursus), and I think there is some empirical knowledge (e.g., knowledge of one's own consciousness) that depends just as strongly on intrinsic conditions as does a priori knowledge. So even if my intrinsic duplicate surrounded by a priori gas lacks a priori knowledge, I think it does not follow that I lack a priori knowledge. Still, the question of whether external constraints such as safety can undermine a priori knowledge is an interesting one. If we allow that the subject surrounded by a priori gas lacks a priori knowledge, then the status of our beliefs as a priori knowledge is at least vulnerable to the state of the environment. That alone does not undermine the existence of a priori knowledge, but it may weaken its epistemic security a little.

I do not think it is obvious that the subject surrounded by a priori gas lacks a priori knowledge, but I also do not think it is obvious that they have a priori knowledge. Rather than settle the matter, I am more interested in whether there is a positive epistemic status that their belief possesses despite the a priori gas. In particular, I am inclined to think that if I have a priori justification for believing p, then so does my twin surrounded by a priori gas. Even if safety is an absolute constraint on knowledge, it is not an absolute constraint on justification. Correspondingly, while the gas may or may not undermine my twin's knowledge, it does not undermine his justification. If there are cases in which intrinsic twins differ in whether corresponding beliefs are a priori justified (see 8.4), I do not think these cases are among them.

If this is right, Hawthorne's arguments do not undermine the existence of a priori knowledge, although they may suggest that the status of a belief as a priori knowledge is extrinsic. They also do not undermine either the existence or the intrinsicness of a priori justification. Hawthorne goes on to argue against a conception of internal a priori justification that depends on an inner 'glow', but he does not argue against other conceptions. So I take it that the existence and even the intrinsicness of a priori justification are left standing.

Williamson (2007, pp. 165–9) argues for a deflationary view of the a priori/a posteriori distinction. He devotes much more space to the analytic/synthetic distinction, arguing that there are no metaphysically or epistemologically analytic truths. I am not committed to analytic truths, and it is clear that Williamson's arguments against them do nothing to undermine the a priori, so I will not engage these arguments here (although see 'Verbal Disputes' and the seventeenth excursus for some relevant remarks). He also devotes a few pages to the a priori/a posteriori distinction, however, arguing that it is not an important or natural distinction, and in particular that it does not yield a natural way to classify the role of experience in certain cases.

Williamson's central case involves knowledge of the counterfactual 'If two marks had been nine inches apart, they would have been at least nineteen centimeters apart'. The subject in question does not know a conversion ratio, but instead imagines two marks nine inches apart and uses visual recognitional capacities to judge that they are nineteen centimeters apart. Williamson argues that sense experience does not play a 'directly evidential' role: one does not recall past experiences, or deploy premises grounded in experience. But he argues that it plays a more than enabling role: one uses skills for judging lengths that are deeply grounded in past experience. So he suggests that the knowledge in question is not naturally classed as either a priori or a posteriori.

Here Williamson focuses on a certain traditional way of dividing the possible roles of experience in belief. Experience might play a merely enabling role, enabling one to possess the concepts involved in a belief, or it might play an evidential role, giving one evidence for the belief. A priori knowledge allows experience to play an enabling role but not an evidential role. I think it is obvious that this distinction is not exhaustive, however. A distinction that is closer to exhaustive is the one I made earlier between causal and justificatory roles. Experience might play all sorts of causal roles in forming a belief that are neither enabling nor evidential: for example, a pang of fear might cause one to think about mathematics and thereby acquire knowledge. A justifying role may come to much the same thing as an evidential role, but importantly, there can be indirect justifying and evidential roles that are not 'directly evidential', as when past experience justifies a pattern of inference used to form a belief. On this picture, the key question for apriority is whether experience plays a justificatory role or a merely causal role (or no role at all).

From this perspective, Williamson's observation that experience does not play a directly evidential role does little to settle the matter. The question is whether experience plays a justificatory role, including indirectly evidential roles. Insofar as we accept Williamson's view that the subject does not have mediating beliefs relating inches to centimeters, then the subject will be deploying some sort of inference from two marks being nine inches apart to their looking a certain way (perhaps invoking a certain mental image), and another inference from their looking that way to the two marks being more than nineteen centimeters apart. It might be natural to hold that these inferences turn on beliefs that nine inches look that way, and so on, but Williamson will presumably deny that such mediating beliefs must be involved. If so, the two inferences will be direct in the sense discussed earlier (under the objection from empirical inference). The key question is then the status of these inferences: are they justified by experience, or not?

Now, I think that Williamson's case is underspecified. There are plausibly versions of the case in which the inference is justified by experience and versions where it is not. If the subject has a deferential conception of a centimeter, roughly picking out a centimeter as what people around here call 'a centimeter', then the inference in question will plausibly be empirical: it will be grounded in evidence that people around here call certain lengths 'a centimeter'. If the subject picks out a centimeter as one-hundredth of the length of the meter stick in Paris, then likewise. If the subject is a nondeferential user of the term who has a conception of one centimeter as a certain visual length, on the other hand, then the inference may well be a priori: experience may have played an enabling role in acquiring the conception and other causal roles, but there is no need to postulate a justificatory role. So in some versions of the case the knowledge is empirical, and in other cases it is a priori, with everything coming down to the justificatory role of experience in acquiring the inferential capacity.

The matter is clearer in another case that Williamson discusses: 'If two marks had been nine inches apart, they would have been further apart than the front and back legs of an ant'. If understood analogously, this case will involve direct inferences between premises about length and conclusions about ants, or perhaps between premises about ants and conclusions about their looking a certain way, or something in the vicinity. In this case, it is plausible that if the inferences are justified, they will be justified by experience: in particular, by one's past experiences of ants and their sizes. So the current framework classifies these cases correctly.

One can count this sort of justificatory role for experience as an evidential role in a broad sense. Williamson suggests that if we count the role of experience as evidential in this case, then one may also have to do so in other cases that are paradigms of the a priori: for example 'It is necessary that whoever knows something believes it'. But even if this case turns on an analogous direct inference between premises about knowledge and conclusions about belief, there is no analogous reason to think that experience plays a justifying role in the inference in this case. At least if we stipulate nondeferential possession of the concepts involved, then in paradigm cases there is no obvious justifying role for experience analogous to the obvious role of experiencing ants. Williamson notes that our judgment depends on the skill with which we deploy concepts, which itself depends on past experience; even so, nothing here begins to suggest a justificatory role for experience. So although the status of this judgment depends on the details of the case, it is prima facie plausible that there are at least some cases in which the inference is justified a priori.[1]

---

[1] Williamson (forthcoming) makes similar arguments about (1) 'All crimson things are red' compared to (2) 'All recent volumes of Who's Who are red'. He invokes a subject who knows both of these things by imagining the relevant objects and judging that they are red, and argues that the role of experience is the same in both cases: 'The only residue of his experience of recent volumes of Who's Who active in his knowledge of (2) is his skill in recognizing and imagining such volumes. That role for experience is less than strictly evidential'. On the present account, past experience plays a justifying role in these skills, most obviously in justifying the imaginative judgment 'Recent volumes of Who's Who look such-and-such'. It need play no analogous role in justifying the imaginative judgment 'Crimson things look such-and-such'.

Of course one can use words such as 'evidential' and 'a priori' as one pleases. The non-verbal point is that a justificatory role for experience in inference clearly renders a resulting belief a posteriori on an extremely natural way of drawing an a priori/a posteriori distinction. Williamson does not consider this sort of justificatory role for experience in his argument. Perhaps he would deny that there is a coherent or natural distinction between cases in which inferences are justified by experience and cases in which they are not, but he has not given an argument against that distinction here.

Williamson suggests at one point that the a priori/a posteriori distinction can be drawn in various ways, but that however it is drawn it will not be an important distinction, because of the similarity between cases of a priori knowledge and cases of a posteriori knowledge. I think the different sources of support make a difference worth marking, however. For my purposes the crucial distinction is that between sentences or propositions that are a priori knowable and those that are not, and especially that between those that have a conclusive a priori warrant and those that do not. These are importantly different classes. The explanatory role of that distinction can be brought out in many ways: for example, by its many applications in the current project.

That said, there are cases that pose a harder problem for the traditional distinction. These cases (discussed briefly in chapter 2) involve mechanisms that deliver reliably true beliefs of the sort that are typically delivered by a posteriori mechanisms, but that are not grounded in the subject's perceptual or introspective evidence. For example, such a system might reliably deliver true beliefs about scientific laws (e.g., the law of gravity) and enable reliable inferences that use those laws. One case involves a *lucky mechanism*: an internal mechanism that develops without any experiential justification and that through luck delivers reliably true beliefs about laws. Another case involves an *evolved mechanism*: an innate mechanism that has been shaped by selection in the evolutionary past so that it reliably delivers true beliefs about laws.[2] Many advocates of the a priori, including me, will not want to count the beliefs produced by these mechanisms as a priori knowledge, but it is not entirely obvious why they do not fit the definition.

These cases will not yield *conclusive* a priori knowledge, as the mechanisms cannot plausibly produce justified certainty. An opponent might suggest that complete reliability in these cases will produce a kind of justified certainty; but I think it is antecedently clear that the paradigmatic sort of conclusive apriority that may be possible in logical cases is not possible here. So the notion of conclusive apriority, which I take to be the most important sort of apriority, is not

[2] Hawthorne discusses lucky mechanisms and evolved mechanisms in his 2002 and 2007 respectively, although he uses them to illustrate consequences of externalist conceptions of apriority rather than to undermine the traditional a priori/a posteriori distinction.

thrown into question by these cases. Still, the question arises of whether these mechanisms produce nonconclusive a priori knowledge. If they do not (as many advocates of the a priori will hold), we need to know why not, given that the subject's experience does not play a justifying role.

A traditionalist may deny that the lucky mechanism produces knowledge, perhaps because it is not appropriately grounded in reasons and evidence. It is harder to take this line for the evolved mechanism, as doing so may undermine much knowledge produced by evolved mechanisms. Still, as in chapter 2, one can at least stipulate a notion of evidentialist knowledge that works this way. Alternatively, one could suggest that the evolved mechanism produces a posteriori knowledge because it is justified by other subjects' past experience. I think there is something to this response, but it requires a greatly elaborated treatment of cross-subject justification. Perhaps the simplest response is to count these mechanisms as producing basic empirical evidence that is not itself experiential evidence. The residual question will then be how to characterize empirical evidence if not in terms of experience. One might try putting weight on interactions with the external world, but the lucky mechanism need not involve such interactions. A better option may be to characterize the a priori in positive rather than negative terms. For example, one might hold (with BonJour 1998) that a priori justification involves justification by reason alone, rather than justification independent of experience. The residual question is then to pin down the notion of justification by reason at least sufficiently well to yield a principled classification of basic evidence as a priori or empirical.

If we were instead to allow that these cases involve nonconclusive a priori knowledge, it might then turn out that most truths can be nonconclusively known a priori. This would suggest in turn that most truths are nonconclusively a priori scrutable from any base, at least in the modal sense where a priori scrutability is understood in terms of the possibility of a priori knowledge. If so, an A Priori Scrutability thesis using the modal notion of nonconclusive a priori knowability would be trivialized. Still, the version of A Priori Scrutability that relies on evidentialist knowledge will not be trivialized, and neither will the version that relies on conclusive a priori knowledge. All this tends to reinforce the view that at least for the purposes I am concerned with, conclusive apriority is the most important notion.

5

Revisability and
Conceptual Change

1 Introduction

Perhaps the most famous attack on Carnap's logical empiricism is W. V. Quine's article 'Two Dogmas of Empiricism'. In the article, Quine argues against the analytic/synthetic distinction that Carnap employs, as well as against his some-time verificationism. The article is widely regarded as much more than an attack on logical empiricism, however. It is often seen as the most important critique of the notion of the a priori, with the potential to undermine the whole program of conceptual analysis.

In this chapter, I address Quine's most influential arguments in 'Two Dogmas'. I do this in part for defensive reasons and in part for constructive reasons. Defensively: Quine's arguments might be thought to undermine my frequent appeals to the a priori, so addressing these arguments helps to support those appeals. Constructively: addressing Quine's arguments in the spirit of the scrutability framework helps to bring out some of the power of that framework. For example, it helps us to analyze notions of meaning in a broadly Carnapian manner, and it helps us to understand the relationship between rationality and conceptual change.

I will address Quine's article construed as a critique of the notions of analyticity and apriority. I am more inclined to defend the notion of apriority than the notion of analyticity, so I will focus more on the former, but the response that I develop can be used to defend either notion from Quine's arguments. I will focus especially on the most influential part of Quine's article: the arguments in the final section concerning revisability and conceptual change.

In addressing these arguments, I will adopt a line of response grounded in Carnap's underappreciated article 'Meaning and Synonymy in Natural Languages'. Carnap's article offers an approach to meaning that is highly congenial to the scrutability framework. I will argue that an analysis inspired by this article, when conjoined with tools drawn from the scrutability framework and from Bayesian confirmation theory, provides just what is needed to reject Quine's argument.

Along the way, I will motivate a Carnap-style analysis of meaning within the current framework. The analysis of meaning is developed further in the tenth and eleventh excursuses. In the ninth excursus I address objections to scrutability from conceptual change.

2 The arguments of 'Two Dogmas'

In sections 1 through 4 of 'Two Dogmas of Empiricism', Quine argues that if one tries to make sense of the notion of analyticity, one ends up moving in a circle through cognate notions (synonymy, definition, semantic rules, meaning), and one cannot break out of the circle. Many philosophers have been unmoved by this worry, as it seems that one finds similar circles for all sorts of philosophically important notions: consciousness, causation, freedom, value, existence. So I will set these criticisms aside here.

In section 5 of the article, Quine makes points that specifically address Carnap's logical empiricism, criticizing his construction of physical concepts from phenomenal concepts in the *Aufbau*, and his verification theory of meaning. I will set these points aside here, as I am not concerned to defend Carnap's phenomenalist construction or the verification theory of meaning.

The extraordinary influence of Quine's article can be traced in large part to its short final section. Part of this influence stems from the positive picture that Quine offers in the first paragraph of the section, characterizing the totality of our knowledge as a 'man-made fabric which impinges on experience only along the edges', in which 'no particular experiences are linked with any particular statements in the interior of the field, except indirectly through considerations of equilibrium, affecting the field as a whole'. This picture serves as a powerful alternative to the verificationist picture provided by some logical empiricists, but it does not contain any direct argument against the analytic/synthetic distinction or the related notion of apriority.

The most influential arguments against an analytic/synthetic distinction are found in the second paragraph, which I quote in full:

> If this view is right, it is misleading to speak of the empirical content of an individual statement—especially if it be a statement at all remote from the experiential periphery of the field. Furthermore it becomes folly to seek a boundary between synthetic statements, which hold contingently on experience, and analytic statements which hold come what may. Any statement can be held true come what may, if we make drastic enough adjustments elsewhere in the system. Even a statement

very close to the periphery can be held true in the face of recalcitrant experience by pleading hallucination or by amending certain statements of the kind called logical laws. Conversely, by the same token, no statement is immune to revision. Revision even of the logical law of the excluded middle has been proposed as a means of simplifying quantum mechanics; and what difference is there in principle between such a shift and the shift whereby Kepler superseded Ptolemy, or Einstein Newton, or Darwin Aristotle? (Quine 1951, p. 43)

I will focus on these critical arguments. There are two crucial points.

(Q1) 'Any statement can be held true come what may, if we make drastic enough adjustments elsewhere in the system.'

(Q2) 'No statement is immune to revision.'

If (Q1) and (Q2) are read as mere psychological claims, saying that as a matter of fact someone might hold onto or revise any statement, then they are highly plausible, but not much of interest will follow from them. Quine is saying something more than this. We can understand (Q1) as saying that any statement can be *rationally* held true come what may, and (Q2) as saying that no statement is immune to *rational* revision. These points have interesting consequences.

Many have taken these points to suggest either that no sentences are analytic, or that no distinction can be drawn between analytic and synthetic sentences. One possible connection goes via the theses that analytic sentences are those that can be rationally held true come what may and that all analytic sentences are immune to rational revision. If so, (Q1) suggests that by the first criterion, all sentences will count as analytic. And (Q2) suggests that by the second criterion, no sentence will count as analytic. Either way, there is no useful distinction between analytic and synthetic sentences to be had. Similarly, if we assume that a priori sentences are those that can be rationally held true come what may and that all a priori sentences are immune to rational revision, (Q1) and (Q2) suggest that there is no useful distinction between a priori and a posteriori sentences to be had.

One common response to the argument from (Q2) is to suggest that revisability is quite compatible with apriority (or analyticity), on the grounds that a priori justification (or the justification we have for believing analytic sentences) is *defeasible*.[1] For example, I might know a mathematical claim a priori, but my justification might be defeated if I learn that a leading mathematician thinks that the claim is false. I think that this response is correct as far as it goes, but to rest entirely on it would be to concede a great deal to Quine. On a common

---

[1] See, for example, Field (1996). Kitcher (2000) defends a conception of the a priori that requires indefeasibility, while Peacocke (2004) defends a conception that does not. For present purposes I will remain neutral on whether apriority entails some sort of ideal indefeasibility; the observation about testimony in section 7 contains some relevant discussion.

traditional conception (not far from the conception of the conclusive a priori outlined in the last chapter), at least some a priori justification (and some justification for believing analytic truths) is *indefeasible*. One might reasonably hold that some a priori justification (in logic or mathematics, say) yields not just knowledge but certainty, at least on ideal reflection. These claims are not obviously correct: for example, a defense of them would have to address worries about metacognitive skepticism. But they are also not obviously incorrect, and I do not think that Quine's argument establishes that they are false. To see why not, we need another line of response.

The response I will develop takes off from the response given by Grice and Strawson at the end of their article 'In Defense of a Dogma'. This response holds that (Q1) and (Q2) are compatible with an analytic/synthetic distinction, for a reason quite different from the one given above. Here is a passage addressing the argument from (Q2):

> Now for the doctrine that there is no statement which is in principle immune from revision, no statement which might not be given up in the face of experience. Acceptance of this doctrine is quite consistent with adherence to the distinction between analytic and synthetic statements. Only, the adherent of this distinction must also insist on another; on the distinction between that kind of giving up which consists in merely admitting falsity, and that kind of giving up which involves changing or dropping a concept or set of concepts. Any form of words at one time held to express something true may, no doubt, at another time, come to be held to express something false. But it is not only philosophers who would distinguish between the case where this happens as the result of a change of opinion solely as to matters of fact, and the case where this happens at least partly as a result of a shift in the sense of the words. Where such a shift in the sense of the words is a necessary condition of the change in truth-value, then the adherent of the distinction will say that the form of words in question changes from expressing an analytic statement to expressing a synthetic statement. . . . And if we can make sense of this idea, then we can perfectly well preserve the distinction between the analytic and the synthetic, while conceding to Quine the revisability-in-principle of everything we say. (Grice and Strawson 1956: 156–7)

Here the central point is that our judgments about any *sentence*, even an analytic sentence, will be revisable if the meaning of the words change. For example, if 'bachelor' changes from a term for unmarried men to a term for sociable men, then we will no longer judge that 'All bachelors are unmarried' is true. But this observation is just what an adherent of the analytic/synthetic distinction should expect. Analytic sentences instead should be understood as those sentences that are immune to rational revision *while their meaning stays constant*. More precisely, they are those that are immune to rational rejection while their meaning stays constant. There is a sense in which an analytically false sentence might be immune to rational revision, but from here onward I will understand 'revision' as requiring rejection.

Following standard practice, we can say that when the meaning of a sentence changes, there is *conceptual change*: some expression in the sentence at first expresses one concept and later expresses another. When the meaning of a sentence stays the same, there is *conceptual constancy*: the expressions in the sentence express the same concepts throughout. Then Grice and Strawson's point could be put by saying that an analytic sentence is one that is immune to revision *without conceptual change*. More cautiously, the point could be put by saying that even if a sentence is analytic, it may still be revisable under conditions of conceptual change. Something similar applies to apriority.[2]

At this point, Quine has two obvious replies. The first is to say that the appeal to meaning in characterizing the class of analytic sentences is circular, as the notion of meaning is as poorly understood as the notion of analyticity. The same could be said for the appeal to concepts and to propositions. This reply would be in the spirit of the first four sections of 'Two Dogmas'. But then this argument will not be much of an advance on the arguments in the first four sections, and anyone who is not moved by those arguments will not be moved by this one.

The second, more interesting reply is to challenge Grice and Strawson to provide a *principled distinction* between cases of revision that involve conceptual change and those that involve conceptual constancy. Quine might argue that cases that are purported to be on either side of this division are in fact continuous with each other, and that there is no principled distinction to be had. Something like this thought might even be read into the last sentences of the paragraph from Quine quoted above.

Now one might suggest that Grice and Strawson are not obliged to provide a reductive characterization of the distinction—that is, one that does not use 'meaning' and cognate notions—any more than they are required to provide a reductive definition of meaning or analyticity to answer the challenge in the first four sections. Again, this suggestion seems correct as far as it goes. Nevertheless, if Quine's opponent cannot say much to characterize the principled distinction

---

[2] We can also allow that there is conceptual change in this sense when the proposition expressed by an utterance of a sentence changes because of a shift in context. For example, 'Someone is bald iff they have no hairs' might be accepted in one context and rejected in another. It is not clear that a mere contextual shift could change the status of a sentence as analytic, as arguably the meaning of such a sentence stays constant throughout. But if we say that a sentence is a priori if it expresses a proposition that is knowable a priori, then it is natural to hold that a sentence might be a priori in one context but not in another. It is for reasons like this that I speak of 'conceptual change' rather than 'meaning change' or 'semantic change'; the latter phrases tend to suggest changes in standing linguistic meaning (thereby excluding mere contextual shifts), but it is changes in the propositions and concepts expressed that matter most for our purposes.

here, he or she is at least in the awkward dialectical position of leaving a challenge unanswered, and of leaving doubts about the distinction unassuaged.

My view is that much can be said to flesh out a principled distinction here. In particular, the scrutability framework provides a way to motivate a principled distinction, building on tools first set out in Carnap's 'Meaning and Synonymy in Natural Languages'.

3 Carnap on intensions

Carnap is Quine's major target in 'Two Dogmas of Empiricism'. It is not always appreciated that 'Meaning and Synonymy in Natural Languages' can be read as a sustained response to Quine, perhaps because Carnap spends little time discussing him explicitly. Nevertheless, Carnap says enough to make clear that a response to 'Two Dogmas' is intended.

Carnap's article sets out to analyze the notion of meaning and related notions such as synonymy. His aim is to provide a 'scientific procedure' by which meaning and synonymy can be analyzed in broadly naturalistic terms. Importantly, he aims to explicate not only the notion of extension but also the notion of intension (the 'cognitive or designative component of meaning'), which he notes has been criticized by Quine as 'foggy, mysterious, and not really understandable'.

Carnap's key idea is that we can investigate the intension that a subject associated with an expression by investigating the subject's judgments about possible cases. To determine the intension of an expression such as 'Pferd' for a subject, we present the subject with descriptions of various logically possible cases, and we ask the subject whether he or she is willing to apply the term 'Pferd' to objects specified in these cases. If we do this for enough cases, then we can test all sorts of hypotheses about the intension of the expression.

In this article Carnap takes the term 'intension' as a primitive and does not build possible cases into the very nature of intensions. But for our purposes it is useful to adopt a suggestion that Carnap makes elsewhere, and simply define an intension as a function from possible cases to extensions. For a term like 'Pferd', the intension will be a function from possible cases to objects characterized in those cases. For a sentence such as 'Grass is green', the intension will be a function from possible cases to truth-values. Then Carnap's procedure above can be regarded as a way of ascertaining the values of the intension that a subject associates with an expression, by presenting the subject with a possible case and noting the extension that the subject associates with the case.

Of course one cannot actually present a subject with all possible cases to determine every aspect of an intension. But Carnap suggests that the intension that a speaker associates with an expression is determined by the speaker's linguistic dispositions. For a given expression E used by a given speaker, the speaker will have the disposition to associate a given extension with E, when presented with a possible case. For example, given a sentence S, the speaker will have the disposition to judge the sentence as true or false of a possible case, when presented with that case. The intension of an expression can then be seen as a function that maps possible cases to the extension that the speaker is disposed to identify, when presented with that case.

In this way, Carnap defines an expression's intension in naturalistic and even operational terms. We can go on to define synonymy: two expressions are synonymous (for a speaker at a time) when they have the same intension (for that speaker at that time). And we can define analyticity: a sentence is analytic (for a speaker at a time) when its intension has the value 'true' at all possible cases (for that speaker at that time).

With this definition in hand, we can go on to provide a principled criterion for conceptual change over time. An expression E undergoes change in meaning between t_1 and t_2 for a speaker iff the speaker's intension for E at t_1 differs from the speaker's intension for E at t_2. If we accept Carnap's dispositional account of intensions, it follows that E undergoes change in meaning between t_1 and t_2 iff there is a possible case such that the speaker is disposed to associate different extensions with E when presented with the case at t_1 and t_2.

There are many immediate questions about Carnap's account. What is a possible case? In what vocabulary are these cases specified? How can we determine whether the meaning of this vocabulary has changed? Cannot speakers make mistakes about intensions? Cannot they change their mind about a case without a change in meaning? Can meaning really be operationalized this easily? And so on. Carnap's account may need to be modified or at least refined to answer these questions.

Before addressing these matters, I will illustrate how Carnap's account might be used to address the challenge in section 6 of 'Two Dogmas' directly. In my view, the essential aspects, if not the specifics, of the resulting response are sound. These essential aspects carry over to more refined analyses couched in terms of the scrutability framework (section 5) and Bayesian confirmation theory (sections 6 and 7).

4 A Carnapian response

In 'Meaning and Synonymy in Natural Languages', Carnap does not mention the arguments in section 6 of 'Two Dogmas', nor does he address revisability or conceptual change. Nevertheless, his framework can be used to give a response to these arguments that is broadly in the spirit of Grice and Strawson's response, fleshed out with a principled criterion for conceptual change.

We can start with Quine's observation that any statement can be held true come what may. This seems correct. Even a paradigmatic synthetic sentence such as 'All bachelors are untidy' can be held true in the face of apparently countervailing evidence, if we allow sufficient adjustment of ancillary claims. The question is whether such adjustments will involve conceptual change, and whether we have a principled criterion for determining this.

We might as well start with a case. At t_1, Fred asserts 'All bachelors are untidy'. At t_2, Fred is presented with evidence of a tidy unmarried man. Fred responds: 'He's no bachelor! Bachelors must be over 30, and he's only 25'. At t_3, Fred is presented with evidence of a 35-year-old with a spotless apartment. Fred responds: 'He's not tidy! Look at the mess in his sock drawer'. In this way, Fred holds the sentence true throughout, and through similar maneuvers he can hold it true come what may.

Does this case involve conceptual change? We can apply Carnap's analysis to see whether Fred's intension for 'All bachelors are untidy' (call this sentence B) changes over the relevant timespan. Suppose that c is a detailed possible case in which there is an unmarried 25-year-old man with a tidy apartment. At t_2, when Fred is presented with the information that c obtains, he responds that 'All bachelors are untidy' is true with respect to c. By Carnap's criterion, Fred's intension for B is true with respect to c at t_2.

What about Fred's intension for B at t_1? The key question is: if Fred had been presented with a description of c at t_1, before he had evidence that the case was actual, would he have judged that 'All bachelors are untidy' was true with respect to c?

If the answer is yes, then Carnap's criterion suggests that there need be no conceptual change involved in the change of judgment between t_1 and t_2. In this case, Fred will simply have had an unusual intension for 'bachelor' all along.

If the answer is no, then Carnap's criterion suggests that there is relevant conceptual change between t_1 and t_2. The intension of 'All bachelors are untidy' will have changed during this time, probably because the intension of 'bachelor' has changed during this time.

The same applies more generally. If a speaker's judgment concerning a case at t_2 is reflected in the speaker's dispositions to respond to such a case at t_1, we can say that the speaker's judgment concerning that case is *prefigured*. If a speaker's judgment concerning a case at t_2 is not reflected in the speaker's dispositions at t_1, we can say that the speaker's judgment concerning the case is *postfigured*. On Carnap's account, postfigured judgments but not prefigured judgments involve conceptual change.

In any case, we have what we need. Carnap's framework allows us to see how any sentence can be held true come what may, while at the same time allowing a principled way to distinguish between those cases of holding true that involve conceptual change and those that do not. Something similar applies to cases of revisability, though I will not go into the details here.

5 Refining Carnap's account

Carnap's account of meaning is remarkably simple, and one might reasonably wonder whether such a simple account can be correct. The questions raised at the end of section 3 still need to be answered. I think that while some of these questions raise problems for the account, they can be addressed in a way that preserves something of the spirit of the account, if not the letter. In particular, the scrutability framework can be used to characterize intensions in a way that meets many of Carnap's needs.

The central idea here is that Carnap's possible cases correspond to scenario specifications such as $PQTI$, and his intensions will be defined by conditional or a priori scrutability with respect to these scenarios. Suppose our subject uses a sentence S. To evaluate the intension of S at a scenario w, specified by a sentence $PQTI^*$, we need only consider whether S is scrutable from $PQTI^*$ for the subject.

We can suppose that our subject is presented with a Cosmoscope carrying the information in $PQTI^*$, and uses it in conditional mode. Under the supposition that the Cosmoscope accurately describes reality (that $PQTI^*$ is true), the scrutability thesis suggests that ideal reasoning should lead the subject to a verdict about S. If this verdict is positive (that is, if S is scrutable from $PQTI^*$ for the subject), then the intension of S is true at w. If this verdict is negative (that is, if $\sim S$ is scrutable from $PQTI^*$ for the subject), then the intension of S is false at w. And so on.

This framework allows us to answer the central questions for Carnap's account. The first two questions concern possible cases: what are they, and how are they specified? For our purposes, possible cases should be epistemically possible scenarios. Scenarios can be specified by $PQTI$-like sets of sentences: $PQTI$ for one's actual scenario, variants on it for scenarios close to home, and sentences using different vocabulary for scenarios of very different sorts. For a full vocabulary for specifying scenarios, we can invoke the Generalized Scrutability thesis.[3] Any scenario will be specified by a maximal epistemically possible set of sentences in a generalized scrutability base, where a set of sentences is epistemically possible when its conjunction cannot be ruled out a priori. Then Generalized Scrutability implies that given any truth-apt sentence S and any scenario w, a truth-value for S will be scrutable from the set of sentences specifying w.

---

[3] This requires an unrestricted scrutability thesis, as opposed to the thesis restricted to ordinary truths that I have argued for so far, but here we can rely on the arguments for an unrestricted thesis in chapter 6.

A third common worry about Carnap-style accounts of meaning is that on the contemporary understanding, intensions are often not accessible to a subject, even by ideal reasoning. For example, if Kripke (1980) is right, the intension of 'water' picks out H_2O in all possible worlds, even for subjects who do not know that water is H_2O. Such subjects will not be disposed to identify H_2O as the extension of 'water' when presented with a possible case, so Carnap's definition will get the intension wrong.

The scrutability framework handles this issue by distinguishing epistemic possibilities from metaphysical possibilities, and by distinguishing epistemic and modal profiles as in chapter 1. Kripke's observation concerns the modal profile of 'water': the way the expression applies to metaphysically possible worlds. Where the modal profile is concerned, we think of possible cases counterfactually: if XYZ *had been* the liquid in the oceans and lakes (as in Putnam's Twin Earth), would water have been H_2O? Kripke and Putnam suggest that we should answer positively here, suggesting that the modal profile of 'water' always picks out H_2O. In the two-dimensional semantic framework, modal profiles correspond to secondary intensions: so the secondary intension of 'water is H_2O' is true at a Twin Earth world. To evaluate a secondary intension at a world, one often first needs empirical information about the actual world (e.g. the knowledge that water is actually H_2O).

By contrast, the intensions we are analyzing here are primary intensions. Primary intensions are more relevant to the a priori than secondary intensions, because they in effect capture an expression's epistemic profile (chapter 1): the way the expression applies to epistemically possible scenarios. Here subjects consider the possible cases as epistemic possibilities: if XYZ *is* the liquid in the oceans and lakes, is water H_2O? If we ask subjects to suppose that XYZ is actually in the oceans and lakes, they should conclude conditionally that water is XYZ (their credence that water is XYZ, conditional on being in a Twin Earth scenario, should be high). This suggests that in a Twin Earth scenario, with XYZ in the oceans and lakes, the primary intension of 'water is XYZ' is true, and the primary intension of 'water' picks out XYZ.

This is just the sort of conditional reasoning familiar from Conditional and A Priori Scrutability. One supposes that a certain scenario actually obtains, and one considers what follows. The arguments of the previous chapters suggest that even if we need empirical information to evaluate secondary intensions, we do not need it to evaluate primary intensions. So the Kripkean worry for Carnap-style accounts does not arise where scrutability is concerned.

A fourth problem for Carnap's account as it stands is that subjects can make mistakes. A subject might miscalculate and judge that $36 + 27 = 73$, and they might even be disposed to judge this to be true with respect to all possible scenarios. On Carnap's account, it will follow that '$36 + 27 = 73$' is analytic for the subject. But this seems the wrong result: on the face of it, the sentence is not even true. Similar mistakes are possible for non-ideal subjects in all sorts of domains.

The scrutability framework handles this problem in a familiar way: by invoking a normative idealization (chapter 2). Instead of appealing to what the subject *would* say in response to the case, we appeal to what the subject ideally *should* say. Or in modal terms: the intension of E maps a possible case c to the extension that the subject would identify for E, if they were to be presented with c and were to reason ideally. In effect, the idealization built into the notions of conditional or a priori scrutability allows these notions to define idealized intensions.

Construed in this idealized way, the account will no longer yield an operational definition of meaning, at least unless we can find an operational criterion for ideal reasoning. But this is not a bad thing for those who are inclined to reject behaviorism in any case. It is also far from clear that this account provides a naturalistic reduction of meaning: it will do so only if we already have a naturalistic reduction of ideal reasoning. But the account need not be a naturalistic reduction to be useful.

Someone might suggest that in these cases, it is facts about meaning that determine facts about ideal reasoning rather than vice versa: it is precisely because we mean such-and-such by 'Pferd' that we should say such-and-such. We need not take a stand on these questions about metaphysical priority here. All we need is that in these cases, there are facts about what subjects should say or about what ideal reasoning dictates, and that we have some pretheoretical grip on these facts. Then we can use these facts to help explicate a corresponding notion of meaning, regardless of which of these notions is metaphysically prior. In effect, we are using an antecedent grip on normative notions to help explicate semantic notions. Of course it remains open to a Quinean opponent to reject normative notions entirely. I discuss opposition of that sort later in the chapter.

A fifth worry for Carnap's account is that subjects might change their mind about a possible case without a change of meaning. Here, one can respond by appealing to Generalized Scrutability as above: then judgments about a sentence are determined by a scenario specification and by ideal reasoning. If so, then if the subject is given such a specification and reasons ideally throughout, there will not be room for her to change her mind in this way. Changes of mind about a fully specified scenario will always involve either a failure of ideal reasoning or a change in meaning. I will return to this issue later.

The model we reach is something like the following. The (primary) intension of an expression for a subject is a function that maps scenarios to extensions. Given a sentence S and a scenario w specified by a set of sentences D, the intension of S is true at w if S is scrutable from D, false at w if $\sim S$ is scrutable from D, and so on. In effect, the intension of S maps a scenario w to what a subject should ideally judge about the truth of S under the supposition that w is actual (or the supposition that all sentences in D are true). Likewise, we can think of the intension of a subsentential expression E as mapping a scenario w to what a subject should ideally judge to be the extension of E under the supposition that w is actual. This is not a perfect definition, but it is good enough for our purposes. This remains very much in the spirit of Carnap's definition, although the invocation of rationality makes it a normative cousin of Carnap's account.

Importantly, we can use this account to respond to Quine with a version of the Carnapian response in the previous section. Conceptual change (of the relevant sort) will occur precisely when an expression's primary intension changes across time. This will happen precisely when the subject's dispositions to judge the expression's extension in a possible case (given ideal reasoning) changes. As in the last section, we can find cases of holding-true where the dispositions change in this way, and cases where they do not. What matters is that we have a principled distinction.

A residual issue concerns the meaning of the basic vocabulary. If cases are specified in this vocabulary, then we need to ensure that the basic vocabulary does not change in meaning throughout the process. If we do not require this, the resulting condition for meaning change will be inadequate: a subject's dispositions to judge that S obtains with respect to a case specified by D might change over time, not because the meaning of S changes but because the meaning of terms in D changes. If we do require this, then it appears that we need some further criterion for meaning change in the basic vocabulary used in D, as the dispositional method would yield trivial results. So it appears that the dispositional method for determining meaning change, even when idealized, is incomplete.[4]

A second residual issue concerns the role of the a priori in characterizing this account. I have so far been vague about whether intensions are defined using conditional or a priori scrutability. For many purposes, it is most natural to appeal to the latter: the primary intension of a sentence S is true at a scenario w if a material conditional 'If D, then S' is a priori, where D is a canonical specification of S. If we appeal to a priori scrutability, however, then we have

---

[4] This objection is related to Quine's argument from the indeterminacy of translation in *Word and Object*. Quine took Carnap's account to be a serious challenge to his arguments in 'Two Dogmas', and the indeterminacy argument can be seen in part as a response to it. Here, Quine argues that no dispositional analysis can settle facts about meaning, because multiple assignments of reference will always be compatible with a subject's behavioral dispositions. This applies even to Carnap's account, if we allow multiple potential assignments of reference to the basic vocabulary. In effect, Carnap's account assumes that the meaning of the basic vocabulary is fixed, but it is not clear why such an assumption is legitimate, and it is not clear how this meaning might itself be grounded in dispositional facts. Thanks to Gillian Russell for discussion here.

arrived at a principled distinction only by helping ourselves to the contested notion of apriority along the way.

As before, it is not clear how bad these residual problems are. One might still see the intensional analysis as demonstrating that the Quinean phenomena of holding-true and revisability are quite compatible with the intensional framework and have no power to refute it. Even if one has to assume some independent grip on the notion of apriority, and on the meaning of expressions in the basic vocabulary, one can still use the framework to provide a reasonably enlightening analysis of relevant cases. Still, we have not broken out of the Quinean circle. It would be nice to be able to characterize the relevant distinctions without such a direct appeal to the contested notions.

I think that such a characterization can be found. At least for the purposes of answering Quine, we can define intensions in terms of conditional scrutability, rather than in terms of a priori scrutability. For example, one can say that the intension of a sentence S is true at a scenario w, for a subject, if $cr^*(S \mid D) = 1$ for that subject, where D is a canonical specification of w.

If we do this, then we will have a principled criterion for conceptual change that does not appeal to apriority. On this criterion, a subject's intension for S will change between t_1 and t_2 iff there is a scenario w with canonical specification D such that $cr^*(S \mid D)$ changes from 1 to 0 or vice versa. One could then run the arguments of the previous section once again using this notion. This will provide a reply to Quine's challenge that gets around the second residual issue above (regarding apriority), though it may still be subject to a version of the first issue (regarding the basic vocabulary).

At this point, however, an alternative analysis involving conditional probability is available. This analysis is closely related to the one just mentioned, and is a descendant of the Carnapian analysis in the previous section, but it does not require this semantic apparatus or the full scrutability framework. Instead of appealing to possible cases and intensions, it proceeds using only standard Bayesian considerations about evidence and updating. In addition to the advantage of familiarity, this approach has other significant advantages in responding to Quine's challenge. By avoiding the need for canonical specifications of complete possible scenarios, it avoids the large idealization needed to handle enormous specifications. As I discuss in section 8, it also has the potential to avoid or minimize the residual issues about apriority and the basic vocabulary discussed above.

6 A Bayesian analysis of holding-true

Let us assume a standard Bayesian model, on which sentences are associated with unconditional and conditional credences for subjects at times. That is, for

a given subject and a given time, a sentence S will be associated with an unconditional credence $cr(S)$, and a pair of sentences S and T will be associated with
conditional credence $cr(S \mid T)$. (These ordinary credences $cr(S \mid T)$ should be
distinguished from the idealized rational credences $cr'(S \mid T)$ and $cr^*(S \mid T)$
defined in chapter 2.) Credences are standardly taken to be real numbers
between 0 and 1, but for our purposes exactitude is not required. It is enough
that some credences be high and others low.

I will also assume a version of the principle of conditionalization: if a subject
has credence $cr_1(S \mid E)$ at t_1, and acquires total evidence specified by the evidence
sentence E at between t_1 and t_2, then the subject's credence $cr_2(S)$ at t_2 should be
equal to $cr_1(S \mid E)$. I will give a more precise version of this principle below. I will
discuss evidence sentences further later in this chapter, but for now we can think
of them as specifying either that certain experiences obtain or that certain observable states of affairs obtain.[5]

We can start with a typical case whereby an apparently synthetic sentence is
held true in the face of apparently countervailing evidence, by appeal to appropriate ancillary theses. As before, suppose that at t_1, Fred asserts 'All bachelors are
untidy'. At t_2, Fred acquires evidence indicating that there is a tidy, unmarried
25-year-old man, and responds by denying that the man is a bachelor, as bachelors must be over 30.

Let B be 'All bachelors are untidy', and let E be Fred's total relevant evidence
acquired between t_1 and t_2. Let $cr_1(B)$ stand for Fred's credence in B at t_1, and
$cr_2(B)$ stand for Fred's credence in B at t_2. Then $cr_1(B)$ and $cr_2(B)$ are both high.

The crucial question is: What is $cr_1(B \mid E)$, Fred's conditional credence in B
given E at t_1, before Fred acquires the evidence in question?

If $cr_1(B \mid E)$ is high, then Fred's judgment at t_2 reflects a conditional credence
that he already had at t_1. In this case, the judgment at t_2 is *prefigured*, in a sense
analogous to the sense discussed earlier. Here, Fred's accepting B in light of E
accords with the principle of conditionalization.

If $cr_1(B \mid E)$ is low, then Fred's judgment at t_2 fails to reflect the conditional
credence that he already had at t_1. In this sort of case, the judgment at t_2 is *postfigured*, in a sense analogous to the sense discussed earlier. Here, Fred's accepting
B in light of E appears to violate the principle of conditionalization.

On standard Bayesian assumptions, there are two central ways in which one
can obtain apparent violations of conditionalization for sentences. First, this can
happen when the subject is not fully rational throughout the process: perhaps at
t_1 Fred has not thought things through properly, or at t_2 he makes some sort of
reasoning error. Second, the content of the key sentence B can change between

---

[5] The arguments I present here can also be run using the principle of Jeffrey conditionalization
(Jeffrey 1983), which allows conditionalization on evidence about which a subject is not certain.

t_1 and t_2. This may happen in cases involving indexicals, which are not relevant here, or in cases of conceptual change. In these cases, it remains possible that Fred's credences in relevant *propositions* obey conditionalization, but that his credences in associated sentences do not, because the association between sentences and propositions changes over time.[6]

We might formulate this as a version of the principle of conditionalization for sentences, making explicit the requirement of meaning constancy that was left implicit in the last chapter:

(CS) If a subject is fully rational, and if the subject acquires total evidence specified by E between t_1 and t_2, and if the content of sentence S does not change between t_1 and t_2, then $cr_2(S) = cr_1(S \mid E)$.

Perhaps the most familiar version of the principle of conditionalization is cast in terms of propositions: if a fully rational subject acquires total evidence specified by proposition e between t_1 and t_2, then $cr_2(p) = cr_1(p \mid e)$. (CS) follows from this claim in conjunction with the plausible claims that when sentence S expresses proposition p for a subject at that time, $cr(S) = cr(p)$ at that time, and that the content of a sentence is the proposition it expresses.

It follows that if Fred in the postfigured case above is fully rational, then this is a case of conceptual change. It might be that Fred is not fully rational, but this is of no help for Quine. It is unremarkable that irrational subjects might hold on to any sentence or reject any sentence, and this observation has no consequences regarding analyticity or apriority. For Quine's observations about revisability and holding-true to have any bite, rational subjects are required. So we may as well assume that Fred is fully rational.

If we assume that the relevant subjects are fully rational, we now have a principled criterion for conceptual change in a case of holding-true. Suppose that our subject accepts S at t_1, acquires apparently countervailing evidence E between t_1 and t_2, and continues to accept S at t_2. Then we can say

---

[6] A potential third way that conditionalization can be violated arises on views where sentences express certain sorts of relativistic contents: for example, a view on which utterances of the sentence 'It is raining' always express the same temporal proposition *It is raining*, which can be true at some times and not at others. On Saturday, I might have a low conditional credence in *It is raining* given *The weather forecast says rain on Sunday*, then on Sunday I might acquire evidence that the weather forecast says rain on Sunday, resulting in high credence in *It is raining*, without irrationality. On a more standard view on which the content of 'It is raining' uttered at t is *It is raining at t*, this will be classified as a change in content, but on the temporal view the content stays the same. For present purposes, we can either count these as changes in content in an extended sense, or we can require in principle (CS) that the content in question is non-relativistic content.

A potential fourth sort of violation arises from cases of self-doubt (e.g. the Shangri-La case of Arntzenius 2003). One could handle these cases by invoking insulated idealizations in the relevant notion of rationality, or simply by noting that the relevant sort of self-doubt is not playing a role in paradigmatic Quinean cases of revisability and holding-true.

(i) If $cr_1(S \mid E)$ is low, this is a case of conceptual change.

(ii) If $cr_1(S \mid E)$ is high, this need not be a case of conceptual change.

One can now ask: is it true that a subject can hold on to any given sentence S come what may, in light of any evidence, *without irrationality or conceptual change*? By this analysis, this claim requires that for any given sentence S and any possible evidence E, $cr(S \mid E)$ is high (or at least is not low). But this claim is obviously false. For rational subjects and most sentences S (including most paradigmatic empirical sentences), there will be evidence sentences E such that $cr(S \mid E)$ is low. So if these subjects conditionalize, they will not be able to hold onto S come what may.

The moral here is that in the general case, Quinean holding-true come what may requires widespread violation of conditionalization, which requires irrationality or conceptual change. But the fact that an irrational subject might reject a sentence is no evidence that it is not analytic or a priori,[7] and the fact that a subject might reject a sentence after conceptual change is no evidence that it is not originally analytic or a priori. So Quine's argument from holding-true fails.

7 A Bayesian analysis of revisability

For our central example of revisability, we can use a familiar case from Hilary Putnam's 'It Ain't Necessarily So' (1962). Let C be 'All cats are animals'. This might seem paradigmatically analytic or a priori. But let E specify evidence confirming that the furry, apparently feline creatures that inhabit our houses are actually remote-controlled robots from Mars, while all the other creatures we see are organic. Putnam argues that if we discovered that E obtains, we would reject C. So let us suppose that Sarah accepts C at t_1, acquires total evidence as specified by E, and rejects C at t_2.

Here, the diagnostic question is: What is Sarah's initial conditional probability $cr_1(C \mid E)$?

If $cr_1(C \mid E)$ is low, then Sarah's judgment at t_2 reflects a conditional credence that she already had at t_1. In this case, the judgment at t_2 is *prefigured*. Here, Sarah's accepting C in light of E accords with the principle of conditionalization.

If $cr_1(C \mid E)$ is high, then Sarah's judgment at t_2 fails to reflect the conditional credence that she already had at t_1. In this sort of case, the judgment at t_2 is *postfigured*. Here, Sarah's accepting C in light of E appears to violate the principle of conditionalization.

---

[7] Perhaps there are certain strong conceptions of analyticity on which an analytic sentence cannot be rejected by any subject, rational or irrational. But these conceptions are not standard, and in any case no such constraint applies to apriority.

For exactly the reasons given before, the postfigured case requires either that Sarah is not fully rational or that her use of C undergoes conceptual change between t_1 and t_2. Cases of this sort are of no help to Quine. Again, the fact that an irrational subject might reject a sentence is no evidence that it is not analytic or a priori, and the fact that a subject might reject a sentence after conceptual change is no evidence that it is not originally analytic or a priori.

For Quine's argument to succeed, he needs to exclude cases of this sort. That is, he needs to make the case that any sentence can in principle be rationally revised without a violation of conditionalization. This requires that for all rational subjects and for all sentences S, there exists an evidence sentence E such that $cr(S \mid E)$ is low.

This claim is not so obviously false as the corresponding claim about holding true come what may. For this reason, one might regard the argument from revisability as a stronger argument than the argument from holding-true. Indeed, supporters of Quine such as Putnam (1962) and Harman (1994) have concentrated on the argument from revisability, and have made claims not far from the claim in question.[8]

Still, it is not clear just what the grounds are for accepting the key claim. At this point, a number of observations can be made.

First, Quine's official grounds for the revisability claim involve the ability to revise ancillary claims when necessary. These grounds are the same as for the holding-true claim, and it is clear that Quine sees the two as continuous. These grounds suggest that *after* obtaining evidence, a subject could use these features to revise a given sentence. But we have seen that revisions of this sort typically involve violations of conditionalization. These grounds do very little to suggest that *before* acquiring the relevant evidence, a subject's conditional credence $cr(C \mid E)$ will be low.

Second, almost any claim could be rationally rejected given testimony of an apparent epistemic superior. But this point has no bearing on apriority: that a claim could be rejected in *this* way is no evidence that it is not a priori. The point also does not establish that any claim is revisable under ideal reflection, as it is far from clear that this sort of revisability applies to ideally rational thinkers.

---

[8] It may be useful to distinguish a pragmatist reading of the arguments in 'Two Dogmas', stressing the freedom to adjust ancillary hypotheses as one chooses, from an empiricist reading, stressing the role of unexpected evidence in driving us to revise our beliefs. Roughly, where the pragmatist reading turns on the claim that one *may* accept or reject certain statements, the empiricist reading turns on the claim that one *should* (or perhaps that one would). A pragmatist reading will put equal weight on the argument from holding-true and revisability, while an empiricist reading will put more weight on the latter. The pragmatist strand is more central in Quine's text, but the empiricist strand has been more influential among later Quineans.

Perhaps these thinkers' grounds for accepting a mathematical claim, for example, will always defeat any evidence concerning an apparent epistemic superior.

Third, even if this sort of consideration applies to many apparent cases of a priori truths, there are a number of cases on which it has no purchase. Some such cases include material conditionals of the form '$D \rightarrow S$' (like those discussed in the previous section), where D is a lengthy specification of an arbitrary scenario, and where S is a sentence such as 'Water is H_2O' such that $cr(S \mid D)$ is high. Assuming a fully rational subject, it follows that $cr(D \rightarrow S \mid D)$ is high, so that $cr(D \rightarrow S)$ is also high. We can stipulate that D includes or entails a full specification of evidence that obtains in the scenario, so that D entails E for any evidence sentence E that obtains in the scenario and D entails $\sim E$ otherwise (setting vagueness aside).[9] A quick two-case argument then suggests that no evidence E could lead us to rationally reject $D \rightarrow S$. First case: if E does not obtain in the scenario, then D entails $\sim E$. In this case, $cr(\sim D \mid E) = 1$, so $cr(D \rightarrow S \mid E) = 1$. Second case: if E obtains in the scenario, then D entails E. Now $cr(D \rightarrow S \mid E)$ must lie between $cr(D \rightarrow S \mid E \& D)$ and $cr(D \rightarrow S \mid E \& D)$. But the former is 1, and the latter is just $cr(D \rightarrow S \mid D)$, which we have seen is high. So $cr(D \rightarrow S \mid E)$ is high. Putting the two cases together, $cr(D \rightarrow S \mid E)$ is high for all E. Importantly, material conditionals very much like these are the a priori truths that are most important in the scrutability framework.

Fourth, once one notes that this argument allows some truths S such that $cr(S \mid E)$ is high for all E, then it is clear that there is no longer a sound principled argument that for all S, there is an E such that $cr(S \mid E)$ is low. As a result, we may expect to find many more exceptions to this claim. Indeed, many Quineans have conceded such objections, for example in the domains of mathematics and logic, and there is no reason not to expect many more.

Fifth, it is worth stressing that even if this line of argument succeeded, it would be much more conservative than Quine's original line. It leads naturally to a view on which there is an analytic/synthetic distinction. At worst, it would be the case that most or all sentences previously regarded as analytic (a priori), such as 'All cats are animals', will be reconstrued as synthetic (a posteriori).[10] But one could still use the current framework to characterize intensions, once one acknowledges that the intensions for sentences such as 'All cats are animals'

---

[9] One can understand entailment here in a variety of ways. For present purposes we need only the claim that if D entails E, then $cr(E \mid D) = 1$ and $cr(\sim D \mid \sim E) = 1$ for a fully rational subject.

[10] Here we can distinguish between radical Quineans, who hold that there is no analytic/synthetic distinction, and moderate Quineans, who hold that there is such a distinction but that very few sentences are analytic. If the analysis given here is right, we would expect this distinction to correlate with the distinction between pragmatist and empiricist Quineans in footnote 8, and this seems to be what we find in practice. For example, Quine in 'Two Dogmas' takes the pragmatist and radical lines, while Putnam (1962) takes the empiricist and moderate lines.

will be false at some scenarios. One will still have a principled distinction between cases that involve conceptual change and cases that do not. In this way, advocates of analyticity, apriority, and conceptual analysis will have much of what they want.

In any case, the Bayesian analysis has given us what we wanted: a principled criterion for identifying cases of conceptual change. It has only given us a sufficient condition, rather than a necessary and sufficient condition, but this is good enough for our purposes. With this analysis in hand, it is clear that Quine's arguments from revisability and holding-true fail.

8 Quinean objections

Objection 1: The Bayesian analysis begs the question

It might be suggested that the Bayesian principle (CS) that I have appealed to simply assumes a notion of conceptual change without argument, and therefore begs the question against the Quinean skeptic about this notion. I do not think that this is quite right. (CS) is itself a consequence of the principle of conditionalization for propositions and of two other weak assumptions, none of which say anything about conceptual change. Still, this line of argument assumes a notion of proposition, about which a Quinean might be skeptical.

Now, Quine's doubts about propositions have been much less influential than his doubts about the analytic/synthetic distinction. It is clear that to get off the ground, Bayesian accounts of confirmation require either something like propositions or something like the notion of conceptual change. Bayesian credences will be assigned either to abstract entities such as propositions, events, or sets, to linguistic items such as sentences, or to mental items such as beliefs. If we take the first route, then we can use these entities just as we used propositions to ground a notion of conceptual change. If we take the second or the third route, we need to require something like conceptual constancy to avoid counterexamples to principles such as conditionalization.

A Quinean might simply reject Bayesianism altogether, along with the associated principle of conditionalization. This would seem rash, however, as Bayesianism is an extremely successful theory with widespread empirical applications. So by a Quinean's own lights, it is hard to reject it. Furthermore, even if one rejects Bayesianism, a successor theory is likely to have corresponding principles of diachronic rationality governing how beliefs should be updated over time in response to evidence. Precisely the same issues will arise for these principles: if they apply to abstract items we can use these to define conceptual change, and if they apply to linguistic items or mental items, we will require a notion of conceptual change.[11]

The deeper moral is that there is a constitutive link between rational inference and conceptual constancy. Issues such as those floated here will arise for any principle of diachronic rationality. If it is a principle that from A and $A \to B$ one should infer B, and if the premises and conclusions here are sentences or mental items, then to avoid obvious counterexamples the principle should require that A and B have the same meaning on each occasion when they occur. And if the principle applies to abstract objects such as propositions, these can themselves be used to define conceptual change. So if we are not skeptics about principles of diachronic rationality, a notion of conceptual change will be hard to avoid.

Objection 2: Rationality presupposes apriority

It might be suggested that in appealing to the notion of rationality, the notion of apriority is smuggled in. For example, someone might hold that all principles of rational inference depend on underlying principles about the a priori: perhaps an inference from some premises to a conclusion is rational precisely if it is a priori that if the premises obtain, the conclusion is likely to obtain. Or perhaps the distinctive idealization made by the Bayesian involves some tacit assumptions about the a priori. For example, perhaps the Bayesian requirement that rational subjects should have credence 1 in logical truths depends in some way on the belief that logical truths are a priori. If so, the appeal to rational principles here presupposes one of the key notions at issue.

The reply here is straightforward. Whether or not the objector is correct that rationality depends in some way on apriority, the appeal to rationality is innocuous in the current dialectical context. The relevant opponents are those who accept the notion of rationality, but who question the notion of apriority. My argument is intended to establish that *if* one accepts certain principles con-

---

[11] A related objection is that the very idea of a credence or a conditional credence presupposes conceptual constancy. After all, one's credence associated with a sentence is arguably determined by one's dispositions to make certain judgments and decisions involving the sentence: for example, the odds one would take on a bet on that sentence if it were offered. But in considering such dispositions, we have to assume that the meaning of the sentence stays constant from the initial moment to the bet. Likewise, a conditional credence $cr(M \mid E)$ is arguably determined by one's dispositions to make judgments about M conditional on the supposition of E. This requires conceptual constancy: if meaning changes between the initial moment and the judgment, a high initial credence might go with a negative judgment. Still, any conceptual constancy needed here is at best very local, within an episode of consciousness. In any case, if it turns out that the notion of apriority is as secure as the notion of a credence, so that the Quinean can reject the former only by rejecting the latter, that should be good enough for the defender of apriority. Thanks to Ned Block and Kelvin McQueen for discussion here.

cerning rationality, then one should reject Quine's argument against the a priori. If this objector is correct, then the opponent should either give up on the principles concerning rationality or accept the notion of the a priori. Either outcome is sufficient for my purposes. I am happy to concede that if an opponent rejects the notion of rationality, or rejects all relevant principles of diachronic rationality, then the current argument has no purchase against her.

It is also worth noting that the principles of rationality that I appeal to are principles that many or most opponents of the a priori accept. Conditionalization has no obvious connection to the a priori, for example. I do not know whether the special status that the Bayesian gives to logical truths has a special connection to the a priori, but in any case this status plays no role in my argument. That is, the argument does not require the Bayesian claim that rationality requires credence 1 in logical truths. In fact, the picture I have sketched appears to be compatible with a view on which logical truths deserve rational credence less than 1, and on which they can be revised given relevant evidence. All that is required is that such a revision should obey conditionalization. Nothing here smuggles in any obvious presuppositions about the a priori.[12]

Objection 3: A principled line between conceptual change and irrationality cannot be drawn

A Quinean may suggest that our concept of rationality is not fully determinate, and that as a result a clear division between cases of irrationality and cases of conceptual change cannot be found. Some hard cases, such as revising logic in light of quantum mechanics, are not easily classified as either.

However, my reply to Quine's argument does not require drawing a line here. It suffices for the purposes of the argument that the violations of conditionalization involve *either* irrationality or conceptual change, and we do not have to classify these violations further. In any case, as long as there are clear cases of rational judgment, the existence of unclear cases entails at worst a vague distinction, not a non-existent distinction.

Objection 4: The argument requires constancy in evidence sentences

Recall the first residual issue for the framework of intensions discussed earlier: the framework assumes conceptual constancy in the base vocabulary, and therefore cannot explain this constancy. One might think that an analogous issue arises here, with

---

[12] My argument appeals to logical claims at various points, but this does not require that logical truths are a priori, or that they are unrevisable. It merely requires that they are true. Likewise, my argument does not require that the principle of conditionalization is itself a priori or that it is unrevisable. It simply requires that the principle is true.

respect to the *evidential* vocabulary: the vocabulary used to specify evidence sentences such as E. After all, conditionalization concerns what to do when one has a certain credence $cr(S \mid E)$ and then learns E. The conditional credence is in part an attitude to a sentence E, and what one learns is also a sentence E. One might think it is required that the sentence have the same meaning on both occasions. If so, then any apparent failures of conditionalization in a rational subject could be blamed on a change in the meaning of terms in E, instead of a change in the meaning of terms in S, and it is not clear that we have a principled way to choose.

As it stands, this picture is not quite right. Learning E does not typically involve the *sentence* E at all. Perhaps if learning were always by testimony, and if E were a sentence used in testimony, then the issue would arise. But for our purposes we can assume that the relevant learning is by perception or by introspection. Here, E will be a sentence characterizing the evidence that one learns, and the learning process need not involve this sentence at all. So there is no use of E at t_2 that needs to be aligned with the use of E at t_1. At best we need to require that E as used at t_1 correctly applies to the evidence acquired at t_2. But this is a much weaker requirement, concerning only the extension of E as used at t_1, with no role for any use of E at t_2.

Still, it can be argued that acquiring evidence requires having certain *attitudes* to the evidence. For example, the rationality of Bayesian conditionalization on new experiences arguably requires not just that one has the experiences, but that one is certain that one has them. If so, one might suggest that the framework tacitly requires that at t_2, one is certain of the evidence statement E (which says that certain experiences obtain). This issue is starker in alternative frameworks such as Jeffrey conditionalization, which accommodate uncertainty about evidence by giving an explicit role to one's credence in evidence statements such as E at t_2. Does this not require some sort of constancy in the meaning of E after all?

The issue is delicate. For the reasons given above, the sentence E as used at t_2 plays no essential role here. However, it is arguably the case that subjects must be certain of (or have other appropriate attitudes to) certain evidential *propositions*, such as the proposition that certain experiences obtain, which were expressed by E at t_1. Or without invoking propositions: the subject must be certain that the relevant evidence obtains (that they are having certain experiences, say), where this is the same evidence concerning which they had conditional credences at t_1. Without this alignment, one could always respond to an apparent failure of conditionalization by saying that although a subject's initial credence was conditional on evidence e obtaining, and although evidence e later obtained, the subject in fact became certain that some *other* evidence e' obtained. If this were so, there would be no violation of conditionalization (the subject would not acquire the evidence e), and there would arguably be no irrationality.

This requirement of alignment provides some room for the Quinean to maneuver, but the room is extremely limited. To eliminate this room altogether, we need only suppose that we have a grip on what it is for a subject to accept or suppose that certain evidence obtains. With this much granted, we can simply stipulate that for our purposes, the conditional credences $cr(S \mid E)$ relevant at t_1 are credences in S conditional on the evidence that is actually obtained at t_2. This removes any loophole, and does so without making any assumptions about constancy in the meaning of language across time. At most, we have to assume an understanding of certain beliefs and suppositions about evidence.

The required assumptions can be reduced further by noting that for our purposes, evidence can be limited to experiences or at least to observational states of affairs. While there is a sense in which empirical knowledge of non-observational states can serve as evidence for other claims, it is plausible that this knowledge is grounded in evidence concerning experiential or observational matters. On a Bayesian view, our credences in these states of affairs must then match those determined by conditionalization on experiential or observational matters. I think it is also plausible that credences in observational states of affairs should match those determined by conditionalization on experiential matters.[13] If the latter claim is granted, then for present purposes we can restrict the relevant evidence in cases of revisability and holding-true to experiential states. Even without it, we can restrict the relevant evidence to observational states. So to answer the Quinean worry, we need only suppose that we have a grip on what it is for a subject to accept or suppose that certain experiential or observational states of affairs obtain. This is something that Quine's arguments in 'Two Dogmas' do not give us any reason to doubt.

The upshot of all this is that the residual issues about a base vocabulary are not eliminated altogether on a Bayesian approach, but they are minimized, in a way that brings out the severe costs of the Quinean position. A Quinean who rejects the notions of analyticity and apriority along present lines must also insist that there is no objective fact of the matter about whether a subject accepts or supposes that a given observational state obtains. This view presumably goes along with a generalized skepticism about the contents of thought, perhaps in the spirit of Quine's skepticism about meaning developed in his arguments concerning radical translation. It likewise requires a certain skepticism about diachronic rationality, for reasons discussed earlier.

Quine himself argues both for skepticism about meaning (in *Word and Object*) and for a sort of skepticism about norms of rationality (in 'Epistemology Naturalized').

---

[13] For example, if one is fully rational, one's credence that there is a red square in front of one should match one's antecedent conditional credence that there is a red square in front of one given that one is having an experience as of a red square. (If norms of rationality do not ensure certainty about the experiences one is having, one can move to a Jeffrey-conditionalization analog.) Theses of this sort have been denied by some dogmatists about perception (e.g., Pryor unpublished), and might also be denied by some who think that perceptual knowledge is more secure than introspective knowledge (e.g. Schwitzgebel 2008).

Few have been prepared to follow him here, and even those who sympathize with the Quine of 'Two Dogmas' have tended to reject these later views. Quine's arguments for these views deserve attention in their own right, but it is clear that the arguments in 'Two Dogmas' provide little direct support for them. Still, the current analysis suggests a deep linkage between these views. Defending the arguments of 'Two Dogmas' against a certain appeal to conceptual change leads naturally to skepticism about diachronic rational principles and about the content of language and thought. Contrapositively, once even minimal claims about rationality and about thought are accepted, the arguments I have considered against analyticity and apriority dissolve.

Objection 5: There can be rational revision by resetting priors

Quineans of a pragmatist stripe often appeal to the underdetermination of theory by evidence: multiple theories are consistent with the same evidence, and we have considerable latitude in choosing between them. In the Bayesian framework, where theory is determined by evidence along with prior probabilities, this underdetermination comes to underdetermination of probabilities that are prior to any evidence. This underdetermination yields a potential way that fully rational subjects might violate conditionalization without conceptual change.

The relevant method here is that of *resetting priors*. This method stems from the observation that most Bayesians allow that there is some flexibility in one's ultimate priors: the prior probabilities that a subject should have before acquiring any empirical evidence. (Of course these priors are something of a fiction.) For example, on Carnap's framework for inductive logic, equally rational subjects may have different values for λ, the parameter that guides how quickly the subjects adjust their beliefs in light of inductive evidence, and this difference can be traced to a difference in ultimate priors. Two such subjects might acquire exactly the same evidence over time, while being led to quite different posterior probabilities. If G is the thesis that a human-caused global warming is occurring, for example, one subject might be led to a high credence in G, while another might be led to a low credence in G.

Now, a subject with a high credence in G might reflect and observe that her high credence is traceable entirely to the value of λ in her ultimate priors, and that this value was quite arbitrary. She may note that it would have been equally rational to start with a lower value of λ and to end up with a lower credence in G. At this point, a bold subject might choose to change her credences wholesale. At least if she has a good enough record of her evidence, she can 'unwind' back to the ultimate priors, reset λ to a lower value, and reintegrate all the evidence by conditionalization. She will end up with a new set of credences, including (among many other differences) a lower value for G.

A Quinean might suggest that there is nothing irrational about doing this, and that this method might be exploited in order that a subject could hold onto almost any sentence come what may and also revise almost any sentence. After all, for most non-observational empirical sentences S and most paths of evidence, there is some ultimate prior that will lead to a high credence in S, and some ultimate prior that will lead to a low credence in S. None of this requires conceptual change. So violations of conditionalization in a rational subject do not provide a sufficient condition for conceptual change after all.

This position requires a rejection or at least a revision of orthodox Bayesianism. On the orthodox view, conditionalization is a constraint on diachronic rationality, and this sort of revision will be irrational. Furthermore, the view tends to lead to an anything-goes view of rational belief. If there are no constraints on ultimate priors, the view entails that at any moment, if $cr(p) < 1$, then one's credence can be rationally revised so that $cr(p)$ is arbitrarily close to zero. And even if there are constraints on ultimate priors, these constraints must be weak enough to vindicate the large violations of conditionalization that the Quinean argument requires, leading naturally to a view on which most beliefs can be rationally revised at any moment into disbelief. Given this much, it is not easy to see how my beliefs can constitute knowledge at all.[14]

Furthermore, it is far from clear that all beliefs can be revised in this way. For example, given that logical beliefs, mathematical beliefs, and evidential statements are constrained to have credence 1, this method will not yield revisability for these beliefs. More generally, there is not much reason to hold that it will yield revisions to those beliefs usually classified as a priori ('All bachelors are unmarried', say), most of which appear not to depend on ultimate priors. So this response is weakest where it needs to be strongest.

Most fundamentally: as long as we have a conceptual distinction between cases in which beliefs are revised by this process and cases in which they are not, we still have enough to draw a distinction between those violations of conditionalization that involve conceptual change and those that do not. The Quinean will have to insist that we do not have a grip on this conceptual distinction, so that there is no distinction to be drawn between cases of resetting priors and cases of conceptual change. I think there is little reason to accept this. Furthermore, even if this line were accepted, it would once again lead to an across-the-board skepticism about principles of belief updating and other forms of diachronic rationality. So if principles of diachronic rationality are allowed at all—even the liberal principles suggested by the current approach—then the distinction between conceptual constancy and conceptual change remains intact.

---

[14] In addition, this method is a sort of belief revision that is not driven by evidence at all. So although this line of reasoning is perhaps the best way of preserving the pragmatist reading of Quine's arguments in light of the present analysis, it does not sit easily with the more influential empiricist reading.

Objection 6: Subjects need not have conditional credences

It might be objected that the Bayesian analysis requires the assumption that for every sentence S used by a subject and every possible evidence sentence E, the subject has a conditional credence $cr(S \mid E)$. But this is an unrealistic idealizing assumption.

In response: the idealization is not enormous. For most S and most E, the subject will have some relevant dispositions involving S and E, for example involving her willingness to accept various bets involving S and E. In many cases, these dispositions will line up in a clear enough way that $cr(S \mid E)$ will be high. In other cases, they will line up in a clear enough way that $cr(S \mid E)$ will be low. In other cases, the dispositions may be enough of a mix that it is hard to say.

Quineans might suggest that if $cr(S \mid E)$ is indeterminate in this way, and the subject later rejects S upon learning E, this should not count as a violation of conditionalization. If so, they might then suggest that for any S, there is some E such that $cr(S \mid E)$ is indeterminate in this way, and such that the subject could later reject S on learning E without violating conditionalization. Perhaps this sort of revisability is enough for their purposes?[15]

I do not think that this is enough, however. Cases of this sort seem to turn essentially on the subject's not being fully rational. If the subject is fully rational, then her dispositions to accept S on supposing E and on learning E should be the same, assuming no conceptual change. That is, if a fully rational subject rejects S on learning E and thinking things through, then if she were to have been initially presented with the *supposition* that E and had thought things through, she should have rejected S conditional on that supposition. To fail to meet this condition is a failure of full rationality, just as is an ordinary violation of conditionalization. So at best the Quinean has presented us with a kind of revisability that can only be exploited by subjects who are less than fully rational. Like the sort of revisability that can be exploited only by irrational subjects, this sort of revisability has no bearing on matters of apriority.

9 Conclusion

Quine is right that any statement can be held true come what may and that no statement is immune to revision. But as Grice and Strawson observe, these phenomena are quite compatible with a robust analytic/synthetic distinction and a robust notion of meaning. A Bayesian analysis reveals that Quine is not right

---

[15] It is especially likely that ordinary subjects will lack credences $cr(S \mid D)$ involving the scenario specifications D discussed earlier, due to the enormous size of these specifications. This observation does not affect the use of conditional credences involving D to define intensions, as these credences used there are always idealized rational credences $cr'(S \mid D)$, for which the current issue does not arise. And where non-idealized credences are concerned, these cases will not yield cases of revisability along the lines in the text, because the subject will be incapable of learning that D.

that any statement can be held true come what may *without conceptual change or irrationality*, and likewise for revision. We can pin down the distinction between cases that involve conceptual change and cases that do not using either the scrutability framework or Bayesian analysis.

The scrutability framework characterizes intensions in terms of scrutability relations, and uses intensions to distinguish cases that involve conceptual change. When intensions are grounded in a priori scrutability, this method assumes the notion of apriority, so it does not provide an independent grounding for that notion. Still, it shows how a framework involving apriority can accommodate all of Quine's data. And for the same reasons that most philosophers reject Quine's arguments in the first four sections of 'Two Dogmas', no independent grounding is required.

The Bayesian analysis takes things a step further and defends the a priori on partly independent grounds. This analysis assumes the notion of conditional probability and the normative notion of rationality to provide conditions for conceptual change, but it does not assume the notion of apriority. In effect, constitutive connections between rational inference and conceptual change are used to make inroads into the Quinean circle.

The conclusion should not be too strong. While I have responded to Quine's arguments against the a priori and the analytic, I have not provided a positive argument for the analytic/synthetic distinction or the a priori/a posteriori distinctions, and I have not tried to ground these notions in wholly independent terms.

One might be tempted to take things a step further still, and attempt to define apriority in terms of conditional probability and rationality. For example, one might suggest that a sentence S is a priori for a subject precisely when the ideal conditional probability $cr^*(S \mid D) = 1$ for all scenario specifications D. But there will be residual issues. For a start, it is not clear that one can define the class of scenario specifications without using the notion of apriority.[16] So much more would need to be said here.

Still, we have seen that these notions can help us at least in diagnosing issues regarding meaning, conceptual change, and the a priori. And we have seen enough to suggest that Quine's arguments in the final section of 'Two Dogmas of Empiricism' do not threaten the distinction between the analytic and the synthetic, or the distinction between the a priori and the a posteriori.

---

[16] One will also need to appeal to an insulated idealization (chapter 2) to handle cases of self-doubt: e.g., the case where S is a mathematical truth, and D specifies a scenario in which one is a poor mathematical reasoner.

Scrutability and Conceptual Dynamics

It is sometimes argued (for example, by Mark Wilson in his 2006 book *Wandering Significance*) that 'classical' models of concepts, stemming from early analytic philosophy and the logical empiricists, are inadequate because they cannot properly accommodate conceptual dynamics: the way that the concepts associated with our expressions develop and change over time. The scrutability framework is at least a relative of these classical models, and similar charges have occasionally been brought against it (for example, by Laura Schroeter, Ned Block and Robert Stalnaker, and Stephen Yablo). The analysis given in this chapter can be used to address these arguments. I will discuss a number of cases of conceptual dynamics that might be thought to pose problems for scrutability.

There is no question that conceptual development is rife and intricate. A paradigmatic case, reflecting a phenomenon common with scientific theories, is given in Joseph Camp's 'The Ballad of Clyde the Moose' (1991). Mary hears something going 'snuff, snuff' in the woods, and introduces the name 'Clyde' for whatever it is. She and her friends set out to track down Clyde, and they find many other strange noises and odd events that they attribute to Clyde. The Clyde theory becomes increasingly complex, until later they discover Clyde. There is a moose who was responsible for most of these events, with a significant exception: the moose did not go 'snuff, snuff' in the woods. So the sentence 'If anyone went 'snuff, snuff' in the night, it was Clyde' (*S*), which may seem to be stipulative and a priori at the first stage, is rejected at the second stage.

Someone might suggest that this is a counterexample to A Priori Scrutability: although *S* initially seems to be a priori scrutable from *PQTI* (or a relevant base), it is not. The framework of chapter 5 handles this case by saying that 'Clyde' undergoes conceptual change. Because of this change, *S* is a priori in Mary's initial context but not in the later context. Suppose that *E* is the evidence acquired by Mary between the first stage and the last. At the earlier stage, Mary presumably has a high conditional credence in *S* given *E*, but after acquiring evidence *E* she rejects *S*. This is a violation of conditionalization. Given that Mary is rational, the violation suggests conceptual change. Indeed, it is plausible that an utterance of *S* at the first stage would be true, but an utterance at the second stage would be false. If so, then even without invoking the principle of conditionalization, there is certainly conceptual change in this scenario. The case brings out the important point that conceptual change can be well-motivated by theoretical change and not at all anomalous or arbitrary. But all this is consistent with the claim that at each stage, true utterances are scrutable from $PQTI$ (or an underlying base), and false utterances are not.

There are also cases in which an original stipulation does not turn out to be false, but moves from a priori to a posteriori. For example, 'Neptune perturbs the orbit of Uranus, if it exists' may initially seem a priori to Leverrier, but after acquiring much further knowledge of Neptune, the same sentence may no longer seem a priori. Suppose that D specifies a scenario in which planet X perturbs the orbit of Uranus, but planet Y plays the rest of the roles that come later to be associated with Neptune. Then if T_1 is 'Neptune is planet X' and T_2 is 'Neptune is planet Y', Leverrier may initially take 'If D then T_1' to be a priori and later take 'If D then T_2' to be a priori. In this case, his conditional credences $cr(T_1 \mid D)$ will move from high to low.

This sort of case yields an indirect violation of conditionalization. Assume that E is Leverrier's total evidence between the stages and that it is consistent with D. Then at stage 1, $cr(T_1 \mid D \,\&\, E)$ is high, but after gaining total evidence E, $cr(T_1 \mid D)$ is low. It is easy to see that this yields a violation of conditionalization. The ratio formula for conditional probabilities entails that at stage one $cr(T_1 \mid D \,\&\, E)$ = $cr(T_1 \,\&\, D \mid E)/cr(D \mid E)$, which by conditionalization should be identical to $cr(T_1 \,\&\, D)/cr(D)$ at stage two, which is just $cr(T_1 \mid D)$.[1] Assuming that Leverrier is fully rational throughout, this is also a case of conceptual change.

In 'Against A Priori Reductions' (2006), Laura Schroeter discusses a hypothetical case of this sort. We first believe that the watery stuff in the oceans is a natural kind before discovering that it is wildly disjunctive. Say that W specifies a world in which the dominant watery stuff is H_2O, and S is 'If W, then water is H_2O'. Schroeter argues in effect that $cr(S \mid W)$ is high at stage one and low at stage two, because at the second stage we no longer think it important that water is a natural kind. The reasoning in the paragraph above shows that this case involves a violation of conditionalization, so that it must involve irrationality or conceptual change.

Schroeter suggests that because we refer to the same thing (a disjunctive kind) by 'water' throughout and the changes are natural, there is no conceptual change.

---

[1] The ratio formula cannot be used if one's initial credence in $D \,\&\, E$ is zero. But in the relevant cases, D and E will at least be mutually consistent, and we will usually be able to coarse-grain them to raise the credence above zero while leaving the same general structure. In any case, the normative quasi-conditionalization principle that after gaining total evidence E, one's posterior credence $cr(T_1 \mid D)$ should be equivalent to one's prior credence $cr(T_1 \mid D \,\&\, E)$ is plausible even independent of the ratio formula.

She suggests that we should individuate concepts in an externalist way so that when reference changes, the concept changes, but when conditional judgments change without reference changing, it need not. I am inclined to individuate concepts differently, but the scrutability thesis and the arguments in this chapter do not depend on how we individuate concepts. If we individuate them Schroeter's way, we will simply conclude that the a priori liaisons (including the scrutability conditionals) associated with an expression can change while the concept stays the same. Importantly, the case gives no reason to doubt that at each stage, when a sentence is true for a speaker, it is scrutable.

Ned Block and Robert Stalnaker (1999) discuss the case of 'jade', in which we discovered two superficially similar substances and decided that there are two sorts of jade. Here it is plausible that even before discovering the two substances, our conditional credence in 'There are two kinds of jade' given D, where D specifies relevant truths about the two substances, would have been high. If a diagnosis of this sort is right, there is no problem for scrutability in these cases. But even if the diagnosis is wrong—if one's credence in 'There are two kinds of jade' given D at the earlier stage was low, for example—then we can say either that this credence was not ideally rational (one had not thought the matter all the way through) and that the utterance was true, or that the low credence was rational, and that the utterance was false. On the latter hypothesis, there will have been conceptual change along the way. But on any of these scenarios, there is no problem for scrutability.

The case of solidity provides another problem case. Let D be 'Apparently solid objects contain mostly empty space', and let S be 'Tables are solid'. It might be held that before discovering the truth of D, then (i) it was reasonable to hold that if D, then $\sim S$, but (ii) S was true all the same. This suggests that even though S was true, $cr'(S \mid PQTI)$ was low and $PQTI \to S$ was not a priori, so that both A Priori and Conditional Scrutability fail. In response, one can note that in the actual world, after discovering D, we affirmed S. This observation combined with (i) yields a violation of conditionalization, so the reasoning in chapter 5 suggests that given rationality throughout, either (i) is false or there was conceptual change here. The former is perhaps the more plausible option: it is arguable that our core concept of solidity all along was tied to functional role (resisting penetration and so on) rather than intrinsic structure. If there was conceptual change, on the other hand, then it is natural to hold that (ii) is false: although S is true of the actual world on its later meaning, it was not true on its earlier meaning. Either way there is no problem for scrutability.

An interesting sort of opposition here invokes epistemic conservatism: roughly, the idea that we ought to hold onto existing beliefs when we can. One might suggest that epistemic conservatism can yield violations of conditionalization without irrationality or conceptual change. On this view, for a proposition p

(concerning solidity, for example) and evidence e (concerning physics, for example), when one thinks that e is very unlikely, one can rationally have a low conditional credence in p given e, but upon discovering to one's surprise that e obtains, epistemic conservatism allows that one can or should rationally retain one's belief in p. I stand with the orthodox Bayesian view that this form of conservatism is irrational: one should either have a high conditional credence at the first stage or a low credence at the second stage.[2] But this sort of opposition should at least be noted.

Another sort of opposition in the solidity case invokes semantic conservatism: roughly, charity principles that suggest that meanings should be assigned to expressions to maximize truth. Here it might be suggested that even if $cr'(S \mid PQTI)$ is low at the first stage, principles of charity might override conditional judgments to dictate that S is true. The diagnosis of this view depends on whether we accept S ('Tables are solid') on discovering D ('Apparently solid objects contain mostly empty space'). If yes (as actually happened), then we have violations of conditionalization, and this view will reduce to a version of the previous view. If no (as might happen in some hypothetical analog case), on the other hand, we have a radically externalist view on which even knowing the relevant underlying truths about the actual world does not put one in a position to know that tables are solid. Strong enough principles of charity might indeed yield a radical view along these lines. As discussed in section 7 of chapter 4, I think that this radical externalism is implausible, but in any case this objection has little to do with conceptual change.

Some tricky cases from the history of mathematics involve conceptual development that is not tied to new empirical evidence. Newton and Leibniz talked of the limit of a series 150 years before Bolzano and Cauchy gave the now-canonical definition of a limit.[3] Take the sentence S: 'The limit of a series S_n is that value a such that for all $\varepsilon > 0$ there exists k such that for all $n > k$, $\mid S_n - a \mid < \varepsilon$'. This sentence is true, and today it seems a priori. But was it a priori for Newton or Leibniz? This is not obvious. To get at this matter, let us suppose that Newton and Leibniz had entertained the sentence and considered whether to accept it. Perhaps the most likely outcome is that on sufficient rational reflection, they would have accepted it. If so, then S was plausibly a priori in their context. But suppose that

---

[2] For example, an epistemic conservative will be vulnerable to a diachronic Dutch book combination of bets (see 4.3), according to which they are guaranteed to lose money in this sort of case. For example, if $cr_1(p \mid e) = 0.1$ and $cr_2(p) = 0.9$, then the subject will bet at 1:2 odds on $\sim p$ conditional on e at stage 1 and at 1:2 odds on p at stage 2. These bets yield a guaranteed loss if e obtains and merely break even if e does not obtain (if e does not obtain, the first bet is refunded and the second is not offered). Furthermore, unlike some other diachronic Dutch book cases (but like the version in chapter 4), this behavior from an epistemic conservative will be predictable in advance, and so can be exploited by a Dutch bookmaker.

[3] For related discussion of this case, see Peacocke 2008.

they would have rejected it. If so, then we must say either that S did not express a truth for them, so that there was conceptual change between them and Cauchy, or that the sentence did express a truth but that they were irrational in rejecting it. Any of these outcomes seems a possibility. It might even be that the actual world was somewhat indeterminate between these possibilities, so that it is indeterminate whether S in the mouth of Newton or Leibniz would have been true.

The indeterminacy hypothesis calls to mind Waismann's 'open texture' of language (discussed in chapter 1): we cannot foresee completely all possible conditions in which words are to be used. Waismann's official point concerns definitions, arguing that no definition of an expression (or rule of verification for a sentence) can cover all unanticipated possibilities. Here even the Gettier case might count as an instance of open texture, and for familiar reasons there will be no obstacle to scrutability. More deeply, however, Waismann also suggests that there are cases in which the application of a concept is not dictated by our previous grasp of the concept at all. ('Suppose I come across a being that looks like a man, speaks like a man, behaves like a man, and is only one span tall—shall I say it is a man?'[4]) In the current framework any such cases are best seen as cases of indeterminacy. It is worth stressing that the scrutability framework is consistent with a good deal of indeterminacy when concepts are applied to previously unanticipated scenarios.

Stephen Yablo (1998; 2002) invokes open texture to suggest that there are cases where rational reflection on qualitative information underdetermines theoretical truth, which is settled only by pragmatic factors. There can certainly be such cases: perhaps at t_1, our credence in S is unsettled, but later one comes to accept S, because of pragmatic factors that are not merely a product of rational reflection. (I leave aside D here on the assumption that the evidence is the same throughout.) But given that the pragmatic factors are rationally underdetermined, so that one's initial *rational* credence in S is not high, then this is best seen as a case in which it is initially indeterminate whether S expresses a truth, and S later comes to express a truth because of terminological evolution. If so, there is no problem for scrutability.[5] Here the pragmatic factors can be seen as producing mild conceptual change, or conceptual precisification: an intension that is initially indeterminate at a scenario becomes determinate at that scenario.

---

[4] The stronger line is more explicit in Waismann's *The Principles of Linguistic Philosophy* (1965): e.g. 'No language is prepared for all possibilities' (p. 76).

[5] It might be suggested that the earlier meaning of M is fixed by its later meaning, so that there is no conceptual change, and M is true but inscrutable at the earlier stage. The mild violation of conditionalization here strongly suggests mild conceptual change, however. There may be cases in which past meaning is fixed by future meaning via a sort of semantic deference to future users, but these cases can be handled as we handle the cases of deference discussed in chapter 6.

Likewise, in *Wandering Significance*, Mark Wilson discusses an enormous number of interesting cases of conceptual evolution, mainly drawn from the history of science and mathematics, in which old concepts are extended in new and unpredictable ways by new developments. I cannot analyze all these cases here, but I think that all are open to diagnoses such as the above.[6] In some cases, the changes in response to new cases are prefigured, in other cases, they are postfigured, and in still others the matter is indeterminate. All of these diagnoses are compatible with a priori scrutability.

If these cases of conceptual evolution pose a problem for the scrutability framework, it is a problem not of incorrectness but of incompleteness. The scrutability framework allows us to associate an expression with an intension at any given time, and indeed to chart the way that the intension changes with time. But it does not provide any explanation of why and how concepts evolve in the way that they do. Indeed, one might think that from the point of view of the scrutability framework, as with classical models of concepts, conceptual evolution should be expected to be rare and anomalous. I think that this is not quite right: there is no reason why the framework should not be combined with a principled account of the dynamics of conceptual change. Indeed, the discussion of conceptual pluralism in 'Verbal Disputes' suggests a view on which conceptual evolution and diversity is constant and ongoing, driven by various practical purposes.[7]

Ultimately we would like a positive theory of conceptual dynamics, answering questions about when, how, and why we can expect concepts associated with an expression to change. In modeling these dynamics, the intensional framework will at least provide a useful tool. For example, the Clyde and Neptune cases above suggest some generalizations about how change in intensions tends to

---

[6] Wilson does not talk much about either apriority or truth (although see his pp. 617–38), so it is hard to know how his arguments apply to a thesis such as A Priori Scrutability. Concerning key questions about whether old sentences are true when applied to a new and extended case, one natural view to extract from his discussion is that there is often no determinate answer: later extensions depend on idiosyncratic developments, and verdicts about such cases are not determinately prefigured in a user's original use of an expression. I think that this view is plausible, especially where the hardest cases are concerned, but as before widespread indeterminacy is quite compatible with the scrutability thesis.

[7] The flipside of the objection from conceptual dynamics is the objection from holism, which says that the framework allows too much rather than too little conceptual change. However, there is no reason to think that the framework leads to extreme holism, on which meanings change whenever beliefs change. Typically, the transition from accepting S to rejecting S (whether 'There is water in this cup' or 'Water is a primitive substance') on this framework will not be accompanied by a change in the scrutability conditionals or the intension associated with S. Certainly there can be changes in intension, sometimes due to changes in the entrenchment of belief (that is, a belief's moving inside or outside the scrutability-determining core for an expression), sometimes due to pragmatic factors, and so on. But some conceptual change of this sort is only to be expected and does not lead to an objectionable holism.

accompany theory development. Other generalizations might concern the relation between intensions and purposes. Intensions need not do all the work. We can be pluralists about concepts and their content. For example, we might invoke coarser-grained features of concepts to analyze what stays constant in some cases where intensions change, and finer-grained features of concepts to analyze what changes in some cases where intensions stay constant. But a positive account of conceptual dynamics within the present framework remains an important open challenge.

Constructing Epistemic Space

In *Meaning and Necessity* (1947), Carnap laid the foundations for much of the contemporary discussion of possible worlds and of intensional semantics. In particular, he developed a notion of 'state-description' that serves as the key to a linguistic construction of possible worlds. He also argued that every expression can be associated with an intension. This extensive modal and semantic project serves as the background for 'Meaning and Synonymy in Natural Languages', in which Carnap engages in the metasemantic project of determining what it is for a subject to use an expression with a given meaning. The modal and semantic projects deserve attention in their own right, however. In this excursus, I focus on analogs of the modal project within the current framework, while in the eleventh excursus, I focus on analogs of the semantic project.

Meaning and Necessity was published two decades after the *Aufbau*, and Carnap does not explicitly connect the projects. But as chapter 5 suggests, it is natural to draw a connection. The basic vocabulary of the *Aufbau* can be used to formulate a set of atomic sentences that characterizes the actual world. In effect, this characterization provides a state-description for the actual world. The definitional elements of the *Aufbau* provide a way to determine the truth of an arbitrary sentence, given the specification of truths in the basic vocabulary. This provides a way of evaluating the intension of a sentence given an arbitrary state-description. In the *Aufbau*, Carnap does not use his basic vocabulary to characterize state-descriptions for non-actual states of the world, but one could certainly do so in principle. In this way, one could use the materials of the *Aufbau* to construct the state-descriptions and intensions that are needed for the project of *Meaning and Necessity*.

Of course there are some differences of detail. Where the *Aufbau* uses an austere basic vocabulary (logic plus a basic relation) and a rich system of semantic rules (arbitrary definitions), *Meaning and Necessity* allows a rich basic vocabulary (atomic sentences containing arbitrary predicates and individual constants) and an austere system of semantic rules (logical relations between atomic and complex sentences). And where the *Aufbau* requires only extensional adequacy of its definitions, *Meaning and Necessity* appeals to a notion of 'L-truth' (truth in virtue of the semantic rules of a language L) that Carnap says is akin to a notion of analyticity or necessity. Still, as discussed in chapter 1, there is a nearby *Aufbau* project that requires something like analyticity of its definitions. This project can be used to ground a nearby *Meaning and Necessity* project that uses austere bases to define state-descriptions and rich definitional connections to define intensions.[1]

Something like this construction is at the heart of contemporary linguistic constructions of possible worlds. In these constructions, metaphysical necessity plays the role that L-truth plays for Carnap, and expressions for fundamental objects and/or properties play the role of the basic vocabulary. One can thereby define possible worlds and intensions for expressions, with the key property that a sentence S is metaphysically necessary iff its intension is true in all possible worlds.

The scrutability project allows us to execute a related but quite different construction: a construction not of metaphysically possible worlds, but of epistemically possible scenarios. On this construction, apriority plays the role that L-truth plays for Carnap, and expressions in a generalized scrutability base play the role of the basic vocabulary. These scenarios can perform a crucial role in the analysis of knowledge, belief, and meaning.[2]

Intuitively, an epistemically possible scenario (or a *scenario* for short) is a maximally specific way the world might be, for all we know a priori. For example, we do not know a priori that gold is an element. For all we know a priori, we could be in a world in which gold is a compound. Correspondingly, there are many scenarios in which gold is a compound, as well as many scenarios in which gold is an element. This already suggests that epistemically possible scenarios are distinct from metaphysically possible worlds. On the usual understanding of metaphysical possibility, it is metaphysically necessary that gold is an element (given that it is actually an element), so there are no possible worlds in which gold is a

---

[1] An austere base might help with certain internal tensions in the *Meaning and Necessity* construction. Carnap says (p. 15) that where '*H*' and '*RA*' are predicates for 'human' and 'rational animal' respectively, $\forall x(Hx \equiv RAx)$ is L-true, on the grounds that '*H*' and '*RA*' are synonymous. But on Carnap's official definitions (pp. 3–4 and pp. 9–10), L-truth requires truth in all state-descriptions, state-descriptions allow arbitrary recombinations of atomic sentences or their negations, and sentences of the form Hc and RAc (for any constant c) are atomic. On these definitions, there will be state-descriptions containing both Hc and $\sim RAc$, so that $\forall x(Hx \equiv RAx)$ will not be L-true. More generally, the rich atomic language along with free recombination has the consequence that all sorts of apparently analytic sentences will be false in some state-description. An *Aufbau*-style version of the *Meaning and Necessity* project with an austere base vocabulary and a rich system of definitions corresponding to a rich notion of L-truth would help to avoid these problems. Alternatively, one could retain the rich base vocabulary but impose a constraint of L-consistency on recombinations of atomic sentences.

[2] Many of the issues discussed below are elaborated at much greater length in 'The Nature of Epistemic Space'.

compound. We have to understand epistemically possible scenarios in different terms.

To construct scenarios, we can start by stipulating that S is *deeply epistemically necessary* when S is conclusively a priori (see the eighth excursus), and that S is *deeply epistemically possible* when $\sim S$ is not deeply epistemically necessary. Note that this stipulative notion of deep epistemic possibility differs from the ordinary notion of what is epistemically possible for a subject, both because it is idealized (all mathematical theorems are epistemically necessary and their negations are epistemically impossible, even if no one has proved them) and because it does not depend on what a given subject knows ('I am not conscious' is deeply epistemically possible, even though I am introspectively certain that I am conscious). For convenience I will abbreviate 'deeply epistemically possible' as 'e-possible' and sometimes as 'epistemically possible' in what follows, but this should not be confused with the non-idealized subject-relative notion. For now we can restrict attention to context-independent sentences S (specifically, epistemically invariant sentences, as discussed in E3), although the definition can naturally be extended to define the e-possibility of a context-dependent sentence S in a context.

We can also stipulate as before that a sentence G is *epistemically complete* when G is e-possible and there is no H such that $G \& H$ and $G \& \sim H$ are e-possible. For example, if a true sentence conjoining all sentences in *PQTI* a priori entails all truths, then that sentence will be epistemically complete.[3] We can also say that two epistemically complete sentences G_1 and G_2 are *equivalent* when $G_1 \to G_2$ and $G_2 \to G_1$ are both e-necessary.

Given Generalized Scrutability, there will be a compact vocabulary that can be used to specify epistemically complete sentences corresponding not just to the actual world but to arbitrary epistemic possibilities. The thesis says that there is a compact class C of sentences such that for all e-possible S, S is a priori scrutable from some e-possible subclass C' of C (where a class of sentences is e-possible iff its conjunction is e-possible). From here, one can argue that for all e-possible S, S is e-necessitated by some epistemically complete sentence in C. In effect, C provides an array of epistemically complete sentences akin to *PQTI*, each of which corresponds to a highly specific epistemic possibility.

---

[3] Indeterminacy raises a few complications. Its treatment will depend on the issue, discussed in the first excursus, of whether the vagueness of epistemic necessity goes along with the vagueness of truth or with the vagueness of determinate truth. If we take the latter route, one should say that S is e-possible when $\sim det(S)$ (rather than $\sim S$) is not e-necessary. Then when G is the conjunction of sentences in an priori scrutability base and H is indeterminate, $G \to indet(H)$ will be e-necessary and neither $G \& H$ nor $G \& \sim H$ will be e-possible. If we take the former route, then under plausible assumptions, each of the two latter sentences will be indeterminately e-possible, but it will be determinately false that both are e-possible. So either way, G will be epistemically complete.

We can then identify scenarios with equivalence classes of epistemically complete sentences in the vocabulary of a generalized scrutability base. Given a scenario w, any sentence D in the corresponding equivalence class is a *canonical specification* of w. For a context-independent sentence S, a scenario w *verifies* S when S is a priori scrutable from a canonical specification of w: that is, when $D \rightarrow S$ is a priori, where D is an epistemically complete sentence corresponding to w. Given a Generalized Scrutability thesis for context-dependent sentences, one can likewise say that w verifies an arbitrary sentence S in a context when S is a priori scrutable from a canonical specification of w in that context.[4]

Given the above, this construction ensures the crucial principle of Plenitude (along with a number of other principles discussed in 'The Nature of Epistemic Space'): S is e-possible iff there exists a scenario that verifies S. Likewise, for context-dependent sentences S, S is e-possible in a context iff there exists a scenario that verifies S in that context. For example, the e-possible sentence 'Gold is a compound' will be verified by many scenarios: intuitively, these are scenarios in which a compound gives rise to the appearances that we associate with gold. Likewise, the e-possible sentence 'Hesperus is not Phosphorus' will be verified by many scenarios: intuitively, these are scenarios in which the relevant bright objects in the evening and morning skies are distinct.

For any subject s (at time t in world w), there will be one scenario that is *actualized* for s (at t in w). This will be a scenario corresponding to an epistemically complete sentence (such as $PQTI$) that is true of w for s at t: specifying the objective character of w (perhaps using P, Q, and T) and the position of s and t within it (using I). The scrutability thesis tells us that a sentence S will be true for s (at t in w) if and only if it is verified by the scenario that is actualized for s (at t in w). Different scenarios will be actualized for different subjects (even within the same world), as reflected in the fact that the I component of $PQTI$ will be different for different subjects.

Scenarios as defined have many applications. They can be used to help understand talk about skeptical scenarios in epistemology, and more generally to serve as 'epistemically possible worlds' in the analysis of knowledge and belief. They can be used to help understand the objects of subjective probability: it is arguable that idealized subjective probabilities are in effect distributed over the space of scenarios. And perhaps most importantly, they can play a key role in the analysis of meaning and content, helping to analyze Fregean notions of meaning and internalist notions of mental content.

---

[4] Here the relevant sort of context-dependence is epistemic context-dependence. Primitive indexicals such as 'I' and 'now' can be taken to be epistemically context-independent. The required Generalized Scrutability thesis then requires a base of epistemically context-independent sentences while allowing context-dependent sentences in the dependent class. See E11 for more on this issue.

For these purposes (which are discussed further in the eleventh excursus and chapter 8), a central role is played by intensions: functions from scenarios to truth-values. The intension of S (in a context) is true at a scenario w if w verifies S (in that context), false at w if w verifies $\sim S$ (in that context), indeterminate at w if w verifies $indet(S)$, and so on. The intension of S will be true at all scenarios iff S is a priori. So the intension of 'Gold is an element' will be true at some scenarios and false at others.

The intension so defined is a version of the primary or epistemic intension familiar from two-dimensional semantics. A sentence's primary intension is its epistemic profile (chapter 1), mapping epistemically possible scenarios to truth-values. A sentence's secondary intension is its modal profile, mapping metaphysically possible worlds to truth-values. A sentence S is a priori (epistemically necessary) iff its primary intension is true in all scenarios, and metaphysically necessary iff its secondary intension is true in all worlds.

When S is an a posteriori necessity, such as 'Hesperus is Phosphorus', its secondary intension will be true at all worlds, but its primary intension will be false at some scenarios. There will be some specifications of scenarios—$PQTI^*$, say—describing a scenario in which the objects visible in the morning sky (around the individual designated by 'I') are entirely distinct from the objects visible in the evening sky. If we discovered that we were in such a scenario, we would accept 'Hesperus is not Phosphorus'. Likewise, conditional on the hypothesis that we are in such a scenario, we should accept 'Hesperus is not Phosphorus'. So 'Hesperus is not Phosphorus' is conditionally scrutable from $PQTI^*$. The arguments earlier in this chapter then suggest that it is a priori scrutable from $PQTI^*$. So the primary intension of 'Hesperus is Phosphorus' will be false at a scenario specified by $PQTI^*$.

More generally, to evaluate the primary intension of a sentence S at a scenario w, one considers w as actual: that is, one considers the hypothesis that w actually obtains, or equivalently, the hypothesis that D is actually the case, where D specifies w. Here we can use conditional scrutability at least as a heuristic guide to a priori scrutability, and ask: conditional on the hypothesis that w is actual, should one accept S? For example, conditional on the hypothesis that a Twin Earth scenario in which the oceans and lakes are filled by XYZ is actual, one should accept 'Water is not H_2O'. So the primary intension of 'Water is H_2O' is false at this scenario.

By contrast, to evaluate the secondary intension of a sentence S at a world w, one considers w as counterfactual: that is, one considers counterfactually what would have been the case if w had obtained, or equivalently, if D had been the case, where D specifies w. Here as a heuristic we can ask: if w had been obtained (that is, if D had been the case), would S have been the case? In the case of a Twin Earth world, we can ask: if the oceans and lakes had been filled by XYZ, would water have been H_2O? Following Kripke and Putnam, the standard judgment about this subjunctive conditional is 'yes'. (By contrast, the intuitive judgment about the indicative conditional 'If the oceans and lakes are filled by XYZ, is water H_2O' is 'no'.) If so, the secondary intension of 'Water is H_2O' is false at the Twin Earth world.

We can also associate subsentential expressions with primary and secondary intensions. In general, a primary intension maps an epistemically possible scenario to extensions—objects for singular terms, properties for predicates, and so on—while a secondary intension maps metaphysically possible worlds to extensions. For example, intuitively the primary intension of 'water' picks out H_2O in the actual scenario and picks out XYZ in a Twin Earth scenario. Making this precise requires us first to make sense of the notion of objects within scenarios, which takes some work (as scenarios have so far just been constructed from sentences), but we can work with an intuitive understanding for present purposes.

The secondary intension of 'Hesperus is Phosphorus' reflects the fact that 'Hesperus' and 'Phosphorus' are *metaphysically rigid*, picking out the same entity—the planet Venus, their referent in the actual world—in all metaphysically possible worlds. By contrast, the primary intension of 'Hesperus is Phosphorus' (in paradigmatic contexts) suggests that 'Hesperus' and 'Phosphorus' are not *epistemically rigid*: they do not pick out the same entity in all epistemically possible scenarios (see E13 for much more here). If they did pick out the same entity in all scenarios, then 'Hesperus is Phosphorus' would be true in all scenarios and therefore a priori, which it is not. Rather, to a rough first approximation, 'Hesperus' picks out a bright object in a certain location in the evening sky in a given scenario, while 'Phosphorus' picks out a bright object in a certain location in the morning sky. In many scenarios, these two objects will be distinct.

This point generalizes to arbitrary names of concrete objects, suggesting that no name for a concrete object is epistemically rigid. By contrast, it is arguable that some names for abstract objects are epistemically rigid: for example, 'o' arguably picks out zero in all scenarios, and 'identity' arguably picks out the relation of identity in all scenarios. One can similarly hold that numerous predicates—perhaps 'conscious', 'causes', and 'omniscient', among many others—are epistemically rigid, having the same property as extension in all scenarios.

Making the notion of epistemic rigidity precise is tricky, in part because we have not yet formally populated scenarios with objects, and in part because it is unclear that there is a coherent general notion of trans-scenario identity: that is, of what it is for entities in two different scenarios to be the same entity. But a useful intuitive gloss on the notion is that an epistemically rigid expression is one that expresses an epistemically rigid concept, and that an epistemically rigid concept is one whose extension we can know a priori. For example, there is an intuitive sense in which we cannot know what water is a priori, and in which we cannot know what Hesperus is a priori, but in which we might be able to know what zero is a priori or what identity is a priori. That is roughly the sense at play here. I discuss this and many other issues about epistemic rigidity at greater length in the fourteenth excursus.

When an expression is epistemically rigid and also metaphysically rigid (metaphysically rigid *de jure* rather than *de facto*, in the terminology of Kripke 1980), it is *super-rigid*. In this case, the expression will pick out the same entity in all scenarios and all worlds. For example, it is plausible that 'o' picks out zero in all scenarios and all worlds. As with epistemically rigid expressions, there are plausibly no super-rigid expressions for concrete objects, but there are plausibly super-rigid expressions for some abstract objects and properties.

What is the relationship between epistemically possible scenarios and metaphysically possible worlds? As I have discussed them so far, these are independent sorts of entities. But it is common to see a close relationship between them, modeling epistemically possible scenarios as centered metaphysically possible worlds. The existence of super-rigid expressions, which function to pick out the same entities in scenarios and in worlds, helps us to explore the connections between these entities. They can also help us to construct scenarios nonlinguistically using worldly entities such as properties and propositions.

To analyze the correspondence between scenarios and worlds it is helpful to highlight two theses about super-rigid expressions that I discuss in the fourteenth excursus and chapter 8. The first is Super-Rigid Scrutability: all epistemically possible sentences S are scrutable from sentences including only super-rigid expressions and primitive indexicals (such as 'I' and 'now').[5] The second is an Apriority/Necessity thesis: when a sentence S contains only super-rigid expressions, S is a priori iff S is necessary. The first thesis is supported by the character of the scrutability bases we arrive at and by general considerations concerning the scrutability of sentences containing epistemically nonrigid expressions. The second thesis is supported by the observation that paradigmatic Kripkean a posteriori necessities all appear to involve epistemically nonrigid expressions.

Super-Rigid Scrutability (and the considerations that support it) suggests that a generalized scrutability base need contain only certain basic super-rigid sentences (that is, sentences containing only super-rigid expressions) and certain indexical sentences such as 'I am F_1' and 'Now is F_2', where F_1 and F_2 are predicates containing only super-rigid expressions. Given this, scenarios can be identified with epistemically complete sentences of the form $D \& I$, where D is a complex super-rigid sentence (conjoining basic sentences) and I is a conjunction of indexical sentences as above. D will say roughly that there exist objects bear-

---

[5] This has roughly the strength of a generalized scrutability thesis, but I omit 'Generalized' here and later for ease of discussion.

ing certain specific properties and relations, and I will attribute certain specific properties and relations of oneself and the current time.

D will express a complex Russellian proposition p, containing properties and relations (perhaps along with other abstract objects) as constituents, connected by logical structure. This proposition is quite reminiscent of a possible world. It is common to regard possible worlds as complex Russellian propositions, specifying the distribution of certain basic properties and relations over objects. If the Apriority/Necessity thesis is correct, then D will be metaphysically possible (as it is super-rigid and epistemically possible), so p will be metaphysically possible. In this case, p will correspond to a metaphysically possible world.[6] If the Apriority/ Necessity thesis is incorrect, then D may be metaphysically impossible, in which case p will correspond to a metaphysically impossible world. But either way p will correspond to a world-like entity involving the distribution of properties and relations over objects.

If a scenario w were specified by D alone, we could then identify the scenario with the world specified by p.[7] Given the additional role of I, which says something like 'I am F_1 and now is F_2', we can instead identify the scenario with a *centered world*. Centered worlds are usually taken to be ordered triples of worlds, individuals, and times. For present purposes, we can take them to be ordered triples of a Russellian proposition p and properties ϕ_1 and ϕ_2 (corresponding to maximally specific properties possessed by the individual and the time respectively). For the scenario in question, we can take ϕ_1 and ϕ_2 to be the properties expressed by the predicates F_1 and F_2 respectively.

---

[6] Strictly speaking, p will correspond either to a complete or an incomplete metaphysically possible world. Which is correct depends on the thesis of Super-Rigid Necessitation (an analog of Super-Rigid Scrutability): for any metaphysically possible sentence S, S is metaphysically necessitated by some sentence T including only super-rigid expressions. If this thesis (along with Apriority/Necessity) is true, the Russellian propositions in the text will be metaphysically complete (by analogy with epistemic completeness) and will specify full metaphysically possible worlds. If this thesis is false, these Russellian propositions may be metaphysically incomplete and will specify incomplete worlds (worlds without all details filled in), which in effect correspond to equivalence classes of of metaphysically possible worlds.

Super-Rigid Necessitation will be false on certain haecceitist views (discussed in E16), on which a super-rigid specification of a world may underdetermine which objects are present in a world. It will also be false on certain quidditist views (discussed in 7.9 and E16), on which a super-rigid specification of a world may underdetermine which intrinsic properties are present in that world. Still, given Apriority/Necessity and Super-Rigid Scrutability, these propositions will correspond at least to incomplete metaphysically possible worlds. Given Super-Rigid Necessitation in addition, the propositions will correspond precisely to metaphysically possible worlds.

[7] This only works when D is super-rigid. If non-super-rigid expressions are involved in the base, identifying scenarios with Russellian propositions will give the wrong results. For example, if 'Hesperus' and 'Phosphorus' are in the base, 'Hesperus is such-and-such' will always specify a Russellian proposition about Venus, as will 'Phosphorus is such-and-such'. So 'Hesperus is Phosphorus will come out true in all scenarios, even though it is not a priori.

If Super-Rigid Scrutability is true, we can always model scenarios as centered worlds in this way. If Apriority/Necessity is also true, scenarios will correspond to centered worlds where the worlds in question are always metaphysically possible.[8]

Take a paradigmatic a posteriori necessity, such as 'Water is H_2O' which is false in a Twin Earth scenario. Super-Rigid Scrutability entails that a Twin Earth scenario can be specified by an epistemically possible sentence $TE \& I$ conjoining a super-rigid sentence TE with indexical claims involving 'I' and 'Now'. Here TE might involve a super-rigid specification of the microphysical and phenomenological character of the world, without using epistemically nonrigid terms such as 'water'. Because TE is super-rigid, it can be used to specify a world: that is, a Russellian complex of objects and properties. Apriority/Necessity entails that TE is metaphysically possible, so that this world is a metaphysically possible world. TE metaphysically necessitates 'Water is H_2O', while $TE \& I$ epistemically necessitates 'Water is not H_2O'. So the primary intension of 'Water is H_2O' is false at the Twin Earth scenario while its secondary intension is true at the Twin Earth world. But there remains a close correspondence between the scenario and the world. The difference in intensions for 'Water is H_2O' arises not so much due to differences between them as due to the difference between epistemic and metaphysical necessitation.

I accept Apriority/Necessity and Super-Rigid Scrutability. (Relatives of these theses play crucial roles in 'The Two-Dimensional Argument against Materialism'.) So I hold that scenarios correspond closely to centered metaphysically possible worlds. In practice, many philosophers already use centered metaphysically possible worlds to model epistemically possible scenarios (this is a standard practice in the literature on subjective probability, for example). The analysis above can be seen as providing a partial grounding for this practice.

At the same time, some philosophers will reject Apriority/Necessity or Super-Rigid Scrutability. If these theses are rejected, the relation between scenarios and possible worlds becomes more complex.

First, consider a view that rejects Apriority/Necessity while retaining Super-Rigid Scrutability: for example, a theist view on which 'There is an omniscient being' is necessary but not a priori. This sentence S plausibly contains only super-rigid expressions. So on the view in question, S will be a counterexample to the Apriority/Necessity thesis. Correspondingly, S will be false in some

---

[8] As before, if Super-Rigid Necessitation is false, scenarios will correspond to centered incomplete metaphysically possible worlds, or to equivalence classes of centered metaphysically possible worlds. If Super-Rigid Necessitation (along with the other two theses) is true, scenarios will correspond near-perfectly with centered metaphysically possible worlds. The only exception involves certain symmetrical worlds, where more than one centered world (centered on symmetrical counterparts) may correspond to the same scenario.

epistemically possible scenario. Given Super-Rigid Scrutability, there will be a sentence D & I specifying such a scenario, where D is super-rigid and I is indexical. D will then specify a world (a Russellian proposition constructed from properties): in effect, a world without an omniscient being. But on the view in question, this world will not be metaphysically possible. So the scenarios here will correspond to centered metaphysically impossible worlds.

Next, consider a view on which Super-Rigid Scrutability is false: for example, a type-B materialist view (discussed in the fourteenth excursus) on which phenomenal concepts are both conceptually primitive and epistemically nonrigid. Then corresponding expressions such as 'consciousness' are needed in a scrutability base, but one cannot know what these expressions pick out a priori: perhaps 'consciousness' picks out a neurophysiological property N empirically. In this case, scenario descriptions (such as $PQTI$) will not be decomposable into a super-rigid part and an indexical part. Even once indexicals are removed, some remaining expressions (such as the phenomenal expressions in Q) will be epistemically nonrigid, so that they will not map a priori onto properties. While the sentence will still correspond empirically to a complex of properties (such as N), the resulting property-involving world will not adequately model the epistemic properties of the scenario. (For example, it becomes hard to see how 'Consciousness is N' can be false at a centered world.) In this case, we can either stay with a linguistic model of scenarios without invoking properties, or perhaps better, we can see scenarios as structures of Fregean senses, where we associate the primitives here with primitive Fregean senses that determine the properties that serve as their referents only a posteriori.

To summarize: if both Apriority/Necessity and Super-Rigid Scrutability are true, as on my view, scenarios correspond closely to centered metaphysically possible worlds. If the former but not the latter is true, scenarios still correspond closely to centered worlds, but the worlds in questions may be metaphysically impossible in some cases. If the latter is false, one has to break the close connection between scenarios and centered (property-involving) worlds, instead constructing scenarios from sentences or from Fregean propositions.

What about two-dimensional evaluation? On the current model, this is tied to epistemic possibilities concerning what is metaphysically possible. For example, someone might hold that it is epistemically possible that there is exactly one metaphysically possible world, and epistemically possible that there are enormously many metaphysically possible worlds. We could model this by a two-dimensional modal structure on which every epistemically possible scenario v is associated with a space of worlds that are metaphysically possible relative to v. If one holds (as I do) that Apriority/Necessity and Super-Rigid Scrutability are both a priori, then every scenario will be associated with a space of worlds such that there is a centered world for every scenario. Under slightly stronger assumptions (which I discuss in 'The Foundations of Two-Dimensional Semantics'), one can use the same space of metaphysically possible worlds to play the role of the putative worlds for each of these scenarios. Under these assumptions one gets a simple 'rectangular' two-dimensional structure, with every scenario corresponding to the same space of worlds. Under weaker assumptions one gets a more complex structure, on which some scenarios may be associated with smaller or larger spaces of worlds, and on which some worlds may be metaphysically impossible (relative to the actual scenario).

Either way, one can use this two-dimensional structure to define two-dimensional intensions for sentences: given a scenario v and a world w that is possible relative to v, the two-dimensional intension of S will map (v, w) to the truth-value of S at w, conditional on the assumption that v is actual. These two-dimensional intensions are a version of the two-dimensional matrices familiar from two-dimensional semantics.

An important residual issue concerns the idealized notion of epistemic possibility that we started with. This works well in modeling the epistemic states of idealized agents, but not as well in modeling the epistemic states of non-ideal agents. For example, a non-ideal agent might disbelieve certain moral or mathematical truths, even though these truths are a priori, or the agent might simply fail to believe these. The current framework does not easily model these states, as a priori truths are true in all scenarios. To model these states, it would be useful to invoke a less idealized notion of epistemic necessity, and a correspondingly more fine-grained space of non-ideal scenarios.

One idea here is that one might understand non-ideal epistemic necessity in terms of a notion of analyticity rather than apriority (discussed in chapter 8) and construct fine-grained scenarios and fine-grained intensions from there. Then insofar as the relevant moral truths (for example) are a priori but not analytic, there will be scenarios where they are false. If so, we may have groups of fine-grained scenarios with the same natural truths and different moral truths. However, it is not clear that this sort of model will help with ignorance of logical truths: these truths are often taken to be analytic, and it is not obvious how best to model scenarios in which they are false. The understanding of non-ideal epistemic space remains open as a challenge for future work.[9]

<hr/>

[9] Jens Christian Bjerring (2010, forthcoming) explores a number of models of non-ideal epistemic space, and demonstrates that there are serious difficulties in developing a model in which complex logical truths are false but simple logical truths are not. As a result, one may be left with a choice between logical omniscience (logical truths are true in all worlds) and triviality (any set of sentences determines a scenario).

Constructing Fregean Senses

Theories of meaning are often classified as Russellian or Fregean. Russellian theories hold that the meaning of simple expressions such as ordinary proper names in natural language is exhausted by their referents. On a typical Russellian view, the meaning of the names 'Hesperus' and 'Phosphorus' is the same, the planet Venus. Fregean theories of meaning hold that the meaning of all such expressions involves not just reference but sense. Sense is tied to cognitive significance, so that expressions that differ in their cognitive roles have different senses. For example, 'Hesperus is Phosphorus' is cognitively significant, so 'Hesperus' and 'Phosphorus' have different senses.[1]

A disadvantage of Frege's own approach to senses is that he says very little about what senses actually are, and he says less than he might about just how senses behave. In *Meaning and Necessity*, Carnap attempted to rectify this problem by constructing entities that behave much like Fregean senses from materials that can be independently understood. In particular, he argued that his intensions could play the role of Fregean senses for names and for other expressions. In later work on possible-world semantics (especially following Kripke), however, intensions and worlds have tended to be strongly separated from epistemological notions, and the intensions that result are more Russellian than Fregean in character.

---

[1] The terminology here is a little awkward in that Russell himself may come out as a Fregean in that he held that the meaning of ordinary proper names such as 'Hesperus' is not exhausted by their referents, as these names are really disguised descriptions. On Russell's own view, the only truly simple expressions are names for sense-data and other entities with which we are directly acquainted. This contrasts with contemporary Russellian views that extend Russell's view to all ordinary proper names. It has become standard to classify Russell's original view as a broadly Fregean view, with content of an associated description playing the role of sense, and I follow that practice here. That being said, there is room for a distinction among broadly Fregean views between 'Russellian Fregean views' that put special weight on Russellian acquaintance and broadly descriptive content, and 'non-Russellian Fregean views' that do not. In some respects, my own view (or at least the view that derives from Super-Rigid Scrutability) is akin to a Russellian Fregean view. I do not take a stand on where Frege's own views fell.

The scrutability framework allows us to reconnect intensions to epistemological notions. To do so, we need only define intensions over epistemically possible scenarios. These are the intensions that I have elsewhere called primary intensions, but for ease of discussion here I will just call them intensions. The epistemological roots of these intensions allow them to once again play some of the roles of Fregean senses. Developing a Fregean account of meaning and content is the main focus of *The Multiplicity of Meaning*, so I will not dwell too long on these issues here. I will provide a brief sketch of how A Priori Scrutability can serve as a foundation for this sort of theory, however, and I will address some potential objections from Russellian opponents.

A Priori Scrutability bears on this debate in part by making the case that most expressions in natural language, at least as uttered by speakers, have substantive and nontrivial a priori connections to other expressions. In particular, they have substantive a priori connections to expressions in a compact base language (the language of *PQTI*, say). Substantive connections of this sort strongly suggest that there is a Fregean aspect of content that is reflected in these connections. This aspect of content is naturally modeled using intensions. For example, we saw in chapter 1 that A Priori Scrutability provides a natural response to Kripke's epistemological arguments against descriptivism. I argued there that Kripke's data can easily be captured by associating a name such as 'Gödel' not with a description but with an intension governing its application to epistemically possible scenarios. This intension can do much of the work that descriptions or Fregean senses were supposed to do.

The scrutability theses we have considered ensure that these intensions are well-defined. The Generalized A Priori Scrutability thesis can be used to make the intuitive notion of a scenario precise, as we saw in the tenth excursus. In particular, scenarios can be understood as equivalence classes of epistemically complete sentences in a generalized scrutability base. We can then define intensions as functions from scenarios to truth-values. The intension of a sentence S (in a context) is true at a scenario w iff S is a priori scrutable from D (in that context), where D is a canonical specification of w (that is, one of the epistemically complete sentences in the equivalence class of w). There are related definitions for falsity at a scenario, indeterminacy at a scenario, and so on. Generalized A Priori Scrutability ensures that whenever a sentence S is epistemically possible (not ruled out a priori), there is a scenario at which its intension is true.

For example, suppose I utter the true sentence 'Gödel proved the incompleteness of arithmetic'. A Priori Scrutability entails that this sentence S is a priori scrutable (for me) from a canonical specification D of my actual scenario, where D is something along the lines of *PQTI*. So the intension of S is true at that scenario. At the same time, S is not a priori, as it is false at a Gödel–Schmidt scenario. Correspondingly, there will be a canonical specification D' of a Gödel–

Schmidt scenario such that ~S is a priori scrutable from D'. So the intension of S is false at this scenario.

These intensions behave in a Fregean fashion. Consider the intension of 'Hesperus is Phosphorus', as uttered in my current context. Because this sentence S is true, its intension will be true at my actual scenario, but given that S is not a priori, its intension will be false at some scenarios. For example, if D' specifies a scenario in which the relevant bright object in the morning sky differs from the relevant bright object in the evening sky, then 'Hesperus is not Phosphorus' will be scrutable from D', so S will be false at that scenario. We can also associate intensions with subsentential expressions such as names (as discussed in E10), so that the intension of a sentence is related compositionally to the intensions of its parts. In a scenario (like the one above) where 'Hesperus is Phosphorus' is false, the intensions of 'Hesperus' and 'Phosphorus' will pick out different referents: the different bright objects in the morning and evening sky. So as used by me, 'Hesperus' and 'Phosphorus' will have different intensions, just as they have different Fregean senses.

This behavior is quite general: whenever '$A = B$' is not a priori (in a context), the names A and B will have different intensions (in that context). The same goes for other expressions: for example, if two general terms are such that 'Everything is an A iff it is a B' is not a priori, they will have different intensions. In general, two expressions (in contexts) have the same intension if and only if they are a priori equivalent. So intensions serve as Fregean semantic values at least in that these semantic values in effect individuate expressions by their epistemological role and by a sort of epistemological equivalence. They also can play another key role of Fregean senses, that of determining reference: the referent of an expression (in a context) is determined by what the expression's intension (in that context) picks out in the scenario corresponding to that context.

Intensions can also play many of the roles that descriptions play in descriptive accounts of meaning. Intensions will not in general correspond to descriptions, for reasons given in chapter 1, but they can at least be approximated by descriptions. For example, the intension of 'water', in a scenario, might very roughly pick out the same thing as 'The clear, drinkable liquid found around here' in that scenario. As usual there will be counterexamples, leading to ever-longer descriptions, but an approximate description can at least capture much of the relevant behavior. And like descriptions, intensions can be seen as capturing criteria that an entity in the environment must satisfy in order to qualify as the referent of a term.

If an opponent wants to resist the case for Fregean theories of meaning, they must do one of three things: (i) resist the case for the scrutability theses, (ii) resist the move from scrutability theses to the existence of intensions, or (iii) resist the claim that intensions so-defined have the key properties required for a successful

Fregean theory of meaning. In what follows I will say something about all three strategies in reverse order. Doing so will help to flesh out the picture of meaning that falls out of the scrutability framework. I will pay special attention to objections that might be mounted by proponents of a Russellian account.

Regarding (iii): There are a number of potential objections to the claim that intensions so-defined have the properties required for a successful Fregean theory of meaning.

A first group of objections derive immediately from a Russellian view. Some Russellians (for example, Scott Soames in *Reference and Description*) hold that intensions across epistemically possible scenarios are well-defined but that co-referential names have the same intension: the intensions for both 'Hesperus' and 'Phosphorus' pick out Venus in all scenarios. However, I have gone to some lengths to define sentential apriority and epistemic possibility so that it is more or less stipulative that 'Hesperus is Phosphorus' is not a priori and that 'Hesperus is not Phosphorus' is epistemically possible. Given these claims, it follows from the construction that the intensions for 'Hesperus' and 'Phosphorus' are distinct and pick out distinct entities in some scenarios. There may be other ways of understanding apriority (for example, in terms of apriority of an associated Russellian proposition) that yield Russellian intensions here. But it is apriority in the sense I have defined that is closely linked to cognitive significance, so it is apriority in this sense that matters for Fregean purposes.

Another Russellian objection is that this account cannot cope with Kripke's modal argument: 'Hesperus is Phosphorus' is necessary, so 'Hesperus' and 'Phosphorus' must have the same intension, while 'Hesperus is visible in the evening sky' is contingent, so that 'Hesperus' cannot have an intension tied to the evening sky. One can deal with this objection by invoking two-dimensional semantics, on which names are associated with two intensions: a primary intension, governing application to epistemically possible scenarios, and a secondary intension, governing application to metaphysically possible worlds. The primary intensions of 'Hesperus' and 'Phosphorus' are distinct, mirroring the fact that 'Hesperus is Phosphorus' is not a priori, but their secondary intensions are the same (both pick out Venus in all worlds), mirroring the fact that 'Hesperus is Phosphorus' is necessary.

On a more refined account (developed in 'Propositions and Attitude Ascriptions'), one can construe the Fregean sense of a term such as 'Hesperus' as an *enriched intension*: an ordered pair of a primary intension and an extension. Then 'Hesperus' and 'Phosphorus' will have distinct enriched intensions that share an extension. Once we combine this with the thesis that modal operators (such as 'Necessarily') are sensitive only to the extension component of the enriched intensions of embedded expressions, whereas epistemic operators are sensitive in addition to primary intensions, this yields the desired result. This hypothesis also has the advantage of yielding an analysis of indexical expressions such as 'I' and 'now' that behaves more like Frege's own account, in that my enriched intension for 'I' will differ from yours and will be an enriched intension that no one else can express.

It is sometimes said (e.g. by Mark Sainsbury and Michael Tye in *Seven Puzzles of Thought*, pp. 33–5) that on the current framework, the referent of a name or natural kind term will not be essential to it: the view predicts that on Twin Earth, the English word 'water' could be used to refer to XYZ. This misunderstanding of the view results from conflating scenarios with contexts of utterance (or equivalently, by running together primary intensions with the 'characters' of Kaplan's 'Demonstratives', construed here as functions from contexts to referents). It is true that the view predicts that 'water' picks out XYZ relative to a Twin Earth scenario (it is a priori that if Twin Earth is actual, water is XYZ), but this does not entail that 'water' could be used in a Twin Earth context to pick out XYZ. The view is quite compatible with the claim that the English word 'water' is associated with an enriched intension that is essential to it (or at least with a referent that is essential to it), that the term picks out H_2O in every context, and that the Twin Earth word 'water' is simply a different word. (There is no contradiction in saying both that 'Heat is whatever causes heat sensations' is a priori and that 'heat' refers essentially to the motion of molecules.) The moral here is that the epistemic dependence inherent in the notion of scrutability has to be sharply distinguished from context-dependence.

Still another Russellian objection (also put forward by Soames) is that these intensions cannot serve as the objects of attitudes in a relational account of attitude ascriptions. One might think that on this account, 'John believes that I am hungry' is true if John stands in the belief relation to the primary intension of 'I am hungry'. John stands in this relation only if he believes that he himself is hungry—which is the wrong result. Now, I do not think the current account stands or falls with its success in giving a solution to the notoriously difficult problem of attitude ascription. Still, I argue in the article cited above that if we invoke enriched intensions (rather than simply primary intensions) in an appropriately flexible account of attitude ascriptions, many of the central problems can be solved.

Another class of objections is more likely to come from Fregean quarters. One such objection suggests that intensions are too coarse-grained to serve as Fregean senses, because of the idealization in the notion of apriority. For example, '$77 \times 33 = 2541$' is a priori, but it is still cognitively significant. So '77×33' and '2541' should have different Fregean senses, but they will have the same primary intensions. One can deal with this objection by holding that the Fregean sense of a complex expression should be seen as a *structured* intension, composed of the (primary or enriched) intensions of its parts, according to the expression's logical form. So '77 × 33' and '2541' will have different structured intensions.

Most potential problem cases can be handled this way. The only remaining problems arise if there are pairs of *simple* expressions 'A' and 'B' such that 'A = B' is a priori while also being cognitively significant. It is unclear that there are any such pairs, however. Someone might suggest that we can stipulate a simple name such as 'Num' whose reference is fixed to be something complex such as 77 × 33; but in such a case it is at least arguable that 'Num' should be understood to have complex structured content. If there are exceptions here, however, then we might try moving to a finer-grained space of scenarios and finer-grained intensions, as discussed at the end of the tenth excursus.

Alternatively, we can simply allow that while intensions are very much like Fregean senses, they are not quite as fine-grained as Frege's own senses. This will be consistent with the intensions playing all sorts of explanatory roles. I am strongly inclined toward a semantic pluralism on which there are many notions of meaning or content playing many different roles. The intensions discussed here are not all there is to meaning and content. They can play many of the relevant roles, but they do not play all the roles. For example, they do not play the 'public meaning' role, where public meanings are associated with expression types rather than expressions in contexts, and while they can play many of the roles of Fregean senses, they may not play the full role of reflecting every difference in cognitive significance.

Another broadly Fregean objection says that these intensions do not determine referents as senses should. One version of the objection is tied to indexicality: two speakers in the same world can have the same intension but a different referent, perhaps for 'I' and 'now'. But although this rules out an absolute determination of referent by intension, it remains compatible with a weaker determination of reference by intension plus the speaker's scenario of utterance, and this sort of determination is good enough for most Fregean purposes. Furthermore, the enriched intensions discussed above allow a stronger sort of determination of reference by sense, one that comports well with Frege's own treatment of indexicals such as 'I'.

Another version of the objection notes that scenarios are linguistic constructions, so that intensions yield only word–word relations (a word picks out a linguistic entity at a linguistic construction), not word–world relations (a word picks out a nonlinguistic entity at a nonlinguistic world such as the actual world). But it is easy to extend these to word–world relations. Most obviously, given that one scenario is actualized for any given speaker, the intension of a sentence at that scenario will determine its truth-value. Now, the notion of actualization of a (linguistically constructed) scenario in effect assumes word–world relations for words in a scrutability base. But as we saw in the tenth excursus, one can also construct scenarios nonlinguistically. For example, given Super-Rigid Scrutability, one can construct scenarios as centered worlds, where worlds are understood as complexes of properties and relations. Alternatively, if we are granted Fregean senses for the expressions in a scrutability base (understood not as intensions but in some other fashion), we can construct scenarios as structures of these senses. There will be a nonlinguistic fact of the matter as to which of these scenarios is actualized for any given speaker, and about which nonlinguistic entity an intension picks out in the actualized scenario, yielding an actual nonlinguistic referent. So these intensions yield word–world relations.

Even without such a construction, the scrutability framework in effect allows word–world relations for all expressions to be fixed by word–world relations for base expressions along with scrutability relations. A Fregean sympathetic with this picture might say that the base expressions have primitive senses, while other expressions have less primitive senses that derive from these. Given scrutability from a base of super-rigid and indexical expressions (as discussed in the tenth and fourteenth excurses), we can construe these primitive senses as super-rigid senses and indexical senses, both of which pick out their referents in an especially direct fashion. If the Fregean is friendly to acquaintance, it might be held that these are special acquaintance-based senses. Even without an appeal to acquaintance or super-rigidity, then as long as we have the materials to account for reference in the scrutability base, scrutability then allows intensions to do the rest of the work.

Finally, many Fregeans resist the idea of constructing senses, or at least constructing them as anything as complex as functions over scenarios. Often senses are held to be primitive abstract objects. Speaking for myself, I find that doing so leaves the character of senses highly obscure, and I think that the detail of a construction is invaluable in understanding just how senses may behave. But if one disagrees, it is also possible to kick away the step-ladder: first use the construction to rebut arguments against Fregean senses and to give a sense of how they behave, then postulate primitive senses that behave in a similar way. We will then have a more detailed picture of how primitive senses are individuated, how they depend on context, how they are related to reference, how they compose with other senses, and so on.[2]

A third class of objection questions whether intensions are suitable to serve as *meanings* or as *semantic contents*. One objection says that meanings are properties

---

[2] A related objection notes that intensions are defined in terms of epistemological properties such as apriority, whereas Fregean senses ought to ground and explain those properties. If one accepts the latter claim (which turns on difficult issues about the priority of the epistemological and the semantic, or of the normative and the intentional) one can either argue that intensions can play this grounding role (distinguishing explication from metaphysical priority as on p. 209) or accept more fundamental Fregean senses as above. It is worth noting that given a nonlinguistic construction of scenarios, intensions can be grounded in properties or relations (e.g., an intension over centered worlds will be determined by a relation to items at the center), which might serve to constitute more fundamental senses.

of expression types in a public language, whereas intensions are not: the same expression can have different intensions in different contexts. In response: it is certainly true that the intension associated with an expression such as 'Gödel' or 'water' or 'tall' or 'that' can vary between contexts: for example, a chemist's intension for 'water' might pick out whatever has a certain molecular structure, while a farmer's might pick out the liquid that falls from the sky when it rains.[3] So *if* 'meaning' is understood to be incompatible with this sort of variation, then intensions are not meanings. However, intensions can still play many of the explanatory roles that meanings are supposed to play—for example, they can serve as truth-conditions for utterances, as referents for 'that'-clauses, and as arbiters of cognitive significance. If they play these roles, little rests on the verbal question of whether they are called 'meanings' or whether we use some other term such as 'content'.

It is worth noting that Frege himself allowed that the sense associated with an expression in natural language can vary between different speakers. Likewise, when Kripke argues against descriptive theories of meaning, he puts no weight on a criterion of constancy between speakers, instead allowing that descriptions might vary between speakers and casting his arguments in terms of what is 'a priori for a speaker'. Furthermore, a plausible moral of much recent discussion of context-dependence is that an enormous amount of explanatory work in the semantic domain is done by context-dependent semantic values, and that less is done by semantic values that are independent of context. There remain some distinctive explanatory projects for the latter (especially in characterizing public languages and in explaining certain aspects of language learning and communication), but these are not the projects that are most of interest here. So while one can reserve the word 'meaning' for the invariant semantic values if one likes, the result may be that semantic values that are not strictly meanings carry much of the explanatory burden.[4]

---

[3] See the discussion of the argument from variability in 'On Sense and Intension' for more on this issue.

[4] How does the epistemic context-dependence in the current framework relate to the extensional context-dependence found with familiar indexicals? For indexicals such as 'I', there is a simple rule of public language for determining how extension depends on context. By contrast, there is no simple rule for determining how the intension associated with a term such as 'Gödel' or 'water' depends on context. Instead it will depend on complex matters involving the speaker's thoughts and intentions. In this respect the context-dependence is more akin to the unruly context-dependence of a demonstrative such as 'that' (or perhaps a predicate such as 'big'), whose referent depends in large part on a speaker's intentions. On the other hand, the way that the intension of a term like 'Gödel' or 'water' behaves for a fixed speaker across time is intermediate between the stable context-dependence of 'I', which always has the same referent for a given speaker, rather than the unstable context-dependence of 'that' or 'big', which are often used with quite different extensions by the same speaker at nearby times. Typically, if the intension associated with a name or natural-kind term changes at all for a given speaker, it will change quite slowly.

It would not be unreasonable to draw a mixed verdict about the debate between the Fregean and the Russellian: the Russellian is right about the semantic values (in a broad sense) of names independent of context, while the Fregean is right about the semantic values of utterances or of names in contexts. This view would be analogous to a 'local descriptivism' where every use of a name is a priori equivalent to a description, and speakers in different contexts have different associated descriptions that share only a referent. Still, it is worth keeping in mind that Frege and Russell themselves allowed their Fregean semantic values to vary, and that local descriptivism is a view that Kripke was arguing against. So this verdict gives traditional Fregeans what they wanted while giving Russellians less than they wanted. The existence of local Fregean senses also suggests that the upshot of Kripke's arguments for other issues in philosophy (the analysis of mental content and the theory of reference, for example) will be less sweeping than it would otherwise have been.

A related question: are these intensions part of semantics or pragmatics? Again, this depends on how the distinction is drawn. If semantics involves only properties of expressions while pragmatics involves properties of utterances, then intensions will be semantically associated only with epistemically context-independent expressions. Where ordinary names and other epistemically context-dependent expressions are concerned, the intensions will be part of pragmatics. If semantics involves truth-conditional properties, however, intensions are part of semantics. Scott Soames once suggested to me that all this is best seen as part of 'epistemics': roughly, the study of those aspects of language tied to knowledge and cognition. I have no objection to seeing the framework in this way, but I think that properties associated with epistemics can do much traditional semantic work.

An opponent may suggest that these intensions are speaker meanings rather than semantic meanings. Again, this depends on how one draws these divisions. If the division is drawn so that semantic meanings are associated with expression types while speaker meanings are associated with utterances, or so that semantic meaning of an expression cannot vary with context while speaker meanings can, then clearly intensions fall on the side of speaker meanings. On the other hand, if the division is drawn so that semantic meanings of an utterance are literal truth-conditions while speaker meanings are not, then intensions fall on the side of semantic meanings. For example, in Donnellan's case (discussed in the third excursus) of someone who uses the false utterance 'Smith's murderer is insane' to convey the true belief that Jones is insane, the primary intension associated with the utterance will be false rather than true. Here the primary intension of the utterance of 'Smith's murderer' picks out what Kripke calls the 'semantic referent' (the murderer of Smith) rather than the 'speaker's referent' (Jones).

A connected objection arises from cases of deference. Take Burge's case of Bert, a non-expert speaker who has not mastered the concept of arthritis and

CONSTRUCTING FREGEAN SENSES

thinks that arthritis can occur in the thighs. Nevertheless, Bert defers to usage in his community, so that his term 'arthritis' picks out the community referent for the term: arthritis, a disease of the joints. On the current account, Bert's term picks out this referent via a *deferential* intension, one whose referent in a scenario depends at least in part on how others within that scenario use the expression in question. In an extreme case of complete deference, the intension will be roughly the same as the intension of 'What others in my community call 'arthritis''. One might object that intensions such as these are certainly not semantic meanings for 'arthritis', even relative to a context. But again, little turns on whether or not these intensions are semantic meanings. The deferential intension here serves as a sort of Fregean content associated with Bert's utterances, one that can play the roles discussed earlier. These are the roles that matter for present purposes.

One might also worry that almost all utterances are deferential, so that almost all utterances will have the metalinguistic intension just mentioned. I think that nondeferential utterances are common in cases of concept mastery. For example, when I say 'P and Q', then even if it turns out that the rest of the community uses 'and' for disjunction, my utterance will be true iff both P and Q are true. Correspondingly, my use of 'and' has an intension corresponding to conjunction rather than a metalinguistic intension. On the other hand, in cases where a concept is not fully mastered, such as the arthritis case above, the deferential intension seems the right one to capture the cognitive role of my use of the expression.

Perhaps most interesting are cases where a speaker has mastered a concept (e.g., *bachelor*), uses a corresponding expression ('bachelor') competently, but still defers to the community in that the referent of her term depends on community usage. Such a speaker's relation to 'bachelor' differs from my relation to 'and': if it had turned out that the community used 'bachelor' for married men (say), her utterances of 'bachelors are unmarried men' would have been false, and she would have deemed them false on idealized reflection. On the current framework, the corresponding intension will have a metalinguistic element as above, one whose referent in a scenario depends on how people use 'bachelor' in that scenario. However, we can also use the framework to associate the mastered concept with a nonmetalinguistic intension: one that picks out the unmarried men in any scenario, perhaps. Given an appropriate expression relation that connects the utterance to the mastered concept, we can thereby associate the utterance with that intension. In cases like this we can associate the utterance with both deferential Fregean content (metalinguistic in character) and autonomous Fregean content (nonmetalinguistic). For epistemically invariant expressions we can also associate the expression (not just the use) with a community Fregean content (also nonmetalinguistic). The framework can easily handle all of these aspects of content.

Regarding (ii): the move from scrutability theses to defining intensions is fairly straightforward. Given Generalized A Priori Scrutability, one can construct scenarios from epistemically complete sentences in the compact base language and define intensions from there. An opponent could in principle resist the move from the scrutability thesis to the existence of epistemically complete sentences, but I do not think this is an especially promising place to resist. There is a good case that every epistemically possible sentence is a priori entailed by an epistemically complete sentence in an ideal language (see 'The Nature of Epistemic Space' for an argument), and even if there were not, one could get much of the force of the intension framework out of intensions defined over evermore-complete partial scenarios.

Why is compactness important here? To see this, suppose we could establish only the trivial scrutability thesis that all truths are scrutable from the class of all truths, perhaps because there are no a priori connections between truths. Given the linguistic construction of scenarios, scenarios will then correspond to something like arbitrary collections of sentences with little interesting structure. The intension of a sentence S would then in effect be the set of sets of sentences that contain S. This would rob the framework of interesting explanatory power. For example, any two names (or any two distinct expressions) will have trivially distinct intensions. More generally, whether a scrutability base is large or small, on the linguistic construction of scenarios the intensions for the expressions in a scrutability base will be fairly uninteresting. So the smaller the base, the more interesting structure one gets for intensions in general. Invoking Super-Rigid Scrutability or primitive senses allows a nonlinguistic construction that will make intensions for base expressions more interesting, but even here, these invocations will be more plausible if we have already established a compact base.

Another way to resist here might be to claim that intensions are sometimes ill-defined because of ineliminable context-dependence in base sentences. If a base sentence G exhibits a certain sort of context-dependence, it can happen that a sentence S is scrutable from G in some contexts and not others. For example, if G is 'Fred is a medium-sized number', then 'Fred is less than 100' may be a priori scrutable from G in contexts with one standard of use for 'medium-sized' but not in contexts with another. Whether 'Fred is less than 100' is then scrutable from G depends on the fine details of how scrutability from sentence types is defined.[5] On the definitions used in chapter 2, all of which are designed for context-independent base sentences, one gets a priori scrutability in this case,

---

[5] The definitions used in chapter 2 yield a priori scrutability but not conditional scrutability in this case, with the status of inferential scrutability being unclear. The main relevant difference in fine details is whether the definition appeals to properties of all thoughts apt to be expressed by G (as in the definition of conditional scrutability), some thought (as in the definition of a priori scrutability), or a nearby thought (as in the definition of inferential scrutability). When base sentences are all context-independent, this difference does not make much difference, but it makes a difference when context-dependent sentences are involved.

and one gets a well-defined intension. But this just shifts the problem. Now it may turn out that 'Fred is greater than 100' is scrutable from G too (in virtue of its behavior in a different context), so that intensions are very ill-behaved.

To avoid worries of this sort, we have stipulated that base sentences must be epistemically invariant, so that their a priori relations to utterances and thoughts do not depend on context. This requirement make the scrutability thesis a stronger thesis: it plausibly excludes most names and natural-kind terms from the base, for example. In addition, the microphysical terms in $PQTI$ are arguably not epistemically invariant: one might competently use 'charge' under some-what different guises with different a priori entailments. As discussed earlier, the differences do not seem to yield cases where S is a priori scrutable from $PQTI$ under some uses but not others: any local differences in the role of 'charge' wash out at the level of scrutability from the whole network in $PQTI$. But to eliminate epistemic variation altogether, we can simply stipulate a certain specific guise for microphysical terms, perhaps by requiring a certain theoretical definition of 'charge' and the like; or we can move straight to a Ramsey-sentence definition, as in chapter 7. It is plausible that the minimal vocabularies canvassed in chapters 7 and 8 can all be understood in epistemically invariant ways (with a minor exception for phenomenal demonstratives that does not greatly affect the application to intensions[6]), so that intensions defined using them will be well-defined.

Regarding (i): the remaining strategy for an opponent is to resist the argu-ments for the scrutability theses. An opponent might resist these via any of the objections I have considered in the last two chapters, but I will focus on forms of resistance that might be distinctively motivated by the Russellian view. While it might suffice to resist only Generalized A Priori Scrutability, in practice it is likely that a Russellian who resists that thesis will also resist A Priori Scrutability. So I will focus mainly on resistance to A Priori Scrutability, with occasional attention to Generalized Scrutability. I will also attend to Inferential and Con-ditional Scrutability, because of their roles in establishing A Priori Scrutability.

As far as I can tell, there is no distinctive reason why a Russellian should resist the Inferential Scrutability thesis. It appears perfectly consistent with a Russel-lian view to hold that if one knows $PQTI$, then one will be in a position to know the truths of one's utterances of sentences such as 'water is H_2O' and 'Gödel proved incompleteness'. Something similar goes for Conditional Scrutability: there is also no clear reason why a Russellian should resist this thesis, or why they

---

[6] For phenomenal demonstratives, here the key expressions will arguably be either epistemically context-dependent ('that') or unshared across speakers ('that$_E$', where E is a token experience). This makes for a very limited lack of alignment between scenarios, but one that still supports a corre-spondence relation. See 'On Sense and Intension' and 'The Nature of Epistemic Space' for discussion.

should resist instances of it such as the claim that the idealized rational credence cr^*('water is H_2O' | $PQTI$) is high.

To be sure, there is a general issue about how Russellians should understand credences, and about whether utterances of sentences such as 'Hesperus is Hesperus' and 'Hesperus is Phosphorus' should be associated with the same credence (because they express the same singular proposition) or different credences (because a subject might be much more confident of the first utterance than the second). If we took the first view, this might lead to doubts about some generalized scrutability claims, such as the claim that there exists some $PQTI^*$ from which the first but not the second is conditionally scrutable. But given that we have defined the credence associated with an utterance in terms of the credence associated with a corresponding mental state, the second view is the natural view to take. Even on a Russellian view, it seems clear that the first utterance may be associated with a state of belief while the second is associated with a state of disbelief. This claim is quite consistent with holding that both mental states involve grasping the same singular proposition. We need only hold that the two states involve grasping the same proposition in different ways, as most Russellians allow.

Some hardline Russellians reject all talk of ways of grasping propositions, and correspondingly may reject the claim that 'Hesperus is Hesperus' and 'Hesperus is Phosphorus' express different mental states. But as discussed in chapter 2, this leads to obvious problems. For example, there is an obvious intuitive sense in which a speaker might express knowledge by uttering the first sentence, while not expressing knowledge by uttering the second sentence. And there is an obvious intuitive sense in which a speaker might have higher credence associated with an utterance of the first sentence than with an utterance of the second. Any Russellian needs to accommodate these intuitions somehow. As discussed in chapter 2, the obvious way to do so is to make distinctions between the token mental states associated with the sentences, distinctions that are compatible with sameness of content. Then however the difference between unconditional credences associated with these utterances is accommodated, we can use the same method to understand the conditional credences used in stating Conditional Scrutability. Once this is done, any obstacle to Conditional Scrutability will be removed. If a Russellian cannot provide a way to understand these credences, on the other hand, then that is a good reason to reject their view.

As for A Priori Scrutability, some of the same issues that come up with Conditional Scrutability also come up here. For example, it might be held that the apriority of a sentence depends on the singular proposition it expresses, so that 'Hesperus is Hesperus (if it exists)' and 'Hesperus is Phosphorus (if it exists)' will both be a priori, and there will be no $PQTI^*$ from which one but not the other is a priori scrutable. But again, we have defined the apriority of a sentence in a context (in E3 and E7) in terms of the epistemic status of an associated mental state, and it is clear that there may be a difference in the epistemic status of the mental states associated with utterances of the two sentences above.

Perhaps the most likely form of Russellian resistance will be to accept Conditional but not A Priori Scrutability. It may be allowed, for example, that a conditional belief in 'water is wet' given *PQTI* is justified only a posteriori. A number of Russellians have argued that purported instances of the contingent a priori, such as 'Stick *S* is one meter long' are known only a posteriori because of the role played by acquaintance. It is natural for the Russellian to take a similar line here, holding that the conditional belief is justified by our acquaintance with water. I have discussed that Russellian line at length under the objection from acquaintance in section 8 of chapter 4. I will not repeat that discussion here, except to repeat the conclusion: it is much more plausible that acquaintance enables us to entertain the relevant conditional thoughts about water than it is that acquaintance justifies those conditional beliefs.

The upshot of the discussion in chapter 4 was that even a Russellian should allow that sentences and beliefs of the relevant sort are a priori. In fact, if we assume Russellianism about belief content, the same considerations tend to suggest that the relevant singular propositions are knowable a priori. If a Russellian insists that the relevant singular propositions cannot be known a priori, I think they might then reconsider the claim that singular propositions are the contents of belief. Such a theorist could still in principle hold onto Russellianism about language, while accepting a non-Russellian view of the contents of thought.

Because of the consistency of views like these, A Priori Scrutability is not outright inconsistent with Russellianism. Still, A Priori Scrutability leads naturally to Generalized A Priori Scrutability, which leads naturally to defining intensions that serve as a Fregean semantic values for sentences in contexts. So once A Priori Scrutability is accepted, it is hard to deny that there is some sort of Fregean content in the vicinity of language and thought.

It remains open to the Russellian to deny that this Fregean content is truly an aspect of meaning: perhaps it is only a content of thought, or a guise rather than a content, or a sort of pragmatic or epistemic content that is nonsemantically associated with utterances. As before, I suspect that claims of this sort will turn on partly verbal issues about what counts as 'meaning' and 'content'. The substantive issues here concern what sorts of explanatory roles these contents can play. What matters at the end of the day is the explanatory work to which these Fregean contents can be put. That work is one of the main foci of *The Multiplicity of Meaning*.

A last place to object is to say that these intensions are fundamentally mental rather than fundamentally linguistic content, being most directly associated with mental items such as thoughts rather than linguistic items such as sentences.

There is something to this: certainly I have defined these intensions in terms of the properties of associated mental states, so that in effect mental content is fundamental and linguistic content is derivative. But I am inclined to think that all linguistic content derives from mental content, so that there is no fundamentally linguistic content. If so, this is not a strike against the account.

In fact, to speculate: the current proposal suggests a certain approach to the grounding of content of all sorts. Linguistic content of expressions in languages is grounded in the content of utterances. The content of utterances is grounded in the content of thoughts they express. The wide content (environment-dependent content such as reference, secondary intensions, and so on) of thoughts and of utterances is grounded in their narrow content (environment-independent content, here primary intensions) along with the environment. Primary intensions of thoughts are grounded roughly in thinkers' dispositions to accept the thought in certain circumstances, as on Carnap's account discussed in chapter 5. Or better: primary intensions of thoughts involving nonprimitive concepts are grounded in their inferential relations to thoughts involving primitive concepts (those expressed by expressions in a scrutability base).[7]

This program in effect reduces the question of what grounds intentionality to two residual questions. What grounds inferential relations? And what grounds the content of primitive concepts? The first question raises difficult issues about the naturalization of normativity, as it is normative inferential relations (what thinkers should infer) rather than descriptive relations (what thinkers do infer) that are at play here. It is not unreasonable, though, to hold that normative inferential relations are grounded at least partly in descriptive inferential relations along with general epistemological norms. The second question raises issues just as deep, but there are some natural options to pursue here: we can look to other aspects of inferential role (such as the 'structural' inferential role of logical concepts), to phenomenology (which may play a role in grounding perceptual or phenomenal concepts), and to relations of acquaintance. It is far from obvious whether this grounding project can be extended all the way to a reductive naturalization of intentionality, but we can at least expect it to yield some insight along the way.

---

[7] On primary intensions as narrow content, see 8.4 and 'The Components of Content'. On the current project as a form of inferentialism, see E17 and the additional excursus on inferentialism. On the grounding project in general, see that excursus and its companion excursus on reference magnets and the grounds of intentionality.

6

Hard Cases

1 Introduction

In this chapter, I consider hard cases: truths about mathematics, morality, ontology, intentionality, modality, and a number of other domains. These all fall outside the scope of the ordinary truths considered in chapters 3 and 4, and there is at least a nontrivial further question about whether all truths in these domains are scrutable from more basic truths or from *PQTI*.

It is easy for the treatment of hard cases to be comically brief. In the *Aufbau*, Carnap's discussions of value and culture get a few pages each. The following passage gives the essence of his treatment of culture:

> The custom of greeting through the lifting of one's hat would perhaps have to be constructed in the following form: 'The custom of 'greeting through the lifting of one's hat' is present in a society (or in some other sociological grouping) at a certain time, if, among the members of this society at that time, there is present a psychological disposition of such a kind that, in situations of such and such a sort, a voluntary act of such and such a sort takes place.' (Carnap 1928, section 150)

My own treatment of hard cases will share something of this comical character. So it is worth saying up front that I am not trying execute a construction or a reduction of truths in these domains, or to develop a positive account of the domains in question. All I will do here is consider, for each domain, whether there is a prima facie challenge to scrutability, and when there is such a challenge, consider the options for answering it. I will outline the views that I think are most plausible in these cases, but I will also indicate how things go under alternative views.

In each case, I will offer reasons to believe in the scrutability of the relevant truths. Often this will be a case for inferential or conditional scrutability in the first instance. As in chapters 3 and 4, this provides the basis of a case for a priori scrutability, and I will consider any specific worries about a priori scrutability where they exist. In some cases, I will also consider how things look if the relevant truths are not scrutable, so that the scrutability base has to be expanded. This discussion will not settle the question of a scrutability base once and for all. But I hope that it gives a sense of the lay of the land, and makes a case that some limited scrutability base will suffice. Readers with different views about specific domains might come to different verdicts about them, and can adjust their results accordingly.

Instead of asking whether all relevant truths are scrutable from *PQTI*, it once again makes sense to ask whether all relevant positive truths are scrutable from *PQI*. This is because if some positive truth *M* is not scrutable from *PQI*, *PQTI* will simply be false, at least if *T* says that all positive truths are scrutable from *PQI*. So when *M* is positive, as it is in most cases below, it makes sense to focus on scrutability from *PQI*. In cases where *M* is negative, we can focus on scrutability from *PQTI* instead.

Faced with a problematic positive sentence *M*—a putative mathematical or moral truth, say—we can first ask whether *M* is scrutable from *PQI*. There are at least five options available here. The first is *rationalism*, holding that *M* is a priori. The second is *empiricism*, holding that *M* is not a priori, but nevertheless is scrutable from more basic truths such as *PQI*. The third is *rejection*, holding that *M* is false and inscrutable from *PQI*, so that (at least if *M* is positive) ~*M* will be scrutable from *PQTI*. The fourth is *indeterminism*, holding that *M* is indeterminate, so that neither *M* nor ~*M* is determinately true or scrutable at all. The fifth is *expansionism*, holding that *M* is true and is not scrutable from *PQI*, so that the scrutability base needs to be expanded.

I think that each of the first four options is right in some cases. These options are clearly no threat to scrutability theses. Even the fifth option does not threaten the compact scrutability thesis as long as the expansion is sufficiently limited, and as long as it is not taken too often. If it turns out that to accommodate three or four problem cases we need to conjoin three or four new families with *PQTI* in the scrutability base, then as long as there are no trivializing mechanisms introduced, the thesis will remain intact. Many of the applications of scrutability theses, especially to issues about meaning and content, will be unthreatened by such an expansion.

Still, I am interested in keeping the scrutability base as small as possible. Some applications of the scrutability thesis depend on a very small base: for example, some applications in metaphysics depend on Fundamental Scrutability, the claim that all truths are scrutable from metaphysically fundamental truths. My own view is that it is not obvious that *PQTI* needs to be expanded at all, and that in any case expansion should be very rare, probably limited to metaphysically fundamental truths and primitive indexicals. I will not now attempt to defend this claim, but I will keep an eye on it in what follows.

Toward the end of this chapter, I will examine the question of whether all truths are scrutable not just from *PQTI* but from a more stripped-down cousin *PQTI–* that dispenses with macrophysical truths and truths about counterfactuals: it contains merely microphysical truths, phenomenal truths, laws involving these, a that's-all clause, and indexical truths. This in effect requires considering the 'hard cases' of macrophysical and counterfactual truths. The project of seeing whether *PQTI–* can be stripped down further still is the subject of the next chapter.

2 Mathematical truths

Perhaps the hardest case for scrutability from *PQI* is mathematics. It is plausible that all ordinary mathematical truths are a priori: at least insofar as they are knowable, they are knowable without justification from experience. But it might be argued that some mathematical truths are not knowable at all, even on ideal rational reflection. If so, then these truths are not knowable a priori, and will plausibly not be a priori at all. Furthermore, empirical information does not seem to help, so if these truths are not a priori, they are also not a priori scrutable from *PQI*.

Most obviously, certain Gödelian statements in arithmetic are not provable from standard axioms, and one might argue that they are not knowable a priori, even under an idealization. Something similar goes for certain statements of higher set theory, perhaps including the Continuum hypothesis or its negation, which do not seem to be provable from obvious axioms. Likewise, in second-order logic there are sentences that are intuitively true, but that do not seem to be provable. If there are sentences in these domains that are true but not a priori, then they are not a priori scrutable from *PQI*.

Still, it is far from clear that there are any mathematical truths that are not a priori. Given a putative example of such a truth, one can argue that either the truth in question is knowable under some idealization of rational reasoning, or that the sentence in question is not determinately true at all.

Take the Gödelian case first. Certainly, the fact that a statement is not provable from the Peano axioms does not entail that it is not knowable a priori. The Gödel sentence of the Peano axioms themselves is not provable from those axioms, but it is plausibly knowable a priori: it is equivalent to the claim that the axioms are consistent, and we plausibly know that the axioms are consistent in virtue of knowing that they are true. All that follows is that the Peano axioms do not encapsulate an axiomatic basis of our mathematical knowledge.

It might be suggested that there are more complex Gödel sentences that we cannot know. For example, if our brains are finite and computational, it is arguable that there is an axiomatic system that either encapsulates or exceeds our arithmetical competence. If that system is consistent, then its Gödel sentence will be a truth that we cannot know. But the construction of this example clearly stems from our contingent cognitive limitations. Just as we can know the truth of Gödel sentences for more limited systems, it is reasonable to hold that reasoners less limited than us could know the truth of this Gödel sentence.

Still, one might wonder whether this will always be so. Might there not be truths of arithmetic that no reasoner could know a priori? I think that there are at least two good reasons to deny this.

First, Feferman's completeness theorem (1962) shows that the truth of any statement of arithmetic can be settled by repeatedly adjoining Gödel sentences to the Peano axioms an infinite number of times. This construction requires an ability to count through sufficiently large infinite ordinals, and for any finite creature this ability will give out at some point. But the ability gives out at different points for different creatures. It is not unreasonable to hold that for any such ordinal, some idealized creature could count that high, and so could know the relevant truth a priori. There is some question about whether the character of the repeated adjoining has to presuppose the arithmetical truths in question, however; if so, it is not obvious that this adjoining should be considered a priori.[1] So I will not rely on the Feferman result here.

More straightforwardly, if more distantly, one can idealize away from our capacity to consider only a finite number of cases at once. Russell famously said that our inability to count through all of the integers is a 'mere medical impossibility'. In *The Logical Syntax of Language* (1934), Carnap himself considered an infinitary inference rule, now usually called the omega rule: from premises $\phi(1)$, $\phi(2)$, and so on for every natural number, infer $\forall n \, \phi(n)$ (where the quantifier ranges over the natural numbers). Then if $\phi(k)$ is a theorem for every natural number k, $\forall n \, \phi(n)$ will be a theorem. This inference rule is plausibly a priori truth-preserving, and even weak systems of arithmetic combined with the omega rule escape Gödel's incompleteness theorem: every statement of arithmetic is settled in them.

Our contingent limitations stop us from following this rule, but we can conceive of a being that lacks these limitations. Consider a creature with an infinite capacity for parallel reasoning: when it has to evaluate the truth of $\forall n \, \phi(n)$, it simultaneously evaluates $\phi(n)$ for each n (perhaps thinking faster for larger n, to ensure a bounded thinking time), and responds with the verdict 'true' if and only if $\phi(n)$ is true for each n. No paradoxes arise here. In fact, there exist programming languages that can specify an algorithm to handle these cases using infinite branching and infinite conjunctions, although the algorithm could not

---

[1] Thanks to Hartry Field for discussion here. See also Torkel Franzen's book *Inexhaustibility* (2004).

be implemented effectively on a finite computer.[2] An infinitary creature like this could know any truth of arithmetic a priori. Correspondingly, an omega-rule proof of an arithmetical proposition provides an idealized a priori warrant for that proposition, so that all arithmetical truths are a priori.

Of course this is a relatively taxing idealization, but it is not out of bounds. It is grounded in familiar cognitive capacities, such as the capacity to evaluate $\phi(n)$ for any given n, and is extended merely by dropping a limitation on parallel processing. One might worry that if we allow idealizations like this, then anything goes. But this seems wrong: even under this sort of idealization, there is no reason to believe that a statement such as 'There is a cup in this room' is knowable a priori. In any case, if the relevant notion of ideal reasoning is stipulated such that idealizations of this sort are allowed, then arithmetical truths will clearly be scrutable from any base.

The case of unprovable statements of higher set theory is murkier. Here, it is not at all clear that the relevant statements are determinately true or false. The most common view among set theorists appears to be that they are indeterminate. Even if they are determinate in some cases, it is not out of the question that further axioms may settle the determinate truths, and that these axioms could be known either by us or by more ideal creatures. In addition, idealizations akin to the one above suggest that relevantly ideal reasoning may take us beyond what is provable from axioms. So at least, there is not much strong reason to believe that some statements of set theory are both determinately true without being a priori, though the matter deserves further investigation.

What about logic, counting this as a branch of mathematics broadly construed? First-order logic is complete, so the standard axioms settle everything, and it is reasonably plausible that the axioms are a priori. Second-order logic is incomplete, so it raises the same sort of issues as arithmetic and set theory. Its diagnosis may involve a mix of the diagnoses in those domains. For some undecidable sentences of second-order logic, we have clear intuitions of truth despite the lack of a proof from standard axioms. In these cases it is reasonable to say, as in arithmetic, that the relevant sentences are both true and knowable a priori. For other undecidable sentences about which we lack clear intuitions, the situation may be more akin to that in set theory. Either the sentences are indeterminate, or an idealization would enable knowledge of these sentences. In any case there is little reason to believe in truths that are not a priori in this domain.

---

[2] See, for example, work on infinitely synchronous concurrent algorithms by McConnell and Tucker 1992, and on deciding arithmetic using SAD computers by Hogarth 2004. Beggs and Tucker (2006) even establish that infinitely parallel computations such as these can be embedded in Newtonian kinematics.

In the worst case, if some mathematical truths are not a priori, then some such truths need to be added to the scrutability base. The precise nature of the needed mathematical sentences and vocabulary will depend on delicate issues involving the treatment of the problematic mathematical domains. The vocabulary expansion needed may be small or even nonexistent, as PQI already includes some mathematical vocabulary (used in stating P, for example). The sentential expansion will be larger: by the nature of the phenomenon of incompleteness, it cannot be removed with finite additions. If the language allows only finite sentences in a countable vocabulary (as on the official restriction discussed at the end of E3), then there will be at most a countable number of sentences to add. If we allowed an infinitary language with expressions for arbitrary sets, then we would perhaps need to add a class of base truths that is larger than any set, leading to some complications. But all this can be seen as an addition within the family of mathematical truths. So the general framework of scrutability will not be threatened.

3 Normative and evaluative truths

What should one say about normative and evaluative truths? I will focus on moral truths to start with. One could ask the question: are moral truths scrutable from PQI? But it is easier to ask the more general question: are moral truths scrutable from non-moral truths? If they are, then moral truths will not pose a distinctive problem for scrutability.

On the face of it, there are good grounds to hold that insofar as there are moral truths and they are knowable, then they are scrutable from non-moral truths. Certainly, given that moral truths are knowable at all, they appear to be inferentially scrutable and conditionally scrutable: given full enough knowledge of the nonmoral properties of a situation, we are in a position to know its moral properties. Applying the argument from chapter 4, if conditional scrutability holds here, a priori scrutability plausibly holds too. Moral truths will be inscrutable from nonmoral truths only if some crucial principles or conditionals governing inferences from nonmoral truths to moral truths are unknowable, or if any inference from nonmoral truths to moral truths has an irreducibly empirical justification. But there is little reason to believe in unknowable moral principles here, and there is little reason to believe in such an irreducibly empirical justification.

Perhaps the best reason to deny that moral truths are a priori scrutable from nonmoral truths arises from the possibility of moral disagreement even among ideal reasoners who agree on the nonmoral truths. It is not obvious that this sort of disagreement is possible: perhaps apparent moral disagreement always involves empirical disagreement, or non-ideal reasoning, or merely verbal disagreement.

But it is also not obvious that this sort of disagreement is impossible. *If* this sort of disagreement is possible, it is not easy to see how the truth of moral claims that are the object of disagreement will be scrutable from nonmoral truths.

However, if this sort of disagreement is possible, then it is natural to hold that there is no fact of the matter about who is correct. That is, one will then naturally embrace a form of moral anti-realism, according to which there are no moral truths. If so, there will be no inscrutable moral truths. Alternatively, one might embrace some form of moral relativism, so that moral sentences are adjudged true insofar as they are true according to an appropriate standard (that of a speaker, or an assessor); but then one can argue that according to that standard, a conditional from nonmoral truths to the moral sentence in question will also be adjudged correct (and a priori). Either way, there is no trouble for scrutability here.

What sort of meta-ethical views are incompatible with a priori scrutability of moral truths from nonmoral truths? Moral rationalism is clearly compatible with scrutability, as are those varieties of moral anti-realism on which moral sentences are not true. Forms of moral anti-realism where moral concepts are response-dependent in some fashion are also compatible: moral truths here will be scrutable from nonmoral facts about causes and responses. Many forms of moral empiricism are compatible: they will typically involve at least the conditional scrutability of moral truths from nonmoral truths, and need not deny the inference to a priori scrutability.

One tricky case arises from forms of moral realism that hold that there are a posteriori necessities of the form 'goodness = X', where X is a nonmoral expression. This claim alone is quite compatible with a priori scrutability of 'moral' truths, just as the a posteriori necessity of 'water is H_2O' is compatible with a priori scrutability of 'water'-truths. For example, as Horgan and Timmons (1992) suggest, such a view is compatible with the apriority of 'If X actually regulates our positive moral responses, then X is goodness'. Then as long as the nonmoral truth that X regulates our positive moral responses is itself scrutable, 'X is goodness' will be scrutable. Of course scrutability is incompatible with a hardline form of this view on which there are no a priori entailments from nonmoral truths to moral truths. But given that moral truths are conditionally scrutable from nonmoral truths, the arguments in chapter 4 can themselves be seen as good reasons to reject such a view.

Another tricky case involves a moral sensibility theory, on which one must have a certain sensibility (certain emotional responses, say) in order to appreciate moral truths.[3] This theory is compatible with scrutability: a proponent of the

---

[3] Thanks to Martine Nida-Rümelin for discussion here. Much the same applies to sensibility theories in aesthetics.

view may hold that moral truths are knowable a priori by those with the right sensibility, or at least that they are conditionally and a priori scrutable from nonmoral truths by those with the right sensibility. Still, it introduces a wrinkle into the picture. On this view, ideal reasoning will require the right sensibility, involving components that one might take to be emotional as well as traditionally rational. (One could say that an ideal reasoner needs a big heart as well as a big brain.) If this view is correct, the scrutability thesis is still fine, but it may have less of a rationalist upshot than one might have supposed.

The meta-ethical view that is most obviously incompatible with scrutability of the moral from the nonmoral is a hardline form of moral realism on which there are moral truths that are not knowable even on full knowledge of nonmoral truths and ideal reflection. Such a view is unattractive, though. The best reason for being a moral realist stems precisely from our apparent knowledge of moral truths. If that knowledge is denied, moral anti-realism seems much the more natural option. Another relevant view is one on which we perceive moral properties directly, so that all moral knowledge is grounded a posteriori in perceptual evidence. However, this view cannot easily account for our ability to know the moral status of hypothetical situations specified in nonmoral terms, even though we have never encountered relevantly similar situations before. Likewise, our ability to have conditional moral knowledge even when we engage in Cartesian suspension of judgment about the external world strongly suggests that this conditional knowledge is justified a priori.

What about truths in other normative domains, such as epistemic truths concerning what is rational or what is justified or what can be known a priori? Here, the situation is much the same as above. If there is a difference, it is that there is less reason to believe in the possibility of significant ideal disagreement in this case. Epistemic disagreement typically appears to be more delimited than moral disagreement, and one can reasonably hope that much of it will disappear on ideal reflection. The issue is delicate, as the notion of ideal reflection is itself an epistemic one, so that an epistemic anti-realist or relativist will hold that the notion of ideal reflection may itself be incoherent or subject-relative. But in any case, there is little reason to believe in inscrutable epistemic truths.[4]

Something similar applies to other evaluative domains, such as the aesthetic domain. In this case, there is perhaps more reason to believe in the possibility of

---

[4] An interesting question: if epistemic anti-realism is true, where does that leave the epistemic conclusions of this book, such as the scrutability thesis? If an epistemic error theory is true, presumably most of these claims are simply false, although perhaps it remains possible that nearby reconstructed claims (such as claims about what is the case in a fiction) could be true. If epistemic expressivism is true, presumably this is compatible with my claims in the same way that meta-ethical expressivism is compatible with claims in normative ethics. I am an epistemic realist, though, and it is arguable that epistemic realism gives the conclusions more interest and weight.

ideal disagreement, and so more reason to accept some sort of anti-realist treatment. But on the assumption that truths in this domain are knowable, the arguments of chapters 3 and 4 suggest that there is little reason to believe in inscrutable aesthetic truths.

If someone disagrees, holding that there are inscrutable truths in one or more of these domains, then one will have to expand the scrutability base, most likely by including some normative or evaluative truths in the base. For example, certain fundamental moral, epistemic, or aesthetic principles might need to be included.[5] Doing so will require a small expansion of the basic vocabulary, perhaps to include normative or evaluative expressions such as 'ought' or 'good'. But this will not pose a threat to the overall scrutability thesis.

4 Ontological truths

Ontological claims are claims about the existence of entities. *PQI* already includes many existence claims. It says there exist entities with various microphysical properties, entities with various phenomenal properties, and perhaps entities with various macrophysical properties too. In effect, it contains ontological claims about microphysical entities, subjects of experience, and possibly macrophysical entities.

Still, an important challenge to scrutability from *PQI* concerns further ontological claims. One such challenge concerns the existence of abstract objects: for example, is the existence of numbers scrutable from *PQI*? One might think that *PQI* itself is irrelevant here as the existence of numbers does not turn on physics or phenomenology (though there will be some views of numbers where these domains matter). One might also think that it is not a priori that numbers exist—perhaps because one thinks it is not a priori that anything exists. Given views like these, then if numbers in fact exist, their existence will not be a priori scrutable from *PQI*. (If they do not exist, on the other hand, their non-existence will be scrutable from *PQTI*, because *T* will rule them out.)

---

[5] Three residual worries here: (i) What if (for example) moral particularism is true, so that there is no finite set of moral principles that generates moral truths from nonmoral truths. Then one will have to include truths about the moral properties of individual cases in the base. (ii) What if moral principles make irreducible appeal to high-level nonmoral notions such as 'kill'? If these are definable in base language, the principles can be stated without them, and if they are not scrutable from base language, they will need to be included in the base anyway. If they are scrutable but not finitely definable, one has the choice between including them in the laws (at cost of vocabulary expansion) or using an equivalent infinitary version of the principles (at cost of much longer base sentences in the original vocabulary). (iii) What about 'thick' moral expressions such as 'brave'? In these cases I think it is plausible that truths involving these expressions are scrutable from (although perhaps not definable in terms of) nonmoral truths and 'thin' moral truths about values and norms.

The existence of macroscopic objects also poses a challenge. *PQI* builds in the existence of macrophysical objects, but if there are macroscopic objects that are not macrophysical objects because they lack shape, mass, and so on (governments, perhaps?), then one might think that *PQI* is a priori compatible with their existence or non-existence. And if we move from *PQI* to the stripped-down base *PQI–*, even macrophysical entities pose a challenge: one might think that *PQI–* is a priori compatible with their existence or non-existence: the existence and distribution of atoms is a priori compatible with either the existence or non-existence of molecules, for example. For example, one might deny that the scrutability conditionals are a priori here on the grounds that from a statement that certain entities exist, it never follows a priori that any other entities exist. If so, then if these entities do exist, their existence will not be scrutable from the relevant base.

We can counter these claims to some extent with the argument from knowability discussed in chapter 3. This argument suggests that insofar as positive ontological truths are knowable at all (even if they are knowable only a posteriori), they are conditionally and a priori scrutable from a limited base such as *PQI*. So if we hold that there are positive ontological truths about numbers, say, and that they are knowable, we should reject the claim that it is never a priori that certain entities exist (perhaps given that other entities exist). For example, one might embrace a view on which it is a priori that there are an infinite number of primes, and therefore a priori that numbers exist. At a more fine-grained level, we might accept a 'lightweight' view of ontology on which existence claims can be analytic, or a rationalist view on which they are synthetic a priori. Alternatively, one can accept an anti-realist view on which there are no ontological truths at all. All of these views pose no problem for scrutability.

Still, there are also important 'heavyweight' views of ontology on which the relevant ontological truths are sometimes not knowable at all, and are correspondingly not a priori scrutable from base truths. There are also other heavyweight views on which ontological truths are knowable only nonconclusively, so that even if they are a priori scrutable from relevant base truths, they are not conclusively a priori scrutable.

In 'Empiricism, Semantics, and Ontology' (1950), Carnap rejected the heavyweight view of ontology. He held that ontological questions can be read in either an 'internal' or an 'external' sense: internal questions are settled analytically or empirically (as on a lightweight view), and external questions do not have objective answers (as on an anti-realist view). My view in 'Ontological Anti-Realism' (2009) has a similar spirit: if existential quantification is understood in a lightweight way, then ontological truths are conclusively scrutable, and if it is understood in a heavyweight way, then ontological claims are indeterminate. Either way, I think that there is little reason to believe in inscrutable ontological truths of the sort that a heavyweight realist requires. If we embrace a view in this vicinity, there is no problem for scrutability.

What if a heavyweight view is correct? In this case the scrutability base may need to be expanded slightly in order to cover positive truths about the existence of macrophysical or abstract objects. The most natural way for this to work is for certain general ontological principles to be added: perhaps principles saying that when certain microphysical conditions obtain, certain macroscopic entities exist. Even here it is not obvious that we need to expand the vocabulary. The crucial expression needed is the existential quantifier, but that is already included in our base.

The only potential expansion here is further vocabulary used to specify ontological principles. For example, the popular principle of universal mereological composition says that for any set of objects, there is a fusion of those objects (an entity with those objects as parts such that any part of the entity overlaps one of the objects). This principle uses mereological vocabulary, requiring especially the crucial notion of 'part'. Now, it is plausible that truths about parthood are scrutable from more basic truths: perhaps a is part of b if b is located at every point where a is located, for example. Correspondingly, it is not out of the question that we can state ontological principles without an expansion of vocabulary: for example, for any objects, there is an object located at all and only points at which one of the original objects is located. But there are certainly views on which mereological or other vocabulary will be essentially required within these principles, in which case there will be a limited expansion. As long as the ontological principles are limited in their extent, however, there will be no threat to scrutability from a compact base.[6]

There are also questions about fundamental natural ontology: roughly, the fundamental concrete entities and properties that populate the world. These questions cannot easily be dismissed in the way that questions about numbers and macrophysical objects can be dismissed, because they clearly affect the character of a scrutability base. If Fundamental Scrutability is true, then there will be a scrutability base made up almost entirely of truths about fundamental entities and properties. And even if Fundamental Scrutability is false, one can expect that there will be a minimal scrutability case containing truths about these entities and properties along with other truths. If physicalism is true, these entities may already be specified by P, and if dualism is true, they may already be specified by P and Q. But if more liberal ontological views are true, we may need to go beyond P and Q.

For example, if a god exists, then the base almost certainly needs to be expanded to specify the god's existence and properties. If libertarian free will

[6] Thanks to Robbie Williams for discussion here.

exists, the base may need to be expanded to include it. If there are angels or nonphysical ectoplasm in another realm, the same applies. If our physics is embedded in a more fundamental 26-dimensional protophysics, then the base may need to include protophysical truths. If there is no god, libertarian free will, angels, ectoplasm, protophysics, and so on, then no such expansion will be required. An especially promising case for expansionism concerns so-called *quiddities*: the intrinsic natures associated with microphysical properties such as mass and charge. I discuss quiddities at length in section 9 of chapter 7, so I defer further discussion until then. For now, I will take it for granted that our scrutability base needs to include all truths about the fundamental properties of fundamental entities.

There are also questions about relative fundamentality, or grounding. For example, metaphysicians debate whether the whole universe is more fundamental than its simple parts: monists hold that the whole grounds the parts, while pluralists hold that the parts ground the whole. Likewise, physicalists hold that the physical is fundamental and grounds the mental, while idealists hold that the mental is fundamental and grounds the physical, and dualists hold that both mental and physical are fundamental. One might hold that *PQTI* does not settle these questions: it is compatible with both monist and pluralist views, and with physicalist, dualist, and perhaps idealist views.

Here Carnap himself appeared to hold that there is no objective fact of the matter between the views in question: he holds that his basic truths are compatible with physicalism, dualism, and idealism. One might also hold that the only truths about relative fundamentality here are scrutable from truths about necessitation or scrutability. On that sort of view, idealism may be ruled out because P is not scrutable from or necessitated by Q, and physicalism is ruled out to the extent that Q is not scrutable from or necessitated by P, but the choice between monism and pluralism is left open, as there is mutual necessitation between properties of the whole and the properties of the parts. This view would reduce the scrutability of truths about relative fundamentality to the scrutability of modal truths, discussed below.

If one thinks that there are truths about fundamentality that go beyond truths about necessitation or scrutability (as I am inclined to), one can build these truths into the base. In fact, there is precedent for doing this already: we saw in the sixth excursus that perhaps the most attractive formulation of the that's-all sentence involves saying 'Those are all the fundamental truths'. If one understands this claim as invoking metaphysical fundamentality, then these truths will be built into the base. *PTI* will in effect settle things in favor of physicalism (in either monist or pluralist form depending on whether P is phrased in terms of properties of the world or of its parts), while *PQTI* will settle things in favor of dualism. And even if one does not understand T in this way (perhaps understanding it in terms of conceptual fundamentality instead), then truths about metaphysical fundamentality may nevertheless be scrutable using T, at least on some views. At worst, one can include certain additional claims about metaphysical fundamentality in the base: perhaps, for example saying that P and Q obtain, that the truths in P are all the metaphysically fundamental truths, and that all positive truths are scrutable from PQ.

In any case, I think it is attractive for multiple reasons to endorse a scrutability base that includes some notion of fundamentality. A world-sentence using such a base might (at least) set out the fundamental truths about fundamental properties and entities, and say that they are the fundamental truths, the fundamental properties, and/or the fundamental entities. I return to the role of fundamentality in scrutability bases in chapters 7 and 8.

5 Other philosophical truths

What about truths in other areas of philosophy? An enormous number of philosophical questions are normative or ontological questions and will be covered by the discussion above: they will be either scrutable from $PQTI$, or at worst from an expanded base that expressions such as 'ought', 'good', 'exists', and/or 'fundamental'. Still, there are other sorts of philosophical questions. To pick just two, the debate between Fregean and Russellian views in the philosophy of language or between internalist and externalist views in the philosophy of mind are not obviously questions about normativity or ontology.

I will not try to go through all philosophical questions here. But I can give a sense of the options. For any given philosophical debate, as before, the options include rationalism (one view or the other can be known to be true a priori), empiricism (neither view is a priori, but one is scrutable from underlying truths such as $PQTI$), indeterminism (there is no objective fact of the matter as to which view is correct), and expansionism (one side is right, and the scrutability base needs to expanded or modified to reflect this).

In addition, where debates are concerned, a fifth option is *pluralism*: both sides are right concerning different notions. I argue in 'Verbal Disputes' that pluralism is often the correct diagnosis of a philosophical debate. This diagnosis typically leads to two or more clarified debates, involving the two or more disambiguated notions. In principle, each of these debates will themselves be subject to the options above. But these debates are usually more tractable than the original debate, so that they will fall more easily under one of the four options above.

I think that all five options are applicable in some cases. On my own view, rationalism holds for fundamental normative questions, empiricism holds for questions about fundamental natural ontology (including questions about phenomenology), and indeterminism holds for ontological questions outside fundamental natural ontology. I think that pluralism holds for debates between the Fregean and the Russellian, the internalist and the externalist, and the compatibilist and the incompatibilist. Expansionism may be correct in some cases (such as the case of quiddities), but as before I would like to think that it is relatively rare.

Some may find the scrutability thesis particularly implausible where philosophy is concerned, given the extent of disagreement even among highly rational philosophers. Here it is worth keeping in mind that we are far from ideal, however, and that our experience of disagreement as non-ideal reasoners is at best weak evidence of what would happen on ideal reflection. And again, it is worth noting that perhaps the deepest debates in philosophy concern the normative and the ontological. In these cases, at worst, if relevant normative and ontological truths are allowed in the base, the disagreements will plausibly be settled by base truths.

I cannot claim to have made a conclusive case here that all philosophical truths are scrutable from a compact base. Still, if all ordinary nonphilosophical truths are scrutable in this way, and if paradigmatic philosophical truths in normative and ontological realms are scrutable too, then the thesis that there are certain special truths in philosophy not scrutable from a compact base begins to look unattractive.

The scrutability thesis yields a distinctive metaphilosophical picture. If the thesis is correct, then all philosophical truths (like all other truths) can be settled by ideal a priori reasoning from base truths. We may be ignorant of these truths because we are ignorant of base truths, or because we are not ideal reasoners. But there is no third form of ignorance. Questions that cannot be settled by a priori reasoning from base truths have no determinate answer.

This principle is structurally analogous to Hume's thesis that claims not involving 'abstract reasoning concerning quantity or number' and 'experimental reasoning concerning matters of fact and existence' involve just 'sophistry and illusion'. Compared to Hume's thesis, the scrutability thesis allows a broader sort of reasoning from a broader base, and where Hume's thesis claims sophistry or meaninglessness, the scrutability thesis merely claims indeterminacy. The scrutability thesis stands to Hume's thesis as it stands to the logical empiricists' verification principle: it is not as strong, but there remains a structural parallel.

Unlike Hume and the logical empiricists, I am not especially inclined to cast my metaphilosophical thesis in a prescriptive voice, at least initially. To the extent that I argue for the scrutability thesis by considering cases, it will have limited prescriptive force when applied to the same cases. And the force of the thesis will in any case depend on the character of the base. Still, once one has made a case for a principled scrutability thesis in many domains, its cumulative support might be seen as carrying at least some prescriptive force when applied to other domains. A sort of philosophical methodology that coheres well with this picture is developed in 'Verbal Disputes'.

6 Modal truths

What about modal truths: truths about what is possible or necessary? Here the analysis depends on what sort of modality is at issue. Where the nomological modality is concerned, fundamental laws of nature are already built into *PQI*. We can stipulate that where *L* is a basic physical or psychophysical law, $\Box L$ is in *PQI*, where the box stands for nomological necessity. It is reasonably plausible that all truths involving nomological necessity can be derived from these, along with the rest of *PQTI*. On some Humean views, as I discuss in the next chapter, truths about nomological necessity will themselves be scrutable from non-nomic truths. But for present purposes there is no need to take a stand on the issue.

What about the epistemic modality, and in particular epistemic modality interpreted as apriority? So far we have usually talked of sentences being a priori, but here it is more natural to phrase relevant claims as 'It is a priori that *S*'. I will assume that sentences of this sort are true (in a context) if and only if the embedded sentence *S* is a priori (in that context). Then it is plausible that a true sentence of this sort is a priori. This follows from an S4 principle for apriority: If it is a priori that *S*, it is a priori that it is a priori that *S*. Here, the thought is that if one can come to know *S* with non-experiential justification, it is a short step to knowing that there is non-experiential justification for *S*, and this step does not require any further experiential justification. If this is right, the S4 principle follows, and all positive claims about apriority are themselves a priori.

What about negative claims about apriority, such as 'It is not a priori that *S*'? Here, the thesis that all true sentences of this sort are a priori requires an S5 principle about apriority: if it is not a priori that *S*, it is a priori that it is not a priori that *S*. This principle is less clearly true than the S4 principle, but reasons for accepting it are given in the sixth excursus.

Finally, what about the metaphysical modality? Here, it is familiar that truths such is 'It is necessary that water is H_2O' and 'It is necessary that Hesperus is Phosphorus' can be true without being a priori. In these cases, though, it is highly plausible that these truths are a priori entailed by nonmodal truths: in particular, by 'Water is H_2O' and by 'Hesperus is Phosphorus'. Given that the relevant expressions are rigid (*de jure*), sentences such as 'If Hesperus is Phosphorus, it is necessary that Hesperus is Phosphorus' is a priori. So as long as the relevant nonmodal truths are scrutable from *PQTI*, the modal truths are scrutable as well.

I think that what applies in these cases applies generally. It is plausible that all modal truths are a priori entailed by nonmodal truths. Some such truths are themselves a priori, while those that are a posteriori typically follow from non-modal identity statements, or perhaps from statements about composition. For example, suppose with Kripke that the following is a modal truth: 'It is necessary that if Elizabeth II exists, she is the daughter of George VI'. This modal truth is arguably implied by the nonmodal truth that Elizabeth II is the daughter of George VI, and the a priori principle that people have their parents essentially. And even if the principle in question is not a priori, perhaps because there could be exceptions in odd hypothetical circumstances, then it remains very plausible that the modal truth at issue is a priori scrutable from *PQTI*.

Some philosophical views involve a stronger separation between the necessary and the a priori than one finds in the cases above. On these views, there may be modal truths that are not scrutable from nonmodal truths. For example, someone may hold that it is necessary that a deity exists, without its being a priori that a deity exists. Perhaps nonmodal properties of the deity will imply that it is omnipotent, omniscient, and so on, and so will imply that it is a deity. But these and all other nonmodal truths could be coherently combined with the claim that the deity exists only contingently. If so, the modal truth is not scrutable, and our scrutability base will have to be expanded by including modal expressions. I reject the existence of modal truths of this sort (for reasons discussed in 'Does Conceivability Entail Possibility?'), but the case in question at least provides an illustration.

7 Intentional truths

Our scrutability base builds in truths about phenomenal states. One might ask: why does it not build in truths about other mental states such as beliefs and desires? This is partly because I think such states are themselves scrutable from *PQTI*, and partly because building them in raises a worry about trivializing mechanisms. I discuss both of these matters below.

Are truths about belief scrutable from *PQI* (or from *PQTI*)? On some reductive views, such as analytic functionalism or logical behaviorism, these truths may even be scrutable from *P*. But no such strong claim is required here. One does not even need the claim that the intentional is scrutable from the non-intentional, since it is plausible that the phenomenal is intentional through and through. This applies both to the phenomenology of perceptual experience and the phenomenology of believing itself, both of which will be specified in *Q*. So it is certainly not out of the question that a base consisting of physical and phenomenal truths will yield truths about beliefs and desires.

Here we can run a version of the Cosmoscope argument. Using the information in *PQI*, the Cosmoscope will give us an image of a subject's behavior and underlying functioning in actual circumstances and many counterfactual circumstances. In addition, it will enable us to know just what it is like to be that subject, and what it would be like to be the subject in various counterfactual circumstances. In addition, it will give us complete information about the subject's environment. Will this be sufficient for us to determine what the subject believes? On the face of it, yes. Though one can reasonably question whether behavioral information alone suffices for 'radical interpretation' of a subject's beliefs, once full phenomenal and environmental information is added, there is no clear reason to think that the subject's mental life is underdetermined. At least, it is not easy to see what sort of mental truth we might remain ignorant of, given all this information.

An opponent might appeal to Kripke's version of Wittgenstein's rule-following argument (Kripke 1982), suggesting that underlying states do not determine what a subject believes. Here, there are at least three relevant observations. First, Kripke understates the role of the phenomenology of cognition (which will be specified within Q), briefly mentioning it and assimilating it to a 'distinctive sort of headache'. But the experience of addition is nothing like this, and arguably involves a cognitive phenomenology that is richly intentional (see Siewert 1998 and Horgan and Tienson 2002). Second, Kripke's argument centrally turns on the idea that there is no reductive analysis of intentionality in non-intentional terms, but no such analysis is needed here, both because the phenomenal is already intentional, and because scrutability does not require explicit analyses. Third, Kripke himself seems to appeal to a version of the scrutability thesis, holding that if truths about belief are not scrutable from the relevant base, then they are not strictly truths at all, at least in the ordinary sense.

One might also object that local physical and phenomenal information underdetermines belief content, due to its dependence on the subject's environment. But PQI will specify the subject's environment, and assuming that ordinary truths about that environment are scrutable from PQI, then insofar as such truths play a role in constituting the belief's content, there is no reason to doubt that the content is scrutable too. For example, knowing the physical and phenomenal truths about a subject might underdetermine whether their beliefs are about water or twin water, but once we know relevant truths about the H_2O in their environment, the matter will be settled.

What if I am wrong, and truths about what a subject believes are not scrutable from PQI? Then one will have to add such truths to the scrutability base. The most obvious suggestion is to initially include arbitrary intentional states along with phenomenal states, yielding $PMTI$ (with M for 'mental'). This would get rid of any gap, but it introduces complications, in the guise of trivializing mechanisms.

The most obvious way to specify intentional states such as beliefs is to use a *propositional* vocabulary. If John believes that the cat is on the mat, then one might say that John stands in the belief relation to the proposition *The cat is on the mat*, or one might use more complex structures to specify Russellian or Fregean propositions that John stands in the belief relation to. But now the danger of trivialization arises. The first of these approaches will end up using arbitrary vocabulary elements, such as 'cat' and 'mat', in the scrutability base, albeit appearing only in certain restricted contexts. The other approaches will require arbitrary objects and properties to be specified in the base (in Russellian propositions), or else arbitrary Fregean senses (in Fregean propositions).

One danger is that once our base vocabulary includes propositions, it is not a large step to the base truths including truths about the *truth* of these propositions, such as '*The cat on the mat* is true', and so on. From such truths, it is plausible that arbitrary truths ('The cat is on the mat') follow a priori. If so, we have trivialization. To deal with this worry, one might initially stipulate that propositional vocabulary can only occur in base truths as objects of attitudes ('John believes p'), and not in any other way ('p is true'). One might also worry about sentences such as 'John believes p, and his belief is true'. Here one can also restrict the places that terms such as 'believe' and 'belief' can occur in base sentences. One can also simply bar terms such as 'true' and other devices of semantic evaluation ('false', 'refers', 'about') from the base vocabulary.

A related worry occurs whether or not we build intentional truths into the base. Suppose that statements about the truth of beliefs are scrutable from base truths, as they must be if the scrutability thesis is true. So 'John believes truly that p' might be scrutable from statements about the success of John's belief that p, or the success of certain p-related behavior, or something much more complicated. Then one will be able to use the scrutability of these truths to yield the scrutability of all truths. In response, I think one can reasonably deny that this is a trivializing mechanism. The most natural way to obtain 'John believes truly that p' is to obtain something like 'John believes p' and 'p'. Even if there is some other way to obtain 'John believes truly that p' without going directly through p, it is plausible that one will have to exploit the same sort of information about the world that one would need to exploit in order to know p. So there is no trivialization here.

A third worry arises if the base includes factive states such as knowledge. From 'John knows p', it follows trivially that p is true. This does not automatically yield all truths, but it yields many, and others might follow using counterfactuals: 'If John considered p, he would come to know p', and so on. In response, I think that factive states can reasonably be excluded from the base. It is plausible that truths about factive states such as knowledge are scrutable from truths about nonfactive states such as belief, along with truths about justification, external facts, and so on. So these need not occur primitively.

A fourth and related worry arises even for nonfactive states, if some sorts of externalism are true. For example, it is often held to be necessary that if a subject believes that water is wet, then water exists, and one might hold that something like this is a priori as well. This is particularly clear if beliefs are stated using Russellian propositions, as the existence of a Russellian proposition involving a certain object or stuff entails that that object exists. One may not be able to recover all truths using this method, but the mechanism still seems overly powerful as a way of recovering some external world truths.

To get around this worry, I think that if intentional states are to be specified in the base, they should be specified in a non-externalist way. A natural suggestion is that one should specify a belief's primary intension, or something along those lines. If primary intensions are indeed narrow content, then this will not yield the worry about externalism. Furthermore, doing this will bypass any worries about vocabulary expansion, as primary intensions can be specified using the same vocabulary that is used to specify scenarios in general. And when primary intensions are combined with sufficient information about the external world, it is plausible that truths about wide content, truth, and so on are thereby scrutable.

A potential problem is that it is not clear that a primary intension can always be finitely specified: it will involve values at an infinite number of scenarios, most of which may have an infinite specification. Perhaps one could allow such long specifications in the scrutability base, but now it will be enormous, and this length will feed back into the size and number of scenarios in turn, which will then feed back into the length of the specification of beliefs. An alternative is to specify primary intensions directly, regarding them as properties or relations and using a rich vocabulary that can pick out such properties. Doing so will avoid the second complication, that of externalism, although it will face the first complication in a significant way. Still, one could argue as before that as long as the rich vocabulary for expressions denoting properties occurs only within belief contexts, and as long as we exclude 'true' and cognates from the base, then there is no danger of trivializing the thesis.

A second potential problem is a threat of dialectical circularity: I need the scrutability thesis to establish that there are primary intensions, but here I am appealing to primary intensions to support the scrutability thesis. I think that the situation is not really circular, though. If it turns out that intentional states are not scrutable from *PQTI* and need to be built into the base, then we can initially build in an expansive class consisting of truths about whatever intentional states (narrow or wide) there are. Then there is no obstacle here to the claim that all truths are scrutable from the expanded base, and there is correspondingly no obstacle to the claim that all beliefs have primary intensions. At most, there is a worry about whether the scrutability base is compact. But once we have established scrutability from the expansive base, and the existence of primary intensions, then (via the scrutability of truths about all intentional states from truths about primary intensions and non-intentional truths), we can establish scrutability of all truths from a base whose intentional truths include at most truths about primary intensions.

Most of the above has been premised on the hypothesis that I am wrong in holding that all intentional truths are scrutable from *PQTI*. It should also be noted that even if I am right, a version of some of these issues may arise from the inclusion of phenomenal truths in the base. If phenomenal truths are themselves intentional truths, then specifying them will involve specifying a certain intentional relation between subjects and intentional contents. And even if they are not themselves intentional truths, it is not implausible that they directly imply intentional truths, for example concerning the content of phenomenal states. Either way, there will be a trivialization worry in the background. For a given *S*, then if there is a phenomenal state *R* whose content is the same as *S*, then one could suggest that *S* might be near-trivially scrutable from a truth like 'If I were to have *R*, it would be veridical'.

This issue is not obviously as broad in its scope as the issue concerning intentional states more generally, as it is far from obvious that for any sentence, there can be a phenomenal state with the same content. On some views, the content of phenomenal states is restricted to low-level properties such as colors and shapes, in which case the threat of triviality is minimized. But on others, phenomenal states can also represent a wide range of high-level properties, perhaps represented in perception (Siegel 2006), or perhaps represented in cognitive phenomenology (Horgan and Tienson 2002, Siewert 1998). Even if this does not extend to all properties and all contents, the scope is broad enough to cause concern.

In any case, one can deal with the issue in the same way as for intentional states in general. If phenomenal states are to be characterized in the base in terms of their intentional content, one can require that these contents occur in base truths only as relata of relevant intentional relations. In addition, whether phenomenal states are so characterized or not, one can exclude notions such as 'veridical' from the base. It is plausible that phenomenal states are narrow states, in which case the worry about the environment does not arise. It is an open question how the narrow contents of phenomenal states are best characterized: perhaps in terms of intentional relations to certain privileged properties (see 'Perception and the Fall from Eden'), or perhaps in terms of something like primary intensions (see 'The Representational Character of Experience'). But as before, there is no obvious problem with building contents such as these into the base if necessary.

Another way to avoid trivialization for intentional truths and phenomenal truths is to appeal to psychophysical laws. It is plausible that intentional and phenomenal properties supervene on physical properties with metaphysical or nomological necessity. If so, there will be psychophysical principles or laws governing this supervenience. Then even if the relevant intentional or phenomenal truths here are not scrutable from physical truths, they will be scrutable from physical truths along with psychophysical laws. It is unlikely that these laws will have special clauses for each intentional content or phenomenal property. Rather, we can expect that the laws will be quite general. The laws might involve intentional or phenomenal notions and might quantify over concepts or contents, but expressing the laws will not require using arbitrary concepts. If so, scrutability from physical truths and psychophysical laws will avoid trivialization and will retain a compact base.

What about intentional states such as desires, hopes, and intentions? So far I have mostly discussed beliefs, but that discussion generalizes to other intentional states. Truths about these states are plausibly scrutable from *PQTI*, and if not, we can include them in the base without trivialization. And what about truths about action, such as 'He is reaching for a cup'? These will plausibly be scrutable from truths about associated mental states (including truths about relevant beliefs, desires, intentions, and the experience of agency), along with macrophysical truths about bodily movements and truths about the environment. If so, these truths do not pose any further obstacle to scrutability.

8 Social truths

There are many expressions that are intimately linked to intentional concepts and terms, such that knowing their extension require knowing various intentional truths. This applies especially to *social* expressions such as 'friend', 'money', 'law', and so on. For John to be Fred's friend, John and Fred must have certain attitudes. For a piece of paper to count as money, people in the community must have certain attitudes. To be a philosopher, one must engage in certain patterns of thought, and so on. Insofar as there is an epistemic gap between *PQI* and intentional truths, there will be a corresponding epistemic gap between *PQI* and truths involving some of these notions. But once intentional truths are within the fold, there is no residual problem.

Here we can picture an extended Cosmoscope that delivers intentional truths to us, allowing us to know what every individual believes, desires, intends, and so on. Given this sort of extended Cosmoscope, there would be no obstacle to determining who is whose friend, who has what sort of money, what the laws of a society are, and so on. All of these phenomena are constituted by attitudes and practices among the members of a society, and the extended Cosmoscope will give us full access to those attitudes and practices.

This does not require us to take a position on questions about holism and individualism in social science. A holistic view holds that truths about societies are not reducible to truths about individuals. But we have seen that scrutability does not require reducibility. Biological truths about life may not be reducible to microphysical or phenomenal truths, but they are scrutable from these all the same. The same goes for social truths and individual truths. Even holists typically endorse some form of supervenience: social truths cannot vary without varying truths about individuals. We can put this claim in an epistemological key: we cannot get an imaginative grip on holding the truths about individuals' attitudes and practices (along with the rest of *PQI*) constant, while varying the social truths. This strongly suggests that (positive) social truths are scrutable from *PQI* and intentional truths. It follows that if the latter are scrutable from the former, then social truths are scrutable from *PQI*.

9 Deferential terms

What about cases in which a speaker uses an expression with deference to one's linguistic community, intending to use it to mean what one's community means with the term? Tyler Burge discusses the case of Bert, who thinks he has arthritis in his thigh, having no idea that arthritis is a disease found only in the joints. Bert has at best a partial understanding of the term 'arthritis'. But because he uses the term with deference to his linguistic community, his utterance of 'I have arthritis in my thigh' is false, and if he were to say 'Arthritis is a disease of the joints', he would say something true. One might think that these cases pose problems for scrutability. After all, Bert does not even know what 'arthritis' means, so it is not obvious how he could come to infer these truths from *PQTI*.

I will say that an expression is used *deferentially* by a speaker when the referent of the speaker's use of the expression depends on how others in the linguistic community use the expression.[7] In the case above, Bert uses 'arthritis' deferentially: the referent of his use depends on others' use. It is certainly possible to use an expression nondeferentially: one can coin an entirely new term (e.g. 'glub'), deliberately use an existing term with a new meaning (e.g., stipulate that 'horse' will pick out the number two), or use a term with its correct meaning but

---

[7] In chapter 3 I stipulated that the scrutability thesis considered there excluded deferential utterances; that restriction is now being relaxed. What about relaxing other stipulations here: that the truths in question must be uttered by the speaker and that the speaker must have normal capacities? On the former: we need in principle to cover any context-independent sentence *M*, whether or not the speaker utters it or even possesses the relevant concepts. On the latter: we need in principle to cover any subject who is capable of thought. In both cases we can invoke an idealization to make the case that *if* the subject were to entertain a thought expressible by *PQTI → M*, the arguments in chapter 3 and 4 suggest that they would be in a position to justify this thought through idealized reasoning, yielding a priori knowledge.

insensitively to the use of others (e.g., stipulate that 'bachelor' picks out unmarried men, regardless of how others use the term). There are also intermediate cases in which a subject has a full understanding of a term (e.g., 'bachelor') without deference, and cases where there is both full understanding and deference. One can test for deference in these cases by asking: if it were to turn out that others use the term 'bachelor' for something other than unmarried males, would the speaker's utterance of 'Bachelors are unmarried men' be true or false? It is plausible that in ordinary language use, many expressions are used deferentially and many are used nondeferentially. Whether an expression is used deferentially or nondeferentially plausibly depends on the intentions and/or dispositions of the speaker, but we need not precisely characterize these intentions and dispositions here.

I think that deferential usage poses no problem for scrutability here, as long as one recognizes that scrutability must proceed through knowing metalinguistic truths about one's community. Once Bert knows what others in his community (and especially the experts in the community) refer to with their uses of the term 'arthritis', then he will be in a position to know that 'Arthritis is a disease of the joints' is true. That is: 'Arthritis is a disease of the joints' will be inferentially and conditionally scrutable for Bert from a base that includes ' "Arthritis" is used by others in my linguistic community to refer to a disease of the joints'. Likewise, 'I do not have arthritis in my thigh' will be inferentially and conditionally scrutable from a base that includes this metalinguistic truth along with underlying truths such as *PQTI*. Then the arguments in the last chapter suggest that there will also be a priori scrutability from this base. Assuming that there are no problems with the scrutability of the relevant metalinguistic truth from underlying truths, then the problem is dissolved.

More generally: let us say that a deferential truth is a true utterance involving an expression used deferentially. Then it is highly plausible that deferential truths are scrutable from nondeferential truths, where the latter class includes nondeferential truths about the use of language. If so, then any problem for scrutability distinctive to deferential truths is removed.[8]

This picture requires that the apriority of a sentence in a context can depend on whether a given expression is used deferentially or nondeferentially in that

---

[8] Block (2006) discusses a case in which a speaker has acquired two terms 'chat' on different occasions and has identical beliefs associated with both, but in which both have different referents due to deference to different speakers or communities. It is not really clear that this case is possible, but if it is, one can handle it as above, with the proviso that scrutability of truths involving a particular token of 'chat' will require tracing the causal history of that token, or of the corresponding concept in thought. Cases in which both concepts are used in language or thought simultaneously can be handled as in the discussion of indexicals and demonstratives below, by adjoining indexicals that pick out relevant concepts, thoughts, or experiences.

context. If Susan fully grasps the concept of *bachelor* and expresses it with a non-deferential use of the term 'bachelor', 'All bachelors are male' may be a priori for her. If Fred only partially grasps the concept *bachelor* and expresses it with a deferential use of the term 'bachelor' (perhaps he has picked up the word from conversation but has no idea that bachelors must be male), 'All bachelors are male' will not be a priori for him. In the latter case, Fred will not be in a position to know the sentence from the armchair at all: at best, he can come to know it by further exposure to the linguistic community. And he certainly will not be in a position to come to know the sentence a priori.

As usual, the difference in the apriority of the utterances mirrors epistemological differences in the thoughts that the utterances expressed: Susan's utterance expresses a thought that constitutes potential a priori knowledge, while Fred's utterance does not. One can find a reverse pattern for other utterances. For Fred, a sentence such as 'Bachelors are what others in my community refer to as 'bachelors'' may be a priori. For Susan, the same sentence may be a posteriori, as knowledge of the sentence depends on empirical knowledge that others use the term the same way. Again, this is just what we should expect when apriority of an utterance is tied to what the speaker is in a position to know a priori.[9]

10 Names

What about names? Here Kripke's epistemological arguments against descriptivism suggest a challenge. Kripke makes the case that someone could use a term such as 'Feynman' or 'Gödel' while being ignorant of or mistaken about any properties of the referent. Given this, it may seem hard to see how truths involving these names will be scrutable.

One can respond to this challenge in exactly the same way as in the case of deferential terms above. In the relevant cases, once the subject knows enough about what *others* refer to with their use of terms such as 'Feynman' and 'Gödel', perhaps along with truths about the causal history of their own use of the relevant names, then they will have no trouble identifying the referent of the term as they use it, and coming to know relevant truths.

---

[9] The trickiest cases are those in which a speaker fully grasps a concept such as *bachelor* but nevertheless expresses it with a deferential use of 'bachelor'. On the current model, these are best regarded as cases in which 'All bachelors are male' is not a priori, as certainty about the sentence will require certainty about usage elsewhere in the linguistic community. Still, there is certainly something a priori in the vicinity for the speaker, and (as discussed in E11) one can develop models on which this sentence is associated with both deferential contents and with nondeferential contents. For present purposes we need not resolve the issue, as there will be no problem for scrutability either way, but I discuss the issue further in *The Multiplicity of Meaning*.

As in Chapter 1, nothing here requires that names are semantically equivalent to descriptions. The scrutability here, as usual, need not be grounded in a description, and any associated descriptive content may vary between different users of a term. Perhaps in some extreme cases of deference, there will be an associated description. If Fred hears the term 'Gödel' for the first time and immediately asks 'Who is Gödel?', it is perhaps not implausible that for Fred, something like the following is a priori: 'If Gödel exists, Gödel is the referent of the term 'Gödel' as used by the speaker from whom I acquired the term'. But other cases may have a more complex mix of deference and other information, so that no clean description like this is available. Either way, there is no problem for scrutability, and for the a priori entailment of sentences involving these names by *PQTI*.

Some object that the relevant sentences involving names cannot be a priori, as they express singular propositions, and these singular propositions cannot be known a priori. For example, in the case of Fred above, the allegedly a priori sentence will express the singular proposition that a certain specific person is the referent of someone's use of a term, and one cannot know such propositions about concrete individuals a priori.

In response: Whether or not these sentences express singular propositions, on the current framework they express thoughts. These thoughts are clearly thoughts that Fred is in a position to know on uttering the sentence, no matter what his relationship is to the individual in question. These thoughts do not require empirical justification: Fred can suspend judgment about the external world, and these thoughts will still constitute knowledge. And it is very difficult to see what the empirical evidence justifying these sentences might be. Someone might suggest, as in the objection from acquaintance in chapter 4, that one's causal acquaintance with the person in question plays an evidential role, but one can respond here as I responded to the objection there. So I think there is not much reason to deny that at least as I have defined apriority, these sentences are a priori. (It remains possible that in some other sense of 'a priori', such as a sense tied to apriority of a corresponding singular proposition, these sentences are not a priori.) I discuss this issue and some related Russellian objections about the a priori scrutability of names at greater length in the eleventh excursus.

11 Metalinguistic truths

On a number of occasions above, I have appealed to knowledge of metalinguistic truths, and in particular to truths about the referents of expressions used by others, such as ''Arthritis' as used by X refers to Y', ''Feynman' as used on occasion O refers to Z', and so on. Is it clear that these truths are scrutable?

In response, I think it is extremely plausible that given (i) the sort of information delivered by a Cosmoscope and (ii) enough intentional truths about speakers in our community, we are in a position to know truths about reference. It is arguable that the first alone is enough. But if not, the first and the second are enough. The details will depend on one's view of the relation between language and thought, though.

Certainly it is plausible that knowing the intentional content of mental states, in combination with knowing base truths about the world, puts one in a position to know the extension of any concepts involved in those mental states. This is straightforward on a view where content is Russellian (here the referents are built in), and it is also straightforward on a view where contents are primary intensions (which in effect yield a function from base truths to extensions). If the content of an utterance always reflects the content of an associated thought, then the same will apply to utterances, and the problem is solved. If the content of an utterance is a more complex function of the contents of associated thoughts, associated intentions, and so on, then it will plausibly be scrutable from these contents. In cases of semantic deference, the content of an utterance depends on a surrounding community, but even in these cases, the primary intension of the utterance plausibly mirrors that of a corresponding thought (both involve functions that pick out what relevant others in the community refer to with 'arthritis', and so on). In any case there is little reason to deny that intentional content of mental states across a community, combined with other qualitative information, will yield scrutability of truths about reference.

In the cases of deference and names above, one also needs to know truths about which others in the community are using the same word as one, or perhaps truths about which others one acquired a word from. Again, it is highly plausible that one could come to know these truths with the aid of a Cosmoscope to examine patterns of linguistic usage and causal connections between speakers, perhaps supplemented by facts about speakers' intentional states.

What about truths about truth? Given that truths about reference are scrutable, it is plausible that truths about truth are scrutable too, or at least that they are scrutable if all other truths are. For example, if in an utterance of 'Bill is Fred' one can know that 'Bill' refers to the D_1 and 'Fred' refers to the D_2, then as long as one can know that the D_1 is the D_2, there is no problem with knowing that the utterance is true. One can also proceed via the primary intension of the utterance (which as above will be determined by the primary intensions of corresponding thoughts, or perhaps thoughts, intentions, and so on), which then in conjunction with base truths will straightforwardly yield a truth-value. So as long as we have intentional truths in the scrutability base, and as long as there is no other problem with scrutability in general, then there is no problem with the scrutability of these metalinguistic truths.

All this applies to the truth and reference of expression tokens. What about expression types? This case must be restricted to cases where the expressions in question are not context-dependent. In these cases, scrutability is straightforward. A metalinguistic truth such as ' 'Philosophers exist' is true' is clearly scrutable from the non-metalinguistic truth 'Philosophers exist' and the Tarskian truth ' 'Philosophers exist' is true iff philosophers exist'. So as long as the Tarskian truth is scrutable from non-metalinguistic truths, metalinguistic truths will be scrutable from non-metalinguistic truths.

What of the Tarskian truth, then? Such truths are often held to be a priori, in which case there is no problem. I think the matter is a little more complicated. A quotational expression such as ' 'Philosophers exist' ' can be understood as picking out an *orthographically* individuated item, in which case it is not a priori that the item means anything at all. Or it can be understood as picking out a *semantically* (and orthographically) individuated item, in which case it is a priori that it means what it does. Understood the latter way, the Tarskian truth is a priori. Understood the former way, the Tarskian truth is not a priori.[10] But it is nevertheless scrutable: the meaning of the orthographic item will be scrutable from intentional states of users of the item, much as with the case of tokens above. So one has scrutability either way.

12 Indexicals and demonstratives

We have seen already that indexical truths such as 'I am Australian' and 'It is now 3 a.m.' are not scrutable from non-indexical truths. To handle these, we added two indexical truths 'I am D_1' and 'Now is D_2' to the base. Are there any others that we need to add?

One might add 'here', but it is arguably equivalent to something like 'The location where I am now'. A complication arises if time travel is possible: then the same person might be in two places now, but intuitively 'here' refers to just one of those places. To handle this, one could add 'here', or perhaps better, have a single indexical that picks out a single local time-slice (or perhaps a single total conscious state) of a person. Then 'I', 'now', and 'here' will all be determined by that time-slice in the obvious way.

What about demonstratives such as 'that'? It is plausible that demonstrative truths such as 'That is a cup' are inferentially and conditionally scrutable given sufficient information about one's experiences and their external causes. So it is plausible that these truths are a priori scrutable as well.

---

[10] This is particularly clear if one thinks about the corresponding thought. Suppose that 'philosopher' and 'wise person' are synonyms. Then ' 'Philosophers exist' is true iff philosophers exist' and ' 'Philosophers exist' is true iff wise people exist' will express the same thought. At the level of thought, any linguistic trapping for the concept expressed by 'philosophers' and 'wise people' is irrelevant. So it is clear that this thought about an orthographic item cannot be known a priori, though it can be known easily by someone who knows the language.

A complication arises due to Austin's 'Two Tubes' puzzle and related cases. I have distinct tubes attached to each eye, and see a dot through each. I experience a symmetrical visual field with two red dots. I might wonder whether the two dots are the same object, and I put this by asking 'Is $that_1$ the same as $that_2$?' I might also wonder whether the two dots are really red. I might hazard two conjectures by saying simultaneously 'That is red' (ostending one dot) and 'That is red' (ostending the other). The first utterance (S_1) is true but the second utterance (S_2) is false.

In this case, it is plausible that S_1 is not scrutable from $PQTI$. From $PQTI$ one can determine that the subject at the center is seeing two dots, one of which is red and the other of which is not. However, one has no basis to tell which of the two dots is *this* one, for the demonstratives above. The situation is entirely symmetrical between the two: for example, one can't appeal to facts about the dot that one is now seeing, or the dot that one is now attending to, as one is seeing and attending to both. One likewise cannot appeal to 'The dot on the left', and so on, at least in the extreme case in which one has a symmetrical history and one has no nondemonstrative way to pick out one side as left or right. (One can also imagine a case where the dots do not seem spatially related in this way, such as a case with two distinct but qualitatively identical visual fields.)

I take the moral to be that as with 'I' and 'now', one needs to add some demonstratives to the base to handle these cases. Which demonstratives? It is plausible that certain *experiential demonstratives*, picking out experiences (or instances of phenomenal properties) will do. In the case above, I will have available two experiential demonstratives '$This_1$ experience' and '$This_2$ experience'. '$This_1$ experience is caused by a red dot' is true, while '$This_2$ experience is caused by a red dot' is false. Given this information and other contextual information, I will have no trouble determining that S_1 is true and S_2 is false. So for each such demonstrative, one can build into the base a truth of the form '$This_n$ experience is D_n', where as with the base truths for 'I' and 'now', D_n is a maximally specific description in the language of $PQTI$ that the experience satisfies. This will then enable inferential, conditional, and a priori scrutability.

One might wonder how a connection between two demonstratives could be a priori. But this is not uncommon. It is possible to use a demonstrative 'that' to pick out an object, and to use a demonstrative 'there' to pick out wherever that object is located (whether or not it is where it seems to be). In such a case, 'That is there (if it exists and is located)' is a priori. Likewise, one can use an experiential demonstrative '$That_1$ experience' to pick out an object, and a perceptual demonstrative '$That_1$ object' to pick out whatever object is perceived with that experience. In that case, '$That_1$ experience is an experience of $That_1$ object (if both exist)' is a priori. A priori links of this sort between demonstratives suffice to ground a priori scrutability.

Experiential demonstratives such as '$That_1$ experience' need not be uttered or even thought. One can think of each such demonstrative as a unique demonstrative in our ideal language, tied to a specific experience: for each experience E, there is a corresponding demonstrative '$This_E$'. The scrutability base for a subject and a time need only involve demonstratives for each of the experiences the subject is now undergoing.[11] And usually, few if any of these demonstratives will be required. If a sentence S involves no demonstratives, one will not need any of these E-sentences for it to be scrutable. And if a sentence involves only one or two demonstratives, then typically one will need only one or two such E-sentences. But arbitrary such E-sentences are available if necessary.

Having such demonstratives available helps with the scrutability of orienting expressions such as 'left' and 'right'. As we have seen, in some symmetrical cases truths about these may not be inferentially or conditionally scrutable from $PQTI$. But if one has experiential demonstratives available, the symmetry is broken, and there is no problem with scrutability: one can determine what is on one's left by determining what is connected to a certain marked experience in one's visual field, or better, by determining what typically causes experiences that bear a certain psychological and phenomenological relation to that experience. If so, there is no need to build in orienting expressions such as 'left' and 'right' in addition.

It is arguable that a similar phenomenon can arise for thoughts as well as experiences. It is not obvious how the referent of expressions such as 'This thought' will be scrutable in general. Here one can construct relevant puzzle cases with multiple thoughts of this form at a single time. How one handles this depends on how one understands the relation between occurrent thoughts and experiences. If occurrent thoughts necessarily involve experience (presumably a phenomenology of thinking), then demonstrative truths about the thought will plausibly be scrutable from demonstrative truths about the corresponding experience. But if they do not, then one may need to build in demonstratives for thoughts into the scrutability base. The same goes for demonstratives for other occurrent mental acts: 'That urge', 'This remembering', and so on. If these acts, or even one's thinking of these acts, necessarily involves experience, then the referents here will plausibly be scrutable, but if not, one may need extra demonstratives for occurrent mental acts in the base. My own tentative view is that occurrent thought always involves experience, so I do not think that the base needs to be expanded with further demonstratives. But the matter is far from obvious, and adding these further demonstratives is not out of the question.

---

[11] Or at least, for each atomic experience, where atomicity is spelled out appropriately: the thought is that any demonstrative truths about composite experiences will be scrutable from truths about atomic experiences along with Q.

13 Vagueness

I have already discussed an objection from vagueness in chapter 2. There the objection was that if S is true iff S is scrutable from $PQTI$, then given that $S \vee \sim S$ is true for all truth-apt S, it seems to follow that for all such S, either S is scrutable from $PQTI$ or $\sim S$ is scrutable from $PQTI$. But in the case of borderline cases of vague expressions, this is perhaps implausible. The solution adopted there was to restrict the scrutability principle to *determinate* truths: S is scrutable iff S is determinately true. Then as long as borderline cases are indeterminate, the problem is removed.

Still, there are other issues concerning borderline cases. One potential objection is that the scrutability thesis requires that whenever S is indeterminate, it is scrutable that S is indeterminate, which might seem far from obvious. In response, however, we need only note that the thesis (at least as formulated in the first excursus) requires only that the indeterminacy of S is scrutable when it is *determinate* that S is indeterminate, and this seems quite plausible.

The biggest objection stems from the epistemic theory of vagueness, according to which vague sentences are true or false even in borderline cases. On this view, in any utterance of 'John is tall', 'tall' expresses a precise property, with a sharp cutoff between cases with the property and cases without it. The utterance will always be true or false, with no intermediate status even in borderline cases. It is just that in borderline cases, we are unable to know the truth-value of the utterance even though we know the subject's height and other relevant facts, because we are unable to know where the sharp cutoff falls. If so, then a sentence such as 'John is tall' can be true even though we cannot know it. And on this view, adding the information in $PQTI$ will not remove the ignorance. If so, then a sentence such as 'John is tall' may be true and inscrutable.

One might try to respond by appealing to the thesis that a truth is scrutable iff it is determinately true, and by giving an epistemological reading of determinacy, for example where determinacy comes to unknowability. If we do this, then this case is not a counterexample. But this epistemological reading of determinacy differs greatly from the original notion, and it tends to trivialize the scrutability thesis, so that the resulting thesis is significantly less interesting. One might also respond by appealing to idealization, and suggesting that even if we cannot know where the sharp cutoff falls, an idealized version of ourselves could. It is true that the epistemic theory itself does not make any claims about what ideal reasoners could know.[12] Still, it would not be contrary to the spirit of the view for a proponent of the theory to deny that the cutoff is knowable even by ideal reasoning. So henceforth I will stipulate this understanding of the epistemic theory.

---

[12] In his discussion of the epistemic theory in *Vagueness* (1994), Timothy Williamson is explicitly agnostic about ideal reasoners.

I think one should accept that *if* this version of the epistemic theory is true, then our central scrutability theses are false. Many truths involving borderline cases of vague expressions will be true but (inferentially, conditionally, and a priori) inscrutable from *PQTI*. One might suggest expanding the scrutability base to include the truths in question, or truths about the cutoff points for vague expressions ('Someone is tall iff their height is greater than...'). But almost all terms in natural language are vague, and any scrutability base that includes all vague terms will certainly not be compact. And it is not clear how one could get around adding an enormous number of such terms: adding truths about the cutoff for 'tall' would seem to leave the cutoff for 'bald' no easier to know than it was before, for example. So it appears that a base vocabulary will have to be enormous. If so, then Inferential, Conditional, and A Priori Scrutability will all be false.

A proponent of scrutability should instead respond by denying the epistemic theory of vagueness. This theory is widely regarded as extremely counterintuitive, so one is certainly not biting a large bullet by denying it. In fact, one might suggest that the implausibility of the epistemic theory is tied in some fashion to the way it denies scrutability, for example in holding that there are truths about someone's tallness that cannot be known even when one knows their exact height and other relevant qualitative truths. Furthermore: if scrutability holds in all other cases, then this fact can be used to argue against the epistemic theory, by establishing that the epistemic theorist must deny a principle that holds everywhere else. So if the epistemic theory is the main potential threat to scrutability, the dialectical situation certainly favors scrutability.

I will not try to argue further against the epistemic theory at this point.[13] For now, this version of the epistemic theory plays the useful role of providing a view according to which the scrutability thesis (whether in inferential, conditional, or a priori form) is false.

14 Secondary qualities

What about truths about secondary qualities, such as the colors of external objects? It is fairly plausible that any truths here are scrutable from truths about the sorts of experiences that these objects cause, along with truths about their physical properties. For example, as long as *PQTI* can tell us that a given apple

---

[13] A more developed argument against the epistemic theory might combine elements from 'Verbal Disputes', suggesting that disputes over what counts as 'tall' against a backdrop of agreement on non-'tall' facts are broadly verbal, with arguments that in such a dialectical situation there is a sort of epistemological transparency. Here the considerations discussed in the last paragraph of 4.7 might play a central role. This way of proceeding suggests a general argument for the scrutability thesis distinct from the main arguments given in this book.

typically causes a certain sort of experience as of red, and that it has a physical property that typically causes experiences of that sort, then one is plausibly in a position to know that the apple is red. This will be so on a wide range of views about color: many physicalist views, dispositionalist views, phenomenalist views, response-dependent views, and so on.

There are some views of color on which this scrutability is not as straightforward. On some primitivist views of colors (discussed at greater length in the next chapter), colors are primitive properties that are quite distinct from any physical, dispositional, or phenomenal properties. On some other views, we have at least primitive *concepts* of color, although these may pick out physical or dispositional properties. On some of these views (as discussed at greater length in the next chapter), one cannot rule out a priori a skeptical scenario on which everything looks to one just as it does, but in which the objects that typically look red have been green all along. On such a view, even all the information in *PQTI* may not rule out such a scenario. So if there are truths about objects' colors, they will be inscrutable from *PQTI*, or at least they will not be conclusively scrutable.[14]

I think it is implausible that there are inscrutable truths of this sort. On my own view ('Perception and the Fall from Eden'), we have primitive color concepts, but these pick out primitive properties that are not instantiated by objects in our world. If so, there are no inscrutable truths about their instantiation. Still, if someone holds that there are inscrutable truths about the instantiation of color, then they can include these truths in the scrutability base. One will presumably have to add corresponding truths for all other secondary qualities, and perhaps for all secondary qualities that might be attributed in some form of perceptual experience. If so, the base will undergo an unattractive expansion, one that arguably reflects an independently unattractive aspect of these views of color. But even if the base is expanded, all these truths fall under a single family, and there seems to be no associated danger of trivialization. So there is no threat to the scrutability thesis here.

15 Macrophysical truths[15]

As defined, *PQTI* contains macrophysical truths: truth about nonfundamental objects in the language of classical physics, including expressions for spatiotemporal properties, mass, and so on. It is natural to ask whether macrophysical truths are

---

[14] Closely related is the view endorsed by Tye (2006) and Byrne and Hilbert (2007), on which there are unknowable truths concerning which objects instantiate unique blue, in light of the fact that the conditions eliciting experiences as of unique blue vary between subjects.

[15] Thanks to Kelvin McQueen for detailed discussion of all the issues in this section. His Ph.D. thesis addresses the scrutability of macrophysical truths in various scientific domains, including the scrutability of macroscopic mass in classical and relativistic physics and the scrutability of macrophysical properties in quantum mechanics, in much more depth than I have here.

dispensable from the base, and in particular whether they are scrutable from a smaller class *PQTI*– which includes microphysical but not macrophysical truths. This issue could be discussed in the next chapter on narrowing the base, but in some respects it is closer to the spirit of this chapter, and it will be convenient to discuss it here.

In considering this question there are really two sets of issues: those that already arise for classical physics and those that arise distinctively for nonclassical physics, including relativity and especially quantum mechanics. I will consider classical physics first. For this purpose I will assume a conception of microphysics on which fundamental objects are characterized by their relative location in a Newtonian spacetime, along with their velocity, mass, and so on. (One could also assume a Bohmian interpretation of quantum mechanics.) I will then relax this assumption in order to consider issues tied to nonclassical physics.

Given a classical conception of microphysics, there is a natural route to the scrutability of macrophysical truths. The simplest suggestion is that the location of a macroscopic object is just the spatiotemporal region consisting of the location of its fundamental parts. The mass of a macroscopic object is just the total mass of its fundamental parts. So to determine the location and mass of a macroscopic object, it suffices to know the location and mass of its fundamental parts. Something similar plausibly applies to velocity, force, momentum, energy, and the like. If so, macrophysical truths are scrutable from (classical) microphysical truths.

One can also make the point by appeal to the Cosmoscope. Suppose that *S* is a sentence about the location, shape, and mass of a macroscopic object. Armed with a Cosmoscope that contained only microphysical and not macrophysical information, one could straightforwardly come to know whether *S* is true. One simply needs to determine whether there is an appropriately located and shaped spatial region at the relevant time, occupied by particles with the appropriate total mass. If the macrophysical truth includes mass density distributions, one can come to know this in a similar way.

There are some residual issues. First, there are questions about just what count as objects. These questions are in effect addressed in the discussion of ontology earlier. Whether we assume a liberal or a restricted view of objects, it is plausible that truths about the existence of macrophysical objects will follow from microphysical truths along with certain principles of composition for macroscopic objects. On my own view, these principles will themselves either be a priori or scrutable from *PQTI*–. If so, there is no problem here. If not, then certain principles of composition may need to be built into the base. With the aid of those principles, there will be no problem in determining just where there are objects.

Second, one could plausibly argue that an object's macroscopic shape is more complex than just the region occupied by its parts: perhaps it includes internal regions of vacuum, for example. Still, however shape is understood, shape should be scrutable from a Cosmoscope. One could suggest that there could be more dramatic failures of the determination of location here: perhaps O is located in Australia although its parts are located in the United States? I think such cases are of dubious coherence, however.

Third, one might argue that it is not a priori that the mass of a macroscopic object is the sum of the mass of its fundamental parts. If one understands mass in terms of resistance of acceleration, it is arguable that there could be fundamental laws that entail that wholes resist acceleration in a manner that is not a linear combination of the way their parts resist acceleration. Something similar applies if one understands mass in terms of its gravitational role. If this is right, then the principle of mass additivity is not a priori. Still, it remains plausible that mass additivity is a priori scrutable from underlying truths. It is notable that hypotheses on which mass additivity is violated require fundamental laws that are distinct from the laws of our (putatively classical) world. In fact, McQueen (2011) makes a strong case that mass additivity is a priori entailed by laws governing the linear composition of forces in classical mechanics (yielding additivity of inertial mass) and in the classical theory of gravitation (yielding additivity of gravitational mass). If so, macrophysical mass truths are scrutable from $PQTI-$. One might also think that P leaves open questions about how macroscopic objects affect mass-measuring instruments. But as with other measuring instruments, once Q is included, then even these facts are settled.

Relativity theory complicates these matters a little, but only a little. The location of macroscopic objects remains derivable from the location of their fundamental parts. The relativistic mass of macroscopic objects remains the sum of the relativistic masses of their parts. Relativistic properties have to be relativized to reference frames, or else determined by one's own reference frame which will itself be determined by one's location and velocity, but either way there is no problem for scrutability. Rest mass is more complicated, but there is still a straightforward formula for inferring macroscopic rest masses from microphysical properties, and this formula can be derived from fundamental laws along with the additivity of energy and momentum (Okun 2009, section V). The status of these additivity principles in relativity theory is plausibly analogous to that of mass additivity in classical physics. If so, truths about macroscopic rest mass are scrutable from $PQTI-$.

It is often suggested that macrophysical phenomena in various domains of science are 'emergent' from lower-level phenomena in a way that renders them unpredictable from microphysical phenomena. However, such cases typically involve *weak emergence*: roughly, cases of unpredictability in practice without unpredictability in principle.[16] The paradigmatic cases of emergence in complex

[16] See Mark Bedau's 'Weak Emergence' (1997) and my 'Strong and Weak Emergence' (2006).

systems are cases in which macroscopic phenomena are hard to predict in practice from a full specification of microscopic phenomena while being predictable
in principle, especially once microscopic boundary conditions are included. In
some extreme cases (Gu et al. 2009), it has been held that macroscopic phenomena may be uncomputable from an infinitary microscopic base, but as in the case
of mathematics, this is no obstacle to scrutability. In other cases of weak emergence, macroscopic *laws* do not seem to follow from microphysical laws, but
once one enhances the base with particular microphysical facts the problem goes
away. None of these cases of weak emergence are a problem for scrutability.

Strong emergence involves macroscopic phenomena that are unpredictable in
principle from microphysical facts and laws. In *The Mind and its Place in Nature*
(1925), C. D. Broad suggested that chemistry and biology (as well as the mind)
involve strongly emergent phenomena. On Broad's view, in order to predict
these phenomena one needs fundamental 'transordinal laws' connecting physics
to these domains. If there are strongly emergent phenomena, then one will have
to expand a scrutability base by including these transordinal laws. However, current orthodoxy holds that there are no strongly emergent phenomena in chemistry, biology, and other macrophysical domains, and there appears to be little
evidence of strong emergence in these domains. If the orthodoxy is right, then
strongly emergent phenomena will be ruled out by *PQTI*–. My view is that consciousness is the only strongly emergent phenomenon, so that while a scrutability base may have to include psychophysical laws, it need not include other
transordinal laws.

Next: issues tied to quantum mechanics. These issues are certainly more complex. For a start, much depends on which interpretation of quantum mechanics
is accurate. The three major options include a Bohmian interpretation on which
particles have classical properties; a collapse interpretation on which wavefunctions evolve in a superposed way and occasionally collapse into a more definite
state; and an Everett (or many-worlds) interpretation on which wavefunctions
evolve in a superposed way and never collapse. The fundamental microphysical
truths in *P* will look quite different depending on which of these interpretations
is correct.[17]

On a Bohmian interpretation there is not much problem for scrutability of
macrophysical truths. Given that the interpretation invokes a fundamental
three-dimensional space in which particles are located (interacting with a wavefunction in a higher-dimensional configuration space), things go through much
as for the classical microphysics described above. On an Everett interpretation,

---

[17] For more on these interpretations, see David Albert's *Quantum Mechanics and Experience*.
On the Everett interpretation, see the articles in Simon Saunders et al., *Many Worlds? Everett,
Quantum Theory, and Reality*.

though, things are complicated, as it is not clear that there *are* any truths about the locations and masses of macroscopic objects on this interpretation. And even on a collapse interpretation, it is not obvious how to move from a wavefunction state to classical macrophysical truths.

The proper treatment of this issue depends on whether there are (positive) macrophysical truths on the relevant interpretation of quantum mechanics, and if so what they are. If there are no such truths, they cannot pose a problem for scrutability. Perhaps their absence could pose a problem for the scrutability of other macroscopic truths from *PQTI–*. But it is far from clear what the problematic macroscopic truths might be, such that they are determinately true where ordinary macrophysical sentences are not. Presumably if it is not determinately true that objects have certain locations, it is also not determinately true that Schrödinger's cat is alive. The status of most other macroscopic sentences will be similar.

For present purposes, I will focus on versions of the Everett and collapse interpretations that accept (i) wavefunction fundamentalism, holding the wavefunction is all there is in the fundamental physical ontology, and (ii) spatial realism, saying that there are macrophysical spatial truths, corresponding roughly to apparent macrophysical truths. For example, for a given object such as a tree or a dog, there will correspond macrophysical truths with the character 'There is an object with such-and-such size, shape, and location'. We can concentrate on truths about location at one of the lowest levels at which there are such spatial truths: perhaps a truth saying that a particle (or a molecule or a cell) is in a certain location. From these, one can recover higher-level spatial truths as in the classical case. The residual question is just how these truths about location are scrutable from truths about the wavefunction.

On the collapse interpretation, a natural interpretive strategy is to say that an entity is located in a certain region of three-dimensional space if a high enough proportion of the (squared) amplitude of its wavefunction is concentrated within that region.[18] Here I assume something like the GRW version of a collapse

---

[18] This interpretive strategy presupposes that we can talk about the amplitude of wavefunctions associated with spatial regions. This raises the prior question (discussed by Monton 2002) of how wavefunction specifications involving a three-dimensional space are recoverable from a specification of a wavefunction in higher-dimensional configuration space. (The same problem arises for the Everett interpretation and even for some versions of the Bohm interpretation.) Existing options here include rejecting the reality of three-dimensional space (Albert 1996), taking the three-dimensional spatial parameters to be built into the fundamental dimensions of configuration space (Lewis 2004), accepting both configuration space and three-dimensional space as fundamental with a fundamental law connecting entities within them (Maudlin 2007), accepting only quasi-classical entities in three-dimensional space as fundamental and treating the wavefunction as a law that governs them (Allori et al 2008), or taking nonseparable states of three-dimensional space to be fundamental (Wallace and Timpson 2010). My preferred option is an appeal to

interpretation (Ghirardi, Rimini, and Weber 1986), on which the post-collapse wavefunction has most of its amplitude concentrated in a small region, with infinite low-amplitude tails extending throughout space. An interpretive principle in involving 'a high enough proportion' will then deliver classical truths at both the microscopic and macroscopic level. If the interpretive principle here were itself a priori, then classical truths at the fundamental level would themselves be scrutable from quantum-mechanical facts. It is implausible that the principle is a priori, but it remains open that the conditional from *PQTI*– to the principle is a priori. The key question is whether it is a priori that *if* we are in a quantum-mechanical world with collapse, the location of objects is determined in this way.

Something similar applies on the Everett interpretation, where the natural interpretive strategy gives a special role to one's own branch of the wavefunction. In ordinary circumstances, the wavefunction can be seen as a sum of branches that have undergone 'decoherence' so that they have little interaction with each other and behave quasi-classically. My own perceived reality is contained within one such branch. We can say that the location of a macroscopic object is its location relative to our own branch. Again, if the interpretive principle here were itself a priori, then classical truths at the macroscopic levels would themselves be scrutable from quantum-mechanical facts. As before, it is implausible that the principle is a priori, but it remains open that the conditional from *PQTI*– to the principle is a priori. Here, the key question is whether it is a priori that *if* we are in an Everett world of the appropriate sort, then the location of objects is determined in this way.

In both cases, I think there is a good case for scrutability of the relevant principle. One natural way that this might go is via the view that in chapter 7 I call spatial functionalism: a roughly, that what it is to be a spatial property is to play the appropriate causal (or counterfactual or nomic) role.[19] In the case of macroscopic spatial properties, it is plausible (as I argue there) that spatial properties can be picked out by spatial concepts as that manifold of properties that serve as

---

the spatial functionalism discussed below, which allows three-dimensional space to be real, non-fundamental, and scrutable. If this is right, then even though the problem here is distinct from the one in the main text (which arises even given a 'spatial' specification of the wavefunction, as on Lewis's conception), the two problems have a common solution.

[19] This appeal to spatial functionalism is roughly in the spirit of David Wallace's (2003) invocation of functionalism about tigers to recover truths about tigers in an Everett ontology. Wallace ties his functionalism to Daniel Dennett's view on ontology in 'Real Patterns', suggesting that only a tiger-like pattern is required for tigers. I think that functionalism understood in terms of causal or counterfactual roles gives a clearer picture, and that its most important locus by far is functionalism about space and related notions (although see Alyssa Ney, forthcoming, for a different perspective). Once we have recovered macrophysical space, time, mass, and so on, recovering tigers is easy, whether or not we are functionalists about tigers.

the causal basis for spatial experience, in much the way that color properties are picked out in the previous section. To simplify, the property of being two meters away from one might be picked out as the spatial relation that normally brings about the experience of being two meters away from one. Something similar goes for properties involving relative length, position, shape, and the like. On this view of spatial concepts, spatial truths will be scrutable from truths about what plays the relevant causal roles.

One can then argue that on a collapse interpretation, the properties and relations that normally bring about the relevant sort of spatial experiences are precisely properties and relations requiring the wavefunction's amplitude to be largely concentrated in a certain area. Likewise, on an Everett interpretation, the relevant spatial experiences will normally be brought about when there is an object that has relevant properties relative to the perceiver's branch of the wavefunction. The details can be argued about, just as in the case of color. But the general point is that *PQTI*– will put one in a position to determine the causal and counterfactual bases of spatial experiences, and that doing so will put one in a position to determine principles connecting quantum-mechanical properties to macrophysical spatial properties of objects.[20]

These spatial functionalist approaches will be rejected if one accepts spatial primitivism (analogous to the color primitivism above, and discussed more in the next chapter), according to which we have primitive spatial concepts that do not pick out spatial properties via the role that they play. On this view, it is much

---

[20] This use of spatial functionalism to defend scrutability of spatial truths relies on the fact that Q specifies spatial experiences as part of the scrutability base. One might worry (with Maudlin 2007) about how the presence of spatial experiences is itself to be explained under these quantum-mechanical ontologies. I attempt a partial answer in chapter 10 of *The Conscious Mind*, using (i) the broadly functionalist principle that consciousness depends (conceptually, metaphysically, or nomologically) on abstract functional organization and (ii) the principle that any abstract functional organization that is implemented in a quasi-classical world will also be present in an Everett world with a 'branch' corresponding to that world. The latter claim is supported by the principle that a superposition of decoherent states implements any functional organization that would be implemented by one of those states taken alone. (In *The Conscious Mind* I omitted 'decoherent' here, leading to problems pointed out by Byrne and Hall [1999]. The restricted claim is all that is supported by my arguments there and is also all that is needed to support (ii).) If these principles are correct, we should expect spatial experience in an Everett world with quasi-classical branches corresponding to spatial perceivers. A related analysis might be applied to a collapse interpretation.

This functionalist approach is compatible with both materialist and dualist approaches to consciousness. One could even combine analytic functionalism about the mental and the spatial to argue that both experiential truths and spatial truths are scrutable without Q in the base, though a residual issue is whether one can make sense of the functional roles associated with mentality without an appeal to spatial notions. An alternative way to avoid appealing to Q in the base that bypasses questions about the mind is to appeal to the nonphenomenal (structural) spatial functionalism discussed in 7.5 and 8.7.

harder to see how apparent macroscopic spatial properties will be scrutable from *PQTI*– where *P* specifies only a wavefunction. But if one is a spatial primitivist, it is hard to see how macroscopic objects have the spatial properties that they appear to have at all, if standard collapse and Everett interpretations that accept wavefunction fundamentalism are true. If those interpretations are true, I think the best thing for a spatial primitivist to say is that objects do not strictly have determinate spatial properties (the molecule is not determinately at a location), but instead have more complex properties best describable in quantum-mechanical terms. But then there is no challenge to scrutability, as the putative macrophysical truths will not be truths at all, and the residual truths will plausibly be scrutable.

Even a spatial primitivist might allow that if we discover that a collapse or Everett interpretation is true, we could come to use spatial vocabulary in a less strict way. We might say for ordinary purposes that an object has a certain location when enough of its amplitude is concentrated there, for example. This would parallel a color primitivist's attitude to our discourse on discovering that objects do not really have primitive colors. Spatial expressions in the new vocabulary might in effect work much as spatial functionalists hold that our existing spatial expressions work, and any spatial truths in the new vocabulary will remain scrutable. But there is not much reason to think that claims in the vocabulary of spatial primitivism, used without conceptual change, will be true in such a situation. (The discussion of solidity and semantic conservatism in the ninth excursus has some relevant observations.)

We can sum up the situation in quantum mechanics by saying that the following four theses are difficult to reconcile: (i) wavefunction fundamentalism, (ii) spatial primitivism, (iii) spatial realism, and (iv) a scrutability thesis holding that all spatial truths are scrutable from fundamental physical truths (perhaps conjoined with *Q*, *T*, and *I*). There will be a problem for scrutability only on a view that combines (i), (ii), and (iii). This view is analogous to the view of color discussed in the previous section that combines color primitivism, color realism, and an underlying physicalism. I think both views involve an uncomfortable combination of claims and should be rejected. I reject (ii), and I think that if one accepts (ii) one should reject (i) or (iii).[21] If a view combining (i)–(iii) is accepted, however, then we need only expand the scrutability base either to include certain

---

[21] Theorists such as Allori et al. (2008) and Maudlin (2007) reject (i), suggesting that to accommodate spatial truths, the wavefunction needs to be supplemented with a 'primitive ontology' of objects in three-dimensional space. This view appears to be motivated by versions of (ii), (iii), and (iv). My view is that the combination of spatial primitivism and spatial realism cannot be taken as a datum any more than can the combination of color primitivism and color realism. But it is interesting to note that these theorists and many other philosophers working on the foundations of quantum mechanics seem to take a version of scrutability as a constraint on correct theories.

claims about macroscopic location, or perhaps better, to include general principles linking quantum-mechanical properties to spatial properties of macroscopic
properties. This will require a more liberal version of P that goes beyond fundamental physical truths, but the vocabulary need not go beyond that of
microphysical properties along with space, time, and mass.

16 Counterfactual truths

$PQTI$ contains true counterfactuals in a microphysical, macrophysical, and phenomenal vocabulary. Still, it is attractive to hold that one can dispense with
counterfactuals, on the grounds that they are scrutable from truths about laws of
nature. This result along with that of the previous section would allow us to strip
down $PQTI$ to its cousin $PQTI-$, which dispenses with macrophysical and counterfactual truths.

To start with, one can make a plausible case that macrophysical counterfactuals are scrutable from microphysical counterfactuals. Here one can use the reasoning in the last section to make the case that the antecedents and consequents
of these counterfactuals are scrutable from specifications of this world and others
using a stripped-down vocabulary that does not use macrophysical notions. One
can then reason as in chapter 3 (on the objection from counterfactuals) to make
the case that the truth-value of these counterfactuals will be derivable from the
truth-value of counterfactuals in the stripped-down language. The same goes for
any counterfactuals connecting the macrophysical with phenomenology.

What about microphysical counterfactuals? It is natural to hold that these are
scrutable from microphysical laws and that the latter are scrutable from psychophysical laws connecting microphysics to phenomenology. When a microphysical counterfactual has a maximally specific antecedent, true in exactly one
nomologically possible world, then one need only apply the laws to the antecedent to determine the status of the consequent. When the antecedent is true in
more than one nomologically possible world, we can still apply the laws to each
world to determine the status of the consequent in that world. Then reasoning
about similarity between the relevant worlds and our own, as in section 9 of
chapter 3, will render the original counterfactual scrutable.

Likewise, counterfactuals connecting microphysics and phenomenology will
be derivable from psychophysical laws. We can assume, as is plausible, that phenomenal truths supervene at least nomologically on microphysical truths. Then
there will be many nomologically necessary conditionals from microphysical
sentences to phenomenal sentences. Assuming that there is some systematicity
to these conditionals, there will be a smaller class of nomologically necessary
psychophysical conditionals from which all of these conditionals follow. On a

dualist view, all the conditionals will follow from fundamental psychophysical laws that have a status similar to fundamental laws of physics. On a materialist view, these conditionals will have a different status, but they remain nomologically necessary (even if they are also metaphysically necessary), and for present purposes we can count them as laws. Then as long as these laws (in a version saying that they are nomologically necessary) are incorporated into *PQTI*–, reasoning of the sort in the previous paragraph suggests that all psychophysical counterfactuals are scrutable from here.

17 Conclusion

We have seen that there is a reasonable case that all truths are scrutable from *PQTI* and from its stripped-down cousin *PQTI*–. In almost all of the hard cases, there are independently attractive reasons for embracing a view on which scrutability holds.

In a couple of cases, there is a relatively strong case for expansion even on my own views. These include the domain of ontology, where there is a case for including any further truths about fundamental natural ontology (such as truths about quiddities, perhaps), and the domain of indexical truths, where there are good reasons to include certain truths involving phenomenal demonstratives. But these expansions are quite compatible with the spirit of the scrutability thesis.

Other significant challenges come from mathematical truths, ontological truths, intentional truths, truths involving vague expressions, and truths about secondary qualities. Handling the mathematical case requires a heavy idealization. In the other cases, there are important philosophical views on which expansion of the base is required. I reject these views, and I think that in each case the rejection can be independently motivated. Still, the views are worth noting.

For most of the hard cases, even if we take an expansionist line, the compact scrutability thesis will not be threatened. Adding mathematical, normative truths, ontological truths, secondary-quality truths, and macrophysical truths will leave the base compact: in fact, in only some of these cases will any new vocabulary be required. Adding intentional truths raises tricky issues because of the threat of trivializing mechanisms, but we have seen that even if these truths are added, the threat can be avoided.

The most significant threat to the compact scrutability thesis in this chapter arises from the epistemic view of vagueness. If an appropriate version of it is true, there might be failures of scrutability for arbitrary expressions. Still, rejecting the epistemic view of vagueness cannot be counted as an implausible move. Some might add further challenges that threaten large classes of expressions, perhaps arising from names, or from expressions used deferentially, or from expressions expressing recognitional concepts. In each of these cases, however, we have seen that the threat can be naturally answered. I conclude that the compact scrutability thesis remains extremely plausible.

What of stronger scrutability theses such as Fundamental Scrutability, holding that all truths are scrutable from metaphysically fundamental truths and primitive indexical truths? The first two expansions above leave this thesis intact, as these expansions concern fundamental truths and primitive indexical truths respectively. If one were to make any of the later expansions, one might have to reject the thesis, at least if one does not take the relevant normative, ontological, or intentional truths (and so on) to be metaphysically fundamental. And there remains a question about whether the base must include phenomenal truths and whether these are metaphysically fundamental. Nevertheless, I think that where the cases we have considered so far are concerned, Fundamental Scrutability remains attractive and plausible. I return to this matter in chapter 8.

What of a stronger A Priori Scrutability thesis that invokes the conclusive a priori, in effect requiring that all truths be a priori scrutable from base truths with certainty? In the discussion in this chapter I have mainly considered ordinary a priori scrutability, not the conclusive variety. Still, in many of the hard cases, the arguments for scrutability can straightforwardly be extended to arguments for conclusive scrutability. One might worry about arguments from knowability to scrutability in the analysis of normative and ontological truths. Even if it is plausible that we can know these truths, it might be denied that we can know them with certainty (even given base facts and insulated ideal reasoning), in which case the arguments in question cannot easily be extended into arguments for conclusive scrutability. I think that there are good grounds for holding that certainty is possible in these domains (given base facts and insulated ideal reasoning), at least to the extent that there are truths in these domains at all. But making this case requires more than I have argued above. In any case, if we allow a somewhat expanded base including normative truths, ontological truths, and the like, the conclusive scrutability thesis will remain plausible.

Scrutability and the Unity of Science

The unity of science was one of the central concerns of the Vienna Circle. Otto Neurath edited the huge, never-completed *Encyclopedia of Unified Science* (see especially Neurath, Carnap, and Morris 1971). In his 1932 article 'The Physical Language as the Universal Language of Science' (translated into English as the 1934 book *The Unity of Science*), Carnap wrote:

> The opinion is generally accepted that the various sciences named [philosophy, formal sciences, natural sciences, social sciences] are fundamentally distinct in respect of subject matter, sources of knowledge, and technique. Opposed to this opinion is the thesis defended in this paper that science is a unity, that all empirical statements can be expressed in a single language, all states of affairs are of one kind and are known by the same method.

There is no single thesis of the unity of science. An *imperialist* unity thesis (embraced explicitly at the end of Carnap's article) holds that all sciences are part of a single science such as physics. A *reductive* unity thesis holds that all correct scientific theories in different domains are somehow reducible to or grounded in a single theory, such as a fundamental physical theory. A *connective* thesis holds that correct scientific theories in different domains have mutually supporting connections between them. A *similarity* thesis holds that correct scientific theories in different domains have some similarity in methods or form. A *consistency* thesis holds only that correct scientific theories should be consistent with each other.

The logical empiricists are often associated with imperialist or reductive versions of the unity of science thesis, although connective and similarity theses are also prominent in their writings.[1] In recent years, the trend among philosophers of science has been to reject strong unity of science theses in favor of weaker theses such as connective theses, or to argue that science is not unified at all. It

---

[1] For analyses of the logical empiricists on the unity of science, see John Symons et al., *Otto Neurath and the Unity of Science*. For recent work favoring the disunity of science, see John Dupré's *The Disorder of Things*, Nancy Cartwright's *The Dappled World*, and Galison and Stump's collection *The Disunity of Science*.

is widely accepted that attention to the scientific practice reveals far more diversity between the sciences than unity.

Scrutability has at least some bearing on the unity of science. The thesis that all truths are scrutable from base truths naturally suggests that all scientific truths are grounded in certain base truths. And the scrutability theses discussed here give a central role in the base to microphysical truths. So this might suggest a commitment to a strong, reductive version of the unity of science thesis. This could be read as a point in favor of the scrutability framework: it reveals a sense in which science is unified. Alternatively, it could be read as an objection to the framework: it is committed to a reductive thesis that the philosophy of science has revealed to be implausible.

The issues here are subtle, but it is worth exploring just what sort of unity thesis might follow from the scrutability thesis. For ease of discussion, I will start by assuming Microphysical Scrutability: the thesis that all truths are scrutable from the microphysical truths P. I will later consider how things are affected by a change to scrutability from $PQTI$. I will discuss both the constructive point (whether scrutability yields some form of unity) and the defensive point (whether objections to unity yield good objections to scrutability).

I will concentrate mainly on reductive unity theses. For any relation of reduction between theories, there is a corresponding unity thesis, holding that there is a single scientific theory to which all theories are reducible. But many notions of reduction and so of unity can be distinguished. One dimension of variation concerns which aspects of theories we are concerned with: their languages, their laws, their methods, their explanations, their true sentences? Another dimension concerns the character of the reduction relation: it might be logical (e.g., entailment), metaphysical (e.g., identity), epistemological (e.g., evidential grounding), or semantic (e.g., meaning equivalence). A further dimension concerns the structure of the reduction relation: it might be conditional (yielding one-way conditionals from the reducing theory to the reduced theory) or biconditional (yielding two-way conditionals from one theory to the other).

The Microphysical Scrutability thesis can be seen as a unity thesis involving epistemological conditional relations among truths: the truths in the languages of all correct theories are epistemologically deducible from the truths of fundamental physics. This thesis has a strong reductive flavor. But it does not entail the traditional unity theses that are now widely rejected.

One aspect of the classical conception of reduction is definitional reduction. Definitional reduction concerns semantic biconditional relations among language: the key claim is that the expressions of the reduced theory can be defined in terms of the expressions in the reducing theory. The corresponding classical unity thesis, found explicitly in Carnap's work on unity, is a definitional unity thesis: the expressions of all correct theories are definable in terms of those of a single theory (such as physics).

The scrutability thesis does not entail the definitional unity thesis for a familiar reason: scrutability does not require definitions. A definitional reduction from economics to physics would require that economic expressions be definable using microphysical expressions, which in turn requires biconditionals connecting economics and physics. By contrast, scrutability requires only one-way conditionals from physical truths to economic truths.

This allows the scrutability thesis to escape perhaps the most well-known objection to classical unity theses: the objection from multiple realizability (e.g. Fodor 1974). On the face of it, economics could be realized in physics or in ectoplasm. Definitional reduction of economics to physics appears to rule out the possibility that economics is realized by anything other than physics. Furthermore, even in a physical world, different instances of an economic kind such as money might be grounded in a heterogeneous and open-ended class of physical realizations, suggesting that any physical definition would be wildly disjunctive. By contrast, the scrutability of economic truths from microphysical truths is quite consistent with the multiple realizability of economic kinds. In fact, the scrutability thesis can allow that in other scenarios, economic truths are scrutable from ectoplasmic truths.[2]

Another aspect of the classical conception of reduction is deductive-nomological reduction, often called Nagelian reduction after Ernest Nagel (1961). Nagelian reduction concerns logical conditional relations among laws. The key claim is that the laws of the reduced theory are entailed by the laws of the reducing theory, perhaps along with bridge laws. We might call the corresponding classical unity thesis a Nagelian unity thesis: the laws of all correct theories are entailed by the laws of a single theory such as physics, along with bridge laws.

The scrutability thesis does not entail the Nagelian unity thesis for a couple of reasons. First, the scrutability relation is weaker than logical entailment. Second, Microphysical Scrutability does not say that all truths are scrutable from microphysical *laws*: it says that they are scrutable from microphysical *truths*, including the distribution of microphysical items throughout space and time as well as microphysical laws. It follows that any true laws in chemistry, economics, and so on are scrutable from microphysical truths, but not that they are scrutable from microphysical laws.

---

[2] When generalized scrutability of B-truths from A-truths obtains, there will be at least approximate definitions of B-expressions using A-expressions. One might think that this is enough for multiple realizability to cause problems. In the case of economics and physics, however, we have scrutability but not generalized scrutability, precisely because there are scenarios in which economics is not grounded in physics. Scrutability alone does not support even approximate definitions of economic expressions in physical terms, at least if definitions are required to be a priori.

This allows the scrutability thesis to escape another objection to classical unity theses: the objection from contingency. On the face of it, there is contingency in biology or sociology that goes beyond the contingency of physics. The principles of neuroscience could easily have been different, even keeping physics fixed. Certain key constants of social network theory appear quite arbitrary. So these principles do not seem to be derivable from the laws of physics alone. To handle this problem, a Nagelian reductionist needs to allow initial conditions and not just laws in the reduction base. There is no analogous problem for the scrutability thesis, which has microphysical truths in the reduction base. The microphysical truths underlying brains and societies will themselves be contingent and arbitrary: even holding physical laws constant, they could have been different. And it is plausible that this contingency matches up well with the contingency of neurobiology and sociology. So for all this objection says, it remains plausible that neurobiological and sociological principles will be scrutable from all the microphysical truths in the vicinity of brains and societies.

Still, the scrutability thesis shares something of the spirit of the Nagelian unity thesis. A priori entailment has something of the spirit of logical entailment: both might be seen as a sort of deducibility. Microphysical truths go beyond microphysical laws, but only so far. If physics is deterministic, microphysical truths are themselves entailed by and scrutable from microphysical laws along with microphysical boundary conditions (the state of the universe at the Big Bang, perhaps). And even if physics is nondeterministic, microphysical truths will be scrutable from these things along with the values of probabilistic variables. So microphysical scrutability might be seen as sharing some of the attractions of this classical unity thesis, without some of its costs.

In one respect, the scrutability thesis is stronger than the Nagelian unity thesis. The classical thesis allows bridging laws in the entailment base: chemical truths are entailed by physical truths plus physical–chemical bridging laws. Scrutability does not allow bridging laws in the base: chemical truths are a priori entailed by microphysical truths. Where logical entailment is concerned, bridging laws play the helpful role of connecting vocabularies. Where a priori entailment is concerned, this role is not needed: truths in one vocabulary can be a priori entailed by truths in a quite different vocabulary. One might think of the framework as akin to one that requires the bridging laws to be a priori, except that as we saw in chapter 1, a priori entailment does not require explicit bridging laws or definitions at all.

This difference is a benefit rather than a cost of scrutability. As Jaegwon Kim (1999) has pointed out, allowing bridging laws makes the Nagelian conception of reduction much too weak. To see this, note that many mind–body dualists (including myself) allow that there are laws connecting physical properties to mental properties, so that mental truths will be logically entailed by physical truths plus psychophysical bridging laws. The Nagelian model appears to predict that on this view, the mental is reducible to the physical. But such a claim obviously mischaracterizes the dualist view. The underlying trouble is that there can be laws connecting entirely distinct domains, each of which is irreducible to the other. So for a connection that deserves to count as reducibility, mere bridging laws do not suffice.

Scrutability invokes the much stronger requirement of a priori entailment, which brings with it a sort of epistemological deducibility of higher-level truths from lower-level truths. It is arguable that something like this is required to satisfy one key desideratum of reducibility: that any epistemologically brute facts in the higher-level domain be grounded in epistemologically brute facts in the lower-level domain. Allowing bridging laws subverts this desideratum. Bridging laws can themselves introduce brute facts, as the case of mind–body dualism suggests. By contrast, scrutability favors the desideratum, at least if we allow that a priori truths are never brute.

There are many different notions of reduction, and there is no point getting into a verbal dispute over what counts as 'reduction'. But the desideratum outlined above corresponds to at least one key notion of reduction, or one key constraint on such a notion. We might call it *transparent bottom-up explanation*: once one has spelled out the lower-level facts, the higher-level facts are rendered transparent. That is, there is no residual mystery about what the high-level facts are or about how the low-level facts give rise to them.[3] This sort of explanation is a goal of many reductive projects in science. A reductive project in chemistry can reasonably aim to ensure that once one has spelled out all the physical facts about an organism, the chemical facts are rendered transparent. If this project succeeds, we may not have explained why all the physical facts obtain, but given that they obtain there will be no residual mystery about why and how they give rise to the chemical facts.

Where scrutability fails, transparent bottom-up explanation fails. This is borne out by the mind–body case. Even after spelling out all the physical facts, the mental facts are not transparent, so there is a residual mystery about how the physical gives rise to the mental. The same applies to options that are intermediate between a priori scrutability and bridging laws. For example, one could appeal to a posteriori identities or a posteriori necessities connecting low-level and high-level domains. But even these leave an element of bruteness in an explanation. If one 'explains' consciousness by saying that it is identical to a certain neural state and leaves it at that, then one has not given a transparent bottom-up explanation. In effect, the identity claim plays the same sort of explanatory function as a bridging law in the case of mind–body dualism. When scrutability fails, there will be a priori coherent scenarios in which the low-level facts are as they are and the higher-level facts are different. These scenarios cannot

---

[3] This intuitive sense of 'transparent' should be distinguished from the technical sense in E14.

be ruled out by the low-level facts alone, so the low-level facts do not transparently explain the higher-level facts. Instead, one needs primitive interlevel bridging principles in one's explanatory theory.

Many cases of reduction involve interlevel identities: the reduction of water to H_2O is one such. But in this case, the identity claim 'water is H_2O' is itself scrutable from lower-level truths.[4] In this sort of case, the high-level truths are scrutable from lower-level truths and are transparently explainable in terms of them. But when the identity claim is not scrutable in this way (as in the consciousness case), it effectively functions as a primitive claim in a bottom-up explanation, playing the same epistemological role as a brute bridging law. To remove this element of bruteness and achieve transparency, something stronger is required. Scrutability can naturally play that role.

It might be argued that scrutability is too weak for transparent bottom-up explanation, on the grounds that a priori entailment can connect distinct domains. For example, if mathematical truths are a priori, then they are priori scrutable from physical truths (or by any other class of truths), but they need not be reducible to physical truths in any reasonable sense. Likewise, two sets of truths can be a priori scrutable from each other, but it seems odd to hold that they can be reducible to each other. I think this is a reasonable criticism, and suggests that scrutability needs to be strengthened to yield the relevant sort of reduction. Here one might strengthen the requirement by moving from a priori entailment to the stronger sort of in-virtue-of claims discussed in chapter 1 and the sixteenth excursus (especially the conceptual grounding relation discussed there), or by moving to more specific models of scrutability-based explanations such as the mechanistic model that follows. In any case, scrutability will still plausibly be a necessary condition for a relevant sort of reduction.

Scrutability is also a weak constraint insofar as good reductive explanations require the low-level phenomena doing the explaining to have a certain internal unity. Scrutability could be satisfied even if microphysical truths were entirely chaotic, non-law-governed, and disunified; but in that case microphysical truths at best explain macrophysical truths in a weak sense. In the actual world, microphysical truths have a certain internal simplicity and autonomy that makes for better explanations than this, but the degree of simplicity will vary from case to case: a reductive explanation of the Second World War might be a poor one,

---

[4] Frank Jackson (1998) gives a nice model of the water/H_2O case, arguing that 'Water is H_2O' can be derived from microphysical facts using the a priori premise 'Water is what plays the water role' and the empirical premise 'H_2O plays the water role', which is itself derivable from microphysical facts. This in effect invokes a definition of 'water' (although a functional rather than a microphysical definition) to ground the derivation. As always, the scrutability framework can dispense with the definition, but 'water is H_2O' will nevertheless be scrutable insofar as it is scrutable that H_2O plays the key roles associated with water.

precisely because of the complexity of the microphysical base. Still, even when the base is arbitrarily complex, scrutability allows a sort of transparent bottom-up explanation: *given* the low-level truths, high-level truths fall out. Good reductive explanation requires something more, but scrutability will again be a necessary condition.

A model of reduction that is quite compatible with scrutability while imposing further constraints is one grounded in *mechanistic explanation*.[5] On this model, high-level phenomena are explained in terms of the orchestrated functioning of a mechanism: a structure performing a function in virtue of its components parts, component operations, and their organization (Bechtel and Abrahamsen 2005). For example, DNA and RNA molecules might serve as a mechanism by which the transmission of hereditary characteristics is enabled, thereby explaining genetic phenomena. Mechanistic explanation typically proceeds via functional analysis of high-level phenomena, casting high-level explananda in terms of functional roles. For example, the genetic phenomena that need to be explained are the functional roles of transmitting hereditary information. One then shows how lower-level mechanisms can play those roles and how DNA can transmit hereditary information. In this way, one achieves transparent bottom-up explanation.

Employing the scrutability model, we can divide this picture into three parts. First, high-level explananda are expressed using functional concepts, or concepts involving functional roles. For example, the concept of a gene can be seen as a concept of an entity that transmits hereditary characteristics in a certain way. Second, one tells a story about how low-level mechanisms play the relevant roles: about how DNA transmits hereditary characteristics, for example. Third, given that the roles in the mechanistic story and the functional analysis match up well enough, high-level truths will be scrutable from the mechanistic story. In effect, functional analysis grounds scrutability from underlying mechanisms.

I do not say that reductive or mechanistic explanation in science requires scientists to demonstrate an a priori entailment from low-level truths to high-level truths. That claim would be much too strong. Still, I think there is an important sort of reductive explanation in science for which scrutability is at least a tacit constraint. That is, it is a tacit desideratum that in principle, a given reductive story could be fleshed out with further lower-level truths, such that higher-level phenomena would be scrutable from there. If it turned out that such scrutability were impossible in principle, then the reductive explanation

---

[5] For my own version of a mechanistic picture of reductive explanation, see section 2 of 'Facing Up to the Problem of Consciousness'. The scrutability model is also compatible with other sorts of reductive explanation, including structural as well as functional explanation, but functional explanation by mechanisms is certainly the most common kind.

could reasonably be regarded as defective, or as failing to satisfy an important desideratum of transparency. In practice, reductive explanations typically proceed by giving just enough detail to make it plausible that a fleshed-out story of this sort could be obtained.

Some will think that scrutability is too strong a constraint on the grounds that the connections between physics and biology, say, are empirical rather than a priori. I have already answered this objection in arguing for scrutability. But it is worth keeping in mind again that scrutability does not require definition of biological notions in microphysical terms, and allows us to appeal to all microphysical truths and not just microphysical laws. And as before, even though bridging principles such as 'water is H_2O' are empirical, this is no bar to the a priori scrutability of the principles themselves from low-level truths.[6] For example, it remains plausible that someone using a Cosmoscope armed with all microphysical truths (along with phenomenal and indexical truths) could ascertain all the 'water' truths and all bridging principles connecting water and H_2O. There are tricky cases here, such as the interface between the quantum and classical domains, but these cases can be handled as in the discussion of macrophysical truths above.

Some may worry that other standard worries for Nagelian accounts of reduction will apply to scrutability. We have seen that standard problems tied to definability, to multiple realizability, and to bridge laws will not arise. Nor will problems tied to logic: some versions of a Nagelian account require that all theories be formulated in first-order logic, but scrutability does not. Another problem for Nagelian reduction concerns the 'reduction' of an old theory to a new one: the old theory contains falsehoods, which cannot be entailed by truths. The falsehoods in the old theory will not be scrutable from truths either, but various nearby truths will be, including claims that those falsehoods are approximately true, or true in certain circumstances.

Another worry concerns the autonomy of the high-level sciences. Cellular biology, cognitive psychology, economics, and paleontology are all enormously different from physics and from one another. It would be crazy to do cognitive psychology by doing physics. These fields have their own methods and their own conceptual and ontological frameworks. Perhaps most importantly, they all have a sort of explanatory autonomy: economic explanations are different in kind from microphysical explanations, and cannot begin to be replaced by microphysical explanations.

[6] Marras (2005) argues against models of reduction in terms of a priori entailment by arguing that bridge laws are empirical and known inductively. I hope it is clear by now that this argument involves a non sequitur.

Scrutability is quite consistent with explanatory autonomy. If an economic truth (say, about the financial crisis in 2008) is scrutable from physical truths, then a weak sort of explanation of the economic truths in terms of physical truths will be possible. Given that the physical truths are as they are, we will be able to derive the existence of the financial crisis and so reductively 'explain' it. But for most purposes this will be a much poorer explanation than an economic explanation (in terms of credit mechanisms, for example). The 'explanation' will presuppose an enormously complex set of physical truths. Even if these truths are grounded in laws and boundary conditions, the boundary conditions and perhaps the laws will involve much irrelevant complexity. This 'explanation' may have little predictive power and little practical use. By contrast, an economic explanation may be far simpler, more systematic, more predictive, and more useful.

In general, I favor explanatory pluralism: there are multiple explanations of most phenomena, and which explanation we choose depends on our purposes. There are causal explanations, historical explanations, reductive explanations, and many others. Reductive explanations are useful for some purposes, espe- cially in trying to get a sense of how the world as a whole hangs together (how could there be economic phenomena in a physical world?). These explanations help to give us a unified picture of the world. But for most purposes, they cannot take the place of other explanations.

Overall, we can see scrutability as a weak sort of reduction, one that is com- patible with various sorts of irreducibility that are manifest in science. One might label it (as I do in *The Conscious Mind*) a sort of reductive explanation without reduction, where the relevant variety of reductive explanation involves transparent bottom-up explanation in terms of underlying truths. At least there is plausibly a notion of reductive explanation here, for which scrutability is a necessary condition.[7]

Correspondingly, the scrutability thesis can be seen as a weak sort of unity thesis that is consistent with the various ways in which science is disunified. It avoids the most prominent objections to classical unity theses, but at the same time shares something of their spirit, and it can do at least some of the work that we might want a reductive unity thesis to do.

Of course microphysical scrutability is false, at least on my view. I think that phenomenal truths, indexical truths, and a that's-all truth are not scrutable from microphysical truths. Correspondingly, I think that these are not explainable in terms of physical truths. But we can add these to the scrutability base, yielding

---

[7] For more on the relationship between a priori entailment and reductive explanation, see chap- ter 2 (sections 2 and 3) of *The Conscious Mind*, and section 6 of 'Conceptual Analysis and Reduc- tive Explanation'.

the thesis that all truths are scrutable from *PQTI*. How does this alter the foregoing?

If phenomenal truths are not scrutable from the microphysical, this brings out a certain disunity of the sciences. If we equate scrutability with reductive explanation, then phenomenal truths will not be reductively explainable in terms of microphysical truths. Nor will truths whose scrutability requires phenomenal truths: perhaps mental truths, social truths, secondary-quality truths, and others. These truths will be explainable in terms of physics and phenomenology, but not in terms of physics alone. Something similar goes for truths whose scrutability requires indexicals. For example, objective physical truths may leave open whether water is H_2O or XYZ, so that a fully transparent explanation of the truth that water is H_2O requires an appeal to indexical claims about our location within the world. Likewise for the that's-all truth: positive truths can be reductively explained in terms of microphysical truths alone, but a full explanation of negative truths requires something more.

Despite this expansion, certain stripped-down analogs of many of these truths will be reductively explainable. As John Searle (1992) has noted, physics can explain the 'objective' aspects of heat and color, if not the 'subjective' aspects. Here we might think of a subjective truth (in the relevant sense) as one with a relevant dependence on phenomenal or indexical truths, and objective truths as those without such a dependence. One might define an objectivized notion of 'heat' solely in terms of an objective causal role (perhaps in terms of expanding metals and the like), leaving out any connection to experience. Then objective truths involving this notion might be reductively explainable in terms of microphysical truths. The same goes for an objectivized notion of 'water', which will apply equally to H_2O and XYZ. Given that all truths are scrutable from *PQTI* and that scrutability entails reductive explainability, it follows that all positive objective truths will be explainable in terms of microphysical truths, and that all objective truths will be explainable in terms of microphysical truths and a that's-all clause. Here the objective truths might be seen as one version of Sellars' 'scientific image' (where subjective truths are part of the 'manifest image'). We will then have a strong unity of the scientific image so conceived.

Still, the scientific image so conceived may be a pale reflection of actual science. Consciousness, mentality, sociology, secondary qualities, and other subjective aspects of the manifest image are all subject matters for science. A unity thesis that covers all of these will need to have more than microphysics in the base: it will need phenomenal and indexical truths too. The role of indexical truths is relatively minor. The most important addition will be certain psychophysical bridging principles: laws, identities, or necessities linking physical properties to phenomenal properties. As long as phenomenal properties supervene on physical properties, this addition will bring phenomenal truths into the fold.

We might put this picture by saying that all scientific truths are grounded in physics and psychophysics. The dual base here is less unified than a purely microphysical base, but it still allows a good deal of unification. We retain a unified scientific picture of the world grounded in a few fundamental properties linked by a few fundamental laws, albeit with more properties and laws than on the physicalist picture. This reinforces the moral of the prior discussion: while various strong unity theses fail, the scrutability framework supports at least a moderate and attenuated conception of the unity of science.

7

Minimizing the Base

1 Introduction

So far, I have argued for scrutability from *PQTI* and from its stripped-down cousin *PQTI–*, where the latter is construed to include microphysical and phenomenal truths, laws involving these, a totality claim, and indexical truths. But if this is a scrutability base, it is almost certainly not a minimal scrutability base. Microphysical truths may well be scrutable from truths characterizing a network of entities in causal or nomic terms, grounded in connections to observable and ultimately phenomenal properties. On some views, truths about laws of nature will be scrutable from underlying truths. Or in reverse, most physical and phenomenal truths may be scrutable from truths about boundary conditions and laws of nature.

In this chapter, I ask how far the scrutability base can be shrunk, aiming to come up with a plausible candidate for a minimal scrutability base. I begin (section 2) by discussing some heuristics that help in determining when the base can be shrunk. In section 3 I argue that many microphysical expressions can be eliminated by the method of Ramsification. In sections 4 and 5 I argue that observational terms involving color, mass, space, and time can also be eliminated. In sections 6 and 7 I discuss nomic and phenomenal expressions, suggesting that some of these must stay in the base. After discussing further compression using laws and boundary conditions (section 8), the tricky case of quiddities (section 9), and miscellaneous expressions (section 10), I bring together all these considerations (section 11) to outline candidates for a truly minimal scrutability base.

As in the last chapter, every topic here could be discussed at much greater length. Even if one accepts the general framework of scrutability, one's verdict about specific cases will depend on one's substantive philosophical views on the corresponding issues. As well as exploring the sort of scrutability bases that my own views favor, I will try to give a sense of the most reasonable overall bases given other views on these issues. The bases arrived at by this issue-by-issue approach will then serve as input to the discussion of principled scrutability bases in chapter 8.

2 Heuristics

We have already seen a number of heuristics that can help in narrowing a scrutability base. Two heuristics used repeatedly in previous chapters, are the *knowledge* heuristic and the *conditional knowledge* heuristic, which correspond to inferential and conditional scrutability respectively. The first heuristic asks: if speakers knew enough S-truths, would they be in a position to know all the T-truths? The second heuristic asks: are speakers in a position to know that *if* certain S-truths obtain, the T-truths obtain. If the answer to these questions is yes, that is the beginning of a case for a priori scrutability of T-truths from S-truths. For reasons we have discussed, satisfying these heuristics is neither necessary nor sufficient for a priori scrutability, but satisfying them will often provide reason to take a priori scrutability seriously. Correspondingly, failing to satisfy them will often provide reason to reject a priori scrutability. When the heuristics are satisfied and certain other conditions obtain (for example, if the conditional knowledge heuristic remains satisfied under suspension of judgment), we have all the more reason to endorse a priori scrutability.

One can apply these heuristics positively, as when one argues from the claim that someone who knows all relevant nonmoral truths will be in a position to know all moral truths to the conclusion that moral truths are a priori scrutable from nonmoral truths. Or one can apply it negatively, as when one argues from the claim that someone (Jackson's Mary in the black-and-white room, say) could know all the physical truths without being in a position to know all the truths about consciousness (even given ideal reasoning) to the conclusion that truths about consciousness are not a priori scrutable from physical truths.

A third heuristic is that of *conceivability*. Let us say that S is conceivable when S cannot be ruled out a priori (that is, when the negation of the thought that S expresses is not a priori). The third heuristic asks: is the conjunction of the S-truths with the negation of a T-truth conceivable? To put it informally: is it conceivable that the S-truths obtain while the T-truths fail to obtain? If so, T-truths are not a priori scrutable from S-truths. If not, T-truths are a priori scrutable from S-truths. This heuristic in effect invokes a notion of idealized conceivability. But one can also give a role to prima facie conceivability, where S is prima facie conceivable if one can imagine the actual world turning out such that S is true. Prima facie conceivability is itself a reasonably good heuristic guide to ideal conceivability, and so is a reasonably good heuristic guide to a priori scrutability.

I will often deploy a useful variant of the conceivability heuristic, using the notion of a *coherent skeptical hypothesis*. When *S*-truths are certain background truths and *T* is something we take ourselves to know, we can think of the hypothesis that the *S*-truths obtain and that *T* fails to obtain as a skeptical hypothesis with respect to *T*. If this hypothesis is conceivable in the sense above, we can call it a coherent skeptical hypothesis. If such a hypothesis is coherent, then *T*-truths are not a priori scrutable from *S*-truths. If such a hypothesis is not coherent, then *T*-truths are a priori scrutable from *S*-truths. Of course our prima facie judgments about coherence of skeptical hypotheses are not perfect, but they can serve as at least a prima facie guide to scrutability.[1]

For example, Descartes' evil genius hypothesis can be seen as a skeptical hypothesis according to which all the experiential truths obtain, but in which positive truths about my body fail to obtain. Many hold that this hypothesis is coherent: if they are right, these positive truths about my body are not a priori scrutable from experiential truths. Likewise, one can think of the zombie hypothesis, according to which all the microphysical truths obtain but in which some positive truths about consciousness fail to obtain, as a skeptical hypothesis about other minds. If this skeptical hypothesis is coherent, as many think, then truths about consciousness are not a priori scrutable from microphysical truths. On the other hand, it is far less clear that there are coherent skeptical hypotheses according to which all the nonmoral truths obtain and the moral truths fail to obtain, or according to which microphysical truths obtain and macrophysical truths fail to obtain. If there are not, then corresponding a priori scrutability claims are true.

The conceivability and coherence heuristics can be seen as a guide to conclusive a priori scrutability. It is arguable that our ordinary notions of conceivability and coherence are tied to conclusive apriority, or a priori certainty. For example, on some views certain skeptical scenarios can be ruled out by nonconclusive a priori reasoning, but cannot be ruled out with a priori certainty. On such a view, the scenario will be naturally counted as conceivable and as a coherent skeptical scenario. I will understand the notions of conceivability and coherence this way in what follows, and so will use these heuristics as a guide to conclusive a priori scrutability. Something similar goes for the analyzability heuristic that follows. By contrast, the knowledge and conditional knowledge heuristics work in the first instances as guides to nonconclusive a priori scrutability, although one can

---

[1] Note that for these purposes we need make no claims about whether conceivability entails possibility and we need make no claims about whether coherent skeptical hypotheses undermine knowledge. It is plausible that at least some skeptical hypotheses, such as 'I am not conscious', can be conclusively ruled out for reasons other than incoherence.

also deploy analog 'certainty' and 'conditional certainty' heuristics as a guide to conclusive a priori scrutability.

A fourth heuristic is that of *approximate definability*. Here the idea is that when one expression is approximately definable in terms of others, this is prima facie evidence that the former is a priori scrutable from the latter. If Definitional Scrutability were true, one could use definability as a guide, but even if it is false, we often find a situation in which there are approximate definitions. If definability requires only that an expression and its definition are a priori equivalent, then approximate definability requires that an expression and its analysis are approximately a priori equivalent: that is, that there are relatively few counterexamples to this equivalence, in some intuitive measure. To improve the heuristic, one might also require that there is a series of refinements of the approximation (approximate definitions of increasing length using the same base vocabulary) with increasing coverage, such that every conceivable counterexample is removed by some refinement in the (perhaps infinite) series. Approximate definability in this sense is a good guide to a priori scrutability.

We cannot expect these four heuristics alone to lead us to a privileged minimal scrutability base. We know that scrutability can be symmetrical: that is, the truths in a set A can be scrutable from those in a set B and vice versa. (For a simple case, we can let A be the set of microphysical truths, and B be a minimal set of conjunctions of microphysical truths.) The heuristics above can also be symmetrical in some cases. For some A and B, knowing A-truths might yield knowledge of B-truths and vice versa, and both A-truths without B-truths and B-truths without A-truths may be inconceivable. Correspondingly, we can expect many minimal scrutability bases, perhaps some more complex than others. If we want to be directed to especially interesting or especially small scrutability bases, we will need further constraints.

One relevant constraint is the suggestion canvased earlier that a scrutability base might involve only concepts that are in some sense primitive. To apply this constraint, we can use a *conceptual priority* constraint as a fifth heuristic: when A is conceptually prior to B, B truths should be scrutable from A truths along with other truths.

The role of conceptual priority is familiar on a definitional model. These models often require that the terms used in a definition (e.g., 'justified true belief') are conceptually prior to the defined term (e.g., 'knowledge'), in one of a variety of senses. One sense holds that a concept C_1 is more basic than another concept C_2 when C_1 is a constituent of C_2. This would be the case if the concept *knowledge* were identical to the complex concept *justified true belief*, which has the concepts of justification, truth, and belief as constituents. Another sense holds that C_1 is prior to C_2 iff possession of C_2 requires possession of C_1 but not vice versa. Another holds that a fully articulate understanding of C_2 will require the use of C_1 but not vice versa. Finally, if one embraces an inferential model of concepts (as I do), one can say that C_1 is prior to C_2 if the constitutive inferential role for C_2 involves C_1.

If the definitional model is wrong, an understanding of conceptual priority in terms of constituency will not be useful for our purposes. But the other models are still available. For example, it is arguable that fully understanding what it is to know something requires understanding what it is to believe something, but not vice versa. Likewise, fully understanding what it is to lie requires understanding what it is to assert and what it is to be true, but not vice versa. And it is arguable that the concepts of assertion and truth are part of the constitutive inferential role of the notion of lying, but not vice versa.

I will not try to settle exactly what conceptual priority comes to here. I am most attracted to a model in terms of inferential role, but I do not want to presuppose that model at this stage. Even without a full model, we often have clear intuitive judgments about conceptual priority. If a robust notion of conceptual priority is viable, it is natural to suggest that a scrutability base involves primitive concepts: concepts such that no other concepts are prior to them. One can then use conceptual priority as a constraint in determining a scrutability base. This heuristic can usefully be combined with the approximate definability heuristic by using conceptual priority as a constraint on the adequacy of approximate definitions.

A priori scrutability does not *require* conceptual priority. Mathematical truths and moral truths may be a priori scrutable from *PQTI*, but it does not follow that the concepts involved in *PQTI* are conceptually prior to mathematical or moral concepts, or even that the latter are approximately definable in terms of the former. Still, where conceptual priority is present, it often goes with approximate definability and with a priori scrutability. So I will use intuitions about conceptual priority at least as a clue to claims about scrutability. When C_1 appears to be prior to C_2, I will take this as a reason to favor C_2 over C_1 as a candidate for a scrutability base. This constraint will certainly help if we want to use a minimal scrutability base as a guide to primitive concepts.

A sixth heuristic concerns *Twin-Earthability*. This name is inspired by Hilary Putnam's Twin Earth thought-experiment. Here, Twin Earth is a planet just like ours except that the watery stuff in that world has a different chemical makeup: it is made of XYZ rather than H_2O. Putnam argues that where Oscar on Earth uses 'water' to pick out H_2O, his functional and phenomenal duplicate Twin Oscar on Twin Earth uses his counterpart term 'water' to pick out XYZ. The difference arises because Oscar's and Twin Oscar's terms are causally connected to different kinds in different environments.

To capture this phenomenon, let us say that two possible speakers are *twins* if they are functional and phenomenal duplicates of each other: that is, their cognitive systems have the same functional organization and are in the same functional states, and they have the same conscious experiences. This is not quite the more standard notion according to which twins are intrinsic duplicates. For a start, Oscar and Twin Oscar are not intrinsic physical duplicates, as their bodies and brains will contain H_2O and XYZ respectively; and later I will consider cases in which one twin is twice the size of another. What matters in practice is that one holds constant functional organization—the abstract pattern of causal transitions between states that generates behavior—and phenomenology.

We can then say that an expression E is Twin-Earthable if there can be a non-deferential utterance of E for which there is a possible corresponding utterance by a twin speaker with a different extension.[2] I will leave the notion of correspondence intuitive, but the idea is roughly that two utterances correspond when they are isomorphic output acts from the twin speakers under a mapping that preserves causal organization. So Oscar's and Twin Oscar's utterances of 'water' will correspond, for example.

Here extension is just reference in the case of kind terms and singular terms: the extension of 'water' (or an utterance thereof in my language) is water, and the extension of 'John' is John. For the purposes of this definition, one should conceive of the extensions of predicates and general terms as the associated property: the extension of 'hot' is the property of being hot (not the class of hot things), and the extension of 'tiger' is the property of being a tiger (not the class of tigers). One can then use Putnam-style cases to argue that expressions such as 'John', 'hot', and 'tiger' are also Twin-Earthable. On the other hand, there are other expressions for which one cannot generate Putnam-style cases: it is hard to see how one would generate such a case for 'zero', for example. So on the face of it, 'zero' is not Twin-Earthable.

A related but importantly different phenomenon has been pointed out by Tyler Burge. If Bert does not fully understand the term 'arthritis', he may believe that arthritis is a disease of the thighs, but his use of the term may nevertheless refer to a disease of the joints, because his utterance is deferential in the sense discussed in chapter 6: the extension of the term as used by him depends on the extension of the term as used by others in his linguistic community. Correspondingly, Bert's duplicate Twin Bert, surrounded by a linguistic community in which 'arthritis' is used differently, may refer to a disease of the thigh. So there is a closely related sense in which 'arthritis' is Twin-Earthable: there can be a *defer-*

---

[2] The definition of Twin-Earthability as well as its relation to issues about internalism and externalism are discussed at much greater length in the additional excursus on twin-earthability and narrow content.

ential utterance of 'arthritis' for which there is a possible corresponding utterance by a twin speaker with a different extension.

Unlike Putnam-style cases, Burge-style cases can be generated for almost any (perhaps any) expression, as almost any expression, even 'zero', can be used deferentially. If so, then if Burge-style cases sufficed for Twin-Earthability, almost every expression would be Twin-Earthable. It is partly for this reason that our definition of Twin-Earthability is cast in terms of nondeferential utterances. Putnam-style cases can be generated even when a key expression (such as 'water') is uttered nondeferentially, but Burge style cases can be generated only when the key expression (such as 'arthritis') is uttered deferentially. The restriction to the nondeferential case focuses the definition on Putnam-style cases, which are the important cases for our purposes, and excludes Burge-style cases, thereby avoiding the threat of trivialization.

There are many expressions whose extension seems to depend on the environment in a way that generates Putnam-style cases: 'water', 'cell', 'human', and even proper names such as 'Gödel'. But there are many other expressions that do not seem to generate Putnam-style cases: 'and', 'zero', 'philosopher', and 'conscious', for example. For any nondeferential utterances of these expressions, it appears that an utterance by a twin will have the same extension. If so, then while expressions such as 'water', 'cell', 'human', and 'Gödel' are Twin-Earthable, expressions such as 'and', 'zero', 'philosopher', and 'conscious' are not.

Twin-Earthability appears to go along with a sort of scrutability. We have seen earlier that 'water'-truths are scrutable from information about the appearance, behavior, composition, and distribution of substances in one's environment. If one uses a Cosmoscope to determine that H_2O is the clear drinkable liquid in one's environment, and so on, then one can conclude that water is H_2O. If one were to determine that XYZ is the clear drinkable liquid in one's environment, and so on, then one would conclude that water is XYZ. Here, the scrutability seems to go along with a sort of approximate analyzability. 'Water', at least as used by a given nondeferential speaker, might be approximately analyzed along the lines of 'the dominant clear drinkable liquid in my environment'. Of course any such approximate analysis is subject to counterexamples, and may also vary between speakers, but the idea is clear.

Something similar applies to other Twin-Earthable terms. We have seen that truths involving 'yellow' and 'hot' are arguably scrutable from phenomenal truths, causal truths, and so on. Correspondingly, 'yellow' might be analyzable to a rough first approximation as 'the normal cause of experiences of such-and-such phenomenal character', and likewise for 'heat'. So it is a priori that if property X is the relevant normal cause, X is yellow, and if property Y is the normal cause, Y is yellow. This mirrors the existence of Twin Earth cases in which twin speakers use their corresponding term 'yellow' to refer to X and Y respectively.

This suggests a heuristic: truths involving Twin-Earthable terms are scrutable from truths involving only non-Twin-Earthable terms. This is not quite right as it stands: certain primitive indexicals, such as 'I' and 'now', are Twin-Earthable but do not seem to be scrutable from non-Twin-Earthable expressions. But we have already seen that these are special cases. So we can suggest a modified heuristic: truths involving Twin-Earthable terms are scrutable from truths involving only non-Twin-Earthable terms and indexical truths.

I will not try to give a conclusive argument for this thesis now. But it is at least useful as a heuristic. In general, where we find Twin-Earthability, it is natural to look for a corresponding sort of scrutability. So I will use this heuristic as a prima facie constraint in looking for a scrutability base, and will return to the underlying thesis later. Attempting to apply the heuristic in the discussion that follows can itself be seen as a way of testing the thesis. We will see later that if the thesis is true, it has significant consequences in the analysis of meaning and content.

3 Microphysical expressions

One might think that microphysical truths, involving specifications of mass, charge, spin, and so on, are especially fundamental and so are essential to a scrutability base. But the analyzability and conceptual priority heuristics suggest that this is not quite right. Microphysical expressions such as these are not plausibly conceptually fundamental, and can easily be approximately defined in other terms. Correspondingly, microphysical truths are plausibly scrutable from other truths.

Terms such as 'charge' and 'spin' are *theoretical* terms, introduced with the introduction of certain physical theories. Like other theoretical terms, they do not seem to be conceptually basic. In fact Ramsey, Carnap, and Lewis, among others have articulated an understanding of theoretical terms according to which they can be analyzed using more basic terms.

On the Ramsey–Carnap–Lewis method, one analyses a theoretical term such as 'electron' by regimenting and Ramsifying. First, one lists the core principles in one's theory of electrons: electrons have negative charge, they surround the nucleus, they play such-and-such role in bonding, and so on. One then Ramsifies the expression 'electron' by replacing it with a corresponding description: perhaps 'that kind E such that objects with E have negative charge, orbit around the nucleus, play such-and-such a role in bonding, and so on'. (More precisely, one first reformulates the 'electron' principles in terms of a property name such as 'electronhood', and then replaces this property name with a description.) Then any sentence containing 'electron' can be translated into a sentence that does not contain 'electron', but will just contain a number of other terms, which Lewis calls 'O-terms' (for 'observational terms' or 'old terms'). We can assume that we have an antecedent understanding of the O-terms.

According to the original Ramsey–Carnap–Lewis method, theoretical terms can be precisely defined in this way. As always, I am skeptical of the claim of precise definition. Given any reasonably simple Ramseyan definition D of 'electron', I suspect that it will not be hard to find counterexamples, by finding scenarios such that if they turn out to be actual, we will say that 'electrons are Ds' is false. Any adequate definition would require an extraordinarily subtle and complex weighting of the various principles governing electrons, and it is not at all clear that such a formulation could be found.

Still, it remains plausible that terms such as 'electron', as used by a given speaker, can at least be approximately defined using the Ramsey method. And whether or not this claim is true, it is extremely plausible that any 'electron'-involving truth S is *scrutable* from truths involving the various O-terms in a Ramsification of 'electron', along with any other vocabulary involved in S, apart from 'electron'. That is, once one knows enough about the existence and properties of various entities playing various roles with respect to the O-terms, one will be in a position to know which entities are the electrons, and what their properties are.

If this is right, then the truths in P (the class of microphysical truths) will be scrutable from truths involving the O-terms in the Ramsifications of microphysical expressions. These O-terms may be other highly theoretical terms in the first instance, including perhaps terms such as 'atom' and 'molecule'. But we can then repeat the Ramsification process until all these theoretical terms are eliminated. It is arguable that through such a process, P will be scrutable from a giant Ramsey sentence specifying the network of microphysical entities and properties with O-terms including observational terms (such as spatiotemporal terms and terms for mass) along with causal and nomic terms and mathematical and logical terms. In effect, this Ramsey sentence for P will specify that there is a large network of objects and properties, standing in certain causal or nomic relations to each other, and to observational properties. (This Ramsey sentence for P, the complete microphysical truth about the universe, should be distinguished from a Ramsey sentence for microphysical theory: where the latter says that there exist certain properties governed by certain laws, the former is a much longer sentence saying in addition that there exist certain objects with a certain distribution of those properties over them.) So this move will transform the scrutability base from $PQTI$ to one involving Q, T, I, observational terms, causal/nomic terms, and logical and mathematical terms.

As part of this process of Ramsification, one may well make reference to various nonfundamental objects (that is, those above the level of microphysics) and perhaps to various nonfundamental properties of these objects. Microphysical entities and properties may be specified in terms of their effects on chemical entities and properties, for example, and so on up the chain. Reference to these entities and properties will itself be Ramsified away, leaving just existential claims about the existence of entities and properties playing relevant roles. This will involve no new vocabulary (apart from O-terms), but it will have the effect of adding existential claims to the Ramsey sentence corresponding to P. Where P made existential claims only about certain fundamental entities, the new sentence will make these claims about nonfundamental entities as well, and it may likewise make existential claims about both fundamental and nonfundamental properties.

However, most of these claims are themselves eliminable. One can limit the Ramsey sentence for P to specify (i) the nomic/causal connections among fundamental entities and fundamental properties, (ii) any properties of these in the O-term vocabulary (including expressions for spatiotemporal properties and mass, as observational properties), (iii) existential specification of certain observed entities and their observational properties, and (iv) any nomic/causal connections to experience. When combined with Q, T, and I, this sentence will be just like $PQTI$, except that specification of some observed entities will be added (itself to be eliminated again shortly), and expressions for non-observational fundamental physical properties ('charge' and 'spin', perhaps) will be replaced by quantified claims about properties playing a certain role in the network. Then the previous arguments for scrutability of the macrophysical from $PQTI$ will still apply to this sentence. The sentence will specify the spatiotemporal properties and the mass of fundamental physical entities, just as before, allowing us to derive the spatiotemporal properties and the mass of arbitrary macrophysical entities. One will be able to determine that a certain property is charge and that another is spin by the same methods that one uses to identify other properties: using a Cosmoscope, for example, will leave no open question here.

4 Color, other secondary qualities, and mass

Which observational terms are needed in the scrutability base? While many notions can in principle be regarded as observational, it is plausible that the central observational notions needed to fix reference to theoretical terms in physics will be notions of primary qualities (space, time, mass, and qualities tied to these) and notions of secondary qualities (color, sound, and so on), perhaps along with causal notions, if one holds that causation is observable. I will discuss spatiotemporal notions and causal notions separately in sections 5 and 6 respectively. In this section I mainly discuss truths involving secondary qualities, and also extend the discussion to truths about mass.

I have already argued in chapter 6 that secondary quality truths are scrutable from phenomenal truths and other truths. Once one knows all the truths about which external objects and properties cause which color experiences under which circumstances, for example, one is in a position to know which objects are red. We can also apply the analyzability heuristic, extending the Ramsey method to cover color terms. To a first approximation, 'red' might be analyzed as 'the property that normally causes phenomenally red experiences in me' (or 'in my community'). A closer approximation might (for example) holistically define all the colors as that manifold of properties that serves as a causal basis for a corresponding manifold of color experiences, while saying more about what counts as 'normal'. If this approach is even roughly on the right track, then color truths will be scrutable from phenomenal truths and relevant truths about the external world. Combining this observation with the results of the previous section suggests that color truths are a priori scrutable from O-truths involving phenomenal terms, causal/nomic terms, and spatiotemporal terms, along with totality and indexical truths.

As I noted in the last chapter, there are views of color on which color terms cannot be analyzed in this way. These include some primitivist views of color on which 'red' expresses a primitive concept of a primitive intrinsic property that is grasped in experience. They also include related physicalist views on which 'red' expresses a primitive concept that picks out a physical property. On views of this sort, any claims about causal relations between red things and red experiences may be regarded as substantive claims that are not a priori.

We can call the two opposing views of color concepts *conceptual primitivism* and *conceptual functionalism* about color. These views about color concepts can be combined with various views about the metaphysics of color. Conceptual functionalism is naturally combined with either dispositionalism about the metaphysics of color or with certain sorts of physicalism (roughly, sorts where color concepts are analyzable as concepts of whatever categorical property plays the appropriate functional role and where physical properties play the role). Conceptual primitivism is naturally combined with either metaphysical primitivism about color, other forms of physicalism about color (sorts where color concepts are not so analyzable) and perhaps other views such as projectivism and even certain forms of dispositionalism.

Everything I have said about color terms applies to terms for other secondary qualities: for any of these, primitivist and functionalist views are available. I think that many of the same points apply in the case of mass, even though mass is typically regarded as a primary quality. It is arguable that our basic conception of mass is functional—mass is what resists acceleration in a certain way, what causes certain experiences and judgments, and so on. If so, truths about mass are eliminable by the Ramsey method in much the same way that truths about color are. Again, one could take a view on which 'mass' expresses a primitive concept, perhaps corresponding to a direct grasp of a certain intrinsic nature, and then one may want to include 'mass'-truths in a scrutability base. But I do not think that such a view is especially plausible. There is a residual issue about whether deleting 'mass' from a scrutability base affects the scrutability of macrophysical from microphysical. I will address this issue alongside the corresponding issue about spacetime at the end of the next section.

A version of the conceivability heuristic can help us to choose between primitivist and functionalist views in these cases. Is it conceivable that all experiences of red (in me, and in every other creature in the actual world) have always been caused by green things, and that correspondingly, all our judgments about color have been massively mistaken? Is it conceivable that all experiences as of an object weighing one gram have always been caused by objects weighing one kilogram, and that correspondingly, all our judgments about mass have been massively mistaken? Or are these further suppositions incoherent, in the sense that they can be ruled out a priori? To sharpen the test (removing worries about brains in vats and the like), and to better assess scrutability from the relevant base, one can require in addition that the causal and spatiotemporal structure of the external world are much as we take them to be (so that objects resist acceleration much as we take them to, for example), and then ask whether the further suppositions above are coherent under this requirement. That is, can the combination of this causal/spatiotemporal specification with either the color supposition or the mass supposition be ruled out a priori?

Taking the case of color: if the skeptical hypothesis here is incoherent, then there are at least a priori constraints on truths about color, grounded in constraints on colors' connections to color experiences along with causal and spatiotemporal truths. These a priori constraints will be most naturally accommodated by a functionalist view, resulting in a view on which color truths are scrutable.[3] On the other hand, if these hypotheses are coherent, then it is most natural to hold that there are few or no such a priori constraints, and to embrace a primitivist view on which truths about color are not scrutable from these other truths, and should be in the scrutability base.

Taking the case of mass: here incoherence suggests a priori constraints on truths about mass grounded in causal connections to phenomenal, causal, and spatiotemporal truths. These constraints are naturally accommodated by a functionalist view of mass concepts. This might be a phenomenal functionalist view, on which it is a priori that mass normally causes certain experiences as of mass,

---

[3] Alternatively, incoherence can be accommodated by some primitivist externalist view, on which color experiences are constituted by relations to color properties that are (normally) instantiated in our environment, and where this constitution is knowable a priori or at least is a priori scrutable from causal, spatiotemporal, and experiential truths. I have argued against this sort of externalism in 'The Representational Character of Experience' and 'Perception and the Fall from Eden'.

or it might be a nonphenomenal functionalist view, perhaps on which it is a priori that mass resists acceleration in a certain way, or it might also combine elements of both. On any of these views, truths about mass will be scrutable from the other relevant truths. By contrast, coherence of the skeptical hypothesis suggests a primitivist view of mass concepts on which truths about mass need to be in the scrutability base.

My own intuitions favor incoherence in both cases, and thereby favor functionalism about both color and mass concepts (with some qualifications, as above), but these are certainly substantive issues.

I am not entirely unsympathetic with a primitivist view. I think that we have primitive color concepts, although I am doubtful that our color terms normally express them. In particular, I think we have a concept of primitive redness, or of *Edenic redness*, in the terminology of 'Perception and the Fall from Eden'. Edenic colors are primitive qualitative properties of the sort that a metaphysically primitivist view of colors invokes. (Fable: in the garden of Eden, apples were primitively red, and color perception worked by direct acquaintance with this redness; then we ate from the Tree of Illusion and the Tree of Science.) On my view, Edenic color properties are presented in perceptual experience, but they are not instantiated in our world. Ordinary color terms such as 'red' work in the functionalist way, so that they typically pick out complex physical properties rather than Edenic properties. So there is still no need for color truths in a scrutability base: sentences about non-primitive colors are scrutable from more basic truths, and sentences about primitive colors are not true. (Though as discussed later, there may be a role within Q for truths about the representation of Edenic colors in color experience.) This view contrasts with stronger primitivist views on which color terms expressing primitive concepts pick out properties (whether primitive properties, physical properties, or something else) that are instantiated. On those views truths about color may well be in a minimal scrutability base.

One point that arguably favors a primitivist view is that it is far from obvious that our concepts of color experience are more primitive than our concepts of color in the external world. Indeed, it is natural to hold the reverse. Certainly, it seems that color concepts are acquired and deployed more easily than concepts of color experience. In ordinary English, concepts of color experience are most naturally expressed by expressions such as 'looks red', and it is natural (although not compulsory) to suppose that a grasp of looking red presupposes a grasp of being red, rather than vice versa. The same goes for philosophical expressions such as 'experience as of red', 'what it is like to see red', and so on. This point can be handled by recognizing primitive color concepts as above, and by analyzing phenomenal concepts in terms of representation of primitive colors. I return to this matter later in the chapter.

5 Spatiotemporal expressions

The case of spatiotemporal terms is complex and important enough to deserve separate treatment.[4] To a first approximation, the core issue here is the same as in the previous section. One can endorse scrutability of spatiotemporal truths from mental and causal truths (perhaps along with other truths), by accepting a broadly functionalist view on which spatiotemporal concepts are concepts of those properties that play a certain functional role (either a phenomenal role, a nonphenomenal role, or a mix of the two, as with the discussion of mass in the last section). Or one can deny the scrutability of spatiotemporal truths here, by accepting a primitivist view on which spatiotemporal concepts are not analyzable at all.

I will focus mostly on spatial concepts, and say a little about temporal concepts (for which closely related issues arise) toward the end. Throughout the discussion, I will use 'spatial primitivism' and 'spatial functionalism' for views about spatial concepts rather than for views of the metaphysics of space.

I suspect that the initial intuitions of many will favor a spatial primitivist view. It is natural to think that spatial concepts involve some sort of direct grasp of spatial properties, and that they are not analyzable in functional terms, especially not in terms of relations to anything mental. And it is not at all obvious that spatial truths are scrutable from non-spatial truths. Still, I favor a functionalist view in this domain, or at least a qualified functionalist view analogous to my view of color. In what follows I will sketch the case for this view.

To loosen intuitions, we can start by noting that physicists have entertained the possibility that spatial properties are not fundamental. On some views, these derive from more basic properties: perhaps those of a quantum-mechanical configuration space, or an underlying space in a theory of quantum gravity such as string theory, or some other 'prespace physics' (see Nathan Seiberg's 'Emergent Spacetime' for a review). If so, spatial properties will not be especially natural properties: like color properties, they may be complex derivative properties. Now, spatial primitivism does not *require* that spatial properties are fundamental properties: it is a thesis about concepts, not properties. Still, insofar as spatial properties are high-level properties, it becomes less obvious that we have an especially primitive grip on them. It also becomes more plausible that spatial

---

[4] I spend more time on this issue compared to others partly because it has not been explored in the literature in nearly as much depth as the corresponding issues concerning color, causation, and the like, and I think that it is very interesting and important in its own right. Here I am indebted to the work of Brad Thompson (e.g., Thompson 2003, 2010) as well as to discussions with him. Thanks also to Robbie Williams for suggesting relativistic adaptations of the relevant cases. I discuss related issues about spatial experience in 'The Matrix as Metaphysics' and 'Perception and the Fall from Eden'.

expressions are Twin-Earthable, perhaps picking out classical properties in a Newtonian world, relativistic properties in a relativistic world, and string-theoretic properties in a string-theory world.

One can also make a case for Twin-Earthability in a more straightforward way. Consider functional and phenomenal twins of us that are twice as large as us, in an environment that is structurally much like ours although twice as large. These twins and us will plausibly pick out different properties with their spatial expressions such as 'one meter long'. So the Twin-Earthability heuristic suggests that these expressions may be scrutable from others. For example, perhaps they are approximately analyzable as invoking a manifold of properties that serves as the sort of causal basis for a certain manifold of experiences, as in the color case.[5]

One can also use conceivability as a diagnostic. To start with perhaps the best cases for a functionalist: is it coherent to suppose that everything that anyone has ever experienced as one meter long, and that we judge to be one meter long, is in fact two meters long? More generally, is it coherent to suppose that our experiences and judgments are massively illusory, in that almost everything that we experience is twice as long as we experience and judge it to be? Note that this differs from the oft-discussed thought-experiment of whether it is coherent to suppose that the universe doubles in size overnight, and even a thought-experiment that asks whether there can be a universe that duplicates ours apart from being twice the size. Here the question concerns our experiences and judgments of our own world. I think that there is a very strong intuition that the supposition is incoherent: prima facie, we do not have a strong enough independent grasp of absolute lengths that we can make sense of the hypothesis that the world is as supposed.[6] As in the case of color and mass, a verdict of incoherence suggests a priori constraints between concepts of absolute length and other concepts (including phenomenal, causal, and structural concepts). This gives prima facie reason to deny primitivism about concepts of absolute length and to accept some sort of functionalism. The most obvious candidate is a sort of phenomenal

---

[5] George Berkeley considers related cases in *Three Dialogues between Hylas and Philonous*, in effect arguing against spatial primitivism about absolute size. In *A Treatise on Human Understanding* (section 2 of book 1), David Hume argues for a sort of spatial functionalism about shape and relative size.

[6] In an informal poll of around 30 philosophers, about 20 responded that the hypothesis is incoherent. Of those who said that it is coherent, most appealed to scenarios in which *relative* lengths are not as we took them to be: for example, in which there is a distinctive illusion involving the meter stick in Paris, or in which everything in the world has been gradually expanding over time. Only two endorsed the coherence of a hypothesis on which relative lengths are as we took them to be but on which absolute lengths were different. It is views of this last sort that suggest primitivism about absolute length concepts, as opposed to primitivism about relative length concepts.

functionalism about these concepts: to a first approximation, our concepts of absolute lengths pick out those properties that normally bring about certain spatial experiences and judgments.

A related question is: can we make sense of the hypothesis that everything (or almost everything) that we have ever experienced as being on our left has in fact been on our right? Again, there is a strong sense of incoherence here. It is natural to hold that what makes a certain relative direction count as being the 'left' direction is precisely that relative direction has been causally correlated with certain sorts of experience and judgment. And it seems implausible with we have some sort of independent grip on the notions of being to the left and being to the right that allows these notions to float free of experiences of left and right as strongly as this. If this is right, then there is a case for a functionalist view of concepts such as *left* and *right*: perhaps one on which it is a priori that things to one's left normally bring about a certain sort of 'leftish' experience.

In the length case, we can certainly make sense of the idea that everything we *now* experience is larger than we think it is. I might recently have undergone a distorting 'shrinkage' process: for example, my body might have doubled in size overnight without my knowing it, or shrinking lenses might have been put on my eyes, with the result that external objects look half as large as they did before. Likewise, we can make sense of the hypothesis that everything that *now* seems to be on our left is on our right. I might recently have undergone a 'flipping' process: for example, left-right flipping lenses might have been put on my eyes, so that I am at least temporarily subject to systematic illusions of orientation. In both cases, we can even suppose that all of our senses (including bodily senses and motor affectors) have recently been subjected to such a process, so that the distortion is undetectable except by comparing perceived objects to our memories of them. But these cases seem coherent precisely because we have concepts of size and orientation grounded in the causal basis of our previous experiences. Once one extends the supposition to the claim that our experiences and judgments have always been illusory in this way, it is no longer clear that the hypotheses are coherent.

What if the flipping process has always been in place? In this case, the right thing to say seems to be: with 'left', I refer to the orientation that if it were not for the flipping process, I would have referred to as 'right'. So this is not a scenario in which my experiences and judgments are massively illusory. In fact, there is actually something of a flipping process in vision, due to inversion of the retinal image. But this gives us not the slightest temptation to say that our experience of up and down is massively illusory. One might suggest that I could suffer permanent illusion if I am 'flipped' with respect to my community. I am doubtful about this, but in any case the view suggests a conceptual functionalism on which orientation concepts are grounded in causal connections to the community. We can bracket this issue by supposing that the flipping process has been in place not just throughout my lifetime but throughout my community.

Something similar applies to a 'shrinking' process. Certainly, there is a possible 'shrinkage' process P such that if we inserted it in the normal visual pathway, it would lead to illusion. But if we were to discover that process P has always been present in normal vision, there will be no temptation to say that vision is illusory. Instead, we will say that our size terms refer to sizes smaller than they would have referred to if process P had been absent.

One could resist these verdicts by embracing a primitivist view of our size and/or orientation concepts, holding that we have a direct enough grasp of specific sizes or orientations that we can make sense of these suppositions. But our difficulty in making sense of the permanent-illusory-flip hypothesis and the permanent-illusory-shrinkage hypothesis suggests that this view is prima facie implausible.[7]

Concepts of shape and relative size are trickier here. Can we make sense of the hypothesis that everything we have experienced as a square has in fact been a rectangle, perhaps whose sides have a ratio of 2-1? Or at least that when an object seems as wide as it is high, it is in fact twice as high as it is wide? There is perhaps less intuitive resistance to this hypothesis than to the hypotheses considered above. In this case, it is perhaps easier to suppose that we have been subject to permanent distortion. Still, I think that on reflection this is far from clear.

One can make the case against primitivism about shape concepts using the theory of relativity. According to special relativity, when an object is accelerated it undergoes Lorentz contractions, contracting in the direction of motion. For example, if a cube with meter-long sides is accelerated to a certain speed s around 87 percent of the speed of light, it will become a mere squashed cuboid whose sides are one meter long in two directions but only a half-meter long in the third. It will be a cube relative to its own reference frame, but relative to our own reference frame, it will not be a cube.

Now consider *Lorentz Earth*: a planet physically just like ours (relative to its own reference frame), containing speakers just like us, except that it is moving at speed s relative to us in the direction of its north pole. To make the case simpler,

---

[7] In the discussion above I have mainly been assuming internalism about spatial experience, so that we can vary environmental properties while leaving spatial experience intact. Externalism about spatial experience complicates things a little. As in the case of color, primitivist externalists could hold that experiences are constituted by relations to spatial properties and relations that are (normally) instantiated in our environment. This view can accommodate the incoherence intuitions above, at least if it holds that the constitution relations are a priori, or a priori scrutable from nonspatial truths. Still, it is hard to see how the spatial experiences of a subject and her permanently doubled twin would differ (perhaps this is easier in the case of permanently left-right flipped subjects). And if their experiences are phenomenally the same, it is hard to see how these experiences would be constituted by and pick out such different properties.

let us suppose that the Earth is exactly spherical.[8] Then where the Earth is spherical, Lorentz Earth is not: it is a mere squashed spheroid, with polar diameter half
as long as its equatorial diameters. So in our mouths, 'spherical' applies to Earth
but not to Lorentz Earth. At the same time, the situation is exactly symmetrical
from a God's-eye point of view. So in the mouths of speakers on Lorentz Earth,
'spherical' applies to Lorentz Earth but not to Earth.

This case is in effect a Twin Earth case for shape terms such as 'spherical'.
Although speakers on Earth and on Lorentz Earth are functional duplicates,
they pick out different properties with 'spherical'. The result is limited, in that
we can also describe the cases by appealing to the notion of sphericalness relative
to a reference frame. Speakers on both planets can correctly allow that each
planet is spherical relative to its own reference frame but not to the other planets.
So the argument does not establish that the relativistic notion of 'spherical-in' is
Twin Earthable. There also remains a relativistic notion of 'rest length', where an
object's rest length is its length in the reference frame where the object is at rest,
and a corresponding notion of 'rest sphericality'. Then accelerated objects do not
change their rest length, and both Earth and Lorentz Earth are rest-spherical.
Still, the orthodox view is that the length of accelerated objects contracts. Given
that this orthodox view is correct when stated in ordinary language, it is clear
that the ordinary notion of length is not that of rest length. Similarly, given that
spheres must have diameters of equal length, it follows that Lorentz Earth is not
spherical in the ordinary sense, so that the ordinary predicate 'spherical' is Twin-
Earthable.

We can extend this Lorentz case to an *absolute* Lorentz case, by supposing,
contrary to the standard understanding of special relativity, that there is a privileged reference frame relative to which absolute motion is measured. We can
further suppose that this privileged reference frame is a frame relative to which
Lorentz Earth is at rest, and relative to which Earth is traveling at 87 percent of
the speed of light. It remains clear in this case that 'sphere' as used on Lorentz
Earth applies to Lorentz Earth but not Earth. But what about 'sphere' as used on
Earth? In particular: if this scenario is actual, do we speak truly when we say
'Earth is spherical'? Likewise, when we look at something we take to be a one-
meter cube, are we correct when we say that it is a cube, or would we be more
correct to say that it is a squashed cuboid?

Intuitions may differ here. Some may take the view that our term 'spherical'
picks out absolute sphericality, and that in this scenario Earth is not absolutely
spherical, so that 'Earth is spherical' is false. The same goes for 'The object is

---

[8] Alternatively, we could run the case using the expression 'near-spherical', where this requires
that diameters are within 1 percent of each other. Then Earth will be near-spherical but Lorentz
Earth will not.

cubical'. Still, I think there is a stronger intuition that the existence of an absolute reference frame does not make a difference to the semantics of our terms
here. If our term 'spherical' applies to Earth in a scenario without an absolute
reference frame, then it equally applies to Earth in a scenario with an absolute
reference frame. Certainly, if we discovered that there is an absolute reference
frame relative to which we are moving fast, it is unlikely that we would concede
that all of our shape judgments have been wrong. More likely, we would say that
our ordinary term 'spherical' picks out something distinct from absolute
sphericality.

We are now close to the nonrelativistic 'El Greco' cases developed by Brad
Thompson (2010), following a related suggestion by Susan Hurley (1998). Let us
say that an El Greco environment is a pocket of the universe in which everything
is stretched 2–1 in a certain direction. For vividness, assume this to be the 'vertical' direction (which I will pretend is a fixed direction throughout the universe).
From a perspective outside the El Greco environment, things in the El Greco
environment will be roughly as depicted in an ordinary movie stretched 2–1
along the vertical axis. The relativistic case above suggests that this supposition is
perfectly coherent. But here we can suppose a nonrelativistic version of the case:
there is no obvious reason why something like this could not also happen in a
nonrelativistic world, due to special forces and the like.[9] Bodies that seem rigid
within the environment will be nonrigid by standards outside the environment,
in that they change their shape when they rotate. And beings in that world will
typically say 'That is a square' when confronted by what outsiders would call a
rectangle that is twice as high as it is tall.

Now, for a twist, let us assume that we are in an El Greco environment relative
to the rest of the world: perhaps the environment covers our galaxy but not
much further. Now the key question is: when we say 'That is a square', confronted with an object that outsiders would call a rectangle, are we speaking
truly? If yes, then terms such as 'square' are Twin-Earthable: our counterparts in

---

[9] It is sometimes asked whether this scenario is coherent, with people finding various ways it
might break down. But the relativistic case provides a straightforward illustration of its coherence.
One simply needs to make an ordinary scenario and contract all of its aspects in a certain direction, as with Lorentz contractions. If there is no principled objection to an absolute Lorentz case,
there does not seem to be a principled objection to an El Greco case in a nonrelativistic world. One
might ask: in virtue of what do these beings count as stretched relative to each other? In a relativistic case, this notion is cashed out in terms of measurement. In a more fanciful nonrelativistic
scenario, we might suppose that there are two sorts of matter, A-matter and B-matter, which are
similar in many respects but which have different relations to space. As it happens, our part of the
universe consists of A-matter, while their part consists of B-matter. But A-matter and B-matter can
in principle interact, while retaining their spatial character. If we were to travel to the B-matter
part of the universe, we would encounter beings who seem to us to be El Greco beings, while they
would perceive us as squashed beings.

El Greco world use corresponding terms with different extensions. If no, then perhaps 'square' is not Twin-Earthable.

I think there is good reason to think the answer is yes. As with the relativistic case, I think that it is clear that if we discovered that our galaxy is unusual in this way, we would not deny that apparently square objects are square, that the earth is spherical, and so on. Rather, experts might distinguish two notions of squareness, perhaps local squareness and global squareness, while holding that our ordinary term 'square' picks out the former. The same goes for notions such as 'length', 'larger', and so on. If these judgments would be correct, and if the corresponding judgments of our counterparts in other parts of the world would also be correct, then these expressions are Twin-Earthable.

Analogously, we might discover that macrophysics has an odd relation to microphysics, so a maximally explanatory microphysics invokes a spatial measure, say 'nanons', such that entities that we typically regard as square measure twice as many nanons in the vertical direction as in the horizontal direction. Would we then say that these entities are not square? I think that we would not. At best, we might distinguish two notions of squareness, perhaps microsquareness and macrosquareness, while holding that our ordinary term 'square' picks out the latter. The same goes for expressions such as 'length', 'larger', and so on. If these judgments would be correct, and if the corresponding judgments of our counterparts for whom macrophysics is more uniformly related to microphysics would also be correct, then these expressions are Twin-Earthable.

Bringing this back to the conceivability case: all this tends to suggest that it is not in fact conceivable that our judgments about shape and about relative length have been systematically incorrect, at least in the scenarios described above. Rather, the case of shape is like the cases of orientation and size. It is conceivable that our shape judgments are wrong *now*, due to some recent distorting effect. But in a scenario in which such 'distorting' processes have always been there, then our judgments will have been largely veridical all along. If so, then primitivism about shape and relative length is false, and some sort of functionalism is plausibly correct.[10]

Some will have different intuitions about the key scenarios (nanons, El Greco, Lorentz with absolute reference frames), holding that our shape judgments are mistaken and our shape experiences are nonveridical in the relevant scenarios.

---

[10] As before, the discussion here largely assumes internalism about experience. An externalist about shape experience might hold that these are constituted by relations to instantiated shapes in a subject's environment, and hold that primitive shape concepts are grounded in these relations. But as in the absolute length case, it is hard to see how the experiences of twin subjects in an El Greco case will differ: will one have an experience as of a rectangle, despite insisting that she is confronted by a square?

But even so, spatial primitivism does not follow. The claim that our judgments are mistaken can also be explained by a sort of nonphenomenal (or structural) spatial functionalism, on which reference to spatial properties is fixed in virtue of their playing certain nonphenomenal roles. In this case, the roles will not involve connections to our spatial experiences, but rather will be structural roles within the physical realm. For example, it might be a priori that spatial location is that property that plays a certain sort of role in certain sorts of physical interaction. (For more on this sort of structuralism about the spatial and about the relevant roles, see section 7 in the next chapter.) That view predicts that we are mistaken about lengths in the cases in question. But this view is not a form of spatial primitivism: it allows that spatial claims are scrutable from claims about the abstract structure of fundamental physics.

To adjudicate the question between spatial primitivism and this sort of structural spatial functionalism, we can consider a specification of the role of space in structural terms, and ask: is it conceivable that something other than space plays the space role? Or better: let us say that P^* is a structuralization of the microphysical truth P if P^* is a Ramsey sentence obtainable from P by replacing all fundamental property terms (such as 'mass') by quantified variables ('ϕ') and by preceding the sentence with a corresponding quantifier of the form 'There exists a fundamental property ϕ'.[11] A structuralization will in effect be a specification of physics in structural terms alone, where these terms may include logical and mathematical terms as well as the notions of law and of fundamentality (for much more on this, see the discussion of structural scrutability in the next chapter). Given such a structuralization P^*, we can consider the full class P^*QTI and a basic spatial truth S using spatial vocabulary, and ask: is $P^*QTI \& \sim S$ epistemically possible?

Some philosophers (quidditists about mass, as discussed later in this chapter) allow that there are metaphysically possible worlds in which properties other than mass play the mass role in physics. Analogously, some philosophers (quidditists about space?) may allow that there are metaphysically possible worlds in which nonspatial properties play the space role, and in which $P^*QTI \& \sim S$ is true. But here we are asking about epistemic possibility. On a standard view, we fix reference to mass as whatever plays the mass role, so it is not *epistemically* possible that something other than mass plays the mass role. Is it epistemically possible that something other than space plays the space role?

[11] For the present purpose of assessing spatial primitivism, we can allow P^* to include temporal expressions without Ramsifying them away: if $P^*QTI \& \sim S$ is epistemically possible when P^* excludes temporal expressions but not when it includes them, the natural upshot is temporal primitivism without spatial primitivism. One could also in principle include expressions for mass, charge, and the like, but in these cases inclusion is unlikely to make a difference.

A yes answer here tends to support spatial primitivism: we have a primitive grasp of spatial properties that is not exhausted by their structural or phenomenal role. A yes answer also strongly suggests that spatial truths are needed in the scrutability base, at least if there are spatial truths at all: any such truths will not be scrutable from structural and phenomenal truths. A no answer tends to support spatial functionalism: roughly, we fix reference to spatial properties as those that play the space role, where this role can be characterized in structural or phenomenal terms. A no answer also strongly suggests that spatial truths are not needed in the scrutability base, as these truths will be scrutable from structural and phenomenal truths.[12] In my experience, a no answer is much more common here, even among those who have a verdict of mistakenness in the El Greco scenarios and the others. All this lends reasonably strong support to spatial functionalism.

As in the case of color, I am not wholly unsympathetic to spatial primitivism. In color experience, I have suggested that we are presented with certain primitive color properties, such as Edenic redness. In spatial experience, I think we are presented with certain primitive spatial properties, such as Edenic squareness (although probably not with Edenic absolute lengths). Just as experience confers a grasp of a certain qualitative properties associated with colors, it also confers a grasp of a certain qualitative properties associated with space. These properties might have been instantiated in the garden of Eden, and perhaps in a classical Newtonian world. But I think that there is little reason to think that they are instantiated in our world. Certainly, it is not easy to see how there could be Edenic squareness in a relativistic world, or in a string-theoretic world in which any spatial properties are complex and derivative. In such a world, the status of primitive spatial properties is much like the status of primitive color properties in a post-Galilean world.

Even if the physics of our world is mathematically Newtonian, this does not entail that Edenic spatial properties are instantiated. We have seen that on a primitivist view, this mathematical structure (as well as our phenomenal states and functional organization) will arguably be compatible with non-Edenic properties playing the relevant roles. So even if physics turned out to be mathemati-

---

[12] These claims are qualified ('suggests' and 'strongly suggests') because of the possibility of alternative views. For example, a yes answer is compatible with a view on which spatial concepts are not primitive and on which spatial truths are scrutable from more primitive 'protospatial' truths that go beyond structural and phenomenal truths. A no answer is compatible with a view on which spatial concepts are primitive, but on which it is a substantive a priori truth that spatial properties are the only properties that can play the space role. A no answer is also compatible with an externalist view on which phenomenal truths about spatial experience are analyzed in terms of awareness of spatial truths, so that phenomenal truths themselves depend on more primitive spatial truths.

cally Newtonian, it is not clear why a primitivist should favor the hypothesis that we are in an Edenic Newtonian world as opposed to a non-Edenic Newtonian world. And given that physics has turned out to be drastically non-Newtonian, there is even less reason to think that Edenic spatial properties are instantiated in our world.[13]

So: insofar as we have reason to think that spatial properties are instantiated, we also have reason to think that they are not Edenic properties. Our ordinary spatial expressions such as 'square' still refer, but they refer to the ordinary nonprimitive properties that serve as the causal basis of our spatial experiences. So even if we possess primitive spatial concepts, these are not needed to express truths about space in this world (at most, they may be needed to properly characterize spatial experience). As in the case of color, all this strongly tends toward the view that spatial expressions are not needed in a scrutability base.

I will not go into the case of time at any length, but I think the situation is similar in at least some respects. The case of absolute temporal duration parallels the case of absolute length. One can generate a Slow Earth case in which beings move through time twice as slowly as we do (Lorentz Earth is such a case; one could also generate nonrelativistic cases). Then our slowed-down functional duplicates (admittedly, it is not entirely obvious whether they will be phenomenal duplicates) plausibly refer to a duration two seconds long with their expression 'one second'. It is correspondingly hard to make sense of the hypothesis that our absolute duration judgments are and have always been systematically off by a factor of two. The case of relative temporal duration parallels the case of relative length. One can generate El-Greco-style scenarios involving beings that regularly speed up and then slow down (by outside standards). If we turn out to be in such a scenario, it is arguable that our ordinary relative temporal duration judgments will nevertheless be correct.

---

[13] These considerations might be extended into a general argument for the scrutability of spatial truths from nonspatial truths, and in particular from structural and phenomenal truths. If scrutability is false, there will be coherent skeptical hypotheses on which structural and phenomenal truths about our world obtain and in which spatial truths about our world do not obtain, presumably because something other than space plays the space role. But if there are such coherent skeptical hypotheses here, it is hard to see how we could know that they do not obtain. Hypotheses involving alternative fillers of the space role would seem to explain our experiences just as well as hypotheses involving space, and would seem to be just as simple. So if scrutability of spatial sentences fails, I think we have good reason to doubt whether those sentences are true. Considerations of this sort might be extended into an argument for the scrutability of all knowable truths from structural and phenomenal truths. Of course there is much more to be said here, especially concerning the extent to which perceptual experience as of primitive space gives reason to support a hypothesis on which there is primitive space over other hypotheses.

There are some mild disanalogies between the spatial case and the temporal case that perhaps make temporal primitivism somewhat more attractive than spatial primitivism. First, although phenomenal truths about spatial experiences intuitively do not imply claims about spatial properties of experiences, it is at least arguable (as alluded to above) that phenomenal truths about temporal experience imply claims about the temporal properties of experiences. Second, the intuition that Edenic properties are presented in experience is especially attractive in the temporal case, where many have noted that experience presents time as passing: it is natural to hold that there was passage of Edenic time in the garden of Eden, even if there is not in our world. Third, even physical theories that give a nonfundamental role to space often give a fundamental role to time (see Seiberg's 'Emergent Spacetime', although see also Julian Barbour's *The End of Time* for a view on which time is not fundamental), so arguments against primitivism based on such theories are somewhat weaker here. Still, I think that there is a reasonable case for a functionalist view of ordinary temporal concepts.

The simplest functionalist view of both spatial and temporal concepts is analogous to the simple functionalist view of color concepts. On such a view, spatial concepts pick out that manifold of properties that serves as the normal causal basis of a corresponding manifold of properties in our spatial experience. Temporal concepts pick out that manifold of properties that serves as the normal causal basis of a corresponding manifold of properties in our temporal experience. On a view of this sort, spatial and temporal truths are a priori scrutable from phenomenal and causal truths, along with other uneliminated background truths.

The simple functionalist view may well need to be refined to handle complex cases, for example incorporating nonphenomenal elements into the relevant roles. For all I have said, there may be further constraints on just what it takes for a manifold of properties that is a causal basis of our spatiotemporal experience to count as the spatiotemporal properties. And it is an open question just how strong these constraints are. A weak sort of spatial primitivism holds that we have a primitive grip on spatiotemporal continuity, at least, and that continuous spatiotemporal intervals should be realized by continuous underlying properties. Another sort holds that we have a primitive grip on spatiotemporal betweenness. I will not discuss these varieties of primitivism here, but I think that one can subject them to arguments akin to the arguments given above.

A key scenario here is one in which we are (and always have been) hooked up to a computer simulation, like the people in *The Matrix*. If we are in this scenario, are our spatiotemporal judgments largely correct? Spatiotemporal functionalism suggests a yes answer: our spatiotemporal expressions will pick out the computational properties and relations that serve as their causal basis, and those properties and relations really are present in the computer. Spatiotemporal primitivism suggests a no answer: the spatial relations that we attribute to entities in our environment are not present in the computer. The considerations in favor of spatiotemporal functionalism tend to suggest that the yes answer is correct, so that beings in a Matrix are not deceived. I have made a more direct argument for that conclusion in 'The Matrix as Metaphysics' and discuss the issue further in the fifteenth excursus.

It remains open to spatial primitivists to deny the claims I have made about shape and relative length, holding that there are no Twin Earth cases here and that the sort of systematic error I have described in El Greco cases and the like is in fact conceivable. If they are right, then primitivism may be right at least about notions in the vicinity of relative length. A harder-line primitivist might deny the claims from earlier and also accept primitivism about absolute size and about orientation. I think that consideration of the cases provides at least prima facie reason to reject all these varieties of primitivism about spatiotemporal notions. But again, this is an issue about which reasonable philosophers may disagree.

It should be noted that for all I have said here, spatiotemporal expressions may still have a role in characterizing phenomenal truths. For example, the phenomenal character of experiences might involve the representation of certain spatiotemporal contents. One may well characterize individuals as instantiating certain phenomenal properties at certain times. If so, then spatiotemporal expressions will at least play an indirect role within Q in a scrutability base $PQTI$. In addition, one still needs a temporal reference to 'now' in the indexical portion I of the base. It may be that these uses of spatiotemporal expressions are also eliminable, but this is not obvious.

A residual issue concerns whether eliminating spatiotemporal expressions (along with mass) undermines the scrutability of the macrophysical from the microphysical, as at the end of the last chapter and again at the end of section 2. In this case, we appealed to claims such as: macroscopic objects are located in the spatiotemporal region where their fundamental parts are located, and their mass is the sum of the masses of their parts. Suppose that fundamental spatial location is characterized by a certain role and that relation x plays that role, so that x is the fundamental spatial location relation. Then one can define a relation x' so that a macroscopic object bears this relation to anything that its fundamental parts bear x to. One can then use the strategy of this section to determine that x' is macroscopic spatial location and to determine the location of various objects. Something very similar goes for mass.

6 Causal and nomic expressions

What about expressions involving causation, lawhood, and the like: for example, 'cause', 'law', 'chance', 'disposition', and 'naturally necessary'? For ease of usage, let us call the expressions in this cluster *nomic* expressions.

Here there are two broad views in philosophy. On what is often called a *Humean* view, nomic truths derive from non-nomic truths, such as truths about regularities in a spatiotemporal mosaic.[14] On a *non-Humean* view, nomic truths do not derive from non-nomic truths, and are in some sense irreducible. Sometimes the issue between Humean and non-Humean views is cast as a metaphysical issue concerning metaphysical and modal relations between nomic and non-nomic properties: hence David Lewis's 'Humean supervenience'. But there is a closely related issue concerning conceptual and epistemological relations between nomic and non-nomic concepts. This is the issue that concerns us.

For present purposes, I will say that a *Humean scrutability* view, or just a Humean view, holds that nomic truths are conclusively a priori scrutable from non-nomic truths, while a non-Humean view holds that nomic truths are not conclusively a priori scrutable from non-nomic truths. Here non-nomic truths are those not involving nomic expressions such as those above, and not involving any related expressions that tacitly involve these notions. Some but not all who are Humeans about the metaphysical issue are also Humeans in this sense: as in the case of the relationship between consciousness and the physical, some philosophers accept supervenience without accepting scrutability. But most or all who are non-Humeans about the metaphysical issue are non-Humeans in this sense: as in other domains, rejecting supervenience leads to rejecting scrutability.

The relevant sort of scrutability here is conclusive scrutability. Even a non-Humean may allow that nomic truths are nonconclusively scrutable from non-nomic truths. It is very plausible that one can know that if certain regularities obtain, certain laws obtain; and if there is any nonconclusive a priori knowledge at all, knowledge of conditionals from regularities to laws is an example. Correspondingly, one can reject supervenience while accepting nonconclusive scrutability. But the non-Humean will reject conclusive scrutability, holding that one cannot have a priori certainty that if the regularities obtain, the laws obtain.

One natural heuristic here is the conceivability heuristic. Can we conceive of a world that is identical to ours in all non-nomic respects while differing in nomic respects? Here, many philosophers have thought that the answer is yes. When it is a law that As are followed by Bs, for example, it is arguably conceivable that Bs follow As just as a matter of coincidence. One could argue that there are lawless worlds in which things happen more or less randomly, and nothing causes anything else. And one can argue that one can at least conceive of a lawless world that through a 'giant cosmic coincidence' produces the regularities in our world. It may be very unlikely that our world is like this, but many hold that we cannot rule this out a priori.

Michael Tooley (1987) gives a related case against Humean supervenience that can be turned into a case against Humean scrutability. Suppose that there are ten pairs of fundamental particles in the world, with 55 fundamental laws that govern their pairwise interaction, and that make no difference to anything else. The 55 laws are associated with 55 independent fundamental constants. Fifty-four of the pairs have in fact interacted, but one pair, as it happens, never interacts in the history of the world. Then on the face of it, any value for the 55th fundamental constant is consistent with the non-nomic facts about the world. If so, then the law governing the 55th interaction is not a priori scrutable from the non-nomic truths about this scenario, so that generalized a priori scrutability of the nomic from the non-nomic is false. This does not yet entail that a priori scrutability is false, given that the scenario in question is not actual. But it at least suggests that in general nomic concepts are not even approximately analyzable in terms of non-nomic concepts. And it tends to suggest that precise values for constants need not be a priori scrutable from non-nomic truths even in the actual world, assuming that there are laws in our world that are as robust as those in the Tooley scenario. So if the Tooley scenario is conceivable and if our world has laws, there is good reason to reject Humean scrutability.

Of course Humeans can deny the intuitions. They might deny that the 'giant cosmic coincidence' world is ideally conceivable: in conceiving of a scenario with those regularities, we are thereby conceiving of a scenario on which the laws obtain. They may also deny that the Tooley scenario is conceivable, holding that a purported 55th independent fundamental constant could not have a value in such a scenario. They may deny that there are laws in our world. Or to avoid a verbal dispute over laws, they might deny that there are 'strong laws' in our world (the sort that might be conceivably absent while the regularities obtain), while allowing that there are 'weak laws' (laws constituted by complex regularities, so that the laws could not be conceivably absent while the regularities obtain).

Here I will only report my own view, which is that there is a sense of 'law' in which the Tooley scenario and the cosmic-coincidence scenario are conceivable, and that our world has laws in that sense. That is, our world has strong laws. To be sure, the hypothesis that our world has only weak laws is coherent, but I think that it is extremely unlikely, as it in effect renders our own world a cosmic-coincidence world on which pervasive regularities are not explained by anything more basic than themselves. A hypothesis on which the pervasive regularities are explained by strong laws is much more likely to be true. So I favor the non-Humean view here.

What applies to laws also applies to causation and the other nomic notions above. In each case there are Humean and non-Humean views, and in each case

conceivability considerations can be used to make a case against Humean scrutability. Humeans can respond by denying conceivability, or by denying that there
are nomic truths of the relevant sort. (Metaphysical Humeans can also respond by
denying that supervenience requires scrutability, but this will not affect the current
issue.) They might back up the first denial by offering an analysis of the relevant
nomic notions in non-nomic terms. Non-Humeans find the denials implausible
and the analyses unacceptable. As before, this is a substantive debate.

I will not try to recapitulate or assess the debate between Humeans and non-
Humeans here. As before, I will just report my view that at least where scrutability is concerned, I think that non-Humeans have the better of the debate. So I
accept a non-Humean view. From this view it follows that a scrutability base
must include some nomic expressions.

The next question is: which nomic expressions? Is one nomic concept fundamental: perhaps that of cause, or law, or power, or chance? Various views are possible here. I think that it is plausible that at least in our world, all causal and
dispositional truths are scrutable from truths about laws (laws that do not mention
causation or dispositions, such as standard microphysical laws), and perhaps truths
about chance, along with non-nomic truths. One cannot conceive of a world in
which the non-nomic truths and the law/chance truths are just as in our world,
but some causal truths or dispositional truths are different. One might argue (following Tooley 1987 and Carroll 1994) that it is at least conceivable that there are
cases of singular causation in which A causes B as a one-off, without any laws or
chances or regularities in the vicinity, and with a corresponding failure of scrutability. Perhaps this is conceivable, in which case a generalized scrutability claim may
fail, but in any case it is reasonable to deny that there are such cases in our world,
so a priori scrutability from law/chance and non-nomic truths is still tenable.

As for chances: if we understand these in a strong sense so that the existence
of nontrivial chances (those not equal to 0 or 1) is incompatible with determinism, it is arguable that all nontrivial chances in our world derive from probabilistic laws. If we understand chances in a weak sense so that the existence of
nontrivial chances is compatible with determinism, it is arguable that all nontrivial chances derive from probabilistic or nonprobabilistic laws (perhaps along
with initial conditions or other boundary conditions). Trivial chances will be
scrutable in the same way that nonprobabilistic laws are scrutable. So if one
knew all the (probabilistic and nonprobabilistic) laws and the non-nomic truths,
one could know all the chances. Again, there may be conceivable chances that
do not work like this, but it is reasonable to deny that there are such chances in
our world.

So I am inclined to think that at least where our world is concerned, the
only nomic truths that need to be included in the scrutability base are statements of fundamental laws, including fundamental probabilistic laws. Here the

fundamental nomic vocabulary may include an operator: 'It is a law that', or perhaps 'It is naturally necessary that'. One may also need to invoke the notion of
chance to state fundamental probabilistic laws, if there are such laws. I am inclined
to think that notions in the vicinity of those expressed by 'law' (or 'naturally necessary') and 'chance' are then conceptually primitive and cannot be analyzed further.
A number of different non-Humean packages are available: for example, one might
take the fundamental notion to be that of a power, a disposition, or a nomic
relation between universals. I cannot hope to settle that substantive issue here.

For a Humean, on the other hand, none of these notions need to be in a scrutability base. Instead such a base will involve only non-nomic notions. One
natural Humean view is the analog with respect to scrutability of Lewis' view of
supervenience. Here, a scrutability base will include truths about the distribution of properties in spacetime. Then truths about laws will be scrutable from
truths about this distribution, especially in virtue of regularities in the distribution. Truths about causation will derive from truths about laws and about the
underlying distribution, and likewise for chance, dispositions, and so on.

This Humean strategy requires that spatiotemporal notions are in the scrutability base. It is not entirely straightforward to dispense with both nomic and
spatiotemporal notions, although various strategies for doing so are discussed
later. If one holds a Humean scrutability view on which spatiotemporal concepts
are prior to nomic concepts and a spatiotemporal functionalist view on which
nomic concepts are prior to spatiotemporal concepts there is a threat of outright
contradiction. Someone who embraces both Humean scrutability and spatiotemporal functionalism might retreat to a position on which they make claims about
a priori scrutability without making claims about conceptual priority. Understood that way, we may have one minimal scrutability base involving nomic truths
and another involving spatiotemporal truths, or we may have an underlying scrutability base that involves neither. I will return to this issue later in the chapter.

In any case, following my own recommendations, we are currently left with a
scrutability base containing phenomenal expressions, nomic expressions, indexical expressions, logical and mathematical expressions, and whatever expressions
are involved in a 'that's-all' truth.

7 Phenomenal expressions

What about phenomenal truths: truths about what it is like to be a conscious
subject? Are these a priori scrutable from nonphenomenal truths? I have already
discussed arguments that phenomenal truths are not scrutable from physical
truths, including conceivability arguments and knowledge arguments. Similar
arguments tend to suggest that they are not scrutable from a base with just
nomic truths, spatiotemporal truths, and other background truths.

Of course some reject these arguments. Most often, materialists accept that phenomenal truths are not scrutable from physical truths, while holding that they nevertheless supervene on physical truths. These 'type-B' materialists do not count as opponents for present purposes, as they accept the failure of scrutability. Less commonly, 'type-A' materialists hold that all phenomenal truths are scrutable from physical truths. One version of this view involves eliminativism, on which there are no phenomenal truths. A more common version is some version of analytic functionalism, on which phenomenal notions are at least approximately analyzable as notions of those states that play a certain functional role. Given analytic functionalism, phenomenal truths will be a priori scrutable from relevant functional truths. If one accepts either of these type-A views, one might well hold that all phenomenal truths are scrutable from nomic truths and spatiotemporal truths, or from spatiotemporal truths alone, or perhaps even from nomic truths alone (along with indexical and that's-all truths). Hard questions then arise as to just what will be in the base, but I will set this sort of view aside for now. I think that both eliminativism and analytic functionalism about the phenomenal are highly implausible, as are other similar views on which phenomenal truths are scrutable from nomic and/or spatiotemporal truths.

Even if one rejects scrutability of this sort, however, some other sorts of scrutability remain open. One general observation is that even on type-B materialist views and many dualist views, phenomenal states will supervene on physical states with nomological or metaphysical necessity: if two (nomologically or metaphysically) worlds have the same physical states, they will have the same phenomenal states. This supervenience will involve psychophysical laws, such that phenomenal truths are scrutable from physical truths and psychophysical laws. Ideally, these laws will be simple and general. If so, a base involving psychophysical laws will be much simpler than one specifying all phenomenal truths, although it will still involve irreducibly phenomenal notions.

As with normative and ontological principles in chapter 6, psychophysical laws bring possible vocabulary expansion. Some potential laws involve high-level expressions such as 'brain' or 'functional organization' or 'information': for example, such-and-such brain state yields such-and-such phenomenal state. If the high-level expressions are definable in microphysical terms, we can state these laws without vocabulary expansion. If the relevant high-level truths are merely scrutable from microphysical truths, however, there may be no simple restatement of the laws in the existing vocabulary. One may be left with the choice between a raft of conditional laws from various microphysical conditions to consciousness, or relatively simple laws that invoke new high-level vocabulary. I think one can reasonably hope for laws that have a reasonably simple specification in microphysical vocabulary, but if not, then to avoid vocabulary expansion we will need added complexity in the base.

There are also views on which most or all phenomenal notions can be eliminated from the base. One is a view on which phenomenal truths are scrutable from *protophenomenal truths*: truths about the distribution of certain protophenomenal properties, properties that are not phenomenal properties but that may somehow add up to phenomenal properties. Here protophenomenal concepts are not physical concepts, and may not be analyzable in nomic or spatiotemporal terms. We might instead think of them as concepts of certain intrinsic natures. It is likely that we do not currently possess these protophenomenal concepts, but we cannot rule out that there are such concepts. At least, conceivability arguments and knowledge arguments do not rule out a view on which phenomenal truths are scrutable from protophenomenal truths. Proponents of this view will hold that given enough protophenomenal information, one could know what it is like to see red and other phenomenal truths. They will also hold that protophenomenal duplicates of us without consciousness are inconceivable. If such a view is correct, we might eliminate phenomenal truths from a scrutability base in favor of protophenomenal truths. This view is extremely speculative, but I leave it on the table as one view that is not ruled out.

Setting this view aside, another relevant view is one on which phenomenal notions are analyzable as having a certain internal structure. For example, a sense-datum theorist might hold that it is a priori that someone experiences phenomenal redness iff they are acquainted with a red sense-datum. A naive realist might hold that it is a priori that someone experiences phenomenal redness iff they are acquainted with a red object. A representationalist might hold that it is a priori that someone experiences phenomenal redness if they represent redness in the right way. Some versions of sense-datum theory, naive realism, and representationalism will deny the claim about apriority, and only make a claim about the metaphysical nature of phenomenal properties. But it is at least possible to hold the a priori versions of these views.

I think that the most plausible version of these views is representationalism, so I will focus on that view here (analogous but somewhat different morals might apply given the other views).[15] I think it is not implausible that it is a priori that

---

[15] On a naive realist view, there is a danger that having phenomenal properties in the base may introduce a trivializing mechanism akin to that introduced by having knowledge in the base, as discussed under 'intentional truths' in the last chapter. On at least some naive realist views, what it is like to veridically perceive a red square differs from what it is like to have an illusion or a hallucination of a red square. If so, the phenomenal property associated with this perception will entail the existence of a red square; indeed, it may be analyzable as (veridically perceiving a red square), or as (seeing the redness of a square), or some such. So some truths about the existence of red squares (at least those that are actually veridically perceived) may be a priori scrutable from these phenomenal truths. If there are also noncore phenomenal properties associated with veridically perceiving (for example) a ripe tomato, and if we also allow counterfactuals about phenomenal properties, then it may be that most or all truths about ripe tomatoes

everyone who experiences phenomenal redness in some sense represents redness (or some property in the vicinity), and that everyone who represents this property in the right way experiences phenomenal redness. Of course 'in the right way' needs some unpacking. It is likely that any given property can be represented unconsciously, for example. So I think one needs to require something like *conscious* representation (equivalently, phenomenal representation or perhaps phenomenal awareness) of the property, or conscious perceptual representation, or perhaps conscious visual representation. Because of this, there is no hope of dropping phenomenal notions entirely. One will need at least a basic phenomenal relation in the base. But at least the structure of these notions may be clarified.

The nature of the represented properties also has to be clarified. I have argued in 'Perception and the Fall from Eden' that the equivalence between phenomenal properties and phenomenal representation of certain properties is only plausible if one takes the represented properties to be primitive (or Edenic) color properties, such as primitive redness. It is arguable that these primitive properties are not instantiated in our world. Still, if this view is correct, we can say that phenomenal redness is a priori equivalent to (something like) phenomenal awareness of primitive redness (or perhaps phenomenal representation of or phenomenal acquaintance with primitive redness).

If this is right, then truths about phenomenal color properties are a priori scrutable from truths about the phenomenal awareness of primitive colors. Something similar may go for the phenomenal awareness of primitive spatiotemporal properties, primitive sound properties, primitive pain properties, and so on. The generalization to nonperceptual domains such as emotion and thought is not as clear, but there is at least something to be said for representationalist approaches here too. But to stay with the perceptual case, if a view like this is right, then it is possible to remove arbitrary phenomenal expressions from a scrutability base, in favor of a generic notion of phenomenal awareness and a class of expressions for properties of which one is aware, such as primitive colors and the like.

Whether or not this is desirable depends on one's ambitions for a scrutability base. If one wishes it to include maximally primitive concepts, then I think there

---

and the like (whether they are actually veridically perceived or not) will be a priori scrutable from these counterfactuals.

As with intentional truths, the trivialization problem can be avoided by an appeal to psychophysical laws. If there are general psychophysical principles specifying when a worldly state of affairs will be associated with a phenomenal state of perceiving it (for example, depending on its connection to a perceptual system), then phenomenal states will themselves be scrutable from worldly truths (including truths about external states of affairs, perceptual systems, and their connections) and psychophysical laws. Then as long as the relevant worldly truths are themselves scrutable from a compact base, there will be no problem for the scrutability thesis here.

is something to be said for the thesis that the concepts of phenomenal awareness and of primitive redness are conceptually prior to that of phenomenal redness. This also allows us to accommodate the observation from earlier that some color concepts are arguably conceptually prior to phenomenal concepts. It remains the case that *physical* color concepts can be analyzed in terms of causal relations to phenomenal properties, but phenomenal properties can be analyzed in turn in terms of the phenomenal representation of *primitive* color properties. This helps us to avoid an implausible picture on which the primitive concepts in a scrutability base are largely inward-directed concepts of mental states. Instead, the primitive concepts will include all sorts of externally-directed concepts such as those of primitive colors, along with a generic notion of awareness.

On the view that I favor, primitive color concepts will enter a scrutability base in the context of representation: the base will include truths about the representation of primitive redness, but not about the instantiation of primitive redness. The same goes for the other primitive concepts. As before, though, if one holds a view on which these concepts pick out primitive properties that are in fact instantiated, then one may also need to include these colors in a nonrepresentational context. For example, truths about the instantiation of primitive redness in the base may not be scrutable from other elements of the base, unless perhaps they are scrutable from more basic constituents, such as primitive hue and primitive brightness. Something similar may apply to views on which these concepts pick out physical properties. Even on my view, primitive color properties and the like may be instantiated in an 'Edenic' scenario: it is just that such a scenario is not actual. So I think that sentences concerning the instantiation of such properties are needed in a generalized scrutability base, although not in a scrutability base for the actual world.

In any case, in what follows I will mainly remain neutral about the possibility of analyzing phenomenal concepts in this sort of way. For present purposes, it is simplest to proceed on the assumption that the scrutability base will include phenomenal expressions, and leave open the possibility that these might be further analyzed.

8 Compression using laws

As things stand, we have a Ramsey sentence R saying (i) that there exist certain properties (one for each fundamental physical property) governed by certain laws connecting these properties to each other and to experience, (ii) that there exist certain objects (one for each fundamental object) with such-and-such properties in that class, (iii) that there exist certain individuals (one for each conscious individual) with such-and-such phenomenal properties, (iv) that I have such-and-such properties in this vocabulary, (v) that now is such-and-such time in this vocabulary, (vi) (optional, for one or more experiences and phenomenal demonstratives 'this' that this experience is such-and-such an experience), and (vii) that all positive truths are implied by (i)–(v).

A natural way to minimize this sentence is to eliminate most or all of the conjuncts in (ii) and (iii) concerning the existence of objects, instead deriving them from statements of laws. After all, if we are non-Humeans, we will already have sentences specifying physical and psychophysical laws in the base. And even if we are Humeans, adding laws to the base will allow a great reduction in the size of the base sentence, if at cost of conceptual priority.[16] This move is in some respects incidental for our main purposes, as it need involve no alteration to the class of expressions used in the base. It nevertheless raises interesting questions concerning the size of the base measured in other respects. In particular, to borrow a term from complexity theory, it bears on the 'compressibility' of the universe.

With regard to physical objects: an obvious way to proceed is to eliminate all reference to these except for specifying certain boundary conditions (perhaps the state of the universe around the Big Bang, for example). Then if fundamental physical laws are specified, and if the physical evolution of the universe is deterministic, all truths about fundamental physical objects will be scrutable from truths about boundary conditions plus truths about laws. Precisely how far one can reduce the specification of boundary conditions is itself an empirical question: insofar as there are laws constraining the distribution of physical entities at a time, or laws constraining boundary conditions themselves, one might be able to reduce these beyond a simple specification of the entire microphysical state of the universe at a time.

If the physical evolution of the universe is nondeterministic, things will be more complicated. One will need some way to specify the results of every fundamental nondeterministic event—that is, every physical state whose character is not determined by preceding states. Depending on how widespread the nondeterminism is, this may require massively expanding the microphysical sentence until it nears the complexity of the original sentence—though it will presumably be somewhat compressed, given the existence of lawful regularities among the microphysical truths.

Alternatively, each nondeterministic event might itself be encoded by a real number between 0 and 1, perhaps attached to a spatiotemporal location (or its equivalent in the Ramsified language), which when combined appropriately

---

[16] Where the non-Humean's law truths will be of the form 'It is a law that P', the Humean's law truths can be of the simpler form 'P', where P specifies regularities, as the Humean but not the non-Humean holds that explicitly nomic truths are scrutable from non-nomic truths about regularities.

with indeterministic laws and preceding conditions will determine the physical state that follows. If there is some way to impose an ordering on these events, one might represent all this nondeterminism with a (perhaps infinite) sequence of real numbers. Then boundary conditions, laws, and this sequence will collectively determine the microphysical state of the universe. In what follows, I will take it that this sequence is subsumed under the label 'boundary conditions'. Then even on a nondeterministic view, laws and boundary conditions determine the microphysical state of the universe.

Something similar applies to psychophysical laws. On the present picture, phenomenal truths are not a priori scrutable from physical truths, but there are psychophysical laws that relate the two. Here I use 'law' in a broad sense: the picture applies equally to dualists, who will hold that these laws are fundamental laws of nature, and to type-B materialists, who will hold that the laws are metaphysical necessities or identities. As long as phenomenal properties globally supervene on physical properties with at least nomological necessity, there will be such laws, and the laws when combined with microphysical truths will determine all phenomenal truths. The microphysical vocabulary used in stating these laws will itself be given in the Ramsified way. The scrutability base need then only consist of the microphysical base (physical boundary conditions and laws) along with psychophysical laws, and the phenomenal truths will follow.

If phenomenal truths do not globally supervene on physical truths with nomological necessity, then the picture will be more complicated. One possibility is that psychophysical laws are probabilistic: this possibility can be handled in much the same way that we handled probabilistic physical laws. Another possibility, perhaps endorsed by some substance dualists, is that the phenomenal domain is autonomous from the physical domain in a way such that the relation between the two cannot be captured even by probabilistic laws. If this is the case, one will probably need to retain a separate specification of the phenomenal character of conscious individuals—although if there are even some regularities connecting these phenomenal characters to physical states, as seems overwhelmingly plausible, then these regularities might be used to at least compress the amount of information required in the description.

All this bears on the question of how 'compressible' the universe is: that is, on how short a description of the universe can be given (in a reasonably natural vocabulary) from which all truths can be derived. On the present picture, the shortest description is likely to involve a specification of microphysical laws (perhaps in the Ramseyan style, although see the following section), psychophysical laws, microphysical boundary conditions, and a little room for indexicals. Each of these elements can itself be compressed as much as possible into a maximally efficient format. It seems reasonably plausible that the laws and the indexical claims can be stated using a reasonably short finite description length, perhaps aside from a few real-number quantities for fundamental constants. Boundary conditions might be finitely stable, if a boundary state involves finite states of a finite number of entities, and if there is no indeterminism or if the extent of the universe is finite. But perhaps more likely, these will require real numbers at least to specify relevant states and relevant indeterministic outcomes.

There is good reason to think that the specification as a whole will be at most countable in extent.[17] The main worry about size above comes from specifying the physical state of the universe, via boundary conditions. But the entire physical state of the world appears to be statable using continuous functions over separable spaces: spaces that have a countable dense subset, in the way that the rationals form a countable dense subset of the reals. Any such function can be specified by specifying the real values of the function at members of the countable subset, and this can always be done using a countable specification. So at least given what we currently know about physics and about consciousness, it is reasonably plausible that a countable specification will suffice.

It is not obvious that a maximally compressed description will itself be a specification of metaphysically fundamental or conceptually primitive truths. For example, on a Humean view, specifying the metaphysically fundamental truths requires specifying the properties of each fundamental entity, whereas a much shorter specification using laws will involve nonfundamental truths. Even on a non-Humean view, it is not clear that initial conditions (for example) should have a privileged status as metaphysically fundamental, or that facts about the properties of fundamental entities are metaphysically or conceptually grounded in facts about laws and initial conditions. So compression should be taken as an interesting project in its own right and not necessarily a guide to fundamentality.

9 Quiddities

A residual question concerns whether the scrutability base should include further truths about the intrinsic nature of microphysical properties. The current Ramsey sentence says that there exist certain properties, playing certain nomic roles with respect to each other and with respect to phenomenal properties. One might wonder: are there truths about *which* properties play these roles? If so, should such truths (or other truths from which these truths are scrutable) be added to the base? Or perhaps, should the existentially quantified truths about properties simply be replaced by unquantified truths using expressions for the relevant properties?

This issue mirrors Russell's famous observation that physics does not tell us about the intrinsic character of the entities and properties that it discusses, but

---

[17] Thanks to Marcus Hutter for discussion here.

merely about their structural relations. In effect, physics characterizes everything by its nomic or causal relation to other entities. But one might think that in order to stand in such relations, entities need to have some further intrinsic character of their own: something to do the causing, perhaps, or something for the laws to relate. Otherwise, as Russell (1927, p. 116) said, we have a 'certain air of taking in each other's washing'. On the present picture, we already have some properties with a specific intrinsic character: the phenomenal properties. But specifying the phenomenal properties of conscious individuals still seems to leave the question of the intrinsic character of microphysical entities wide open.

In recent years, following Lewis (2009), this issue has been discussed under the label of 'Ramseyan humility'. Rae Langton (1997) attributes a related idea to Kant under the label of 'Kantian humility'; Lewis transposes this idea into the domain of Ramsey sentences. Lewis argues that there are different structurally isomorphic worlds in which different fundamental properties play the roles specified by the Ramsey sentence, and that we cannot know which such world we are in. If so, then there are truths about the nature of the properties that play these roles that we cannot know.

The term 'quiddity' is sometimes used for these potentially hidden fundamental properties that play the causal/nomic role specified in microphysics.[18] If Lewis and Russell are right, there are truths about quiddities that physics alone does not reveal. Where do these truths fit into the scrutability picture? Here, I think there are at least four different reactions to the humility claim, each with different consequences for scrutability.

The *no quiddity* picture rejects quiddities entirely. On this picture, there is no strong distinction to be drawn between fundamental properties and the causal/nomic roles that they play. On the most common version of this picture (e.g. Bird 2009), fundamental properties in physics are themselves powers or dispositions to

[18] The word 'quiddity' was first used in these contexts by David Armstrong (1989) for certain second-order properties: the intrinsic natures of properties. On Armstrong's use, quidditism for properties is parallel to haecceitism for universals: just as haecceities are those features of objects that make objects the objects that they are, quiddities are those features of properties that make properties the properties that they are. I use 'quiddity' for certain first-order properties, however. On this usage, quiddities are not intrinsic properties of properties, but rather certain intrinsic properties of (microphysical) things: in particular those (arguably hidden) categorical properties that play certain microphysical roles. While this differs from the original use, the two notions are closely connected, and in practice most discussions of quidditism are concerned more with quiddities in this sense than in the original sense. For example, Dustin Locke (forthcoming) argues that the core thesis of quidditism does not require Armstrong-style quiddities but rather turns on the connection between first-order properties and their roles. Hawthorne 2001, Lewis 2009, and Schaffer 2005 also in effect understand quidditism in this way. So I think the revised usage is justified by the ethics of terminology (see 'Verbal Disputes'): the first-order properties here are much more important than the second-order properties, we badly need a label for them, and 'quiddity' is nearby and apt.

affect other properties. Given that the other properties are themselves powers, the powers will themselves form a sort of circular structure that is not grounded in something other than a power. Some reject this picture along the lines of Russell's remark above, finding that the world it describes is too insubstantial to be a world, but others find it acceptable. On this picture, our existentially quantified claims about the existence of properties that play certain roles can be replaced by the claim that such-and-such powers (corresponding to these roles) are instantiated by entities in our world. On this picture, there will be no unknown truths about the properties that play these roles, and no need to add anything to a scrutability base.

On the other three pictures, there is a substantial distinction to be drawn between the roles and the properties that play the roles. But these pictures differ in what they say about the relevant properties.

The *thin quiddity* picture accepts that the various roles are played by numerically distinct properties, but there is no more to the difference between the properties than their numerical distinctness. (There might also be certain structural differences, for example if we allow both binary properties and real-valued 'properties', but for simplicity I will set these aside here.) So in particular, these properties do not have a distinct 'intrinsic character' to search for. Fundamental property 1 plays the charge role, fundamental property 2 plays the spin role, and that is that. On this picture, I think that all truths are scrutable from the truths that there are distinct properties playing these roles, along with the 'that's-all' truth. One might think that there is a further truth to worry about here—the truth that property 1 plays the charge role, for example. But there is no truth here that we do not know: we know that the charge role is played by a property distinct from the properties played by the other properties, we can use the term 'property 1' for it if we like, and there is nothing else here to know.[19] So on this picture, the standard Ramsey sentence will yield the scrutability of all truths.

---

[19] I think that the thin quiddity picture is very close to Lewis' own picture, as well as to the picture of Armstrong (1997). Why, then, does Lewis say that there are unknown truths here? I think that Lewis makes an invalid inference from the claims (1) there are distinct metaphysically possible worlds in which the relevant properties are permuted (this will be possible if one allows transworld identity for properties) and (2) our knowledge does not distinguish between these worlds to (3) we are ignorant of which properties are instantiated in our world. Inferences of this sort sometimes break down in circumstances I discuss in 'The Nature of Epistemic Space', wherein multiple metaphysical possibilities correspond to a single epistemic possibility. Another such case arises if one allows a reasonably strong transworld identity for individuals. Suppose one inhabits a world with two duplicate balls. Then (1) there will be a world qualitatively just like ours in which the two balls are permuted, and (2) our knowledge does not distinguish between these worlds. But it is not true that (3) we are ignorant of any truths concerning which ball is which. There are two distinct balls with the relevant properties in our world, and that is all there is to know. Given the existence of the distinct balls and the relevant sort of transworld identities, one can construct new qualitatively identical possible worlds, but one should not mistake these worlds for distinct epistemic possibilities. The same goes in the case of properties. See E16, footnote 5, for some related considerations.

The third and fourth pictures are versions of a *thick quiddity* picture on which quiddities have a substantial nature of some sort and are not merely numerically distinct from each other. The *graspable thick quiddity* picture holds that there are truths about thick quiddities that we can entertain, or at least that some being could entertain. One version of the third picture is a version of panpsychism on which fundamental microphysical entities have experiences and the various roles are played by distinct phenomenal properties. To take an oversimple version: the charge role might be played by phenomenal redness, while the spin role might be played by phenomenal painfulness. Microphysical entities will have intrinsic phenomenal properties corresponding to these roles. On this picture, we can certainly entertain truths about which properties play which roles, though it may be difficult to know these truths (except perhaps by some complicated inference to the best explanation of the association between physical properties and our own conscious experiences).

On almost any view that acknowledges quiddities, we will at least be able to *refer* to quiddities, for example as 'the property that plays such-and-such role'. So on any such view there is a weak sense in which we can form concepts of these properties and grasp them. For graspability in the sense of the third picture, however, a stronger relation is required. The property must be picked out by a *quiddistic concept*: intuitively, one that picks out the property not by its role but by its intrinsic character. In the framework of the fourteenth excursus, we can require that a quiddistic concept picks out a quiddity *super-rigidly*, so that someone who possesses the concept can know a priori what it picks out.[20] For example, on the panpsychist picture, a phenomenal concept will pick out a phenomenal quiddity super-rigidly. This sort of direct grasp enables us to entertain hypotheses about which quiddities play which roles, hypotheses that may turn out to be true or false. And we can use quiddistic concepts to state truths about quiddities and their connections to roles.

There are also nonpanpsychist views on which thick quiddities are graspable. There is a version with protophenomenal properties playing the roles; there is a version with primitive color properties playing the roles (e.g., the Edenic color properties discussed earlier, and likewise for other primitive secondary qualities); and there is a version on which the properties playing the roles have nothing to do with conscious experiences or their contents. What matters for graspable thick quiddities is that we (or our idealized counterparts) can form quiddistic concepts of these properties.

[20] Quiddistic concepts are roughly the same as Daniel Stoljar's 'O-concepts' in 'Two Conceptions of the Physical' (2001). Instead of super-rigidity, one could also require only epistemic rigidity or conceptual transparency, in the framework of E14.

Will quiddistic truths be scrutable from the truths in the Ramsey sentence? This will be so only if the association of quiddities with roles can be determined a priori. It is most natural (although not obligatory[21]) for a proponent of graspable thick quiddities to hold that multiple hypotheses about which quiddities play which role are epistemically possible, in which case truths about quiddities will not be scrutable. One could then simply adjoin truths about which quiddities play which roles. But it is simplest just to replace the existentially quantified claims that there are properties that play the roles by claims to the effect that such-and-such properties play the roles, where 'such-and-such' expresses quiddistic concepts of these properties. In effect, the Ramseyan nomic structure in the scrutability base will be replaced by a number of claims about the nomic relations that these quiddities bear to each other. The Ramseyan truths will then be scrutable from the relevant quiddistic truths, whether the quiddistic truths are themselves scrutable from the Ramseyan truths or not.

Finally, on the *ungraspable thick quiddity* picture, there are quiddities with a substantial nature, but we cannot form quiddistic concepts of them (we can only conceive of them as the properties that play such-and-such roles), and neither can our idealized counterparts. One might say that on this view there are no quiddistic concepts, at least if one takes a psychological or Fregean view of concepts on which concepts are essentially graspable. On this picture, there is a sense in which there are facts and true Russellian propositions about these properties that one cannot derive from the truths in the scrutability base. But the underivability of these propositions will not be reflected by the underivability of any true sentence that any possible being can utter: in a certain sense, the propositions will be inexpressible. As discussed in the third excursus, phenomena of this sort yield counterexamples to propositional scrutability theses (at least construed in terms of Russellian propositions) but not to a sentential scrutability thesis: all true sentences will still be scrutable from the previous Ramsey sentence. Still, as with other cases of this sort, it is arguable that this fourth picture goes against an aspect of the spirit of the scrutability thesis if not its letter.

There are also pictures on which elements of these four pictures are combined. For example, one could combine the third and fourth picture by holding that

---

[21] John Heil (2003), C. B. Martin (1997), and Galen Strawson (2008) hold a thick quiddity view on which quiddities and dispositions are identical or at least necessary connected. One version of this view involves an a posteriori necessity, so that quiddistic truths are not scrutable from dispositional truths or vice versa. Another version involves an a priori connection, in which case there may be scrutability one or both directions. For example, it is open to a panpsychist to hold that is a priori that a given phenomenal property plays a certain causal roles (it is a priori that pain causes aversive reactions, for example), so that dispositional truths are scrutable from quiddistic truths and perhaps (given further commitments) vice versa.

one can grasp some truths about quiddities without being able to grasp their entire nature. Or one could combine elements of the no quiddity picture with elements of one of the others by holding that some fundamental powers have quiddities as bases while others have none. Here, the consequences for scrutability will be correspondingly combined.

The label *quidditism* is often used for views that accept quiddities and that accept a certain independence between them and the associated roles. At least four theses of roughly decreasing strength might be distinguished. *Epistemological quidditism* holds that there are truths about quiddities (that is, about which quiddities play which roles) that are not a priori scrutable from truths about the roles. (*Strong* epistemological quidditism holds that these truths are unknowable.) *Conceptual quidditism* holds that there are quiddistic concepts of quiddistic properties. *Modal quidditism* holds that facts about quiddities are not necessitated by facts about the roles. *Metaphysical quidditism* holds that there exist quiddities distinct from the associated roles and powers. Of the four pictures above, the no quiddity picture rejects all four varieties of quidditism. The thin quiddity pictures and the ungraspable thick quiddity picture accept modal and metaphysical quidditism, but (at least on my analysis) not conceptual or epistemological quidditism.[22] Only the graspable thick quiddity picture accepts conceptual quidditism, and this picture is naturally (although not compulsorily; see footnote 21) combined with epistemological quidditism.

I am uncertain which of these four pictures is correct, and I cannot rule any of them out conclusively. I am most sympathetic with the graspable thick quiddity picture, in a form that accepts epistemological quidditism, although I am far from certain about this. On this picture, the scrutability base will need to include *quiddistic expressions*, expressing the relevant quiddistic concepts, and used in truths specifying the distribution and roles of the associated quiddities.

On some forms of this picture, the quiddistic expressions will be included in the base already, and will simply need to be redeployed. This may apply to views on which quiddities are phenomenal properties, protophenomenal properties, or

---

[22] Epistemological quidditism comes in two varieties, depending on whether the truths in question are understood as sentences or propositions. The ungraspable thick quiddity picture above may accept the propositional version (at least for Russellian propositions) while rejecting the sentential version, by holding that there are inscrutable propositions about quiddities that we cannot entertain or assert. So if epistemological quidditism is understood propositionally, it need not entail conceptual quidditism. Lewis' version of the thin quiddity picture, as Lewis himself understands it, might also be seen as a version of propositional epistemological quidditism without sentential epistemological quidditism or conceptual quidditism (one might think of it as a sort of ungraspable thin quiddity picture). If I am right in the earlier footnote on Lewis, though, the thin quiddity picture is best not understood in this way. Where the ungraspable thick quiddity picture involves some ignorance of the way our world is, the thin quiddity picture does not involve any such ignorance. The distinction is very delicate, however.

primitive qualities analogous to color qualities. On some versions of this picture, phenomenal truths about conscious individuals such as ourselves will themselves be implied by quiddistic truths (about the fundamental phenomenal, protophenomenal, or primitive properties). This will greatly simplify the scrutability base, so that it need only specify nomic relations (corresponding to laws of physics) among these fundamental properties. On other versions of the picture, one will still need to specify 'psychophysical' laws relating the fundamental quiddities (phenomenal, protophenomenal, or primitive properties) as specified in physics to 'high-level' phenomenal properties in individuals such as ourselves.

On other forms of the picture, entirely new quiddistic concepts and expressions will be required. Then our base sentence will consist in specifying the nomic relations (corresponding to laws of physics) among the quiddities, and the nomic relations (corresponding to psychophysical laws) connecting these quiddities with phenomenal properties, along with the usual boundary conditions, indexicals, and the like. On any form of conceptual quidditism, we can replace quantification over properties with quiddistic expressions for properties, thus simplifying the logical form of sentences in the scrutability base, although on the picture in this paragraph (as opposed to the last), this simplification will come at the cost of expanding the vocabulary used in the scrutability base.

It is worth noting that issues parallel to those for quiddities also arise for haecceities. For any given object (such as the Eiffel tower), the object's haecceity is the property of being that object. Metaphysical haecceitism holds that haecceities are distinct from any qualitative (non-object-involving properties), and modal haecceitism holds that facts about haecceities are not necessitated by facts about qualitative properties. In the spirit of such a view, one might suggest an epistemological haecceitism on which haecceitistic truths are inscrutable from qualitative truths. However, while it is possible to refer to haecceities ('the property of being John'), this sort of reference involves no more of a problem for scrutability than ordinary sentences involving names or descriptions. Any problem for scrutability here would require haecceitistic concepts: distinguished concepts (akin to quiddistic concepts) that pick out haecceities in an especially direct manner (super-rigidly, in the language of the fourteenth excursus). It seems that we have no terms expressing such concepts, and that we do not grasp any such concepts. Furthermore, this does not seem to be a contingent limitation on our part: it is plausible that there are no such (graspable) concepts to grasp. If so, epistemological haecceitism is false, and there is no threat to scrutability arising from haecceities.

10 Other expressions

Given my own views, we are currently down to a base that includes phenomenal, nomic, indexical, logical, and mathematical expressions, perhaps quiddistic expressions, and whatever expressions are needed to state a 'that's-all' truth. Can there be further minimization here? How small a base can we use?

Indexical expressions: As discussed in the last chapter, a natural package is 'I', 'now', and some phenomenal demonstratives. To handle time-travel cases in which the same person exists in more than one place at once, one might add 'here', or perhaps better, replace 'I' and 'now' by an expression '[I]' that serves to pick out the current time-slice of a person. One could then use truths involving '[I]' to recover truths about 'I', 'now', and 'here' in an obvious way. Another alternative is to always include phenomenal demonstratives in the base, construed as picking out token momentary experiences. One could then reconstruct 'I' and 'now' as the subject and the time of that demonstrated experience. I will not do this here, in part because I do not think that phenomenal demonstratives are prior to notions such as 'I' in this way. But if one is looking for a truly minimal base, this is one way to go.

Logical expressions: So far, I have assumed the use of connectives (and, or, not) and quantifiers (existential, universal). Conjunctive and disjunctive sentences will be scrutable from simpler sentences without conjunction or disjunction and negated sentences are arguably scrutable from non-negated sentences and 'that's-all'. But there may still be a need for connectives inside the scope of quantifiers, laws, and a that's-all sentence. In a familiar way one could reduce the connectives required to one (the Sheffer stroke, perhaps), or even reduce connectives and quantifiers to a single operator (Schoenfinkel's not-exists-and, perhaps). If conceptual priority is required, though, there is a case that negation is conceptually primitive, perhaps along with conjunction (or perhaps conjunction and disjunction are equally conceptually primitive, in case one can choose one and omit the other).

There is an interesting question about whether all quantified truths are scrutable from nonquantified truths. It is tempting to say that existential truths are scrutable from truths about their instances, and that universal truths are scrutable from truths about each instance along with a that's-all truth. This would require, though, that we have a way of referring to each instance. If we were to refer to each instance via a description, then at least on a standard understanding of descriptions, this would involve a sort of quantification in any case. And if we were to refer to each instance via a name, the base would need a name for every object in the universe, yielding an extremely expansive base. Furthermore, there can always be multiple names for concrete objects, where no such name is canonical or primitive, and it appears that names for concrete objects are always Twin-Earthable. So our heuristics suggest that these are not good candidates for a scrutability base.

Furthermore, one can argue that in the general case, it is impossible to have a name for every object in the universe. There may be objects that we have no way of picking out uniquely, due to symmetries in the world. For example, there is no way to refer uniquely to either of the square roots of −1: we can just refer to them jointly by a description (or perhaps a descriptive name such as 'i') that applies equally to both. The same could apply to fundamental concrete objects in certain scenarios. For example, if our world consisted of three spatiotemporally disjoint components, and the two components aside from our own were qualitative duplicates of each other and were symmetrically placed with respect to us, then we might not be able to refer uniquely to objects in either component. If so, there is no avoiding the use of quantification in the general case.

If we cast scrutability in terms of Russellian propositions, this problem might be avoided: even in a symmetrical universe, quantified propositions would be scrutable from nonquantified singular propositions (about i and −i, for example) along with a that's-all proposition. For anything analogous to work at the level of sentences, we would need names expressing haecceitistic concepts (as discussed at the end of the last section), which might serve as canonical names for objects and ground unique reference. But it seems that there are no (graspable) haecceitistic concepts, and so no canonical names. So where sentential scrutability is concerned, existential quantification plays a fundamental role in a scrutability base.

This leaves open meta-ontological questions about whether there is a single conceptually primitive concept of existential quantification that will be used in the base vocabulary, and if so what it applies to. In 'Ontological Anti-Realism', I suggested that there may be multiple equally primitive concepts of existential quantification: perhaps a quantifier that ranges just over fundamental entities, one that ranges over arbitrary mereological sums of such entities, one that ranges just over stuff, and so on. If our base includes one of these quantifiers, it is likely that arbitrary truths using the other quantifiers may be scrutable from it, but the choice of quantifiers to use in the base may be arbitrary. On alternative views (e.g. the ontological realism of Sider 2009), there is a privileged quantifier that corresponds to a metaphysically fundamental aspect of the world. It is natural for such a view to hold that such a quantifier expresses a privileged primitive concept, so that it plays a special role in a scrutability base. I will set aside this meta-ontological issue for now.

What about modal operators? The discussion in the last chapter suggests that truths about apriority (that is, truths of the form 'It is a priori that such-and-such') are themselves a priori, and that truths about metaphysical necessity are scrutable from nonmodal truths. One may well need a nomological necessity operator, but this is counted under the class of nomic truths. One interesting residual case is the use of an apriority operator in stating the 'that's-all' truth—I revisit this below.

What about identity? Are truths about identity scrutable from truths about objects and their non-identity-involving properties and relations, along with a that's-all clause? This is a tricky issue. It is arguable that claims of the form '$A = B$'

are so scrutable. If we know $F(A)$ and $F(B)$ for some maximally specific non-identity-involving positive predicate F, then these imply the positive truth 'There is at least one F' but they do not imply the positive truth 'There are at least two Fs'. So if $A = B$, then $F(A)$ and $F(B)$ plus a that's-all clause (saying that they imply all positive truths) imply 'There is exactly one F', and so imply '$A = B$'. Something similar will apply to more expansive bases. Claims of the form '$A \neq B$' are trickier. These will usually be scrutable from claims of the form $F(A)$ and $\sim F(B)$. But *if* there can be a case in which $F(A)$, $F(B)$, and $A \neq B$, for a maximally specific non-identity-involving predicate F, then one will need at least need a claim such as 'There are two objects with F' in the base—which is arguably identity-involving.

Mathematical expressions: I argued in the last chapter that mathematical truths are all a priori, so need not be in the scrutability base. There remains an interesting question about how much mathematics one needs to state physics (and perhaps to state phenomenology). Any mathematics needed here is likely to remain once one moves to a Ramsey sentence. I take it to be plausible that some mathematics is needed here, though perhaps the fundamental mathematics required might be statable using set theory.

Categorical expressions: Do we need expressions such as 'object' and 'property'? Any work done by 'object' can arguably be done by quantifiers. As for 'property', depending on how we handle issues about quiddities we may want to be able to say things like 'There exists a property ϕ such that'. For these purposes, one either needs something like 'property', or a second-order quantifier that quantifies only over properties, or perhaps a term such as 'instantiates' one of whose places applies only to properties. If we think that the universe may fundamentally contain certain stuffs, the same issues may arise: we may need a stuff quantifier in the base, or else a term such as 'stuff'. Of course all of these issues interact with one's substantive metaphysical views.

That's-all: The central that's-all truth in chapter 3 might be put as: 'For all p, if p and pos(p) then $A(B \rightarrow p)$', where p ranges over propositions, 'pos' is a positiveness operator or predicate, A is an apriority operator, and B is a conjunction of the other base truths. This requires a propositional quantifier, the notion of positiveness, and the notion of apriority. One can probably do better than this, however.

One might try to define a that's-all truth wholly in terms of logical notions and other expressions already in the base. For example, one version might say that every entity and property is identical to one of the entities or properties specified by the base truths. But if 'specified by' here requires explicit introduction by existential base truths, then this will let in fundamental microphysical entities and conscious beings, but it will not let in other entities such as chairs and universities. It is not clear how one might rephrase a purely logical that's-all truth to let in these other derivative entities while ruling out other entities such as ghosts.

Alternatively, as discussed in chapter 3, we might obtain a that's-all truth by casting it in terms of fundamental properties: for example, the only fundamental properties and entities are those specified by the base truths. This requires that a version of the Fundamental Scrutability thesis itself is a priori. But if one thinks this is plausible (as I do), then the extra vocabulary required here might be restricted to the notion of fundamentality. If one is doubtful about this, there may well be other options in the vicinity, including options that appeal to conceptual fundamentality instead and options that appeal to various in-virtue-of relations.

I think it is plausible that at least one such distinctive expression may be required to specify a that's-all truth. In what follows I will refer to expressions utilized to play this role as *totality* expressions, and the concepts they express as totality concepts. Candidates for totality concepts include those of metaphysical and conceptual fundamentality, various notions of in-virtue-of, notions of positiveness or intrinsicality, and the notion of apriority. In what follows, for concreteness, I will usually take the concept of fundamentality to be the key totality concept.

11 Packages

I have in effect argued that there is a minimal scrutability base of a certain sort, expressing microphysical and psychophysical laws and boundary conditions along with indexical and that's-all truths in a certain vocabulary. This vocabulary uses only nomic expressions ('It is a law of nature that'), phenomenal and/or quiddistic expressions, along with logical, mathematical, indexical, and totality expressions.

Still, other packages are available to those with other views, at least if they do not reject the scrutability thesis entirely. What are the most likely packages?

In the current chapter, perhaps the most important choice points have concerned nomic concepts (Humeanism or non-Humeanism), spatiotemporal concepts (functionalism or primitivism), phenomenal concepts (phenomenal realism or anti-realism), and quiddities (quidditism or nonquidditism). Other choice points in this chapter and the last have concerned secondary quality concepts, intentional concepts, normative concepts, and modal concepts, as well as mathematical truths and ontological truths. (The latter two need not involve new concepts in the base, but could lead to further truths using existing concepts.)

Many combinations of views at these choice points are possible. Here I will set aside most of these choice points, and focus on four central cases: nomic concepts, spatiotemporal concepts, phenomenal concepts, and quiddistic concepts. In each case one has the choice between inclusion in a base (non-Humean-ism, spatiotemporal primitivism, phenomenal realism, quidditism) and exclusion (Humeanism, spatiotemporal functionalism, phenomenal anti-realism, anti-quidditism). I will usually also assume that logical, mathematical, indexical, and totality concepts are included in the base. In principle this yields sixteen possible packages. But not all of these packages are obviously available.

The most austere package takes the exclusion option at all four choice points. The most extreme version here is Logical Scrutability, with only logical expres-sions in the base, but we saw in chapter 1 that this view leads straight to New-man's problem. Base truths of this sort are satisfied by any set of an appropriate cardinality, so in effect they constrain only the cardinality of the world. One might try to save an austere package by adding mathematical and indexical expressions, but a moment's reflection suggests that these will do very little to constrain the world beyond its cardinality. One might also suggest a package that adds normative, intentional, modal, and/or secondary quality expressions, but it is hard to see how these will yield a rich enough base from which one can reconstruct microphysical truths and everything else, unless perhaps these are presented as candidates for quidditstic concepts.

An important austere package that takes all four exclusion options is one that exploits the concept of fundamentality. That concept is already playing a role in a that's-all clause, but one might give it a wider role. For example, the base truths may say that there exist *fundamental* objects and entities satisfying a certain structure. This leads to the thesis of Fundamentality Scrutability: all truths are scrutable from truths about fundamentality, perhaps combined with logical, mathematical, and indexical expressions. This austere view is interestingly related to Carnap's own view, and I discuss it in section 7 of the next chapter.

The next most austere packages each include logical, mathematical, indexical, and fundamentality expressions along with one of the four main families above, excluding the other three. We might call the four corresponding theses Nomic, Spatiotemporal, Phenomenal, and Quidditstic Scrutability. Each of these four theses is arguably at least coherent, given appropriate philosophical commit-ments concerning the four choice points.

According to Quidditstic Scrutability, all truths are scrutable from a complete specification of the quidditstic properties and relations instantiated by funda-mental entities in our world (along with indexical and that's-all truths), specified using quidditstic concepts. Certainly this specification would in effect yield a large mosaic full of regularities. Given a Humean view, this might yield truths about nomic and causal relations among the quiddities. One could also perhaps infer truths about nomic and causal relations between macroscopic entities, cast in terms of the quiddities or higher-level properties that derive from them. On a deflationary view of experience or on a protophenomenal view of quiddities, this might suffice to yield phenomenal truths. And on a functionalist view of space-time, these materials might suffice to yield spatiotemporal truths.

According to Nomic Scrutability, all truths are scrutable from a specification of the world as containing entities with certain nomic or causal powers in relation to each other, perhaps with distinct powers corresponding to distinct fundamental properties in physics. Such a world of pure powers or pure causation may seem insubstantial, but it is not obviously incoherent. On the most natural version of this view, there are no quiddities. Given a deflationary view of experience, it is at least arguable that one can use this nomic structure to infer phenomenal truths, if there are such truths. Then given a functionalist view of spacetime, one can use nomic relations to phenomenal truths (along with indexicals) to infer spatiotemporal truths.

According to Spatiotemporal Scrutability, all truths are scrutable from truths specifying that there are entities with certain spatiotemporal properties, standing in certain spatiotemporal relations. Exploiting the Ramsey method, the base truths may also specify that there exist certain further properties (corresponding to nonspatiotemporal fundamental properties in physics such as mass, but without using terms such as 'mass') that are distributed in a certain way over objects. These properties can be seen as quiddities (e.g., mass is the property that plays the mass role), but there will be no inscrutable quiddistic truths about them, so they will probably be either thin quiddities or ungraspable thick quiddities. A Humean view of laws will then yield nomic or causal truths among the fundamental properties. One can also infer spatiotemporal properties of high-level entities, and given a deflationary view of experience, one can infer phenomenal truths. This view is a sort of epistemological analog of Lewis' 'Humean supervenience' picture, on which all truths are necessitated by truths about the distribution of numerically distinct fundamental properties in a spatiotemporal mosaic.

According to Phenomenal Scrutability, all truths are scrutable from truths about what it is like to be certain conscious beings. For this view, the main challenge is seeing how microphysical truths could be scrutable from phenomenal truths, but there are perhaps two different ways this could work. If panpsychism (the view that everything is conscious) is true, truths about the phenomenal properties of microphysical entities could play the role of the quiddistic truths above. And if certain forms of phenomenalism or idealism are true, all nonphenomenal truths would be scrutable from phenomenal truths about the experiences of observers. This view seems to require something like panpsychism or phenomenalism. Without something like panpsychism or phenomenalism, the view is subject to a version of Newman's problem, in that truths in logical and phenomenal vocabulary are compatible with all sorts of variation in truths about the nonphenomenal world. So if one is not a panpsychist or a phenomenalist, phenomenal concepts need to be supplemented with nomic, spatiotemporal, and/or quidditic concepts.

In any case, we have four reasonably austere packages available here. There are also combined views, combining elements of all four packages. There is nothing incoherent about a position that combines Humeanism, phenomenal realism, quidditism, and spatiotemporal primitivism, so that all four classes of concepts will be included in a minimal scrutability base. All sorts of intermediate positions are also possible. Overall, there are sixteen possible combinations ranging from Fundamentality Scrutability through Nomic/Phenomenal/Quidditic/ Spatiotemporal Scrutability, with the four austere options above and various combinations of two or three of them along the way.

Speaking for myself, I am most attracted by Nomic/Phenomenal Scrutability, or perhaps Nomic/Quidditic or Nomic/Phenomenal/Quidditic Scrutability. I think that there is an overwhelmingly strong case for phenomenal realism, a very strong case for non-Humeanism, a reasonably strong case for spatiotemporal functionalism, and an inconclusive case for quidditism. The main open choice points for me concern the truth of quidditism, the relation of quiddities to the phenomenal, and the question of whether phenomenal truths are themselves scrutable from more basic protophenomenal truths.

On a non-quidditic version of the view I favor, the most natural result is a scrutability base specifying the nomic structure and boundary conditions among existentially specified microphysical entities and microphysical properties, along with nomic connections to phenomenal properties and indexical and that's-all truths. This view is a sort of Nomic/Phenomenal Scrutability. I also do not rule out a view on which there are laws connecting microphysical properties to (non-quidditic) protophenomenal properties, which then constitute phenomenal properties. We might think of this view as a sort of Nomic/Protophenomenal Scrutability.

On a quidditic version of the view I favor, a scrutability base will at least include a specification of nomic structure and boundary conditions among quiddities and existentially specified entities that instantiate those quiddities. On some but not all versions of quidditism (in particular, versions of what I have elsewhere called Russellian monism), these quidditic/nomic truths will imply all phenomenal truths. One of these versions is a panpsychist view on which the quiddities are themselves phenomenal: this is a sort of Nomic/Phenomenal Scrutability. Another version holds that the quiddities are protophenomenal: this is perhaps a version of Nomic/Quidditic Scrutability, or alternatively, Nomic/Protophenomenal Scrutability.

On other versions of quidditism, the quidditic and nomic truths will not imply all phenomenal truths. Here we will also need quiddity-phenomenal laws in the base. Views of this sort might be represented either as Nomic/Phenomenal

Scrutability (for a panpsychist view with laws connecting 'microphenomenal' and 'macrophenomenal' properties) or Nomic/Phenomenal/Quiddistic Scrutability (for views with laws connecting nonphenomenal quiddities to phenomenal properties). There will also be versions of the last view on which phenomenal properties are replaced by protophenomenal properties, yielding Nomic/Protophenomenal/Quiddistic Scrutability.

For all I have said, pluralism about base vocabularies remains possible. One can allow that more than one of the sixteen options above forms a minimal scrutability base. *If* one requires that the elements of a minimal scrutability base be conceptually primitive, and if one holds that there is a fact of the matter about conceptual priority in each of the four issues above (Humeanism and so on), then pluralism will be ruled out. But if one rejects either of these claims, for example requiring only a priori entailment rather than conceptual priority, then multiple options may remain open. One might, for example, allow that nomic and phenomenal truths imply all spatiotemporal truths while also allowing that spatiotemporal truths imply all nomic and phenomenal truths. Still, it is natural to understand each of the four issues as an issue about conceptual priority, in which case this sort of flexibility is excluded.

From the *Aufbau* to the Canberra Plan

One the nearest analogs of the *Aufbau* in contemporary philosophy is the so-called Canberra plan. This broadly naturalistic program is associated with Australian philosophers such as Frank Jackson and with Australia-associated philosophers such as David Lewis. It aims to exploit the method of Ramsification (discussed in section 3 of chapter 7) to deliver a conceptual, metaphysical, and epistemological reduction of all sorts of complex concepts and properties to simpler concepts and properties. Here, the thought is that the Ramsey–Carnap–Lewis method can be applied to almost any expression: not just theoretical terms from science such as 'electron' or 'charge', but also philosophical notions such as 'free will' or 'belief', and ordinary notions such as 'water' and 'Gödel'.

As before, the key thought is that one first regiments certain core principles regarding an expression: for example, 'freedom is required for moral responsibility', 'freedom requires the ability to do otherwise', and so on. One then conjoins these principles, yielding a sentence of the form 'P(freedom)'. One can then analyze 'freedom' as 'that property ϕ such that $P(\phi)$', analyze 'x is free' as '$\exists \phi(\phi(x)$ & $P(\phi))$', and so on. This analysis will involve many O-terms, but one can repeat the process, eventually analyzing most of the O-terms away.

The nature of a Ramseyan analysis will depend on just what one takes to be the core principles regarding freedom. The key claim of the Canberra plan is that in most cases there is some core theory such that the Ramseyan analysis of 'free' (or whatever) according to that theory is a priori equivalent to 'free' itself. Just as electrons were previously understood as whatever plays the electron role, freedom is understood as whatever plays the freedom role. Likewise, belief is whatever plays the belief role, water is whatever plays the water role, and Gödel is whatever plays the Gödel role. So one in effect has definitional analyses of all these expressions in terms of O-terms that do not include the expressions.

As before, I am doubtful about the availability of definitions like these, so I am doubtful about the Canberra plan construed in this way. Still, the scrutability framework is at least a close relative of the Canberra plan. So I will temporarily set aside my skepticism about definitions to explore consequences of the Canberra plan. Many of the issues from chapter 7 recur here in a slightly different key. In particular, it is natural to wonder whether the Canberra plan might be used to successively define arbitrary terms, yielding a limited class of basic O-terms, and a very close relative of the *Aufbau* project. This matter has received surprisingly little discussion in the literature, but it deserves attention.[1]

How far can this program go? The Canberra plan holds that a very large class of expressions—perhaps most expressions—can be analyzed using the Ramsey method in principle. It may be, though, that some terms cannot be so analyzed, or at least that they cannot be so analyzed in conjunction with the analysis of other analyzed terms. If so, then these terms will serve as ultimate O-terms. And in effect, all expressions will be analyzed in terms of logic and ultimate O-terms. Once this is done, it is plausible that all truths will be scrutable from truths involving logic and ultimate O-terms.

An extreme version of the Canberra plan embraces *global Ramsification*: every expression, or at least every non-logical expression, can be given a Ramseyan analysis, and furthermore every such expression can be Ramsified at once. If this program worked, then there would be no ultimate O-terms outside logic. Our theory of the world could then be represented as a giant Ramsified statement, saying that there exist objects, properties, and relations standing in certain patterns of instantiation. This program would be very much like the pure structuralism that Carnap momentarily embraces in the *Aufbau* (see chapter 1), and like Carnap's pure structuralism, it falls victim to Newman's problem. At least assuming that we take a liberal view of properties and relations, then the Ramsified statement will be satisfied near-vacuously. So it is not plausibly equivalent to our theory of the world.

The moral is that not every nonlogical expression can be Ramsified, or at least that not every nonlogical expression can be Ramsified simultaneously. Some nonlogical terms must serve as ultimate O-terms, in order to avoid Newman's problem. Perhaps the ultimate O-terms will express non-theoretical concepts of which we have a particularly direct grasp, a grasp that does not depend on the grasping of an associated role.

The question then arises: what are the ultimate O-terms? Or at least, how small can a package of ultimate O-terms be, while still delivering an analysis of all other terms? Different philosophers will give different answers to these questions, but there are certain natural constraints on the answers.

---

[1] One of the few discussions of basic O-terms is given by Peter Menzies and Huw Price (2009), who consider whether causal expressions need to be among the basic O-terms. They argue that they need not be, as causal terms can themselves be Ramsified away. They also hold that if causal terms are not among the basic O-terms, then their role as 'ID tags' in picking out Ramsified entities (as those that play a certain causal role) will have to be played by semantic notions instead (picking out entities as the referents of certain expressions). Menzies and Price do not consider the natural alternative on which the role of ID tags is played by spatiotemporal expressions instead.

A paradigmatic Canberra planner (such as Jackson or Lewis) holds that terms for theoretical entities in science are analyzable in terms of nomic and causal connections between these entities and between these entities and observable entities. Natural kind terms such as 'water' and 'gold' might be analyzed (very roughly) in terms of the dominant bearers of certain observable properties. Names are analyzable in terms of descriptions: often descriptions specifying relevant causal connections to one's use of a term. The use and meaning of language might itself be analyzed in terms of behavior, mental states, and so on. Expressions for secondary qualities such as colors can be analyzed in terms of causal connections to experience. One is left with a view on which very many expressions can be analyzed in terms of a base that includes expressions for primary qualities, mental states and behavior, and causal and nomic expressions (plus logic, mathematics, categorical expressions, and indexicals). From here, moves depend on the philosopher.

Many Canberra planners are analytic functionalists about the mental, holding that concepts of various mental states can be analyzed in terms of causal connections among these states and between these states, perceptual input, and behavioral output, perhaps along with certain connections to the environment. The correct analysis of perceptual inputs and behavior is not obvious, but perhaps these are to be specified in terms of primary qualities. Regarding the nomic or causal: someone like Lewis analyzes causal notions in terms of counterfactual notions, and analyzes counterfactual notions in terms of modal and nomic notions. Nomic notions are analyzed in terms of regularities in spacetime. For Lewis (although not most other Canberra planners), modal notions are analyzed in terms of concrete possible worlds.

Lewis is not explicit on the question of ultimate O-terms. But a natural package suggests itself, on which spatiotemporal notions are basic, perhaps along with logic, mathematics, indexicals, and so on. A world sentence specifies that there are certain perfectly natural properties (where each property is specified only existentially) distributed in a certain pattern in spacetime. All other expressions are definable using these notions, and all other truths are scrutable from these truths. Certainly these semantic and epistemological theses comport with Lewis' metaphysical thesis of Humean supervenience, according to which all truths supervene on the distribution of qualities in spacetime. And it is notable that Lewis does not anywhere attempt to analyze spatiotemporal notions.[2] Still, as discussed in the summation after chapter 8, it is not out of the question that he might have analyzed these notions, yielding an even more austere package of

---

[2] The closest that Lewis comes to an analysis of spatiotemporal notions is a passage in *On the Plurality of Worlds* (pp. 75–6) in which he discusses the 'analogically spatiotemporal' and gives a few constraints on the notion.

O-terms in which spatiotemporal notions are eliminated in favor of the notion of fundamentality or naturalness.

Other packages of O-terms are available. Non-Humeans, phenomenal realists, and spatiotemporal functionalists will go in different directions here, yielding O-term packages analogous to those in the last section. Given my own views, a natural package would include nomic and phenomenal notions (as well as logical, mathematical, and indexical notions). Canberra planners with other philosophical views might also embrace various combinations of the nomic, the phenomenal, and the spatiotemporal, including just one of these, or including all three. A package with no non-logical O-terms is implausible for Newman's reason, but beyond this no option is obviously ruled out. Two natural packages—the austere package involving just fundamentality, and my favored package involving nomic and phenomenal expressions—are discussed in the summation after the next chapter.

Epistemic Rigidity and Super-Rigidity

In *Naming and Necessity*, Saul Kripke introduced the idea of a rigid designator: an expression that picks out the same thing in every possible world. He held that names are rigid designators: for example, 'Hesperus' picks out the same planet (Venus) in all possible worlds. Natural kind terms are also rigid designators: 'water' picks out the same kind, H_2O, in all possible worlds. By contrast, many descriptions are nonrigid: 'The greatest cricket player' picks out Bradman in our world, but it picks out someone else in a world where Bradman died in his youth.

Kripke's notion of rigidity is sometimes called *metaphysical rigidity*: an expression is rigid iff it picks out the same entity in all metaphysically possible worlds. It might more aptly be called counterfactual or subjunctive rigidity, as what really matters here is stability of reference in counterfactual or subjunctive contexts: if a Twin Earth situation had obtained, it still would have been the case that water is H_2O, and the liquid in the oceans and lakes would not have been water. But I will use the more standard term here.

In the tenth excursus, I introduced the parallel notion of *epistemic rigidity*. Epistemic rigidity and the related notion of super-rigidity play an important role in some parts of this book. These notions are related to but importantly distinct from the notion of non-Twin-Earthability discussed in chapter 7. In this excursus I discuss the notions in detail.

To a first approximation, an epistemically rigid expression is one that picks out the same thing in every epistemically possible scenario. As we saw earlier, 'water' is not epistemically rigid: it picks out H_2O in an Earth scenario and XYZ in a Twin Earth scenario. Similarly, names such as 'Hesperus' are not epistemically rigid: 'Hesperus' picks out Venus in the actual scenario, but in a scenario where a star (rather than a planet) is visible in the evening sky at the relevant location, 'Hesperus' will pick out that star. If we construe predicates as picking out properties, then a predicate such as 'hot' is not epistemically rigid: it picks out a property involving molecular motion in our scenario, but in a scenario where a different property X plays the role of heat (in causing experiences, expanding metals, and so on), it will pick out X. The same goes for general terms such as 'tiger', if these are construed as picking out properties.

By contrast, numerical expressions such as 'zero' are epistemically rigid: 'zero' picks out 0 in every scenario. The same plausibly goes for various property terms, predicates, and relations: perhaps 'consciousness', 'wise', 'part', and 'cause', for example. And the same goes for various general terms: perhaps 'philosopher', 'friend', and 'action', for example.

Of course there are scenarios within which a word pronounced 'zero' picks out other things, but those scenarios are irrelevant to epistemic rigidity. What matters here is the intension of the actual word 'zero' and the way that this intension is evaluated at other scenarios. This intension is defined in terms of a priori entailments involving the actual word, not in terms of of the way that the word or others that sound like it behave when uttered in other scenarios.

The definition of epistemic rigidity given above is intuitively useful, but as a formal definition it has a couple of problems. First, it presupposes the notion of what an expression picks out in a scenario. On some approaches to epistemic space (as in E9), the notion of epistemic rigidity is used to help characterize evaluation in scenarios, with an ensuing danger of circularity. Second, it invokes the notion of trans-scenario identity: the relation whereby an object in one scenario is the same object as an object in another. But it is not entirely clear how to make sense of trans-scenario identity.[1] One could invoke an intuitive conception of these things, but there is another approach.

As an alternative, one can define an epistemically rigid expression as one whose extension can be known a priori. For example, there is an intuitive sense in which one can know the referent of 'zero' a priori, and in which one cannot know the referent of 'Hesperus' a priori (although there is some delicacy in understanding this sense, as we will see). It is natural to expect that if one can know an expression's extension a priori, it will pick out the same extension in all epistemically possible scenarios and vice versa. Likewise, if one cannot know an expression's extension a priori, it will pick out different extensions in different scenarios, and vice versa.

What it is to know an expression's extension is not entirely clear, as we saw in the second excursus. For current purposes, we should understand it in much the same way that we understood knowing that a sentence is true (in 2.2), so that metalinguistic knowledge is not required. To know what 'zero' refers to is just to know what zero is, where zero is presented under the guise of 'zero'. Intuitively, one can know a priori what zero is (where zero is presented under the guise of

---

[1] See 'The Nature of Epistemic Space' for a discussion of trans-scenario identity.

'zero'). By contrast, one cannot know a priori what Hesperus is (where Hesperus is presented under the guise of 'Hesperus').

In addition, to say that one can know the extension of 'zero' priori is not simply to say that there is a truth 'Zero is such-and-such' that one can know a priori. The most obviously relevant truth around here is just 'Zero is zero', but the existence of an a priori truth of that form does not suffice for epistemic rigidity. It is true that one can know 'Zero is zero' a priori while one cannot know 'Hesperus is Hesperus' a priori, because one cannot know 'Hesperus exists' a priori. But one can also know 'The number of stars is the number of stars' a priori, and 'The number of stars' is not epistemically rigid.

A more promising suggestion is that 'zero' is epistemically rigid iff one can know a priori (*de re*) of zero that it is zero (where zero in its predicative role is presented under the guise of 'zero'). Generalizing this pattern plausibly excludes both 'Hesperus' and 'The number of stars'. Tricky issues still arise, though. Someone might suggest that there is a name 'Starnum' whose reference is fixed to be the number of stars, and that by knowing 'Starnum is Starnum' we thereby know of Starnum that it is Starnum. To exclude this case, one requires a strong reading of *de re* knowledge in which one does not know *de re* of Starnum that it is Starnum simply in virtue of knowing that Starnum is Starnum.[2] I think that there is a natural way of reading *de re* attributions so that the definition gets the right results. But for present purposes I will leave the idea of knowing an extension a priori as intuitive.

All this can be extended naturally to the key case of properties and relations. A predicate is epistemically rigid when one can know a priori what it is for something (or some things) to satisfy the predicate. Intuitively, we know a priori what it is for one thing to be part of another thing. Arguably, we know a priori what it is for something to be conscious. But we do not know a priori what it is for something to be human, or what it is for one object to be more acidic than another. Correspondingly, we might say that we can know a priori (*de re*) of the parthood relation that it is the parthood relation, but we cannot know a priori of the more-acidic-than relation that it is the more-acidic-than relation. The idea of knowing a priori what it is for something to have a certain property is perhaps the most intuitive understanding, though.

There are numerous epistemically rigid expressions for abstract objects such as numbers ('zero'), properties ('conscious'), and relations ('part'). By contrast, it is

---

[2] For example, Scott Soames (2004) suggests an exportation principle that allows names (but not descriptions) to be exported from *de dicto* knowledge attributions to yield *de re* attributions. Then if one can know a priori that Starnum is Starnum, one can know a priori of Starnum that it is Starnum. I argue against exportation principles of this sort toward the end of 'Propositions and Attitude Ascriptions: A Fregean Account'.

arguable that there are no epistemically rigid expressions for concrete objects. For any expression E for a concrete object e, it is hard to see how we could know the extension of E a priori. On the face of it, for all we know a priori, E refers to e or to some quite distinct object f. Correspondingly, any ordinary expression for a concrete object picks out what seem to be different entities in different scenarios.

Another way to bring this out: any true identity statement in which both sides are epistemically rigid, such as '2 + 2 = 4', is a priori. This is a consequence of both the intuitive definition above and the definition in terms of scenarios: such an identity statement will be true at all scenarios and will therefore be a priori. By contrast, most true identity statements involving ordinary proper names for concrete objects, such as 'Mark Twain is Samuel Clemens', are not a priori. It follows from this that at least one of the names is epistemically nonrigid. Furthermore, the two names seem on a par, so that if one is epistemically nonrigid, both are epistemically nonrigid. In the case of abstract objects, there will also be a posteriori identity statements such as 'o is the number of phlogiston atoms'. But here the two expressions are plausibly not on a par. Numerical representations have a special status as designators for numbers, so that the left side is epistemically rigid while the right side is not.[3]

When an expression is epistemically rigid and also metaphysically rigid *de jure* (roughly, one can know a priori that it is metaphysically rigid), we can say that it is *super-rigid*.[4] A super-rigid expression has the same extension in all scenarios and in all possible worlds. We can know its extension a priori, and we can even know its extension in all possible worlds a priori.

In practice, most epistemically rigid expressions in natural language are also super-rigid. There are some fairly artificial expressions that are epistemically rigid but not super-rigid. Consider 'Whether (P iff actually P)', where P is any contingent sentence, and 'whether' is an operator that serves to pick the truth-value of the embedded sentence. Then this expression picks out *true* in all scenarios, but it picks out *false* in some non-actual worlds. One can even devise expressions that are epistemically rigid and metaphysically rigid *de facto* without being super-rigid. Still, any epistemically rigid expression E can easily be turned into a super-

---

[3] One might suggest that there are some similarly privileged designators for concrete objects: for example, 'I' for oneself, and/or expressions that pick out concrete objects by their essences. I discuss suggestions of this sort in 'The Nature of Epistemic Space' and argue that they do not yield epistemically rigid expressions.

[4] The term 'super-rigid' is due to unpublished work by Martine Nida-Rümelin (2002). A published article in German (Nida-Rümelin 2003) uses the equivalent German term 'superstarrer', and also uses 'absolut starrer' ('absolutely rigid'), with credit to Ulrike Haas-Spohn (1995).

rigid expression E' by rigidifying it *de jure*. For example, one can simply take E' to be 'the actual E'. Then $E = E'$ will be a priori, although it will not be necessary unless E is metaphysically rigid. So where epistemic (although not modal) matters are concerned, one can move easily between epistemic rigidity and super-rigidity.

These distinctions can naturally be represented in the two-dimensional semantic framework (discussed in E10 and E11), according to which expressions have primary intensions (functions from scenarios to extensions), secondary intensions (functions from worlds to extensions), and two-dimensional intensions (functions from scenario–world pairs to extensions). An epistemically rigid expression is an expression with a constant primary intension. A metaphysically rigid expression is one with a constant secondary intension. A super-rigid expression is one with a constant two-dimensional intension.

A closely related notion is that of semantic neutrality. An expression is semantically neutral roughly when its extension in any given possible world is independent of which scenario is actual.[5] Every super-rigid expression is semantically neutral, but the reverse is not the case. For example, 'the only conscious being in the world' is semantically neutral but not super-rigid (it picks out different entities in different worlds, but in a way that can be known without knowing which world is actual). Still, any semantically neutral expression is equivalent to a compound of super-rigid expressions. For example, the semantically neutral description just mentioned can be decomposed as 'the F', where the predicate F super-rigidly expresses the property of being the only conscious being in the world, and where 'the' contributes logical expressions that can be regarded as super-rigid. So there is little difference for our purposes between the class of sentences containing only super-rigid expressions and the class containing only semantically neutral expressions.

Epistemic rigidity is highly reminiscent of non-Twin-Earthability. The epistemically rigid expressions I have discussed here are roughly the same expressions as the non-Twin-Earthable expressions discussed at the start of chapter 7. The epistemically nonrigid expressions correspond to the Twin-Earthable expressions. Still, the two notions are not quite the same. A non-Twin-Earthable expression is roughly one whose extension does not depend metaphysically on the environment (all possible duplicates use corresponding expressions with the same extension). An epistemically rigid expression is roughly one whose extension

---

[5] Nida-Rümelin (2007) calls semantic neutrality 'actuality-independence'. In other work on these topics I have given semantic neutrality a larger role. Here I put more weight on super-rigidity as I think the notion is both more fundamental and easier to grasp.

does not depend epistemologically on empirical evidence. The application of these two notions coincides in many cases, but they can come apart.[6]

Consider the expression, 'Fred', stipulated to pick out 1 if there are any thinkers and 0 if not. Then 'Fred' is non-Twin-Earthable: any token of 'Fred' picks out 1. The same applies at the level of thought: any user of a *Fred* concept picks out 1. Still, 'Fred' is not epistemically rigid: it picks out 1 in scenarios containing thinkers, and 0 in scenarios not containing thinkers. Likewise, subjects are not in a position to know its referent a priori. 'Fred = 1' is true but not a priori: to know it, subjects need either introspective evidence that they are thinking or non-introspective knowledge that others are thinking. So non-Twin-Earthability and epistemic rigidity come apart here.[7]

Something similar goes for concepts of other intrinsic properties (for a notion of Twin-Earthability tied to intrinsic duplicates) or functional and phenomenal properties (for a notion tied to functional and phenomenal duplicates). For example, if 'Bill' is stipulated to pick out the phenomenal color in the center of my visual field, then 'Bill' will not be Twin-Earthable (in every duplicate the corresponding token will pick out phenomenal blueness), but 'Bill = phenomenal blueness' is still not a priori.

In the other direction: it is plausible that in our world, any epistemically rigid expression is non-Twin-Earthable. But in some possible worlds, this might not be so. For example, if there are Edenic worlds (see 7.4 and 'Perception and the Fall from Eden') in which subjects are directly acquainted with instances of primitive redness in their environments, then their expression 'redness' or 'primitive redness' may be Twin-Earthable (for reasons discussed in 8.4), at least in a sense where Twin-Earthability is tied to intrinsic duplication. But our expression 'Edenic redness' is plausibly epistemically rigid, and the same goes for the corresponding expressions in the Edenic world: Edenic subjects are in a position to know just what property they are talking about, simply by possessing the concept of Edenic redness. So this is at least a potential case of epistemic rigidity without non-Twin-Earthability.

---

[6] Epistemically nonrigid but semantically neutral expressions such as 'The only conscious being' will be extensionally Twin-Earthable but not intensionally Twin-Earthable, in the sense defined in the additional excursus on Twin-Earthability. Roughly, epistemic rigidity stands to extensional non-Twin-Earthability as semantic neutrality stands to intensional non-Twin-Earthability. Another approximate parallel is that epistemic rigidity stands to Twin-Earthability roughly as scenarios stand to contexts of utterance (although see footnote 8).

[7] I discuss cases like this in 'Does Conceivability Entail Possibility?' and 'The Two-Dimensional Argument against Materialism' as counterexamples to George Bealer's thesis that there are no a posteriori necessities involving semantically stable expressions. Semantic stability is a sort of non-Twin-Earthability (closest to the intensional Twin-Earthability discussed in the additional excursus). This putative role for semantic stability is better played by semantic neutrality or super-rigidity.

I think that epistemic rigidity is clearly the more fundamental of the two concepts here. At least where epistemological and modal matters are concerned, epistemic rigidity and super-rigidity cut things closer to the joints. Non-Twin-Earthability is interesting for these purposes to the extent that it approximates epistemic rigidity, and is independently interesting for its connections to internalism and externalism about content, but epistemic rigidity runs deeper.

Epistemic rigidity should also be distinguished from context-independence.[8] It is arguable that ordinary proper names such as 'Gödel' are extensionally context-independent: they pick out the same referent in every context. They are not epistemically rigid, however: they do not pick out the same referent in every scenario. In reverse, a term such as 'small' (construed as a predicate of numbers) may be context-dependent while being epistemically rigid in every context. Some terms ('small' as a more general predicate, perhaps) may even be epistemically rigid in some contexts but not others

We can think of epistemically rigid expressions as *referentially transparent* expressions, and epistemically nonrigid expressions as *referentially opaque* expressions. As defined earlier, an epistemically rigid expression is one whose extension is available on ideal a priori reflection, while the extension of an epistemically nonrigid expression is not knowable a priori. Correspondingly, we can think of epistemically rigid expressions as expressing referentially transparent concepts—concepts whose extension is knowable a priori—while epistemically nonrigid expressions express referentially opaque concepts. Referentially transparent concepts come with an especially direct grip on the corresponding entities in the world.

What sorts of expressions are epistemically rigid? We can approach the question by first examining epistemically nonrigid expressions. Analyzed from within the scrutability framework, the obvious examples fall into two classes. The first class includes indexicals: primitive indexicals, such as 'I', 'now', and phenomenal demonstratives, along with other less primitive indexicals that derive from these, such as 'today', 'here', and ordinary demonstratives. These are epistemically nonrigid because they function indexically to pick out a certain ostended entity—the current time, the present subject, and so on—and the subject is not in a position to know a priori what the ostended entity is.

---

[8] Context-dependence should also be distinguished from Twin-Earthability. 'Gödel' is Twin-Earthable: a corresponding expression could be used by a twin with a different referent. It is also arguably context-independent: the English word 'Gödel' picks out the same referent in every context. The difference arises from the fact that the corresponding expression on Twin Earth need not be the English word. In reverse, 'small' might be context-dependent without being Twin-Earthable, as long as any pairs of contexts in which it is uttered with different referents are not contexts involving twins.

The second class includes *role-scrutable* expressions: roughly, expressions whose extension is a priori scrutable from more basic truths by determining what plays a certain role (typically although not necessarily a causal role). For example, the extension of 'water' is a priori scrutable by determining what plays the role of (roughly) being the clear drinkable liquid that we have seen in our environment. The extension of 'Gödel' is a priori scrutable by determining what plays the role of being called 'Gödel' by others and of being at the other end of a causal chain.

Within a definitional framework, epistemically nonrigid expressions will include primitive indexicals (such as 'I' and 'now') and definite descriptions 'the D' (for example, 'the watery stuff around here'), where D is made up of primitives and it is not a priori what is the D. They will also include certain descriptive predicates (for example, 'has my favorite property') and general terms. In some cases D may include only epistemically rigid expressions: for example, 'The most friendly being in the universe'. These cases will turn on the fact that even if we know a priori what property a predicate F refers to, we often are not in a position to know which entities satisfy F. In other cases D will also include primitive indexicals: 'today' corresponds roughly to 'the day including now'.

In all of these cases, the definitional framework provides a clear explanation of epistemic nonrigidity: we would expect primitive indexicals to be epistemically non-rigid, and we would expect the relevant descriptions to be epistemically nonrigid also. We might say that in the definitional framework, these expressions are *conceptually opaque*: their referential opacity is apparent through conceptual reflection, so that their conceptual structure guarantees that they are referentially opaque.

Within the scrutability framework, something similar applies. We will still have primitive indexicals in the first class. The expressions in the second class will no longer be precisely equivalent to descriptions, and there may not be a simple specification of the relevant role. But if we follow the approximate definition model of chapters 1 and 8, a role-scrutable expression will be at least approximately a priori equivalent (in a given context) to certain descriptions of the form 'the thing that plays such-and-such complex role'. And even if we eschew approximate definitions, the relevant expressions will still be scrutable from truths about the various roles that the extension plays, just as truths such as 'water is H_2O' are scrutable from truths about the various properties of H_2O.

As with the definitional framework, the scrutability framework provides a natural explanation of epistemic nonrigidity. As before we would expect primitive indexicals to be epistemically nonrigid, and we would expect the relevant role-scrutable expressions to be epistemically nonrigid also. These expressions can also reasonably count as conceptually opaque: their referential opacity is apparent through conceptual reflection, so that their conceptual structure and role guarantees that they are referentially opaque.

If these are the epistemically nonrigid expressions, which expressions are epistemically rigid? If we buy into the version of the scrutability framework that involves conceptual priority, the most obvious candidates are the non-indexical primitive expressions in a scrutability base. For example, 'and', 'zero', 'law', 'fundamental', and 'consciousness' are all plausible candidates to be in a scrutability base. Other candidates are expressions that derive from these non-indexical primitives, either through definition or scrutability, as long as we avoid role-scrutability. For example, other logical expressions ('some'), mathematical expressions ('plus'), mental expressions ('believe'), and nomic expressions ('cause') are also plausible candidates to be epistemically rigid, as are various expressions that derive from a combination of these (e.g., 'friend' or 'philosopher', at least on certain readings).[9]

Unlike the epistemically nonrigid expressions considered above, none of these expressions appear to be conceptually opaque (at least granted views on which they are conceptually primitive). They are *conceptually transparent*, in that conceptually they appear to be transparent: no referential opacity is revealed by conceptual reflection. On the face of it, 'zero' transparently picks out zero, and 'consciousness' transparently picks out consciousness. In effect, these expressions at least *seem* to be epistemically rigid. That is, they seem to give a direct grip on their referent in the world (phenomenal properties, fundamentality, lawhood, addition, and so on), whether or not they really do.

On the face of it, it is most plausible to hold that these expressions are epistemically rigid. That is, it is plausible to endorse a Conceptual/Referential Transparency thesis: all conceptually transparent expressions are referentially transparent. This thesis has the consequence (given the above) that all non-indexical primitive expressions are epistemically rigid. I will stipulate that conceptually transparent expressions must also be metaphysically rigid *de jure*. Then the thesis allows us to conclude that conceptually transparent expressions are super-rigid.

There will be philosophical views that deny this thesis. For example, some type-B materialists may hold both that 'consciousness' is conceptually primitive and that it is epistemically nonrigid: it refers to a certain physical property, even though one could not know that a priori.[10] Some 'type-B color physicalists' who

---

[9] In some of these cases one may need to disambiguate, precisify, or fix a context first.

[10] Not all type-B materialists will deny the Conceptual/Referential Transparency thesis. One sort of type-B materialist holds that phenomenal properties are necessitated by physical properties but are not identical to them; this version can accept the thesis and will probably instead deny the Apriority/Necessity thesis below. A second sort holds that phenomenal properties are identical to physical properties while holding that all physical expressions for those properties are epistemically nonrigid. That view can accept both of these theses, although doing so probably leads to a version of Russellian monism. A third sort holds that 'consciousness' is a primitive indexical or derives from primitive indexicals such as demonstratives. A fourth sort holds that 'consciousness' is role-scrutable from more basic primitives, although here the issue will recur for the more basic primitives.

are primitivists about color concepts but not about color properties may hold a simi-lar view of color expressions.[11] An analogous view about spatial expressions, nomic expressions, and others is possible at least in principle. These views can still agree that the relevant expressions are conceptually transparent in the sense above, while hold-ing that conceptual transparency does not entail referential transparency.

We might usefully divide the corresponding concepts into three groups. Expressions that are both conceptually and referentially transparent express *transparent* concepts: concepts that reveal their referents. Expressions that are both conceptually and referentially opaque express *opaque* concepts: concepts that obscure their referents, at least in the sense that they do not reveal their referent. Expressions that are both conceptually transparent but referentially opaque express *pseudo-transparent* concepts: concepts that appear to reveal their referents but in fact obscure them. The type-B theorists in the previous para-graph are naturally allied with the view that phenomenal concepts or color con-cepts are pseudo-transparent.[12]

These views are varieties of *primitive externalism*: externalism about reference for (non-indexical) primitive concepts. These will often be externalist in the sense that the referent of a primitive concept is determined by factors outside the skin, but they need not be: a type-B theorist might hold that 'consciousness' refers to an internal neurophysiological property, for example. But they will be externalist in at least the sense that their referent lies outside our immediate cognitive grasp: even when full a priori mastery of the relevant primitive concept does not yield knowledge of what it picks out. Primitive externalism is naturally allied with an externalist account of what grounds reference for primitive expres-sions: perhaps a causal, teleological, or reference-magnet account.

A full assessment of primitive externalism is a substantial project in its own right. For now, I note that the major arguments for externalism are not argu-ments for primitive externalism. Putnam-style arguments apply best to role-scrutable expressions, and Burge-style arguments apply to expressions used deferentially. A quite new sort of argument would be needed to establish primi-tive externalism. So following the methodology laid out in the introduction, I take the default view to be primitive internalism.

Someone might argue for primitive externalism by appealing to the causal theory of reference or some other externalist theory. As in the previous para-graph, though, I think the arguments for the causal theory are grounded in the

---

[11] Here I have in mind Byrne and Hilbert 2007, who seem to treat color concepts as primitive and hold that at least some color truths are inscrutable from underlying physical truths while hold-ing that colors are physical properties. By contrast Jackson (1998) holds what we might think of as type-A color physicalism, involving functionalism about color concepts.

[12] Philip Goff (2011) uses the terminology of transparent and opaque concepts for a similar distinction.

cases of role-scrutable expressions and expressions used deferentially and do not have much purchase on the case of primitive expressions. There is little reason to accept a causal theory of reference for expressions such as 'zero' or 'part', so there is little reason to think these theories are universal. In fact, one can argue (as I do on the additional excursus on reference magnets and the grounds of intentionality) that the role of causation and other apparently externalist factors in reference is grounded in certain features that are internal to a subject's grasp, suggesting that the purely external role needed for primitive externalism would require a distinct mechanism that there is not much positive reason to believe in.

Most fundamentally, I think that primitive externalism is to be rejected because it gives us too little grip on what we are thinking and saying. We have a substantial grasp of what we are talking about when we talk about laws of nature or parthood or consciousness, and primitive externalism is not in a position to explain that substantial grasp. That issue requires a sustained investigation in its own right, though. In the meantime, I flag the issue and I register my own view, which rejects primitive externalism and accepts the Conceptual/Referential Transparency thesis.

Epistemic rigidity can help us to analyze Kripke's examples of the necessary a posteriori. We have already seen that true identity statements involving epistemically rigid expressions are a priori. Correspondingly, any a posteriori identity statement must involve at least one epistemically nonrigid expression. This is just what we find in Kripke's examples of necessary *a posteriori* identity sentences: 'Hesperus is Phosphorus', 'heat is the motion of molecules', 'water is H_2O', and so on. In each of these cases, a key term is metaphysically rigid but not epistemically rigid.

We can put the point by saying that identity sentences involving super-rigid expressions on each side are a priori iff they are necessary. This thesis follows immediately from the definition of super-rigidity. Similarly, any necessary a posteriori identity sentence must involve at least one expression that is not super-rigid. Assuming that both expressions are metaphysically rigid, as in the paradigm cases, then at least one expression must be epistemically nonrigid. In a sense, the combination of epistemic nonrigidity and metaphysical rigidity can be seen as the source of the necessary a posteriori.

This trivial thesis can be strengthened in a couple of ways. First, if we accept the Conceptual/Referential Transparency thesis, then we can derive the thesis that all identity statements involving conceptually transparent expressions on each side are a priori iff they are necessary. In effect, on this view conceptual opacity is the source of epistemic nonrigidity, and the combination of conceptual opacity and metaphysical rigidity is the source of necessary a posteriori identity statements. This model certainly fits all the a posteriori identity statements that Kripke discusses.

Second, one could strengthen the thesis in a different direction by generalizing from a posteriori identities to all a posteriori necessities, as follows:

Apriority/Necessity Thesis: If a sentence S contains only super-rigid expressions, S is a priori iff S is necessary.

This thesis is trivially true when S is an identity statement, and nontrivial but plausible when S is not. Certainly, all of Kripke's examples of the necessary a posteriori involve epistemically nonrigid expressions. Still, some philosophical positions will deny the thesis. For example, 'An omniscient being exists' plausibly involves only super-rigid expressions, and some theist views entail that this sentence is necessary but not a priori. Likewise, some views of mathematics (as discussed in chapter 6) may allow that there are mathematical truths that are necessary but not a priori. Once again, however, the Apriority/Necessity thesis fits the a posteriori necessities that Kripke discusses, all of which involve epistemically nonrigid expressions.

Finally, one can make both strengthenings at once, holding that if a sentence S contains only conceptually transparent expressions, S is a priori iff S is necessary. We might call this the Strong Apriority/Necessity thesis: it follows from the original Apriority/Necessity thesis and the Conceptual/Referential Transparency thesis. The Strong Apriority/Necessity thesis in effect says that all necessary a posteriori sentences and all contingent a priori sentences involve conceptually opaque expressions.

A counterexample to the Strong Apriority/Necessity thesis would be a necessary a posteriori or contingent a priori sentence involving only conceptually transparent expressions. Such a sentence would be what I have elsewhere called a *strong* a posteriori necessity (as opposed to Kripke's weak a posteriori necessities involving conceptually opaque expressions), or a strong priori contingency. I have argued at length (in, e.g., 'The Two-Dimensional Argument against Materialism') that there are no strong a posteriori necessities, and those arguments apply equally to strong a priori contingencies. So I accept the Strong Apriority/Necessity thesis.

A key thesis about super-rigidity that I discuss elsewhere in this book (tenth and sixteenth excursuses and chapter 8) is the following.

Super-Rigid Scrutability: All truths are scrutable from super-rigid truths and indexical truths.

There is also a generalized version: all epistemically possible truths are scrutable from epistemically possible super-rigid sentences and indexical sentences. Here super-rigid sentences are those containing only super-rigid expressions, and indexical sentences are those of the form 'E is D' where E is a primitive indexical and D contains only super-rigid expressions.

Generalized Super-Rigid Scrutability is a consequence of the thesis that all epistemically nonrigid sentences are scrutable from epistemically rigid sentences and indexical sentences. One can also derive a version of Super-Rigid Scrutability from Conceptual/Referential Transparency, along with the theses that all truths are scrutable from truths involving conceptual primitives and that all non-indexical conceptual primitives are conceptually transparent. In practice, the most important sort of challenge to Super-Rigid Scrutability (from those otherwise sympathetic with the scrutability framework) is likely to come from primitive externalism.[13]

As before, I think that primitive externalism is false: all epistemic nonrigidity derives from either primitive indexicality or role-scrutability. So I hold that all epistemically nonrigid sentences are scrutable from epistemically rigid sentences and indexical sentences, and therefore accept Generalized Super-Rigid Scrutability.[14] I return to the issue in chapter 8.

[13] A tempting argument for Generalized Super-Rigid Scrutability runs as follows. Even if we cannot know the extensions of our expressions a priori, we can know their primary intensions a priori. So we can refer super-rigidly to primary intensions. But then all truths will be scrutable from truths of the form 'p is true', where p specifies the primary intension of a truth in the scrutability base. Similarly, we can refer super-rigidly to scenarios, so all truths will be scrutable from 's is actualized', where s specifies a scenario super-rigidly. However, an opponent can note that if Super-Rigid Scrutability is false, primary intensions and scenarios are best understood as linguistic or Fregean entities (E10). They can then hold that 'true' and 'actualized' as predicates of these entities are not super-rigid. Because the properties picked out by the basic linguistic or Fregean entities can be known only empirically, the reference relation involving these entities can be known only empirically, and likewise for truth and actualization.

[14] One can develop a weak sense in which even pseudo-transparent concepts count as epistemically rigid. There is an intuitive sense in which 'consciousness' at least picks out the *feature* of consciousness in every scenario, whether or not it picks out the property of consciousness. Here features are roughly projections of conceptually transparent concepts: they correspond to the way that properties would be if those conceptually transparent concepts were referentially transparent, as they seem to be. They are abstract objects that are akin to properties in that they can be predicated of objects, but they are individuated by the transparent or pseudo-transparent concepts that pick them out. Then we can say that phenomenal features are distinct from neural features, even if phenomenal properties are identical to neural properties. On my view, features correspond one-to-one with properties, so these two will stand and fall together. But for someone who believe in pseudo-transparency, distinctness of features does not lead to dualism about the mind-independent world, as features are in the relevant sense mind-dependent. We can then say that phenomenal concepts are weakly epistemically rigid in that they pick out the feature of consciousness in every scenario, and color concepts are weakly epistemically rigid in a similar way. The same goes for weak super-rigidity. This would then allow even those who believe in pseudo-transparent concepts to accept Generalized (Weak) Super-Rigid Scrutability. This may be useful for allowing them to accept some applications of Generalized Super-Rigid Scrutability: for example, we could then use features instead of properties to construct scenarios in the fashion of the tenth excursus.

8

The Structure of the World

1 Principled scrutability bases

In their constructions of the world, Carnap and Russell imposed principled constraints on what sort of expressions might enter the basic vocabulary. Carnap held that truths in the basic vocabulary must be objective and communicable, and so required that the basic vocabulary be a structural vocabulary. Russell held that all propositions are composed of elements with which we are directly acquainted, and so required that the basic vocabulary be an acquaintance-based vocabulary. These principled constraints were important for Carnap's and Russell's wider philosophical purposes.

So far, I have proceeded in a relatively unprincipled way. We started with the base *PQTI* of physical, phenomenal, and indexical truths along with a 'that's-all' truth. In chapters 3, 4, and 6 I argued that all truths may well be a priori scrutable from such a base (perhaps with mild expansions, depending on one's views). In chapter 7, I attempted to minimize this base, for example Ramsifying physical truths in order to replace them with conceptually more fundamental truths. Various candidates for a minimal base have emerged.

All of our candidates for such a base include certain background expressions: logical, mathematical, indexical, and totality expressions. The other leading candidates are nomic expressions (concerning lawhood), phenomenal expressions (concerning consciousness), quiddistic expressions (characterizing the unknown categorical properties underlying microphysical dispositions), and spatiotemporal expressions (concerning the distribution of entities in space and time). Various combined packages with some or all of these candidates are possible, as are expanded versions including expressions for secondary qualities, and perhaps normative and intentional expressions. The scrutability bases that result are compact, but they are not yet principled.

Imposing a principled constraint on a scrutability base yields a principled scrutability thesis. We have spent time on at least one such thesis already: Fundamental Scrutability, according to which all truths are scrutable from metaphysically fundamental truths. Other principled theses, analogous to Russell's and Carnap's theses above, include Structural Scrutability (only structural expressions in the base), and Acquaintance Scrutability (only expressions for entities with which we are acquainted). Still others include Primitive Scrutability (only expressions for primitive concepts), and Narrow Scrutability (only narrow, non-environment-dependent expressions).

These principled scrutability theses are highly relevant to applications of the framework. Fundamental Scrutability has important consequences in metaphysics. Structural Scrutability can be used to support a sort of structural realism in the philosophy of science and to support a reply to external-world skepticism. Acquaintance Scrutability can be used to argue for Russellian theses in epistemology. Primitive and Narrow Scrutability have consequences for debates about primitive concepts and internalism in the philosophy of mind and language.

In what follows, I will step back and consider the prospects for these principled scrutability theses. I will assess how each of them stands in virtue of the scrutability bases in previous chapters; I will examine arguments for the theses; and I will draw conclusions for substantive issues in philosophy: the mind–body problem, narrow content, structural realism, and so on. Of necessity, this discussion will only scratch the surface of some deep issues, but I hope that the preliminary charting here points to some promising areas for further exploration.

I will also assess the prospects for scrutability theses involving relations that differ from the a priori scrutability relation that has been the main focus so far. These include Definitional Scrutability (scrutability via definitions), Analytic Scrutability (scrutability via analytic truths), and Generalized Scrutability (scrutability in all epistemically possible scenarios). Using this assessment I will draw out conclusions for philosophical issues concerning conceptual analysis, primitive concepts, and Fregean sense.

All this will give us a better sense of the landscape that results from the discussion so far. It offers the promise of characterizing scrutability bases in independent terms, and helps us to assess various potential applications of the scrutability base. It also helps us to see how close the current framework might get to delivering on Carnap's aims in the *Aufbau* and to delivering on related projects by Russell and others. As we will see, versions of the current framework can come surprisingly close to delivering on some of these claims.

2 Definitional Scrutability (and conceptual analysis)

Carnap's project in the *Aufbau* centrally involves the thesis of Definability, according to which all expressions are definable in terms of a limited class of expressions. This thesis leads naturally to the thesis of Definitional Scrutability, according to which all truths are logically entailed by a compact class of base truths along with definitions. We saw in chapter 1 that these two theses are questionable, because finite definitions seem to be unavailable for many natural-language expressions. We have also seen that A Priori Scrutability does not require Definitional Scrutability. Still, it is interesting to ask: given that A Priori Scrutability obtains, how close can we get to a version of Definitional Scrutability and to a version of Definability?

I will assume initially that the criteria of adequacy for definitions require that they be a priori, and will consider other criteria shortly. I will also assume that we have established Generalized A Priori Scrutability, which connects more easily to Definitional Scrutability than does A Priori Scrutability alone. I will initially set aside issues about context-dependence, assuming that all relevant sentences are context-independent. We can then suppose that a compact class C of sentences, involving a limited class of base expressions, makes up a generalized scrutability base for all sentences. Can we recover a claim about the definability of all expressions in terms of base expressions?

There are a few ways to proceed.

(i) *Infinitary definitions.* If definitions can be infinite, adequate definitions may be possible. An extreme definition will go scenario by scenario: for example, 'For all x, x is a cat iff $(D_1$ & $\phi_1(x))$ or $(D_2$ & $\phi_2(x))$ or...'. Here D_1, D_2, and so on are full canonical specifications of scenarios (conjunctions of base truths), and for each specification D_i, ϕ_i is a predicate made up of base expressions such that 'x is a cat iff $\phi_i(x)$' is implied by D_i. It is reasonable to expect that there will be such predicates ϕ_i for every D_i, at least if we set aside vagueness and we allow ϕ_i itself to be infinitary if necessary. The resulting definition will involve an infinite disjunction of infinite (and finite) conjunctions, but it will plausibly be a priori, at least if the disjunction of the specifications D_i is a priori, as it should be. Its right-hand side will involve only logical expressions and expressions in the scrutability base. For typical expressions there will also be shorter infinitary definitions, for example by taking the limit of an appropriate sequence of long finite approximate definitions.

(ii) *Long finite definitions.* We have seen that short finite definitions for natural-language expressions are usually unavailable, and that attempts at refining the definitions usually meet with counterexamples. Still, these attempts usually give up at a short finite length, often within a few lines of text, and almost always within a page or so. So the possibility is left open that some much longer finite definition (pages long? book length?) might be a priori equivalent to the original expression. Given that there is a large amount of vagueness in most of our concepts, one might reasonably expect to at least be able to eventually find a definition that correctly classifies the determinate cases. With enough further work one might extend this to a definition that classifies indeterminate cases correctly as well, perhaps eventually getting higher-order determinacy right. The existence of a long finite definition of this sort might even be thought to follow from the fact that the brain is a finite computational system and has the capacity to classify cases correctly.[1]

The long finite definitions that result from this process will not usually be in the vocabulary of a scrutability base. But if we re-apply the process to the non-base expressions used within the definition, with a long finite definition for each that avoids circularity, this will yield an even longer finite definition for the original expression. Repeated application of this process (assuming a finite number of steps without circularity) will yield a long finite definition in the language of a scrutability base.

As with infinitary definitions, the long finite definitions that result from a specification of this sort may violate various traditional criteria of adequacy for definitions. They may be too long, they may not give any sort of perspicuous analysis, they may not be the sort of thing that we know when we know what a word means, and so on. But they might at least be definitions to which there are no counterexamples, and that idealized a priori reflection could reveal to be correct.

(iii) *Approximate definitions.* We have already seen that one can often find a sequence of ever-longer putative definitions of the same expression (such as 'knows'), where each definition has exceptions (both actual exceptions and epistemically possible exceptions) but each has fewer exceptions than the last. It is not unreasonable to hold that for any natural-language expression, there is a sequence of approximate definitions that at least converges on correctness.[2] Such

---

[1] If the brain is a finite computational system, there will be some finite algorithmic specification that mirrors any one subject's judgments about an expression's extension in various scenarios. The same goes for a community's collective judgment. Of course there are limits on the size of the inputs that subjects and communities can consider, and they can make mistakes that would be corrected on ideal reflection, so these specifications need not be a priori equivalent to the original expression. Still, if our own classificatory capacities can be finitely captured, this undermines any objection to definitions based on our own responses, and leaves the claim that finite definitions are unavailable in need of further motivation.

[2] Here we can say that a sequence of purported definitions of E *weakly converges on correctness* iff for every counterexample to a definition in the sequence, there is a point in the sequence after which all definitions classify the example correctly. If we have some reasonable measure over the set of possible cases (where the full set has measure 1), we say that a sequence *strongly converges on correctness* iff the sequence weakly converges and for every $\phi < 1$ there is a point in the sequence after which all definitions classify at least a measure-ϕ subset of cases correctly. I think the considerations below tend to motivate both weak and strong convergence.

a claim can be motivated by considerations about the finiteness of language users, for example. While there are possible expressions in hypothetical possible languages for which there is no such sequence (certain uncomputable predicates of real numbers, for example), there is little reason to think that these expressions are available to finite language users.

The claim can also be motivated by our experience with attempting to define expressions such as 'know' or 'lie', where counterexamples to successive definitions tend to become more and more abstruse and isolated. A definition of knowledge in terms of justified true belief already gets things right most of the time: Gettier cases are fairly rare. (If we measure beliefs by measuring utterances, for example, it seems unlikely that more than 1 percent of our utterances express Gettiered beliefs.) A definition as 'justified true belief not inferred from a false belief' gets even more cases right. Perhaps there is an intuitive measure by which there are very short definitions that get 90 percent of cases right, reasonably short definitions that get 99 percent of cases right, longer definitions that get 99.9 percent of cases right, and so on. We should not put too much stock in the figures, but the pattern is at least suggestive. Furthermore, these sequences of definitions tend to at least be somewhat perspicuous rather than wholly opaque. So there is some hope for converging approximate definitions that at least approximate some traditional criteria of adequacy. All this might motivate an Approximate Definability thesis, where this requires that for any given level of accuracy, any term of natural language has a finite approximate definition that meets that level of accuracy.

(iv) *Revisionary definitions.* In his later work, Carnap put heavy weight on explications, or revisionary definitions. These explications did not need to capture the exact contours of an existing concept, as long as they could do the central work of the old concept. Approximate definitions can often serve as revisionary definitions. An approximate definition of 'table' is not a perfect definition of table, but it is a perfect definition of a nearby possible expression 'quasi-table'. And while the concept of a quasi-table differs from that of a table, the differences are fairly insignificant: a community that talked about quasi-tables rather than tables would be for most practical purposes indistinguishable from our own.

For certain philosophical purposes, revisionary definitions are suboptimal. If we want to use definitions to give a semantics for natural language as it now exists, then an approximate definition will always be imperfect. Likewise, if we want to use definitions for epistemological purposes, to help analyze justification of our existing beliefs, an approximate definition may miss a few subtleties in our existing concepts. For many other purposes, though, a revisionary definition may be all we need. For the purposes of constructing the world out of a fundamental base, for example, it does not matter much whether we construct quasi-tables or tables. If we show how truths about quasi-tables can be grounded in certain primitive truths, and if the great majority of quasi-tables are tables and vice versa, then there may not be much further reason to worry about tables. For the purposes of unifying science, if we can show how the study of quasi-genes is unified in a certain way with physics, then the same moral will plausibly generalize to genes. Even for coarse-grained epistemological purposes (defeating the skeptic, for example), if we can show that we can have knowledge of quasi-tables, we have shown most of what we need to show.

(v) *Context-dependent definitions.* Context-dependence (especially epistemic variance) complicates all four of the projects above, in that when an expression-type is context-dependent, no definition in terms of invariant base expressions can be adequate. Still, given Generalized A Priori Scrutability for tokens, we can at least apply the methods above to tokens of context-dependent expressions, yielding the sorts of definition above for any given token. So for a name such as 'Gödel', we may not find a single description D that is a priori equivalent to all uses of 'Gödel', but for any given use there will be such a description. It may be that more systematicity than this is possible. For example, it may be that when the original base expressions are conjoined with a relatively small class of context-dependent base expressions, all or most context-dependent expressions in natural language can be defined (context-independently) in terms of these. But just how much systematicity is possible here remains an open question.

Overall, it seems to me that while Carnap's definitional project in the *Aufbau* was a failure, the truth of A Priori Scrutability suggests that many closely related definitional projects have a chance of success. Furthermore, these definitional projects can play at least some of the key roles that Carnap wanted definitions to play. I think that many of those roles can be played by a priori scrutability even without definitions, so I have not attempted to set out even approximate definitions in this work. Still, the reasoning here suggests that a version of the *Aufbau* that starts with a base vocabulary (perhaps a nomic and a phenomenal vocabulary) and that constructs successive expressions (such as spatiotemporal expressions, mental expressions, social expressions, or at least approximations to them) via approximate definitions should be viable.

All this has consequences for the project of conceptual analysis. Construed as a search for perfect definitions, contemporary conceptual analysis has been a failure. But construed as an attempt to better understand various specific concepts, it has arguably been a success. We have certainly come to understand the contours of concepts such as 'know', 'cause', and 'lie', for example, much better than we did previously. In part, this is because the intensional model can at least yield better and better approximate definitions (chapter 8), and better and better ways to chart the broad patterns of application that a concept involves. All this in effect yields a way to chart the structure of a concept.

Following this mode, we might understand conceptual analysis as a quasi-scientific process of conjecture, refutation, and refinement.[3] A purported analysis is put forward, counterexamples are found, and a refined analysis is discovered that avoids the counterexamples. Further counterexamples can be found in turn, and we do not in practice reach a perfect definition, but we make progress all the same. The phenomenon is analogous to that found in the high-level sciences, in which counterexample-free principles and laws are almost never found, but in which one can nevertheless state approximate principles that get most cases approximately right, and in which one can refine these principles via successive improved principles, gradually converging on the truth. If there are converging approximate definitions for our concepts, then we should expect that something similar may be possible in the process of conceptual analysis. So I am inclined to think that at least some version of the program of conceptual analysis is viable.[4]

3 Analytic and Primitive Scrutability (and primitive concepts)

Definitions are commonly required to be more than a priori. It is common to hold that definitions should be analytic, or true in virtue of the meanings of the terms involved. It is also common to require the expressions used in the definition to be conceptually prior to the defined expression. Correspondingly, while A Priori Scrutability supports the thesis that all expressions are (approximately) definable when definitions are required to be a priori, it does not support this thesis on stronger conceptions of a definition. The stronger definability claims requires claims akin to Analytic Scrutability (all truths are analytically scrutable from a compact class of base truths), Primitive Scrutability (all truths are a priori scrutable from base truths involving primitive concepts), and perhaps Analytic Primitive Scrutability (all truths are analytically scrutable from base truths involving primitive concepts). In what follows I will investigate the prospects for theses like these, starting with Analytic Scrutability.

---

[3] Magdalena Balcerak Jackson develops this sort of understanding in her forthcoming 'Conceptual Analysis and Epistemic Progress'.

[4] That said: we should distinguish the viability of conceptual analysis from its philosophical importance. I am not inclined to think that all philosophy is conceptual analysis or even that the core of philosophy is conceptual analysis. The conceptual analysis of specific expressions can easily lead to a sort of ordinary language philosophy whose consequences are limited. I think the most important sort of conceptual analysis is what we might think of as global conceptual analysis, involving the analysis of conceptual spaces rather than of specific expressions. For more on these themes, see 'Verbal Disputes' and the additional excursus on conceptual analysis and ordinary language philosophy.

If all a priori truths are analytic truths, then A Priori Scrutability entails Analytic Scrutability. Logical empiricists such as Carnap were inclined to identify the two categories. Carnap talks more about analyticity and necessity than apriority, but he emphatically rejects the synthetic a priori, and gives no evidence of believing in analytic truths that are not a priori. But many contemporary philosophers believe that there are synthetic a priori truths. If they are correct, the two theses come apart.

It is common to hold that synthetic a priori truths include mathematical, normative, and metaphysical truths. On such a view, '5 = 13 − 8' will be a priori but not analytic. On a common normative view, 'An act is right iff it maximizes utility' is a priori but not analytic. On a common metaphysical view, 'Any two objects have a mereological sum' is a priori but not analytic. Correspondingly, a priori truths in these domains will not yield analytic definitions. This comes out when we look at cases.

Let us suppose that there are moral truths and that the truth of moral sentences is a priori scrutable from base sentences in all epistemically possible scenarios. Then we can use the method of successive approximation in the last section to articulate a sequence of converging definitions of a moral term such as 'right'. These will be definitions that get the extension of the term right in successively more cases. They might reflect the sort of theorizing one finds in normative ethics, for example with successively refined versions of the principle that an act is right if it produces the greatest amount of happiness or if it is the product of an appropriate sort of will. Or it might proceed by compiling an ever greater list of causes and cases. The definition that results may be a priori, but many will deny that it is analytic. On the face of it, the definition will encapsulate moral principles and judgments that are substantive in a way that analytic truths are not supposed to be.

I have made little use of the notion of analyticity so far in this book, and I do not think it is obvious how to make sense of the notion. Still, I think I have a reasonable grasp in extension and perhaps even in intension of the sort of truths that people typically label analytic. To a first approximation: while both concepts and reason play a role in knowledge of any a priori truth, concepts play the more significant role in knowledge of putative analytic truths, while reason plays the more significant role in knowledge of putative synthetic a priori truths. I have suggested (E4, E17) that an analytic truth might be characterized as one that subjects have a conceptual warrant to believe, where a conceptual warrant is one that derives from the concepts involved. For now, I will not rely on a definition of analyticity, but I will proceed on the assumption that there are analytic truths and that while all analytic truths are a priori, some a priori truths (mathematical and normative truths, for example) are not analytic.

Given this much, it follows that any analytic scrutability base will be an a priori scrutability base but an a priori scrutability base need not be an analytic scrutability base. In particular, the minimal a priori scrutability bases that we have considered will almost certainly not be analytic scrutability bases. Given a mathematical truth M that is a priori but not analytic, then M will be a priori scrutable from nonmathematical base truths, but there is little reason to think that it will be analytically scrutable from them. Something similar applies to normative truths that are a priori but not analytic. Even for normative truths that are a posteriori but a priori scrutable from base truths ('Hitler was bad', for example), there is little reason to think that they are analytically scrutable from base truths.

The key question then is: what must we add to a minimal a priori scrutability base to yield a minimal analytic scrutability base? It is natural to add some mathematical truths to the base in order to render mathematical truths analytically scrutable. How many? One will presumably add at least fundamental axioms to the base: for example, Peano axioms or the axioms of ZFC or both, if one does not think that the connection between numbers and sets is analytic. One will also need a raft of further mathematical truths, such as Gödel sentences, in order that various truths that are unprovable from these axioms are rendered analytically scrutable from the base. Whether this is enough to bring in all mathematical truths depends on whether logical consequence suffices for analytic scrutability: if Q is provable from P via some series of steps, is Q analytically scrutable from P? If the answer is yes in general, a provability base will be an analytic scrutability base. If the answer is no, then more will need to be added. Clearly the answer here depends on just how analyticity is understood. In the extreme case, one could simply add all mathematical truths to the base, though this may be overkill: perhaps it is analytic that $100 + 1 = 101$, for example? If so, then something intermediate may be required.

If there are normative truths, it is also natural to add some of them to the base. How many? If there is a true and complete moral theory, one should presumably add the fundamental principles of such a theory to the base. Something similar goes for normative claims in other domains such as epistemology. If we have such a theory, then any normative truth will presumably follow logically from certain non-normative truths and normative principles. If logical consequence suffices for analytic scrutability, and if all non-normative truths are analytically scrutable from the base, it follows that all normative truths will be too. If normative theories are not codifiable in this way, or if logical consequence does not suffice for analytic scrutability, then more must be added to the base.

Is more needed in the base? It is possible that what goes for mathematical and normative truths goes for truths in other domains: perhaps aesthetic truths, metaphysical truths, modal truths, and so on. In these cases it is perhaps less clear that there are synthetic a priori truths, but if there are, we can handle them in much the same way as in the previous cases.

What about ordinary truths such as 'Water is H_2O' and 'The cat sat on the mat'? Suppose that arguments in chapters 3 and 4 succeed in making the case that these are a priori scrutable from the base. Once again, whether they are analytically scrutable depends on just what analyticity comes to. But there is at least a case for regarding them as analytically scrutable. One could suggest that in using a Cosmoscope to determine the truth of these sentences, it is our conceptual capacities rather than reason that are playing the central role. Once the whole world is revealed to us with the Cosmoscope, certain verdicts regarding these truths seem to flow naturally from our concepts of 'water' and 'cat'. If we adopt the casewise model of conceptual analysis discussed earlier, a view like this is natural: possessing a concept conveys a conditional ability to classify cases, one that plays the central role in using the Cosmoscope. Certainly highly complex capacities are need to keep track of information and so on, but it is arguable that these are playing essentially a storage and control role, rather than a substantive rational role. All this is far from clear, but there is at least a case for analyticity here.

The case of names such as 'Gödel' is even less clear. Certainly, analyticity will have to be relativized to tokens rather than types, but this is not unreasonable if analyticity is understood in the epistemological terms I have suggested. But there is at least a reasonable case that our judgments regarding who counts as Gödel in a given scenario rest on the same sort of capacities as our judgments regarding what counts as water in a given scenario, and that these judgments flow naturally from an individual speaker's concept of Gödel.

If something like this is right, there is at least a chance of keeping the expansion of the base limited. We will have to add some mathematical truths, but mathematical expressions were already being used in the base. We will have to add some normative truths and a limited number of normative expressions, such as one or more version of 'ought'. If there are other synthetic a priori truths, we might have to add further expressions: other evaluative expressions (such as aesthetic expressions), perhaps, or more widespread use of existential quantifiers and modal operators. But the expansion does not obviously need to go far beyond that.

All this connects to the thesis of Primitive Scrutability: all truths are scrutable from truths involving primitive concepts. Once again, the issues here are fairly obscure due to the obscurity of the key notion, that of a primitive concept. Here a primitive concept can be understood as one that no other concepts are conceptually prior to, but this just raises the issue (discussed in the last chapter) of how to understand conceptual priority. On various understandings of that notion, a primitive concept might be one whose grasp does not require a grasp of any other concepts, or that does not have a constituent concept, or whose understanding is not best articulated in terms of other concepts, or (perhaps best, on my view) that does not have a constitutive inferential role that essentially involves other concepts.

If there is a distinction between primitive and nonprimitive concepts, there is at least a reasonable case that the concepts in our a priori scrutability base fall on the primitive side. Certainly indexical concepts such as *I, now,* and a basic *this* seem to qualify. It is not unreasonable to suggest that basic logical concepts such as those of conjunction and existence are primitive, or at least that they belong to primitive families of connective and quantificational concepts. The same goes for key mathematical concepts such as basic set-theoretical concepts. For phenomenal realists, the same is plausible for phenomenal concepts, or for something in the near vicinity such as phenomenal relations and secondary quality concepts. For non-Humeans, the same goes for key nomic concepts such as the concept of lawhood. For spatiotemporal primitivists, unsurprisingly, spatiotemporal notions are primitive. On a view with nonphenomenal quiddistic concepts, it is natural to take these concepts or something in the vicinity as primitive.

Furthermore, something similar applies to the expressions that we have added to yield an analytic scrutability base. Normative concepts are plausible candidates to be primitive concepts, as are certain evaluative concepts, and perhaps modal and existential concepts (especially on views on which there are synthetic a priori modal and metaphysical truths). So where the initial base suggests that all truths are a priori scrutable from truths involving primitive concepts, the expanded base suggests that all truths are analytically scrutable from truths involving primitive concepts.

It is natural to suggest that when a concept is not primitive, truths involving it are scrutable from truths involving more basic concepts. This principle follows directly from certain models of primitiveness, such as those on which primitiveness is understood in terms of definability or constituency. Even without those models, it is not implausible that nonprimitiveness goes along with at least approximate definability in terms of more basic concepts. If that is right, and if approximate definability goes with scrutability, then the principle follows. All this applies whether we are invoking a priori scrutability or analytic scrutability.

From this principle, it follows that any nonprimitive concept is dispensable from a scrutability base in favor or more basic concepts. If we assume that descending chains of more basic concepts ultimately terminate in primitive concepts, it follows that there will be a scrutability base that involves primitive concepts alone. This seems to reflect what we find.

A minimal a priori scrutability base need not include all primitive concepts: normative concepts may be dispensable, for example. This reflects the fact that there may be a priori connections among primitive concepts, and that a primitive normative concept may be approximately 'definable' if definitions are required only to be a priori. But if definitions are required to be analytic, or if terms in the definition are required to be conceptually prior to defined terms, then the definitions here will not qualify.

It is tempting to say that a minimal analytic scrutability base will include all primitive concepts. But this will be false if there are primitive concepts that are not needed to state base truths. For example, I have suggested (chapter 7) that we have primitive concepts of Edenic space, time, and color, although none of these are instantiated in our world. If so, we will not need truths about the distribution of these properties in an analytic scrutability base. As long as it is epistemically possible that they are instantiated, they will be needed in a generalized analytic scrutability base, though. It may even be that there are primitive concepts for which it is a priori that corresponding properties are not instantiated: perhaps moral concepts on some error-theoretic views, or perhaps the concept of Edenic pain, as I suggest in 'Perception and the Fall from Eden'. If so, these will not be needed in a generalized analytic scrutability base, but they will be primitive all the same.

In any case, it is plausible that the class of primitive concepts will constitute an analytic scrutability base, an a priori scrutability base, and generalized versions of these, whether or not it constitutes a minimal such base. If something like this is right, it fits nicely with the definitional program in the previous section. Arbitrary expressions can be (approximately) defined in terms of the primitive expressions. While the definitions in the last section need not meet the requirements of analyticity and conceptual priority, these definitions will meet these requirements (perhaps modified to allow approximate analyticity). This fits with the commonsense idea that one needs normative notions to define normative notions, while holding out the hope that a small number of basic notions (basic oughts, for example) might be used to approximately define all the others. The same goes for mathematical expressions, which are plausibly best defined in mathematical terms.

Putting all this together, an explicit list of primitive concepts on the current approach might include something like the following. The list is extremely tentative, and I do not have clear views about just which concepts from each family should be included, so I will just list relevant families and an example or two from each.

Logical: e.g., *not, there exists*
Mathematical: e.g., *set*
Phenomenal: e.g., *conscious*
Spatiotemporal: e.g., *space, time*
Secondary qualities: e.g., *color*
Nomic: e.g., *law*
Fundamentality: e.g., *in virtue of*
Normative/evaluative: e.g., *ought*
Indexical: e.g., *I, now, this*

There is much room for flexibility here. Some might add further families: modal concepts (*might* or *possibly*), mereological concepts (*part*), semantic concepts (*true*), or other mental concepts (*believe, intend*). Some might subtract families: phenomenal and nomic concepts, perhaps. One could invoke other basic nomic concepts (e.g., *cause* or *chance*) and other normative/evaluative concepts (e.g., *good* or *reason*). One may well need to invoke specific secondary quality or phenomenal concepts, corresponding to primitive dimensions of color space such as *red* for example. The spatiotemporal properties (and secondary qualities) I have invoked are those most directly presented in experience: I think these are Edenic spatiotemporal properties, but others will think they are ordinary spatiotemporal properties. I have not included quiddistic concepts on this list, as these plausibly either coincide with concepts on the list (such as phenomenal concepts) or are concepts that we do not currently possess. The list is perhaps best seen as a tentative list of primitive concepts possessed by humans, but there is certainly room for further 'alien' primitive concepts that we do not possess.

The issues here are murky, in part because of the murky notions of analyticity and conceptual priority. Still, in 'Verbal Disputes' I approach issues related to analyticity and primitive concepts from a quite different direction, and reach conclusions that tend in the same direction as the conclusions here. In particular, the list of leading contenders for primitive concepts as characterized there is quite similar to the list above. Perhaps that is a sign that this approach is on the right track.

I have arrived at the list above largely through a priori means, and I have not made strong psychological claims about the concepts on this list. Nevertheless, it is at least tempting to construe this is a list of the basic dimensions or building blocks of thought, and it is interesting to see how this project squares with empirical projects concerning primitive concepts, most obviously in linguistics and psychology.

In linguistics, we can compare this list to Anna Wierzbicka's list of primitives in chapter 1.[5] Wierzbicka's list contains many expressions that are not listed here, in part because Wierzbicka is much more specific about the primitive expressions in a family, and in part because she includes numerous expressions (e.g., *people, know, live*) that I think are analytically scrutable from others and so can be approximately defined. In reverse, mine contains some expressions (e.g., *color*) that I think are not scrutable but that Wierzbicka takes to be definable by her standards. Mine also contains expressions (e.g., *ought, law, in virtue of*) that are

---

[5] Related projects of analysis in lexical semantics have been developed by Ray Jackendoff (1990) and James Pustejovsky (1995), among others. These projects have less clearly delimited sets of primitives than Wierzbicka's framework, however, so they are harder to assess in the current context.

have less technical and perhaps more linguistically universal counterparts on Wierzbicka's list (e.g., *good*, *bad*, and *because*, where the later arguably comes in both causal and in-virtue-of varieties). These differences are no surprise, as the lists are subject to very different constraints: for example, Wierzbicka requires definability and linguistic universality where I do not, and her adequacy constraints for definitions appear to differ from the usual philosophical constraints. Still, there is at least some convergence among the families on the lists.

In psychology, there is a large recent literature on primitive concepts. Here concepts are typically taken to be psychological entities (mental representations) rather than abstract entities, and I will follow this practice in what follows. Empiricist theorists such as Lawrence Barsalou (1999) and Jesse Prinz (2002) hold that all concepts are grounded in perception, and take primitive concepts to be restricted to perceptually acquired concepts. By contrast, nativist theorists such as Susan Carey (2009), Alan Leslie (2004), and Elizabeth Spelke (2000) have postulated innate 'core systems' for dealing with certain special nonperceptual domains such as the domains of causation, objects, number, and other minds. Here concepts such as *cause*, *object*, and *number* are taken to be primitive.

The primitive concepts at play in this literature are usually *acquisitionally* primitive concepts: very roughly, concepts whose acquisition does not derive from acquisition of other concepts. By contrast, Wierzbicka's project and my own is concerned with something more like *semantically* primitive concepts: very roughly, concepts whose meaning or content does not derive from the meaning or content of other concepts. So it is tricky to draw connections here. On the face of it, a semantically nonprimitive concept (*life*, perhaps) could be innate and acquisitionally primitive, while a semantically primitive concept (*law*, perhaps) might be acquired or isolated by abstraction from a semantically nonprimitive concept (such as *cause*). Still, one might expect at least a correlation between the two sorts of primitiveness, and it is interesting that the central families of primitive concepts in this literature (perceptual concepts, objects, causation, number, mind) correspond at least roughly to families on the list above.

Recent psychology has not focused much on semantically primitive concepts, perhaps associating them with the widely rejected classical model of concepts where most concepts are composed from other concepts. Still, one can make sense of semantically primitive concepts even on other models. Prototype or exemplar models often invoke an underlying feature space within which prototypes or exemplars are placed. We can then think of prototype concepts as semantically dependent on concepts of the underlying features, and we might see primitive concepts as serving as dimensions of a most basic feature space. In a theory-based model of concepts, we can think of a concept as semantically dependent on the concepts in terms of which an associated theory is cast. Primitive concepts might then be seen as the basic concepts in which an underlying theory of the world is cast. So there is certainly no tension between these ways of understanding concepts and the existence of primitive concepts.

A promising general model here is an *inferentialist* model of concepts, where most concepts are characterized by their inferential role with respect to other concepts. For example, concepts will be characterized by how they are applied to specific cases that are characterized using other concepts. On a classical model, the key inferences will involve definitions; on a prototype model, the key inferences will involve prototype structure; on a theory-based model, the key inferences will be theory-based. Primitive concepts will not be characterized by their inferential role with respect to other concepts, but in some other way.

Despite these connections, the scrutability framework does not immediately entail claims about psychological implementation. Scrutability involves normative inferential roles for concepts, concerning how they should be applied. Psychological models of concepts are often seen as descriptive frameworks, concerning how they are actually applied. One cannot simply read off the latter from the former. Still, it is plausible that there are strong mutual constraints between normative and descriptive inferential roles, especially in beings with a modicum of rationality. If so, we might expect the normative conceptual structure revealed here to stand in at least some rough correspondence to psychological structure. Just how strong a correspondence one can expect depends in part on the strength of the mutual constraints. Mapping out this correspondence remains an important open question for further investigation.

4 Narrow Scrutability (and narrow content)

We saw in the last chapter that many expressions are wide, in that their extension depends on the environment. As I put it there, these expressions are Twin-Earthable, in that there can be nondeferential utterances of them that have corresponding possible utterances by functional and phenomenal twins with different extensions. Here prime cases include natural-kind terms such as 'water' and names such as 'Gödel'. By contrast, non-Twin-Earthable expressions include those such as 'zero', 'plus', and perhaps 'philosopher' and 'action': their referents (when used nondeferentially) depend only on the speaker's functional and phenomenal states. Given that functional and phenomenal states are intrinsic states of a speaker, it follows that these referents depend only on speakers' intrinsic properties. We can say that they are *narrow* expressions, where narrow expressions are defined to be non-Twin-Earthable expressions or primitive indexicals such as 'I' and 'now'.[6]

We can likewise talk about Twin-Earthable concepts, where a concept is Twin-Earthable if there are possible functional and phenomenal twins one of whom has mastered the concept and one of whom has not. We can define narrow concepts similarly: these are either primitive indexical concepts or concepts such that there are no possible intrinsic twins one of whom has mastered the concept and one of whom has not. Then it is plausible that for a narrow concept there will be a corresponding narrow expression (one that always expresses that concept) and vice versa.

In the last chapter I canvassed the attractive thesis that truths involving Twin-Earthable expressions are always scrutable from corresponding truths without those expressions, and ultimately from truths involving only non-Twin-Earthable expressions and primitive indexicals. Given that these expressions are narrow, this thesis yields a Narrow Scrutability thesis: all truths are scrutable from truths involving only narrow expressions.

How does this thesis hold up in light of the scrutability bases considered here? Logical and mathematical expressions are very plausibly narrow. Indexical expressions also count, and it is difficult to generate Twin Earth cases for totality expressions such as 'fundamental'. It is common to hold that phenomenal expressions are narrow, although there are some views on which they are wide.

Nomic expressions such as 'it is a law that' are plausibly narrow. At least, it is not easy to generate Twin Earth cases involving them. Perhaps one could suggest that 'law' picks out something Humean in Humean worlds and something non-Humean in non-Humean worlds. But then we need only stipulate a more demanding term 'law' that always demands a non-Humean referent. Some Humeans may not accept that there is any such non-Humean concept, but on their view nomic concepts are dispensable from the scrutability base. On the non-Humean view, it is natural to hold that the core nomic expressions are narrow.

What about quiddistic expressions and concepts? If we follow the phenomenal or protophenomenal model for quiddistic concepts, they will be plausibly narrow. The same goes for a model on which they are seen as something like Edenic secondary qualities. And on any model, it is natural to hold that insofar

---

[6] More precisely, we can define narrowness in terms of non-Twin-Earthability understood in terms of intrinsic twins rather than functional/phenomenal twins: a (non-indexical) expression is narrow when for any nondeferential utterance of it, any corresponding possible utterance by an intrinsic twin has the same extension. Here I pass over some subtleties about just how to understand the notion of twin (tied, for example, to anti-internalist arguments by Clark and Chalmers 1998 and by Fisher 2007). These subtleties and much more concerning the relations among narrowness, Twin-Earthability, and internalism are discussed in the additional excursus on twin-earthability and internalism.

as we can form these concepts at all, it will be in virtue of some sort of direct understanding of the properties in question, with causal connections to instances being largely irrelevant. It is natural to expect them to be narrow.

My own view is that spatiotemporal expressions are wide, or at least Twin-Earthable, in that there can be Spatial Twin Earth cases of the sort discussed in chapter 7. But I think this width reflects the fact that spatiotemporal truths are scrutable from nomic and phenomenal truths and so are dispensable from a scrutability base. A spatiotemporal primitivist, by contrast, will hold that spatiotemporal expressions are not dispensable in this way. But it is natural for a spatiotemporal primitivist to hold that spatiotemporal expressions are not Twin-Earthable: two functional and phenomenal duplicates will have a primitive grasp of the same properties. This view is not compulsory for spatiotemporal primitivists, who may hold that we primitively grasp a causally connected property in a way that is not analyzable in causal terms or scrutable from causal truths (although see the discussion that follows). Or they may hold that spatial experience itself depends on the environment, so that spatiotemporal expressions are not Twin-Earthable but are nevertheless wide. But we saw in the last chapter that it is not at all clear how to develop these views in a reasonable way. So I think that the narrow version of spatiotemporal primitivism is the most natural.

As for other candidates for a scrutability base: it seems hard to construct a Twin Earth case for basic intentional and normative notions, so there is a good case that these are narrow. As for secondary quality concepts, these parallel the spatiotemporal case. On many views these concepts will be wide and correspondingly not needed in a scrutability base. There will be views on which they are wide and nevertheless primitive. But the most natural view on which they are primitive is one on which they are narrow.

What explains the phenomena here? I think the key observation is that paradigmatic Twin-Earthable expressions are all conceptually opaque in the sense of the fourteenth excursus: they are either primitive indexical expressions (such as 'I') or expressions whose referent is scrutable from truths about what role it plays, so that they are at least approximately analyzable as 'the entity that plays such-and-such role'. We would expect any such expression to be Twin-Earthable, at least given an appropriate role. So in these cases, conceptual features explain Twin-Earthability. Where primitive non-indexical expressions are concerned, however, these explanations do not apply. So we are left with no reason to think that these are Twin-Earthable.

This line of reasoning does not prove that no primitive expression is Twin-Earthable. As discussed in the fourteenth excursus, an opponent might embrace primitive externalism, holding that certain primitive concepts (primitive spatiotemporal or color concepts, perhaps) are Twin-Earthable, even though they are not causally analyzable and are not primitive indexicals. But establishing this conclusion would take arguments very different from the standard Putnam and Burge arguments, and I have never seen an argument with this sort of force. So following the methodology laid out at the end of the introduction, I will take it that in the absence of such arguments, we have default reason to think that the primitive non-indexical concepts in a scrutability base are not Twin-Earthable, so that the Narrow Scrutability thesis is true.

At the same time, I do not think that Narrow Scrutability is a priori, or even that it is a priori that the relevant concepts are narrow. For example, in an Edenic scenario, phenomenal states are constituted by direct acquaintance with instances of Edenic color in the environment. Intrinsic twins acquainted with different colors in such a scenario will have different phenomenal states and correspond-ingly different phenomenal and color concepts. In this scenario, phenomenal expressions and concepts will not be narrow. Still, I do not think that this is a plausible model of our relation to colors and phenomenal states in our world. In our world, unlike an Edenic world, our possession of phenomenal and primitive color concepts is constituted by factors independent of the environment. If this is right, phenomenal concepts are wide in some worlds but narrow in our world.

All this suggests that Narrow Scrutability is not a truly fundamental thesis. Indeed, I think it is best understood as a consequence of a more fundamental thesis, such as the Acquaintance Scrutability thesis in the next section, com-bined with a contingent claim about our world (such as the thesis that acquaint-ance in the relevant sense is always narrow). Correspondingly, the conclusion that there is a narrow scrutability base is not irresistible. There are views on which phenomenal, spatiotemporal, quiddistic, and secondary-quality concepts are conceptually primitive, and even involve acquaintance, but in which they get their content from causal connections to instances and so are Twin-Earthable all the same. Still, I think that there are good reasons to deny these theses as theses about our world. So I think there is good reason to accept Narrow Scrutability in our world.

The Narrow Scrutability thesis has important consequences for the the-ory of content. In particular, it can be used to support the claim that arbi-trary expressions and thoughts have *narrow* content, a sort of content that is independent of the environment. Narrow content will be shared between corresponding utterances and thoughts by any possible speakers who are intrinsic twins. To make the case for narrow content, we use the scrutability framework to associate utterances and thoughts with primary intensions (intensions defined over epistemically possible scenarios, as in E10) and use Narrow Scrutability to argue that these intensions are a sort of narrow content.

An argument runs as follows. Suppose we have established Generalized Narrow Scrutability: there is a generalized scrutability base consisting of narrow expressions. And suppose we have established the Narrowness of Scrutability: scrutability relations are themselves narrow, roughly in that if A-utterances are scrutable from (epistemically invariant) B-sentences for one nomologically possible speaker, then A'-utterances are scrutable from B'-sentences for a twin speaker, where A'-utterances correspond to A-utterances and B'-sentences to B-sentences (two sentences correspond when for any utterance of one there is a corresponding utterance of the other). Then it is not hard to make the case that for any nomologically possible utterance E, the intension of E defined over epistemically possible scenarios is narrow. By Generalized Narrow Scrutability, every scenario has a complete narrow specification. When D is a narrow sentence, D for one speaker will correspond to D for any twin speaker. By the Narrowness of Scrutability, if E is scrutable from a narrow scenario specification D, then for any corresponding utterance E' by a twin speaker, E' is also scrutable from D. So E and E' have the same primary intension. So primary intensions are a sort of narrow content.[7]

The Narrowness of Scrutability also needs defense. At least in the version of this thesis that involves a priori scrutability, it is natural to see the thesis as a consequence of the Narrowness of Apriority: if S is a priori for a (nomologically possible) speaker, then a corresponding sentence S' is a priori for a twin. This thesis can in turn be seen as a consequence of a thesis about thought: if a thought T is a priori for one (nomologically possible) thinker, then any corresponding thought T' is a priori for a twin.[8] Here corresponding thoughts in twins should be understood by analogy to corresponding utterances. Oscar's thoughts about water and Twin Oscar's thoughts about twin water are corresponding thoughts, for example.

---

[7] A loophole in this argument concerns phenomenal demonstratives in the scrutability base: these are indexicals and count as narrow by our definition, but they are not as well-behaved as standard indexicals such as 'I' and 'now'. Consider a symmetrical speaker using 'that' twice for symmetrically corresponding experiences in their visual field, as in the Two Tubes case of chapter 6. Call these utterances 'that$_1$' and 'that$_2$'. A twin speaker will make two utterances that we can call 'that$_3$' and 'that$_4$'. Then 'that$_1$' will correspond to both 'that$_3$' and 'that$_4$' under different mappings, and so will 'that$_2$'. If we see these four as utterances of different expressions (typed by their referents), then D for one speaker will correspond to a different expression D' for another speaker. If we see them as utterances of the same epistemically context-sensitive expression 'that', then we will need to formulate the Narrowness of Scrutability in terms of corresponding expressions-in-contexts (in order to apply it to yield narrow contents), and a similar issue will arise. The upshot is that the primary intensions of 'that$_1$ is red' and 'that$_2$ is red' are not narrow by the current definition, although they share a sort of structural coarse-grained content. For more on this case see 'The Nature of Epistemic Space'.

[8] See also 'The Components of Content' and 'The Nature of Epistemic Space'.

I think that these Narrowness of Apriority theses are prima facie attractive and that nothing in the strongest arguments for externalism gives reason to doubt them. In Putnam's cases, an utterance such as 'Water is a liquid' will plausibly be a priori for both twins or for neither. In Burge's cases, sentences such as 'Arthritis is a disease of the joints' may be a priori or analytic in one community but not the other. But the twins' utterances of the sentence and the corresponding thoughts will not be a priori as understood here: as with all deferential thoughts, conclusive justification of them will require empirical evidence about usage in the community. So if there are reasons to reject the Narrowness of Apriority theses, the sources of these reasons will at least differ from these sources.[9] So Narrow Scrutability can be used to motivate a notion of narrow content that is not undermined by the most common arguments for externalism.

The upshot is that primary intensions of utterances and thoughts serve as a sort of narrow content. For example, Oscar and Twin Oscar share a primary intension for their expressions 'water' that picks out (very roughly) the dominant clear, drinkable liquid in the environment around the core subject in a scenario. Likewise, the primary intension of my term 'Hesperus' may pick out something like the object visible at a certain location in the evening sky in a given scenario, and any twin of mine will have a term with the same primary intension. Even in the case of 'arthritis', Burge's two deferential users will share a primary intension that picks out (very roughly) the disease called 'arthritis' in the linguistic community around the core subject in a scenario.

Of course utterances and thoughts also have various sorts of wide content, for example corresponding to associated Russellian propositions and secondary intensions. Linguistic items may also have various sorts of wide content associated with use by a subject's linguistic community, and thoughts can be associated with wide content of this sort as well. Oscar and Twin Oscar's utterances and thoughts will certainly have different wide contents, as will Burge's user of 'arthritis' and his twin.

While there are many sorts of content, the narrow contents defined above can play many important roles.[10] This sort of narrow content reflects the rational relations between thoughts and utterances, reflects a thought's role in reasoning much more closely than non-narrow content does, and also plays a primary role in the explanation of behavior. As well as shedding light on the Putnam and

---

[9] The arguments of Clark and Chalmers 1998 and of Fisher 2007 are relevant here, but can be accommodated by properly understanding the notion of twin. Another worry concerns cases in which a priori justification of a thought depends on its history (inference from a priori justified premises, for example). This sort of case does not seem to yield a difference in idealized a priori justifiability, however.

[10] See 'The Components of Content' for more on this sort of narrow content and on the roles that it can play.

Burge cases, the framework can also shed light on indexical thought and on modes of presentation in thought. This account of the content of thought also coheres well with an account of ordinary propositional attitude ascriptions, which can be seen as attributing a combination of narrow and wide content. The scrutability framework, via theses such as Narrow Scrutability and the Narrowness of Apriority, serves as a foundation for this sort of narrow content.

Even if Narrow Scrutability is false and primitive externalism is true, the Narrowness of Apriority might deliver a sort of narrow content. Here we need only identify a sort of content associated with primitive concepts that is shared between the corresponding primitive concepts of duplicates. Perhaps even if we are externalist spatial primitivists, for example, there is a sort of quasi-spatial Fregean sense that is shared between our spatial concepts and the corresponding concepts of duplicates (a sense that determines different referents in different environments, of course). Given this much, we could then construct scenarios from these Fregean senses (as discussed briefly in E10), and use scrutability to associate arbitrary thoughts with sets of scenarios. Given the Narrowness of Apriority, it will follow that corresponding thoughts in duplicates will be associated with the same sets of scenarios. So in effect we will have defined a sort of narrow Fregean content. A related approach constructs scenarios from the 'features' discussed at the end of E14.

5 Acquaintance Scrutability (and Russellian acquaintance)

Russell famously advocated a Principle of Acquaintance: every proposition which we can understand must be composed wholly of constituents with which we are acquainted. He took this thesis to be central to his semantic, epistemological, and metaphysical projects. All expressions were ultimately to be analyzed in terms of expressions standing for entities with which we are acquainted. All knowledge was ultimately grounded in knowledge of entities with which we are acquainted. And in his metaphysical projects, Russell sought to construct the world out of entities with which we are acquainted.

We can put Russell's views in the cognitive and linguistic mode by saying that there is a special class of *acquaintance concepts*, concepts of entities with which we are acquainted, presented under the acquaintance mode of presentation. Likewise, there is a special class of *acquaintance expressions* (either types or tokens) that express acquaintance concepts. Then Russell's linguistic view might be put as the claim that all expressions are definable in terms of acquaintance expressions. His epistemological view might be put as the claim that all truths are knowable given knowledge of acquaintance truths (truths involving acquaintance expressions). His constructive view might be put as the claim that we can wholly specify the world in terms of acquaintance expressions.

The notion of acquaintance itself is vexed. But one central idea is that 'we have acquaintance with anything of which we are directly aware, without the intermediary of any process of inference or any knowledge of truths' (Russell 1912, chapter 5). Another central idea is that anyone who stands in an acquaintance relation to an entity knows (or is in a position to know) what that entity is. Correspondingly, an acquaintance concept is one such that anyone who possesses the concept knows (or is in a position to know) its referent.

Russell held that we are acquainted at least with sense-data and certain universals, and perhaps with the self. On Russell's view, acquaintance expressions may include 'I', 'this' (primitive demonstratives for sense-data), and perhaps expressions standing for certain universal properties and relations, such as 'red', 'before', and 'aware'.

Russell's views about acquaintance are widely rejected today. But the present framework has the potential to vindicate some of them. The obvious analog of Russell's views in the current framework is the thesis of Acquaintance Scrutability: all truths are scrutable from acquaintance truths. The sort of expressions that we have entertained for a scrutability base are strikingly reminiscent of Russell's class of acquaintance expressions: 'I', 'now', phenomenal demonstratives, and expressions for various universals such as phenomenal properties, nomic and spatiotemporal relations, and fundamentality. These are all at least candidates for being acquaintance expressions on a Russellian view.

As it stands, the Acquaintance Scrutability thesis suffers from the unclarity of the notion of acquaintance. But we can approach the matter indirectly, by invoking the notion of epistemic rigidity.

To recap discussion from the fourteenth excursus, an epistemically rigid expression is one whose referent can be known a priori by (nondeferential) users. Alternatively, it is an expression that picks out the same referent in every epistemically possible scenario. We cannot know what water is a priori, and we cannot know who Gödel is a priori, so 'water' and 'Gödel' are not epistemically rigid. But we can arguably know what zero is a priori, and we can arguably know what friendliness is a priori, so 'zero' and 'friendly' are epistemically rigid.

Epistemic rigidity is strikingly reminiscent of the concept of acquaintance. Epistemically rigid expressions need not be acquaintance expressions in the strong sense in that (nondeferential) possession of the corresponding concept entails knowledge of its referent. A simple epistemically rigid expression such as '2' may be an acquaintance expression in this sense, but a complex epistemically rigid expression such as '1008/7' is probably not. But epistemically rigid expressions are acquaintance expressions in the weaker sense that (nondeferential) possession of the corresponding concept entails being in a position to know its referent, at least if 'in a position to know' involves a sufficient idealization. In fact, such possession entails being in a position to know the referent a priori.

Epistemic rigidity is much stronger than the watered-down notion of acquaintance (operative in section 4.8, for example) that has become familiar in recent discussions of reference. On the watered-down notion, a perceptual connection or even a distant causal connection suffices to ground acquaintance, so that almost any ordinary proper name is an acquaintance expression. For example, 'Einstein' may be an acquaintance expression simply because I have heard of Einstein. Acquaintance in this sense certainly does not require that reference is a priori knowable, and correspondingly 'Einstein' is not epistemically rigid. The difference in strength is brought out by the fact that there can be true a posteriori identity statements involving acquaintance expressions in this watered-down sense, but there are no true a posteriori identity statements involving epistemically rigid expressions. The current notion of acquaintance is much closer to Russell's notion than to the watered-down notion.

The notion of epistemic rigidity fits some of Russell's paradigm examples of acquaintance better than others. It fits well for certain universals, such as consciousness or causation or friendliness. It also fits well for certain *properties* of sense-data, such as redness and roundness. Against the background of a Russellian ontology, it is natural to hold that expressions for these are epistemically rigid. But it does not fit so well with reference to the self, or to particular sense-data. On the current framework, an expression such as 'I' is not epistemically rigid: it picks out different individuals in different scenarios. And it is not especially plausible that I can know who I am a priori. Likewise, phenomenal demonstratives (the nearest equivalent to sense-datum demonstratives in the current framework) are not epistemically rigid: they pick out different experiences in different scenarios.[11]

Still, there is something special about reference to the self and to one's current experiences, in the current framework. 'I' and phenomenal demonstratives (along with 'now') are built into a scrutability base. They are primitive indexicals that appear to be unanalyzable. It is natural to hold that they operate by a sort of direct acquaintance with certain concrete parts of reality: oneself, the current moment, and one's experiences.[12] This sort of acquaintance differs from the sort

---

[11] Although see 'The Nature of Epistemic Space' for some discussion of a version of the current framework on which 'I' and related indexicals are treated as epistemically rigid.

[12] Actually, it seems less obvious that one is acquainted with the current time than it does that one is acquainted with oneself and one's experience. But the discussion in 6.12 already gives reason to say that the truly primitive indexicals are indexicals for either one's current time-slice or for one's current experience. It seems reasonable to say that these involve acquaintance. One might even hold that they involve strong acquaintance in the sense that whenever one possesses the concept one knows what it refers to—though this knowledge will be empirical (grounded in introspection) rather than a priori.

involved in the cases above (it does not confer a priori knowledge of the referent), but it can plausibly be regarded as a sort of acquaintance all the same.

Here one can suggest that there are two sorts of acquaintance. There is
acquaintance with concrete entities (oneself, one's experiences, the current time),
which involves a sort of immediate indexical ostension of them. And there is
acquaintance with abstract entities (properties, relations, and other abstract
objects), which involves a sort of full understanding of them. In the current
framework, acquaintance of the first sort can be cashed out in terms of primitive
indexicality, and acquaintance of the second sort can be understood in terms of
epistemic rigidity.

One can then suggest that an acquaintance expression is either a primitive
indexical expression or an epistemically rigid expression. Acquaintance Scrutability then comes to the thesis that all truths are scrutable from truths involving
only primitive indexicals and epistemically rigid expressions. Given that every
epistemically rigid expression is a priori equivalent to a super-rigid expression,
one can equivalently formulate Acquaintance Scrutability as the thesis that all
truths are scrutable from truths involving only primitive indexicals and super-
rigid expressions. I will go back and forth between these formulations in what
follows.

How plausible is this Acquaintance Scrutability thesis? In the scrutability
bases we have been considering, 'I', 'now', and phenomenal demonstratives
are plausibly primitive indexicals. Logical and mathematical terms are plausibly epistemically rigid: at least insofar as they have extension at all, their
extension is constant across scenarios. Phenomenal expressions and primitive secondary quality expressions are plausibly epistemically rigid, as we
have seen. Nomic expressions are also plausibly epistemically rigid: at least
given the relevant non-Humean concept, there is not much reason to think
that the extension of 'law' will vary across scenarios. Spatiotemporal expressions are epistemically nonrigid on my own view, but on a spatiotemporal
primitivist view it is natural to regard them as rigid. The same goes for quiddistic expressions and expressions for fundamentality. So there is a good case
for Acquaintance Scrutability.

As discussed in the fourteenth excursus, there are primitive externalist views
that will deny that non-indexical primitives are epistemically rigid. For example,
some type-B materialists hold that phenomenal concepts are primitive and that
phenomenal properties are identical to certain physical properties, where one
cannot know which property a priori. Likewise, some theorists hold that spatiotemporal concepts or secondary-quality concepts are primitive and that truths
involving them are not scrutable from more basic truths, while still holding that
they are epistemically nonrigid. I reject these views. But if these views are cor-

rect, and if these epistemically nonrigid concepts are thereby not acquaintance concepts, then Acquaintance Scrutability will be false.[13]

What about Russellian acquaintance? We might define a strong acquaintance concept as either a primitive indexical or a concept for which possession of the concept entails a priori knowledge (not merely a priori knowability) of its referent. The second disjunct is the stronger Russellian analog of epistemic rigidity discussed above, and primitive indexicals also are standardly regarded as involving Russellian acquaintance. Correspondingly, all strong acquaintance concepts are acquaintance concepts but not vice versa. The current framework is not committed to strong acquaintance. But if one believes in strong acquaintance concepts, the expressions in our putative scrutability base are all reasonable candidates for expressing them. So a Strong Acquaintance Scrutability thesis is at least on the table.

Russellian acquaintance is usually construed even more strongly, in that it is construed not just as acquaintance or strong acquaintance as defined, but as a substantive epistemic relation (perhaps primitive, perhaps nonconceptual) between a subject and an entity in virtue of which other epistemological and conceptual relations obtain. For example, it is because one is acquainted with one's sense-data in this substantive way that one knows (or is in a position to know) what they are. Furthermore, it is in virtue of these acquaintance relations that acquaintance concepts and acquaintance expressions have their content.

My official definition of acquaintance expressions invokes epistemic rigidity, which one might think of as a sort of weak acquaintance rather than strong acquaintance or Russellian acquaintance. One can consistently hold that epistemically rigid and primitive indexical concepts do not get their content through Russellian acquaintance with their referents. Still, if one is friendly to Russellian acquaintance, it is not out of the question to hold that the most primitive concepts in these classes all involve Russellian acquaintance, so that a Russellian Acquaintance Scrutability thesis is true. A role for acquaintance seems especially apt for phenomenal concepts (acquaintance with consciousness), for primitive perceptual concepts (acquaintance with primitive redness), and perhaps for primitive indexicals (acquaintance with oneself). In these cases there is perhaps

---

[13] If one accepts the relevant views, one might still retain a version of Acquaintance Scrutability by understanding acquaintance in a different way. For example, one might understand it in terms of the weak epistemic rigidity discussed at the end of E14. It seems natural to say that even on the type-B views where phenomenal or color concepts are pseudo-transparent, we are acquainted with phenomenal or color properties: it is just this this form of acquaintance does not bring revelation of the property with it. We might say that we have nonrevelatory acquaintance with the property. Alternatively, we could say that we have revelatory acquaintance with the corresponding feature (E14).

some phenomenological plausibility to a claim of acquaintance. Acquaintance is less obviously apt for logical, mathematical, nomic, and fundamentality concepts. Perhaps one could hold that these concepts are based on (intellectual?) acquaintance with their referent, but any acquaintance here seems further from the phenomenological surface. For now, I will be agnostic about whether Russellian acquaintance is involved in these cases.[14]

Acquaintance Scrutability follows from the following thesis: if an expression E is epistemically nonrigid, then E is scrutable from epistemically rigid expressions and primitive indexicals, in that any set of truths involving only E and certain other expressions E' is scrutable from a set of truths involving E' along with epistemically rigid expressions and primitive indexicals. I will not attempt a rigorous argument for that thesis here, but it certainly fits the behavior of paradigm epistemically nonrigid expressions that we have examined.

Acquaintance Scrutability provides a natural explanation of Narrow Scrutability. Given (i) the thesis that every epistemically rigid expression in our world is non-Twin-Earthable, (ii) the definitional claim that narrow expressions are non-Twin-Earthable expressions or primitive indexicals, and (iii) the definitional thesis that acquaintance expressions are epistemically rigid expressions or primitive indexicals, it follows that every acquaintance expression in our world is a narrow expression. So if Acquaintance Scrutability is true in our world, so is Narrow Scrutability. Insofar as there are worlds (such as Edenic worlds) where some epistemically rigid expressions are Twin-Earthable, then Acquaintance Scrutability may be true in those worlds even though Narrow Scrutability is not. I am inclined to think that Acquaintance Scrutability is necessary and a priori, while Narrow Scrutability is contingent and a posteriori. But the connection between acquaintance and narrowness gives us a good explanation of when the latter thesis does and does not hold.

6 Fundamental Scrutability (and the mind–body problem)

The Fundamental Scrutability thesis says that all truths are scrutable from metaphysically fundamental truths. This thesis, and other theses like it, have played a central role in various metaphysical debates, including the debate over the mind–body problem. In light of where we have gotten to, is this thesis plausible?

---

[14] In 'The Content and Epistemology of Phenomenal Belief', I defend a model of phenomenal concepts that involves something like Russellian acquaintance. I am inclined to think that Edenic perceptual concepts also involve something like Russellian acquaintance with universals. It is much less clear to me whether logical, mathematical, nomic, and fundamentality concepts involve something like Russellian acquaintance, or whether inferential role does the crucial work instead.

One obvious issue at the start is that a scrutability base requires indexical truths, and indexical truths are not plausibly metaphysically fundamental. To finesse this issue for now, I will understand Fundamental Scrutability as the thesis that all truths are scrutable from metaphysically fundamental truths plus indexicals. I will revisit the underlying issue later.

Another issue: presumably metaphysically fundamental truths will involve expressions for fundamental properties and the like. But fundamental properties, such as mass and charge, can in principle be picked out under many different modes of presentation, not all of which seem relevant to the thesis, and indeed some of which might trivialize the thesis.[15] The natural response is to constrain the modes of presentation here, perhaps requiring that the expressions used in these truths are super-rigid. But now a worry is that on some views (versions of quidditism without quidditistic concepts, for example) there may be no super-rigid expressions that pick out fundamental properties such as mass and charge. To handle this, we can stipulate that if this view is correct, we can instead characterize fundamental truths by using a Ramsey sentence using existentially quantified properties in place of expressions for these fundamental properties. Such a Ramsey sentence may then involve only super-rigid expressions. The Ramsey sentence may not consist in truly fundamental truths, but intuitively it is an immediate consequence of fundamental truths and is good enough for our purposes.

Somewhat more rigorously: let us say that a class of truths is a *necessitation base* if it necessitates all truths. A super-rigid necessitation base is a class of super-rigid truths that necessitates all super-rigid truths. It is trivial that there exist bases of this sort: the classes of all truths and all super-rigid truths will qualify, for example. If there are super-rigid expressions for all fundamental properties (as on some no-quiddity and quiddistic-concept views), then fundamental truths involving these expressions will plausibly also comprise a super-rigid necessitation base. And if there are not super-rigid expressions for all fundamental properties (as on the views above), then the Ramsey sentence above will qualify as a super-rigid necessitation base. We could then replace the Fundamental Scrutability thesis by the thesis that all truths are scrutable from any super-rigid necessitation base plus indexical truths.

One can argue for Fundamental Scrutability in two ways. One can argue from prior principles, or one can argue from data about cases: that is, from the conclusions we have established about scrutability bases. I will briefly discuss arguments of both sorts in what follows.

---

[15] For example: for any truth Q, there is an expression E that picks out electrons iff Q is true and otherwise picks out nothing. So without constraints on modes of presentation, all truths are scrutable from electron-truths.

One argument from prior principles proceeds as follows. Here F is any super-rigid necessitation base, and F-truths are the truths in F.

1. All super-rigid truths are necessitated by F-truths, which are super-rigid.
2. When S is super-rigid, S is necessary iff S is a priori.

3. All super-rigid truths are a priori scrutable from F-truths.
4. All truths are a priori scrutable from super-rigid truths and indexical truths.

5. All truths are a priori scrutable from F-truths and indexical truths.

Here, premise 1 is a definitional consequence of the stipulation that F is a super-rigid necessitation base. Premise 2 is the Apriority/Necessity thesis introduced in the fourteenth excursus. The intermediate conclusion 3 follows by applying premise 2 to the necessary conditionals involved in premise 1. Premise 4 is the Acquaintance Scrutability argued for in the last section. The conclusion 5 follows from 3 and 4 given the transitivity of a priori scrutability.

The Apriority/Necessity thesis and the Acquaintance Scrutability thesis are substantive principles and can be denied. The Apriority/Necessity thesis will be denied by those who hold that there are a posteriori necessities that involve only super-rigid expressions: for example, 'There is an omniscient being' (on certain theist views) and 'Any two objects have a mereological sum' (on certain ontological views). The Acquaintance Scrutability thesis will be denied by primitive externalists (E14): for example, certain type-B materialists and certain spatial or color primitivists. I think that all these views should be rejected, but the issue is substantive.

We can also argue from cases, using the scrutability bases established to date. An obvious problem here is that most type-B materialists will reject Fundamental Scrutability out of hand, because they hold that phenomenal truths (which they take to be nonfundamental) are not scrutable from microphysical truths (which they take to be the fundamental truths) plus indexical truths. Now, I think that if Fundamental Scrutability is plausible when considerations about consciousness are set aside, this gives us good reason to reject type-B materialism. So at the outset I would like to set aside issues about consciousness, and see whether Fundamental Scrutability is plausible. The easiest way to do that is to build phenomenal truths into the scrutability base. To do this, we can say that Fundamental+ Scrutability is the thesis that all truths are scrutable from a class of fundamental truths plus phenomenal truths and indexical truths.

Now, if all truths are scrutable from $PQTI$, as I argued earlier, then Fundamental+ Scrutability is highly plausible. On a physicalist view, there will be a necessitation base involving a conjunction of microphysical truths plus a that's-all truth, perhaps to the effect that those truths are all the fundamental truths. Prima facie, this base plus phenomenal and indexical truths yields $PQTI$, which is a scrutability base, so Fundamental+ Scrutability is true. On a dualist view, on which phenomenal truths are fundamental, the thesis that all truths are scrutable from *PQTI* also leads directly to Fundamental+ Scrutability. On nonphysicalist ontologies with further fundamental elements, then there will perhaps be truths not scrutable from *PQTI*, but the resources for a scrutability base will correspondingly go beyond *PQTI*, in what will prima facie be a parallel way. So there is a strong prima facie case for Fundamental+ Scrutability.

There are some subtleties here. One pertains to that's-all truths. Prima facie, physicalism requires a metaphysical that's-all truth, while scrutability requires an epistemological that's-all truth. We have seen that it is not unreasonable to suppose that one truth can play both roles: assuming physicalism, this might be $F(P)$, the metaphysical that's-all truth saying that P includes all the (positive) metaphysically fundamental truths. If an appropriate version of Fundamental Scrutability (for positive truths) is a priori, it will follow a priori that P (and indexical truths) comprise a scrutability base for positive truths, so that $F(P)$ is also an epistemological that's-all truth. If this version of Fundamental Scrutability is not a priori, however, then different that's-all theses may be needed. Still, if this version of Fundamental Scrutability is not a priori, there will certainly be epistemically possible obstacles to Fundamental Scrutability other than the that's-all clause. It follows that the that's-all truth cannot be the *only* epistemically possible obstacle to Fundamental Scrutability. So if the thesis is acceptable in other respects, we should accept it. In the worst case we can simply allow an epistemic that's-all truth in the statement of Fundamental Scrutability, as we allow indexicals.

Other issues pertain to quiddities. Depending on whether we embrace quiddistic concepts, quiddities without quiddistic concepts, or a no-quiddity view, the fundamental truths will be specified either using quiddistic concepts, using a Ramsey sentence, or using a specification of dispositions and powers. On any of these specifications, P (a characterization in the vocabulary of theoretical physics) will at least be scrutable from this specification. On the quiddistic-concept view, the specification will go beyond P, and there will be corresponding truths that are not scrutable from *PQTI*, but they will be scrutable from the expanded fundamental base all the same. And on the other views, scrutability from *PQTI* yields scrutability from the fundamental base directly.

The issues regarding nomic truths are largely straightforward. On paradigmatic Humean views, minimal necessitation bases and minimal scrutability bases need not include nomic truths. On paradigmatic non-Humean views, minimal bases of both sorts must include nomic truths. Either way, P will be scrutable from the base and there will be no problem. The only potential problem comes from a view that embraces Humean supervenience without Humean scrutability: the analog of type-B materialism in the domain of the nomic. A view like this will probably deny Fundamental Scrutability. But I think that there is little reason to accept this sort of view in any case. Much the same analysis applies to spatiotemporal truths: there will be problems only if spatio-temporal truths supervene on non-spatiotemporal truths without being scruta-ble from them. Again, there is little reason to find this sort of view attractive.

Some views deny scrutability from *PQTI*– not because they think that there are further fundamental truths, but because they think that some nonfundamen-tal truths are inscrutable from *PQTI*–. These include versions of views discussed in chapter 5 maintaining the inscrutability of mathematical truths, normative, ontological, intentional, vague, or macrophysical truths. On some versions of such views, the further truths may be fundamental, but on many they will not be. I have given reasons for rejecting all these views in chapter 5, but it is useful to have them on the table as views that will deny Fundamental Scrutability.

Overall, I think the case for Fundamental+ Scrutability is strong. And given Fundamental+ Scrutability, the case for Fundamental Scrutability is strong. To maintain the former but not the latter, a proponent needs to maintain that phe-nomenal truths are the only exception to Fundamental Scrutability, or at least that all exceptions to Fundamental Scrutability are so closely associated with phenomenal truths that adding phenomenal truths to the base removes the exceptions. This sort of exceptionalism is unattractive and requires a great deal of explanation and motivation.

An opponent could reasonably respond that we have already in effect allowed one exception to the thesis that all truths are scrutable from fundamental truths: the case of indexicals. Once we have allowed one exception, why not allow one more? I think the case of indexical truths is special, though, in that one can straightforwardly explain why even in a world that is fundamentally objective, one would expect there to be inscrutable indexical truths. It is an objective truth that there are inscrutable indexical truths, and this objective truth (like all others) is itself scrutable from fundamental objective truths. So a basic thesis of scrutabil-ity from fundamentals can itself explain the existence of this exception.

It then remains open to an opponent to do the same for phenomenal truths: that is to explain why, even in a world that is fundamentally physical, one would expect there to be inscrutable phenomenal truths. This is precisely the strategy taken by proponents of the so-called phenomenal concept strategy for respond-ing to anti-materialist arguments. I think that this is a powerful strategy, but I have argued in 'Phenomenal Concepts and the Explanatory Gap' that it cannot work. In particular, the thesis that there are inscrutable phenomenal truths (or even that there are inscrutable quasi-phenomenal truths, where these truths are cast in topic-neutral nonphenomenal terms) is not scrutable from fundamental physical truths. If this is right, the analogy with indexical truths cannot be main-tained, and the opponent must once again postulate a unique and unexplained exception.

Accepting Fundamental Scrutability does not settle the issue between materialism and dualism. But it does effectively rule out type-B materialism, leaving a choice between type-A materialism (eliminativism, analytic functionalism), Russellian monism, and various varieties of dualism. And if one is convinced that there are phenomenal truths that are not scrutable from physical truths (that is, from truths in the language of microphysics) and indexical truths, then one is left with a choice between Russellian monism and dualism.

There is much more to say about this issue. A proper defense of Fundamental Scrutability requires an analysis of issues about the connection between epistemic and metaphysical possibility that I cannot resolve here. As usual in this book my primary concern is with epistemological and conceptual theses, rather than metaphysical theses. But the connection between the epistemology and the metaphysics here remains an interesting and important issue in its own right.

7 Structural Scrutability (and structural realism)

In the *Aufbau*, Carnap insisted that his basic truths be *structural* truths, characterizable in terms of certain sorts of relational structure. This requirement arose because Carnap held that only structural truths are truly objective, only these are intersubjectively communicable, and only these are fit to be the subject matter of science. This objective structural picture of the basic truths is very different from Russell's picture, on which all basic expressions are grounded in a sort of direct subjective acquaintance.[16]

Carnap's ideal is *pure structuralism*, on which the basic vocabulary is limited to logical expressions alone. We saw in chapter 1 that this thesis is undermined by Newman's problem. But this leaves open the possibility of *weak structuralism*, on which the basic vocabulary may include a limited number of expressions for relations (such as phenomenal similarity) plus logical expressions.

Both theses have analogs in the domain of scrutability. The analog of pure structuralism is Logical Scrutability: the thesis that all truths are scrutable from truths using logical vocabulary alone. The analog of weak structuralism is Structural Scrutability: roughly, the thesis that all truths are scrutable from truths using logical vocabulary plus structural expressions, where (to a first approximation) a structural expression is one that expresses a basic relation. Logical Scrutability is undermined by Newman's problem, but Structural Scrutability remains on the table. The content of the Structural Scrutability thesis is somewhat unclear, because it is somewhat unclear just what counts as a structural expression. If we use the definition in terms

---

[16] For discussion of the relation between Carnap's and Russell's projects, see Alan Richardson's 'How Not to Russell Carnap's *Aufbau*' (1990), Christopher Pincock's 'Russell's Influence on Carnap's *Aufbau*' (2002), and his 'Carnap, Russell, and the External World' (2007).

of relations, we run up against the problem that any expression for a property (e.g., 'red') can trivially be turned into an expression for a relation (e.g., 'R', where $R(a,b)$ holds iff a is red). And many true relational expressions, such as 'redder', are arguably too closely tied to subjective experience to count as 'objective'. So we need some way to restrict the relevant class of relations. Furthermore, we may wish to count some nonrelational expressions as structural: the notion of lawhood, for example. In practice, what counts as a structural expression will be determined by the purposes for which we are interested in the structural scrutability thesis: for example, purposes tied to objectivity and communicability. In what follows, I will not try to define a structural expression, but I will keep the criteria of objectivity and communicability in mind. I will return to the question of what counts at the end of this section.

I will stipulate that mathematical, totality, and indexical expressions are structural expressions. Mathematical and totality expressions are intuitively used to characterize the structure of the world, and they do not pose obvious obstacles to objectivity and communicability. There is a sense in which indexical truths are non-objective, so there is perhaps a sense in which indexical expressions such as 'I' and 'now' are nonstructural. Still, indexical expressions function in an objectively definable and highly constrained way in communication, and we know that we need them in a scrutability base, so it makes sense to count them as structural for present purposes.

Given the varieties of scrutability that we have seriously entertained, there are a number of natural paths to a version of Structural Scrutability. Most obviously, one might appeal to nomic, spatiotemporal, or phenomenal structure, or to some combination of these.

(i) *Spatiotemporal structuralism.* The Spatiotemporal Scrutability thesis already discussed yields one obvious route. Here, the base truths specify that there exist entities with certain spatiotemporal properties, bearing certain existentially quantified further properties. On the face of it, there is no need to include specific monadic spatiotemporal properties, such as absolute spatiotemporal position, in a scrutability base. Assuming a classical conception of spacetime for simplicity, it is arguable that there are no such truths, or at least that any such truths that we can entertain are all scrutable from truths about spatiotemporal relations. So it is natural for the base truths here to simply specify spatiotemporal relations among the fundamental entities, to specify fundamental spatiotemporal structure. The resulting view holds that all truths are scrutable from truths involving expressions for spatiotemporal relations and background expressions. This is a sort of spatiotemporal structuralism.[17]

---

[17] An awkwardness here is that 'spatiotemporal structuralism' can in principle be used either for the claim that the primitive structure is spatiotemporal or for the diametrically opposed claim that spatiotemporal notions can be analyzed in more fundamental structural terms. Here I am using it the first way. As in chapter 7, I use 'spatiotemporal functionalism' or sometimes 'structural spatiotemporal functionalism' for the second claim.

Which spatiotemporal relations will be included in the base, and how do we specify them? On a Newtonian picture, these might include relations of spatial and temporal distance, or better, relative spatial and temporal distance, as there is not obviously a need for notions of absolute distance in a scrutability base. More straightforwardly, though, one can specify the relevant structure using something like a co-ordinate representation of space and time (there is an entity with properties P and Q at point (x, y, z, t)). A co-ordinate system is not absolute, but one can choose an arbitrary system and simultaneously specify the allowable transformations into other systems (e.g., rotating or rescaling the spatial co-ordinates, rescaling the temporal co-ordinate). If one holds that truths about velocity are not scrutable from truths about spatiotemporal location, one can straightforwardly build them in within the same framework. It will be part of the basic specification that the first three co-ordinates are *spatial* co-ordinates and that the final co-ordinate is a *temporal* co-ordinate. This sort of explicit specification saves the construction from Newman's problem.

This sort of mathematical approach has the advantage of generalizing to nonclassical pictures of spacetime. For the framework of special relativity, for example, one can use a co-ordinate system with more allowable transformations, reflecting the fact that there is no absolute reference frame. For general relativity, one can use a mathematical specification of a four-dimensional differential manifold. For a quantum-mechanical framework, one can specify a mathematical structure corresponding to that of a wavefunction in the relevant mathematical space. All of these can be seen as broadly structural specifications.

It is important that these specifications not be *purely* mathematical. If they were, we would run into the threat of vacuity posed by Newman's problem. In effect, the specification would say simply that reality can be described by that structure: roughly, that there is a structure-preserving mapping from various parameters in reality to parameters of the model. With no constraints on the choice of parameters, then as long as the world has the right cardinality, we can always find such a mapping. According to spatiotemporal structuralism, the relevant constraints come from our (primitive) concepts of space and time. So in the classical specification, it will be specified that the first three parameters are spatial parameters and that the last parameter is a temporal parameter. Something similar applies on the nonclassical specifications: certain dimensions within these models will be specified as spatial and temporal dimensions.

These nonmathematical constraints, here appealing to notions of space and time, allow us to avoid the threat of vacuity. As usual, these constraints force us to give up on pure structuralism, but we are still left with a sort of weak structuralism, in effect specifying the structure of the world with the help of appeal to spatiotemporal structure. At the same time, this picture requires spatiotemporal primitivism, a view I argued against in the last chapter. It is not easy to see how this picture will work for physical theories that do not give a fundamental role to spacetime, for example. But it at least gives an example of one sort of weak structuralism in the current framework.

(ii) *Nomic structuralism.* Another route to weak structuralism is provided by Nomic Scrutability. According to this thesis, the base truths specify a world of entities and properties connected by certain nomic relations. On one version, fundamental properties are specified as powers to affect other properties (as when mass is specified as a power to resist acceleration and to attract other masses), and the states of fundamental entities (in initial conditions, perhaps) are specified in terms of a distribution of these powers over those entities. On another version, it is specified that there exist distinct properties related by certain laws, and it is specified that there are certain entities (in initial conditions, perhaps) with a certain distribution of these properties. On this version, the extra nonlogical vocabulary is strictly speaking an operator ('It is a law that') rather than a relation, but the operator in effect serves to relate the relevant properties. These views are versions of nomic structuralism.

Nomic structuralism can be combined with the sort of mathematical specification of microphysics discussed above. The difference will be that instead of labeling certain parameters or dimensions as spatiotemporal, we will instead require that certain connections among these parameters are laws of nature. This specification will avoid the threat of vacuity. One might think that this specification will still be open to multiple realization, and that it will leave certain truths about the nature of these parameters unsettled (as spatiotemporal properties, phenomenal properties, or certain quiddities, for example). The nomic structuralist will reply that this claim requires false doctrines such as quidditism, or spatiotemporal primitivism, or phenomenal realism. There are no such unsettled truths: there are simply properties related in the relevant nomic pattern, and that is all we can say.

(iii) *Phenomenal structuralism.* A third route to weak structuralism is provided by Phenomenal Scrutability. We saw in the last chapter that there are both phenomenalist and panpsychist versions of Phenomenal Scrutability, with base truths specifying phenomenal properties either of observers or of microphysical entities. As I have put things so far, base truths about phenomenology may involve the specification of properties such as phenomenal redness. This sort of characterization is hard to square with weak structuralism. But it is also possible to characterize phenomenal properties in structural terms, and there are views on which all phenomenal truths and even all truths are scrutable from such a characterization. We might call such views phenomenal structuralism.

Carnap's view for much of the *Aufbau* is a sort of phenomenal structuralism. He characterizes experiences wholly in terms of the relation of phenomenal similarity among them, and he argues in effect that all phenomenal truths are scrutable from there, and that all truths are scrutable from these phenomenal truths in turn. These last two claims are questioned by Goodman and Quine respectively. Goodman's basic worry is that a single phenomenal similarity relation is not rich enough to recover the full character of phenomenology. Here, I think that the phenomenal structuralist has various options. Even if Carnap's account of phenomenal structure is deficient, other characterizations may be available.

At this point, a natural move for the phenomenal structuralist is to move from a single phenomenal similarity relation to multiple such relations, each corresponding to different respects or dimensions of phenomenal similarity. For example, distinct color experiences can be similar in red-green respects (having the same amount of redness), yellow-blue respects, or brightness respects. Visual experiences can also be similar in various spatial respects. Still, residual problems in the spirit of Goodman's may remain. For example, mere similarity information among a set of experiences may not suffice to recover structure when the number of total experiences is limited. If we are told that there are two experiences that are different in all relevant respects, this seems to leave their character underdetermined. A move to graded similarity relations may help to some extent, but problems will remain. The picture also gets complicated when we move to more complex experiences, such as that of a full visual field.[18]

A better move for the phenomenal structuralist is to move from respects of phenomenal similarity to parametric information about locations along phenomenal dimensions. All this is most straightforwardly done by using quasi-mathematical specifications of phenomenal states analogous to the mathematical specifications of physical states discussed above.

For concreteness, let us adopt the fiction that phenomenal states are entirely visual and that (as on Carnap's own model) visual phenomenal states involve only the distribution of phenomenal colors in a two-dimensional visual field. On this model, locations in the visual field can be represented by (x, y)

---

[18] To handle a visual field in this framework (where visual fields have the structure characterized below), one might appeal to an entire manifold of graded similarity relations, three for each location in the visual field, corresponding to similarity in the redness, blueness, and brightness respects at that location. One could then have three higher-order similarity relations that hold along these relations: an on–off relation that holds iff the lower-order relations involve sameness in the same color respect, and two graded relations that measure similarity of the two points corresponding to the two lower-order relations in left–right respects and up–down respects respectively. From here, given a sufficiently rich set of total experiences one could recover much of the geometric structure of the parametric model below. The similarity-based model is arguably somewhat closer to the spirit of Carnap's method of 'quasi-analysis', but the parametric model is much more straightforward, and is also somewhat more powerful (it allows one to more easily capture the distinct status of unique hues, for example).

co-ordinates, where x is intuitively a left–right co-ordinate and y is an up–down co-ordinate. Phenomenal colors can be represented as (a, b, c) co-ordinates, corresponding to locations on a red-green axis, a yellow-blue axis, and a brightness axis. We can assume that each of these five co-ordinates is constrained to lie between -1 and 1 inclusively. Then if A is $[-1, 1]$, the set of real numbers between -1 and 1 inclusively, locations in the visual field can be represented as members of A^2 and phenomenal colors can be represented as members of A^3. The total phenomenal state of a subject can then be represented as a function from A^2 to A^3, in effect assigning a phenomenal color to each location in the visual field.[19]

What sort of additional constraints are needed to characterize the dimensions? The strongest constraints specify explicitly that the three dimensions of A^3 represent degrees of phenomenal redness, phenomenal blueness, and brightness respectively, and that the two dimensions of A^2 represent location on a left–right axis and an up–down axis in the visual field. This treatment makes it reasonably plausible that the full character of the total phenomenal state will be scrutable, but its credentials as a variety of structuralism are dubious. The notions of phenomenal redness and phenomenal blueness are intuitively far from structural notions, and they seem to pose the sort of problems for objectivity and communicability that structuralist views are supposed to avoid. It is arguable that something similar applies to primitive concepts of (phenomenal) left and right, and up and down.

The weakest constraints here will simply specify that the dimensions are *phenomenal* dimensions, and will say nothing beyond that. This sort of specification requires an unanalyzed notion of phenomenology, or of a phenomenal dimension, just as nomic and spatiotemporal specifications require unanalyzed notions of lawhood and spacetime, but it plausibly counts as (weakly) structural to roughly the extent that these do. It likewise counts as structural to the extent

[19] Of course visual experiences have a much more complex structure than this, but the phenomenal structuralist can reasonably hold that this structure can be characterized in more complex mathematical terms. The same goes for other perceptual experiences. Some putative experiences, such as the experience of thinking, or the experience of perceptually recognizing a given person, seem harder to characterize in mathematical terms, but the phenomenal structuralist could adopt a 'thin' view of experience on which it is exhausted by the experience of low-level features such as color, shape, and location. The temporal aspects of consciousness raise further issues: here the phenomenal structuralists might appeal to phenomenal temporal qualities analogous to phenomenal spatial qualities (alternatively, a phenomenal/temporal structuralist could appeal to the temporal properties of experience). Phenomenal structuralism can also be adapted to a representationalist framework, characterizing experiences in terms of phenomenal awareness of certain properties (color and spatiotemporal properties, for example), where these properties are characterized in the structural terms above. Such a framework may invoke a primitive concept of awareness as well as concepts for relations among various primary and secondary qualities, so we can think of it as phenomenal/quality structuralism.

that Carnap's own specification in terms of phenomenal similarity does. The most obvious problem for the weak model is one of underdetermination. It is natural to suggest that merely specifying that a phenomenal state is characterized by a certain function from A^2 to A^3 leaves open whether it involves phenomenal color (for example) at all. For example, perhaps there can be a phenomenal state isomorphic to this one involving the distribution of auditory qualities in a two-dimensional field. Still, a certain sort of structuralist about phenomenal properties will deny that this is possible, holding that the difference between visual and auditory phenomenal properties is ultimately a matter of their structure.[20]

An intermediate model specifies that the dimensions of A^3 are color dimensions and that the dimensions of A^2 are spatial dimensions, but does not specify their nature beyond this. As one might expect, the intermediate option is subject to watered-down versions of the objections to the weak and strong models. First: the notions of phenomenal color and phenomenal space are not structural notions, although perhaps they are less objectionable to a structuralist than phenomenal redness or phenomenal blueness. Second: specifying a phenomenal color in terms of its locations along three dimensions leaves open whether it is phenomenal redness or phenomenal blueness. For example, unique phenomenal redness and unique phenomenal blueness can both be represented as $(1, 0, 1)$ in the different co-ordinate systems: the [red, blue, brightness] and the [blue, red, brightness] systems respectively. So the mere claim that a given phenomenal state can be represented as $(1, 0, 1)$ along phenomenal color axes does not enable one to determine whether it is phenomenal redness or phenomenal blueness.

The second underdetermination problem is a version of the problem of the inverted spectrum, which plagues all structuralist accounts of phenomenology. A structuralist may reply by appealing to further structural constraints that distinguish the various dimensions. But it is arguable that related problems will always arise. One way to see this is to note that Frank Jackson's Mary in her black-and-white room (chapter 3) could in principle be told any set of mathematical and structural facts about the phenomenal state someone is in when they see roses, but she still would not be in a position to know what it is like to see roses. So she will not be in a position to know that a certain mathematically specified state is a certain sort of phenomenal redness (specified under a pure phenomenal concept). Even if she is told that certain parameters represent locations along phenomenal dimensions, or along phenomenal color and space

---

[20] Leitgeb (2011) makes a different phenomenal structuralist proposal on which there is a single basic property of 'qualitative overlap' applied to sets of experiential tropes, for example when they all involve the same shade of red in the same area of the visual field. In effect overlapping sets will correspond to Carnap's phenomenal quality circles while avoiding Goodman's problems of companionship and imperfect community. The respects of overlap are specified only as phenomenal respects, so this specification imposes a version of the weak constraints in the text.

dimensions, this will not help. If she is told that these represent locations along phenomenal redness and blueness dimensions, where she somehow has mastered the pure phenomenal concepts of phenomenal blueness and redness, then she will be in a position to know what the state is like. But assuming that this sort of characterization in terms of specific phenomenal dimensions does not count as structural, then the considerations here suggest that certain phenomenal truths are simply not scrutable from truths about phenomenal structure, and that any form of phenomenal structuralism is false.

Still, a phenomenal structuralist is likely to be deflationary about phenomenal knowledge. Carnap himself would probably not have been too worried about inverted spectrum hypotheses or about Mary's new phenomenal knowledge: these are precisely the sorts of putative hypotheses and knowledge that he wants to reject as meaningless. I think that the most consistent line for the phenomenal structuralist is to adopt only the weak constraints on which it is simply specified that the relevant parameters are phenomenal dimensions, and to deny the claim that this phenomenal structure leaves some phenomenal truths underdetermined.[21] This model shares much of the spirit of Carnap's model in the *Aufbau*. In effect, Carnap's single relation of phenomenal similarity has been expanded into many such relations (corresponding to unspecified respects of similarity), and these have then been reconstrued as parametric phenomenal dimensions.

Phenomenal structuralism is also subject to worries about whether truths about the external world are scrutable from truths about phenomenology. As we saw in the last chapter, the latter thesis seems to require either a version of phenomenalism or a version of panpsychism. Carnap in the *Aufbau* in effect took the phenomenalist approach, defining all external-world notions purely in terms of phenomenology. This phenomenalist program here is subject to familiar criticisms by Quine and others, and the appeal to fine-grained phenomenal structure above does little to help. This leaves open a panpsychist version of phenomenal structuralism, on which one in effect specifies the properties of microphysical entities by specifying the total experiences of those entities in terms of their phenomenal structure. This panpsychism is unlikely to have much appeal for a logical empiricist such as Carnap, and the sorts of consideration that lead to panpsychism are not easily reconciled with the considerations that lead to structuralism. But I leave the view on the table as a point in logical space.

[21] If phenomenal dimensions are too cheap, then a version of Newman's problem will arise. For example, if any function from total phenomenal states to $[-1, 1]$ counts as a phenomenal dimension, then given any set of phenomenal states of cardinality no greater than the continuum, there will be phenomenal dimensions under which these states can be mapped to A^3. Something similar applies to mappings from phenomenal states to functions from A^2 to A^3. These structural specifications will be satisfied by any set of phenomenal states of small enough cardinality. To avoid this problem, there must be constraints on phenomenal dimensions, perhaps requiring them to correspond to natural or fundamental aspects of phenomenology.

Alternatively, the problems about the external world can be handled by supplementing phenomenal structure with some other sort of structure, such as nomic or spatiotemporal structure. The result will be nomic/phenomenal structuralism or phenomenal/spatiotemporal structuralism. Either of these would be reasonably close to the spirit of the *Aufbau*, and would straightforwardly avoid Quine's problem and other problems associated with phenomenalism. Views like this would also avoid some of the problems of nomic and spatiotemporal structuralism in accommodating for phenomenal truths, although they would still face the problems of phenomenal structuralism in underdetermining phenomenal truths.

(iv) *Quiddistic structuralism.* As with panpsychist structuralism, quiddistic structuralism is a combination that is unlikely to be held, as the motivations for the two halves of the view stand in strong tension with each other. On many standard treatments, quiddities are invoked precisely to go beyond structure, and it is not easy to see how quiddistic concepts would qualify as structural concepts. There are views (involving thin quiddities or ungraspable thick quiddities, in the terms of chapter 7) on which quiddities are specified merely as certain numerically distinct properties that play certain roles. But these views will not need quiddistic concepts in the base, so they count for present purposes as nonquiddistic. (Indeed, this template fits certain versions of the nomic, spatiotemporal, and fundamentality structuralism discussed elsewhere in this section.) Perhaps one could have a single broad quiddistic concept Q (analogous to the concept of phenomenology), that we use to specify quiddistic states in terms of mathematical structures along dimensions of Q (analogous to phenomenal structuralism). This is not an especially attractive view for structuralists or for nonstructuralists, however. So I will set quiddistic structuralism aside.

(v) *Fundamentality structuralism.* According to fundamentality structuralism, we dispense with nomic, spatiotemporal, phenomenal, and quiddistic expressions, and appeal only to the notion of fundamentality (along with logical, mathematical, and indexical expressions). This view can appeal to the same base truths as logical structuralism, except that it will be stipulated that all properties and relations quantified over are fundamental properties and relations. For example, base truths might say that there are certain entities and certain fundamental properties and relations such that the properties and relations are distributed in such-and-such a way over the entities. Or on a mathematical version of the view, base truths might give a mathematical specification of reality (perhaps along the lines of the mathematical specifications of microphysics discussed above), and it will be stipulated in addition that certain dimensions of the model (those corresponding to fundamental physical properties, for example), are *fundamental* dimensions.

This view is closely akin to Carnap's final view in the *Aufbau*, substituting the notion of fundamentality for his notions of naturalness and foundedness, and dropping his dubious claim that these notions are logical notions. As in the *Aufbau*, this leaves open the question of how fundamentality is to be understood. It might be understood as various varieties of metaphysical or conceptual fundamentality, for example. We might also choose to define fundamentality in terms of a more basic in-virtue-of or grounding relation: if we take this route, we might strictly speaking obtain *grounding structuralism* rather than fundamentality structuralism. However we understand fundamentality, it is arguable that we have a reasonable grasp of some notions in this vicinity, and we have also seen that notions along these lines may already be needed in stating a that's-all truth.

As in the *Aufbau*, the appeal to fundamentality is intended to evade Newman's problem for logical structuralism. The standard objection to Carnap's final view is that fundamentality is not a logical notion, but once the structuralist project is freed of a tie to logic, this is no longer an objection. One may object that the view requires a primitive grasp of the notion of fundamentality, but it is not obvious why this is any more problematic than a primitive grasp of the notions of conjunction and existential quantification. There remain the usual worries about whether we can recover nomic, phenomenal, or spatiotemporal truths from here, but one can at least give some motivation to the view.

For example, one can motivate fundamentality structuralism by starting from spatiotemporal structuralism and eliminating spatiotemporal vocabulary via a structural version of spatiotemporal functionalism. Spatiotemporal structuralism holds that all truths are scrutable from a mathematical specification of reality along with the claims that certain dimensions in this model are spatial or temporal. Fundamentality structuralism holds that all truths are scrutable from the same mathematical specification along with the claim that certain dimensions are fundamental. Spatiotemporal structuralism will support fundamentality structuralism as long as the truths that certain dimensions are spatial and temporal are themselves scrutable from the fundamentality specification. For this purpose, it suffices if one can define the spatiality and temporality of a fundamental dimension in relevant structural terms.

Here we could invoke certain mathematical properties of being spacelike and timelike. These might be characterized in terms of the core functional roles of spatial and temporal parameters in familiar physical theories, or perhaps in our folk conception of the physical world. For example, a timelike parameter might be one with certain sorts of determination of world-slices in one direction ('future') by those in the other direction ('past'), with certain sorts of dynamics. A spacelike parameter might just be a non-timelike parameter (the parameters that in effect specify the character of the slices), or it might invoke a substantive analysis. The notion of spacelikeness in relativity theory yields one example of a substantive analysis. Another is given by David Albert (1996), who in effect gives a functional analysis of space in terms of interactive distances defined using Hamiltonians. Further analyses are certainly possible, though the character of the best such analysis for present purposes remains an open question. One could then argue that it is a priori that any spacelike dimension is a spatial dimension, or perhaps that it is a priori that any spacelike dimension that stands in the relevant indexical relation to us is a spatial dimension. One could argue for a similar a priori relation between being a timelike dimension and being a temporal dimension.

If this sort of structural analysis of space and time is possible, then spatiotemporal structuralism will yield fundamentality structuralism. At least, given that there are fundamental spatial and temporal dimensions in our world, what is scrutable from the spatiotemporal description will be scrutable from the corresponding fundamentality descriptions. If spatial and temporal dimensions are nonfundamental, then perhaps a similar analysis applied to spacelike and timelike nonfundamental dimensions could succeed.

Defining spatiality and temporality in purely structural terms raises difficult philosophical and technical issues that I will not try to adjudicate here. Philosophically, one might reasonably worry that these analyses will not fully capture our concepts of space and time, and that there will always be counterexamples involving unusual spacetimes. Still, it appears the project is at least a promising one for the structuralist. The resulting view will still suffer from the problems of spatiotemporal structuralism in accounting for truths about laws of nature and about consciousness. But if the view is combined with Humeanism about laws and phenomenal deflationism, there is at least a chance that it could account for these truths and ultimately for all truths.

One might also try to develop a version of fundamentality structuralism that takes off from nomic structuralism instead of from spatiotemporal structuralism, for example by analyzing laws of nature in terms of regularities over fundamental properties. It is arguable that this would end up at much the same place as the previous version. One could also attempt a version that takes off from phenomenal structuralism, via a structural analysis of what it is to be a phenomenal dimension, although it is less clear how this might go.

Of all the structuralist views I have discussed, fundamentality structuralism is clearly the view that is most in the spirit of Carnap's final view in the *Aufbau*. By my own lights it cannot succeed, because of problems with recovering laws of nature and phenomenology from a fundamentality specification. But if one is antecedently a Humean and a phenomenal deflationist (as Carnap plausibly was), then it is a promising approach. If one is a non-Humean and phenomenal deflationist, one might also consider nomic/fundamentality structuralism, which adds specifications of nomic relations among fundamental properties to a fundamentality specification. It is arguable that something like this yields the most powerful version of nomic structuralism. One could also combine either or both of these elements with elements of phenomenal or spatiotemporal structuralism, yielding combined versions of structuralism.

Overall: the issue of what it takes to be a version of structuralism remains imprecise. Some criteria that we might invoke for a structural expression include: (i) that the expression intuitively characterizes structural and relational aspects of reality, (ii) that it is not specific to any domain, (iii) that it can be grasped in principle by any intelligent human subject, (iv) that it can be used unproblematically to communicate truths between intelligent human subjects, and (v) that sentences involving only these expressions have an objective truth-value.

Here, logical expressions such as 'and' seem to satisfy all of (i)–(v). Expressions for fundamentality and lawhood satisfy (i) and (ii) and at least arguably (iii)–(v). Indexical expressions satisfy (iii) and (iv) although not obviously the others. Spatiotemporal expressions satisfy (i), (iii), (iv), and a version of (v) (setting aside worries tied to nonclassical physics), although perhaps not (ii). Something similar applies to general phenomenal expressions of the sort invoked by phenomenal structuralism. Specific phenomenal expressions such as that of phenomenal redness arguably violate (i)–(iv). So overall, the purest forms of structuralism are arguably logical structuralism followed by fundamentality and nomic structuralism. Spatiotemporal and phenomenal structuralism are intermediate cases, while a version involving specific phenomenal concepts is a very weak case. The inclusion of indexicals arguably weakens structuralism a little, but not too much.

My own view is that no robust version of structuralism along these lines is correct, because of problems associated with consciousness. If a structural specification is something that Mary can grasp from inside her black-and-white room, as criterion (iii) above suggests, then it is likely that many phenomenal truths (for example, that what it is like to see roses is such-and-such) will be inscrutable from this specification. And if a specification cannot be grasped by Mary inside her black-and-white room (for example, because it uses the notion of phenomenal redness), then it will be structural in at best a highly attenuated sense.

Still, to say this much is compatible with holding with Carnap that structural expressions play a special role in science and in communication. One might hold that nonstructural concepts, such as that of phenomenal redness, pose special problems for science and communication, in that grasp of these expressions depends on one's prior history, and in that one cannot be certain that others are using their corresponding expressions to express the same concept. Nevertheless, it is plausible that science can say a good deal about phenomenal redness in structural terms, as when phenomenal colors are decomposed along three basic dimensions. There is a core part of the science of color experience that can be understood by Mary inside her black-and-white room, just as there is a rich science of nonhuman sensory modalities that can be understood by human scientists. This core part can be cast largely in terms of phenomenal structure. Grasp of specific phenomenal dimensions such as phenomenal redness certainly enriches our grasp of the science, but it is not obviously necessary in order for the science to proceed. For that purpose, structural notions are enough.

All this connects interestingly to the thesis of structural realism in the philosophy of science, which says roughly that scientific theories concern the structure of reality.[22] It is standard to distinguish ontological structural realism, according to which reality (as described by science) is wholly structural, from epistemological structural realism, according to which we can know (through science) only structural aspects of reality. As an epistemological thesis, structural scrutability is more akin to epistemological structural realism, but it is somewhat stronger. We might see structural scrutability as a form of *conceptual* structural realism, holding that the only true hypotheses that we can entertain about reality are structural (here I assume that a hypothesis can be entertained iff it can be expressed, and that any truth scrutable from a structural truth is itself a structural truth). Conceptual structural realism is intermediate in strength between the ontological and epistemological varieties. It is plausibly entailed by ontological structural realism but not vice versa: the two will come apart if there is a nonstructural character to reality that we cannot entertain hypotheses about. And it plausibly entails epistemological structural realism but not vice versa: the two will come apart if there are true nonstructural hypotheses that we can entertain without knowing them to be true.

A further complication is the issue of whether the notions of structure at play here and in the debate over structural realism coincide. This issue is complicated by the fact that so many notions of structure are at play on both sides. The strongest form of structural realism requires a characterization of reality using logical expressions alone, but this version leads directly to Newman's problem. I think it is reasonable for a structural realist to appeal to a broader notion of structure that allows nomic expressions and expressions for fundamentality to count as structural. If so, Newman's problem is avoided.

The consciousness-based objections to structural scrutability do not apply to all versions of structural realism. It is common to cast structural realism as a claim about the *non-observational* aspects of reality, staying neutral on whether the considerations that apply to scientific theories also apply to observation.

---

[22] Structural realism was introduced under that name by Grover Maxwell in 'Structural Realism and the Meaning of Theoretical Terms' (1970). For the distinction between epistemological and ontological structuralism, James Ladyman's 'What is Structural Realism?' (1998). For discussions of Newman's problem as a problem for structural realism, see Ainsworth 2009, Ketland 2004, and Melia and Saatsi 2006.

These views in effect allow that reality more broadly can be characterized in structural and observational terms, in effect allowing certain observational expressions in the base. On this reading, structural realism is somewhat weaker than structural scrutability, which does not make special allowance for observational expressions. Corresponding, even if phenomenal truths count against structural scrutability (as I have suggested), they need not count against structural realism so understood, as long as one counts phenomenal expressions as observational expressions. Something similar applies to secondary qualities: even if these pose an obstacle to structural scrutability, they do not pose an obstacle to this variety of structural realism.

The upshot is that at least some version of structural realism looks promising in light of the current discussion. If we allow structural truths to include nomic, fundamentality, and logical expressions, then the thesis that all truths are scrutable from structural truths and phenomenal truths is not implausible. This yields a version of conceptual (and therefore epistemological) structural realism about non-observational reality. If there are no ungraspable quiddities or other inexpressible nonstructural aspects of the world, then we can even make the step to ontological structural realism about non-observational reality. The obstacles posed by consciousness make the further step to ontological structural realism about all of reality more difficult, but one who adopts a deflationary and perhaps structuralist view of consciousness might make this step.

Perhaps the biggest remaining challenges for structural realism arise from quiddities and from spacetime. Ungraspable quiddities would undermine ontological structural realism (even about non-observational reality), while graspable quiddities would undermine both ontological and conceptual structural realism. These quiddities need not undermine epistemological structural realism, however, as long as the distribution of the quiddities is not knowable. Spatiotemporal primitivism would tend to undermine all three forms of structural realism, unless we broaden the concept of structure to include primitive spatiotemporal structure. Still, it is not biting a large bullet for the structural realist to reject quiddities and to reject spatiotemporal primitivism, instead understanding the spatiotemporal domain in structural terms as I have suggested.

Even if one accepts nonstructural aspects of reality such as consciousness, quiddities, and primitive spacetime, it is plausible that there will at least be a structural core to our scientific theories. As in the case of the science of consciousness above, this structural core will capture the structural aspects of these phenomena and abstract away from nonstructural aspects. Such a theory will not be a complete theory of reality, but it will do much of the work that a complete theory can do. Speaking for myself: as long as the structural realist accepts a conception of structure that includes nomic and fundamentality structure, I think it is quite possible that some version of structural realism is true.

8 Generalized Scrutability (and Fregean content)

What about Generalized Scrutability: roughly, the thesis that there is a compact class of base sentences such that it is a priori that all truths are scrutable from sentences in that class, or the thesis that scrutability holds across all epistemically possible scenarios? For any ordinary scrutability thesis, there is a generalized counterpart. So one can ask about Generalized A Priori Scrutability, Generalized Definitional Scrutability, Generalized Analytic Scrutability, as well as generalized versions of Primitive Scrutability, Narrow Scrutability, Acquaintance Scrutability, Fundamental Scrutability, and Structural Scrutability.

Focusing mainly on Generalized A Priori Scrutability: what needs to be in a generalized scrutability base? Some expansion of an ordinary a priori scrutability base is plausibly required. If one holds (as I do) that there are primitive color concepts and primitive spatiotemporal concepts that pick out properties that are not instantiated in our world, but that are instantiated in other worlds (e.g., an Edenic world) and whose instantiation we cannot rule out a priori, then these primitive concepts will need to be included in a generalized scrutability base. Likewise, one might hold that even if there are no quiddities in the actual world, there are quiddistic concepts, and one cannot rule out a priori that the corresponding quiddities are instantiated. Similarly, some Humeans about nomic concepts and some deflationists about phenomenal concepts may allow that we also have non-Humean and inflationary concepts in the vicinity, which may pick out nothing in the actual world, but which may pick out something in some epistemically possible scenarios. Given these views, relevant quiddistic, nomic, and phenomenal concepts may need to be added to yield a generalized scrutability base.

On my own view, it is likely that a generalized scrutability base will include nomic concepts, primitive spatiotemporal and secondary-quality concepts, and phenomenal concepts. Where phenomenal concepts are concerned, one may need only the relation of phenomenal awareness, which might then combine with the other primitive concepts to yield phenomenal properties. There may or may not be quiddistic concepts beyond these. One interesting possibility is that all quiddistic concepts pick out properties that can be objects of phenomenal awareness, and so are analogous to the primitive concepts above. But perhaps there can be quiddistic properties that we can grasp only in thought, in which case further concepts are needed.

There may well also be alien concepts that we have not yet dreamed of. I cannot rule out that there are an enormous infinity of primitive alien concepts, picking out properties, relations, and other entities that we cannot even conceive. I am inclined to suspect, though, that there will be some order in this space, and that even alien concepts might be regimented into some limited number of types. It is hard to assess this claim, though.

We should also consider ordinary expressions such as 'water'. 'Water'-truths are scrutable from more basic truths in the actual world, but are there scenarios in which they are not so scrutable? Is it a priori that they are so scrutable? Can we rule out the epistemic possibility that there is water but that there is nothing more basic from which it is scrutable? I cannot really make sense of the hypothesis that water does not appear in any way, does not behave in any way, does not affect us in any way, and so on. So it seems to me that in any epistemically possible scenario in which there is water, there would be truths about the corresponding appearance, behavior, and so on, from which the claim that there is water is scrutable. Something similar goes for 'Gödel', 'philosopher', and other terms. So I am inclined to think that in any scenario, truths involving these nonprimitive terms are scrutable from more basic sentences.

I suspect that the most fundamental scrutability theses hold a priori. The most fundamental scrutability thesis may well be some variety of Acquaintance Scrutability, whose apriority yields the thesis of Generalized Acquaintance Scrutability. If this thesis holds, it would explain the truth in our world of Generalized Narrow Scrutability (given the thesis that every acquaintance concept in our world is a narrow concept). If we assume that there are some primitive acquaintance concepts (perhaps strong acquaintance concepts?) from which all acquaintance concepts are scrutable, then Generalized Acquaintance Scrutability can also help explain the truth of Generalized Primitive Scrutablity. I do not have a knockdown argument for Generalized Acquaintance Scrutability at this point, however.

As for Generalized Fundamental Scrutability: my view is that there is an a priori connection between epistemic and metaphysical possibility. In particular I think that the Apriority/Necessity Thesis, holding that any sentence composed of super-rigid expressions is a priori iff it is necessary, is itself a priori. If this is right, then it is a priori that any minimal super-rigid necessitation base is also a minimal super-rigid scrutability base. Given that it is a priori that the class of fundamental truths forms a minimal super-rigid necessitation base, it is then also a priori that they form a super-rigid scrutability base. If we combine this with the Generalized Acquaintance Scrutability thesis, holding that it is a priori that there is a scrutability base consisting of super-rigid expressions and indexicals, it follows that it is a priori that fundamental truths and indexicals form a scrutability base. So Generalized Fundamental Scrutability follows from Generalized Acquaintance Scrutability and the apriority of the Apriority/Necessity thesis.

As we saw in the tenth and eleventh excursuses, Generalized Scrutability theses allow us to define the space of epistemically possible scenarios and to define intensions over these scenarios for sentences and thoughts. As seen there, these intensions serve as a sort of Fregean or cognitive content. Different theses entail that the intensions have different features. We have already seen that Generalized Narrow Scrutability yields a sort of narrow intension. Generalized Acquaintance Scrutability yields a sort of Russellian intension, grounded in items with which we are acquainted. Generalized Super-Rigid Scrutability allows us to construct these scenarios from worldly entities such as properties. Generalized Fundamental Scrutability allows us to treat these scenarios as metaphysically possible worlds, so that intensions over centered worlds can serve as Fregean contents. Generalized Structural Scrutability would suggest that these intensions can all be seen as structural contents. As with their non-generalized counterparts, I am inclined to think that all of these theses except the last are true.

Summation: Whither the *Aufbau*?

What, then, of the *Aufbau*? Given where we have come, is Carnap vindicated? Even if the actual *Aufbau* was a failure, is there a nearby possible *Aufbau* that succeeds?

It is clear that there are many possible *Aufbau*s. They vary with their basic class of expressions, and their mode of construction. Some are closer to Carnap than others. Some are more successful than others. In what follows I will outline two. The first is one that stays close to the spirit of Carnap. The second is one that fits my own philosophical beliefs.

The first *Aufbau* starts with just logical and mathematical expressions, the indexicals 'I' and 'now', and an expression for fundamentality. Its base truths mainly purport to limn the structure of physics. The rest of the world is built up from there, through analytic definitions.

Assuming classical physics, the base truths might say: there are some fundamental properties (perhaps mass and charge, though not specified as such) and some fundamental relations (spatial and temporal relations, though not specified as such), and some objects over which these properties and relations are distributed in such-and-such way.[1] Those are all the fundamental truths. I now have such-and-such among these properties.

Assuming nonclassical physics, the base truths might say: the world has such-and-such mathematical structure, perhaps involving a function from such-and-such mathematical space into such-and-such space, with such-and-such course of values. Such-and-such dimensions of this space are fundamental. These are all the fundamental truths. I am now located at such-and-such point in this space.

From there, a spatial relation (on the classical model) might be defined as a relation whose distribution (with respect to the other properties and relations)

---

[1] The first *Aufbau* is grounded in the fundamentality structuralism of section 8.7, where this picture is laid out in somewhat more detail.

has such-and-such structural properties. A temporal relation might be defined in the same sort of way. Likewise, spatial and temporal dimensions on the second model might be defined as dimensions with such-and-such mathematical properties with respect to other dimensions and the function.

From there, laws of nature might be defined in terms of certain sorts of regularities among objects, properties, relations, or values in these spaces, perhaps analyzed via a best system principle. Causal, dispositional, and counterfactual expressions might be defined in terms of laws of nature. Macroscopic objects might be introduced as sums of the entities specified in the original space, or as certain abstractions from the function. Spatial and temporal predicates of macroscopic objects might be defined in terms of corresponding predicates of the basic entities. Crude behavioral predicates might be defined in spatiotemporal terms. Mental predicates might be defined functionally, in terms of their causal relations to behavior and to each other. Secondary qualities might be defined in terms of their causal relations to certain mental states. Social and linguistic expressions might be defined in terms of mental and behavioral properties, along with primary and secondary quality properties. Normative expressions might be defined in terms of mental states. Natural kind terms might be defined in terms of spatiotemporal properties, secondary qualities, causal relations to mental and linguistic properties, and fundamentality. Names might be defined similarly, with a special emphasis on causal relations to linguistic items. Cultural notions might be defined in terms of everything that came before.

Carnap could have written a version of this *Aufbau*. He says many times that he could have chosen a physical rather than a phenomenal basis. Presumably his final base expressions would have involved logic and 'foundedness', just as in the real *Aufbau*, perhaps along with mathematical expressions. He had some but not all of the other materials. There is no analysis of nomic or dispositional notions in the *Aufbau*, for example. His behavioral analysis of mental expressions was crude, and he had nothing to say about a number of the topics above. But the basic shape of the package seems available to him.

The shape of this package is familiar. It is closely akin to a package of views presented in the work of David Lewis. There are some differences: Lewis usually took spatiotemporal notions as basic, rather than attempting to analyze them in terms of structure and fundamentality; and the package above omits Lewis' distinctive metaphysics of modality and of mathematics. Still, Lewis's life's work can be seen as an attempt to construct the world, and to carry out Carnap's project where Carnap failed. Viewed through this lens, Lewis came remarkably close to succeeding.

This Carnap/Lewis *Aufbau* would avoid many criticisms of the original *Aufbau*. There would be no analog of Goodman's or Quine's problems. As in the original *Aufbau*, Newman's problem would be avoided by the appeal to fundamentality, and this *Aufbau* might eschew the unnecessary claim that fundamentality is a logical notion. Criticisms tied to definitions and the analytic/synthetic distinction would still arise, but it is not clear how deep these criticisms go.

For my part, I think that while the Carnap/Lewis *Aufbau* draws a beautiful picture of the world, it is not a correct picture of the world. The two largest reasons are that no structuralist account can adequately account for phenomenal truths and that no Humean account can adequately account for nomic truths. I also have doubts about the appeal to definitions, at least if these are supposed to be finite and precise. And questions can be raised about various steps along the way. Still, these are largely matters of substantive philosophy over which serious contemporary philosophers disagree. They are not clear internal fatal flaws of the sort often ascribed to the *Aufbau*.

The second *Aufbau* starts with logical and mathematical expressions, indexical expressions 'I', 'now', and 'this', an expression for fundamentality, an expression for lawhood, and phenomenal expressions, where the latter are characterized in terms of phenomenal awareness and expressions for primitive primary and secondary qualities. Its base truths purport mainly to characterize physical and psychophysical laws, along with physical boundary conditions. The rest of the world is built up from there, through a priori scrutability, and perhaps through approximate a priori definitions.

The base truths will say: the (physical) world has such-and-such mathematical structure, perhaps involving a function from such-and-such mathematical space into such-and-such mathematical space. This function is governed by such-and-such laws, and it has such-and-such boundary conditions. Such-and-such dimensions are fundamental. There are such-and-such laws connecting this space to entities that are phenomenally aware of such-and-such qualities distributed by such-and-such function over such-and-such space. These are all the fundamental truths. I am now phenomenally aware of such-and-such.

There are variations on this project. Instead of specifying that certain (physical) dimensions are fundamental, we could specify that they are certain quidditistic or phenomenal dimensions. We could represent phenomenal structure in various different ways, and on some versions we might have laws connecting a physical space to a protophenomenal rather than a phenomenal space.

From here, causal, counterfactual, and dispositional truths are scrutable from truths about laws and non-nomic truths. The spatiality and temporality of certain dimensions is scrutable from their causal and counterfactual relations to certain sorts of spatiotemporal phenomenal properties. Microphysical and then macrophysical spatiotemporal properties are scrutable from there. The existence and spatiotemporal properties of microscopic objects are scrutable from the fundamental physical truths, and the existence and spatiotemporal properties of macroscopic objects are scrutable from those of microscopic objects. Truths about secondary qualities are scrutable from causal and counterfactual connections to certain phenomenal states. Truths about intentional and other mental states are scrutable from phenomenal and causal truths. Truths about behavior are scrutable from truths about mental states and spatiotemporal truths. Linguistic and social truths are scrutable from mental, behavioral, and spatiotemporal truths. Normative truths are scrutable from mental truths, behavioral truths, and other truths. And so on.

Carnap could in principle have written this version of the *Aufbau*, but he would have been unlikely to. The unreduced appeal to specific phenomenal qualities does not fit the structuralist program of the *Aufbau*. The unreduced appeal to lawhood does not fit the generally reductionist spirit of the *Aufbau*. Still, in certain respects, this version can be seen as an extension of the phenomenological program in the *Aufbau*, starting from a much richer characterization of phenomenal states, and building in explicitly nomic connections to other aspects of the world.

The shape of this package is at least somewhat familiar. It has something in common with the constructive projects of Bertrand Russell, especially in the periods when he leaned more heavily on acquaintance and less heavily on structure. There are a number of differences: awareness of (represented) qualities stands in for Russell's awareness of sense-data, and where Russell gives a basic role to spatiotemporal relations, this project gives a basic role to nomic relations. It is less phenomenalist in character than many of Russell's constructions, building in a key role for the structure of physics from the start. All the same, both are ways of building up the world's structure from acquaintables, and especially from features of experience, the self, and certain key universals.

This quasi-Russellian project avoids Goodman's and Quine's objections to the *Aufbau*. It also avoids Newman's objections to Russell's structuralism, and the many objections associated with his phenomenalism. The view can be subjected to objections of its own, especially from philosophers with different substantive views. But again, this is largely a matter of substantive philosophy.

We might call the first *Aufbau* here a structuralist *Aufbau*, in the spirit of Carnap, and the second *Aufbau* an acquaintance *Aufbau*, in the spirit of Russell. But I prefer to think of the second *Aufbau* as a structural/acquaintance *Aufbau*, with both structural elements (logic, mathematics, law, fundamentality) and acquaintance-based elements (phenomenal and perhaps perceptual qualities) in the base.

I have not written either of these *Aufbau*s here. That is, I have not tried to carefully and explicitly lay out the basic vocabulary and the form of the basic truths, and I have not tried to construct other truths from these step by step. But I have argued that such an *Aufbau* is possible. Many of the elements of the first *Aufbau* are already present in the work of Carnap and Lewis. Some elements of the second *Aufbau* are sketched at various places in this book.

As long as the A Priori Scrutability thesis is true, some *Aufbau* like these will be possible. There will be a limited basic vocabulary in which base truths can be stated. Other truths will be derivable from these, either by a priori entailment, or through approximate definition. The overall structure will depend on one's philosophical views about phenomenology, spacetime, laws of nature, quiddities, normativity, intentionality, ontology, and so on. The details will depend on empirical matters about physics, phenomenology, and other domains. But we have reason to believe that a successful *Aufbau* exists, somewhere in philosophical space.

A project of this sort has many uses. Semantically: it can be used to construct Fregean semantic values and notions of mental content, and a reconstrued project of conceptual analysis. Epistemologically: it can vindicate an attenuated knowability thesis and help in responding to the skeptic. Metaphysically: the bases in the projects above can be construed as metaphysical bases, and if we accept a fundamental scrutability thesis, many metaphysical conclusions will follow. Scientifically: these *Aufbaus* might help us to discern the unity within science, and elements of them might be used to vindicate Carnap's structuralist approach to science. Metaphilosophically: an *Aufbau* project might help us to dissolve many questions and clarify many others.

I conclude that constructing the world is possible, and that it has philosophical value.

The Structuralist Response to Skepticism

One aim of the logical empiricists was to defeat epistemological skepticism. Traditional skepticism holds that we cannot know that external-world truths ('I have hands', 'That is a table', 'We live on a planet') are true, because we cannot exclude certain skeptical scenarios: scenarios in which we are having the same experiences that we are currently having, but in which these hypotheses do not obtain. One skeptical scenario is Descartes' evil genius scenario, in which we are entirely disembodied and in which our experiences are produced by an evil genius. Another is the Matrix scenario, in which we are brains in vats and our experiences are produced by a computer simulation to which our brains are hooked up.

Carnap does not discuss skepticism at length in the *Aufbau*, but in its later sections (part E, especially section 180), he argues for an anti-skeptical conclusion: that there is no question whose answer is in principle unattainable by science.[1] (The 'in principle' sets aside practical obstacles due to separation in space and time.) He reaches this conclusion by arguing that any question can be reformulated in terms of the primitive elements of elements, so that it comes down to a question about the distribution of basic relations among experiences. And he argues that all questions about the distribution of basic relations can be settled. If so, all questions can be settled.

This can be seen as an attempt to defeat skepticism through structuralism. Carnap held that all our hypotheses about the external world are in effect structural hypotheses, concerning the existence of objects satisfying a certain structure. And he held that we can know in principle whether any structural hypothesis obtains. If so, then we can know that the external-world truths obtain. Even if we are in the evil-genius scenario, or the Matrix scenario, the relevant structure among our experiences obtains. So even if we inhabit these scenarios, we should allow that we have hands, that there are tables, and that we live on a planet.

One way of putting a structuralist response to skepticism along these lines is as follows:

[1] See Friedman 1992 for discussion of other epistemological issues in the *Aufbau*.

(1) Ordinary beliefs have (only) structural contents.

(2) The structural contents of most ordinary beliefs are justified.

(3) Most of our ordinary beliefs are justified.

An anti-skeptical argument of this sort can be made whether we construct the world from structure through definitions or through scrutability. For example, if all truths were scrutable from truths about phenomenal structure, and if we could know all relevant truths about phenomenal structure, then we would be in a position to know all truths.

Importantly, the anti-skeptical force of structuralism does not require Carnap's austere logical or phenomenal structuralism. In particular, I think key elements of the anti-skeptical force apply to nomic structuralism, as well as to fundamentality or grounding structuralism, and to combined views. In fact, one can gain anti-skeptical purchase even if one gives a role to some nonstructural elements such as phenomenal and indexical truths.[2] In effect, a structural scrutability base or a limited extension thereof gives us the materials to make large inroads against the external-world skeptic, although perhaps not enough to defeat skepticism entirely.

The argument here is a version of an anti-skeptical argument I have made elsewhere, in 'The Matrix as Metaphysics'. That argument did not appeal explicitly to structuralism as a premise, but instead made arguments that in effect supported a sort of structuralism along the way, and used it to argue against skepticism. Because of this, I think the Matrix argument is somewhat stronger dialectically than the present argument. Nevertheless, the argument from structuralism helps to bring out some of the underlying issues that are at play in the original Matrix argument, so I will here try to develop the argument from structuralism explicitly.

We can start with nomic structuralism. The central thought here is that our conception of the external world is grounded in a conception of a network of entities and properties connected by relations of causation and laws. To put things simply, we conceive of entities and properties in terms of the nomic or causal roles that they play. Electrons are what play the electron role. Mass is what plays the mass role. Space is what plays the space role. Consciousness is what plays the consciousness role. And so on. All this yields a giant network of entities characterized ultimately in terms of their nomic and causal relations to each other.

---

[2] In part for this reason, the scrutability version of the response does not require a premise as strong as premise (1) above. Another reason is that what matters for the purposes of this response is that primary intensions are (largely) structural. One can allow that beliefs have other sorts of content (such as secondary intensions and Russellian content) that are nonstructural. But the initial form captures something of the spirit of the response, at least.

On this view, a complete specification of the universe will say that there exist certain properties that stand in certain nomic relations to each other, and that there exists a network of entities that instantiate these properties and that thereby stand in certain causal and nomic relations. The properties in question will correspond to mass, charge, spatiotemporal properties, or whatever are the fundamental properties in physics, while the entities will correspond to fundamental particles or fields, or whatever are the fundamental entities in physics. These labels—mass, charge, quarks—will not enter the fundamental description. The base truths just say that there are properties and entities satisfying a certain nomic structure. From a description of the world in these nomic terms, all ordinary truths about the world are scrutable.

The central thought behind the structuralist response to skepticism is that even if the allegedly skeptical scenarios obtain, much or all of the relevant nomic structure still obtains. In the Matrix scenario, for example, there is a computer running a complete simulation of the physical universe. This computer will have a causal complexity of the same order as the universe that it simulates, with concretely implemented data structures for each fundamental particle, and computational properties of these structures for each fundamental property. When we take it that one particle affects another in our world, the data structure corresponding to the first particle really does affect the data structure corresponding to the second. A macroscopic object in our world, such as a table, corresponds to a complex of data structures, or perhaps to a macroscopic data structure or an entity supervening on data structures (just as one might say a table is related to particles on a more standard metaphysics). When we take it that we see a table, this computational entity really is affecting our experience, just as a table does on a more common picture. Likewise, causal connections among planets or billiard balls will be reflected in causal connections among data structures in the computer. All in all: the computer instantiates all of the nomic and causal structure of the world that it is simulating.

We can put the basic structure of the structuralist response here as follows. We are presented with a putatively skeptical scenario, such as a Matrix scenario. A standard skeptical argument says something along the following lines:

(1) Most of my ordinary beliefs are false if this scenario is actual.
(2) I do not know that this scenario is not actual.

———————————————————————

(3) Most of my ordinary beliefs do not constitute knowledge.

For example, one familiar version of this argument says:

(1) If I am in a Matrix, then I do not have hands.
(2) I do not know that I am not in a Matrix.

———————————————————————

(3) I do not know that I have hands.

The most common responses to skepticism attempt to reject the second premises of these arguments. A structuralist response in the spirit of Carnap rejects the first premises, as follows.

(1) The content of ordinary beliefs is structural.
(2) The structural content of most ordinary beliefs is true if this scenario is actual.

(3) Most of my ordinary beliefs are true if this scenario is actual.

In this anti-skeptical argument, premise (1) is grounded in structuralist theses such as structural scrutability, while premise (2) is grounded by reasoning about the structure of putative skeptical scenario. If this argument is sound, then the belief that I have hands will have structural content (by (1)) that is true with respect to the Matrix scenario (by (2)). If this is right, then even if I am in a Matrix, I still have hands. So skeptical arguments like those above will fail.

Focusing on the special case of nomic structuralism and Matrix scenarios, we can flesh out the argument more explicitly. Let us say that a Matrix scenario and a non-Matrix scenario *correspond* when the former involves a perfect computational simulation of the latter, bringing about a stream of experiences in the core subject that duplicate those of the core subject in the latter.[3] And let us say that a skeptical scenario is a scenario in which most of our ordinary beliefs are false (or perhaps: sufficiently many are false, for some relevant threshold). Then given the reasoning above, and given pure nomic structuralism, it follows that if I am in a Matrix scenario (as the subject with the experiences in question), my ordinary beliefs are just as true as they would be if I was in the corresponding non-Matrix scenario. After all, the truth of these beliefs can be determined from nomic structure alone, and the Matrix scenario instantiates the nomic structure of the non-Matrix scenario. So if the non-Matrix scenario is not a skeptical scenario, neither is the corresponding Matrix scenario.

We may put this in the form of an argument.

(1) All ordinary truths are scrutable from truths about nomic structure.
(2) All truths about nomic structure in a non-Matrix scenario are also truths in a corresponding Matrix scenario.

(3) All ordinary truths in a non-Matrix scenario are also truths in a corresponding Matrix scenario.

---

[3] Here, scenarios should be understood as epistemically possible scenarios (not as metaphysically possible worlds), along the lines discussed in the tenth excursus. A scenario corresponds to an extremely detailed hypothesis about how the world might turn out to be, for all we know a priori. The core subject is the referent of 'I' in a scenario. A sentence is true in a scenario when it is scrutable from a canonical specification of the scenario. Truth at a scenario differs from truth at a

Corollary: If a non-Matrix scenario is not a skeptical scenario, neither is a corresponding Matrix scenario.

If this is right, the Matrix scenario has no special force to support skepticism. If we start from a non-Matrix scenario that is much as we take our ordinary world to be, our ordinary beliefs and sentences will be mostly true in that scenario. If we now consider a Matrix scenario in which that world is simulated, it follows from the above that our ordinary beliefs and sentences will be true in the Matrix scenario too.

Premise (1) is a statement of nomic structuralism. One could try to deny (2), perhaps holding that the structure in the computer is not real nomic structure (because it was programmed?), or perhaps holding that the computer has some extra nomic structure (in its implementing machinery?), undermining the parity between the two. But even if (2) is false for this sort of reason, a nearby argument will go through. After all, it could turn out that our world is a physical and spatial non-Matrix world whose nomic structure is 'programmed' by and at the mercy of a creator, and it could turn out that it has additional nomic structure beyond the sort of structure we think it has. If these non-Matrix scenarios turned out to be actual, most ordinary beliefs would not be undermined. At most, we would undermine a few theoretical beliefs, such as 'The laws of physics are not programmed' or 'Microphysical laws are the fundamental laws'. It follows that most ordinary truths in an ordinary non-Matrix scenario will also be true in the 'programmed' non-Matrix scenario. This programmed scenario will share its nomic structure with a Matrix scenario corresponding to the original scenario, so truths in the former will also be true in the latter. So most truths in the original scenario will be true in the Matrix scenario, and the Matrix scenario will not be a skeptical scenario.

One can resist by denying (1) and denying nomic structuralism. My view is that nomic structuralism is false. A complete specification of reality requires more than nomic truths: it requires indexical truths, that's-all truths, phenomenal truths, and maybe even quiddistic truths. Nevertheless, the structuralist response to skepticism is robust enough that these additions do not undermine it.

For a start, the addition of indexical truths to the scrutability base will not change much here. When skeptical scenarios are set up, they are set up so that crucial indexical truths such as 'I am having such-and-such experiences' are true in the relevant non-Matrix and Matrix scenarios alike.

world, which requires necessitation by a canonical specification of that world. I do not say that all ordinary truths would be true in a Matrix world: that would depend on the claim that all truths are necessitated by nomic truths, which is a quite different claim.

The addition of a that's-all truth, and of fundamentality truths in general, is a small complication. It is arguable that the Matrix and non-Matrix scenarios differ in matters of fundamentality: the Matrix scenario may have a further layer of more fundamental truths realizing the computation, and perhaps truths about the world outside the computation. Still, this matter can be handled straightforwardly by introducing an extended non-Matrix scenario, as above, that mirrors these features of the Matrix scenario. The extended scenario will have a more fundamental layer underlying truths that were fundamental in the original non-Matrix scenario, and will extend much further than the original scenario. Despite these changes, most of our ordinary beliefs will be true in this non-Matrix scenario. Furthermore, the nomic and fundamentality truths that hold in this scenario will also hold in the Matrix scenario. So if all truths are scrutable from nomic and fundamentality truths, our ordinary beliefs will also be true in the Matrix scenario.

What about the addition of phenomenal truths to the base? One might object that there is no guarantee that these will be reproduced in a Matrix. A modified version of the argument will still go through, however. Corresponding Matrix and non-Matrix scenarios are already stipulated to share first-person phenomenal truths (truths such as 'I am having such-and-such experiences'), and these are the most crucial phenomenal truths required for the scrutability of ordinary truths. As for phenomenal truths about others, one might modify the notion of correspondence to build these in too: corresponding scenarios must have corresponding phenomenal truths. The skeptic might then reply by noting that the conclusion (3) that results from this modification is more limited than before. For example, there may be Matrix scenarios in which others lack experiences: these will correspond not to ordinary non-Matrix scenarios, but to non-Matrix scenarios in which other people lack experiences. And these latter non-Matrix scenarios are indeed skeptical scenarios, at least with regard to beliefs about other minds. But even so, one can note that at best this scenario gives rise to skepticism about other minds (and to phenomena deriving from other minds), and not about the external world in general.

What if the scrutability base includes quiddities: the intrinsic properties that serve as the basis for all this nomic structure? Of course quiddities are not at all in the spirit of structuralism. But adding them to the base does not undermine the argument. Even if there are quiddistic truths, knowledge of these is inessential to knowledge of ordinary truths such as 'I have hands' or 'That is a table'. Likewise, quiddistic truths are inessential to the scrutability of ordinary truths. There will be multiple scenarios in which the same nomic and phenomenal structure is associated with a different distribution of quiddities, but these ordinary truths will have the same truth-value in all of them. At most, what will vary is the truth-value of theoretical claims, such as 'Quiddities have such-and-such protophenomenal nature'.[4]

The best way to resist the argument is to focus on the spatiotemporal, arguing that spatiotemporal truths are not scrutable from the scrutability bases above. If this is right, then a Matrix scenario will not preserve the spatiotemporal structure of a corresponding non-Matrix scenario, and many ordinary truths in the latter may be false in the former. On the current framework, the natural way to do this is to endorse spatiotemporal primitivism, on which we have a primitive grip on certain spatiotemporal properties and/or relations, and our fundamental conception of the world requires that a certain spatiotemporal structure involving these properties and relations obtains.

Still, I argued in chapter 7 that spatiotemporal primitivism is false: ordinary spatiotemporal truths do not involve primitive spatiotemporal concepts. Instead, I think that ordinary spatiotemporal notions function to pick out whatever properties and relations play a certain role within physics and with respect to our spatiotemporal experience. One way to bring this out is to note that physicists seriously entertain the hypothesis that fundamental physics may be computational and that spatiotemporal notions may play no role at the fundamental level. It is implausible that these physicists are entertaining a skeptical hypothesis on which ordinary spatiotemporal claims (that a certain person is over six feet tall, for example) are false. It is also implausible that given the truth of such a hypothesis, there are spatiotemporal constraints on how the computational structure must be realized in order to avoid a skeptical scenario. This is prima facie evidence that if we have the right nomic/computational structure, we have sufficient structure for the scrutability of ordinary truths, even without further primitive spatiotemporal constraints.

What goes for the Matrix also goes for other skeptical scenarios. If the evil genius simulates every particle in the universe, she is in effect acting as a Matrix, and the same analysis applies to her. If I am dreaming and simulating the whole universe, then my unconscious mind is acting as a Matrix, and the same applies to it.

What about versions of all these hypotheses on which the simulator simulates only some local part of the universe or only the macroscopic level? The point still

---

[4] It should be noted that the Matrix hypothesis can itself be regarded as a hypothesis about quiddities. Russell and others observe that science does not reveal the intrinsic properties that underlie microphysical structure. If the Matrix hypothesis is right, these intrinsic properties are themselves computational properties, deriving from a computational system in the 'next universe up'. Viewed though this lens, the Matrix hypothesis changes from being an illustration of Descartes to an illustration of Kant: it is not a skeptical hypothesis but rather a hypothesis about the unobservable noumenal properties of reality. In the movie, taking the red pill allows us to outsmart Kant: we can look at the computer and thereby see the 'things in themselves' for the first time. Of course Kant will then outsmart us in turn: even underlying this next level of reality, there may be quiddities that we cannot observe.

applies: these scenarios will have the same nomic structure as a nonsimulated world in which only the local part of our world exists, or only the macroscopic level is as it seems and in which physics is different or nonexistent. In these non-simulated scenarios, we would certainly have false beliefs about the far away and about the very small. Many of our ordinary beliefs would be correct, however, so these are not fully skeptical scenarios. The same goes for the simulated scenarios. Likewise, a scenario in which we have recently entered a Matrix will produce false beliefs about the present, but will still allow many true beliefs about the past, so this is not a fully skeptical scenario.

To get a fully skeptical scenario, one may need to move to one on which experiences are produced at random, and by huge coincidence produce the regular stream of experiences that I am having now. This scenario cannot be excluded with certainty, but (unlike the Matrix scenario) it is reasonable to hold that it is extremely unlikely.

The anti-skeptical conclusion is limited. Many local skeptical scenarios cannot be excluded. For this reason, any individual belief about the external world can still be cast into doubt. For example, beliefs about the present and the recent past can be cast into doubt by a recent Matrix scenario, while beliefs about the distant past can be cast into doubt by a local Matrix scenario. Beliefs about other minds and about the future can certainly be cast into doubt. But at least it is hard to cast all our external-world beliefs, or even all our positive external-world beliefs, into doubt all at once via a single global skeptical scenario. On the current picture, it is reasonable to assign an extremely low probability to such a global skeptical scenario.

The picture that results here is in some respects reminiscent of Hilary Putnam's externalist response to skepticism in *Reason, Truth, and History*. On the current picture, it is natural to hold as Putnam does that many concepts deployed by a brain in a vat refer to entities in its environment (the entities that play the relevant nomic roles): computational structures if in a Matrix scenario, structures within the evil genius if in Descartes' scenario. But it is important to note that my argument has not assumed anything about externalism or about the causal theory of reference. This is a good thing, as it is far from clear that these premises alone warrant the anti-skeptical conclusion. For example, no one thinks that a mere causal connection between word and object suffices for reference; many further constraints are required. And it is entirely unclear whether the relevant entities in a vat-brain's environment satisfy the further constraints. So one cannot argue straightforwardly from a causal theory of reference to the anti-skeptical conclusion.

Instead, my structuralist response to skepticism has proceeded from independently motivated structuralist premises. By contrast with generic externalist premises, these premises make a direct case that the relevant entities in the environment satisfy the relevant constraints. So these premises more strongly support the anti-skeptical conclusion.

I have laid out a simple version of the structuralist response here, but my view of matters is a little more complicated. As I suggested in chapter 7, I think that we have primitive representation of space and time as well as of secondary qualities such as color. At some level, perception and belief represent our world as an Edenic world, with primitive colors distributed over objects in primitive space, passing through primitive time. If we are in a Matrix, then these Edenic contents are certainly false. In effect, the Matrix serves as a sort of fall from Eden. Does this mean that the Matrix is a skeptical scenario after all?

Even in the ordinary world revealed by science, however, there has been a fall from Eden. Since Galileo, science has suggested ours is not a world with Edenic colors. Since Einstein, science has suggested that ours in not a world with Edenic space. I argued in chapter 7 that even if physics is mathematically Newtonian, it is not at all clear that it involves primitive space. And in the complex physics of quantum mechanics and string theory, there is even less reason to think that there is primitive space in our world. So while it is true that our perception and belief has nonstructural content that is false in a Matrix scenario, this content is equally false in the world revealed by modern science.

One could take the view that modern science has revealed us to be living in a skeptical scenario in which there are not colored objects laid out in space and time. I think it is much better to hold that even after Galileo, ordinary claims such as 'The apple is red' are true. The apple is not Edenically red, but it is structurally red: that is, it has the property that plays the structural role associated with redness in causing experiences and the like. Likewise, ordinary claims such as 'The apple is round' are true. The apple is not Edenically round, but it is structurally round: that is, it has the property that plays the structural role associated with roundness, in causing experiences and the like.[5] Our ordinary terms such as 'red' and 'round' are best taken to pick out the structural properties, not the Edenic properties.

The Matrix scenario is on a par with the post-fall scenarios here. If we are in a Matrix, apples are not Edenically red and round, but they are nevertheless structurally red and round. If claims such as 'The apple is red' and 'The apple is round' are true in a post-fall non-Matrix scenario, they are also true in a Matrix scenario. So there is not a distinctive skeptical problem raised by the Matrix scenario.

The upshot here is to concede a little to the skeptic: the Edenic contents of our beliefs are unjustified, and indeed they are probably false. Nevertheless, we retain a significant bulwark against the skeptic: the structural content of our beliefs is justified and is probably true.[6] We can put this by saying that while our model of

---

[5] For more on the Edenic picture, see 'Perception and the Fall from Eden'.

[6] Even in a recent Matrix, a local Matrix, and other skeptical scenarios, it is arguable that the structural content of our beliefs is largely true. On these hypotheses, most of the causal structure that we attribute to the world is present. It is just divided into components, so that the structure

the world is not perfectly veridical, it is at least imperfectly veridical, both in a post-fall world and in a Matrix world. Given that our most important beliefs and utterances are true in a post-fall world, the most important content of beliefs and utterances is their structural content rather than their Edenic content.

More speculatively, one might also use the structuralist framework to analyze the justification of perceptual beliefs. Where the contents of perception are concerned, structural contents are in effect response-dependent contents. To a first approximation, experiences as of red pick out whatever normally causes experiences as of red, experiences as of a location pick out whatever normally causes experiences as of that location, and so on. Assuming such experiences have causes in normal circumstances, these contents will be true in normal circumstances. One might speculate that we have a weak default justification to believe that we are in normal circumstances (roughly, circumstances normal within our not-too-distant past), at least in the absence of reasons to believe otherwise. Given this much, and given that one is justified in believing that experiences have these contents and that experiences normally have causes, it will be possible to have justified perceptual beliefs about the external world.

Now, most of our ordinary perceptual beliefs are not formed by a complex process of inference along the lines above, but simply by taking a perceptual experience at face value. What can we say about their justification? The inferential justification will yield at least a propositional justification for these beliefs. It is perhaps arguable that taking a structural content at face value will yield doxastic justification in virtue of encapsulating the result of the inference, even for a subject who does not go through the inference. If so, then ordinary perceptual beliefs will be justified in virtue of their structural content.[7]

---

is realized one way in the distant past and another way in the present, for example. This still leads to significant falsity in our beliefs, due to the structural fact that the realizers are different in both cases, but it enables us to see how a core of these beliefs—both about the present and about the past—remains true.

[7] How does this response to skepticism relate to the dogmatist view of perception discussed in chapter 3, according to which experiences as of p directly justify beliefs that p? We might approach things by saying that an experience is *proto-justified* when any belief that results from taking that experience at face value is prima facie justified. I suggested earlier (chapter 3, section 8) that some noncore experiences may be proto-justified in virtue of being grounded in prior evidence. Dogmatism holds that all experiences (or perhaps all core experiences) are proto-justified. While dogmatism captures some intuitions in 'folk epistemology'—our natural judgments about justification, at least when in a nonskeptical mode—it is far from obvious that these intuitions are correct. Certainly, any special justificatory powers of experience require explanation.

The view in the text has the potential to provide such an explanation: all perceptual experiences are proto-justified in virtue of their structural content (although not in virtue of their Edenic content). In effect, the propositional justification for the perceptual belief derives from an inferential justification for the belief that the experience is veridical. At the same time, doxastic justification for the former belief need not derive from doxastic justification for the latter belief. If so, then while the view is not dogmatist about propositional justification, it agrees with dogmatism that perceptual experiences are proto-justified and that perceptual beliefs have a prima facie doxastic justification that need not derive from the doxastic justification for any other belief.

Scrutability, Supervenience, and Grounding

Our central scrutability theses have been epistemological theses, not metaphysical theses. But it is natural to ask about the metaphysical upshot of these scrutability theses. For example: does a minimal scrutability base serve as a guide to the fundamental metaphysical structure of the world?

To ask this is to ask about the reach of conceptual metaphysics. In the introduction I said that conceptual metaphysics investigates the structure of our conception of reality, with one eye on how well this structure corresponds to reality itself. At a finer grain, conceptual metaphysics divides into four parts. The first focuses on the *structure of concepts*: relations among the concepts involved in our conception of the world, unconstrained by external reality. The second focuses on the *structure of belief*: roughly, the structure of our model of reality, constrained by our beliefs (and perhaps also by other states such as perceptual experiences) but not directly constrained by external reality. The third focuses on the *conceptual structure of reality*: conceptual relations among truths about reality. The fourth focuses on the *metaphysical structure of reality*: using conceptual relations as a guide to metaphysical relations among truths about reality. The third and fourth projects are constrained by external reality, while the first and second projects are largely constrained by psychological reality.

I have occasionally engaged in the first project in this book. For example, discussions of generalized scrutability and the class of primitive concepts are largely unconstrained by external reality. Some of our primitive concepts may have no application to the actual world: it may be that our basic conception is of an Edenic world that is very different from reality. Still, the structure of concepts at least serves as a constraint on the conceptual structure of reality.[1]

---

[1] The first two projects are closely related to P. F. Strawson's descriptive metaphysics, characterized in *Individuals* (1959) as describing 'the actual structure of our thought about the world', whereas revisionary metaphysics is characterized as 'concerned to produce a better structure'. The structure of concepts and the structure of beliefs might both be seen as aspects of the structure of thought. It is not out of the question for parts of the first project to be revisionary, however, in that some primitive concepts may be unfamiliar concepts that are not manifest in our ordinary thought about the world.

I have not really engaged in the second project in this book. Insofar as I have focused on our representations of the world, the focus has been on the concepts involved rather than on our beliefs and other representations of how the world is.

I have mainly engaged in the third project in this book. Ordinary scrutability theses reflect conceptual and epistemological relations among truths about the world. The focus on truths means that the project is constrained by empirical reality. For example, the base truths include truths from physics, and an important constraint is that all truths about reality be scrutable. In effect, we isolate conceptually and epistemologically fundamental truths about the world, helping to understand the structure of reality as reflected in our concepts.

I have only rarely engaged in the fourth project in this book. That is, I have largely been unconcerned with how well the conceptual and epistemological relations reflect metaphysical relations. The main exception has been the discussion of whether all truths are scrutable from metaphysically fundamental truths (especially in 8.6). I think that there is a great deal of promise in the fourth project, however. Metaphysical relations among truths about reality do not float free of conceptual relations, but are heavily constrained by them. So we should expect conclusions about the conceptual structure of reality to have at least some consequences for the metaphysical structure of reality.

We might think of the fourth project as *conceptually guided global metaphysics*: using concepts as a guide to the global metaphysical structure of reality.[2] This project, like the third, involves a heavy interplay of the conceptual and the empirical. Empirical methods such as those of physics play an enormous role in delivering fundamental truths and in delivering nonfundamental truths. But the relation between the fundamental and the nonfundamental requires careful philosophical analysis. The analysis of this relation can play a significant role in constraining which truths are fundamental in turn. In this excursus, I concentrate on the role that scrutability and related notions can play in this project.

We can approach the question by comparing scrutability to two related notions often thought to do metaphysical work in connecting the fundamental and the nonfundamental. One notion is *supervenience* (Kim 1993): B-properties supervene on A-properties when any two possible worlds that are indiscernible with respect to their A-properties are indiscernible with respect to their B-properties. Another notion is *grounding* (Fine 2010; Schaffer 2009): B-properties are

---

[2] For closely related projects in conceptually guided global metaphysics, see Frank Jackson's *From Metaphysics to Ethics* (1998) and Amie Thomasson's *Ordinary Objects* (2007). For recent projects in global metaphysics that are not especially conceptually guided, see Jonathan Schaffer's 'On What Grounds What' (2009) and Ted Sider's *Writing the Book of the World* (2011).

grounded in A-properties when B-properties are instantiated in virtue of A-properties being instantiated.[3]

I will start with supervenience. Where Scrutability is the thesis that B-truths are scrutable from A-truths, Supervenience is the thesis that B-properties supervene on A-properties. How are these two theses related? The most obvious difference here is that Scrutability concerns truths (sentences or perhaps propositions) while Supervenience concerns properties. A second difference is structural: roughly, Supervenience concerns the whole space of possible worlds, while Scrutability concerns entailment within a world. The third and most important difference is that Scrutability is cast in terms of the a priori (an epistemological notion) whereas Supervenience is cast in terms of possibility (a modal notion). I will take these differences one at a time.

Truths vs. properties. On the first difference, we can line up truths and properties by saying that some sentences (e.g., the A-sentences) *characterize* some properties (e.g., the A-properties) when the sentences fully specify the instantiation of the properties. More precisely, A-sentences characterize A-properties when two worlds are indiscernible with respect to the A-properties iff the same A-sentences hold in them. The following discussion will focus on pairs of scrutability theses and supervenience theses satisfying a characterization assumption: the scrutability thesis holds that B-truths are scrutable from A-truths and the supervenience thesis holds that B-properties supervene on A-properties, where the A-truths are just the true A-sentences, A-sentences characterize A-properties, and B-sentences characterize B-properties.

The characterization assumption serves largely as a formal rather than a substantive constraint on the scrutability theses at issue: roughly, they have to concern truths about the instantiation of properties. Most of the scrutability theses we are concerned with can be put into this form straightforwardly. But the assumption also builds in a substantive claim about the expressibility of the properties involved in the supervenience thesis. If there are A-properties that cannot be referred to by any expression, then there may be two A-discernible worlds in which the same sentences are true. If so, there will be no A-sentences that characterize the A-properties. This sort of inexpressibility provides one way in which Supervenience (a thesis about properties) and Scrutability (a thesis

---

[3] A third notion is that of *metaphysical definition* (Fine 1994; Sider 2011): B-properties are metaphysically definable in terms of A-properties when for each B-property, there is a metaphysical definition of it that appeals only to A-properties. Unlike the definitions on which I have focused in this book, metaphysical definitions are usually not constrained to be conceptual or a priori truths. Still, I think the counterexample problems outlined in chapter 1 also pose problems for metaphysical programs grounded in metaphysical definition. In any case, the three metaphysical projects (metaphysical definition, supervenience, metaphysical grounding) can be seen as analogous to the three epistemological/conceptual projects (definitional scrutability, a priori scrutability, analytic scrutability or conceptual grounding).

about sentences) can come apart. I will set worries about inexpressibility aside for now and return to them later.

Possible worlds vs. entailment. To address this structural difference between scrutability and supervenience, it is useful to first abstract away from the third difference involving apriority and necessity. We can do this by comparing Supervenience not to A Priori Scrutability but to its modal counterpart, Necessitation: the thesis that all B-truths are necessitated by A-truths. In chapter 1 I called this thesis Necessary Scrutability, as it shares a common structure with scrutability theses. It is not cast in epistemological terms, however, so it is really a scrutability thesis only in a weak sense.

Supervenience and Necessitation are closely related. Where Supervenience says that all A-indiscernible worlds are B-indiscernible, Necessitation says in effect that in every possible world where all the (actual) A-truths are true, all the (actual) B-truths are true. Given the assumptions above, Necessitation is very nearly a consequence of Supervenience. One might reason: a world w where all the actual A-truths are true will be A-indiscernible from our world, so (by Supervenience) w will be B-indiscernible from our world, so all the actual B-truths will be true at w.

The only questionable step here is the first: perhaps all actual A-truths are true at w but some other A-sentences are true there as well. This cannot happen if we assume that the A-sentences are closed under negation (setting aside indeterminacy), so that A-truths include both positive and negative A-truths, that is, truths about both the instantiation and non-instantiation of A-properties. If they include only the former, it will also suffice to assume that the A-sentences include a 'that's-all' truth saying that these are the only instantiations of A-properties. Call the assumption that the A-sentences are either closed under negation or include a that's-all truth the completeness assumption. Given the completeness assumption (along with the characterization assumption), Supervenience entails Necessitation. Without the completeness assumption, the entailment will not quite go through. The number of apples plausibly supervenes on applehood: two worlds with the same distribution of apples have the same number of apples. But the number of apples is not necessitated by positive truths about applehood: the positive truths about seven apples are consistent with there being eight apples.

In the reverse direction, Supervenience is not a consequence of Necessitation, even given the characterization and completeness assumptions. Necessitation says that actual A-truths necessitate actual B-truths, but it makes no such claim about A-sentences and B-sentences in other worlds. While the connections between the actual A-truths and the actual B-truths must be necessary, the thesis itself may be contingent. For example, a version of Necessitation holding that all truths are necessitated by physical truths may be true in some physicalist worlds and false in other nonphysicalist worlds. By contrast, supervenience theses as defined so far are not tied to the actual world, and (at least given S5) will be necessary if true at all.

Necessitation is more closely analogous to a weaker sort of supervenience thesis (Lewis 1983, Chalmers 1996) tied to a specific world. These are sometimes called contingent supervenience theses, although they might more accurately be called worldwide supervenience theses, as the relation may or may not hold contingently. We can say that B-properties c-supervene on A-properties in world w if any world that is A-indiscernible from w is B-indiscernible from w. Given the characterization and the completeness assumptions, Necessitation is equivalent to C-Supervenience in the actual world. Without the completeness assumption, Necessitation will be slightly stronger than C-Supervenience.

Another way to draw the notions more closely into alignment is to move from Necessitation to the stronger Generalized Necessitation (that is, Generalized Necessary Scrutability): the thesis that in every world, the A-truths in that world necessitate the B-truths in that world. Supervenience is certainly a consequence of Generalized Necessitation. Under the characterization and completeness assumption, supervenience will be equivalent to Generalized Necessitation. Without the completeness assumption, Generalized Necessitation will be slightly stronger than supervenience.

What goes for Necessitation goes also for A Priori Scrutability, once the modalities are changed. The moral of the discussion above is that as long as the modalities of scrutability and supervenience theses are aligned, ordinary scrutability theses have approximately the same strength as contingent supervenience theses (at least given the relevant assumptions), and ordinary supervenience theses have approximately the same strength as generalized scrutability theses. So we can compare a priori scrutability to epistemic supervenience, where B-properties epistemically supervene on A-properties when all epistemically possible scenarios that are A-indiscernible are B-indiscernible. (To avoid worries about reidentifying properties across scenarios, one might also cast such a thesis in terms of concepts or expressions.) These epistemic supervenience theses have roughly the same force as generalized a priori scrutability theses, while ordinary a priori scrutability theses have roughly the same strength as (epistemically) contingent supervenience theses.

Why not cast scrutability theses as epistemic supervenience theses from the start? One reason is that I have been most concerned with ordinary rather than generalized scrutability theses, and these align less well with the most familiar supervenience theses. Another is that I have not wanted to presuppose the relatively unfamiliar apparatus of epistemically possible scenarios. Casting supervenience theses in terms of possible worlds rather than in terms of necessity is useful because worlds are so familiar and vivid, but it is more straightforward to cast scrutability theses in terms of the a priori.

In any case, c-supervenience is arguably the most important sort of superveni-ence for discerning the metaphysical character of the actual world. For example, it is plausible that the metaphysical thesis of physicalism does not require that mental properties supervene on physical properties, but it requires (at least) that mental properties c-supervene on physical properties. Physicalism is a thesis about the actual world, and is consistent with various supervenience-falsifying claims: for example, it is consistent with the claim that there are two non-actual worlds that are physically indiscernible and differ in that one world has additional nonphysical minds. So in what follows I will compare A Priori Scrutability to C-Supervenience, or equiv-alently (given the characterization and completeness conditions) to Necessitation.

Apriority vs. necessity: We can now abstract away from the structural differ-ences, comparing the epistemological thesis that B-truths are a priori scrutable from A-truths to the modal thesis that B-truths are necessitated by A-truths. If apriority and necessity were equivalent, then these two theses would be equiva-lent. But given that there are truths that are necessary but not a priori, or vice versa, the theses come apart. For example, 'There is water' is necessitated by but not scrutable from 'There is H_2O'.

Still, a weaker link between scrutability and necessitation remains tenable. It is arguable that the gap between apriority and necessity in 'water' cases and the like arise because 'water' is not super-rigid. The Apriority/Necessity thesis dis-cussed earlier (in 8.5) says that sentences composed of super-rigid expressions are necessary if and only if they are a priori. If one accepts this thesis, it follows that if A- and B-truths involve only super-rigid expressions, B-truths will be neces-sitated by A-truths iff they are scrutable from A-truths.

A complication arises because the scrutability bases we have considered have not been restricted to super-rigid expressions: they also involve primitive indexi-cals such as 'I' and 'now'. These indexicals can generate a gap between necessita-tion and scrutability. Still, one might suggest a weaker link:

Linking Thesis: For any class of super-rigid A-truths, all truths are necessi-tated by the A-truths iff all truths are a priori scrutable from the A-truths plus indexical truths.

The Linking Thesis articulates a strong link between supervenience and scru-tability theses. Roughly, any (contingent metaphysical) supervenience base yields an (a priori) scrutability base and vice versa, as long as the relevant base expres-sions are super-rigid, and the scrutability base is augmented by indexical truths. So I will spend some time assessing the prospects for this thesis, and for theses in the vicinity.

I have already in effect given an argument for the left-to-right direction of the Linking Thesis in the argument for Fundamental Scrutability in chapter 8. The key premises there were the Apriority/Necessity thesis (super-rigid truths are necessary iff they are a priori) and the Acquaintance Scrutability thesis (all truths are a priori scrutable from super-rigid truths plus indexical truths). Suppose all truths are necessitated by the A-truths, which are super-rigid. Then by Apriority/Necessity, all super-rigid truths are scrutable from the A-truths. By Acquaintance Scrutability, all truths are scrutable from these super-rigid truths plus indexical truths, so all truths are scrutable from A-truths plus indexical truths.

As in Chapter 8, one can deny this link from Necessitation to Scrutability by denying one of the key premises. Some theists, some ontologists, and some type-B materialists may deny the Apriority/Necessity thesis, while other type-B materialists may deny the Acquaintance Scrutability thesis. Still, these two theses have significant support. I have argued for relatives of these theses in 'The Two-Dimensional Argument against Materialism' and elsewhere.

What about the right-to-left direction of the Linking Thesis? If all truths are scrutable from super-rigid A-truths plus indexical truths, then are all truths necessitated by the A-truths? We could derive this claim by assuming the Apriority/Necessity thesis along with the auxiliary claims that (i) if a super-rigid truth is scrutable from the super-rigid A-truths plus indexical truths, it is scrutable from the A-truths alone, and (ii) all truths are necessitated by super-rigid truths.

The first auxiliary claim is a consequence of the rules for indexical truths in scrutability bases (in the fifth excursus). If a super-rigid truth S is scrutable from 'I am ϕ' and super-rigid A-truths, it will be scrutable from 'Something is ϕ' and A-truths. The rules require that 'Something is ϕ' is scrutable from the non-indexical truths in the base in any case, so it will be scrutable from A-truths. So S will be scrutable from A-truths.

The second auxiliary claim, Super-Rigid Necessitation (discussed briefly in E9) is not obvious, however. Potential counterexamples will arise on haecceitistic views (Adams 1979), on which certain truths about concrete objects are not necessitated by underlying 'qualitative' truths. On such a view, there can be a world that is qualitatively identical (microphysically and phenomenally identical, for example) to our world but in which different objects exist: where our world contains Obama, the other world contains Twin Obama. Given the plausible claim that there are no super-rigid expressions that refer to concrete objects, so that super-rigid truths are all qualitative, the actual truths about Obama will not be necessitated by super-rigid truths.

One could reply by simply denying the relevant haecceitistic view. The view is controversial and to deny it is not to pay a large cost. But if one accepts haecceitism, one can weaken the Linking Thesis by retreating to the claim that if all truths are scrutable from super-rigid A-truths plus indexical truths, then all *qualitative* truths are necessitated by A-truths. Here qualitative truths are understood to exclude object-dependent truths (this might involve a ban on singular terms, along with certain restrictions on predicates and the like). This weaker claim can then be defended by replacing auxiliary thesis (ii) with a weaker thesis (iii), which we might call Super-Rigid/Qualitative Necessitation: all qualitative truths are necessitated by super-rigid truths. Haecceitistic views will not pose an objection to these weaker theses.

Another potential counterexample arises if truths about quiddities are not necessitated by truths about non-quiddities and if there are no super-rigid expressions for quiddities. If one accepts a no-quiddity or a graspable-thick-quiddity view (as discussed in 7.9), one will reject these claims. If one accepts a thin-quiddity view or an ungraspable-thick-quiddity view, on the other hand, one may well accept these claims. If so, one could always retreat to the thesis that if all truths are scrutable from super-rigid A-truths plus indexical truths, then all *super-rigid* truths are necessitated by A-truths. Alternatively, we can expand the class of qualitative truths above to exclude quiddity-involving truths. In what follows, I will assume the Super-Rigid/Qualitative Necessitation thesis, and readers can adjust the notion of qualitativeness, perhaps to exclude object-involving and/or quiddity-involving truths, according to their own views of whether this is needed.

Where does this adjustment leave the connection between scrutability bases and supervenience bases? In chapter 8, we saw that there is plausibly a scrutability base involving just super-rigid expressions and indexicals. If we assume Apriority/Necessity along with Super-Rigid/Qualitative Necessitation, it follows that these super-rigid truths form a necessitation base for qualitative truths: all qualitative truths will be necessitated by the super-rigid truths in such a base.[4] Furthermore, given that the super-rigid truths and indexicals form a minimal scrutability base, the super-rigid truths in question will form a minimal qualitative necessitation base: a minimal class of truths such that all qualitative truths are necessitated by those truths. So the scrutability base yields a sort of supervenience base: the properties involved in the super-rigid truths will in effect be a supervenience base at least for qualitative properties.

Scrutability and metaphysical fundamentality. Given this connection between scrutability and supervenience, we can then ask about the place of metaphysical fundamentality. For example, can we conclude that the super-rigid truths in such a scrutability base are the metaphysically fundamental truths: that is, the

---

[4] This claim requires only the less controversial direction of the Apriority/Necessity thesis: if a super-rigid sentence is a priori, it is necessary. The claim about minimality in the next sentence requires both directions, however.

metaphysical grounds for all truths? There are a few obvious obstacles to this thesis: one involving nonqualitative truths, one involving inexpressible properties, and one involving metaphysical priority. Addressing these obstacles can help us to better understand the connection between scrutability and metaphysical fundamentality.

The first obstacle is posed by nonqualitative truths. We know that the super-rigid truths in question necessitate all *qualitative* truths, but one might think that the metaphysically fundamental truths should necessitate *all* truths. Matters are not entirely clear here, however. In practice, many philosophers at least implicitly take it that necessitation of object-involving truths is not required. For example, physicalists often allow that microphysical truths do not necessitate object-involving truths (that is, they allow that there are microphysically identical possible worlds involving different objects) without taking this to threaten physicalism. The issue is subtle. If the stronger thesis is required, then the move from necessitation to fundamentality will require either ruling out haecceitism or else fleshing out the necessitation base with certain object-involving truths (object-involving truths about certain microphysical objects, for example) so that the base becomes a full necessitation base. For present purposes, however, I will take it that at least one interesting sort of metaphysical fundamentality is compatible with failure to necessitate object-involving truths.[5]

An analogous worry arises if there are no super-rigid expressions for quiddities, as on views with ungraspable thick quiddities and with thin quiddities. On these views, quiddistic truths will not be necessitated by the super-rigid truths in a scrutability base. Most believers in quiddities take at least some of them to be metaphysically fundamental, so this problem cannot be dismissed as with haecceities above. Rather, the super-rigid truths involved in a scrutability base will have to be augmented by non-super-rigid truths concerning quiddities in order

---

[5] See Hofweber 2005 and Almotahari and Rochford 2011 for differing perspectives on this matter. My view is that even if object-involving truths are not necessitated by underlying qualitative truths, they may nevertheless be grounded in underlying qualitative truths. For example, suppose there are just two particles. Then the fundamental truth about the world (that's-all truth aside) might take the form $\exists x \exists y (x \neq y \ \& \ Fx \ \& \ Gy)$. There may also be object-involving truths about this world of the form Fa and Gb, but I do not think it is compulsory to see Fa and Gb as the fundamental truths here. Instead, they may themselves be grounded in the existential truths. This 'qualitativist' view of grounding (Dasgupta forthcoming) requires rejecting the standard view that existential truths are always grounded in object-involving truths. This view is consistent with a haecceitistic view of modality on which there is a distinct world in which $Fb \ \& \ Ga$. In effect, once there are objects in our world, we can use them to characterize various counterfactual possibilities involving them, but the original objects are nevertheless grounded in qualitative matters. More deeply, I think one can distinguish notions of prior and posterior metaphysical possibility here, depending on whether possibility is prior or posterior to actuality. There are multiple posterior metaphysical possibilities consistent with the existential truths, but only one prior metaphysical possibility. While haecceitism may be true of posterior metaphysical possibility, it is prior metaphysical possibility that is relevant to questions of grounding.

to yield a necessitation base for all truths. Then the truths involved in this necessitation base (or perhaps a minimal subset of it) may well be metaphysically fundamental, at least as far as quiddities are concerned.

The second obstacle is posed by the possibility that certain metaphysically fundamental truths are inexpressible. If the problem is just that they are not expressible super-rigidly, as for quiddities and haecceities, then as in the previous paragraph we will need some non-super-rigid fundamental truths. But now the worry is that they are not expressible by sentences at all. Perhaps there are fundamental properties in other realms that we cannot even refer to, for example. If there are such properties, then there will also be inexpressible propositions concerning them. Then our necessitation base for sentences will not yield a necessitation base for propositions and will not yield a base of metaphysically fundamental properties. Still, if we make the fairly weak assumption that we can refer to all fundamental properties, then (given Super-Rigid/Qualitative Necessitation) truths about these properties will either be in our necessitation base or will be necessitated by our base, and this obstacle will be removed. If we make the stronger assumption that we can refer super-rigidly to all fundamental properties, then we do not need Super-Rigid/Qualitative Necessitation. Given the Apriority/Necessity thesis and (i), scrutability of all truths from super-rigid A-truths plus indexical truths yields scrutability of all super-rigid truths by A-truths (by (i)), which yields necessitation of all super-rigid truths by A-truths. Given the assumption, there will be super-rigid truths corresponding to every instantiation of a fundamental property. We can call these the fundamental super-rigid truths. Given that these fundamental truths necessitate all truths (perhaps setting aside object-involving truths) and are necessitated by the A-truths, the A-truths necessitate all truths.

The third and most important obstacle arises from metaphysical priority. Being a member of a minimal necessitation base (or even a super-rigid member) does not suffice for fundamentality. To see this, we can note that given a nonfundamental truth such as 'There are philosophers' (which is plausibly super-rigid), there will be a large class of bases including that truth. Some of these bases will be minimal among this class, in that they do not include any other bases in that class. Some of these bases will have the further property that if one subtracts 'There are philosophers', one would no longer have a necessitation base. These necessitation bases will be minimal in that no subset of them is a necessitation base, and they will include 'There are philosophers'. But 'There are philosophers' is not plausibly fundamental. The moral where matters of fundamentality are concerned, we need to appeal to a relation more fine-grained than necessitation.

Necessitation and grounding. The fine-grained relation that is most directly connected to fundamentality is the relation of grounding. Here the thought is that B-truths are grounded in A-truths when B-truths hold *in virtue of* A-truths holding. A metaphysically fundamental truth will then be a truth that is not grounded in any other truths. Under certain assumptions, the metaphysically fundamental truths will form a minimal grounding base: a minimal set of truths that ground all truths. Likewise, any minimal grounding base will be the set of metaphysically fundamental truths.

Grounding can be understood as a relation among propositions, facts, properties, or objects. I will use grounding relations among sentences as a stand-in for all of these. If grounding is understood as a relation among true propositions (perhaps Russellian propositions), we can translate by saying that sentence S_1 grounds sentence S_2 iff the proposition expressed by S_1 grounds the proposition expressed by S_2. One can do the same if grounding is construed as a relation among facts. Grounding relations among properties will correspond to grounding relations among sentences that characterize those properties. Something similar applies to grounding relations among objects, depending on how those relations are understood. So my talk of grounding relations among sentences can be translated to apply to these other sorts of grounding, though as before we need to keep worries about inexpressibility in mind.

It is tempting to hold that if A-truths ground B-truths, A-truths necessitate B-truths, but this is not entirely obvious. For example, some hold that the collection of fundamental positive truths grounds all truths, both positive and negative, even though it does not necessitate all negative truths. On the view in question, a that's-all truth needs to be added for necessitation, but this truth is itself grounded in the collection of positive truths. On some haecceitistic views, as discussed above, one might also hold that object-involving truths are grounded in qualitative truths even though they are not necessitated by those truths. I will not take a stand on these matters here. I am more sympathetic with the second point than the first (I am inclined to think that a that's-all truth is itself metaphysically fundamental), but these points will make only a minor difference for present purposes.

More importantly, it is not the case that if A-truths necessitate B-truths, A-truths ground B-truths. For example, if A, B, and C are microphysical truths, then A is necessitated by $A \& (B \lor C)$, but it is not plausible that A is grounded by $A \& (B \lor C)$. More plausibly, the latter truth is grounded in some combination of A, B, and C. Likewise, the minimal necessitation base including 'There are philosophers' necessitates all truths but does not ground all truths. It may even be that some necessary truths, such as mathematical truths, are not grounded by any other propositions, even though they are necessitated by all other propositions. If so, they will be in a minimal grounding base, although they are not in any minimal necessitation base. These phenomena arise because grounding requires a much stronger connection between truths than necessitation.

Because of this, even if one can argue from super-rigid A-truths plus indexicals forming a minimal scrutability base to their forming a minimal qualitative necessitation base, one cannot argue directly from here to their forming a minimal grounding base. There will certainly be nonfundamental super-rigid truths. Some of these will be in minimal scrutability and necessitation bases without being in minimal grounding bases. At best, we might be able to move in reverse and hold that a minimal grounding base (perhaps with the addition of a that's-all truth) will itself be a minimal qualitative necessitation base and will therefore, if it involves only super-rigid truths, be a minimal scrutability base (with the addition of some indexical truths). That is in effect a version of the argument for Fundamental Scrutability offered earlier.

We have seen how to move from premises about scrutability to conclusions about supervenience and vice versa, at least given certain assumptions. We have also seen how to move from premises about fundamentality to conclusions about supervenience and scrutability. But this leaves open the question raised above: can we move from premises about scrutability to conclusions about fundamentality?

Conceptual and metaphysical grounding. To properly connect scrutability and fundamentality, I think we have to appeal to a more fine-grained relation that stands to scrutability roughly as grounding stands to necessitation. We might call the more fine-grained relation *conceptual grounding*. We have investigated relations in this vicinity when discussing the thesis that all truths are analytically scrutable from truths involving primitive concepts. One might hold that one truth is conceptually grounded in other truths when it is analytically entailed by those truths and those truths are conceptually prior to it. Or perhaps better, one might understand it in terms of the notion of 'translucent settling' discussed in 'Verbal Disputes'. The discussion there and in chapter 8 gives at least some plausibility to the claim that there is a notion of conceptual grounding in this vicinity.

In what follows, I will assume that we have pinned down a conceptual grounding relation, although the matter requires a more sustained analysis than I have given. To get a rough grip on it, we can work with the approximate definition picture, so that when E is approximately definable as D (under criteria of adequacy that include conceptual priority), truths involving E are conceptually grounded in truths without E involving the terms in D. So truths about bachelors will be conceptually grounded in truths about gender and about marriage, while truths about electrons will be conceptually grounded in truths about playing the electron role. I will also take it that standard logical grounding relations yield conceptual grounding: so A and B jointly ground A & B, A or B separately ground $A \lor B$, and so on.

The discussion in chapter 8 (and also in 'Verbal Disputes') makes a case that there is a minimal conceptual grounding base such that all truths are conceptually grounded in those truths. These truths will involve primitive concepts: perhaps some or all of nomic, phenomenal, spatiotemporal, and quiddistic concepts, as well as normative and mathematical concepts, perhaps among others. The inclusion of normative and mathematical truths in a minimal conceptual grounding base makes clear that such a base can go well beyond a minimal scrutability base.

Can one make inferences from claims about conceptual grounding to claims about metaphysical grounding? Certainly, the claim that A conceptually grounds B does not seem to be equivalent to the claim that A metaphysically grounds B. For example, a claim about a table might be metaphysically grounded by microphysical truths about charge, spin, and the like, but it is not plausibly conceptually grounded in those truths. The truth that an entity has a certain charge may be conceptually grounded in the claim that it has a property that plays a certain role, but (at least on some views) it will not be metaphysically grounded in that truth.

Correspondingly, charge and spin may be metaphysically fundamental, but the concepts *charge* and *spin* are certainly not conceptually fundamental. In the reverse direction, some may hold that *conscious* and *I* are conceptually fundamental, while denying that consciousness and I are metaphysically fundamental. So fundamentality of a concept need not go along with fundamentality of its referent.

Still, all these problems also arose when considering the relation between apriority and necessity, and there is a familiar diagnosis: 'charge', 'spin', and 'I' are not epistemically rigid. For a more plausible thesis, we can restrict the thesis to super-rigid truths as follows. The case of consciousness is still a potential exception, to be sure, but this case is controversial, and as before one might use the restricted thesis to argue for the metaphysical fundamentality of consciousness.

Conceptual/Metaphysical (C/M) Thesis: When A and B are super-rigid truths, A conceptually grounds B iff A metaphysically grounds B.

On the left-to-right direction: it is very plausible that when A conceptually grounds B for super-rigid A and B, A metaphysically grounds B. The obvious candidates for conceptual grounding without metaphysical grounding all involve non-super-rigid expressions: for example, truths involving natural kind terms ('charge', 'electron') or names ('Jack the Ripper'). If we take a conceptually grounded super-rigid expression, such as 'friendly' perhaps, it is highly plausible that those expressions involved in its conceptual grounds (for example, expressions involving certain mental states and dispositions to behave) are equally involved in its metaphysical grounds. Certainly, when A is definable super-rigidly as D (where super-rigidity excludes devices of a posteriori rigidification and the like within D), we can expect D-truths to metaphysically ground A-truths: truths about unmarried males plausibly ground truths about bachelors, for example. Something similar goes for approximate definitions and for logical grounding. So there is a strong prima facie case for the left-to-right direction here.

The right-to-left direction is clearly more controversial, as the case of consciousness illustrates. But setting aside that case and related controversial cases for now, are there any clear exceptions? One might worry that super-rigid microphysical truths will metaphysically ground super-rigid high-level truths without conceptually grounding them. After all, microphysical truths seem far from being conceptually primitive.

To assess this matter, we should first consider what super-rigid microphysical truths will involve. This class will include broadly structural truths, cast in terms of logical, mathematical, nomic, and perhaps spatiotemporal vocabulary. An example is the truth that there exists an entity with a property that plays a certain specified nomic role with respect to other properties. On some views there will also be a distinct class of super-rigid quidditic truths, characterizing intrinsic quiddities of microphysical entities. The broadly structural truths are cast in conceptually primitive vocabulary, and they are plausible candidates to be conceptually primitive truths, not grounded in any further truths. The main exception is that on a quidditic view, certain existential claims within them (there exists a property that plays a role) may be grounded in a corresponding quidditic truth (quiddity Q plays that role). As for quidditic truths, quidditic concepts are certainly unfamiliar, but it is natural to hold that basic quiddities can serve as conceptual grounds for higher-level quiddities.

Next, we should consider what super-rigid high-level truths will involve. Most high-level expressions are not super-rigid, and the super-rigid expressions derive from a limited number of categories: causal, spatiotemporal, mathematical, quidditic, phenomenal, normative, and a few others. In the case of causal and spatiotemporal high-level truths (truths involving 'computer' or 'square' perhaps), it is plausible that these truths will be both conceptually and metaphysically grounded in structural microphysical truths. In effect, fine-grained nomic and spatiotemporal microphysical structure will serve as conceptual and metaphysical grounds for coarse-grained macrophysical nomic and spatiotemporal structure. In the case of high-level quidditic truths (if any), these are again unfamiliar, but there is no obvious reason to doubt that if they exist, they are both conceptually and metaphysically grounded in microphysical quidditic truths.

In the case of pure mathematical truths, it is arguable that these are neither conceptually nor metaphysically grounded by microphysical truths. On the face of it, the microphysical truths are simply irrelevant to pure mathematical truths, and play no role in grounding them. One could hold that mathematical truths are conceptual truths and that conceptual truths need no grounds: they are not fundamental, but they are conceptually grounded in an empty base. If they are not conceptual truths, however, then one could hold either that they are meta-physically grounded in an empty base, or that they are not metaphysically grounded in microphysical truths at all. I think that the last view is perhaps the most plausible of these options.

As for phenomenal truths: some type-B materialist views will reject the Conceptual/Metaphysical Grounding thesis, just as they reject the Apriority/Necessity thesis, but we can set those views aside for now. On type-A materialist views such as analytic functionalism, phenomenal truths (if super-rigid at all) will be both conceptually and metaphysically grounded in structural microphysical truths. On dualist views, phenomenal truths will be grounded in neither way in microphysical truths. On a Russellian monist view, phenomenal truths are meta-physically grounded in certain quiddistic truths: either phenomenal or proto-phenomenal truths. It might seem odd to suggest that familiar phenomenal truths are conceptually grounded in much less familiar protophenomenal truths; but this is not much odder than the plausible claim that truths about phenom-enal color are conceptually grounded in truths about phenomenal hue, satura-tion, and brightness. It is certainly possible for unfamiliar primitive concepts that play a role in conceptually grounding truths involving familiar concepts. Here it is worth keeping in mind that primitive concepts may be quite different from the concepts that we first acquire.

An especially tricky case is that of normative truths. Basic normative expres-sions are arguably super-rigid. If one is a naturalist normative realist, one will hold that normative truths are metaphysically grounded in non-normative truths. But we have seen that (setting aside normative descriptivism and the like) it is arguable that normative truths are not conceptually grounded in non-nor-mative truths. One could respond by embracing normative irrealism, normative non-naturalism, or normative descriptivism. I am inclined to think that the moral is that one should be either a normative irrealist or a weak sort of norma-tive non-naturalist who holds that normative truths are partly grounded (con-ceptually grounded and metaphysically grounded) in fundamental normative moral principles, which are not themselves conceptually grounded or metaphys-ically grounded in non-normative truths (although they are necessary and there-fore necessitated by those truths). In this way, fundamental normative truths are akin to fundamental mathematical truths. But if one rejects non-naturalism, irrealism, and descriptivism, one may need to allow that there are cases of super-rigid metaphysical grounding without conceptual grounding.

Something very similar goes for the case of ontological truths. We saw earlier (chapter 6) that some ontologists hold that the existence of a mereological sum (say) is necessitated but not a priori entailed by the existence of its parts. Likewise, some will hold that the existence of the sum is metaphysically grounded but not conceptually grounded in the existence of its parts. I am inclined to reject these views, holding that one should be either an ontological irrealist (so there is no truth to ground) or an ontological deflationist (so the truth is conceptually grounded in truths about the parts). An ontological realist could also preserve the C/M thesis by endorsing ontological nonreductionism and holding that the existence of the sum is not entirely metaphysically grounded in truths about its parts. But if one rejects these three views, one might allow that there are cases of super-rigid metaphysical grounding without conceptual grounding.

Overall, the moral of this discussion is that there are no clear exceptions to the C/M thesis. Certain philosophical views entail the existence of exceptions: type-B materialism, some strong forms of naturalist normative realism, and some strong forms of ontological realism. But these views are all controversial and far from obviously correct (although to be fair, their negations are also controversial, and the views are far from obviously wrong). Good reasons to accept the C/M thesis will also be good reasons to reject these views.

I will not try to argue for the C/M thesis at any length here. I think that one can argue for it in ways parallel to arguments for the Apriority/Necessity thesis. In the latter case, one can argue that any a posteriori necessities involving super-rigid expressions (such as putative necessities connecting consciousness and physical properties) will be brute necessities (Chalmers 1996, 2010). One can likewise argue that any a posteriori, and perhaps any nonconceptual, grounding claims involving super-rigid expressions (such as grounding claims connecting consciousness and physical properties) will be brute grounding claims. And one can argue that there can be no brute necessities and no brute grounding claims. More strongly, one can argue that our modal concepts are grounded in epistemic concepts, so that we do not have a grip on a notion of metaphysical necessity that is not tied to epistemic necessity in the way that the Apriority/Necessity thesis suggests. In the same way, one can argue that we do not have a grip on a notion of metaphysical grounding that is not tied to conceptual grounding in the way that the C/M thesis suggests. For now, however, I simply note that the C/M thesis remains on the table as a highly attractive view about grounding.[6]

If the C/M thesis is true, then a minimal conceptual grounding base for super-rigid truths is also a minimal metaphysical grounding base for super-rigid truths, and vice versa. If the right-to-left half of the C/M thesis is false but the left-to-

---

[6] Even if the C/M thesis is false, some sorts of conceptually guided global metaphysics will be possible. For example, we can still do *feature metaphysics*, where features are understood as at the end of E14. Conceptual grounding relations between concepts will then reflect metaphysical grounding relations between features if not between properties. On a type-B materialist view, for example, the primitiveness of the concept of consciousness will reflect the metaphysical primitiveness of the feature of consciousness. Here features are tied to concepts, so we can see this feature structure of reality as an aspect of the conceptual structure of reality. If one accepts the C/M thesis, one can read the property structure of reality off the feature structure of reality. If not, there will be a gap between the two.

SCRUTABILITY, SUPERVENIENCE, AND GROUNDING

right half is true, then a conceptual grounding base for super-rigid truths is also a metaphysical grounding base for super-rigid truths (although a minimal conceptual grounding base need not be a minimal metaphysical grounding base).

What about the stronger claim that any conceptual grounding base for *all* truths is also a metaphysical grounding base for all truths and vice versa? This does not follow immediately from the C/M thesis, as we now have worries about non-super-rigid expressions to contend with. For the left-to-right direction, the biggest worry concerns object-involving truths. (Related issues arise for other non-super-rigid truths such as kind-involving truths, but the issues are largely parallel.) For example, perhaps existential truths such as '$\exists x Fx$' collectively serve as conceptual grounds for singular truths such as 'Fa' (as discussed in 7.10), while the latter collectively serve as metaphysical grounds for the former. If so, conceptual and metaphysical grounding bases will look quite different. To respond, one could take the line discussed earlier (footnote 5) according to which even a metaphysical grounding base involves the existential truths here. Alternatively one could weaken the thesis to the claim that any conceptual grounding base *corresponds* to a metaphysical grounding base, where correspondence requires replacing existential truths by singular truths of an otherwise similar form.

As for the right-to-left direction, there is an obvious worry about indexical truths. Given the C/M thesis, a super-rigid metaphysical grounding base for all super-rigid truths will also conceptually ground all super-rigid truths, but it will not conceptually ground indexical truths. One needs to add indexical truths to obtain a full conceptual grounding base. If the right-to-left direction of the C/M thesis is false, one may need to add further truths (perhaps phenomenal truths, normative truths, and so on) to obtain a full conceptual grounding base.

So if the C/M thesis is correct, a minimal conceptual grounding base will not be a minimal metaphysical grounding base: one will have to subtract indexical truths for that purpose. One may also have to convert existential truths to singular truths, depending on one's view of the role of these truths in grounding. In the reverse direction, to go from a minimal metaphysical grounding base to a minimal conceptual grounding base, one will need to add indexical truths, and perhaps convert singular truths to existential truths. If the C/M thesis is false, one will need to add or subtract further truths (such as phenomenal truths and normative truths) along with the indexical truths. On my own view, the only difference between the two bases will be the inclusion or exclusion of indexical truths. These aside, metaphysically fundamental truths will be conceptually fundamental truths and vice versa.

It might seem surprising to say that metaphysically fundamental truths, such as those in physics, are conceptually primitive truths. But once one reflects on the fact that metaphysically fundamental truths in physics will themselves either involve quiddities (perhaps with nomic and spatiotemporal links) or else nomic profiles, powers, and the like, this no longer seems so surprising. If there are concepts of these quiddities at all, they will be novel concepts and we should not be surprised that they are primitive. Concepts of nomic profiles and powers, expressed in an appropriately structural way, themselves appear to be good candidates to be conceptually primitive truths. Finally, if phenomenal truths are metaphysically fundamental, it is no surprise that they should also be conceptually fundamental.

Grounding grounding. Given this close a connection between metaphysical and conceptual grounding it is natural to ask about the relation between the two: are the two identical, is one grounded in the other, or are they more independent than that? An unrestricted identity thesis seems unlikely, because of the way the two relations come apart for non-super-rigid truths. Furthermore, conceptual grounding seems to apply most directly to concepts (or perhaps Fregean propositions) where metaphysical grounding applies to objects and properties (or perhaps Russellian propositions). But links are still on the table.

One linking strategy stems from the idea (common among deflationary metaphysicians) that the most basic principles of metaphysical grounding are themselves conceptual truths. For example, one could hold that it is a conceptual truth that all true propositions p metaphysically ground propositions $p \lor q$, thereby explaining the metaphysical grounding claim above via a conceptual truth. Perhaps it is also a conceptual truth that true Russellian propositions about mereological sums are metaphysically grounded in true propositions about their parts. One could then say that it is a conceptual truth that one sentence (super-rigid or not) metaphysically grounds another when the Russellian proposition expressed by the former metaphysically grounds the Russellian proposition expressed by the latter. Then one could argue that less basic truths about metaphysical grounding themselves follow from conceptual truths and fundamental truths.

This line of thinking suggests the intriguing idea that conceptual truths along with fundamental truths conceptually ground all truths about metaphysical grounding, and thereby metaphysically ground those truths. If we see conceptual truths as corresponding to conceptual grounding claims, we might put this pithily as: conceptual grounding grounds metaphysical grounding. One could then suggest that conceptual truths do not themselves require explanation or grounding (perhaps they are grounded in the empty set). If so, this provides perhaps as good an explanation of metaphysical grounding as we will get.

On another intriguing view, metaphysical grounding grounds conceptual grounding. For example, one could hold that at least for non-indexical acquaintance concepts, to grasp the concept depends on being acquainted with its referent. Then one could suggest that grounding relations about the concepts reflect metaphysical relations among the referents. For example, a hue concept may ground a color concept in virtue of a hue property grounding a color property. If so, then conceptual grounding relations among the concepts are grounded in metaphysical grounding relations among the properties. This strategy works best for super-rigid concepts, but it might be extended to non-super-rigid concepts at least given a view where primary intensions and the like are constructed from properties and relations: then conceptual relations among these concepts might be grounded in metaphysical grounding relations among the corresponding properties and relations.

Both of these views are attractive, and I do not know which is correct. It would not surprise me if elements of both of them are correct. Either way, there will be a close and even constitutive connection between conceptual grounding and metaphysical grounding.

An opponent might say that metaphysical grounding is mind-independent while conceptual grounding is mind-dependent, so the two cannot be as closely connected as this. One response here would be to adopt the broadly Kantian idea that metaphysical grounding is itself mind-dependent and depends on our contingent cognitive scheme. I am inclined to the opposite response, however: conceptual grounding is mind-independent. That is, conceptual grounding relations among truths do not depend on our cognitive apparatus at all. On this view, the primitiveness of a concept is not a fact about humans. Of course our grasping of these concepts is mind-dependent, as are the beliefs we form with them. To the extent that we are well-functioning, the relations among concepts may be reflected in various contingent cognitive relations in us. But there are mind-independent truths about conceptual relations, just as there are mind-independent truths about numerical relations.[7] If this is right, conceptually guided metaphysics can lead us to mind-independent metaphysical truths.

Conclusion. Overall, we have seen that the relationships between scrutability, supervenience, and grounding are complex, but they can be drawn. The most important principles in drawing these connections are epistemological/modal bridging principles for super-rigid truths. The Apriority/Necessity thesis connects supervenience and scrutability, while the C/M thesis connects conceptual and metaphysical grounding. Smaller obstacles along the way include structural differences, worries about non-super-rigidly expressible propositions, and the status of indexical and that's-all truths. Given the major principles, the smaller obstacles can be handled in reasonably straightforward ways, leaving a fairly strong connection between the theses in place. If all this is right, we may truly

---

[7] This not to endorse Platonism about concepts, any more than to hold that it is a mind-independent truth that 2 < 3 is to endorse Platonism about numbers.

say that scrutability and conceptual grounding are guides to the structure of the world.

I have not argued at any length for the Apriority/Necessity thesis or the C/M thesis. I have just tried to make the case that they have some plausibility, and that standard worries about the connection between apriority and necessity (and so on) are not worries for these theses. I have argued for the former thesis elsewhere, and I am more confident of it than of the latter thesis. I think that both deserve further investigation, which I leave to future work.

Explaining Scrutability

I have argued that various scrutability theses are true, but I have not yet explained why they are true. I have argued for them mainly by attending to truths about the world and arguing that they are all scrutable from various limited bases. This provides an argument, but it does not yet provide an explanation. I do not have a conclusive explanation of scrutability, but I have some relevant thoughts of a sketchy and speculative character. It is likely that much of what follows is wrong, but it may at least suggest some directions for exploration and help to stimulate alternative explanations.

Why are scrutability theses true? Of course these could be brute facts that are not to be further explained, but they are too complex for this to be a plausible diagnosis. If they are true, there are surely simpler principles in terms of which they can be explained. Given this much, explanatory pluralism suggests that there are probably multiple explanations to be found.

In chapter 8 (especially section 8), I have done some preliminary charting of the explanatory relations *between* scrutability theses. There I suggested that Acquaintance Scrutability may be especially fundamental. When combined with the thesis that acquaintance concepts are narrow concepts (in our world), it can explain the truth (in our world) of Narrow Scrutability. When combined with the claim that there are primitive acquaintance concepts (perhaps strong or Russellian acquaintance concepts) from which all acquaintance concepts are scrutable, it can help explain the truth of Primitive Scrutability.

We have also seen that Acquaintance Scrutability along with the Apriority/Necessity Thesis entails Fundamental Scrutability. Furthermore, Fundamental Scrutability, combined with the thesis that the class of expressions for fundamental properties (plus indexicals) is compact, entails Compact Scrutability. If all this is right, we might see Acquaintance Scrutability, along with the ancillary theses mentioned here, as explaining the other four theses. That reduces the question as explaining those theses to that of explaining Acquaintance Scrutability, and perhaps explaining the ancillary theses.[1]

---

[1] My best attempt at both explaining the Apriority/Necessity thesis and providing an a priori argument for it is in the full version of 'The Two-Dimensional Argument against Materialism'.

We still need to explain Acquaintance Scrutability, however. And if one rejects the Apriority/Necessity thesis and Fundamental Scrutability, one will also need to explain Compact Scrutability in some other way.

What about explaining scrutability relations? I think that A Priori Scrutability (in its conclusive version) can explain Conditional Scrutability and Inferential Scrutability, insofar as these are true. A Priori Scrutability theses might themselves be explained in terms of Analytic Scrutability theses. Assuming that analyticity entails apriority, then analytic scrutability entails a priori scrutability. Analytic scrutability theses seem more basic in some respects: in particular, analytic scrutability bases seem to better reflect the class of primitive concepts. So it is arguable that Analytic Acquaintance Scrutability can explain A Priori Acquaintance Scrutability, and that Analytic Compact Scrutability can explain A Priori Compact Scrutability. But the explaining theses themselves need explanation.

At this point, it is natural to try explaining these theses in terms of the character of our concepts. For example, one might invoke *conceptual descriptivism*: the thesis that every concept is composed from a compact set of primitive concepts. (Here I construe concepts as types of mental representations, though something similar will apply if one construes concepts as abstract objects.) Given that thoughts are composed from concepts, and given that sentences express thoughts and subsentential expressions express concepts, it follows that every expression is equivalent to one composed of expressions that express primitive concepts. If this is right, then all truths will be analytically entailed by truths involving expressions that express primitive concepts alone.

So conceptual descriptivism might be taken to ground a Primitive Analytic Scrutability thesis. Given the further theses that there is a compact class of primitive concepts, or that primitive concepts are all acquaintance concepts, this thesis might also explain Compact Analytic Scrutability and Acquaintance Analytic Scrutability.

I think that conceptual descriptivism is probably false, for reasons discussed in chapter 1. Just as most expressions are not definable from a limited class of primitive expressions, most concepts are not equivalent to complexes composed from a limited class of primitive concepts. But I think that a sort of inferentialism about concepts can avoid these problems while at the same time providing a promising explanation of scrutability.

According to inferentialism, concepts are grounded in their inferential roles.[2] If we construe concepts as a certain sort of mental state (or mental representation),

---

[2] Inferentialism can be traced back at least to *The Logical Syntax of Language* (1934), in which Carnap develops a broadly inferentialist view of language. In that work the meaning of a sentence is understood in terms of its consequences with respect to certain primitive sentences, as captured by certain transformation rules. Inferentialist views of linguistic content have been developed by Sellars (1953), who was strongly influenced by Carnap's inferentialism, Field (1977), Harman (1982), and Brandom (1994). Inferentialist views of mental content have been developed by Harman, Block (1986), and Peacocke (1993), among others.

this thesis can be seen as a thesis about the existence and content of concepts: a state counts as a concept in virtue of its inferential role, and a concept has its content in virtue of its inferential role. If we construe concepts as abstract objects, we can construe the thesis as a thesis about the individuation and possession of concepts: concepts are individuated by inferential roles and subjects possess these concepts in virtue of having states with the relevant inferential role.

According to *anchored* inferentialism, there is a limited set of primitive concepts, and all other concepts are grounded in their inferential role with respect to these concepts.[3] The view is neutral on how primitive concepts are grounded. Anchored inferentialism is compatible with a primitive externalist view (E14) on which primitive concepts are grounded in causal connections to their referents. In the present context, an especially natural view holds that they are grounded in acquaintance with their referents. The scrutability framework fits anchored inferentialism especially well: nonprimitive concepts are grounded in their inferential relations to primitive concepts, and primitive concepts are grounded some other way.

The inferential role of a concept can be construed as a normative role, constituted by *good* inferences that the concept might be involved in. On one construal, the inferential role will be an a priori role, involving the a priori justified inferences that the concept is involved in. On another, it will be a sort of analytic role, involving the trivial or cognitively insignificant inferences that the concept is involved in. Either way, inferentialism will give special weight to *entry inferences*: good inferences from thoughts constituted by primitive concepts alone to thoughts involving the concept in question. There may also be a role for *exit inferences*: involving good inferences from thoughts involving the concept to thoughts involving primitive concepts alone. Typically, however, a pattern of entry inferences will itself fix a pattern of exit inferences. If so, one can hold that concepts are individuated by entry inferences alone.[4]

This model fits the scrutability framework well. Entry inferences can be represented as inferences from sets of sentences composed of expressions for primitive concepts to sentences that also involve nonprimitive concepts. Under certain reasonable assumptions, the pattern of entry inferences for a nonprimitive con-

---

[3] Anchored inferentialism is discussed in 'Verbal Disputes' and at greater length in the additional excursus on inferentialism and analyticity.

[4] How does this inferentialism square with the claim in excursus 9 that there are many ways to individuate concepts? Certainly there are many ways to classify mental representations under types (by their referents, for example), and there are many corresponding sorts of abstract objects. But if we are interested in epistemological properties and the epistemological semantics of mental representations, inferentialism provides the best individuation. One might think the claim is trivial: individuating by inferential role best explains inferential role. However, substantive claims include (i) all or most mental representations have a core inferential role: entry and exit inferences with respect to a limited set of primitive concepts, (ii) this core inferential role grounds overall inferential role, and (iii) core inferential role grounds truth-conditional cognitive content.

cept *C* will itself fix a pattern of scrutability inferences: inferences from certain complete sets of sentences involving expressions for primitive concepts (where these sets correspond to full scenarios) to sentences also involving *C*. And in the reverse direction, these scrutability inferences will fix the pattern of entry inferences. So on this model, the content of any concept corresponds to a pattern of scrutability inferences.

If this is right, then the inferential role associated with any concept will fix the scrutability inferences it is involved in. If we grant that inferences fixed by constitutive inferential roles are a priori or analytic, then this will explain a priori and analytic scrutability from the relevant bases. I think it is most natural to appeal to a sort of analytic scrutability here, but this requires first unpacking a relevant notion of analyticity.

Here we can invoke the framework of warrants discussed in fourth excursus. Following the discussion there, we can say that *S* is warrant-analytic for a subject if there is a conceptual warrant the subject to accept *S*. We can say that *S* is warrant-analytic (not relative to a subject) when *S* is warrant-analytic for any subject who uses the expressions in *S* with full competence.[5]

Here, intuitively, a conceptual warrant for accepting a sentence is one that derives wholly from the concepts expressed by the expressions in that sentence. For example, it is natural to hold that there is a warrant for accepting 'Vixens are female foxes' that derives from the concept expressed by 'vixens', 'foxes', and so on. The existence of a warrant does not entail that any given subject will use the warrant. So the warrant-analyticity of a sentence *S* does not entail that *S* is epistemologically analytic in the sense that anyone who grasps the relevant concepts knows *S*. Correspondingly, warrant-analyticity is not subject to the critique of epistemological analyticity by Williamson (2007). But it is still an epistemological notion, and is one that may be able to play some roles of the traditional notion of analyticity.

Can we characterize conceptual warrants more precisely? Here the inferentialist analysis of concepts provides some potential tools. On this view, most concepts can be characterized by certain inferential roles with respect to other concepts. One might suggest that there is a conceptual warrant to accept a proposition *p*, constituted by various concepts, when *p* is warranted in virtue of the constitutive inferential roles of the concepts that constitute it.

For example, suppose that the inferential role of *vixen* is constituted by the obvious inferential relations to *female* and to *fox*. Then it is natural to hold that

[5] Warrant-analyticity is a relative of the notion of positional analyticity discussed in 'Verbal Disputes': *S* is positionally analytic if any subject who uses the expressions in *S* (with full competence) is in a position to know *S*. Warrant-analyticity cashes out 'in a position to know' in terms of warrants, as in the fourth excursus, and more importantly, it constrains the sort of warrants that are relevant to a special sort: conceptual warrants.

an inference from *x is a vixen* to *v is a female fox* is warranted in virtue of these constitutive inferential relations.[6] It is not a large step from there to hold that *vixens are female foxes* is warranted in virtue of these inferential relations (perhaps along with inferential relations deriving from *are* and from various logical concepts). If this is right, then there is a conceptual warrant to accept *vixens are female foxes*. As before, none of this entails that a subject possessing the concepts must accept the proposition: constitutive inferential roles are normative rather than descriptive. But the roles nevertheless provide a warrant.

Much more would need to be said to make this picture fully precise. As well as spelling out the rules as to what can be a constitutive inferential role, we would need a precise account of just how these inferential roles have to be related to a proposition to warrant it. There are also questions about how precisely to represent conceptual warrants in the framework of support structures: they might be seen as a sort of basic warrant, providing basic a priori evidence, or alternatively they might be seen as grounded in concepts somehow. But we have enough on the table here to provide the basic picture.

Given that all nonprimitive concepts have constitutive inferential roles connecting them to primitive concepts, one can then see the outlines of an explanation of why all truths are analytically scrutable from primitive truths. Take a sentence *S* expressing (or apt to express) a thought *T*. Every nonprimitive concept involved in *T* will be associated with entry rules endorsing inferences from thoughts involving primitive concepts to thoughts involving it. If we put together the inference rules for all nonprimitive concepts in *T*, we can expect these entry rules to determine inferences from certain sets of thoughts *T'* involving only primitive concepts to *T*. If *S'* expresses a conjunction of the thoughts in *T'*, then these constitutive inferences will also determine a conceptual warrant for inferences from a sentence *S'* to *S*. Likewise, they will also provide a conceptual warrant for accepting a conditional 'If *S'*, then *S*'. So that conditional will be warrant-analytic. So *S* is analytically scrutable from the conjuncts of *S'*, if analytic scrutability is understood in terms of warrant-analyticity. This reasoning applies to any sentence *S*, so it follows that any sentence is analytically scrutable from some set of sentences expressing primitive concepts. This explains a generalized version of Analytic Scrutability.

This explanation is congenial to the basic picture of conceptual application set out in section 3 of chapter 1. On that picture, grasp of a concept goes along with

---

[6] This is an instance of what Paul Boghossian (2003) calls the Meaning–Entitlement Connection: any inferential transitions built into the possession conditions for a concept are eo ipso entitling. Boghossian worries that defective concepts (such as Prior's 'tonk') provide a counterexample. I would instead restrict the thesis to concepts that can be possessed and deny that defective concepts can be possessed (or perhaps better, hold that all concepts can be possessed and deny that 'tonk' expresses a concept).

a conditional ability to identify an expression's extension, given sufficient information about how the world turns out and sufficient reasoning. We can now see how such a conditional ability might fall out of constitutive inferential connections to primitive concepts, along with the claim that subjects are always in a position (ideally) to make the constitutive inferences. When they do, the inferences will have a conceptual warrant. Once a picture of this sort is granted, analytic scrutability from primitive concepts is only to be expected.

What are the primitive concepts? A natural hypothesis is that they are acquaintance concepts. On a strong view of acquaintance, the primitive acquaintance concepts are strong acquaintance concepts: those for which possession entails knowledge of reference. On an especially strong view, these strong acquaintance concepts are always Russellian acquaintance concepts, so that the concept and the strong acquaintance are grounded in a substantive nonconceptual relation between subject and referent. It could also be that primitive acquaintance concepts are grounded some other way: for example, one can make a case that logical concepts are grounded in structural aspects of inferential role. It could also be that some primitive acquaintance concepts are grounded in Russellian acquaintance whereas other structural concepts (e.g., logical, nomic, and fundamentality concepts) are grounded in other ways. In what follows I will assume the strong Russellian view for the purposes of exploration, but I think that elements of the story might also be adapted to other views.

Let us say that *acquaintance inferentialism* is an anchored inferentialism on which the primitive concepts are acquaintance concepts. This hypothesis coheres well with the scrutability theses: given acquaintance inferentialism, analytic acquaintance scrutability is only to be expected. Acquaintance inferentialism tells us that there are the sorts of normative relations between all concepts and acquaintance concepts that will ground acquaintance scrutability. One might reasonably object that the distance between the two theses is too small for the latter to do much work in explaining the former. The same objection may apply to explaining scrutability in terms of inferentialism in general. Still, the step from scrutability to inferentialism helps us to at least narrow down the explanatory project and localize the residual explanatory questions.

Even granted acquaintance inferentialism, a residual question is why the scrutability base is compact. Here one could suggest that there is only a compact class of (strong) acquaintance concepts. Alternatively, one could allow that there are many possible acquaintance concepts but that only a few of them are needed to describe the actual world, due to its limited structure. Other more complex scenarios may require acquaintance concepts of all sorts of alien properties. If this is right, then generalized scrutability will require something more than a compact class of primitive concepts (although perhaps still a relatively compact class, compared to the class of all concepts), but a compact class will suffice for actual-world scrutability.

It remains to explain acquaintance inferentialism itself. In particular, why do all concepts have entry and exit inferences connecting them to acquaintance concepts? I do not have a definitive answer to this question. But to speculate: I am inclined to think that without some role for acquaintance (that is, strong acquaintance and perhaps Russellian acquaintance), we are not really thinking at all. To be sure there are forms of representation that do not involve acquaintance, as when a thermostat represents temperature or a computer processes my tax return. But we would not classify these forms of representation as involving thinking or understanding. We might here distinguish intentionality from mere representation, where intentionality requires a grounding in acquaintance. Not every thought must involve acquaintance with a referent, but without at least an inferential connection to concepts involving acquaintance, a representation would be too ungrounded to count as being genuinely intentional.

We might cast the distinction between intentionality and representation in terms of the associated forms of normativity. Where representational processes are subject to norms of reliability, intentional processes are subject to a sort of robust normative assessment that goes beyond assessment of reliability. This sort of robust normativity includes norms that are often classified as internalist norms: the not-merely-reliable grounding of belief in reasons and evidence, for example. Here again, I am tempted to suppose that some role for acquaintance is required for this sort of robust normative assessment. Judgments involving acquaintance concepts are subject to these norms, and only a state with inferential connections to these judgments could be subject to these norms. Representation without acquaintance is in a certain sense blind. If this is right, then acquaintance is a condition on the possibility of thought and justification.

It then remains then to explain how acquaintance and normativity are possible. One might speculate further that one of the functions of consciousness is to enable acquaintance and thereby to enable normativity and intentionality. But at this point I have speculated enough.

Glossary

Glossary entries are provided for key expressions that occur in more than one location, with a reference to a location where the fullest explanation can be found. Following the convention established at the start of chapter 2, scrutability theses are capitalized ('A Priori Scrutability') while scrutability relations are not ('a priori scrutability'). In what follows S is a sentence, C is a class of sentences, s is a subject, and p is a proposition.

A priori: S is a priori (for s) iff S can be known a priori (by s) (or: if there is an a priori warrant (for s) to believe S). A subject s knows S a priori iff s knows S with justification independent of experience; s knows S is a posteriori iff s knows S with justification dependent on experience. [E8]

A priori scrutability: S is a priori scrutable from C (for s) iff a material conditional 'If C', then S' is a priori (for s), where C' conjoins sentences in C. [2.5]

A Priori Scrutability: The thesis that there is a compact class C of sentences such that for all subjects, all truths are a priori scrutable from truths in C. [2.5]

Acquaintance expression: A super-rigid expression or a primitive indexical expression. [8.5]

Acquaintance Scrutability: The thesis that all truths are scrutable from truths involving only acquaintance expressions. [8.5]

Alethically fragile truth: See Fitchian truth. [2.3]

Analytic: A sentence S is analytic when it is true in virtue of the meanings of the expressions involved. Alternatively, S is analytic when there is a conceptual warrant for accepting S, one that derives from the concepts expressed by S. [8.3, E17]

Apriority/Necessity thesis: The thesis that if a sentence S contains only super-rigid expressions, S is a priori iff S is necessary. [E10, E14]

Canonical specification: See scenario. [E10]

Certainty: Absolute confidence that p, or degree of belief 1 in p. Epistemological certainty (or knowledge with certainty, or conclusive knowledge) that p is justified absolute confidence in p, or rational degree of belief 1 in p. [2.1, E8]

Compact: A class of sentences is compact iff it involves expressions from only a small number of families and does not involve any trivializing mechanisms. [1.5]

Conclusive knowledge: Knowledge with certainty. Conclusive a priori knowledge is a priori knowledge with certainty. Conclusive scrutability theses replace 'know' with 'know with certainty'. [2.1, E8]

Conditional credence: $cr(P \mid Q)$ is a subject's credence in P's being the case conditional on Q's being the case. [2.4]

Conditional scrutability: A sentence S is conditionally scrutable from C for s iff s is in a position to know that if C', then S (or: if s's insulated rational credence $cr^*(S \mid C') = 1$), where C' conjoins the sentences in C. [2.4]

Conditional Scrutability: The thesis that there is a compact class C of sentences such that for all subjects, all truths are conditionally scrutable from truths in C. [2.4]

Conditionalization: If a subject's rational credence $cr'(S|E) = \phi$ at t_1, and the subject acquires total evidence E between t_1 and t_2, then at t_2, the subject's rational credence $cr'(S) = \phi$. [4.2, 5.6]

Context-dependence: A context-dependent expression is one whose content depends on the context in which it is uttered. An extensionally context-dependent expression is one whose extension depends on context. An epistemically context-dependent expression is one whose a priori inferential role (or whose associated primary intension or mode of presentation) depends on context. [E3]

Core Evidence thesis: The thesis that all knowledge is grounded in core evidence: introspective evidence about phenomenal states (and perhaps intentional states) and perceptual evidence about the distribution of primary and secondary qualities in the environment. [3.4]

Core Knowability thesis: The thesis that all knowable (non-Fitchian) ordinary truths are knowable with grounds in core evidence. [3.4]

Cosmoscope: A virtual-reality device for conveying the physical, phenomenal, and indexical information in *PQI*. [3.2]

Credence: A subjective probability (or degree of belief, between 0 and 1 inclusive) that a proposition or a sentence is true. A subject's credence in a sentence S is represented by '$cr(S)$', while her rational credence (credence she should ideally have) and her insulated rational credence (credence she should ideally have on an insulated idealization) in S are represented by '$cr'(S)$' and '$cr^*(S)$'' respectively. [3.4, E5]

Deferential use of an expression: A use of an expression such that the referent of the expression as used depends on how others in the linguistic community use the expression. [6.9]

Definability: The thesis that there is a compact class of primitive expressions such that all expressions are definable in terms of that class. [1.1]

Definitional scrutability: S is definitionally scrutable from C (for s) if S is logically entailed by members of C and adequate definition sentences (for s). [1.1]

Definitional Scrutability: The thesis that there is a compact class of sentences C such that (for all subjects) all true sentences S are definitionally scrutable from truths in C. [1.1]

Descriptivism: The view that ordinary proper names (and perhaps other expressions) are equivalent to definite descriptions: expressions of the form 'The F' for some predicate F. [1.4]

Edenic properties: Edenic redness is primitive redness of a sort that is arguably presented to us in perceptual experience. Such Edenic properties might be instantiated in some possible worlds (akin to the Garden of Eden), but are arguably not instantiated in our world. [7.4]

Epistemic and extensional context-dependence: See context-dependence. [E3]

Epistemically complete: S is epistemically complete iff S is epistemically possible and there is no T such that $S \& T$ and $S \& {\sim}T$ are both epistemically possible. [E10]

Epistemically invariant: An epistemically invariant expression is an expression that is not epistemically context-dependent (see context-dependence): that is, its associated a priori inferential role does not depend on context. [E3]

Epistemically possible: S is epistemically possible if $\sim S$ is not a priori. C is epistemically possible if a conjunction of all sentences in C is epistemically possible. [E10]

Epistemically possible scenario: See scenario. [E10]

Epistemically rigid expression: One whose referent can be known a priori. Alternatively: one that picks out the same referent in every epistemically possible scenario. [E14]

Extension: The extension of a sentence is its truth-value (the extension of 'Sydney is in Australia' is true). The extension of a singular term, such as a name, is its referent (the extension of 'Canberra' is Canberra). The extension of a predicate is either a class or a property (the extension of 'hot' is either the class of hot things or the property of being hot). Extensions for other expressions are analogous entities on which the truth-value of a sentence depends. [1.1, 7.2]

Externalism: Most commonly (in this text), content externalism, which says that the contents of thought depend on features extrinsic to the thinker (or on another understanding, on features that are not accessible to the thinker). [8.4]

Fitchian truth (or alethically fragile truth): A truth S such that properly investigating the truth-value of S will change the truth-value of S. [2.3]

Fregean proposition: A proposition made up of Fregean senses. [2.2, E11]

Fregean sense: A meaning or content associated with an expression that captures its cognitive significance. In a nontrivial true identity statement such as 'Hesperus is Phosphorus', the two names have the same referent but different senses. [2.2, E11]

Fundamental Scrutability: The thesis that all truths are scrutable from metaphysically fundamental truths plus indexical truths. [8.6]

Fundamentality Scrutability (also fundamentality structuralism): The thesis that all truths are scrutable from truths about fundamentality plus indexical truths. [8.7]

Generalized Scrutability: The thesis that Scrutability holds not just in the actual world but in all epistemically possible scenarios. More precisely: there is a compact class C of sentences such that for all sentences S, if S is epistemically possible, then there is an epistemically possible subclass C' of C such that S is scrutable from C'. There are also generalized versions of numerous other scrutability theses: e.g., Generalized Narrow Scrutability requires that C contain only narrow expressions rather than being compact. [2.6]

Grounding: Given truths A and B, A is metaphysically grounded in B when A is true in virtue of B being true. A is epistemically grounded in B (for a subject) when a justification for B is part of a justification for A (for that subject). A is conceptually grounded in B, when (roughly) the concepts in B are prior to those in A and B analytically entails A. [E18]

Haecceity: An object's haecceity is the property of being that object. Varieties of haecceitism hold that haecceities are not reducible (in various ways) to non-object-involving properties. [7.9]

Humean Scrutability: The thesis that all nomic truths are conclusively scrutable from non-nomic truths. [7.6]

Indexical truths: Truths of the form 'X is...', where X is a primitive indexical ('I', 'now', or a phenomenal demonstrative). [3.1, E6, 6.12]

Inferential scrutability: S is inferentially scrutable from C for s iff, were s to come to know C, s would be in a position to know S. [2.3]

Inferential Scrutability: The thesis that there is a compact class C of sentences such that for all subjects, all truths are inferentially scrutable from truths in C. [2.3]

Inferentialism: The view that concepts are individuated by their inferential roles, or that they get their content in virtue of their inferential roles. [E17]

Insulated idealization: An idealization of rationality that sets aside level-crossing principles whereby first-order reasoning is insulated from higher-order beliefs about one's cognitive capacity; so mathematical reasoning will be insulated from doubts about one's mathematical competence, for example. [E5]

Intension: See primary intension. [1.4, 5.3, E11]

Intentional truths: Truths about intentional mental states, mental states (including but not limited to beliefs and desires) that are about other entities. [6.7]

Internalism: Most commonly (in this text), content internalism, which says that the contents of thought depend only on a thinker's intrinsic properties (or on another understanding, on features that are accessible to the thinker). [8.4]

Knowability thesis: The thesis that all true propositions (or true sentences) are knowable. [E1]

Logical empiricism (also logical positivism): A philosophical movement active in Vienna and elsewhere in the 1920s and 1930s, with leading figures including Rudolf Carnap, Otto Neurath, Moritz Schlick, and others. [1.2]

Macrophysical truths: Truths about any entities, including macroscopic entities, in the language of classical physics. [3.1]

Microphysical truths: Fundamental physical truths in the language of a completed physics. [3.1]

Modal truths: Truths about what is possible or necessary. [6.6]

Narrow expression: One whose content does not depend on a speaker's environment. Narrow expressions include non-Twin-Earthable expressions (where twins are understood as intrinsic duplicates) and primitive indexicals. Narrow content is a sort of mental content that does not depend on a thinker's environment. [8.4]

Narrow Scrutability: The thesis that all truths are scrutable from truths involving only narrow expressions. [8.4]

Newman's problem: A problem for constructions of the world using purely logical vocabulary. Any specification of the world in such a vocabulary is near-vacuous in that if it is satisfied by a world, it is satisfied by any world containing the same number of entities. [1.2]

Nomic Scrutability (also nomic structuralism): The thesis that all truths are scrutable from nomic truths, plus indexical and that's-all truths. [7.11, 8.7]

Nomic truths: Truths about laws of nature, and associated truths such as those about causation, dispositions, chance, and the like. [7.6]

Normative truths: Truths about what one ought to do and what one ought to believe. On a broad usage, also includes evaluative truths: truths about values, such as about what is good or bad. [6.3]

Ontological truths: Truths about the existence of entities. [6.4]

Ordinary truths (or ordinary macroscopic truths): Truths about the macroscopic natural world, such as 'Water is H_2O' and 'Life on our planet is based on DNA'. This class excludes hard cases such as mathematical, mental, metaphysical, modal, moral, and social truths, truths involving proper names, and borderline cases of vague sentences. Also excludes deferential utterances and may be restricted to positive truths. [3.1]

PQI: A version of *PQTI* without the 'that's-all' sentence. [3.1]

PQTI: A set containing all microphysical, macrophysical truths, and phenomenal truths (including any true laws and counterfactuals involving these), some designated indexical truths, and a 'that's-all' sentence.

PQTI–: A stripped-down version of *PQTI* without macrophysical truths or counterfactuals: just microphysical and phenomenal truths (including laws involving these), indexical truths, and a 'that's-all' sentence. [6.1]

Panpsychism: The view that everything has a mind, or at least that fundamental microphysical entities are conscious. [7.9]

Phenomenal realism: The thesis that phenomenal truths are not scrutable from physical truths (perhaps along with indexical and that's-all truths). [7.7]

Phenomenal Scrutability: The thesis that all truths are scrutable from phenomenal truths, plus indexical and that's-all truths. [7.11]

Phenomenal truths: Truths about conscious experience, and in particular about what it is like to be a conscious subject. [3.1]

Phenomenalism: The thesis that all expressions can be defined in terms of phenomenal expressions (expressions for conscious experience). [1.2]

Positive sentence: A sentence *s* such that if *s* holds in a world (or scenario) *w*, it holds in all worlds (or scenarios) that outstrip *w*. One world (scenario) outstrips another when the first contains an intrinsic duplicate of the second as a proper part. [3.1, E6]

Primary intension: The primary intension (or epistemic profile) of a sentence *S* (in a context) is a function from scenarios to truth-values, true at a scenario *w* if *S* is scrutable (in that context) from a canonical specification of *w*. The primary intension of a subsentential expression is a function from scenarios to extensions. [E10, E11]

Primary qualities: Spatiotemporal properties and mass properties. [3.4]

Primitive concept: A concept such that no concept is conceptually prior to it. [7.2, 8.3]

Primitive externalism: Externalism about primitive concepts. More precisely, the thesis that some non-indexical primitive concepts are not epistemically rigid. [E14]

Primitive indexicals: 'I', 'now', and phenomenal demonstratives ('this'). [3.1, 6.12]

Primitive Scrutability: The thesis that all truths are scrutable from truths involving only primitive concepts. [8.3]

Quiddistic Scrutability: The thesis that all truths are scrutable from truths about quiddities, plus indexical and that's-all truths. [7.9]

Quiddity: The categorical basis for microphysical dispositions; for example, the (arguably unknown) intrinsic nature of mass or charge. Varieties of quidditism hold that quiddities can come apart (in various ways) from the associated dispositions. Quiddistic concepts and expressions are concepts and expressions that pick out quiddities super-rigidly. [7.9]

Ramsification: The process of replacing sentences containing certain theoretical expressions (e.g. sentences about charge) to sentences without them (e.g. sentences about the property that plays a certain role within physical theory). The result is a *Ramsey sentence* that captures the content of the original sentence. [7.3, E13]

Russellian proposition: A proposition made up of objects, properties, and other worldly entities. [2.2, E11]

Scenario: An epistemically possible world. Can be modeled as an equivalence class of epistemically complete sentences in a generalized scrutability base. The sentences in this class serve as canonical specifications of the scenario. [E10]

Scrutability: Used alone, either a generic term for various scrutability relations, or (when capitalized) for A Priori Scrutability. [Introduction, 2.1]

Scrutability base: A class of sentences from which all truths are scrutable. [1.5]

Secondary intension: The secondary intension of a sentence S (in a context) is a function from metaphysically possible worlds to truth-values, true at w iff S is true at w (i.e., if S is necessitated by a canonical specification of w) in that context. The secondary intension of a subsentential expression is a function from scenarios to extensions. The secondary intension of an expression can be seen as its modal or counterfactual profile. [E10]

Secondary qualities: Color properties and their analogs in other sensory modalities. [3.4, 6.14, 7.4]

Semantically fragile sentence: A sentence S such that investigating whether S is true changes the proposition S expresses. [E3]

Spatiotemporal functionalism: The thesis that our ordinary spatiotemporal concepts pick out spatiotemporal properties as the properties that play a certain role (typically either a role within physics or a role with respect to experience or both). [7.5]

Spatiotemporal primitivism: The thesis that we have primitive spatiotemporal concepts (and perhaps that these are expressed by our ordinary spatiotemporal expressions and are instantiated in our world). [7.5]

Spatiotemporal Scrutability (also spatiotemporal structuralism): The thesis that all truths are scrutable from spatiotemporal truths plus indexical and that's-all truths. [7.11, 8.7]

Structural expressions: Expressions characterizing structure. On different understandings structural expressions may include only logical expressions, or these plus nomic/causal and fundamentality expressions, perhaps along with further relational expressions. [8.7]

Structural realism: Roughly, the thesis that scientific theories concern structural aspects of reality. Ontological structural realism says that scientific reality is wholly structural. Epistemological structural realism says that we can know (through science) only structural aspects of reality. [8.7]

Structural Scrutability: The thesis that all truths are scrutable from truths containing only structural expressions. [8.7]

Structuralism: All truths (or all truths in a certain domain) are reducible (in some sense) to structural truths: truths involving only structural expressions. Pure structuralism says that all expressions are definable in terms of logical expressions alone. [8.7]

Super-rigid expression: An expression that is epistemically rigid and metaphysically rigid *de jure*. [E10, E14]

Super-Rigid Necessitation: The thesis that all truths are necessitated by super-rigid truths. [E10, E14]

Super-Rigid Scrutability: The thesis that all truths are scrutable from super-rigid truths and indexical truths. [E10, E14]

Supervenience: B-properties supervene on A-properties when any two possible worlds with the same distribution of A-properties have the same distribution of B-properties. [E16]

Synthetic a priori: S is synthetic when it is not analytic. S is synthetic a priori when it is a priori but not analytic. [8.3]

That's-all sentence: A sentence saying that one's actual scenario is a minimal scenario satisfying some other sentence or sets of sentences (such as *PQI*). For example, it may say that all positive truths are scrutable from *PQI*. [3.1, E6]

Thought: A state or act of entertaining a proposition, where entertaining is the maximally general propositional attitude with a mind-to-world direction of fit. [E3]

Totality expression: An expression needed especially to state a that's-all sentence. [7.10]

Twin-Earthable expression: An expression E such that there is a nondeferential utterance of E that has a possible twin utterance (a corresponding utterance made by a functional and phenomenal duplicate of the speaker of E) with a different extension. Named after Hilary Putnam's Twin Earth, where our duplicates use 'water' to refer to the indistinguishable liquid XYZ. [7.2]

Type-A materialism: A materialist view on which phenomenal truths are a priori scrutable from physical truths. [7.7]

Type-B materialism: A materialist views on which phenomenal truths are necessitated by but not a priori scrutable from physical truths. [7.7]

Verificationism: The thesis that all meaningful sentences are verifiable. [E1]

Warrant: A conclusive justification for believing a proposition or a sentence (whether or not one already believes it), or a justification suitable for knowledge. Understood as a support structure. [E4]

Warrant-analytic: A sentence S is warrant-analytic when there is a conceptual warrant for believing it: that is, a warrant deriving from the concepts expressed by expressions in S. [E17]

Wide expression: One whose content depends on a speaker's environment. Wide content is a sort of mental content that depends on a thinker's environment. [8.4]

Bibliography

Adams, R. M. 1979. Primitive thisness and primitive identity. *Journal of Philosophy* 76: 5–26.

Ainsworth, P. 2009. Newman's objection. *British Journal for the Philosophy of Science* 60: 135–71.

Albert, D. 1994. *Quantum Mechanics and Experience*. Harvard University Press.

——1996. Elementary quantum metaphysics. In J. Cushing, A. Fine, and S. Goldstein, eds., *Bohmian Mechanics and Quantum Theory: An Appraisal*. Kluwer.

Allori, V., Goldstein, S., Tumulka, R., and Zanghi, N. 2008. On the common structure of Bohmian mechanics and the Ghirardi–Rimini–Weber theory. *British Journal for the Philosophy of Science* 59: 353–89.

Almotahari, M. and Rochford, D. 2011. Is direct reference theory incompatible with physicalism? *Journal of Philosophy* 108: 255–68.

Armstrong, D. M. 1989. *A Combinatorial Theory of Possibility*. Cambridge University Press.

——1997. *A World of States of Affairs*. Cambridge University Press.

Arntzenius, F. 2003. Some puzzles about conditionalization and reflection. *Journal of Philosophy* 100: 356–70.

Austin, D. F. 1990. *What's the Meaning of 'This'?* Cornell University Press.

Balcerak Jackson, M. forthcoming. Conceptual analysis and epistemic progress. *Synthese*.

Barbour, J. 1999. *The End of Time*. Oxford University Press.

Barsalou, L. 1999. Perceptual symbol systems. *Behavioral and Brain Sciences* 22: 577–609.

Bechtel, W. and Abrahamsen, A. 2005. Explanation: A mechanist alternative. *Studies in History and Philosophy of Biological and Biomedical Sciences* 36: 421–41.

Bedau, M. 1997. Weak emergence. *Philosophical Perspectives* 11: 375–99.

Beggs, E. J. and Tucker, J. V. 2006. Embedding infinitely parallel computation in Newtonian kinematic systems. *Applied Mathematics and Computation* 178: 25–43.

Benacerraf, P. 1965. What numbers could not be. *Philosophical Review* 74: 47–73.

Bird, A. 2007. *Nature's Metaphysics: Laws and Properties*. Oxford University Press.

Bjerring, J. C. 2010. Nonideal epistemic spaces. Ph.D. dissertation, Australian National University.

——forthcoming. Impossible worlds and logical omniscience: An impossibility result. *Synthese*.

Block, N. 1986. Advertisement for a semantics for psychology. *Midwest Studies in Philosophy* 10: 615–78.

——2006. Max Black's objection to mind–body identity. *Oxford Review of Metaphysics* 2: 3–78.

——and Stalnaker, R. 1999. Conceptual analysis, dualism, and the explanatory gap. *Philosophical Review* 108: 1–46.

Boghossian, P. 2003. Blind reasoning. *Proceedings of the Aristotelian Society*, Supplementary Volume 77: 225–48.

BonJour, L. 1998. *In Defense of Pure Reason*. Cambridge University Press.

Brandom, R. 1994. *Making it Explicit*. Harvard University Press.

Broad, C. D. 1925. *The Mind and its Place in Nature*. Routledge & Kegan Paul.

Burge, T. 1979. Individualism and the mental. *Midwest Studies in Philosophy* 4: 73–122.

Byrne, A. 1999. Cosmic hermeneutics. *Philosophical Perspectives* 13: 347–83.

——and Hall, N. 1999. Chalmers on consciousness and quantum mechanics. *Philosophy of Science* 66: 370–90.

——and Hilbert, D. 2007. Truest blue. *Analysis* 67: 87–92.

Camp, J. L. 1991. The ballad of Clyde the moose. In T. Horowitz and G. Massey, eds., *Thought Experiments in Science and Philosophy*. Rowman and Littlefield.

Carey, S. 2009. *The Origin of Concepts*. Oxford University Press.

Carnap, R. 1923. Über die Aufgabe der Physik und die Anwendung des Grundsatzes der Einfachstheit. *Kant-Studien* 28: 90–107. Translated as 'On the Task of Physics and the Application of the Principle of Maximal Simplicity' in A. Carus, M. Friedman, W. Kienzler, and S. Schlotter, eds., *Collected Works of Rudolf Carnap. Volume I: Early Writings*. Open Court, 2009.

——1928. *Der logische Aufbau Der Welt*. Leipzig: Felix Meiner Verlag. Translated as *The Logical Structure of the World*, University of California Press, 1967.

——1932. Die physikalische Sprache als Universalsprache der Wissenschaft. *Erkenntnis* 2: 432–65. Translated as *The Unity of Science*, University of Chicago Press, 1934.

——1932. Psychologie in physikalischer Sprache. *Erkenntnis* 3: 162–76. Translated as 'Psychology in physical language' in A. J. Ayer, ed., *Logical Positivism*. Free Press, 1959.

——1934. *The Logical Syntax of Language*. University of Chicago Press.

——1936. Testability and meaning. *Philosophy of Science* 3: 419–71.

——1947. *Meaning and Necessity: A Study in Semantics and Modal Logic*. University of Chicago Press.

——1950. Empiricism, semantics, and ontology. *Revue Internationale de Philosophie* 4: 20–40.

——1955. Meaning and synonymy in natural languages. *Philosophical Studies* 6(3): 33–47. Reprinted as Appendix D of *Meaning and Necessity*. University of Chicago Press, 1956.

Carroll, J. 1994. *Laws of Nature*. Cambridge University Press.

Cartwright, N. 1999. *The Dappled World: A Study of the Boundaries of Science*. Cambridge University Press.

Chalmers, D. J. 1995. Facing up to the problem of consciousness. *Journal of Consciousness Studies* 2: 200–19.

——1996. *The Conscious Mind: In Search of a Fundamental Theory*. Oxford University Press.

——1999. Materialism and the metaphysics of modality. *Philosophy and Phenomenological Research* 59: 473–96.

——2002. The components of content. In D. J. Chalmers, ed., *Philosophy of Mind: Classical and Contemporary Readings*. Oxford University Press.

——2002. Does conceivability entail possibility? In T. Gendler and J. Hawthorne, eds., *Conceivability and Possibility*. Oxford University Press.

——2002. On sense and intension. *Philosophical Perspectives* 16: 135–82.

——2003. Consciousness and its place in nature. In S. Stich and F. Warfield, eds., *The Blackwell Guide to Philosophy of Mind*. Blackwell.

——2003. The content and epistemology of phenomenal belief. In Q. Smith and A. Jokic, eds., *Consciousness: New Philosophical Perspectives*. Oxford University Press.

——2004. Epistemic two-dimensional semantics. *Philosophical Studies* 118: 153–226.

——2004. The representational character of experience. In B. Leiter, ed., *The Future for Philosophy*. Oxford University Press.

——2005. The Matrix as metaphysics. In C. Grau, ed., *Philosophers Explore the Matrix*. Oxford University Press.

——2006. The foundations of two-dimensional semantics. In M. Garcia-Carpintero and J. Macia, eds., *Two-Dimensional Semantics: Foundations and Applications*. Oxford University Press.

——2006. Perception and the fall from Eden. In T. Gendler and J. Hawthorne, eds., *Perceptual Experience*. Oxford University Press.

——2006. Strong and weak emergence. In P. Clayton and P. Davies, eds., *The Re-Emergence of Emergence*. Oxford University Press.

——2007. Phenomenal concepts and the explanatory gap. In T. Alter and S. Walter, eds., *Phenomenal Concepts and Phenomenal Knowledge*. Oxford University Press.

——2009. Ontological anti-realism. In D. Chalmers, D. Manley, and R. Wasserman, eds., *Metametaphysics: New Essays on the Foundations of Ontology*. Oxford University Press.

——2010. The two-dimensional argument against materialism. In *The Character of Consciousness*. Oxford University Press. Abridged version in B. McLaughlin, A. Beckermann, and S. Walter, eds., *The Oxford Handbook of Philosophy of Mind*. Oxford University Press, 2009.

——2011. Actuality and knowability. *Analysis* 71: 411–19.

——2011. The nature of epistemic space. In A. Egan and B. Weatherson, eds., *Epistemic Modality*. Oxford University Press.

——2011. Propositions and attitude ascriptions: A Fregean account. *Noûs* 45: 595–639.

——2011. Verbal disputes. *Philosophical Review*, 120: 475–513.

——and Jackson, F. 2001. Conceptual analysis and reductive explanation. *Philosophical Review* 110: 315–61.

Chisholm, R. 1948. The problem of empiricism. *Journal of Philosophy* 45: 512–17.

Christensen, D. 2007. Does Murphy's Law apply in epistemology? Self-doubt and rational ideals. *Oxford Studies in Epistemology* 2: 3–31.

Clark, A. and Chalmers, D. 1998. The extended mind. *Analysis* 58: 10–23.

Coffa, A. 1985. *The Semantic Tradition from Kant to Carnap: To the Vienna Station*. Cambridge University Press.

Dasgupta, S. forthcoming. On the plurality of grounds.

Demopolous, W. and Friedman, M. 1985. The concept of structure in *The Analysis of Matter*. *Philosophy of Science* 52: 621–39.

Dennett, D. C. 1991. Real patterns. *Journal of Philosophy* 87: 27–51.

Donnellan, K. 1966. Reference and definite descriptions. *Philosophical Review* 75: 281–304.

——1979. The contingent a priori and rigid designators. In P. French, T. Uehling, and H. Wettstein, eds., *Contemporary Perspectives in the Philosophy of Language*. University of Minnesota Press.

Dorr, C. 2003. Vagueness without ignorance. *Philosophical Perspectives* 17: 83–113.

Dowell, J. L. 2008. Empirical metaphysics: The role of intuitions about possible cases in philosophy. *Philosophical Studies* 140: 19–46.

Dupré, J. 1993. *The Disorder of Things: Metaphysical Foundations of the Disunity of Science*. Harvard University Press.

Edgington, D. 1985. The paradox of knowability. *Mind* 94: 557–68.

Evans, G. 1979. Reference and contingency. *The Monist* 62: 161–89.

Feferman, S. 1962. Transfinite recursive progressions of axiomatic theories. *Journal of Symbolic Logic* 27: 259–316.

Field, H. 1977. Logic, meaning, and conceptual role. *Journal of Philosophy* 74: 379–409.

——1996. The aprioricity of logic. *Proceedings of the Aristotelian Society* 96: 359–79.

Fine, K. 1994. Essence and modality. *Philosophical Perspectives* 8: 1–16.

——2010. Some puzzles of ground. *Notre Dame Journal of Formal Logic* 51: 97–118.

Fisher, J. 2007. Why nothing mental is just in the head. *Noûs* 41: 318–34.

Fitch, F. B. 1963. A logical analysis of some value concepts. *Journal of Symbolic Logic* 28: 135–42.

Fodor, J. A. 1974. Special sciences (or: the disunity of science as a working hypothesis). *Synthese* 28: 97–115.

——1998. *Concepts: Where Cognitive Science Went Wrong.* Oxford University Press.

——Garrett, M. F., Walker, E. C. T., and Parkes, C. H. 1980. Against definitions. *Cognition,* 8: 263–67.

Franzen, T. 2004. *Inexhaustibility: A Non-Exhaustive Treatment.* Association for Symbolic Logic.

Friedman, M. 1992. Epistemology in the *Aufbau. Synthese* 93: 15–57.

——1999. *Reconsidering Logical Positivism.* Cambridge University Press.

Galison, P. and Stump, D. eds. 1996. *The Disunity of Science: Boundaries, Contexts and Power.* Stanford University Press.

Gettier, E. 1963. Is knowledge justified true belief? *Analysis* 23: 121–3.

Ghirardi, G. C., Rimini, A., and Weber, T. 1986. Unified dynamics for microscopic and macroscopic systems. *Physical Review D* 34: 470–91.

Goddard, C. 2003. Whorf meets Wierzbicka: Variation and universals in language and thinking. *Language Sciences* 25: 393–432.

Goff, P. 2011. A posteriori physicalists get our phenomenal concepts wrong. *Australasian Journal of Philosophy* 89: 191–209.

Goldman, A. 2011. Toward a synthesis of reliabilism and evidentialism. In T. Dougherty, ed., *Evidentialism and its Discontents.* Oxford University Press.

Goodman, N. 1951. *The Structure of Appearance.* Harvard University Press.

Grice, H. P. and Strawson, P. F. 1956. In defense of a dogma. *Philosophical Review* 65: 141–58.

Gu, M., Weedbrook, C., Perales, A., and Nielsen, M. A. 2009. More really is different. *Physica D* 238: 835–9.

Haas-Spohn, U. 1995. *Versteckte Indexikalität und subjektive Bedeutung.* Akademie Verlag.

Hájek, A. 2003. What conditional probability could not be. *Synthese* 137: 273–323.

Harman, G. 1982. Conceptual role semantics. *Notre Dame Journal of Formal Logic* 23: 242–56.

——1994. Doubts about conceptual analysis. In M. Michael and J. O'Leary-Hawthorne, eds., *Philosophy in Mind.* Kluwer.

Hawthorne, J. 2001. Causal structuralism. *Philosophical Perspectives* 15: 361–78.

——2002. Deeply contingent a priori knowledge. *Philosophy and Phenomenological Research* 65: 247–69.

——2004. Why Humeans are out of their minds. *Noûs* 38: 351–8.

——2005. Vagueness and the mind of God. *Philosophical Studies* 122: 1–25.

——2007. A priority and externalism. In S. Goldberg, ed., *Internalism and Externalism in Semantics and Epistemology.* Oxford University Press.

Heil, J. 2003. *From an Ontological Point of View*. Oxford University Press.

Henderson, D. and Horgan, T. 2000. What is a priori and what is it good for? *Southern Journal of Philosophy* 38: 51–86.

Hofweber, T. 2005. Supervenience and object-dependent properties. *Journal of Philosophy* 102: 5–32.

Hogarth, M. 2004. Deciding arithmetic using SAD computers. *British Journal for the Philosophy of Science* 55: 681–91.

Horgan, T. 1984. Supervenience and cosmic hermeneutics. *Southern Journal of Philosophy Supplement* 22: 19–38.

——1986. Psychologism, semantics, and ontology. *Noûs* 20: 21–31.

——and Tienson, J. 2002. The intentionality of phenomenology and the phenomenology of intentionality. In D. Chalmers, ed., *Philosophy of Mind: Classical and Contemporary Readings*. Oxford University Press.

——and Timmons, M. 1992. Troubles on Moral Twin Earth: Moral queerness revived. *Synthese* 92: 221–60.

Hurley, S. 1998. *Consciousness in Action*. Harvard University Press.

Ichikawa, J. and Jarvis, B. 2009. Thought-experiment intuitions and truth in fiction. *Philosophical Studies* 142: 221–46.

Jackendoff, R. 1990. *Semantic Structures*. MIT Press.

Jackson, F. 1982. Epiphenomenal qualia. *Philosophical Quarterly* 32: 127–36.

——1998. *From Metaphysics to Ethics: A Defence of Conceptual Analysis*. Oxford University Press.

Jeffrey, R. 1983. *The Logic of Decision*. University of Chicago Press.

Kaplan, D. 1989. Demonstratives. In J. Almog, J. Perry and H. Wettstein, eds., *Themes From Kaplan*. Oxford University Press.

——1995. A problem in possible-world semantics. In W. Sinnott-Armstrong, D. Raffman, and N. Asher, eds., *Modality, Morality and Belief: Essays in Honor of Ruth Barcan Marcus*. Cambridge University Press.

Ketland, J. 2004. Empirical adequacy and Ramsification. *British Journal for the Philosophy of Science* 55: 287–300.

Kim, J. 1993. *Supervenience and Mind*. Cambridge University Press.

——1999. Making sense of emergence. *Philosophical Studies* 95: 3–36.

Kitcher, P. 2000. A priori knowledge revisited. In P. Boghossian and C. Peacocke, eds., *New Essays on the A Priori*. Oxford University Press.

Kripke, S. 1980. *Naming and Necessity*. Harvard University Press.

—— 1982. *Wittgenstein on Rules and Private Language*. Harvard University Press.

Ladyman, J. 1998. What is structural realism? *Studies in the History and Philosophy of Science* 29: 409–24.

Langton, R. 1997. *Kantian Humility: Our Ignorance of Things in Themselves*. Oxford University Press.

Leibniz, G.W. 1679–81. De alphabeto cogitationum humanarum. In *Sämtliche Schriften und Briefe*, Series VI, vol. 4, pp. 270–3. Akademie Verlag.

Leitgeb, H. 2011. New life for Carnap's *Aufbau*? *Synthese* 180: 265–99.

Leslie, A., Friedman, O., and German, T. P. 2004. Core mechanisms in 'theory of mind'. *Trends in Cognitive Sciences* 8: 528–33.

Lewis, D. 1976. Probabilities of conditionals and conditional probabilities. *Philosophical Review* 85: 297–315.

——1983. New work for a theory of universals. *Australasian Journal of Philosophy* 61: 343–77.

Lewis, D. 1984. Putnam's paradox. *Australasian Journal of Philosophy* 62: 221–36.

——1986. *On the Plurality of Worlds.* Blackwell.

——1993. Many, but almost one. In J. Bacon, ed., *Ontology, Causality and Mind: Essays in Honour of D. M. Armstrong.* Cambridge University Press.

——1994. Reduction of mind. In S. Guttenplan, ed., *A Companion to the Philosophy of Mind.* Blackwell.

——2009. Ramseyan humility. In David Braddon-Mitchell and Robert Nola, eds., *Conceptual Analysis and Philosophical Naturalism.* MIT Press.

Lewis, P. 2004. Life in configuration space. *British Journal for the Philosophy of Science* 55: 713–29.

Locke, D. forthcoming. Quidditism without quiddities. *Philosophical Studies.*

Locke, J. 1690. *An Essay Concerning Human Understanding.*

McConnell, B. and Tucker, J. V. 1992. Infinite synchronous concurrent algorithms: The algebraic specification and verification of a hardware stack. In F. Bauer, W. Bauer, and H. Schwictenberg, eds., *Logic and Algebra of Specification.* Springer.

McQueen, K. 2011. A priori entailment and mass additivity. Manuscript.

Malmgren, A.-S. 2011. Rationalism and the content of intuitive judgements. *Mind* 120: 263–327.

Marras, A. 2005. Consciousness and reduction. *British Journal for the Philosophy of Science* 56: 335–61.

Martin, C. B. 1997. On the need for properties: The road to Pythagoreanism and back. *Synthese* 112: 193–231.

Maudlin, T. 2007. Completeness, supervenience, and ontology. *Journal of Physics A: Mathematical and Theoretical* 40: 3151–71.

Maxwell, G. 1970. Structural realism and the meaning of theoretical terms. In S. Winokur and M. Radner, eds., *Analyses of Theories and Methods of Physics and Psychology.* University of Minnesota Press.

Melia, J. and Saatsi, J. 2006. Ramseyfication and theoretical content. *British Journal for the Philosophy of Science* 57: 561–85.

Melnyk, A. 2008. Conceptual and linguistic analysis: A two-step program. *Noûs* 42: 267–91.

Menzies, P. and Price, H. 2009. Is semantics in the plan? In D. Braddon-Mitchell and R. Nola, eds., *Conceptual Analysis and Philosophical Naturalism.* MIT Press.

Monton, B. 2002. Wave function ontology. *Synthese* 130: 265–77.

Mormann, T. 2003. Synthetic geometry and the *Aufbau.* In T. Bonk, ed., *Language, Logic, and Truth: Contributions to the Philosophy of Rudolf Carnap.* Kluwer.

——2004. A quasi-analytic constitution of physical space. In S. Awodey and C. Klein, eds., *Carnap Brought Home: The View from Jena.* Open Court.

Moss, S. forthcoming. Epistemology formalized. *Philosophical Review.*

Nagel, E. 1961. *The Structure of Science: Problems in the Logic of Scientific Explanation.* Harcourt, Brace & World.

Neurath, O., Carnap, R., and Morris, C. F. W. 1971. *Foundations of the Unity of Science.* University of Chicago Press.

Newman, M. H. A. 1928. Mr. Russell's causal theory of perception. *Mind* 37: 137–48.

Ney, A. forthcoming. The status of our ordinary three dimensions in a quantum universe. *Noûs.*

Nida-Rümelin, M. 2002. Phenomenal concepts and phenomenal properties: An argument for property dualism. Presented at NEH Institute on Consciousness and Intentionality, July 2002. <http://consc.net/neh/papers/nidarumelin.htm>.

——2003. Phänomenale Begriffe. In U. Haas-Spohn, ed., *Intentionalität zwischen Subjektivität und Weltbezug*. Mentis.

——2007. Grasping phenomenal properties. In T. Alter and S. Walter, eds., *Phenomenal Concepts and Phenomenal Knowledge: New Essays on Consciousness and Physicalism*. Oxford University Press.

Okun, L. 2009. Mass versus relativistic and rest masses. *American Journal of Physics* 77: 430–1.

Peacocke, C. 1993. *A Study of Concepts*. MIT Press.

——2004. *The Realm of Reason*. Oxford University Press.

——2008. *Truly Understood*. Oxford University Press.

Pincock, C. 2002. Russell's influence on Carnap's *Aufbau*. *Synthese* 131: 1–37.

——2007. Carnap, Russell, and the external world. In M. Friedman and R. Creath, eds., *The Cambridge Companion to Carnap*. Cambridge University Press.

Pollock, J. 1974. *Knowledge and Justification*. Princeton University Press.

Prinz, J. 2002. *Furnishing the Mind: Concepts and their Perceptual Basis*. MIT Press.

——2012. *The Conscious Brain*. Oxford University Press.

Pryor, J. 2000. The skeptic and the dogmatist. *Noûs* 34: 517–49.

——2007. Uncertainty and undermining. <http://www.jimpryor.net/research/papers/Uncertainty.pdf>.

Pustejovsky, J. 1995. *The Generative Lexicon*. MIT Press.

Putnam, H. 1962. It ain't necessarily so. *Journal of Philosophy* 59: 658–71.

——1975. The meaning of 'meaning'. *Minnesota Studies in the Philosophy of Science* 7: 131–93.

——1981. *Reason, Truth, and History*. Cambridge University Press.

Quine, W. V. 1951. Two dogmas of empiricism. *Philosophical Review* 60: 20–43.

——1960. *Word and Object*. MIT Press.

——1967. Epistemology naturalized. In *Ontological Relativity and Other Essays*. Columbia University Press.

——1990. *Pursuit of Truth*. Harvard University Press.

Ramsey, F. P. 1931. General propositions and causality. In R. B. Braithwaite, ed., *The Foundations of Mathematics and Other Logical Essays*. Routledge & Kegan Paul.

Reimer, M. 2004. Descriptively introduced names. In M. Reimer and A. Bezuidenhout, eds., *Descriptions and Beyond*. Oxford University Press.

Richardson, A. 1990. How not to Russell Carnap's *Aufbau*. *PSA: Proceedings of the Biennial Meeting of the Philosophy of Science Association*: 3–14.

——1998. *Carnap's Construction of the World: The Aufbau and the Emergence of Logical Empiricism*. Cambridge University Press.

Russell, B. 1911. Knowledge by acquaintance and knowledge by description. *Proceedings of the Aristotelian Society* 11: 108–28.

——1912. *The Problems of Philosophy*. Williams and Norgate.

——1913. Theory of knowledge. Unpublished manuscript, later published as *Theory of Knowledge: The 1913 Manuscript*. Allen & Unwin, 1984.

——1914. *Our Knowledge of the External World*. Open Court.

——1918. The philosophy of logical atomism. *The Monist* 28: 295–527. Reprinted as *The Philosophy of Logical Atomism*. Taylor and Francis, 2009.

——1927. *The Analysis of Matter*. Kegan Paul.

Sainsbury, M. and Tye, M. 2012. *Seven Puzzles of Thought and How to Solve Them*. Oxford University Press.

Salerno, J. 2009. *New Essays on the Knowability Paradox*. Oxford University Press.

——2009. Knowability Noir: 1945–1963. In J. Salerno, ed., *New Essays on the Knowability Paradox*. Oxford University Press.

Salmon, N. 1986. *Frege's Puzzle*. MIT Press.

——1988. How to measure the standard metre. *Proceedings of the Aristotelian Society* 88: 193–217.

——1993. Relative and absolute apriority. *Philosophical Studies* 69: 83–100.

Saunders, S., Barrett, J., Kent, A., and Wallace, D. 2010. *Many Worlds? Everett, Quantum Theory, and Reality*. Oxford University Press.

Schaffer, J. 2003. Is there a fundamental level? *Noûs* 37: 498–517.

——2005. Quiddistic knowledge? *Philosophical Studies* 123: 1–32.

——2009. On what grounds what. In D. Chalmers, D. Manley, and R. Wasserman, eds., *Metametaphysics: New Essays on the Foundations of Ontology*. Oxford University Press.

Schroeter, L. 2006. Against a priori reductions. *Philosophical Quarterly* 56: 562–86.

Schwitzgebel, E. 2008. The unreliability of naive introspection. *Philosophical Review* 117: 245–73.

Searle, J. R. 1992. *The Rediscovery of the Mind*. MIT Press.

Seiberg, N. 2006. Emergent spacetime. <http://arxiv.org/abs/hep-th/0601234>.

Sellars, W. 1953. Inference and meaning. *Mind* 62: 313–38.

Shope, R. K. 1983. *The Analysis of Knowing: A Decade of Research*. Princeton University Press.

Sider, T. 2009. Ontological realism. In D. Chalmers, D. Manley, and R. Wasserman, eds., *Metametaphysics: New Essays on the Foundations of Ontology*. Oxford University Press.

——2011. *Writing the Book of the World*. Oxford University Press.

Siegel, S. 2006. Which properties are represented in perception? In T. Gendler and J. Hawthorne, eds., *Perceptual Experience*. Oxford University Press.

——2011. *The Contents of Visual Experience*. Oxford University Press.

——forthcoming. The epistemic impact of the etiology of experience. *Philosophical Studies*.

Siewert, C. 1998. *The Significance of Consciousness*. Princeton University Press.

Soames, S. 2002. *Beyond Rigidity: The Unfinished Semantic Agenda of Naming and Necessity*. Princeton University Press.

——2004. *Reference and Description: The Case Against Two-Dimensionalism*. Princeton University Press.

Spelke, E. 2000. Core knowledge. *American Psychologist* 55: 1233–43.

Stoljar, D. 2001. Two conceptions of the physical. *Philosophy and Phenomenological Research* 62: 253–81.

Strawson, G. 1989. *The Secret Connexion: Causation, Realism, and David Hume*. Oxford University Press.

——2008. The identity of the categorical and the dispositional. *Analysis* 68: 271–82.

Strawson, P. F. 1959. *Individuals: An Essay in Descriptive Metaphysics*. Methuen.

Symons, J., Pombo, O., and Torres, J. M. (eds.) 2011. *Otto Neurath and the Unity of Science*. Springer.

Thomasson, A. 2007. *Ordinary Objects*. Oxford University Press.

Thompson, B. 2003. The nature of phenomenal content. Dissertation, University of Arizona.

——2010. The spatial content of experience. *Philosophy and Phenomenological Research* 81: 146–84.

Tooley, M. 1987. *Causation: A Realist Approach*. Oxford University Press.

Tye, M. 2006. The puzzle of true blue. *Analysis* 66: 173–8.

Uebel, T. 1992. *Overcoming Logical Positivism from Within: The Emergence of Neurath's Naturalism in the Vienna Circle's Protocol Sentence Debate*. Rodopi.

Waismann, F. 1945. Verifiability. *Proceedings of the Aristotelian Society*, Supplementary Volume 19: 119–50.

——1965. *The Principles of Linguistic Philosophy*. St. Martin's Press.

Wallace, D. 2003. Everett and structure, *Studies in the History and Philosophy of Modern Physics* 34: 86–105.

——and Timpson, C. G. 2010. Quantum mechanics on spacetime. I: Spacetime state realism. *British Journal for the Philosophy of Science* 61: 697–727.

Weatherson, B. 2007. The Bayesian and the dogmatist. *Proceedings of the Aristotelian Society* 107: 169–85.

White, R. 2006. Problems for dogmatism. *Philosophical Studies* 131: 525–57.

Wierzbicka, A. 1972. *Semantic Primitives*. Athenaeum-Verlag.

——2009. *Experience, Evidence, and Sense: The Hidden Cultural Legacy of English*. Oxford University Press.

Williamson, T. 1994. *Vagueness*. Routledge.

——2000. *Knowledge and its Limits*. Oxford University Press.

——2007. *The Philosophy of Philosophy*. Blackwell.

——forthcoming. How deep is the distinction between a priori and a posteriori? In A. Casullo, ed., *Essays on the A Priori*. Oxford University Press.

Wilson, M. 1986. *Wandering Significance: An Essay on Conceptual Behavior*. Oxford University Press.

Wittgenstein, L. 1921. *Tractatus Logico-Philosophicus*. Routledge.

——1953. *Philosophical Investigations*. Macmillan.

Wolpert, D. H. 2008. Physical limits of inference. *Physica D* 237: 1257–81.

Wright, C. 2007. The perils of dogmatism. In S. Nuccetelli and G. Seay, eds. *Themes from G.E. Moore*. Oxford University Press.

Yablo, S. 1998. Textbook Kripkeanism and the open texture of language. *Philosophical Quarterly* 48: 98–122.

——2002. Coulda, woulda, shoulda. In T. Gendler and J. Hawthorne, eds., *Conceivability and Possibility*. Oxford University Press.

Index

inferential role 70–1, 173–6, 187, 258, 316, 393, 462–7
inferential scrutability 40–1, 41, 47–53, 57–8, 66, 77, 81, 84, 94, 106, 127, 134–9, 471
Inferential Scrutability xiv–xv, 41, 47–53, 134–8, 471
inferentialism 462–7, 471
　acquaintance 466–7
　anchored 463–7
infinitary definitions 381
infinitary thought 62, 65
infinitism 98
innate concepts 147, 392
innate knowledge 128
innate process 67, 99 n. 8, 197
inscrutability of reference 34–8
inscrutable truth 30–1, 32, 69, 88, 176, 230 n. 5, 259–300, 352 n. 22, 353, 359, 375 n. 11, 408
insulated idealization 101–7, 123, 125, 136, 191–2, 213 n. 6, 225 n. 16, 471
insulated rational credence 85 n. 11, 105–6, 138
insulated warrant 105
intension 16–19, 27, 69–71, 204–11, 216, 219, 224–5, 231–2, 233–58, 424–5, 471
　deferential 252–3
　enriched 247–9
　epistemic, see primary intension
　idealized 69–71, 209
　metalinguistic 253
　primary 18 n. 20, 69–71, 144 n. 24, 208–11, 237–58, 277, 284, 367–71, 378 n. 13, 396–8, 432 n. 2, 459, 472
　secondary 208, 237–43, 247, 370, 473
　structured 248–9
　two-dimensional 242–3, 370
intention 251 n. 4, 279, 281, 284
intentional truths 112, 128–9, 150, 274–9, 280, 283–4, 299–300, 342 n. 15, 471
intentionality 27, 274–9
　grounds of 258, 462–7
internalism, see externalism
intrinsic properties 88, 152–3, 240 n. 6, 322, 348 n. 18, 357, 371, 393–4, 436–7
introspection 85, 96–9, 103–5, 116, 130–4, 136, 141, 144, 154, 172, 180, 190, 235, 401 n. 12
intuition 63, 97, 126, 128
inverted spectrum 415–16
irrationality 102–4, 214, 219

Jackendoff, R. 391 n. 5
Jackson, F. xxi–xxii, 12 n. 17, 22, 109, 112 n. 5, 169 n. 7, 306 n. 4, 313, 362, 364, 375 n. 11, 415, 442 n. 2
Jarvis, B. 15 n. 18
Jeffrey, R. 163 n. 4, 212 n. 5, 220–1

justification
　a posteriori 27, 99, 179, 185–98
　a priori xv, 99, 157, 179–80, 185–98, 468
　classical 96
　direct/indirect 95–6
　doxastic 92–9, 440
　non-inferential 95–9, 130
　partial/full 96
　propositional 92–9, 440
　proto- 146 n. 25, 440 n. 7

Kaplan, D. 89, 248
Kent, A. 293 n. 17
Ketland, J. 421 n. 22
Kim, J. 304, 442
Kitcher, P. 201 n. 1
knowability
　argument from 125–34
　non-modal conception 92–100
　paradox of xv, 29–33, 50–2, 89, 106
Knowability thesis xvi, 26, 29–33, 471
　Core 131–4, 161–2, 469
knowledge
　analysis of 11–19, 383
　conditional 53–6, 59, 133, 158–69, 313
　of reference 34–8, 173–6, 466
　reliabilism about 66–9
knowledge argument 109, 313, 415–16, 420–1
Kripke, S. 179, 186 n. 1, 208, 239, 252, 274, 275, 366
　epistemic argument 10–11, 17–19, 282
　modal argument 10–11, 17–19, 247

Ladyman, J. 421 n. 22
Langton, R. 348
language of thought 75–6
Laplace, P.-S. xiii, xiv, xviii, 41, 62
Laplace's demon xiii–xviii, 7, 41, 51, 62, 109, 118, 136
Laplacean Scrutability xiv–xvi, 62
Leibniz, G.W. 1, 229–30
Leitgeb, H. 9 n. 13, 25 n. 27, 415 n. 20
Leslie, A. 392
level-crossing principle 103–5
Lewis, D. 35, 53, 76, 149, 174, 319–20, 337, 340, 348, 349 n. 19, 352 n. 22, 362, 364, 427–8, 445
Lewis, P. 294 n. 18
Liar paradox 32–3
limit 229–30, 381
Linking thesis 446–8
Locke, D. 348 n. 18
Locke, J. 1–2
logic 263, 354–6
logical empiricism 9–10, 26, 199–200, 471
logical expressions 354–6